Susan Hawthorne is a feminist activist, author and (co-)editor of numerous books. Her recent work has focused on the impact of globalisation on women, and her book *Wild Politics* suggests new ways of thinking about long-term solutions to environmental and political problems. She has worked across a number of disciplines in academia and considers herself an independent scholar. She is also a poet, novelist and circus performer. She works in a freelance capacity at Victoria University, Melbourne.

Bronwyn Winter is a Senior Lecturer in the Department of French Studies at the University of Sydney. She is also a feminist and lesbian activist. Her work on feminist theory, women in international and national politics, human rights, women and the politics of race, nation and culture, Islamism, globalisation, and critiques of liberalism has been widely published in Australian and international journals and anthologies. She considers her academic work and her feminist activism as feeding each other rather than being separate, and writing as a personal and political necessity. She is also active in the National Tertiary Education Union. This is another political necessity, particularly given the current Australian government's negative and punitive attitude towards higher education, or indeed towards any human endeavour which might sow the seeds of intelligence and respect for others.

T0159863

SEPTEMBER 11, 2001: FEMINIST PERSPECTIVES

Edited by
Susan Hawthorne
and Bronwyn Winter

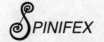

Spinifex Press Pty Ltd
504 Queensberry Street
North Melbourne, Vic. 3051
Australia

women@spinifexpresss.com.au
http://www.spinifexpress.com.au

First published 2002

Cover design by Deb Snibson, Modern Art Production Group
Typeset in Sabon by Palmer Higgs Pty Ltd
Printed and bound by McPherson's Printing Group

National Library of Australia
Cataloguing-in-Publication data:
September 11, 2001 : feminist perspectives.

  Bibliography.
  Includes index.
  ISBN 1 876756 27 6.

1. September 11 Terrorist Attacks, 2001. 2. September 11
Terrorist Attacks, 2001 – Personal narratives. 3. Feminism.
I. Hawthorne, Susan, 1951– . II. Winter, Bronwyn, 1955– .

973.931

To women who have struggled to perfect
the difficult and valuable skill of surviving,
who refuse to be overwhelmed by the overwhelming,
and who continue to hope against hopelessness.

Contents

Whose Peace? 14 November to 8 March

PART TWO: REFLECTIONS

Acknowledgements

First and above all, thanks to Véronique Delaunay who had the idea for this book and entrusted it to Bronwyn to bring to fruition—and had no doubt that we would. Thanks to Renate Klein who encouraged the growth of this book even when the number of contributors expanded to an unforeseen extent.

We would like to thank the many contributors to this book. First of all to those whose words were published in print, on the internet and on e-mail lists in the days, weeks and months following September 11. It takes courage to speak against the mainstream, especially in times of violence and war, and many of our contributors have "copped flak" for their words. To those authors who have written pieces specifically for the volume, thank you for meeting our very short deadlines, answering our questions and finding those last reluctant references. We would also like to thank those contributors and publishers who have waived fees which has helped to make this book possible. We appreciate your generosity.

Without the work of Belinda Morris on e-mail and internet, we would never have managed to track down so many of the contributors, and we thank her for her resourcefulness and persistence. We would also like to thank Janet Mackenzie for her editing which has made the book work as a whole; and to Kerry Biram for proofreading. Merilyn Whimpey took on the arduous job of typesetting, and we thank her for her work. Thanks, once again, are due to Deb Snibson for her cover design.

Susan would like to extend her thanks to the Diverse Women for Diversity email list, <divwomen@vsnl.com>. It was a source of sanity in the weeks following September 11, knowing that so many women in so many places were responding differently to the events than was suggested by the mainstream media. The conversations on this list alerted me to the possibility of this book once the seed had been sown.

Robin Morgan's enthusiasm for the project was important. Her work on terrorism a decade earlier meant that her postings on events in New York in the first week came edged with a feminist critique. Cynthia Enloe's work on militarism over years has shaped many of my views, and I thank her for that and for her interest in the volume, with the hope that it will be adopted on courses from Women's Studies to Politics, International Relations and Military Studies!

Renate Klein, who has read all the different versions behind what finally appears, has contributed significantly to the development of my ideas. A session at the National Women's Studies Association conference on 15 June 2002 in Las Vegas brought new issues to the fore, and I thank the audience present on that day. I would also like to thank Coleen Clare who has impressed upon me the importance of this book; Suzanne Bellamy who made me laugh about nationalism in the USA when the alternative was to cry.

Bronwyn would like to extend her thanks, firstly, to Véronique Delaunay who provided supportive and constructive feedback as she struggled with complex thoughts and against impossible deadlines to write something that would approach clarity and resonance in the middle of the mess of this world. Thanks also to Genée Marks, Sherri Hilario and Robin McLaughlin for their rapid and constructive feedback on various drafts of "Dislocations", and to a number of other friends and colleagues for their personal support and patience with me during the often heart-wrenching and nerve-wracking process of co-editing this book.

I would in particular like to thank those many individuals and organisations, located in Australia, Pakistan, Afghanistan and France, who assisted me in connection with my research in Afghanistan and Pakistan during June 2002. They are far too numerous to name here, but many women and some men, working in universities, feminist organisations, non-governmental aid organisations, the trade union movement and the UN, were generous with their time and expertise when I sought information and assistance, and a number of them also helped me with the logistics of travelling to and within Afghanistan and Pakistan at such a difficult time.

I would especially like to thank all those Afghan and Pakistani people who have made the intelligent choice of refusing to punish individual Australian citizens for the reprehensible actions of the Australian government. If only the Australian government and sections of the Australian population could act as intelligently and show as much compassion and generosity. Among those intelligent and generous people I had the privilege to meet are the many many Afghan women, a number of whom remain nameless, who shared their stories with me and with the other women of the French delegation to Kabul, who welcomed us to their schools and, in one case, into their home. Acknowledgement is also due to the refugees in Shalman camp whose privacy is precious and rare but who nonetheless were willing to meet me and to be photographed.

I acknowledge also the financial support of the University of Sydney, my employer, and the Australian Research Council, as well as the enthusiastic support of my colleagues and academic managers in my School, Faculty and

College for my research in both practical and moral terms, at a time when the Australian government is seeking to close minds rather than open them.

Finally our joint thanks to all the women at Spinifex Press, Johanna de Wever, Laurel Guymer, Maralann Damiano, Belinda Morris and Jo O'Brien for their continuing faith and commitment.

Susan Hawthorne and
Bronwyn Winter
July 2002

Glossary

Burqa or chadri: the long, conical-looking garment worn by Afghan women that covers their head and whole body, with only a small grille for them to see through. Some burqas are worn shorter in front (above the knee). They are usually light blue but may also be white, dark blue, fawn or olive green.

Hammam: bath-house.

Hezb-e Wahdat-e Islami: Islamic Unity Party, Afghanistan. It is led by Karim Khalil and is supported by Iran.

Jamiat-e Islami: Society of Islam. It is the largest Islamist party in Afghanistan and was the party of the Rabbani government.

Jehadi: the Afghan term for *mujahideen*.

Kia ora: Maori for "greetings, good luck".

Mujahideen: from *jihad*, "just struggle" or "holy war" (itself from *jahada*, to endeavour or strive or struggle, or to wage battle against infidels). The *mu-* prefix denotes some sort of agent, a person who does. *Mujahideen* is masculine plural.

Negar: Persian for "deep or close friendship", can be translated as "love" as well. It is also the imperative of the verb "write" and is used as a woman's first name

Salwar kameez: literally "trousers and shirt". They are the knee-length shirt and loose trousers, usually in a light colour (mostly white) worn by Pakistani and Afghan men. A more "feminine" version is worn by Pakistani women, along with a *dputa*, a long scarf women draped around the head or across the chest. The terms are originally from the Arabic *sirwal* and *qamis*.

Taliban: from the Pashto plural of *talib*, Arabic for student.

Abbreviations

ABC	American Broadcasting Corporation
ALP	Australian Labor Party
AMBO	Albanian–Macedonian–-Bulgarian Oil Pipeline Corporation
AMEWS	Association for Middle East Women's Studies
ANZUS	Australia, New Zealand, United States (treaty)
ASAP	Acting in Solidarity with Afghan People
AWORC	Australian Women's Research Centre, Deakin University
BBC	British Broadcasting Corporation (UK)
CEDAW	Convention on the Elimination of all Forms of Discrimination Against Women
CEO	chief executive officer
CIA	Central Intelligence Agency (USA)
CNN	Cable News Network (US)
DAR	Democratic Republic of Afghanistan
DOAR	Democratic Organisation of Afghanistan
DWD	Diverse Women for Diversity
FAO	Food and Agriculture Organisation (of the United Nations)
FBI	Federal Bureau of Investigation (USA)
FIS	Islamic Salvation Front (Algeria)
FLQ	Quebec Liberation Movement
FTAA	Free Trade Area of the Americas
FUWBOIA	Federation of Uganda Women of Business Organisations, Industry and Agriculture
GMO	genetically modified organism
IDF	Israeli Defence Force
ILO	International Labour Organisation
IMF	International Monetary Fund
ISI	Inter-Services Intelligence (Pakistan)
IUD	intra-uterine device
KGB	Komitet Gosudarstvennoy Bezopasnosti (Committee for State Security) (USSR)
KKK	Ku Klux Klan
MAI	Multilateral Agreement on Investment
MAPA	Mine Action Programme for Afghanistan (of the United Nations)
MD	Missile Defence
NA	Northern Alliance

NAC	National Action Committee (Canada)
NAFTA	North American Free Trade Agreement
NATO	North Atlantic Treaty Organisation
NGO	non-government organisation
NWC	National Commission for Women (India)
NYC	New York City
OSW	Office of the Status of Women (Australia)
PDPA	People's Democratic Party of Afghanistan
PLO	Palestine Liberation Organisation
POTO	Prevention of Terrorism Ordinance (India)
RAWA	Revolutionary Association of the Women of Afghanistan
ROTC	Reserve Officers Training Corps
SANG	Saudi Arabia National Guard
UAW	Union of Australian Women
UNDP	United Nations Development Program
UNESCO	United Nations Educational, Scientific and Cultural Organisation
UNFPA	United Nations Population Fund
UNHCR	United Nations High Commissioner for Refugees
UNICEF	United Nations International Children's Emergency Fund
UNIFEM	United Nations Development Fund for Women
UNTAET	United Nations Transitional Administration in East Timor
USA PATRIOT (Act)	Uniting and Strengthening America by Providing Appropriate Tools Required to Intercept and Obstruct Terrorism
WAPHA	Women's Association for Peace and Human Rights in Afghanistan
WILPF	Women's International League for Peace and Freedom
WLUML	Women Living Under Muslim Laws
WTO	World Trade Organisation

Currencies

A$	Australian dollar
US$	US dollar
Rs	Rupees

Susan Hawthorne and Bronwyn Winter

Introduction

"The day that shook the world". This is how the BBC characterised September 11, 2001, in the title to its book documenting the events from September 11 until the Northern Alliance entered Kabul on 13 November (Baxter and Downing 2001).

The world was indeed shaken. There is no doubt as to the magnitude of the events of that day. The United States, the tower of might and self-proclaimed right, was suddenly and unequivocally demonstrated to be vulnerable. What more symbolic target than the Twin Towers of the World Trade Center, which, along with the New York Stock Exchange, were a monument to global capitalism and to the USA's preponderant role in its development? What more symbolic place than Manhattan, the cultural hub of the New World, of North America at its most cosmopolitan, its most refined, its most culturally vibrant? What more potent message of warning to send than to attack the Pentagon, the symbolic heart of the US military?

Reactions were instantaneous and extreme, both governmental and non-governmental. On the evening of September 11, George W. Bush claimed, in a speech delivered on national television, that the USA was the "brightest beacon for freedom and opportunity in the world", reassured the American public that it was "business as usual" down at Wall Street, and vowed retaliation, making "no distinction between the terrorists who committed these acts and those who harbor them". He then quoted Psalm 23 to add an extra touch of Christian reassurance (Address to the Nation, 8.30 pm US EDST). The next day, Bush vowed to "rally the world" in the fight against "evil"; this would take "time and resolve", but he assured "the world" that he would win ("Remarks in Photo Opportunity with the National Security Team", 10.53 am US EDST).

Over the days that followed, Bush appeared regularly on US national television, repeating the same litany of might is right and God is on our side, promising victory but only after a long hard fight which would leave no resource unspent, no "enemy" free from attack. This against the backdrop of television stations showing action replay after action replay of the World Trade Center collapsing—edited to appear to happen in a matter of minutes and not hours—then poring, along with New Yorkers, over the rubble.

September 11 became the world's latest, and biggest, disaster movie—complete with its trick cinematography.

Many other voices throughout the USA, and throughout the West, were raised in jingoistic support of Bush. None was more jingoistic or more violent than the voice of the Australian government, led by Prime Minister John Howard. Less than a month after having lied to the Australian people over asylum seekers (the now notorious "children thrown overboard" fabrication),[1] this government once again lied to us, as George Bush was lying to the people of the USA, over the "war against terror". On the basis of those compounded lies, on calls to a misguided "patriotism" and on manipulated national fears of a demonised Islam, Howard's government was re-elected in November 2001. That government has proceeded to introduce "anti-terrorism" legislation of which any dictator would be proud, and which is being debated in parliament as we write this Introduction. It also continues to breach the 1951 Geneva Convention either by turning away asylum seekers—a number of them Afghan—without processing, or by detaining them in conditions that resemble those of the worst prisons.

Such abuses are not occurring only in Australia. Tony Blair is using Australia's immigration policies as a model; Dutch extreme-right leader Pym Fortuyn, before being murdered, was doing much the same, and French extreme-right leader Jean-Marie Le Pen has also stated that Australia's policies are a model for other governments. And the USA's treatment of prisoners (not considered prisoners of war) at Guantanamo Bay, as well as of those civilians arrested since September 11, denying them the usual rights that most Americans claim to defend, challenges most of the assumptions about "freedom" that are promoted officially and unofficially within the US. These

---

1 On 26 August 2001, the Norwegian container ship *Tampa* rescued 438 asylum seekers (most of them Afghan) from a sinking Indonesian vessel. The Australian government refused to let the refugees land on Australian soil (on Christmas Island), even though they had been picked up in Australian waters: the Australian government thus flouted its obligations under the 1951 Geneva Convention and 1967 Protocol on the treatment of asylum seekers. In October, it accused the asylum seekers of deliberately throwing children overboard in order to force the Australian government to pick them up. (In November, these allegations were exposed as false, and it was made clear that members of the government had been told they were false by senior Navy officials.) The government arranged for the asylum seekers to be sent to the Pacific island state of Nauru for detention and processing—the so-called "Pacific solution"—and in early 2002 came under further fire for having mounted a surveillance operation targeting the *Tampa* during the asylum seeker crisis. The Australian government has met widespread international condemnation over the *Tampa* incident.

assumptions are similarly challenged by the USA PATRIOT Act, discussed by Diane Bell, which has become the template for so-called "anti-terrorist" legislation that governments elsewhere in the West have introduced or attempted to introduce.

Bush, like Blair and Howard, remains oblivious to the waves of national protest and international condemnation that their actions have prompted. Yet there has been no lack of such protest. Immediately and forcefully, voices were raised in opposition to Bush's response to the events of September 11: those of journalists, political commentators, intellectuals, and of countless "ordinary" people, who communicated their concerns, both in the media and in public and private communiqués and correspondence over the internet. Some of these voices have been grouped together in the "protest anthologies" that began to appear as early as December 2001—a collection of interviews with Noam Chomsky (2001) being no doubt one of the earliest and best-known. Others ranged in stance from liberal (Talbott and Chanda 2001) to more radical (Burbach and Clarke 2002; Parenti 2002; AbuKhalil 2002; Zinn 2002). Some of them contained articles by feminists (Burbach and Clarke 2002), but we know of only one other anthology in production which presents a feminist perspective on the events before and after September 11: *Femininist Perspectives on War and Violence*, edited by Kalpana Sharma, Ammu Joseph and Ritu Menon, published in India by Kali for Women. There were also special issues of journals such as *Meridian* and *Granta* 77 (2002). These "protest anthologies" were followed, inevitably, by counter-protests criticising the anti-American left, such as Salusinszky and Melleuish (2002).

Many of the lesser-known of these voices of protest, however—and practically all female voices—were all but drowned out in the weeks and months following September 11, as governments and mainstream media indulged in the hyperbolic machismo of the "Terror War".

One of the very first responses to September 11 to circulate through the world from the island of Manhattan, and to register extreme concern at anticipated retaliation by the USA, was from Robin Morgan, well-known feminist and author of, among other works, *Demon Lover* (1989, 2001)—the book to which many of us turned in trying to deal with the events of September 11 and their aftermath.

A couple of days later, the Revolutionary Association of the Women of Afghanistan (RAWA) published its own statement: "Bin Laden Is Not Afghanistan". It is fitting that *September 11, 2001: Feminist Perspectives* opens with these two feminist statements, emanating from the countries that became the protagonists of the "War on Terror/Terror War".

It is appropriate that feminist responses in the days and weeks following September 11 are brought together and documented, so there may be no mistake as to the fact that women's voices *were* raised, publicly and massively across the world. But they were not listened to. Even those women on whose behalf Bush's war was supposedly waged—Afghan women—were not listened to.

Documenting feminist voices against the war, and feminist analyses of the masculinist ideology behind it, is, then, the reason for this book's existence. It is those voices, and those analyses, that continue to be alarmingly lacking in public fora, as the daily and weekly press reports of terror and war are superseded by anthologies and commemorations, and as the USA no doubt prepares another performance of media-hyped public grieving for the anniversary of September 11. Very few women's voices have made it into either the press or the anthologies. Even fewer of those voices have been feminist, with hardly any non-Western—or, indeed, non-US—ones. Among the small and remarkable minority of strong women's voices of protest that achieved public prominence is that of Democrat Congresswoman Barbara Lee, a lone and brave voice against Bush's war. Among the even smaller, and hence more remarkable, minority of non-Western voices is that of Tahmeena Faryal from RAWA, whose speech to a US Congress sub-committee was published, along with Barbara Lee's statement and texts by Arundhati Roy, Margot Pepper, Kinda Burnham, Barbara Kingsolver, Susan George and Aurora Levins Morales. Faryal, Lee, Roy and Kingsolver have all also contributed to this book.

Yet at the same time as feminist voices were being marginalised, women became the alibi for Bush's war against the Taliban: the acceptable human-itarian face of unacceptable aggression. Through a sleight of discourse, the Northern Alliance or Jihadi went from being the former ex-mujahideen oppressors of Afghan people, and in particular of Afghan women, to being their liberators. Christine Delphy's article "A War for Afghan Women", which appears for the first time in English in Part Two of this book, is a powerful indictment of this cynical use of "women's rights" and of the deep hypocrisy of US and Western governments and large sections of the media. Delphy's article is complemented by Valentine M. Moghadam's historical analysis of the background of the current political situation in Afghanistan, and in particular the situation of its women. Diane Bell picks up some of the same issues and, with an anthropologist's eye, critiques the shifting sands of US culture as an outsider living inside the USA. Together, these articles demonstrate strongly that there is much of the story of Afghanistan, and of US involvement there for at least the last two decades, that has not been fully nor clearly told.

This is not, however, for want of trying. Even before the Soviet invasion of Afghanistan in 1979, RAWA, formed in 1977, was campaigning for democracy and women's rights in Afghanistan. Even before the Soviets were chased out and the Jihadi came to power, RAWA was warning of the dangers of fundamentalism. During the Jihadi rule and the ensuing Taliban rule, RAWA protested to the world via statements and petitions sent out across the Internet and via its representatives and supporters in the West. But its protests were largely ignored. Buddhist statues appeared more worthy of public outcry—not to mention of a US presidential visit.

Now RAWA is once again urging the world not to believe US and Jihadi lies. We hope that this book will help them gain a better hearing this time around.

September 11, 2001: Feminist Perspectives is both a testimony—a documentation of many of the feminist responses in the days, weeks and months following September 11—and an attempt, to paraphrase Cynthia Enloe's famous title, to "make feminist sense of international events" that have unfolded since the attack on the World Trade Center.[2] It is, above all, a call for widespread resistance to the masculinist politics of war.

The book is divided into two sections: the first is made up of women's responses to and analysis of events as they unfolded, from 12 September 2001 to 8 March 2002; the second contains longer analytical pieces, many of which frame their analysis within deeply personal reflections and experiences. A number of the articles appearing in Part Two (those by Lentin, Abdo, Accad, Akhter, Bell, Hawthorne and Winter) have been written especially for the book.

In tracing the chronology of events as seen through feminist eyes, Part One takes up the key questions raised within the pieces included therein: "Whose Terrorism?" (12 September to 7 October: the day the USA started bombing Afghanistan), "Whose War?" (8 October to 13 November, the day Northern Alliance troops entered Kabul), and "Whose Peace?" (14 November to 8 March 2002). It is logical that the chronology of feminist responses should end on International Women's Day, and fitting that the women's day message that closes Part One should be delivered by RAWA.

The pieces in Part One were written by women from many different national, cultural and professional backgrounds. They come from countries as far apart, and as different, as Uganda and the Philippines, as Aotearoa

---

2   Enloe's book *Bananas, Beaches and Bases: Making Feminist Sense of International Politics* (1989) was a groundbreaking work in feminist international relations. Along with *Does Khaki Become You?* (1983), *Bananas, Beaches and Bases* demonstrated how both international politics and the military are gendered, and that, far from being at the periphery of international politics, women are central to its dynamics.

(New Zealand) and India. The pieces come from journalists, academics, feminist activists, writers, publishers, politicians, human rights workers, and a woman who simply identifies herself as a widow. Amber Amundson, widow of a member of the US military who died in the Pentagon attack on September 11, calls on her country's government not to use her husband's death and those of others to justify actions of violence and hatred, and on the responsibility of US leaders to be a force for peace, not for war.

Her call for peace, and for resistance to acts of violence by the US state, echoes throughout the pieces appearing in Part One. Many of them were first published in newspapers and magazines, including feminist media (such as Carol Anne Douglas' piece "A World Where Justice Brings Peace", first published in the US radical feminist monthly *off our backs*, and statements by Women Living Under Muslim Laws, reproduced in the feminist media in a number of countries). Others, like Theresa Wolfwood's "Resistance is Creative" and Sunera Thobani's "It's Bloodthirsty Vengeance", were first delivered as speeches. Many, many pieces first appeared as communiqués or personal reflections posted to feminist e-mail discussion lists such as Ausfem-Polnet or Diverse Women for Diversity, or on various feminist or antiwar websites. Other pieces were originally submissions to national governments or to the UN: Rigoberta Menchú Tum's letter to President Bush, the Federation of Uganda Business Women's letter to Kofi Annan, Tahmeena Faryal's submission on behalf of RAWA before a subcommittee of the US Congress, and the letter from the Women's International League for Peace and Freedom to the Labor Party Opposition in the Australian parliament to urge a vote against the government's Anti-Terrorism Bill.

A number of pieces were written by feminist organisations: RAWA, GABRIELA, Women Living Under Muslim Laws, Bat Shalom, The Federation of Uganda Business Women, the Union of Australian Women, the Women's International League for Peace and Freedom, Women Making Peace, Diverse Women for Diversity. Others were collectively written by groups of individuals who came together for the purpose of making a statement, such as the Transnational Feminist Statement Against the War and the Delhi Women's Petition.

Many feminists got severe flak for speaking out. Sunera Thobani was one of them. She came under attack in Canada following her speech to a women's meeting, "It's Bloodthirsty Vengeance", denouncing US foreign policy following September 11. These attacks included investigation by the Canadian police for "a potential violation of Section 319 of the Canada Criminal Code —inciting hatred against an identifiable group". No formal charges were made, however. Those vilifying Thobani on racial and gendered grounds in the Canadian media were not investigated. Nor were those (including some academics) who called for her dismissal from her tenure-track position at the University of British Columbia and subsequent barring from holding tenure at a Canadian university. There was immediate and widespread international support for Thobani, with petitions and messages of protest defending her right to speak out and defending academic freedom.

But feminists will always get flak for speaking out, because, as Diane Bell writes in her article "Good and Evil: At Home and Abroad", feminists excel in asking "awkward questions"—the questions no-one else will ask, let alone attempt to answer. Practically all the contributions in this book both ask and answer those questions. They make, explicitly or implicitly, connections between war and masculinism, and, conversely, between feminism and peace. As many contributors to this book, such as Judith Ezekiel, Carol Anne Douglas, Ronit Lentin and Bronwyn Winter, point out, this does not mean that men are "naturally" warmongering or women are "naturally" peaceful. Such biologising arguments are not a useful means of addressing political questions. When we, and the contributors to this book, use the terms "masculinity" and "masculinism", we use them as political concepts. And, as Cynthia Enloe cogently argues in her contribution, "Masculinity [is] a foreign policy issue", militarisation is a key element in the male supremacist construction of masculinity. Although, like Valentine M. Moghadam's article, Enloe's piece was written prior to the events of September 11, it is an appropriate introduction to Part Two of the book. In retrospect, it appears to be a prophetic warning against the extreme militarisation of US society and politics that has occurred since September 11, 2001.

While Enloe discusses the way in which masculinity is implicated in foreign policy, Moghadam traces the impact internationally of masculinism as well as many of the feminist resistances to it over the past thirty years. Catharine A. MacKinnon draws parallels between the casualties of war and the casualties of women during so-called peace time. Susan Hawthorne notes that we are "caught in the same old mythic pattern" of men struggling for power among themselves. Similar analyses come out in the immediate responses to September 11 and the escalation of violence through war (Susanne Martain, Kalpana Sharma, Zelda D'Aprano, Jennie Ruby, Nikki Craft).

Within and alongside this broad theme of linking war and masculinity, the contributors to the book make many other connections, such as those between the events of September 11 and aftermath and other events occurring in the world. The Middle East conflict in particular has come to feature strongly in many of the contributions written expressly for the book, which appear in Part Two. Nahla Abdo's "Eurocentrism, Orientalism and Essentialism", Ronit Lentin's "Feminist Snapshots from the Edge" and Evelyne Accad's "The Phallus of September 11", all draw connections between September 11 and the Middle East crisis, on which they primarily focus, as does Bronwyn Winter's "Who Will Mourn on October 7?"

Many of the pieces in Part One and practically all of the articles in Part Two connect war and global capitalism. Karen Talbot's article in particular details the pursuit of increased oil profits in the wars the USA has engaged in since 1990. With the bugbear of communism gone, security of oil supply and profits have taken over as justifications for aggression. The connection between the pursuit of profit and the pursuit of war is a theme developed in many of the contributions in Part One (Vandana Shiva, Theresa Wolfwood, Susan Hawthorne, Jen Couch). The continuing economic colonisation of so-called Third World countries and the double standards applied to the citizens of the Third World is explored by Urvashi Butalia and Mythily Sivaraman, while yet others speak of racism and the demonisation of Islam.

Several authors comment on the way in which the media has represented both the events and the commentary (Madeleine Bunting, Ameena A. Saeed, Naomi Klein, Cynthia Peters, Diane Bell).

The women of Afghanistan, their victimisation, their liberation and the silencing of their voices, is a theme that arises in many of the articles, from RAWA's outspoken stance to pieces which describe life experiences in Afghanistan (Janelle Brown, Cilocia Zaidi, Lesley Garner, Anuradha M. Chenoy, Sonali Kolhatkar, Bronwyn Winter).

The range of issues covered by contributors to the volume is an indicator of the interlinking of politics, economics, violence and international relations as they impact on the daily lives of women, whether this is the effect of population control policies pursued by the West at the expense of poor women (Akhter), or whether it is the part played by Western consumerism in creating demand for cheap products (including oil) form the colonised world (Klein, Talbot).

Peace is demanded by women from South Korea, Uganda, Israel, Australia, Aotearoa, Pakistan, India, Afghanistan, Palestine, the USA, Canada, the UK, France, Ireland, Lebanon, and many other places torn apart by war or by those horrified at the prospect of war.

Introducing each section in the book are poems written in response to September 11. Patricia Sykes' "Log of Impacts" records her reactions to the events as they happened, and as viewed from the other side of the world. She calls on us to "unpeel terrorism's winding/sheets", and if we do not she wonders "who will provide/the next welcome planet?" Suheir Hammad writes from the midst of the experience as one "born Black, born Palestinian" living in Brooklyn. She frets about the effect events will have on those close to her. She writes: "There is no poetry in this./There are causes and effects./ There are symbols and ideologies,/mad conspiracy here and information we will never know." Ani di Franco muses that "people are just poems/we're 90% metaphor", and we follow her rollercoaster ride through wars from Noah to El Salvador, and we listen for the train, the peace train. Bronwyn Winter's "Dislocations" opens the final section, moving between images of Peshawar "Before The War/Before The World Changed/Before New York realised It Too was Vulnerable" to images of Peshawar and Kabul now and the cities of Afghanistan, cities that "Do not have buildings jobs homes".

In the short weeks before this book goes to press, we are reflecting on our recent impressions of the two cities most centrally involved in the "War on Terror": New York and Kabul. Susan Hawthorne visited New York in May 2002, and Bronwyn Winter visited Kabul in June 2002.

New York, May 2002

New York City in May 2002 still carries the wounds of the attack as if it had been the very first attack in the history of the world. This is not to suggest that the grief is unwarranted, far from it. But the promotion of grief as a commodity for tourists is problematic. There were street stalls selling uncredited photographs to the public, along with instant publishing products, such as one entitled Day of Terror (published in September 2001). The book proclaims that "America will not forget what happened here" (Shangle 2001: 29). And nor should it. Indeed, such a memory should inform its future actions. But what strikes me is that "America", and by that I mean a series of US governments, media organisations and transnational companies, appear to believe that people in other countries do somehow forget the atrocities committed against them in the name of US freedom. Nationalism is rife with US flags hanging from many windows or in the entrances to stores. I saw only one resistance to this phenomenon, a small Palestinian flag stuck to the window of a Brooklyn residence.[3] The tourist shops sell T-shirts with NYPD and FDNY emblazoned across them. At least the T-shirts commemorate the courage of those who went into the World Trade Center soon after the attacks. The same cannot be said for the "Osama bin Laden, Wanted Dead or Alive" posters, which hark back to an era regarded as heroic in the American mainstream, that of colonising the "West" without due regard to its prior habitation by Native Americans (see Judith Ezekiel's article).

Heroism, nationalism, and enormous media push for war, mixed with sentimental emotion, is what is served up to the desperate American public.

---

3 Had I not known the owner of the apartment, the incipient nationalism of the flag would have troubled me as much as did the flying of the US flag. Knowing the owner of the apartment was Jewish, I was struck more by her empathy and courage.

Visiting the USA results in a sense of having landed on the wrong planet, as stories that would get at least some counterweight to them in the media of other democratic countries run unchallenged in the US media. But who can see the missing analyses when one is sitting in the midst of it?

And this is precisely one of the values of *September 11, 2001: Feminist Perspectives*. Enloe and Moghadam signal such analyses with their feminist take on the masculine system which they *can* see because they are not implicated in its maintenance. In addition, the wide range of contributors from many different countries and cultures allows the reader to see the world differently: as Makere Stewart-Harawira from Aotearoa (New Zealand) writes, "I too am a Muslim, a Hindu, an Arab." In this collection writers proclaim in addition, I am a Jew, a Christian, an Indigenous woman, a non-believer and more; but most of all, I am a woman, a feminist.

Kabul, June 2002

I visited Kabul and parts of the surrounding region in June 2002: impressions and thoughts from that experience are included here in my poem "Dislocations" and in the final article in this book, "If Women Really Mattered ...". What struck me time and again in Afghanistan—as well as in the neighbouring North-West Frontier Province of Pakistan on the two occasions I visited it, in March 2000 and June 2002—is that women *don't* really matter. Of course, I did not need to leave Sydney to come to that conclusion. But it is glaringly, painfully, confrontingly obvious in Afghanistan. Men have waged war, devastating a country that miraculously manages to remain magnificent despite the widespread destruction of land and lives. And women and children are left to pick up the pieces.

The rubble of the World Trade Center left a peculiar and tragic hole in a small part of one of the US's major cities. Imagine, then, an entire country that is one big gaping hole. Imagine the whole of the US razed, its buildings blown away, its homes reduced to rubble, its cities gutted, its arable land mined, its water cut off, its people either dead, maimed (physically or emotionally), or riddled with disease. Or if the enormity of this is too much to contemplate, imagine Manhattan. Imagine the theatres of Broadway abandoned and desolate, the Guggenheim and the Met great gutted hangars, Central Park a pile of rubble. Imagine the fine aparments of the Upper East and Upper West Side reduced to broken skeletons. Imagine Brooklyn Bridge blown away and the restaurants and galleries of SoHo, the cafés and bookshops of Greenwich Village, reduced to empty and forlorn little shells of places, like so many ruined cells of ancient monasteries. Imagine the Lower East Side and Alphabet City a sea of UNHCR tents amidst the remains of something that was once a place.

Take these imagined snapshots of devastation and multiply them through-out the country. Then you will begin to have a picture of what Afghanistan is like. Except that Afghanistan started from much lower down the scale, there was so much less there to destroy. And there are far fewer voices raised to protest or arms raised to retaliate. Not to mention the considerable help from within, in pursuing an agenda of belligerence. A much easier job all round.

Our own recent experiences of New York and Kabul, along with conversa-tions we have had in various fora across the world, have reaffirmed our conviction that this book is necessary. They have reaffirmed our conviction that, unless feminist analysis of male violence is taken seriously, there will be no end to war. And women will continue to pay the highest price.

The stories told in *September 11, 2001: Feminist Perspectives* are painful, often tragic. The voices of their authors resonate with sorrow and with anger. But above all, they resonate with the rage and passion of resistance. This gives us great hope.

References

AbuKhalil, As'ad. (2002). *Bin Laden, Islam and America's New "War on Terrorism"*. New York: Seven Stories Press.

Baxter, Jenny and Macolm Downing. Eds. (2001). *The Day that Shook the World: Understanding September 11th*. London/Sydney: BBC Books/ABC Books.

Burbach, Roger and Ben Clarke. Eds. (2002). *September 11 and the US War: Beyond the Curtain of Smoke*. San Francisco: City Lights.

Chomsky, Noam. (2001). *September 11*. Sydney: Allen and Unwin.

Enloe, Cynthia. (1983). *Does Khaki Become You? The Militarisation of Women's Lives*. London: Pluto Press.

——. (1989). *Bananas, Beaches and Bases: Making Feminist Sense of International Politics*. London: Pandora.

Morgan, Robin. (1989). *Demon Lover: The Sexuality of Terrorism*. New York: W. W. Norton & Company.

——. (2001). *The Demon Lover: The Roots of Terrorism*. London: Piatkus.

Parenti, Michael. (2002). *The Terrorism Trap: September 11 and Beyond*. San Francisco: City Lights.

Salusinszky, Imre and Gregory Melleuish. Eds. (2002). *Blaming Ourselves: September 11 and the Agony of the Left*. Sydney: Duffy and Snellgrove.

Shangle, Robert D. (2002). *Day of Terror: September 11, 2001*. Beaverton, OR: American Products Publishing Company.

Sharma, Kaplana, Ammu Joseph and Ritu Menon. Eds. (2002). *Femininist Perspectives on War and Violence*. New Delhi: Kali for Women.

Talbott, Strobe and Chanda, Nayan. (2001). *The Age of Terror: America and the World after September 11*. New York: Basic Books and the Yale Center for the Study of Globalization.

"What We Think of America." *Granta 77*, Spring 2002.

Zinn, Howard. (2002). *Terrorism and War*. New York: Seven Stories Press.

PART ONE

REACTIONS

Whose Terrorism?

12 September to 7 October

Patricia Sykes

Log of Impacts: As It Happened

1 September 11, 2001, southern hemisphere

light explodes inside the skull
do hours weep?   these ones are grey

shocked off-course like whales
forced off their migrations

the eyes of witness can save
nothing   nor their hands

unpeel terrorism's winding
sheets   is it possible

to still save the moon?
fuel-soaked

the death cloths
give rise to suspicion

of each incognito breath
faces interrogate the mirror

shoes do not care
where they were born

it is feet that drive the flags
as now they turn the clock

from year of the snake
to year of *infinite justice*

2 *fractured dawn*

the New York skyline smoke-plumed
like a Nostradamus prediction

a terror loose as ash   the take
after take of two hijacked

jets thrusting their suicide murders
into trade's glittering towers

the gross hunger of replay
like a magnet to disbelief

bodies plummet and plummet
as the stock markets will

this is gravity
the horror of pity

makes its own descent
in the space of a week

relics will entrepreneur
a tee shirt recovery

3 *aurora borealis*

electricity cannot do it
grief is wholly alight

in votive candles
technology's primitive fire

its tapers of wax
sealing their sad tributes

as hope's eternal blister
keeps mouth room

for the missing
to arrive from the rubble

like miracles sniffed out
by stressed dogs

or barely alive in the arms
of firefighters

who take time out to weep
legions of love burn here

out of this a world
agitates for tooth and claw

can candle wax
be so flammable?

4 confetti

a byline offering up a *poetry*
of paper   the brutal fact

of its bountiful survival
above the vapourised:

the bodies the concrete
the glass the asbestos

the specks of steel more like
evidence than structure

it's the way of words to insist
on living longer than the tongue

the ash holds these   the body
bags inflate with absence

or yield up parts as in a single hand
its nails bitten to the quick

like presentiment its fingers
gesturing towards a future

pared to loss
as faith buys allies

against a man accused
of more than *gentle eyes*

5 the four corners

meeting at the lip
the death toll as envelope

80-odd nations as *family of man*
joined in capital

no global flowers were
and no days of mourning

for the Rawandas the East
Timors the etceteras

as if blood leaps truest
for higher fidelities

the efficiency of ties
rewards us   we melt

each other on the tongue
of a dreadful communion

to fly now is for the birds
and refuge is all at sea

shores are withdrawing
and withdrawing

who will provide
the next welcome planet?

Robin Morgan

New York City: The Day After

12 September 2001

Dear Sisters and Friends,

Forgive the mass e-mailing of this letter, but in this situation it seems more important to get some personal, basic lower-Manhattan news/impressions to you all than take the time to reply one-on-one to each of your many, many, moving e-mails. I've received e-mails and phone calls from women in 18 different countries over the last 24 hours—from South Africa to Jordan, Malaysia to Brazil, Nepal to Canada, Australia to the Caribbean, The Philippines to Peru, all across Europe and the US—and from the West Bank and the Gaza Strip. I also know that many of you tried to telephone all day yesterday but couldn't get through—although e-mail seems to be working even when the land-phone lines are clogged; cell-phones have been working only erratically.

First, thank you from my heart for all your thoughts, concerns, invitations to come stay with you, expressions of sadness, solidarity, and political anxiety. So many, many of you have astonishingly cited my book *The Demon Lover* as the essential expression/analysis of what has just happened (as well as the background and underlying conflicts) that even in the midst of deep sorrow and grief you have renewed my belief that art, an attempted clarity of thought, and a stubborn politics of transformation do make a contribution, make a difference. But so far, as we know all too hideously, not enough.

I am well and safe, as are those dearest to me. (I've also been in touch with dear friends who were in transit around the US, who are safe, though some stranded in hotels and airports.) Here in Greenwich Village we are, as many of you worried, in lower Manhattan, but north—about a mile and a half—of the catastrophic area. We have electric power, water, the basics. Friends who live(d) much closer to it staggered here yesterday morning, covered with ash, shaking with fear, and spent the day and last night here. It is bizarre that my city garden is untouched by all this: late summer roses blossoming, finches singing, vegetables ready to harvest. But you can hear fighter jets overhead now and then. From my street corner, looking south down Seventh Avenue, I had a clear view of both towers; I went out yesterday morning and saw the first tower burning—and actually stood there watching while the second plane hit the second tower; later on, I stood and watched the first tower collapse with my own eyes. It strikes one as totally surreal— as if Hollywood had produced yet another special-effects blockbuster. This morning early I went for a walk, looked down Seventh Avenue and saw nothing but massive billows of smoke—no towers anymore.

The city is holding together superbly; New Yorkers rise to such an occasion like the British did during the blitz. I live only one and a half blocks from St Vincent's Hospital—which is the closest triage center to the disaster—so all day yesterday and last night the ambulances have been wailing; that and the planes overhead remind me of the sounds of Beirut at the height of the war there. All streets and avenues below Fourteenth Street (for those of you who know New York City) have been cleared of all traffic, but evacuation has been enforced only for those below Canal Street. (Both *Ms Magazine* and the Ms Foundation for Women have offices below Canal, not far from the site itself—and were evacuated with all hands now accounted for; thanks to those of you who expressed concern for them. As for me, I live below Fourteenth but above Canal.) You can walk right down the middle of major lower Manhattan avenues with only emergency vehicles whizzing by now and then. People are volunteering all over the city, very touchingly; those of us near St Vincent's Hospital have brought homemade food and coffee and cold drinks to the workers and the people milling about hoping for news of lost relatives. There's a doctors' conference in town, by fortunate coincidence—so a great many MDs have responded to hospitals' calls for help, even more have shown up apparently than the emergency rooms can use; same with nurses. Yesterday and last night I tried to give blood but there were by formal count over 1000 people lined up ahead of me, with an estimated 7-hour wait, so I decided to try again in a day or two. The infrastructure of the city is holding extraordinarily well: subways and busses are already running again (though not south, near the site itself); there was a brief run on the banks and food stores but that seems to have passed. (Personally, I'm supplied enough even to be able to help others; have garden vegetables growing plus leftover Y2K water, candles, and canned goods—but that seems probably unnecessary.) No food shortages have been felt—yet—but since many bridges and tunnels and other approaches to Manhattan are closed or limited except for emergency vehicles, that may change. Still, people are calm, helping one another, not panicking—though they're clearly in a state of disbelief. I personally know three people who apparently have lost friends or family— ordinary folks, secretaries, working in the twin towers. It's the stories about people hunkered down at the back of the hijacked planes, whispering into their cell phones "I love you" one last time, that bring tears. It's the children who will lose/have lost parents who especially crack one's heart. The hospitals are now announcing that they are concerned—had expected thousands of emergency cases but are treating only hundreds—which means more fatalities than injuries. Emergency morgues are now being set up in ten locations around Manhattan. Already known dead approaches 1000—mostly firefighters, emergency personnel, and police. Apparently 800 died in the Pentagon attack, and the passenger manifests of the four planes add another almost 300. It appears that there will be massive fatalities, easily topping Pearl Harbor's 2500.

The site itself has rubble as deep as 100 feet high, with breakaway fires still burning, some underground, making rescue of those trapped even more difficult, especially since the twin towers foundation went down 70 feet below ground and, apparently, people are still trapped there, calling out on cell-phones. It sears the brain just to think about it. Good news: six fire-fighters have just been pulled from the rubble ...

This morning the National Guard arrived—and on my dawn walk I could just as well have been walking through a military state: police, state troopers, and emergency personnel on every corner below Fourteenth Street, with trucks filled with Guardsmen, rifles bayoneted and at ready, beginning to roll through the streets. Since this area is uptown from the site itself, you can imagine how tight security is closer to the World Trade Center. We must be calm but truly vigilant, since in such a time of crisis, the danger of a turn to the extreme Right is genuinely real. The press continues to roll, though no newspapers could be delivered below Fourteenth Street. Where I am, we've been fortunate, in that the winds have been prevailing to blow the dense smoke southeast out to sea—so although we could see the smoke plumes, there has been no stench or fallout of concrete or contaminants in my immediate vicinity. But just now the wind changed, and a smell like burning rubber or electrical wire pervades Greenwich Village.

Media coverage has been nonstop, and relatively cautious to avoid rumors (especially in the wake of misreporting the election results last year). As of this morning (first day "after") the expectable patriotic blabber and religious jargon had started, along with pundits and politicians issuing media clichés about "beginning the healing process" and seeking "closure". Maddeningly, there have been frequently repeated airings of film clips of some Palestinian men in West Bank celebrating the attack with laughter, dancing, and V-signs—but unfortunately there have *not* been as frequently repeated press airings of Palestinian leaders, Arab leaders, and leaders of the Arab American community deploring it; equal time has *not* been given; only once in 24 hours have I heard major media announce the official statement of the Muslim community in the US that heatedly denounced the attack. But there *has* been heartening journalistic comment—including from the mayor of New York City—warning against bigoted responses to this tragedy.

As those of you with whom I've managed to speak know, in fact, that has been one of my great worries, because a few years ago, in the 48 hours after the Oklahoma City bombing (before it was discovered that the perpetrator was a white Christian right-wing male) three Arab Americans were lynched in the Midwest of the US. Already, mosques are being defaced and Internet chatrooms spewing hate against "all Arabs". We (feminists, progressives, etc.) are doing everything we can to avoid this kind of escalating nightmare— and a network of safe houses is already being set up to shelter and help innocent Arab or Muslim civilians who might be persecuted in the wake of this tragedy. This morning I was touched to learn that the Pagan and Wiccan community is doing the same thing, in the name of religious freedom from persecution. We are also trying to organize a press conference of support— but whether that will be covered or not is questionable, given the major news that breaks every hour or so.

Politically—well, it's too early to say, of course. But some things can be hypothesized. It may be heartening that this disaster might deter Bush's star wars anti-missile fantasy—since, as so many of us have said for so long, *this* kind of attack, not missiles, is the real twenty-first century threat (and it was amazingly "low-tech": ceramic knives, commercial flights, three to five men ready to die for a cause: simple). Furthermore (despite the expectable "let's all stand together behind our president" rhetoric) general press analysis plus public reaction seems fairly critical of Bush's handling so far, noting (1) Bush's policy of withdrawal from Mideast peace process talks, (2) Bush's adminis-tration having ignored warnings three weeks ago of a major "unprecedented" attack to come, and (3) Bush being incapable of projecting leadership or even a sense of basic competence. In talking with colleagues in feminist leadership, a number of us have noted that for years we've tried everything to get the US to move forcibly against the Taliban, given the literal attempted genocide of women and girls in today's Afghanistan—and each time we've been impeded by the powerful boys of Big Oil—who care only for their beloved pipelines. Perhaps this may finally make a difference.

As I write this, news breaks that the FBI has picked up possible "suspects" in Florida and in Boston ... but that kind of story you will hear or read as it evolves, in your own press, or if you can access CNN, where you are.

So I will sign off for now. Feel free to share this communiqué with your own networks. I trust with all my heart that you will each do all you possibly can in your own countries, cities, and situations to educate people as to *why* this kind of tragedy happens—that it is *not* just "madmen" or "monsters" or "subhuman maniacs" who commit dramatic violence, but that such acts occur in a daily climate of patriarchal violence so epidemic as to be invisible in its normality—and that such tactics as this attack come from a complex set of circumstances, including despair over not being heard any other way; desperation over long-term, even generational, suffering; calcification of sympathy for "the other"; callousing of sensibilities, blatant economic and political injustice, tribal/ethnic hatreds and fears, religious fundamentalisms, and especially the eroticization and elevation of violence as a form of "manhood" and "solution." Violence *is* psychosis—but it's a psychosis that contemporary incumbent leaders of most nations share with their insurgent opponents.

Even as we mourn, we somehow must continue to dare audaciously to envision and revision a different way, a way out of this savage age, to a time when our species will look back and gasp, recoiling at its own former barbarism. Even as we weep, we must somehow reorganize to reaffirm our capacity to change the world, each other, and ourselves—to insist, even in the teeth of despair, on a politics that is possible and necessary: a politics not of Thanatos and death, but of Eros and joy. I send each of you my gratitude and my deep affection.

Robin Morgan

Revolutionary Association of the Women of Afghanistan

Afghani Women's Resistance Organization: Bin Laden Is Not Afghanistan

14 September 2001

On September 11, 2001 the world was stunned with the horrific terrorist attacks on the United States. RAWA stands with the rest of the world in expressing our sorrow and condemnation for this barbaric act of violence and terror. RAWA had already warned that the United States should not support the most treacherous, most criminal, most anti-democracy and anti-women Islamic fundamentalist parties because after both the Jihadi and the Taliban have committed every possible type of heinous crimes against our people, they would feel no shame in committing such crimes against the American people whom they consider "infidel". In order to gain and maintain their power, these barbaric criminals are ready to turn easily to any criminal force.

But unfortunately we must say that it was the government of the United States who supported Pakistani dictator General Zia-ul Haq in creating thousands of religious schools from which the germs of Taliban emerged. In the similar way, as is clear to all, Osama Bin Laden has been the blue-eyed boy of CIA. But what is more painful is that American politicians have not drawn a lesson from their pro-fundamentalist policies in our country and are still supporting this or that fundamentalist band or leader. In our opinion any kind of support to the fundamentalist Taliban and Jihadis is actually trampling democratic, women's rights and human rights values.

If it is established that the suspects of the terrorist attacks are outside the US, our constant claim that fundamentalist terrorists would devour their creators, is proved once more.

The US government should consider the root cause of this terrible event, which has not been the first and will not be the last one too. The US should stop supporting Afghan terrorists and their supporters once and for all.

Now that the Taliban and Osama are the prime suspects by the US officials after the criminal attacks, will the US subject Afghanistan to a military attack similar to the one in 1998 and kill thousands of innocent Afghans for the crimes committed by the Taliban and Osama? Does the US think that through such attacks, with thousands of deprived, poor and innocent people of Afghanistan as its victims, will be able to wipe out the root-cause of terrorism, or will it spread terrorism even to a larger scale?

From our point of view a vast and indiscriminate military attack on a country that has been facing permanent disasters for more than two decades will not be a matter of pride. We don't think such an attack would be the expression of the will of the American people.

The US government and people should know that there is a vast difference between the poor and devastated people of Afghanistan and the terrorist Jihadi and Taliban criminals.

While we once again announce our solidarity and deep sorrow with the people of the US, we also believe that attacking Afghanistan and killing its most ruined and destitute people will not in any way decrease the grief of the American people. We sincerely hope that the great American people could *differentiate* between the people of Afghanistan and a handful of fundamentalist terrorists. Our hearts go out to the people of the US.

Down with terrorism!

Please circulate this statement.

Kathleen Barry

Non-Selective Compassion

14 September 2001

To say that we are one in spirit, interconnected in being means right now that we are one with the victims of the Tuesday attack, one with the grieving families. Moreover, if there is a lesson for us as Americans to be learned from this attack it is that we must be one with those who are the victims of US bombing and US-sponsored attacks on human life throughout the world.

We are now given a special opportunity to transform the raw grief we feel, our own vulnerability being under attack within our own country, our own fears, our sense of terror that there may be other strikes—we don't know where, we don't know when. For we are experiencing the very grief, the same fear, the unknown terror that is the daily life experience of everyday people in Palestine, in Iraq, whose terror is supported by the US, in Northern Ireland and in Israel, and other places where bombing and shooting are everyday events. We now have the opportunity to exit from American isolation and from our own pain and in our own grief to identify with those victims, those families who suffer from loss, repeatedly at US hands, from other male-dominated aggressors.

When we look at the lines of people with photographs of loved ones held to their hearts, looking and waiting for word, hoping for life, we can immediately be reminded of the mothers of the "disappeared" who carried those pictures for years, in Argentina and in Chile after the bloody US-sponsored coup that set up the vicious dictator, Pinochet, or in Guatemala, in East Timor and many other countries.

And when we take this next step in our grief, from our own fears and pain, we will become intolerant of any act of terror, state sponsored or para-militaries, or individual. When we are intolerant of terror we will have to call upon our government as we did during the war in Vietnam to cease and desist—not only its plans for revenge attacks, but its own state-sponsored terror. Only then will we begin to heal, for we can only heal together as one.

This is the lesson I have learned from this week's attack. I send it on to you in the hope that it makes sense, as I look for any evidence of like-minded consciousness from which we can begin, once again, to make change. Please share this as you see fit.

Love and peace,

Kathleen Barry
Santa Rosa, California

Candlelight Vigil for Restraint and Peace

19 September 2001

Friends

We are shocked and pained by the recent terrorist violence in the US in which thousands of innocent people belonging to many nationalities and religions died. We were equally shocked and pained in the past when some other countries attacked, bombed or starved thousands of innocent people in different parts of the world. Like millions of others, we feel this spiral of violence and terrorism of all kinds must stop. But we are horrified to see and hear the language of war and hatred being used by the US and many other governments. Preparations seem to be going on for an all-out war against nations and religious groups, even before anyone knows conclusively who was behind the attacks in the US. As a result of this kind of unrestrained official reaction, killing of innocent people has already started in the US.

We feel war and retaliatory violence are not the answer to terrorism, as they have never resolved any conflict. This incident should not be used as an excuse for increased militarization and more business for the weapons industry. The Indian Government should also exercise caution and not commit India to any US initiated military action. We believe, what we need, at this moment is restraint, reflection and all round condemnation of violence, terrorism, militarization, intolerance and hatred.

To express our grief at violence and death and to demand peace we are organizing a Candlelight Vigil on 19th September at 1730 (5.30 p.m.) at India Gate (entry from Copernicus Marg side).

Do join us with candles, banners and placards on peace, for peace.

Action India, AIDWA, Akhil Bharat Rachnatmak Samaj, Ankur, Anuradha Chenoy, Association of People's of Asia, Bindia Thapar, Brinda Singh, Guild of Service, Indian Social Action Forum (INSAF), Jagori, Joint Womens' Programme, Kali for Women, Kamal Chenoy, Lawyers Collective, Mahila Chetna Kendra, Muslim Women's Forum, Nirantar, Nirmala Deshpande, North East Network, PEACE, Radical Humanist Association, SAHMAT, South Asian Network of Gender Activists and Trainers (SANGAT), Women's

Coalition for Peace and Development with Dignity, Women's Initiative for Peace in South Asia (WIPSA).

(These are the organizations and persons who have already expressed their support for this vigil. Many more are expected to support and participate.)

PS: It will be very good if friends in other parts of India and South Asia can organize similar vigils, preferably on the same day and time. Do inform us if you are able to do anything.

Susanne Martain

Rancid Social Soup

18 September 2001

"God continues to lift the curtain and allow the enemies of America to give us probably what we deserve," said Falwell ...

whose side is god—now a terrorist mastermind—working on then this supports osama bin l's statements that god is against usa chrisendom/jewry/? and is siding with not islam but sharia law ie misogyny to the max not classed but most definately gendered

cant see the goddess in any of this whilst transcontinental willy jousting prevails locally women are being tortured raped and murdered—generationally only the depth varies around the globe

isnt there something that will calm an aggressor ie treat it as if it was a family issue—maybe siblings fighting
—no intention of murdering/or harming anyone
—no depleted uranium in their wheaties
—no land mines in the bathroom
—no napalm dropped on their room

what would each do what outcomes are immediately/longterm best practice is there any common ground is it possible for humanity to stop spilling its own blood including women and men killing themselves, each other or their children a vet would firstly tranquilise the aggressive then tend to their needs

democracy has failed the peoples—everywhere
it is but a blanket
—to throw over primary votes
—to throw over dissent
—to colonise others—geographically—socially—economically ...
—for capital and government to walk on so they dont stain their shoes with the lives of the peoples

—to throw over the corporates as they rapidly stockpile even more of the planet's resources/first peoples' existence just for profit

what is possible in this rancid social soup
where is all the money coming from to fund the global military response/support
why wasnt that spent on resolving what brings this level of desperation/hatred about

government is in the process of becoming a privatised democracy
this structure has produced the only "business" that doesnt think assets are an asset
—does anyone have schedules of public assets and details of their acquisition depreciation disposal?
—prior to public privatisaton—this behaviour was know in the corporate as "bottom of the harbour"

meanwhile locally
—it mainly means an increase in aggressively posturing males now split by more than their cricket/football team
—women and children begin to suffer an increase in domestic misogynist war crimes
—stereotype rules on the streets as well as in decision making places

peoples need to find the brakes

in hope
susanne

Robin Morgan

Week One: Ghosts and Echoes

19 September 2001

Dear Friends,

Your response to the e-mail I sent on Day 2 of this calamity has been over-whelming. In addition to friends and colleagues, absolute strangers—in Serbia, Korea, Fiji, Zambia, all across North America—have replied, as have women's networks in places ranging from Senegal and Japan to Chile, Hong Kong, Saudi Arabia, even Iran. You've offered moving emotional support and asked for continued updates. I can't send regular reports/alerts as I did during the elections last November or the cabinet confirmation battles last year. But here's another try. Share this letter as you wish.

I'll focus on New York—my firsthand experience—but this doesn't mean any less anguish for the victims of the Washington or Pennsylvania calam-ities. Today was Day 8. Incredibly, a week has passed. Abnormal normalcy has settled in. Our usually contentious mayor (previously bad news for New Yorkers of color and for artists) has risen to this moment with efficiency, compassion, real leadership. The city is alive and dynamic. Below Fourteenth Street, traffic is flowing again, mail is being delivered, newspapers are back. But very early this morning I walked east, then south almost to the tip of Manhattan Island. The 16-acre site itself is closed off, of course, as is a perimeter surrounding it controlled by the National Guard, used as a com-mand post and staging area for rescue workers. Still, one is able to approach nearer to the area than was possible last weekend, since the law-court district and parts of the financial district are now open and (shakily) working. The closer one gets the more one sees—and smells—what no TV report, and very few print reports, have communicated. I find myself giving way to tears again and again, even as I write this.

If the first sights of last Tuesday seemed bizarrely like a George Lucas special-effects movie, now the directorial eye has changed: it's the grim lens of Agnes Varda, juxtaposed with images so surreal they could have been framed by Bunuel or Kurosawa.

This was a bright, cloudless, early autumnal day. But as one draws near the site, the area looms out of a dense haze: one enters an atmosphere of dust, concrete powder, and plumes of smoke from fires still raging deep beneath the rubble (an estimated 2 million cubic yards of debris). Along lower Second Avenue, ten refrigerator tractor-trailer trucks are parked, waiting; if you stand there a while, an NYC Medical Examiner van arrives—with a sagging body bag. Thick white ash, shards of broken glass, pebbles, and chunks of concrete cover street after street of parked cars for blocks outside the perimeter. Handprints on car windows and doors—handprints sliding downward—have been left like frantic graffiti. Sometimes there are messages finger-written in the ash: "U R Alive." You can look into closed shops, many with cracked or broken windows, and peer into another dimension: a wall-clock stopped at 9:10, restaurant tables meticulously set but now covered with two inches of ash, grocery shelves stacked with cans and produce bins piled high with apples and melons—all now powdered chalk-white. A moonscape of plenty. People walk unsteadily along these streets, wearing nosemasks against the still particle-full air, the stench of burning wire and plastic, erupted sewage; the smell of death, of decomposing flesh.

Probably your TV coverage shows the chain-link fences aflutter with yellow ribbons, the makeshift shrines of candles, flowers, scribbled notes of mourning or of praise for the rescue workers that have sprung up everywhere—especially in front of firehouses, police stations, hospitals. What TV doesn't show you is that near Ground Zero the streets for blocks around are still, a week later, adrift in bits of paper—singed, torn, sodden pages: stock reports, trading print-outs, shreds of appointment calendars, half of a "to-do" list. What TV doesn't show you are scores of tiny charred corpses now swept into the gutters. Sparrows. Finches. They fly higher than pigeons, so they would have exploded outward, caught midair in a rush of flame, wings on fire as they fell. Who could have imagined it: the birds were burning.

From a distance, you can see the lattices of one of the Towers, its skeletal bones the sole remains, eerily beautiful in asymmetry, as if a new work of abstract art had been erected in a public space. Elsewhere, you see the trans-formation of institutions: The New School and New York University are missing persons' centers. A movie house is now a rest shelter, a Burger King a first-aid center, a Brooks Brothers clothing store, a body parts morgue, a record shop a haven for lost animals. Libraries are counseling centers. Ice rinks are morgues. A bank is now a supply depot: in the first four days, it distributed 11,000 respirators and 25,000 pairs of protective gloves and suits. Nearby, a mobile medical unit housed in a McDonald's has administered 70,000 tetanus shots. The brain tries to process the numbers: "only" 50,000 tons of debris had been cleared by yesterday, out of 1.2 million tons. The medical examiner's office has readied up to 20,000 DNA tests for unidentifiable cadaver parts. At all times, night and day, a minimum of 1000 people live and work on the site.

Such numbers daze the mind. It's the details—fragile, individual—that melt numbness into grief. An anklet with "Joyleen" engraved on it—found on an ankle. Just that: an ankle. A pair of hands—one brown, one white—clasped together. Just that. No wrists. A burly welder who drove from Ohio to help, saying softly, "We're working in a cemetery. I'm standing in—not on, in—a graveyard." Each lamppost, storefront, scaffolding, mailbox, is plastered with homemade photocopied posters, a racial/ethnic rainbow of faces and names: death the great leveler, not only of the financial CEOs—their images usually formal, white, male, older, with suit-and-tie—but the mailroom workers, receptionists, waiters. You pass enough of the missing posters and the faces, names, descriptions become familiar. The Albanian window-cleaner guy with the bushy eyebrows. The teenage Mexican dishwasher who had an American flag tattoo. The janitor's assistant who'd emigrated from Ethiopia. The Italian-American grandfather who was a doughnut-cart tender. The 23-year-old Chinese American junior pastry chef at the Windows on the World restaurant who'd gone in early that day so she could prep a business breakfast for 500. The firefighter who'd posed jauntily wearing his green shamrock necktie. The dapper African-American midlevel manager with a small gold ring in his ear who handled "minority affairs" for one of the companies. The middle-aged secretary laughing up at the camera from her wheelchair. The maintenance worker with a Polish name, holding his newborn baby. Most of the faces are smiling; most of the shots are family photos; many are recent wedding pictures ...

I have little national patriotism, but I do have a passion for New York, partly for our gritty, secular energy of endurance, and because the world does come here: 80 countries had offices in the Twin Towers; 62 countries lost citizens in the catastrophe; an estimated 300 of our British cousins died, either in the planes or the buildings. My personal comfort is found not in ceremonies or prayer services but in watching the plain, truly heroic (a word usually misused) work of ordinary New Yorkers we take for granted every day, who have risen to this moment unpretentiously, too busy even to notice they're expressing the splendor of the human spirit: firefighters, medical aides, nurses, ER doctors, police officers, sanitation workers, construction-workers, ambulance drivers, structural engineers, crane operators, rescue worker "tunnel rats" ...

Meanwhile, across the US, the rhetoric of retaliation is in full-throated roar. Flag sales are up. Gun sales are up. Some radio stations have banned playing John Lennon's song, "Imagine." Despite appeals from all officials (even Bush), mosques are being attacked, firebombed; Arab Americans are hiding their children indoors; two murders in Arizona have already been categorized as hate crimes—one victim a Lebanese-American man and one a Sikh man who died merely for wearing a turban. (Need I say that there were not nationwide attacks against white Christian males after Timothy McVeigh was apprehended for the Oklahoma City bombing?)

Last Thursday, right-wing televangelists Jerry Falwell and Pat Robertson (our home-grown American Taliban leaders) appeared on Robertson's TV show "The 700 Club", where Falwell blamed "the pagans, and the abortionists, and the feminists and the gays and lesbians ... the American Civil Liberties Union, People for the American Way" and groups "who have tried to secularize America" for what occurred in New York. Robertson replied, "I totally concur." After even the Bush White House called the remarks "inappropriate", Falwell apologized (though he did not take back his sentiments); Robertson hasn't even apologized. (The program is carried by the Fox Family Channel, recently purchased by the Walt Disney Company—in case you'd like to register a protest.)

The sirens have lessened. But the drums have started. Funeral drums. War drums. A State of Emergency, with a call-up of 50,000 reservists to active duty. The Justice Department is seeking increased authority for wider surveillance, broader detention powers, wiretapping of persons (not, as previously, just phone numbers), and stringent press restrictions on military reporting.

And the petitions have begun. For justice but not vengeance. For a reasoned response but against escalating retaliatory violence. For vigilance about civil liberties. For the rights of innocent Muslim Americans. For "bombing" Afghanistan with food and medical parcels, *not* firepower. There will be the expectable peace marches, vigils, rallies ... One member of the House of Representatives—Barbara Lee, Democrat of California, an African American woman—lodged the sole vote in both houses of Congress against giving Bush broadened powers for a war response, saying she didn't believe a massive military campaign would stop terrorism. (She could use letters of support: e-mail her, if you wish, at barbara.lee@mail.house.gov)

Those of us who have access to the media have been trying to get a different voice out. But ours are complex messages with long-term solutions—and this is a moment when people yearn for simplicity and short-term, facile answers.

Still, I urge all of you to write letters to the editors of newspapers, call in to talk radio shows, and, for those of you who have media access—as activists, community leaders, elected or appointed officials, academic experts, whatever—to do as many interviews and TV programs as you can. Use the tool of the Internet. Talk about the root causes of terrorism, about the need to diminish this daily climate of patriarchal violence surrounding us in its state-sanctioned normalcy; the need to recognize people's despair over ever being heard short of committing such dramatic, murderous acts; the need to address a desperation that becomes chronic after generations of suffering; the need to arouse that most subversive of emotions—empathy—for "the other"; the need to eliminate hideous economic and political injustices, to reject all tribal/ethnic hatreds and fears, to repudiate religious fundamentalisms of every kind. Especially talk about the need to understand that we must expose the mystique of violence, separate it from how we conceive of excitement, eroticism, and "manhood"; the need to comprehend that violence differs in degree but is related in kind, that it thrives along a spectrum, as do its effects—from the battered child and raped woman who live in fear to an entire populace living in fear.

Meanwhile, we cry and cry and cry. I don't even know who my tears are for anymore, because I keep seeing ghosts, I keep hearing echoes.

The world's sympathy moves me deeply. Yet I hear echoes dying into silence: the world averting its attention from Rwanda's screams ...

Madeleine Bunting

Women's Voices Silenced in the Enthusiasm for War

20 September 2001, *The Guardian*, London.

Not for over a generation has an event so transfixed the world. Everywhere, on buses, at corner shops, offices, school gates and hairdressers, men and women seem able to think and talk of only one thing—the terrorist attacks on America. Yet, what is rapidly becoming clear is that in a crisis like this, many of the gender differences between men and women are thrown into sharp relief. The most striking of these is the different attitudes towards a military attack on Afghanistan as revealed in recent polls. The Guardian's ICM poll on Tuesday showed a remarkable consistency of attitudes across age and political affiliation; the one big gap was between men and women: 74 per cent of men support air strikes and only 58 per cent of women. Whereas 55 per cent of men were prepared to contemplate war, 32 per cent of women opposed any military action if it meant war.

This isn't a one-off. Polls in both the 1990 Gulf War and the 1999 Kosovo War showed the same gap. In 1990, 61 per cent of men and only 39 per cent of women thought Britain should agree to using British troops to get Iraq to withdraw from Kuwait; nearly half of women (49 per cent) opposed military action. In Kosovo, the gap between men and women narrowed after atrocities against Kosovan Albanians were broadcast: 76 per cent of men were in favour of air strikes and 62 per cent of women. A few days later, after Nato mistakenly bombed a convoy of refugees, women's support for air strikes fell sharply to 56 per cent while men's held steady. Equally intriguing is how women have been wiped off many newspaper pages and television screens. Despite significant advances in the number of women in the media, the crisis has exposed how many of them are in the "softer" areas of news such as features and domestic stories. In a major crisis such as this, virtually all the reporters have been men.

An analysis of the first five pages of five newspapers (the *Sun*, *Daily Mail*, *Guardian*, *Daily Telegraph* and *Times*) on Thursday and Friday, September 14 and 15, bore this out. The *Sun* had no women writing on the crisis on either day compared to their writing about a third of the front of the paper on the previous Friday. Likewise, the *Mail* on the Thursday, but by the Friday, it had shifted to roughly 50/50 across the front pages and comment with a strong human interest emphasis. This was still a steep decline; in comparison the previous Friday was dominated by women reporters (2703 words to men's 874) and comment pages were written entirely by women.

The *Times* and the *Guardian* showed a similar sharp drop in women writing; the former had no women in the first five pages or on the comment page on Friday, and the *Guardian* had only one (1215 words) which represented a sharp drop from the previous week, when women wrote 5850 words. Only the *Telegraph* recorded little change in the number of articles—it was consistently low—although the word count doubled, almost all of which was accounted for by men.

This rough snapshot confirms what editors were becoming increasingly aware of, but attempts to find women to write were often frustrated. It wasn't just a shortage of female diplomatic correspondents—it was across the board. One female novelist, when approached to write a piece, said she was too upset to do so, but male novelists had no such hesitations. The consequence is a curious, lopsided, mutated version of the event in which men have dominated the debate, shaping our understanding of what happened, how it happened and what should happen next. Women have been marginalised in a way which would have seemed barely possible only two weeks ago.

This is reinforced by the impression that virtually all the people involved in handling this crisis are men. It is men who perpetrated this violence and men who organise the response. The power structure is exposed at such times, as the token women slide into the background, leaving war to men. Condoleezza Rice seems to be the one exception. Virtually the only female faces in the media at the moment are the victims; women are cast as passive. The polls, the media coverage, the absence of major women politicians in this crisis, breathe new life into old debates. The polls seem to bear out some of the oldest gender stereotypes about women's tendency to nurture life rather than destroy it. It takes you back to the long-running and unprovable theses about nurture versus nature: how little boys play war games and bomb their Lego buildings while little girls look after babies.

Psychologist Oliver James argues that one persistent difference between the genders across cultures is attitudes towards violence. Women are less interested in it and less likely to be violent, and he points to the fact that, while young women have caught up with their male counterparts on a range of behaviour from drugs to cigarettes, they are dramatically less violent. Women are far more likely to internalise anger in depression, from which they are twice as likely as men to suffer.

Also significant in explaining how men have dominated the coverage, James believes, is the way men are socialised to intellectualise the world, analyse and objectify it, in a bid to emotionally distance themselves and control it. Women, brought up to empathise, have fewer such distancing techniques. As Alice Miles in the *Time*s suggests, for many women the "extent of the horror was in itself a bar to certainty", while men have translated their "outrage into concrete demands".

Women Living Under Muslim Laws

Statement on Attacks in the USA

21 September 2001

The network Women Living Under Muslim Laws (WLUML) wishes to extend its deepest condolences to the aggrieved, their families and the people of America following the crimes against humanity that were committed on 11 September 2001. Our sorrow is particularly heartfelt because many of those linked through the WLUML network have directly experienced terror and the devastation that goes with it. And also because of our links of solidarity with allies in the women's movements and other progressive people in the US.

We know that indiscriminate violence and terrorism by state and non-state actors are a global phenomenon. We are particularly aware of the human cost of terrorism and war frequently perpetrated in the name of religion or belief systems. However we regard all of these as assaults on the principle of respect for civilian life.

Vengeance Is Not Justice

We urge the US and their allies not to pursue fruitless retaliation with military force. The world must focus on transparent investigation and bring the perpetrators to justice under the principles of international law through an appropriate forum such as an International Criminal Court (ICC).

Violence cannot eradicate terrorism. Many people in our communities are deeply distressed by these events but many are at the same time also angered by the poverty and deprivation, injustice and exploitation they experience; they are also angered by domestic and foreign policies that they perceive to be hypocritical. All of this can fuel extreme and violent attitudes. Ending terrorism requires addressing the roots of global inequality.

Misguided Retaliation?

It is WLUML's experience that terrorism in the name of Islam is a transnational force. Politico-religious movements across the world are reinforcing each other through funding, military training, educational exchanges, joint international lobbying, etc. The profound impact on women can be seen, for example, through restrictions on access to education and limitations imposed on freedom of movement as well as changes in family laws that severely curtail women's legal rights.

And yet the current focus of retaliation is against one person and one country. If the US is talking about taking action against "those harbouring terrorists" it should consider that the US and the UK have both become safe havens for those who openly advocate violence against those who do not share their opinions. For example, Anouar Haddam, a leader of the Algerian Islamic Salvation Front, is currently seeking asylum in the US and numerous politico-religious extremists are operating out of the UK. Human rights concepts such as freedom of expression have been misused by some international human rights organisations as well as manipulated by governments and co-opted by politico-religious extremists, thereby giving unwarranted space and credibility to such views. Also Saudi Arabia has been bankrolling extremist madrassahs (seminaries) in Pakistan where many Taliban supporters are being trained. It should be remembered that Bin Laden and the Taliban emerged in the context of Cold War confrontation and the vacuum of its aftermath. Global reaction should not be determined by US political and economic interests alone.

We are concerned that legitimate grief is being exploited as a cover for increased military spending—weapons that are aimed mainly at civilian populations. Such military action will cause further suffering to civilians elsewhere. After twenty years of war, Afghanistan is already destroyed while the intended "targets" have fled. Furthermore, Bin Laden and the Taliban are not Afghanistan.

The Consequences

The demonising of "the other" has already increased, resulting in violent attacks on innocent individuals. Talk of "crusades" is buying into the agenda of the perpetrators, at the risk of world war. Already the situation has given public exposure to previously unheard of fringe groups. And already there have been moves towards sweeping restrictions on civil liberties under the guise of this crisis. In those countries which will bear the brunt of any military action, the space for alternative positions will vanish. People may find themselves forced to make choices which they had no say in formulating. Any military action will destabilise an already unstable and nuclearised region. Women in Muslim countries and communities in particular may suffer the direct impact of militarisation and a potential backlash from politico-religious movements.

Susan Hawthorne

Terrorism, Globalisation, Bio/diversity, Survival: A Feminist Perspective

21 September 2001

I have been thinking the last two weeks about the destruction of the twin towers of the World Trade Center in New York and the Pentagon in Washington. Even more, I have been thinking about the wanton destruction of life which is really the key loss in all of this. Buildings can be rebuilt, lives cannot be revived.

I have been researching globalisation for some years now, and writing my ideas about the connections between feminism, globalisation and biodiversity for a PhD I have completed entitled *Wild Politics* (Spinifex Press, 2002). The research has forced me to rethink a lot of things and it has reinforced some ideas. It has forced me to read economics and consider the different positions of peoples in different parts of the world, and in different social settings in Australia and the wider Western world.

I am truly horrified by the devastation in New York and Washington. I know parts of these cities and know people living there whose shock, grief and loss affects me. But what horrifies me even more is the potential, not for one or two cities and their inhabitants to go up in flames, but the prospect that it could affect huge numbers of people across the world.

I deplore statements such as George W. Bush's "this is the first war of the twenty-first century". Where has he been? Does he see nothing outside his own tiny dominant culture (wealthy, white, male, American) experience? How insulting is his statement to the many thousands who have died in Palestine/Israel, Serbia/Kosovo, Macedonia/Albania, Sierra Leone, Fiji, West/East Timor, Aceh, Ambon, Afghanistan, just to name a few of the places most prominent in violent clashes around the world (although not all have had formal declarations of war). Beyond that, there are then the many millions whose lives have been made worse, not better, under the new multilateral globalisation regimes which create more and more wealth for the US and US-based companies. There are victims—and they are dead, or living lives filled with horror and sadness—in every poor country, and among the poor of the wealthy countries too. They are slaves—many of them women and girls; they are the workers in the Export Processing Zones—many of them women and girls; they are those trafficked for the sexual pleasure of mobile men—the vast majority are women and girls; they are dependent on drugs, or handouts; they are starving, or homeless, or landless, or countryless; they have had their possessions, their land, their knowledge, their plants, their culture, even parts of their bodies stolen, appropriated, pirated, commodified. These people too are victims of another undeclared war in which the rich stand to gain, and the poor lose almost everything. And many of these people are women and girls, for whom the "war against women" as Marilyn French called it, has never really ceased, indeed it appears to have gained momentum.

War, formal declared war, will make the suffering of those already victim-ised by America's corporate self-seeking attitude even greater. Those who stand to gain are overwhelmingly men. They are rich men, mostly white, but male elites from other cultures are welcome to join the club. They represent a very narrow view of the world, one which has little contact with real life, with daily activities such as buying milk or bread, such as staying up with a sick child, such as talking with a friend about relationships or politics, such as comforting another who has suffered loss, such as planting trees or flowers or harvesting fruits or milking the goats. This narrow view is what I have come to call Dominant Culture Stupidities: the more dominant cultures one belongs to, the more socially and politically insensitive and stupid one is. American corporate, military and mainstream political culture tends to think that the rest of world wants what they value.

The military might of the US is intimately connected with its corporate might. Their economies feed one another with goods and multimillion-dollar contracts. General Electric did not get rich on refrigerators or kitchen appliances; its nuclear plants are much more profitable.

Where are the women in the structures of power? They are not there (even with the few tokens who are). They do not have decision-making power. They do not provide the financial backing. No, the women—even the captains of industry or law—are outside this place of hyperpower. Under the Taliban, women are rendered invisible, covered up. In the highest offices of the US corporate and military decision-making boardrooms, it is much the same.

So what does biodiversity have to do with all of this? I suggest, that were the planet to shift its focus from profit-making (and war-mongering is a part of that, as economists such as Marilyn Waring have shown) to biodiversity, many of these things would be undoable, unthinkable. To focus on life—an inherent feature of sustaining biodiversity—is to change scale, to change direction, and to change all the basic aspects of life activities. If biodiversity were our inspiration, we would not be building 110-storey buildings for people to die in. We would not be dispossessing people on the other side of the globe just so that we can have that cheap T-shirt, that computer on which I'm writing this, that next trip with its seductive frequent flyer rewards, that strawberry grown out of season and trucked or flown to me thousands of miles away. The garments industry, the electronics industry, the tourism industry, the industrialised farming industry are interfaces of globalisation. They are the small, incremental cuts supported by the American way of life. They—along with the bombs and economic sanctions—are the makers of despair.

We do not yet know who is responsible for the huge acts of violence, but it does appear likely that they are male; that they are backed by wealth; that they are highly mobile. If, and I say this with caution, if they are connected to CIA-trained Osama Bin Laden, they too will have been surrounded by a grossly masculinised culture, one in which aggression is valorised, and death for a higher good seen to be the highest honour. If they have come from the madrassahs for orphaned boys, then their education too is pure masculinity. The boys passing through the madrassahs are mostly war orphans; they do not know the company of mothers or sisters or aunts or grandmothers, or possibly even the woman passing on the street. Madrassahs are intended to be places of education and peace, but in recent years some of them have been turned instead to educating for disconnection and violence. The boys inside some of the madrassahs have been politicised for violence, for unemotion-ality, and for reward in the afterlife. If they could turn their heads towards biodiversity, to the earth's context now, towards growing things, towards caring, towards sustenance and a belief in life, then the world would be a different place. The next step would be to move toward a principle based on biodiversity, a philosophy based in the local, in contextual richness which includes the principle of diversity—social, political and cultural diversity—alongside biodiversity. They would have to move outside their narrow groove—whether they are George W. Bush or a Taliban-educated boy (the girls are never educated under the Taliban); they would have to learn to appreciate the small things, the ecosystems, the community arts program, the local shopping area or market, the garden.

Biodiversity is an inspirational concept. Unlike diversity it is not easily appropriated and turned to utilitarian ends. One can appropriate the concept of diversity to market baseball caps, but biodiversity just is. If, and it's a big if, biodiversity were to become the inspiration of the culture a whole raft of things become undoable, some even impossible to think about. Monocultures would be unthinkable, as would be the things that support monocultures, including US-style patents, the fake-neutral language of mulilateral agree-ments, as well as all attempts to colonise people and shape them in the mould of the dominating culture.

Biodiversity means that one has to return to the local, to connections between ourselves, to relationship with those who live in the same commun-ities—even some of the ones we don't much like. I think that a community which is based on recognising people's diverse skills and talents, interests and strengths—even our weaknesses—and which also values the specialness of everyone is important. I do think it is time men started to take more account of these issues; women have long been the mainstay of community networks and relationships. But it is also more, because it relates to the way the culture is structured—cars, displacement, disconnection, dislocation and the kind of mobility that gives those of us who fly frequent flyer points. It's hard not to participate—I recognise this—which is why the inspiration of the culture has to shift. From profit to biodiversity again.

Disconnection is critical for a system based on profit. It allows govern-ments to kill people in other countries; it allows for widespread theft through colonisation and globalisation; it allows for profit at the expense of children's lives; it allows environmental degradation, including nuclear dumps in poor countries; it allows for the dumping of refugees in other countries; and it makes violence possible. Disconnection is intimately associated with a separation of means and ends, and with a basic utilitarian philosophy, whereby the ends justify unjustifiable means. By contrast, biodiversity relies on connection and on relationship. It also demands accountability, since one's actions are visible to those who feel the consequences. Biodiversity ap-proaches social and cultural life as an ecosystem, with immediate feedback within the system. Violence might not be entirely eliminated, but it would be dealt with more productively and effectively, instead of simply passing it on to the next victim or generation. Connection requires thinking about process, about how we move through one social structure into another, about means as well as ends, and about the context in which these things take place. Biodiversity, then, is an important inspiration for changing how we think and how we act. There is a long way to go. Getting there won't be achieved by bombs, or reconstructing 110-storey buildings. It will be achieved by those in the diversity sector who see life with greater richness than those who inhabit the masculinised world of war, profit and globalisation.

Afterword: 24 September 2001

The connection between biodiversity and feminism as forces opposing global corporate greed appeared in an e-mail on my computer this morning. The alliance between those who favour military retaliation and globalisation (with its attendant promotion of biotechnology and GMO rhetoric "to feed the hungry of the world") is shown by the nastiest kind of slippage such as that promulgated by Andrew Apel's (agbionews@earthlink.net to AgBioView, Subject: The Face of Terrorism) accusation that anti-globalisation activists and those of us who are against industrialised farming practices are terrorists. This is the usual kind of reversal (in Mary Daly's sense) that we can expect from the hypermasculine ideology of corporate and military men. Feminists and ecological activists are not war-mongers, neither is there much profit to be gained; by contrast those who favour global corporate power—whether it be directed to war contracts or industrialised farm contracts—reap huge profits, and are the ones whose minds are focused on destroying or distorting life.

Barbara Kingsolver

A Pure, High Note of Anguish

23 September 2001, *Los Angeles Times*.

TUCSON—I want to do something to help right now. But I can't give blood (my hematocrit always runs too low), and I'm too far away to give anybody shelter or a drink of water. I can only give words. My verbal hemoglobin never seems to wane, so words are what I'll offer up in this time that asks of us the best citizenship we've ever mustered. I don't mean to say I have a cure. Answers to the main questions of the day—Where was that fourth plane headed? How did they get knives through security?—I don't know any of that. I have some answers, but only to the questions nobody is asking right now but my 5-year old. Why did all those people die when they didn't do anything wrong? Will it happen to me? Is this the worst thing that's ever happened? Who were those children cheering that they showed for just a minute, and why were they glad? Please, will this ever, ever happen to me?

There are so many answers, and none: It is desperately painful to see people die without having done anything to deserve it, and yet this is how lives end nearly always. We get old or we don't, we get cancer, we starve, we are battered, we get on a plane thinking we're going home but never make it. There are blessings and wonders and horrific bad luck and no guarantees. We like to pretend life is different from that, more like a game we can actually win with the right strategy, but it isn't. And, yes, it's the worst thing that's happened, but only this week. Two years ago, an earthquake in Turkey killed 17,000 people in a day, babies and mothers and businessmen, and not one of them did a thing to cause it. The November before that, a hurricane hit Honduras and Nicaragua and killed even more, buried whole villages and erased family lines and even now, people wake up there empty-handed. Which end of the world shall we talk about? Sixty years ago, Japanese airplanes bombed Navy boys who were sleeping on ships in gentle Pacific waters. Three and a half years later, American planes bombed a plaza in Japan where men and women were going to work, where schoolchildren were playing, and more humans died at once than anyone thought possible. Seventy thousand in a minute. Imagine. Then twice that many more, slowly, from the inside.

There are no worst days, it seems. Ten years ago, early on a January morning, bombs rained down from the sky and caused great buildings in the city of Baghdad to fall down—hotels, hospitals, palaces, buildings with mothers and soldiers inside—and here in the place I want to love best, I had to watch people cheering about it. In Baghdad, survivors shook their fists at the sky and said the word "evil". When many lives are lost all at once, people gather together and say words like "heinous" and "honor" and "revenge", presuming to make this awful moment stand apart somehow from the ways people die a little each day from sickness or hunger. They raise up their compatriots' lives to a sacred place—we do this, all of us who are human—thinking our own citizens to be more worthy of grief and less willingly risked than lives on other soil. But broken hearts are not mended in this ceremony, because, really, every life that ends is utterly its own event—and also in some way it's the same as all others, a light going out that ached to burn longer. Even if you never had the chance to love the light that's gone, you miss it. You should. You bear this world and everything that's wrong with it by holding life still precious, each time, and starting over.

And those children dancing in the street? That is the hardest question. We would rather discuss trails of evidence and whom to stamp out, even the size and shape of the cage we might put ourselves in to stay safe, than to mention the fact that our nation is not universally beloved; we are also despised. And not just by "The Terrorist", that lone, deranged non-man in a bad photograph whose opinion we can clearly dismiss, but by ordinary people in many lands. Even by little boys—whole towns full of them it looked like—jumping for joy in school shoes and pilled woolen sweaters.

There are a hundred ways to be a good citizen, and one of them is to look finally at the things we don't want to see. In a week of terrifying events, here is one awful, true thing that hasn't much been mentioned: Some people believe our country needed to learn how to hurt in this new way. This is such a large lesson, so hatefully, wrongfully taught, but many people before us have learned honest truths from wrongful deaths. It still may be within our capacity of mercy to say this much is true: we didn't really understand how it felt when citizens were buried alive in Turkey or Nicaragua or Hiroshima. Or that night in Baghdad. And we haven't cared enough for the particular brothers and mothers taken down a limb or a life at a time, for such a span of years that those little, briefly jubilant boys have grown up with twisted hearts. How could we keep raining down bombs and selling weapons, if we had? How can our president still use that word "attack" so casually, like a move in a checker game, now that we have awakened to see that word in our own newspapers, used like this: Attack on America.

Surely, the whole world grieves for us right now. And surely it also hopes we might have learned, from the taste of our own blood, that every war is both won and lost, and that loss is a pure, high note of anguish like a mother singing to any empty bed. The mortal citizens of a planet are praying right now that we will bear in mind, better than ever before, that no kind of bomb ever built will extinguish hatred.

"Will this happen to me?" is the wrong question, I'm sad to say. It always was.

Barbara Lee

Why I Voted against War

24 September 2001, *San Francisco Chronicle*. Barbara
Lee, a Democrat, represents the 9th Congressional
District (which covers parts of California) in the US
Congress. She was the only member of Congress to
vote against going to war.

WASHINGTON—On September 11, terrorists attacked the United States in an
unprecedented and brutal manner, killing thousands of innocent people,
including the passengers and crews of four aircraft.

Like everyone throughout our country, I am repulsed and angered by these
attacks and believe all appropriate steps must be taken to bring the perpetrators to justice. We must prevent any future such attacks. That is the highest
obligation of our federal, state and local governments. On this, we are united
as a nation. Any nation, group or individual that fails to comprehend this or
believes that we will tolerate such illegal and uncivilized attacks is
grossly mistaken.

Last week, filled with grief and sorrow for those killed and injured and
with anger at those who had done this, I confronted the solemn responsibility
of voting to authorize the nation to go to war. Some believe this resolution
was only symbolic, designed to show national resolve.

But I could not ignore that it provided explicit authority, under the War
Powers Resolution and the Constitution, to go to war. It was a blank check
to the president to attack anyone involved in the September 11 events—
anywhere, in any country, without regard to our nation's long-term foreign
policy, economic and national security interests, and without time limit.

In granting these overly broad powers, the Congress failed its responsibility to understand the dimensions of its declaration. I could not support
such a grant of war-making authority to the president; I believe it would put
more innocent lives at risk.

The president has the constitutional authority to protect the nation from
further attack, and he has mobilized the armed forces to do just that. The
Congress should have waited for the facts to be presented and then acted with
fuller knowledge of the consequences of our action.

I have heard from thousands of my constituents in the wake of this vote.

Many—a majority—have counseled restraint and caution, demanding that we ascertain the facts and ensure that violence does not beget violence. They understand the boundless consequences of proceeding hastily to war, and I thank them for their support.

Others believe that I should have voted for the resolution, either for symbolic or geopolitical reasons or because they truly believe a military option is unavoidable.

However, I am not convinced that voting for the resolution preserves and protects US interests. We must develop our intelligence and bring those who did this to justice. We must mobilize—and maintain—an international coalition against terrorism.

Finally, we have a chance to demonstrate to the world that great powers can choose to fight on the fronts of their choosing and that we can choose to avoid needless military action when other avenues to redress our rightful grievances and to protect our nation are available to us.

We must respond, but the character of that response will determine for ourselves and for our children the world that they will inherit. I do not dispute the president's intent to rid the world of terrorism, but we have many means to reach that goal, and measures that spawn further acts of terror or that do not address the sources of hatred do not increase our security.

Secretary of State Colin Powell himself eloquently pointed out the many ways to get at the root of this problem—economic, diplomatic, legal and political, as well as military.

A rush to launch precipitous military counterattacks runs too great a risk that more innocent men, women and children will be killed. I could not vote for a resolution that I believe will lead to such an outcome.

Amber Amundson

A Pentagon Widow Pleads for Non-violence

25 September 2001, *Chicago Tribune*. Amber Amundson is the widow of the late Craig Scott Amundson, an enlisted specialist in the US Army.

My husband, Craig Scott Amundson, of the US Army, lost his life in the line of duty at the Pentagon on September 11 as the world looked on in horror and disbelief. Losing my 28-year-old husband and father of our two young children is a terrible and painful experience. His death is also part of an immense national loss and I am comforted by knowing so many share my grief. But because I have lost Craig as part of this historic tragedy, my anguish is compounded exponentially by fear that his death will be used to justify new violence against other innocent victims.

I have heard angry rhetoric by some Americans, including many of our nation's leaders, who advise a heavy dose of revenge and punishment. To those leaders, I would like to make clear that my family and I take no comfort in your words of rage. If you choose to respond to this incomprehensible brutality by perpetuating violence against other innocent human beings, you may not do so in the name of justice for my husband. Your words and imminent acts of revenge only amplify our family's suffering, deny us the dignity of remembering our loved one in a way that would have made him proud, and mock his vision of America as a peacemaker in the world community.

Craig enlisted in the Army and was proud to serve his county. He was a patriotic American and a citizen of the world. Craig believed that by working from within the military system he could help to maintain the military focus on peacekeeping and strategic planning—to prevent violence and war. For the last two years Craig drove to his job at the Pentagon with a "Visualize World Peace" bumper sticker on his car. This was not empty rhetoric or contra-dictory to him, but part of his dream. He believed his role in the Army could further the cause of peace throughout the world.

Craig would not have wanted a violent response to avenge his death. And I cannot see how good can come out of it. We cannot solve violence with violence. Mohandas Gandhi said, "An eye for an eye only makes the whole world blind." We will no longer be able to see that we hold the light of liberty if we are blinded by vengeance, anger and fear. I ask our nation's leaders not to take the path that leads to more widespread hatreds—that make my husband's death just one more in an unending spiral of killing.

I call on our national leaders to find the courage to respond to this incomprehensible tragedy by breaking the cycle of violence. I call on them to marshal this great nation's skills and resources to lead a worldwide dialogue on freedom from terror and hate.

I do not know how to begin making a better world: I do believe it must be done, and I believe it is our leaders' responsibility to find a way. I urge them to take up this challenge and respond to our nation's and my personal tragedy with a new beginning that gives us hope for a peaceful global community.

Makere Stewart-Harawira

I Too Am a Muslim, a Hindu, an Arab ...

26 September 2001

Kia ora

Today the juncture of capital and militarism has given rise to renewed ideologies and practices of racism, discrimination and otherness which throughout history have legitimated hatred, violence and genocide in all its forms. And once again they are again being manifested in calls for identifying labels and insignia, in the Taliban's instructions for Hindus to be identified with a yellow patch "for security reasons", in the calls of everyday Americans for the identification of Arab-Americans, in the burnings and lootings of Islamic places of worship, in the terrorising of Islamic and Arab children, in the planned strikes against Afghanistan and in the demands of George Bush to "chooose—for or against".

At present I am unable to march against war and violent retaliation or to bring relief to thousands of terrified Afghan people and so I have asked myself this question—in addition to countering militaristic terrorism with the strongest thoughts of love that I am capable of, love, what else is there that I can do?

This morning part of an answer came to me. I can wear a yellow patch with words that identify me as

Moslem
Arab
Hindu

and perhaps in some small way demonstrate the injustice and insanity of practices that categorise, that exclude, that deny and invalidate the legitimate right of other civilisations, other belief systems, and other ways of being.

Perhaps you, too, could do likewise.

loving greetings,
Makere

Theresa Wolfwood

Resistance is Creative:
False Options and Real Hope

27–29 September 2001. Draft for speech at Resisting
Global Militarism conference, Victoria, BC, Canada

This summer I was driving behind a tourist bus here in Victoria with a big ad for McDonald's potato chips which said, "Resistance is Futile". I was so angry that I nearly went off the road. How dare they steal and corrupt our slogans? I went home and made the banner that says, "Resistance is Fertile". Now we need that resistance more than ever. (And the need is urgent as we bomb, as predicted and feared, the suffering people of Afghanistan [added after 7 October].)

Today we are facing in this terrible global situation a polarization of false choices that leaves out the possibility of democratic civil resistance. We are told we must support the military terrorism of USA and its allies, including Canada. If we don't the US President says we are supporting this unnamed, unidentified terrorism of the tragedy in the USA. Those are false options which can only lead to more violence.

They remind me of the Cold War when again we were told to support the militarism of our side, state capitalism, against the militarism of the other side, state communism. In those days peace activists were harassed and investigated, ridiculed and called reds or commie sympathizers. During the FLQ crisis in Canada (Quebec Liberation Movement in 1971), the War Measures Act was used as an excuse to round up intellectuals, workers and artists who wanted peaceful change. It is happening again: this year special police and spy networks were set up to track anti-globalization activists and these networks will be directed against all of us. We can expect opportunists, provocateurs and spies. So we must be very clear and open about our work at all times. And we need to form affinity and support groups for those who are most likely to be the focus of attention.

Globalization, the power of a few enormous corporations to exploit the world, can only flourish with the military force of the world's richest nation and its sycophants. In post-Cold War politics, the Pentagon stated in a policy document that its role is to defend the USA's economic superiority, the world's only superpower. Now as the economies of globalization, the G-8, are failing their own agendas of growth and power, the City of Calgary wants $18 million to protect itself from protestors next year who plan to question this failed agenda in public. In USA military stocks rise as that country prepares for war. (The economies of the Minority World are all in recession— just like 11 years ago when we had the Gulf War.) Let us face it, war is good for business, it has always been the panacea for bad economics.

Peaceful resistance to the evils of any kind of terrorism, by states, groups or individuals, is all that will save the world. Violence is elitist, anti-people and shows a lack of trust in humanity and lack of faith in collective social change. We have a big task to challenge these death ideologies—but we have a big movement. We will expose the lie that there are good and bad kinds of violence and that we must choose between them. As Bill Phipps (moderator of the United Church of Canada, at Resisting Global Militarism conference) told us on Thursday, now is the time, we must seize the day, the global powers are in disarray. We reject all violence that kills innocent people wherever they are. Ninety per cent of the victims of modern state military warfare are unarmed civilians. The rich are getting richer and the poor are getting poorer—everywhere. Eighty per cent of the earth's resources are consumed by 20 per cent of its population. Starvation, homelessness, grinding poverty and landlessness are also forms of violence.

Resistance is more than protest. Resistance is a locally rooted, globally connected life time project that seeks and speaks the truth about evil and violence. Resistance unites diverse people in the work for peace and justice. Resistance makes the connections between military oppression, the rule of elites, the oppression of the poor and dispossessed, the consolidation of power in international alliances like NATO, WTO, FTAA, and the destruction of our planet's biodiversity.

Our lives are filled with the culture of consumerism and the glorification of violence. We must take back our space and fill it with hope. Our task is to overcome the brutal injustice and appalling inequality that the ideologies of death have wrought. We will have to reject, unplug, turn off the corporate media of advertising, manipulated news, violent and mindless entertainment. This is how they obliterate creativity, memory and discernment.

We need to create and strengthen our own means of communication, with each other and the world; take the time, as Rosa Luxemburg (German socialist in the early twentieth century) said, to find new forms and new language. (And I wish resisters would not use words like "march" and "target" and we need to reclaim "security" from the military and talk about real human security.) To do that we need to reclaim the space in our minds, senses and lives that have been jammed full with the trivialization of consumerism and violence. Jose Bove, the French activist, told me this year that one of the great dangers of militarism is that it is used to impose the standardization of the culture of the strong on the weaker. We see today the results, everywhere, of that imposed oppression. Let's overturn it, overcome passive alienation and let's create a culture of peace.

Our resistance is creative. We take the inspiration of the Zapatistas (I use them because I was a human rights observer in a village there, a few years ago) peacefully creating local autonomy in Mexican villages, growing their crops, using their own languages, true to their non-commercial subsistence life, even as the military returns to their homeland. Their uprising started the day NAFTA came into force, the day the indigenous people would lose their communal land and be forced by the military to leave their subsistence farms. Their resistance grows—can we do less?

Creative resistance is the wisdom of saying many "No's".

No to nuclear testing in the South Pacific.
No to genetically modified organisms.
No to oil exploration on sacred or ecologically sensitive lands.
No to the trade agreements that favour and strengthen the military industries and forces.
No to speculation on the stock market—where military stocks soar.
No to the loss of civil liberties everywhere.
No to intolerance and violence against different ethnic and religious groups.

We have many No's, but only one Yes, as the Zapatistas say. Yes to peace with justice!

We need to root our Yes in our own community. Build bridges with people in poverty. Support native land claims. Shut down Nanoose Bay Testing Range (US military test range for maritime weapons systems, near Victoria, BC). End US military tourism and adventurism in our ports and waters. Connect with the local environmental movements, war is the greatest destroyer of our planet. Paving paradise is a precursor to bombing babies. The global can undermine the local—biodiversity is threatened on every level. Let us work in solidarity with groups in struggle against oppression around the world. In the words of Kay Macpherson (late Canadian feminist/peace activist), "when in doubt, do both".

Again, we need to be creative about our response to media manipulation. Not only what we see and read, but why some stories and not others. We should question and doubt everything we are fed. The images of September 11 will stay with us, not only because the events were so terrible, but because 80 per cent of the world's media repeated and repeated the images of the events.

But I want to tell you about some images that are burned into my brain.

On 11 September 1973, the democratically elected government of Chile was overthrown and President Allende was assassinated. Thousands of citizens were herded into a stadium by the military. The popular singer, Victor Jarra, was among them. He started to sing, was ordered to stop, he continued, they cut off his hands; bleeding, he sang until they killed him—and thousands more.

In Baghdad this year, I stood in a children's hospital ward, filled with still, silent little bodies, grasping for life. The doctor said to me wearily, "They will all die." Indeed 5000 of them die every month.

I just received a photo from my friend, Wanjiku Kironyo in Kenya. She runs a refuge for women and children in need. The photo showed two forlorn children, AIDS orphans, abandoned on the doorstep of her already bulging building. Thousands of children die in Africa every day—from the diseases of poverty.

I ask—why aren't those images beamed around the world?

In the creativity of resistance, "we can be our own media", as Rosalie Bertell (a Canadian scientist and anti-nuclear expert) says. We can choose and seek to know what is important to us, and support and participate in our own independent media and networks.

In creative resistance we examine in our own lives—personal and local violence and inequality. We can plant our creativity in our homes, workplaces, school and churches. These are still influential institutions where ideas and attitudes are born. When we oppose nuclear pollution and radioactive contamination, we say that all the people of tomorrow are carried by in the eggs of women today. We can also say that all the ideas and inspiration of tomorrow are also in hearts and minds of people today. Birth and life are creative!

In our personal, community and global reality we will have to address the appalling inequality between men and women—in life conditions, wealth and freedom. And we must question the differences in values between men and women. Violence is glorified in sport and entertainment, an almost total male monopoly. Women and children are the main victims of domestic violence. Women own 10 per cent of the world's property, produce 70 per cent of our food and do most of the work. Another image I see in my mind: the streets of Managua, Addis Ababa, Manila, many cities, are filled with idle men. Women are invisible—they are working or confined to home—to work there, also.

The global factories that produce our cheap clothes, computers, weapons systems and toys are staffed by women—abused, raped and harassed by a few male supervisors. The sex trade exploits millions of women. They are trapped in their need to support whole families. Those idle men on the streets lack status, work and self-worth. Violence is often their only means of self-expression. They are ripe easy picking for ideological, ethnic and civil wars. Give them a uniform and a gun—and they are someone. Here too in Canada, the military lure the unemployed into the killing life. Our society and men, especially, must recognize the particularity of violence against women. Men do most of the killing—women do most of the dying. Yet all research shows that women, even in hawkish England, are less likely to support war and violence and more likely to care about the victims of violence. Where are the women's voices in this war situation? Why are the commentators and speakers usually men? Men and women everywhere need meaningful and dignified work. This is a project for our creative resistance—even as we examine our own relationships within movements. The resistance movement can become a microcosm of the world we build together. Gandhi said, "We must be the change we want to see in the world."

Resistance is an open borderless country which we can only create if men and women are equal, a community where people of all colours and backgrounds are at home, where nature is respected for its abundance, where we "put life in the centre" (Maria Mies, German author-activist), and where creativity blooms in everyone. A collective and united resistance liberates from our fears. We are not trapped between the terror of a great power and the terror of rage against that power. Pessimism is not an option; despair is a useless luxury. As Swiss anti-NATO activists say, solidarity, not war. Happiness is the best revenge for violence and hatred.

Resistance nourishes us and gives us a place and a purpose in life. We create that country by walking there together, smoothing the roads for those who come after us.

Resistance is creative, fertile, fruitful and "resistance is the secret of joy". (Alice Walker, Afro-American writer.)

Jen Couch

So the Party Is Over? The Global Justice Movement after September 11

30 September 2001

It was September 2001 and fighting for global justice had become an extreme sport with a tough-edged street quality. Such was the level of police repression, that you wouldn't even consider turning up to an "anti-globalisation" protest without the activist "uniform" of gas mask, helmet, raincoats and padding. The usual activist attire of vinegar-soaked bandanas offered little protection from the enduring physical consequences of such excessive tear gas, and without padding you would be likely to be hurt by rubber bullets.

In the same month I was due to fly to New York to take part in the protests against the IMF and the World Bank in Washington. I wanted to join a group of New York activists to take part in a group they had named the Masquerade Project. The activists who had created the project had been bothered that, with all the focus on defending themselves against extreme police repression, they felt that a focus of aesthetics had been forgotten, that the global justice movement's most powerful weapons in the fight for global justice—ridicule, theatre, performance and humor—had been lost.

Thus, the Masquerade Project was formed. The aim was simple. Buy and distribute hundreds of free gas masks to those attending the Washington DC protests. But first, decorate them in bright colors, with sparkles, tinsel, and diamantes, and thus transform them into symbols of the creativity, diversity, resilience and ingenuity of the global justice movement.

But of course that was before September 11. In the days that followed the World Trade Center attack I received e-mails from my friends. Initially they spoke of the horror, mixed with exhaustion of attending quickly called meetings, handing out leaflets for peace rallies, developing and pasting up posters, all in a city where toxic smoke covered the sky, papers and news headlines yelled *War!*, where Muslims were being threatened and where "missing" posters were everywhere.

And then there were the boxes and boxes of decorated gas masks that sat in activists' apartments. They pulled off all the decorations, and took them to Ground Zero, the same place where days before they had been meeting to plan a shutdown of the financial district in November as part of the protests against the WTO meeting in Qatar.

It would be an understatement to say that September 11 put a spanner in the works of the global justice movement. In the days that followed, a demonisation of anti-globalisation activists occurred. One of the greatest symbols of global capitalism had been blown off the world stage. Accusations abounded in mainstream media, surely it must have been masterminded by an anti-globalisation/anti-capitalist activist? After all, were we not also enemies of Western Civilisation? Wanting to turn back the clock to some golden age? Did we not also want to confine the forces of modernity? Are we not a movement, as was suggested by *New Republic* editor Peter Beinart, united by hatred of the United States?

The protests that were planned in Washington DC were predicted to be the most diverse, broad and intense protests since Seattle. The labor movement, communities of faith and NGOs had activated thousands of people, who were to attend, many who hadn't attended such demonstrations before. Additionally, there was continuing discussion regarding a "diversity of tactics", respecting those activists that chose to move away from traditional non-violent forms of protest that have dominated movements for the previous few decades.

Those tactics now seem somewhat inappropriate. Attacks on the symbols of capitalism now require care in a substantially altered landscape. I doubt whether smashing corporation windows in New York City or our most infamous identifying symbol, the mask, will now be received very well, even by the most sympathetic of citizens.

This is not to say that the global justice movement is no longer viable or necessary, or does not have a place. Mind you, you wouldn't get this picture from the media. The same pundits that were so quick to dismiss the protestors in Seattle as a "kooky crowd", a "circus", a "motley crew" or as "misguided youth living out an 'inauthentic' version of the 60s rebellion", and who even went so far as to compare the smashing of the windows of corporations in Seattle to the actions of the Nazis in attacking Jews across Germany in 1938, now proclaim the movement as dead, in tatters or "just so yesterday".

These comments are nothing new, and have all been said before. The movement was meant to be dead after the A16 protests in Washington DC in 2000, and as Naomi Klein perceptively wrote, "it has been declared with ritualistic regularity before and after every mass demonstration: our strategies apparently discredited, our coalitions divided, our arguments misguided".

But what perhaps is the most worrying is that these very comments are now coming from activists themselves. "The movement is dead, it really is", an activist wrote to me today.

Yes, the picture is sobering. The attacks that occurred on September 11 not only essentially mean a crackdown on any dissent that will happen in the future, and as Naomi Klein comments, it could "cost us our few political victories". Klein bleakly points out that funds that were committed to the AIDS crisis in Africa will now disappear and soon behind it, commitments to expand debt cancellation, not to mention the rights of refugees and asylum seekers. And perhaps in one of the biggest ironies, "free trade, long facing a public relations crisis, has been rebranded as a patriotic duty". We now consider in our repertoire of September 11 heroes, those workers of the stock market who bravely went back to work, despite their coworkers, virtual "practitioners of liberty", having died.

The message is clear: advocate for free trade and you are a freedom fighter; don't and you are a fundamentalist.

There's no doubt that such a radically altered landscape provides opportunities and challenges. However, I have a problem with Northern activists announcing the movement is dead. Says who? I feel like asking. Wasn't this meant to be *global* resistance to globalisation, aren't we part of a *global* movement? Haven't we all mumbled many times before, "It didn't begin in Seattle and it won't end in Quebec, Prague, Melbourne"?

Wasn't the Battle of Seattle and those that proceeded it merely reflecting the "core issues" that had been resisted by Third World activists for decades? The "enormous discontent" against the reign of international capital has its origins in the many rebellions that have taken place in the Third World against neoliberalism, embodied in so-called structural adjustment policies, Third World debt, the MAI, World Bank projects and NAFTA. Examples include (and are not limited to) the "Zapatista uprising in 1994, the protests in India against the Namarda Dam, the strikes and uprisings in Indonesia and South Korea in 1997 due to the Asian financial crisis, and the more recent revolts in early 2000 of Ecuadorian Indians and Bolivians against neoliberal austerity policies". Rather than the starting point, the Battle of Seattle showed that what we witnessed was a consolidation of a "truly diverse movement capable of challenging the most powerful institutions on the planet" that in fact was already in existence.

I hope some Northern activist remembers to tell the Zapatistas, the landless peasants of Brazil, the people fighting the Narmada Dam and the majorities of the planet who are suffering under and consequently resisting neoliberalism (and who many claim to have been acting on behalf of) that the party is over.

Perhaps the biggest challenge facing the global justice movement therefore lies in remembering why and how the movement came about in the first place and to remember that these factors are still relevant. One of the major points that makes the Seattle protests so unique was the supposed emergence in the North of a movement for *global* justice, otherwise known as the anti-globalisation movement. This swelling *global* justice movement did not emerge organically, but was a coalition of many of the same groups who have been mobilising previously against NAFTA, neoliberal globalisation and flawed development strategies, and its uniqueness partly rests on the variety of causes and groups it represents.

Many of the issues that the global justice movement has demanded responses to are situated in the Third World. These are sites of lands in crisis, since they have often been arenas of international conflict and lands conquered and reconquered, first by European colonialism and later by the power that has come to define the modern project of development. Today's crises of development in the Third World occur as part of a long history of transgressions, including the penetration of imperial interests, which have been the sites of much resistance. Consequently, it is not surprising that in these places, we find long histories of collaboration and resistance against the current dilemmas posed by neoliberalism.

It is essential that we now listen to these voices on the margins of social justice, and that the *global* justice movement continues to move forward in solidarity with those that can show us examples of "plurality, progress and deep democracy". As Naomi Klein writes, "Our task, never more pressing, is to point out that there are more than two worlds available, to expose all the invisible worlds between economic fundamentalism of McWorld" and the religious fundamentalism of "Jihad".

Perhaps the uncritical acceptance and endorsement of the *global* movement construct was problematic. Perhaps what will be revealed is that this is a term fraught with ambiguity, contradictions, biases, gaps and Eurocentric assumptions that are rarely explored further by activists. Perhaps we should ask ourselves what the various motives and intentions were that lay behind our sudden embrace of a global movement, post-Seattle. Who defined that construct? Which groups were included and excluded in our definition of global? What are the biases, gaps and assumptions? Does the idea of a global movement represent the interests of both the North *and* the South—in other words, how *global* is the global movement?

There is a tendency to deny the significance of these issues, and blindly submit to the universal altruistic project of a global movement and subsequently global civil society instead. This romanticised image of the construct as a people-powered panacea to globalisation is reinforced by sweeping assumptions of the term's emancipatory potential and only token inclusion of any discrepancies, gaps and contradictions. Hence engaging in a project to critique and challenge the notion of a global movement or civil society is resisted by many activists, considering it as a counter-productive attack on well-intentioned efforts.

One of the accusations leveled towards the global justice movement was that it had a lack of in-depth analysis in a movement so focused on direct action. Perhaps this was warranted criticism, for our lack of incorporation of concrete and critical analysis allowed us to advance a simplistic, haphazard adoption of the global construct.

Now that we Northern activists have decided it's all over, perhaps the term *global* movement is more problematic than useful in order to explain the processes of international activism and resistance to globalisation. By not prioritizing issues of power imbalances, resource inequities, North–South ideological and political tensions, the "globality" of the movement and trans-national activism, this construct must be questioned. It is becoming increasingly worth consideration that the agendas and issues we have prioritised on the agenda of anti-globalisation protest mirror the interests of the North, despite the rhetoric of global solidarity.

With any emergency there is emergence and with any crisis there is always change and opportunity. Maybe it's the opportunity for some deep reflection.

Urvashi Butalia

The Price of Life

30 September 2001. A shorter version of this article appeared in *New Internationalist*, No. 340, November 2001.

More than 6000 people died in the recent attacks on what has come to be known as 'black Tuesday'. Each of them came from a home, a family, a relationship. Each was someone's parent, child, sibling, partner. Would it be any comfort to them, I wonder, to know that their deaths will, in all probability, lead to a war against a devastated, starving people, and result in many more violent, inhuman deaths? For those who will be killed in this war—proudly claimed as the first war of the twenty-first century—will the American soldier with his guns and missiles not be a terrorist?

Would those who died have appreciated hearing their President, supposedly the upholder of law, speaking of "revenge" and "retaliation", demanding someone "dead or alive", flouting every principle of law, plotting openly—and with the support of the media—to kill the presumed perpetrator without even waiting for him to be proved guilty?

More than 6000 people died on that day. Last week, in India, we were asked to observe two minutes of silence in solidarity with them. Wherever you are, whatever you are doing, our Prime Minister told us, stop all activity and stand in silence. No matter how much I mourned those deaths, I could not bring myself to do this. More than 3000 people died in anti-Sikh riots in Delhi in 1984. More than 2000 died in the anti-Muslim riots in Bombay in 1993. More than 10,000 died in the final tally as a result of a gas leak in the Union Carbide factory in Bhopal in India. And this does not even touch the tip of the iceberg.

Why were we not asked to stand in silence for them? Perhaps because they weren't all killed in what are strictly defined as terrorist attacks. In Delhi and Bombay the killers (terrorists?) had the tacit support of the State. Did that make them better? In Bhopal, Union Carbide had the might of America behind it. And yet, I wonder, did not the victims of the Bombay and Delhi riots feel terror when facing their killers? Did not mothers in Bhopal feel terror as they watched the gas waft in and take away the lives of their children?

I never thought the day would come when I would feel ashamed to be an Indian. I remember being enraged by the paltry compensation Union Carbide offered to the Bhopal victims, and complaining about this to an American at a seminar. "But my dear," he said to me with an arrogance I now recognize as typical, "don't you know that the price of an Indian life is much less than that of an American one?"

I realize now, as America prepares to fight its war in our region, on our soil, how true his words were. But I did not expect that we in India would so willingly subscribe to such ideas. But here we are, offering all help to America. You want air space? Air bases? Take them. We haven't even waited to be asked. We know only too well the exploitation, the widespread instances of rape, the arrogance of American soldiers in air bases all over the world, and here we are, laying ourselves open to this. Why? Not because we care for those who died—by now they have been forgotten—but because we want to prove Pakistan is worse than us. And because we want to turn attention away from the real issues: starvation deaths in the face of overflowing food stocks, a shaky economy, civil unrest, to name only a few.

Suddenly, India and Pakistan are at the heart of this impending war. And I think, how tragic that the goodwill, the momentum, albeit slow, of the painful process of dealing with the bitter legacy of the past, has suddenly been lost, bartered away. For what? Why should we be implicated in an American war?

Even as I ask this question, I know. This war is "good' for us: for our Hindu government, what better than to have international validation of its representation of the Muslim as terrorist, of Islam as the enemy? For Pakistan, what better than to have America conveniently forget its stance on the nuclear explosions and lift sanctions? You've been a good boy, you'll get all sorts of prizes. And as for the people who died, well, who cares?

It's easy to fight a war that's not on your own soil, easier still to pretend to be the guardian of all morality, when you are the one responsible for creating the problem in the first place. It's much more difficult to self-reflect, to analyse, to be honest and realize that if you were to try to locate the real sources of terrorism, they would lead right back to you; whether it is in Afghanistan, or Pakistan, or Nicaragua, or Cuba, or Chile, the route points to only one nation: America. But that would mean confronting the devil within.

Yet, it's not too late for that. As women who have lived through the terrible war in Kosovo say in a moving message:

American politicians and decision-makers, grieve for your dead and find ways to protect the living! We ask you not to put us and your citizens at more risk ... Please remember your past and learn from ours to leave a legacy of justice and peaceful construction, not of revenge, destruction and war.

I don't know what will happen to us in South Asia if the American war takes off. Will we survive or die? But I do know that both inside America and in our region, we'll be much more vulnerable to further violence. I do know that the hatred for minorities nurtured by our fundamenalist majoritarian politics will only get worse. As Mahatama Gandhi once said: an eye for an eye only makes the whole world blind. I fear that is what is happening to us today.

Diverse Women for Diversity

Statement

1 October 2001, New Delhi, India. Drafted at a conference on Globalisation, Environment and People's Survival.

....

We, Diverse Women for Diversity, committed to a peaceful world, celebrate our differences. From our differences come our strengths. We come from all the continents, and from different cultures and races, and are united in our vision for peace and justice for the world today. We want to leave a peaceful and just world for our children and for the generations to come. We celebrate and uphold cultural and biological diversity. We will defend all forms of diversity and resist all forms of monoculture, fundamentalism and violence from which intolerance and hatred arise.

The tragedy on September 11 has shown us another face of terror.

We join in the pain of all people who have faced the terror of those who do not value the sanctity of human life. We especially abhor the use of human beings themselves as weapons. In this regard the terror of September 11 cannot be viewed as a lone event. Many acts of such terror have been inflicted on the peoples of this earth. The sacredness and dignity of life, and the right to peaceful existence and justice have been destroyed through imperialistic globalization and all forms of fundamentalism.

Among the many tools of terror in the modern world are:

- economic sanctions and structural adjustment policies by the World Bank, IMF, WTO, the transnationals, and their accomplices in the different governments that lead to starvation and disease epidemics;
- biotechnologies that threaten the roots of life;
- monocultures that destroy social and biological diversity;
- degradation of the environment for monetary gain;
- widespread application of pesticides that lead to deformities, illness and death;
- pollution of soils, water and ecosystems at large;
- the pursuit of profit by global corporations which is the driving force behind terrorism—terrorism which destroys sustainable livelihoods, cultural identities and the right of people to basic necessities of life;
- the marginalization of indigenous peoples through continuing colonization, and the loss of sovereignty;

- the growing disparity between the rich and the poor between countries, and within countries, including countries of the "developed" nations;
- the US-led NATO alliance with its new strategy which is fostering war all over the globe, with other governments being blackmailed to join in— this leads to further militarization and violence within all countries.

Given the extent of such structural terror in the world, it is perhaps surprising that direct terrorist attacks, like that of September 11, are not more common. If we want to end terrorism we must pay attention to all sources of injustice that widen the gap between rich and poor, men and women, nature and human beings, and which create the hopelessness that can lead to terrorism. We stand with those who are working to remove the structural causes of injustices.

Women, children, the differently-abled and the aged are the worst victims of this reign of terror:

- the terror of not having water to drink and food to eat;
- the terror of food and water contamination;
- the terror of loss of livelihood;
- the terror of losing home, homeland, family and community and becoming a refugee;
- the terror of persistent poverty that leads to the sale of life and body organs;
- the terror of being forced into prostitution as a means of survival;
- the terror of living in communities where drug abuse has become a way of life;
- the terror of losing our children to a culture of violence;
- the terror of increased violence, in all forms, against women;
- the terror of patriarchy, racism, and casteism which affects the vast majority;
- the terror of living in a society where basic human rights for women are not respected.

We, Diverse Women for Diversity, pledge to overcome this capitalist patriarchal terrorism. We will work towards a world free of war, hunger and social and economic injustices. We condemn all acts of war and call on all nations to boycott pacts of aggression. We invite all women of the world to join with us in stopping governments from rushing into a mindless global war. Together, we will find peaceful, creative and non-violent ways to end terrorism in all its forms.

We ask all peoples of the world to stand with us in defending and celebrating diversity, peace and hope.

Transnational Feminists

Transnational Feminist Practices Against War

October 2001. A Statement by Paola Bacchetta, Tina Campt, Inderpal Grewal, Caren Kaplan, Minoo Moallem, and Jennifer Terry.

As feminist theorists of transnational and postmodern cultural formations, we believe that it is crucial to seek non-violent solutions to conflicts at every level of society, from the global, regional, and national arenas to the ordinary locales of everyday life. We offer the following response to the events of September 11 and its aftermath.

First and foremost, we need to analyze the thoroughly gendered and racialized effects of nationalism, and to identify what kinds of inclusions and exclusions are being enacted in the name of patriotism. Recalling the histories of various nationalisms helps us to identify tacit assumptions about gender, race, nation, and class that once again play a central role in mobilization for war. We see that instead of a necessary historical, material, and geopolitical analysis of September 11, the emerging nationalist discourses consist of misleading and highly sentimentalized narratives that, among other things, reinscribe compulsory heterosexuality and the rigidly dichotomized gender roles upon which it is based. A number of icons constitute the ideal types in the drama of nationalist domesticity that we see displayed in the mainstream media. These include the masculine citizen-soldier, the patriotic wife and mother, the breadwinning father who is head of the household, and the properly reproductive family. We also observe how this drama is racialized. Most media representations in the US have focused exclusively on losses suffered by white, middle-class heterosexual families even though those who died or were injured include many people of different races, classes, sexualities, and religions and of at least 90 different nationalities. Thus, an analysis that elucidates the repressive effects of nationalist discourses is necessary for building a world that fosters peace as well as social and economic justice.

Second, a transnational feminist response views the impact of war and internal repression in a larger context of global histories of displacement, forced migrations, and expulsions. We oppose the US and European sponsorship of regimes responsible for coerced displacements and we note how patterns of immigration, exile, and forced flight are closely linked to gender oppression and to the legacies of colonialism and structured economic dependency. Indeed, history shows us that women, as primary caretakers of families, suffer enormously under circumstances of colonization, civil unrest, and coerced migration. Taking this history into account, we critique solutions to the contemporary crisis that rely on a colonial, Manichean model whereby "advanced capitalist freedom and liberty" is venerated over "backward extremist Islamic barbarism". Furthermore, we draw upon insights from post-colonial studies and critical political economy to trace the dynamics of European and US neocolonialism during the Cold War and post-Cold War periods. Thus questions about the gendered distribution of wealth and resources are key to our analytical approach. Neo-liberal economic development schemes create problems that impact women in profound and devastating ways in both the "developing regions" as well as the "developed world". So while middle-class Euro-American women in the United States are held up as the most liberated on earth even while they are being encouraged to stand dutifully by their husbands, fathers, and children, women in developing regions of the world are depicted as abject, backward, and oppressed by their men. One of the important elements missing from this picture is the fact that many women in Afghanistan are starving and faced with violence and harm on a daily basis not only due to the Taliban regime but also due in large part to a long history of European colonialism and conflict in the region. The Bush administration's decision to drop bombs at one moment and, in the next, care packages of food that are in every way inadequate to the needs of the population, offers a grim image of how pathetic this discourse of "civilization" and "rescue" is within the violence of war. We see here a token and uncaring response to a situation to which the US has contributed for at least twenty years, a situation that is about the strategic influence in the region and about the extraction of natural resources, not the least of which is oil.

Third, we want to comment on the extent to which domestic civil repression is intrinsically linked to the violence of war. Thus the effects of the current conflict will be played out in the US and its border zones through the augmentation of border patrolling and policing, as well as in the use of military and defense technologies and other practices that will further subordinate communities (especially non-white groups) in the US. Such state violence has many gendered implications. These include the emergence of patriarchal/masculinst cultural nationalisms whereby women's perspectives are degraded or wholly excluded to create new version of cultural "traditions". And, for many immigrant women, other devastating effects of state repression include increased incidents of unreported domestic violence, public hostility, and social isolation. In practical terms, policing authorities charged with guaranteeing national security are likely to have little sympathy for the undocumented immigrant woman who is fleeing a violent intimate relationship, unless her assailant fits the profile of an "Islamic fundamentalist". Thus we need an analysis and strategy against the "domestication" of the violence of war that has emerged in these last few weeks and whose effects will be felt in disparate and dispersed ways.

Fourth, we call for an analysis of the stereotypes and tropes that are being mobilized in the current crisis. These tropes support, sustain, and are enabled by a modernist logic of warfare that seeks to consolidate the sovereign (and often unilateral) power of the First World nation-state. When President Bush proclaims that "terrorist" networks must be destroyed, we ask what this term means to people and how it is being used to legitimate a large-scale military offensive. The term is being used to demonize practices that go against US national interests and it permits a kind of "drag-net" effect at home and abroad which legitimates the suppression of dissent. We also want to inquire into constructions of "terrorism" that continue to target non-native or "foreign" opposition movements while cloaking its own practices of terror in euphemisms such as "foreign aid". Deconstructing the trope of "terrorism" must include a sustained critique of the immense resources spent by the US in training "counter-terrorists" and "anti-Communist" forces who then, under other historical circumstances, become enemies rather than allies, as in the now famous case of Osama Bin Laden. We are concerned about the ways in which the "war against terrorism" can be used to silence and repress insurgent movements across the globe. We also emphasize how racism operates in the naming of "terrorism". When the "terrorists" are people of color, all other people of color are vulnerable to a scapegoating backlash. Yet when white supremacist Timothy McVeigh bombed the Murrah federal building in Oklahoma City, killing 168 men, women, and children, no one declared open season to hunt down white men, or even white militia members.

The production of a new racial category, "anyone who looks like a Muslim", in which targets of racism include Muslims, Arabs, Sikhs, and any other people with olive or brown skin, exposes the arbitrary and politically constructed character of new and old racial categories in the US. It also reveals the inadequacy of US multiculturalism to resist the hegemonic relationship between being "white" and "American". Finally, the short memory of the media suppresses any mention of the Euro-American anti-capitalist and anti-imperialist "terrorist" groups of the 1970s and 1980s. A critical attention to the idioms of the present war mobilization compels us to deconstruct other politically loaded tropes, including security, liberty, freedom, truth, civil rights, Islamic fundamentalism, women under the Taliban, the flag, and "America".

Fifth, we recognize the gendered and ethnocentric history of sentimentality, grief, and melancholy that have been mobilized in the new war effort. We do not intend to disparage or dismiss the sadness and deep emotions raised by the events of September 11 and its aftermath. But we do think it is important to point out that there has been a massive deployment of therapeutic discourses that ask people to understand the impact of the events of September 11 and their aftermath solely as "trauma". Such discourses leave other analytical, historical, and critical frameworks unexplored. Focusing only on the personal or narrowly defined psychological dimension of the attacks and the ensuing war obscures the complex nexus of history and geopolitics that has brought about these events. We are not suggesting that specific forms of therapy are not useful. But the culture industry of "trauma" leads to a mystification of history, politics and cultural critique. Furthermore, therapeutic discourse tends to reinforce individualist interpretations of globally significant events and it does so in an ethnocentric manner. Seeking relief through a psychotherapeutic apparatus may be a common practice among Euro-American upper- and middle-class people in the United States, but it should not be assumed to be universally appealing or an effective way to counter experiences of civil repression and war among people of other classes, ethnicities, and cultural backgrounds. Signs of the current trauma discourse's ethnocentricity come through in media depictions staged within the therapeutic framework that tend to afford great meaning, significance, and sympathy to those who lost friends and family members in the attacks on the World Trade Center and the Pentagon. By contrast, people who have lost loved ones as a consequence of US foreign policy elsewhere are not depicted as sufferers of trauma or injustice. In fact, they are seldom seen on camera at all. Similarly, makeshift centers in universities around the US were set up in the immediate wake of September 11 to help college students cope with the psychological effects of the attacks. They tended to assume that September 11 marked the first time Americans experienced vulnerability, overlooking not only the recent events of the Oklahoma City federal building bombing, but moreover erasing the personal experiences of many immigrants and US people of color for whom "America" has been a site of potential or realized violence for all of their lives.

Sixth, our transnational feminist response involves a detailed critical analysis of the role of the media especially in depictions that include colonial tropes and binary oppositions in which the Islam/Muslim/non-West is represented as "uncivilized" or "barbaric". We note the absence or co-optation of Muslim women as "victims" of violence or of "Islamic barbarism." We note as well the use of those groups of women seen as "white" or "Western" both as "rescuers" of non-Western women but also as evidence of the so-called "civilizing" efforts of Europe and North America. We see these discursive formations as a result not only of colonialism's discursive and knowledge-producing legacies, but also of the technologies and industrial practices that produce contemporary global media, and transnational financing of culture industries. We seek especially to analyze the participation of women in these industries as well as the co-optation of feminist approaches and interests in the attack on a broad range of Islamic cultural and religious institutions, not just "Islamicist/extremist" groups. Thus we point out as a caution that any counter or resistance media would need to have a firm grasp of these histories and repertoires of practice or risk reproducing them anew.

Seventh, we call for a deeper understanding of the nature of capitalism and globalization as it generates transnational movements of all kinds. Thus, we seek to counter oppressive transnational movements, both from the "West" as well as the "Non-West", with alternative movements that counter war and the continued production of global inequalities. We note in particular that religious and ethnic fundamentalisms have emerged across the world within which the repression of women and establishment of rigidly dichotomized gender roles are used both as a form of power and to establish a collectivity. Such fundamentalisms have been a cause of concern for feminist groups not only in the Islamic world but also in the US. Feminist and other scholars have noted that these movements have become transnational, through the work of nation-state and non-governmental organizations, with dire consequences for all those who question rigid gender dichotomies. Since these movements are transnational, we question the notion of isolated and autonomous nation-states in the face of numerous examples of transnational and global practices and formations. The recent displays of national coherence and international solidarity (based on nineteenth- and twentieth-century constructions of inter-national relations), cannot mask the strains and contradictions that give rise to the current crisis. Thus, we need an analysis of the numerous ways in which transnational networks and entities both limit and at the same time enable resistance and oppression. That is, the complex political terrain traversed by transnational networks as diverse as Al-Qaeda and the Red Cross must be understood as productive of new identities and practices as well as of new kinds of political repression. Transnational media has roots in pernicious corporate practices yet it also enables diverse and contradictory modes of information, entertainment, and communication. Feminist analysis of these complex and often contradictory transnational phenomena is called for.

In closing, we want to make it very clear that we oppose the US and British military mobilization and bombing that is underway in Afghanistan and that may very well expand further into the West, Central, and South Asian regions. We are responding to a crisis in which war, as described by the George W. Bush administration, will be a covert, diversified, and protracted process. At this moment we call for a resistance to nationalist terms and we argue against the further intensification of US military intervention abroad. We refuse to utilize the binaries of civilization versus barbarism, modernity versus tradition, and West versus East. We also call for an end to the racist scapegoating and "profiling" that accompanies the stepped up violations of civil liberties within the territorial boundaries of the US. We urge feminists to refuse the call to war in the name of vanquishing a so-called "traditional patriarchal fundamentalism", since we understand that such fundamentalisms are supported by many nation-states. We are also aware of the failures of nation-states and the global economic powers such as the IMF and the World Bank to address the poverty and misery across the world and the role of such failures in the emergence of fundamentalisms everywhere. Nationalist and international mobilization for war cannot go forward in our name or under the sign of "concern for women". In fact, terror roams the world in many guises and is perpetrated under the sign of many different nations and agents. It is our contention that violence and terror are ubiquitous and need to be addressed through multiple strategies as much within the "domestic" politics of the US as elsewhere. It is only through developing new strategies and approaches based on some of these suggestions that we can bring an end to the violence of the current moment.

Sunera Thobani

It's Bloodthirsty Vengeance

1 October 2001, Ottawa, Canada. An edited transcript
of a speech at a conference on Women's Resistance:
From Victimization to Criminalization. For a description
of subsequent attacks on Professor Thobani, see the
Introduction: xxii-xxiii.

We, and this "we" is really problematic. If we in the West are all Americans
now, what are Third World women and Aboriginal women to do? If
Canadians are Americans now, what are women of colour to do in this
country? And I'm open to suggestions for changing this title, but I thought I
would stick with it as a working title for getting my ideas together for making
this presentation this morning.

We are living in a period of escalating global interaction now on every
front, on every level. And we have to recognize that this level and this
particular phase of globalization is rooted in the colonization of Aboriginal
peoples and Third World peoples all over the world. That is the basis. Globalization continues to remain rooted in that colonization, and I think, recognizing that we are on Aboriginal land is a very, very important starting point for
any one of our movements. But that cannot be the end point. And we have
to recognize that there will be no social justice, no anti-racism, no feminist
emancipation, no liberation of any kind for anybody on this continent unless
Aboriginal peoples' demand for self-determination is resolved.

The second point I want to make is that in the global order that we live
in, there are profound injustices. Profound injustices. Third World women—
I want to say for decades, but I'm going to say for centuries—have been
making the point that there can no women's emancipation, in fact no
liberation of any kind for women will be successful, unless it seeks to
transform the fundamental divide between the North and the South, between
Third World people and those in the West who are now calling themselves
Americans. There will be no emancipation for women anywhere on this
planet until the Western domination of this planet is ended.

Especially as all of us are being herded into the possibility of a massive war
at the behest of the United States. We need to hear those words even more
clearly today. Today in the world the United States is the most dangerous and

the most powerful global force unleashing prolific levels of violence all over the world.

From Chile to El Salvador, to Nicaragua to Iraq, the path of US foreign policy is soaked in blood. We have seen and all of us have seen, felt, the dramatic pain of watching those attacks and trying to grasp the facts of the numbers of peoples who died. We feel the pain of that every day, we have been watching it on television constantly.

But do we feel any pain for the victims of US aggression? Two hundred thousand people killed only in the initial war on Iraq. That bombing of Iraq has continued for ten years now. Do we feel the pain of all the children in Iraq who are dying from the sanctions that were imposed by the United States? Do we feel that pain on an everyday level? Share it with our families and our communities and talk about it on every platform that is available to us? Do we feel the pain of Palestinians who now for fifty years have been living in refugee camps?

US foreign policy is soaked in blood. And other countries of the West—including, shamefully, Canada—cannot line up fast enough behind it. All want to sign up now as Americans and I think it is the responsibility of the women's movement in this country to stop that, to fight against it.

These policies are hell-bent on the West maintaining its control over the world's resources. At whatever cost to the people ... Pursuing American corporate interest should not be Canada's national interest.

This new fight, this new war against terrorism, that is being launched, it's very old. And it is a very old fight of the West against the rest. Consider the language which is being used. ...

Calling the perpetrators evildoers, irrational, calling them the forces of darkness, uncivilized, intent on destroying civilization, intent on destroying democracy. They hate freedom, we are told. Every person of colour, and I would want to say also every Aboriginal person, will recognize that language. The language of us versus them, of civilization versus the forces of darkness, this language is rooted in the colonial legacy. It was used to justify our colonization by Europe.

We were colonized in the name of the West bringing civilization, democracy, bringing freedom to us. All of us recognize who is being talked about when that language is being used. The terms *crusade*, *infinite justice*, the cowboy imagery of dead or alive posters, we all know what they mean. The West, people in the West also recognize who this fight is against. Cries heard all over the Western world, we are all Americans now. People who are saying that recognize who this fight is against. People who are attacking Muslims, any person of colour who looks like they could be from the Middle East, without distinguishing, recognize who this fight is against. These are not slips of the tongue that Bush quickly tries to reject. They reveal a thinking, a mindset. And it is horrific to think that the fate of the world hangs on the plans of people like that. This will be a big mistake for us if we just accept that these are slips of mind, just slips of the tongue. They're not. They reveal the thinking, and the thinking is based on dominating the rest of the world in the name of bringing freedom and civilization to it.

If we look also at the people who are being targeted for attack. A Sikh man killed. Reports of a Cherokee woman in the United States having been attacked. Pakistanis being attacked. Hindu temples attacked. Muslim mosques attacked regardless of where the Muslims come from. These people also recognize who this fight is against. And it is due to the strength of anti-racist organizing that Bush has been forced to visit mosques, that our prime minister has been forced also to visit mosques and say, no, there shouldn't be these kinds of attacks. We should recognize that it is the strength of anti-racist organizing that is forcing them to make those remarks.

But even as they visit mosques, and even as they make these conciliatory noises, they are talking out of both sides of the mouth because they are officially sanctioning racial profiling at the borders. In the United States, for entrance into training schools, for learning to become pilots, racial profiling is being used at every step of the way. On an airplane, who is suspicious, who is not? Racial profiling is being officially sanctioned and officially introduced. In Canada we know that guidelines—leaked by the *Globe and Mail* were given to immigration officers at the border to decide against whom to step up security.

So on the one hand, they say no, it's not all Muslims; on the other hand they say yes, we are going to use racial profiling because it is reasonable. So we have to see how they are perpetrating the racism against people of colour, at the same time that they claim to be speaking out against it. And these are the conditions, the conditions of racial profiling. These are the conditions within which children are being bullied and targeted in schools, women are being chased in parking lots and shopping malls, we are being scrutinized as we even come to conferences. That extra security, you can feel the coldness when you enter the airport. I was quite amazed. I have been traveling in this country for ten years, and I have never had the experience that I had flying down here for this conference. All of us feel it. So this racial profiling has to be stopped.

Events of the last two weeks also show that the American people that Bush is trying to invoke, whoever they are these American people—just like we contest notions of who the Canadian people are, we have to recognize that there are other voices in the United States as well, contesting that.

But the people, the American nation that Bush is invoking, is a people which is bloodthirsty, vengeful, and calling for blood. They don't care whose blood it is, they want blood. And that has to be confronted. We cannot keep calling this an understandable response. We cannot say yes, we understand that this is how people would respond because of the attacks. We have to stop condoning it and creating a climate of acceptability for this kind of response. We have to call it for what it is: bloodthirsty vengeance.

And people in the United States—we have seen peace marches all over this weekend—they also are contesting this. But Bush is developing the definition of the American nation, and the American people need to be challenged here. How can he keep calling it democracy? How can we keep saying that this response is understandable after Bush, of all people, who stole the election, how can we ever accept that this is democracy?

Canada's approach has been mixed, it has said yes, we will support the United States but with caution. It will be a cautionary support. We want to know what the actions will be before we sign on and we want to know. This has been Canada's approach. And I have to say we have to go much further. Canada has to say we reject US policy in the Middle East. We do not support it.

And it's really interesting to hear all this talk about saving Afghan women. Those of us who have been colonized know what this "saving" means. For a long time now, Afghan women, and the struggles that they were engaged in, were known here in the West. Afghan women became almost the poster child for women's oppression in the Third World. And rightfully many of us were in solidarity with them. Afghan women at that time were fighting and struggling against the Taliban. They were condemning the Taliban's particular interpretation of Islam. Afghan women, Afghanistan women's organizations were on the front line of this. But what did they become in the West? In the West they became nothing but poor victims of this bad, bad religion, and of these backward, backward men. The same old colonial construction. The women were in the front line, but we did not take the lead from them then. We could see them more as victims, only worthy of our pity. And today, even in the United States, people are ready to bomb those same women, seeing them as nothing more that collateral damage. You see how quickly the world can change on you. And I say that we take the lead from the Afghan women. They fought back against the Taliban, and when they were fighting back they said that it is the United States that is putting this regime in power. That's what they were saying. Look at US foreign policy!

They were trying to draw out attention to who was responsible for this state of affairs, to who was actually supporting repressive regimes, as women all over the world have been doing. So I say we take the lead from them and even if there is no American bombing of Afghanistan—which is what all of us should be working on right now, to stop any move to bomb Afghanistan—even if there is no bombing of Afghanistan, hundreds of thousands, if not millions, of people have already been displaced, fleeing the threat of war—you see the power of America here, right? One word in Washington and millions of people are forced to flee their houses, their communities. So even if there is no bombing, we have to bear in mind how many women's lives have already been disrupted, destroyed, and it will take generations for them to put back them together again.

Inevitably, and very depressingly, Canada is of course turning to the enemy within—immigrants and refugees. Tighter immigration laws, all the right-wing forces in this country are calling for that kind of approach. This is depressing for women of colour, immigrant and refugee women. If anything happens, even if George Bush was to get a cold, we know somehow it'll be the fault of immigrants and refugees in Canada, and our quote-unquote lax border policies. So I'm not going to say much about it, but I just want to ask you to think about how this anti-immigrant sentiment continues to be resurrected anytime over anything in the world.

In terms of any kind of military action, Angela Davis (an American activist) asked in the 1970s, "Do you think the men who are going to fight in Vietnam, who are going to kill Vietnamese women and children, who are raping Vietnamese women, do you think they will come home and there will be no effect of all of this? On women in the United States?" She was asking this in the 1970s. That question is as relevant today. All these soldiers that are going to be sent there, we think there will be no effect?

For women, when they come back here? This is something that we need to think about, as we talk about the responses, as we talk about this kind of jingoistic militarism. And recognize it as the most heinous form of patriarchal, racist violence that we're seeing on the globe today. The women's movement , we have to stand up to this. There is no option. There's no option for us, we have to fight back against this militarization, we have to break the support that is being built in our countries for this kind of attack. We have to recognize that the fight is for control of the vast oil and gas resources in Central Asia, for which Afghanistan is a key, strategic point!

There's nothing new about this, this is more of the same, this is more of the same that we have been now fighting against, for so many decades. And we have to recognize that the calls that are coming from progressive groups in the Third World, and from their supporters, their allies, in the rest of the world, the three key demands they are asking for are: End the bombing of Iraq, lift the sanctions on Iraq, who in this room will not support that demand? Resolve the Palestinian question, that's the second one. And remove the American military bases, everywhere in the Middle East. Who will not support these demands? We have to recognize that these demands are rooted in anti-imperialist struggles and that we have to support these demands. We need to end the racist colonization of Aboriginal peoples in this country, certainly, but we need to make common cause with women across the world who are fighting to do this. Only then can we talk about anti-racist, feminist politics. Only then can we talk about international solidarity in women's movements across the world.

And in closing, just one word—the lesson we have learned and the lesson that our politicians should have learned, is that you cannot slaughter people into submission. For 500 years they have tried that strategy. The West for 500 years has believed that it can slaughter people into submission and it has not been able to do so. It will not be able to do so this time either.

Janelle Brown

"Fatima" Speaks: Resisting the Taliban

2 October 2001, Salon.com

The film footage is wobbly and blurry but stunning: A soccer stadium in Afghanistan is packed with people, but there is no match today. Instead, a pickup truck drives into the stadium with three women, shrouded in burqas, cowering in the back.

Armed men in turbans force a woman from the truck, and make her kneel at the penalty line on the field. Confused and unable to see, the woman tries to look behind just as a rifle is pointed against the back of her head. With no fanfare whatsoever, she is shot dead. The shaky video camera captures the cheering crowd as people rise to their feet, hoping to get a better view of the corpse on the ground. The blue folds of the burqa begin to stain red with blood.

This public execution is some of the most shocking film ever seen on television; it is perhaps the best document that the West has of atrocities committed by the Taliban. It is just one part of an astonishing hour-long documentary called *Beneath the Veil*, currently in heavy rotation on CNN. Filmed by the half-Afghan British reporter Saira Shah, who traveled undercover to Afghanistan last year, *Beneath the Veil* neatly captures the horror of life under the Taliban—the public executions for infractions as minor as prostitution or adultery, the brutality of fundamentalist police, the slaughter of civilians unlucky enough to live on the front line of the civil war with the Northern Alliance.

In documenting life under the Taliban, Shah went into the homes of the Afghan people and onto the battlefields, cleverly evading the Department of Vice and Virtue, which would have thrown her in jail for filming illegally (all unsanctioned filming is forbidden). She visited territory occupied by the Northern Alliance, and visited a village where the Taliban had brutally murdered dozens of civilians just weeks earlier—a local wedding photographer had filmed the scene as villagers buried rotting bodies that had been scalped and mutilated. There, Shah also interviewed three teenage girls whose mother had been shot dead by the Taliban. They were so traumatized by the atrocities that the Taliban subsequently inflicted upon them that two of them would no longer speak.

But some of the most heartstopping footage in *Beneath the Veil*, including film of the execution of the women in the soccer stadium, was captured not by Shah but by an Afghan underground organization which assisted her in her work. Indeed, Shah's documentary would not have been possible were it not for the Revolutionary Association of the Women of Afghanistan (RAWA), an underground organization whose members risk their lives every day in attempts to undermine the Taliban and publicize its brutality.

RAWA was originally founded in 1977 as an Afghan feminist group focused on women's rights, but its mandate broadened when fundamentalists rose to power. Determined to expose the frightening abuses of the Taliban, women in the group began to hide video cameras under their burqas and document the executions and public floggings which take place every day under the Taliban. They also smuggle female journalists like Saira Shah and Eve Ensler, writer/director of *The Vagina Monologues*, into the country, in hopes of bringing attention to their cause. In defiance of the Taliban's law forbidding education for women, RAWA also runs clandestine home-based schools for girls; for women, who are forbidden to work, RAWA teaches handicrafts and sells them online. In the refugee camps in Pakistan, RAWA also provides medical assistance, housing and education for impoverished and terrified fugitives of Taliban rule.

RAWA, the most prominent Afghan-run organization to oppose the Taliban, has become one of the fundamentalists' greatest enemies. Perhaps the aspect of the group most infuriating to its opponents—and a surprising key to its effectiveness—is that it consists entirely of women, nearly 2000 in Afghanistan and Pakistan, who use the cover of their burqas and the seeming powerlessness of their status to strategic advantage.

By traveling with RAWA, Shah got a first-hand view of what it's like to be a woman living under the Taliban, and she was invited into RAWA's secret schools and illegal meetings. She also got access to its library of video footage—which includes not just the film of the execution of the women, but footage of the public hanging of three men in the same soccer stadium. (The soccer stadium was funded by international aid groups who wanted to raise the spirits of the Afghan people; instead, the Taliban is using it only for executions. One Taliban official told Shah that if the aid groups felt that the stadium should be used for soccer, they should build the Taliban an extra stadium for executions.)

Beneath the Veil was filmed long before the attacks of September 11, and, according to RAWA members, the situation in Afghanistan has since become more dire. Because the borders between Pakistan and Afghanistan have closed, the Afghan people are now trapped in their own country—enduring the oppressive rule of the Taliban while waiting for US bombs to drop from the sky. RAWA, meanwhile, says it is running out of money and can't afford to educate, feed and treat the millions of refugees massed along the border. The Pakistani police, which are sympathetic to the Taliban, regularly target RAWA members; and since communication with Afghanistan has been cut off, the RAWA members in Pakistan know little about what is happening to their members across the border.

In a telephone interview from Islamabad, a 26-year-old member of RAWA, identified only as "Fatima", spoke about RAWA's work in Pakistan and Afghanistan, its position on war and the Northern Alliance, and its "uncompromising attitude" toward fundamentalism. A seven-year veteran of the group's dangerous brand of activism, Fatima is a member of the RAWA political committee that has been trying to rally both Afghan women and the international media to its agenda.

What is your life story, and what do you do for RAWA?
I'm from Kabul. I started to work with RAWA when I was nineteen years old. There has been war in our country for more than twenty-three years; my generation was born with war, we've experienced just crimes, just blackness, just sorrow in our country. We never saw happiness or democracy. I lived in shock, because every day there were tragic stories in my neighborhood around me.

When I was young I decided to do something about this. A lot of young girls commit suicide because they are helpless and hopeless. But some, like me, choose the way of struggle. We accept that we want to serve our people— that this is the best way to bring justice to our country.

When I was twenty years old, I left Afghanistan; my job for RAWA was to come here to Pakistan and work in the refugee camps. I had to cross the border often and go back into Afghanistan to organize women for demonstrations; and to bring RAWA's publications into Afghanistan. We would go secretly and without documents—no one asks you for them because you are a woman. I wear the burqa then, because this is the only visa required for women to enter Afghanistan for women. When I cross the border, no one can know that I am in RAWA.

Why do you use the pseudonym "Fatima"?
We all use different names all the time, because we have a lot of security problems. Our leader Meena and her bodyguards were assassinated in Pakistan in 1987 by the Islamic fundamentalists and the KGB. Our members are always attacked and injured—we receive death threats by e-mail and letters

and telephone, telling us to stop what we are doing or they will kill us. So we are working clandestinely in Afghanistan, and in Pakistan we are half-secret.

Have you ever been personally attacked by the Taliban?
I was flogged three times in the streets, for stupid reasons. They will flog women that don't have the veil on, or aren't with their male relative, or are talking to a male shopkeeper, or are out on the streets during the evening. There are always people sobbing in the streets because they are being beaten. This is normal.

In Pakistan in 1999, I was injured at a RAWA demonstration. Pakistan is one of the countries that officially recognizes the Taliban government; so when we take our anti-Taliban slogans into the streets, they try to stop us. During the demonstration, we were fighting—we wanted to go in front of the United Nations building, but the Pakistani police wanted to stop us. During the fighting, they beat me and broke my hand.

What has been RAWA's most crucial activity in Afghanistan?
We teach hundreds of women and children in the underground schools in Afghanistan. For children, we teach mathematics, physics, chemistry, Persian, science, social studies and the history of Afghanistan; also, the geography of the world. For women, we just teach them two main subjects—mathematics and Persian. When our women go to the shops, they don't know how to pay the shopkeeper and get change, because they haven't had an education.

We also bring in video cameras to expose the crimes of the Taliban. It's risky work. We filmed the execution of the women that you saw in *Beneath the Veil*. Also, we've filmed hangings in Kabul and several other cities, taken pictures of Afghans who have had their hands cut off for stealing, or their necks cut. There are photos on our web site.

We make a hole in the burqa and film through it. That's why the quality of our films is very bad; it's very difficult. No one has ever been caught doing it; but execution is the only punishment if you get caught, especially if the Taliban knew we were RAWA.

What are you doing in the refugee camps in Pakistan?
We have schools for girls in the fugitive camps; but in some we have problems because of the influence of the fundamentalists. We have handicraft projects for women; we run chicken farms, a jam-making business and carpet-weaving projects. We also have mobile medical teams that go in to the camps one or two days a week to give free medicine. We had a hospital called Malalai, but it closed because of our financial problems; one of our very urgent projects is to reopen it.

What are your feelings about the attack on America?
We are so sorry for the victims of this terrorist attack. We want to shower them with deep solidarity. We can understand their sorrow because we also suffered this terrorism for more than twenty-three years. We were already victims of this tragedy.

On the other hand, unfortunately, we warned the United States government about this many, many times; as well as the other countries that are supporting and creating the fundamentalist parties. They helped create these terrorists during the Cold War; they supported Osama Bin Laden [during the Russian occupation of Afghanistan]. Fundamentalism is equal to terrorism; it's equal to crime. We said, this germ won't just be in Afghanistan, it will spread out all over the world. Today we can see this with our own eyes. We warned them but they never listened to our cry, to our voice.

How is the crisis in America affecting your work at RAWA?
Thousands of families are escaping from Afghanistan, leaving everything behind because they are afraid of war. Thousands of others that are living in Afghanistan don't have the possibility to immigrate here; and now, even the borders are closed. That means that our people have to burn in the flame of war and all the doors are closed.

In fugitive camps it's really hard to work, especially hard because millions of fugitives have just arrived. They are in shock, and have nothing but themselves and the clothes on their back. I met a family yesterday that wanted help from RAWA, they cried and said they walked through the mountains because the border was closed. Their child fell down the mountain and died, but they couldn't stop because they had to escape. Our people escape from Afghanistan because of the fear of killing and rape and torture, but they will die in the refugee camps because of lack of food, jobs and healthcare. Even here the situation is not good. We are in a crisis in the camps; thousands have contacted us for help and we don't know how to help them. At every moment they want their children to be in our orphanages or our schools; they want a house, medicine—they need everything, and we have no money. Also we are so worried about our members inside Afghanistan, about their lives.

Are you concerned about a war with the United States?
We are condemning an attack of the US on Afghanistan, because it won't be the Taliban but our people who will be the victims. The United States should decry these terrorist groups in Afghanistan; but not through an attack. Maybe through commando attacks, though. We do want the United Nations to be more active—their rule is very important in this moment. We also want

to convey a message to the American people that there's a difference between the people of Afghanistan and the criminal government of Afghanistan. There is a river of blood between them.

Do you support the Northern Alliance?
We condemn the cooperation of the United States with the Northern Alliance. This is another nightmare for our people—the Northern Alliance are the second Taliban. The Northern Alliance are hypocrites: They say they are for democracy and human rights, but we can't forget the black experience we had with them. Seventy-year-old grandmothers were raped during their rule, thousands of girls were raped, thousands were killed and tortured. They are the first government that started this tragedy in Afghanistan.

What government do you support, then?
We are ready to support the former king. It doesn't mean that the king is a very ideal person for us. But in comparison to the fundamentalist parties, we prefer him. The only condition we have for the king is that he must not cooperate with the Northern Alliance.

What does RAWA need right now?
We are in a very bad financial condition. We need anything we can get—for our mobile team, for medicine, for our schools. Maybe $1 is nothing for them, but for us it means a lot. To run our struggle with empty hands is impossible for us. (To donate to RAWA, visit the Web site of RAWA, The Afghan Women's Mission, or The Feminist Majority.)

Do you want to go back to Afghanistan?
I miss Afghanistan very much, it's my country. I love my city and my country a lot. I am a fugitive here. Whenever there is peace in Afghanistan we will never go to another country—we will go back to rebuild Afghanistan and experience good days, I hope.

GABRIELA Network

Justice, Not Revenge; Peace, Not War; Civil Liberties and Human Rights, Not Fascism

October 2001

GABRIELA Network, a US–Philippine women's solidarity organization, grieves with the families of those who perished in the September 11, 2001 attacks on the cities of New York and Washington, DC. We grieve most profoundly for the loss of Americans of Philippine ancestry, and the deaths of Filipino migrant workers who held jobs at various establishments at the World Trade Center. We extend our condolences and our support to the bereaved families.

In the aftermath of these tragedies, we ask that the public bear in mind that the dead of the World Trade Center twin-tower collapse came from sixty-two countries. To use their deaths for xenophobia and anti-immigrant hysteria is to disrespect their suffering and those of their families.

It is a matter of grave concern that within hours of the attacks, we witnessed and continue to witness an assault on civil liberties and human rights within the US itself. Militarization has proceeded apace, attended by mobilization, overseas deployment, police and military barricades, wiretaps, raids, the zoning off of neighborhoods, "detention",—all wrapped in secrecy and the legal fiction of "sealed documents" violative of due process. "Immigration questions" is the excuse used for arrest and interrogation, a phrase designed to quell any question regarding the processes by which investigation surrounding the tragedies are carried out.

That little time has been spent in asking questions—why the choice of targets, why such an acceptance of "collateral damage", why such disregard for human life, etc.—and even less time in seeking for answers add to our sorrow. We urge that time be spent in understanding the source of such rage towards the US, the role of the US outside its borders and finally, the role of the US in fostering the very climate in which massive death and destruction are acceptable. The root causes of the attacks have to be understood, so that the events of September 11, 2001 are never again repeated, whether the victims be people of the United States or peoples of Asia, Africa or the rest of the Americas. Osama Bin Laden, the Al-Qaeda, the Taliban, and others accused of terrorism did not spring full-blown; nor did they develop in a vacuum. Certainly, the acute disparity in wealth, power and even in how grievances are heard create a fertile source of recruits for those who would commit such acts of despair as the attacks on the Twin Towers of New York City. Certainly, encouragement and support for their violence did not come from one culture or one religion or one system of beliefs alone. Indeed, the US itself was and continues to be instrumental in the creation and shaping of the Taliban, in the fostering of fundamentalism and fanaticism. And certainly, the US has been a prime creator of a world climate wherein the large-scale slaughter of civilians has become acceptable. The very term "collateral damage", to objectify the death of civilians, emerged from US military history.

Moreover, US transnational corporations, with their ruthless drive for profit, have been instrumental in creating a value system which ranks human lives as not even a poor second to the accumulation of wealth. Where medicine vital to survival becomes priced out of reach of the majority of the sick, where medicine is not manufactured because the sick poor does not constitute a market, where the food self-sufficiency of nations is compromised to maintain a world trading system, and where the most fundamental needs of human beings are ignored in favor of "globalization", not only despair but also a vast reservoir of hatred becomes the constant emotion of daily existence of the populations of the world.

We therefore urge that the response to the attacks be predicated on justice, not revenge; that it be predicated on the resolution of long-standing conflicts in various regions of the world, in lieu of war; that militarism be curbed, if not totally eradicated; that solutions to disparities in wealth and development be actively sought and implemented; and that the people of the US hold even more strongly and with greater fervor to civil liberties, due process and the respect for human rights.

We call on everyone to resist and oppose the current xenophobic and anti-immigrant hysteria. We call for an end to general public apathy and ignorance of the international situation, so carefully cultivated in the mass culture of the US. We call for even greater effort towards knowledge and the understanding of peoples, cultures and conditions outside US borders, and even firmer solidarity with those struggling for economic and social justice, independence, national liberation and genuine democracy.

We must do this in commemoration of the thousands who died in those attacks and toward the single objective that similar attacks not happen again, whether the victims be people of the US or people of Asia, Africa and the rest of the Americas.

Betty McLellan

Another Feminist Response to the Terrorist Attacks

5 October 2001

Dear All,

In the early 1970s, when I "discovered" the Women's Liberation Movement, the thing that impressed me so much and gained my absolute commitment to the cause was the fact that the Movement's aim was no less than: bringing about a New World Order. One based on justice, equality and peace.

The events of 11 September reminded me tragically and forcefully that that aim was never achieved. Why not? Three reasons, as I see it:

- The male machine in every country is so powerful and so ruthless that it is prepared to destroy everyone and everything that stands in its way. (In Western countries, the male machine is comprised of powerful government members together with wealthy corporate executives—working hand-in-glove.)
- Liberalism took over the feminist movement, silenced radical voices within the movement and encouraged women in general to "be more understanding" of men, to "forgive", to "accommodate" and "work with" them.
- Left-leaning feminists didn't work hard enough at encouraging cooperation between all groups working for social justice, e.g., environment groups, socialist groups, peace groups, some unions, etc.

So, where does the feminist movement stand today in relation to the aim of bringing in a New World Order? In my despair over the terrorist attacks and my fear about US reprisals, I've struggled in recent weeks to formulate my own feminist response. One of the reasons for my despair was that I was not able, immediately, to develop a feminist analysis that satisfied me. As a matter of fact, I wasn't able to convince myself that feminism had anything significant to say that was any different from all other movements for social justice. And, I said to myself, if feminism has nothing specifically feminist to say in response to violent acts of such magnitude, then we should be honest and admit that feminism is now irrelevant and put our energy into other social justice movements. But I wasn't convinced. So I set about to analyse this horrific event for myself. What is it about? It sounds too simple to say that it's about male violence on a huge scale. But it is! It's about competition between men, men getting even, men humiliating each other. It's about men not losing face, men raising the stakes, meeting the challenge, coming out on top. And it's also about the total invisibility of women. It's important not to forget that this violent, horrendous game of tit for tat is one that masculinist society is comfortable with, challenged by and prepared for. And an added bonus is that they don't have to include women in any aspect of it. For most women, and those men who don't fit with the masculinist desire to be conquerors, this is foreign territory. So, we shrink from it and are thereby not a problem to the men who own the game.

In the days following September 11, as I immersed myself (compulsively) in the horror of it all—glued to the TV, talking about it as if there was no other topic available, reading all the newspapers, consuming all the excellent commentaries posted on the e-mail list Ausfem, attending a special church service—the one thing that stood out like a beacon was that this whole thing, in all its aspects, was indeed totally dominated by men. Women and children were among the victims, of course (nothing new about that), and women and children featured among the mourners. But every other role in this tragic drama was played by men. Even the church service I attended was led by eight men and one woman (a young woman with an American accent).

The perpetrators were men (as far as we know), the "experts" interviewed on TV are men, most of the commentators (including those posted on this list) are men, those making decisions about how the world should respond are men, those leading memorial services and conducting funerals are men. Did George W. Bush or his advisers seek advice from any group of women before formulating the US response? Did they seek advice from RAWA? Did Tony Blair seek advice from British women? Did John Howard consult with the Office of the Status of Women or the Women's Electoral Lobby or any other group of women before committing Australia to join the US in *whatever* retaliatory action they may decide to take? Of course not! Since the terrorist attacks, it has been demonstrated very clearly what some of us have known for a long time—that the short period when men and governments paid lip-service to the inclusion of women, to justice and equality for women, was but a blip on the history of *man*kind. What ever happened to the New World Order? Some feminists thought they saw glimpses of it in the 1980s but, really, there was never anything very convincing. To topple or to change the present World Order seems impossible because the culture of masculinity, the culture of violence, the culture of greed are so ingrained. But, we have to try—again and again.

This time, I suggest that we:

- develop a stronger and even more comprehensive analysis of men's violence (we did pretty well last time, but more is needed)
- take a *radical* stand against men's violence and domination, rather than a watered-down, let's-be-nice, let's-be-careful-not-to-alienate-men, liberal stance
- find the courage, in greater numbers than ever before, to speak and act (in other words, those feminists who want to see a New World Order must stop being lurkers and spectators in the drama of life, and begin speaking out and expressing their rage like never before)
- make a concerted effort to work with those men and groups that have a similar interest in social justice and in replacing the existing World Order with something better (this is always a difficult one for me because even the most "aware" men seem to have a blind spot when it comes to women —and are totally blind when it comes to feminists. But still, I think we have to make the effort).

There are other things I want to say in relation to my own feminist response to the terrorist attacks, but I'll stop here. It would be great if we could have a discussion on this list about the terrible tragedy we've all been through. Our own thoughts, I mean. Our own attempts at a feminist analysis of the events. Susan Hawthorne's response, the other day, was very important. I look forward, now, to more discussion. Our task is no less than that of saving the world!!

All the best,
Betty

Carol Anne Douglas
A World Where Justice Brings Peace

October 2001

I am deeply saddened by the hijackings and the attacks on the World Trade Center and, yes, even the Pentagon. Even if one could argue that the Pentagon is the center of a neoimperialistic military, the passengers on the airplane that was forced to crash into it (one of whom was the wife of a man at my workplace) were civilians and many of the people who were killed were probably clerical workers.

If the reason for these attacks was retaliation for the suffering of the Palestinians, which it is true that the world has largely ignored, this helps them not at all. If anything, they are likely to face greater hostility from administration of Bush, who has seen fit to meet only Israel's Sharon, and not Palestinian leader Arafat, since he has taken office. The United States is likely to back Israel more than it did before in its occupation of the Palestinian territories and repression of Palestinians. And Sharon has been attacking the Palestinians more fiercely than ever since the US tragedy.

I think how differently women handle anger. I remember when women surrounded the Pentagon with ribbons and chanted to overcome military power.

In the early 1980s, filmmaker Lizzie Borden produced a movie, *Born in Flames*, in which a mostly African–American and Latina group of radical and lesbian feminists stages a rebellion in New York City: the climax was bombing the World Trade Center. But they did it at night, and supposedly no one was hurt (although in real life cleaning people would be there). It is amazing to think now that anyone could have thought (as the women in the movie did) that such a bombing could be a cause for celebration. The reality of people jumping from the 80th floor because they preferred a death by falling to a death by fire is gut-wrenching.

Today, it is fortunately almost impossible to imagine a group of feminists bombing a building, although some in the 1970s did support bomb- and gun-toting leftist men. In her book *The Demon Lover*, Robin Morgan has examined male violence, including the violence of leftist men, many of whose other beliefs we might share though we reject the idea that "all power grows out of the barrel of a gun" (a quote from Mao, I think).

I do not believe that women are intrinsically nonviolent or that men are intrinsically violent. I know that most women have been socialized to turn their anger inward, which is not good either. Nevertheless, I think nonviolent tactics offer the greatest hope for the future. But I am not a pacifist.

I am saddened that the Bush administration is apparently preparing to bomb Afghanistan in retaliation and "go to war" (it probably will happen before you read these words) and that all of Congress and most of the nation's people support such action. I could support killing Osama Bin Laden, if he is indeed behind these attacks, and the heads of the brutal fundamentalist Afghan Taliban, for they are likely to continue to kill and cause suffering. However, they are not the ones who are likely to suffer. They are reportedly well hidden, and I fear that thousands of Afghan civilians, including the women who have been forced to give up their jobs and to stay in their houses, will be the ones to suffer. I fear that the United States government's reaction will continue to strengthen the hand of the fundamentalists, helping them perpetuate and spread the most extreme doctrine and practice of male supremacy in a world that already suffers from many forms of male supremacy.

We should remember what Americans do not always remember—that everyone suffers just as much when they are attacked. Too many people in this country gloated over the bombing of Iraq as if it didn't kill thousands of innocent people. Too many Americans seemed to learn from the Persian Gulf War that it is possible to wage war without suffering many casualties. It is not good to imagine that war can be painless for any side.

Let us condemn all forms of male supremacy, militarism, racism, and exploitation, the kind practiced in the West as well as that of the men who planned and carried out these attacks. And let us work for a world where justice brings peace and no one's suffering is ignored.

Azra Talat Sayeed

Reflections on "Infinite Justice"

October 2001

....

Not more than a generation ago, the Pakistan Military had come to the rescue of the American Interest. The enemy at that time was the Soviet threat to "world peace and democracy". Now just twenty or some years later, we enter another such event, again under the leadership of a military rule. This time the war is on terrorists, ironically the same ones who had been in the last war termed as heroes by the Americans.

It is well known that the "Afghan War" had been fought by the American by creating the Mujahideen, the leaders representing Osama Bin Laden and many of his type. Billion of dollars had been provided to the Mujahideen for training and supply of the latest weapons and warfare technologies, all done under the aegis of the United States CIA and the British MI6.

According to Moran of www.msnbc.com, the CIA had understood that Arabs might create a problem for later on, but at the moment they were serving their purposes in fighting the anti-Soviet war. Islamic militants from many Islamic states including Pakistan were bosom brothers of the Americans then; now the very same are terrorists wanted "dead or alive".

The question which we need to ask ourselves is, what did we "gain" from "hosting a war against the Afghans" especially so in the light of the fact that, shamefully, we are bent on doing it once again. That our country has been given no other choice (except of course being smashed into a time zone some four centuries back) is another matter. Are threats like these not terrorism? Maybe as a mere woman from a "backward, barbaric" country, I am just too dumb and don't understand world politics and the diplomacy that captitalist patriarchs work out for our protection and long-term prosperity.

Is it not interesting that if you ask the common person he will blame the "weaponization" of Pakistan on the Americans? As they were equipping the Mujahideen for fighting the Soviets in Afghanistan, many of the weapons delivered reached hands of many in Pakistan. With violent reper-cussions for the Pakistani population. Of course. Weapons are for violence, and no hands in the world are safe for their use. How come rules are written such that in the hands of our "heroes" they are "safe" and in the hands of "terrorists" not so. But then in this rather confusing world how do we know who is "the terrorist" of the moment? The same who were our "Mujahideen brothers" just twenty years or so ago are now terrorists. Some fifty years ago the Japanese had to be "taught a lesson", hence no less than nuclear bombs were used. So what if millions were killed then and generations to this day pay the price of their "sins". Maybe this is what "infinite justice" means.

What other thoughts come to the mind of a person who has lived in a country in the aftermath of "hosting a war"? The hundreds of homes that now bear the very visible wounds of a destroying demeaning evidence of drug addiction. The hopelessness, the misery, the fear, the weariness in the eyes of many, many women who now live side by side with this filthy devil. In other words, drug trafficking was the poisonous fruit which came along as a product of war in Afghanistan. Now there is just about no squatter settlement in this country which does not house this ever-present enemy. Women are afraid to walk those narrow dark alleys, scared of being pulled in, used and sold by those who are lost to all sense and decency of human life.

And what was the fate of the Afghani people on whom the war was waged? Pakistan housed four million Afghan refugees, the largest number of refugees to be housed by any country ever, at least according to CIA reports. A country already poor, with meager resources to feed its own, the burden was awesome. The result has been the presence of massive poverty and misery on the streets of our country. It has been a common sight for the past twenty years or so to see young Afghan boys scavenging garbage dumps looking for food and recyclable material so that they could earn some meagre sum to feed their stomachs and that of their families. What of the Afghani women? Not seen or heard, as usual the invisible presence, but who cares? They are only worth mentioning as a victim of the "fundamentalist Islamic faith". Their daily existence is seldom mentioned or thought of.

The Afghan people seeking refuge in any part of the world are facing not only the loss of a homeland, but fighting racist discrimination. Remember the Norwegian ship carrying 400 Afghan refugees seeking a refuge? Does anyone know what will be their plight after the New York and Washington DC tragedies? This no doubt reflects the plight of many other millions across the globe.

And what of Pakistan? For us, offspring of the Afghan War are the Taliban and with them the tightening grip of fundamentalism in our country. What has this fundamentalism done to our children? Religious madrassahs (seminaries) abound. It has now become common for children to be sent to these madrassahs rather than school. Children have been the tools of these militant groups, taught to hate all that defy the narrow confines of religious purity as defined by them. One can only imagine the horrors awaiting us when these children turn into adults and start practicing what has been taught to them. Girls, even as young as six and seven years old, are made to wear hijab. Who knows what is in store for them? Though one can almost predict the wrath of the "pious" will fall on their unprotected heads.

We have become used to walking with our heads down, scurrying through our streets, ashamed to be seen, guilty of our very existence. Hatred towards women knows no bounds. All atrocities under the pious flag of religion and conservatism are practised. Pakistan is constantly under criticism by the so-called civilized world for honor killings practised widely in this country. Much of this is part and parcel of the values that have increased with fundamentalism. In the end, we are left facing the criticism of the "civilized" North of our "harsh, fundamentalist, backward" culture, but never any acknowledgement from them about their "crowning role" in proliferation of these "fundamentalist" practices.

And now once again our country has been forced to have a central place in a war that should never be fought. What will this new "crusade" deliver? What will this "new friendship" bring in its wake? What new weapons will be developed to bring "infinite justice" by the hands and minds of the insane capitalist gods of our "global village"?

Whose War?

8 October to 3 December

Suheir Hammad

First Writing Since

Suheir Hammad is a black Palestinian woman, based in Brooklyn. One of her brothers is in the US Navy and due to be called up for active duty.

....

1. There have been no words.
I have not written one word.
no poetry in the ashes south of Canal Street.
no prose in the refrigerated trucks driving debris and DNA.
not one word.

Today is a week, and seven is of heavens, gods, science.
evident out my kitchen window is an abstract reality.
sky where once was steel.
smoke where once was flesh.

Fire in the city air, and i feared for my sister's life in
a way never before.
and then, and now, i fear for the rest of us.

First, please God, let it be a mistake, the pilot's heart
failed, the plane's engine died.
then please God, let it be a nightmare, wake me now.
please God, after the second plane, please, don't let it
be anyone who
looks like my brothers.

I do not know how bad a life has to break in order to kill.
I have never been so hungry that i willed hunger
I have never been so angry as to want to control a gun over a pen.
not really. even as a woman, as a Palestinian, as a
broken human being.
never this broken.

More than ever, I believe there is no difference.
The most privileged nation, most Americans do not know
the difference between Indians, Afghanis, Syrians, Muslims, Sikhs, Hindus.
more than ever, there is no difference.

2. *Thank you Korea for kimchi and bibim bob, and corn*
tea and the genteel smiles of the wait staff at Wonjo
The smiles never revealing the heat of the food
or how tired they must be working long midtown shifts.
Thank you Korea, for the belly craving that brought me
into the city late the night before
and diverted my daily train ride into the World Trade Center.

There are plenty of thank yous in NY right now.
thank you for my lazy procrastinating late ass.
thank you to the germs that had me call in sick.
thank you, my attitude, you had me fired the week before.

thank you for the train that never came,
the rude NYer who stole my cab going downtown.
thank you for the sense my mama gave me to run. thank you for my legs,
my eyes, my life.

3. *The dead are called lost and their families hold up*
shaky printouts in front of us through screens smoked up.
We are looking for Iris, mother of three.
please call with any information.
we are searching for Priti, last seen on the 103rd floor.
She was talking to her husband on the phone and the line went.
please help us find George, also known as Adel.
his family is waiting for him with his favorite meal.
i am looking for my son, who was delivering coffee.
i am looking for my sister girl, she started her job on monday.

I am looking for peace.
I am looking for mercy.
I am looking for evidence of compassion.
any evidence of life.
I am looking for life.

4. Ricardo on the radio said in his accent thick as yuca,
"I will feel so much better when the first bombs drop over there, and
my friends feel the same way."

On my block, a woman was crying in a car parked and stranded in hurt.
I offered comfort, extended a hand she did not see before she said,
"We're gonna burn them so bad, I swear, so bad."
My hand went to my head, and my head went to the numbers within it of the
dead Iraqi children, the dead in Nicaragua.
the dead in Rwanda who had to vie with fake sport wrestling for
America's attention.

Yet when people sent e-mails saying, this was bound to happen, lets not
forget US transgressions,
for half a second I felt resentful.
hold up with that, cause I live here, these are my friends and family,
and it could have been me in those buildings, and we're not bad people,
do not support america's bullying.
can I just have a half second to feel bad?

If I can find through this exhaust people who were left behind to mourn
and to resist mass murder, I might be alright.

Thank you to the woman who saw me brinking my cool
and blinking back tears.
She opened her arms before she asked "Do you want a hug?"
A big white woman, and her embrace was the kind only people with the
warmth of flesh can offer.
I wasn't about to say no to any comfort.
"My brother's in the Navy," I said. "and we're Arabs".
"Wow, you got double trouble."

5. If one more person asks me if I knew the hijackers,
one more motherfucker asks me what navy my brother is in.
one more person assumes no Arabs or Muslims were killed.
one more person assumes they know me, or that I represent a people,
or that a people represent an evil,
or that evil is as simple as a flag and words on a page.

We did not vilify all white men when McVeigh bombed Oklahoma.
America did not give out his family's addresses or where he went to church,
or blame the Bible or Pat Robertson.
When the networks air footage of Palestinians dancing in the street,
there is no apology that hungry children are bribed with sweets that
turn their teeth brown,
that correspondents edit images,
that archives are there to facilitate lazy and inaccurate journalism.

When we talk about holy books and hooded men and death,
why do we never mention the KKK?

If there are any people on earth who understand how New York is feeling
right now,
they are in the West Bank and the Gaza Strip.

6. *Today it is ten days.*
Last night Bush waged war on a man once openly funded by the CIA.
I do not know who is responsible.
I read too many books, know too many people to believe what
I am told.
I don't give a fuck about bin Laden.
His vision of the world does not include me or those I love,
and petitions have been going around for years trying to get the US
sponsored Taliban out of power.
Shit is complicated, and I don't know what to think,
but I know for sure who will pay.
in the world. It will be women, mostly colored and poor.
Women will have to bury children, and support themselves
through grief.

"Either you are with us, or with the terrorists"
—meaning, keep your people under control and your resistance censored.
Meaning we got the loot and the nukes.

In America, it will be those amongst us who refuse blanket attacks on
the shivering,
those of us who work toward social justice, in support of civil
liberties, in opposition to hateful foreign policies.

I have never felt less American and more New Yorker, particularly
Brooklyn, than these past days.
The stars and stripes on all these cars and apartment windows represent
the dead as citizens first, not family members, not
lovers.

I feel like my skin is real thin, and that my eyes are only going to get darker.
The future holds little light.

My baby brother is a man now, and on alert,
and praying five times a day that the orders he will take in a few days'
time are righteous
and will not weigh his soul down from the afterlife he deserves.

Both my brothers—my heart stops when I try to pray—not a beat to
disturb my fear.
one a rock god, the other a sergeant, and both
Palestinian, practising
Muslims, gentle men.
Both born in Brooklyn, and their faces are of the
archetypal Arab man,
all eyelashes and nose and beautiful color and stubborn hair.

What will their lives be like now?

Over there is over here.

7. *All day, across the river, the smell of burning*
rubber and limbs
floats through.
The sirens have stopped now.
The advertisers are back on the air.
The rescue workers are traumatized.
The skyline is brought back to human size,
no longer taunting the gods with its height.

I have not cried at all while writing this.
I cried when I saw those buildings collapse on themselves
like a broken heart.
I have never owned pain that needs to spread like that.
and I cry daily that my brothers return to our mother
safe and whole.

There is no poetry in this.
There are causes and effects.
There are symbols and ideologies,
mad conspiracy here, and information we will never know.

There is death here, and there are promises of more.

There is life here.
Anyone reading this is breathing, maybe hurting, but
breathing for sure,

and if there is any light to come,
it will shine from the eyes of those who look for peace
and justice.
after the rubble and rhetoric are cleared, and the phoenix
has risen.

Affirm life.
Affirm life.
We've got to carry each other now.
You are either with life, or against it.
Affirm life.

Revolutionary Association of the Women of Afghanistan
Statement on the US Strikes on Afghanistan

11 October 2000

Taliban should be overthrown by the uprising of Afghan nation. Again, due to the treason of fundamentalist hangmen, our people have been caught in the claws of the monster of a vast war and destruction.

America, by forming an international coalition against Osama and his Taliban-collaborators and in retaliation for the September 11 terrorist attacks, has launched a vast aggression on our country.

Despite the claim of the US that only military and terrorist bases of the Taliban and Al-Qaeda will be struck and that its actions would be accurately targeted and proportionate, what we have witnessed for the past seven days leaves no doubt that this invasion will shed the blood of numerous women, men, children, young and old of our country.

If until yesterday the US and its allies, without paying the least attention to the fate of democracy in Afghanistan, were supporting the policy of Jihadis-fostering, Osama-fostering and Taliban-fostering, today they are sharpening the dagger of the "Northern Alliance". And because of this policy they have plunged our people into a horrific concern and anxiety in fear of re-experiencing the dreadful happenings of the years of the Jihadis' "emirate".

Afghans, while keeping in mind the tremendous disasters they faced at the hands of Jihadi and Taliban vultures, just hang onto their hope for the return of the ex-king. However, if he comes to the scene while relying on the "Northern Alliance" and so-called "moderate" Taliban, he not only will lose his reputation among the people but it will endanger the stability and success of whatever set-up he forms.

In the time of the Taliban's medievalist domination, no Afghan and no honorable and mindful Muslim will be deceived by the "nationalistic" gestures of Taliban who invite the Afghan people and even the whole Muslim world for "Jihad" against America. Any person, group or government that supports the Taliban, no matter under what pretext, is the enemy of the Afghan people, the people who also hate the "anti-Osama" and "anti-terrorism" acts of the "Northern Alliance" murderers. Our people not only have not forgotten the five years after the collapse of the puppet regime of Najib—the most horrible years of terrorism and unchastity—but as well they don't forget the time when the Jihadis themselves were the cheap servants of Abdullah Ezam and Osama Bin Laden.

Now the "Northern Alliance" groups lie in ambush like hungry wolves so they, while riding the guns of the US, can assault and swarm into Kabul and in proportion to the depth and width of their "conquests", besides committing vandalism like the years before, gain ground in order to bargain for position in the second "emirate", and as a consequence again spoil the aspiration of the people for the establishment of a stable and democratic government acceptable to all.

The continuation of US attacks and the increase in the number of innocent civilian victims not only gives an excuse to the Taliban, but also will cause the empowering of the fundamentalist forces in the region and even in the world.

Our people have two options: Either the eradication of the plague of Taliban and Al-Qaeda—though they (our people) didn't have any part in its cultivation and germination—and the establishment of a government based on democratic values, or to hand over Afghanistan to these forces who have dependence, looting, crime and national treason as the main components of their perfidious entity. Our compatriots, therefore, must rise up for a thorough demolition of Taliban and their Osamas so the world should understand that the tired, wounded, mournful and deserted Afghans not only in word, but practically too, have no connection with the criminals and don't regard a handful of Arab or non-Arab terrorists as "honorable guests".

Only an overall uprising can prevent the repetition and recurrence of the catastrophe that has befallen our country before. With, or even without, the presence of the UN peace-keeping force this uprising can pave the way for the establishment of an interim government and preparation for elections. We believe that once there is no foreign interference, especially of a fundamentalist type, all ethnic groups of all religions, with no regard to the devilish designs of the fundamentalists, will prove their solidarity for achieving the most sacred national interests for the sake of a proud and free Afghanistan.

The Revolutionary Association of the Women of Afghanistan (RAWA) asks that all anti-fundamentalist, freedom and democracy-loving and pro-women's rights forces and also the ex-king of Afghanistan, before it is too late, must play their role in the organizing of mass-uprising and as well thwart the plans of the internal and external enemies of Afghanistan. The peace- and justice-loving people of the world will be on the side of the Afghan people.

Mythily Sivaraman

Women Oppose War

11 October 2001

> We have all been overwhelmed by the attacks in the USA ... But the Timorese never called for Jakarta to be bombed when their whole country was destroyed by Indonesian forces two years ago ... The US President could learn from them.
>
> Janet Hunt, Dili, East Timor

Jingoism in America, following the September 11 massacre, appeared to be getting somewhat tempered prior to the strikes on Afghanistan which began on 7 October. The inhumanity of a military assault on a miserably impoverished country did not seem to be exercising the sensibilities of Washington very much.

From a civilisational viewpoint, the voices raised across the globe, counselling sanity and human decency—even if not the dominant ones—are truly encouraging. It stands to reason that many women's groups and movements in different countries should have reacted strongly against military retaliation, as women have been the worst sufferers of war. Since war broke out in the Balkans in 1992, more than 20,000 women and girls are said to have been raped, followed by 15,700 in Rwanda, in one year. A UN study also shows, ironically, that the arrival of UN peacekeeping troops has been associated with a rapid rise in child prostitution! (And far more children are said to die of disease and malnutrition caused by war than from direct attack.) It is also claimed that close to 90 per cent of current war casualties are civilians, the majority of whom are women and children, compared to a century ago, when 90 per cent of the dead were army men.

Hence the increasing awareness and critical responses from the global women's movements that see war even in a distant continent as a concern for them, a concern that impacts gender justice and calls for intervention. Women from war-battered countries are, understandably, very vocal in their views and forthright in expressions. For instance, the Revolutionary Association of the Women of Afghanistan (RAWA), vehemently opposed to the Taliban, cautioned the US against military attacks, for three reasons: "further trauma and misery for the hapless Afghans will not in any way decrease the grief of the Americans"; the hope that "the great American people could

differentiate between the people of Afghanistan and a handful of fundamentalist terrorists" and that America would be able to "wipe out the root cause
of terrorism" by armed action which would render thousands of deprived,
poor and innocent people of Afghanistan as its victims, might, in fact, "well
spread terrorism even to a larger scale".

The Women of Kosovo, even today living with war-induced trauma, share
their own experiences and lessons drawn: "We have lived through war. We
know what it is like to be attacked, to grieve, and to feel anger. We understand the urge for revenge is strong. And we know that it must not be given
in to. Violence kills more innocent victims and gives birth to new holy
avengers." They offer an advice the US could well take in large doses:
"Terrorists are not nations. And nations must not act like terrorists."

Many social scientists and scholars do point out that if terrorism is defined
as violence against civilians for political ends, then the US is guilty of it
more than anyone else. Ms Asma Jehangir, veteran human rights activist from
Pakistan, the one country facing a massive influx of refugees from Afghanistan, says: "As victims of terrorism for a long time, we know very well what
it means to humanity. But, no terrorism against terrorism. It solves nothing."
Women from Canada are aghast: "How does it increase our security to bomb
countries into the Stone Age?"

The not-so-humble political and military establishments of the US would
be well advised—for themselves and for others—to listen to the words of
women, who are humble and willing to learn from experience, and thereby
wiser than the imperial powers with noses in the cloud. On the contrary, they
stubbornly refuse to recognise that the dastardly acts that led to the
September 11 massacre could largely be of their own making. RAWA states
this sharply:

> it was the Government of the US that supported Pakistani dictator General Zia-ul
> Haq in creating thousands of religious schools from which the germs of Taliban
> emerged ... Osama Bin Laden has been the blue-eyed boy of CIA ... any kind of
> support to the fundamentalist Taliban and jihadis is actually trampling ... human
> rights values. The US should examine the root cause of this terrible event, which
> has not been the first and will not be the last one too.

Groups from Spain point out that the West never cared when the Taliban
attacked women's rights or extremists in Algeria kidnapped, raped, killed and
"ripped to pieces scores of women". Presumably, such atrocities did not merit
being termed "barbaric" when superpower interests were not affected and
when the socially radical were not also politically convenient. Many concerned women's organisations such as the Women's International League for
Peace and Freedom (WILPF) hold that if the present "gross iniquities in
distribution of the world's wealth" were to continue, "people in the affluent

nations of the West must continue to expect anger and resentments to be directed against ordinary citizens." To quote further:

> If world leaders truly value human security as they proclaim, then they will have to abandon their cant about "barbaric" acts of terrorism against "civilised" nations. To use such rhetoric and to try to posit an "enemy" other than the real culprit is to mislead people. To permit such racism to flourish is to further undermine our collective security.

Women in Black, a British peace movement, now being nominated for the Nobel Prize, also reiterates that feelings of genuine despair in many parts of the world will lead to hatred of the superpowers whose policies are seen to contribute to them. In such a situation created by itself, for the West to resort to military means for conflict resolution would be another means of diverting wealth to the arms manufacturers by creating a "white elephant missile shield".

The British section of the WILPF goes one step further and calls the US proposal of a missile shield "not merely worthless, but a threat to world stability" and demands that the British Government not support it. Unilateral retribution by the US and its allies are opposed by the Violence Against Women in War Network, Japan, and several others who want the United Nations to establish an International Criminal Tribunal to prosecute terrorists instead of a few countries taking "justice"—infinite or otherwise—into their own hands. An impressive array of women organisations met in New Delhi last week and declared:

> If we are to live as one world it must be a world that respects diversity and does not insist on a single path or single ideology. We must search for a solution to these seemingly intractable issues in a manner that upholds the rights of all people to live in peace and dignity.

The US President, Mr George W. Bush, has spoken, much like the Oracle of Delphi, "If you are not with us, you are with the terrorists" and had threatened action even against "those harbouring terrorists". Referring to this, Women Living Under Muslim Laws International Solidarity Network (WLUML) reminds the US and the UK that they themselves have become safe havens for terrorists today.

The most moving plea against retaliatory violence comes, uncommonly, from an American couple whose son fell victim to the September 11 massacre; in a letter to Mr Bush, the Rodriguez couple said:

> the Government is heading in the direction of violent revenge, with the prospect of sons, daughters, parents, friends in distant lands dying, suffering and nursing further grievance against us. It will not avenge our son's death. It is not the time to act like bullies. Let us not as a nation add to the inhumanity of our times.

Judith Ezekiel

Un Pavé dans la mare, or Rocking the Boat: September 11 Viewed from France

11 October 2001. A letter to the editorial board of the *European Journal of Women's Studies,* after a few weeks of discussion of a possible special issue on September 11 and the war. Translated from French by Bronwyn Winter.

I've been in and out of Toulouse these days and have only just had time to sit down to read the texts you've been sending. I agree with the idea of us doing something for the journal, with the one concern of being able to produce something sufficiently solid and original not to be redundant by publication. However, I (and some friends here) have some reactions to this war that may not be very popular, that I want to put forward.

Perhaps, since you do not know my past very well, I ought to mention that my radical record goes back a long way: for more than thirty years I've been involved in feminist, anti-racist and anti-imperialist activism. The current situation seems to me to be different to many of those being evoked from the past by feminists and progressives.

First, I was appalled by the almost instant reaction of many people in my/our extended circles to the September 11 terror—one of horror and condemnation *but* ...! The "but" was almost always followed by a condemnation of America/the US. Note—they say America, not the US government, a specific administration, or specific acts. Sometimes, lip service was paid to "our" responsibility, "our" meaning other Western Europeans, but mostly we are talking about the US here. The critiques vary from CIA support of the Taliban, to Vietnam atrocities, to the genocide of Native Americans—often a full-blown list of every horror committed by anything American. I have seen dozens of texts of this kind. And this started before the strikes on Afghanistan.

This reaction nauseated me for many reasons. First, and this has been confirmed repeatedly in the interim, it set up a symmetry between "two evils". In fact, as anybody who's taught rhetoric knows, it actually gives more weight to the second of the evils, America. Second, it is a remarkable, glaring example of victim-blaming. Have we not learned from decades of feminism (and anti-racist and anti-poverty work before that) that the victim is not the guilty party? Over five thousand people have died in utterly horrifying circumstances, and many, many others are suffering. Even the richest capitalists among them did not deserve to be executed without a trial. (An amusing phenomenon, observed repeatedly: when I point to the numerous foreigners and no doubt poor cleaning women who were in the World Trade Center, not to mention offices of a number of progressive groups, suddenly the critiques ease up. Has violent class struggle started, and nobody told me? Or have we just abandoned our commitment to a fair judiciary? And against the death penalty?) Furthermore, although many rightly demanded proof of who was behind these acts, it appeared that these victims were murdered by—all the more when viewed through a feminist lens—some of the most odious people on the planet. So why do we immediately concentrate on Americans' "guilt"?

The reaction is particularly understandable in the US. When faced with the flood of jingoism—the flags everywhere, the media bandwagon, etc.—I, too, would probably have reacted similarly. Like the Jewish joke that needs to be told by a Jew, I think Americans can be forgiven for even unthinking anti-Americanism. For critical thinkers in the rest of the world, feminists included, I would suggest that this anti-Americanism is an abomination from a human point of view—imagine how you'd feel if it were a major landmark in your country in which your friends worked, and if, as I encountered the other day, an acquaintance cheered. More importantly, I suggest that it is clouding our vision politically.

One example. On 18 September in Paris (NB: before any "retaliation"), I was at a preparatory meeting for a long-planned demonstration to support Afghan women, organized by a broad coalition of feminist, female labor and political activists. Although it was a mere week since the World Trade Center attack, not a single woman, many of whom I've known for decades, came over to me to see if my US friends and family were okay. Five minutes later, an Afghan woman walked in and the meeting was stopped while everyone hugged and kissed her. The meeting centered on writing a press release, in the new context, for the demo. A draft spoke of the "terrorist attack against the US that caused many deaths". The assembly decided to eliminate the word "terrorist" since it was not used for US state terrorism, but then equally rejected the term "murderous attack". The short text included several references to many of the bad things that "America" has done, and the assembly massively rejected targeting the "American government" or even "*le pouvoir americain*" (American power), although the distinction was of course made between the Afghan people and the Taliban. In the end, as one person even dared to state outright, great care was taken not to criticize the Taliban more than America. To top this off, there is actually a group of American women in Paris, which has been working for Afghan women for far longer than most of the women present at this meeting. Some of them had actually organized a convoy to Afghanistan last year to meet with women resistance leaders. The Americans had not been invited to the meeting, nor were they mentioned.

Islam, of course, is not the guilty party. However Islamic fundamentalism and the upsetting increase of anti-Semitism lurking behind the righteous anger at the Israeli regime need to be examined, and examined [by us] as feminists. As do the sexual politics involved. The golden-boy terrorists could have been in a Geneva nightclub picking up attractive women, but they preferred waiting for the seventy virgins in the hereafter (whether or not blowing up Americans for sexual pie-in-the-sky is a founded interpretation of the Koran).[1] A journalist friend, who has just returned from an assignment in Magreb, interviewed Moroccans who cheered when the Towers fell. Against the backdrop of the common rumor that their king is gay, and in anger at his reinstating his father's Jewish adviser, they see in Bin Laden a real man to redeem Islam, reactions that blend homophobia and anti-Semitism.

When we cite figures about women being against war, what do we mean? First, is it true? And is this some glorious female quality, as many feminists are suggesting? The most recent Gallup poll I was able to find, from 5 October, shows no significant gendered difference in support of military retaliation in the US. Women's support drops once specific repercussions are mentioned, for instance, if it resulted in a gas [petrol] shortage or if 1000 American troops were to die. Is this positive? Mightn't this mean that it's fine to kill Afghanis as long as "we" don't have to suffer? Of course, this is not 1933, but can we really think about women and war, particularly one involving the Taliban, without thinking back to feminist pacifists' shortsightedness during the rise of Nazism?

Now don't get me wrong. I am the first to say that US foreign policy has nearly always been catastrophic and contrary to its avowed goals. When

---

1   Editors' note: The *houris*, the eternal virgins available to believers in the Islamic afterworld, are mentioned in two *sura* or chapters of the Koran, both of which deal with the conditions of life in paradise. Sura 44, "The Smoke", Verse 54: "Thus [shall it be], and We will wed them with Houris pure, beautiful ones." Sura 56, "The Event", Verses 36–38: "Then We have made them virgins/ Loving, equals in age/ For the sake of the companions of the right hand." There was subsequently a considerable body of erotic and mystical writing by Muslim scholars and poets on the *houris*, the divine, eternal and eternally available virgins.

interviewed by the radio straight after the attack, I immediately spoke of my fear that the US government would curtail civil liberties domestically, and predicted that the Bush administration would bomb Kabul, killing people who were already victims of the vicious Taliban regime, making martyrs of the perpetrators, polarizing the world even more, and leading to even more terror. But this will not happen because evil "America" massacred Native Americans or because the US government razed large parts of South-East Asia, or even because of a general anger at the effects of globalization, but because of specific actions by specific people, in which all sides—not just the US government, but also the Taliban and Bin Laden—are active players. And, my dear feminists and progressives, Bin Laden and others involved in this terror are not a National Liberation Front, deserving of our sympathy and support.

Love to all
Judith

Rigoberta Menchú Tum

Letter to President George W. Bush

12 October 2001 (unofficial translation).

Honorable Mr President:

I wish, firstly, to reiterate to you the solidarity and condolences which I expressed to your people last Tuesday, September 11, after hearing of the painful events in your country, as well as to share my indignation and to condemn these acts of terrorism.

These last days, I have been monitoring the evolution of events, convinced that the best reaction to these is reflection, not rigidity; measured wisdom, not anger; the search for justice, not revenge. I have asked that the conscience of the peoples of the world, the media, the eminent personalities with whom I share the ethical mission for peace, the Chiefs of State and the leaders of international organizations, that serenity enlighten our acts.

Nevertheless, Mr President, hearing the speech which you gave to your Congress last night, I have not been able to repress my fear for what your words may bring. You call on your people to prepare for "a large campaign as we have never before seen". And to your military to be proud, marching into a war in which you intend to involve all of the peoples of the world.

In the name of progress, of pluralism, of tolerance and liberty, you leave no option for those of us who do not share the benefit of the liberty and the fruits of the civilization which you wish to defend for your people and those of us who never sympathized with terrorism, as we have been its victims. Those of us who are proud expressions of other civilizations; who live day by day with the hope of turning discrimination and discard into recognition and respect; those of us who carry in our souls the pain of genocide perpetrated against our peoples; those of us who are fed up with placing the dead in foreign wars, we cannot share the arrogance of your infallibility nor the sole road which you wish to push us toward when you affirm that "all nations in all regions of the world must now make a decision: either you are with us or you are with the terrorists".

At the beginning of this year, I invited men and women of the planet to share a Code of Ethics for a Millennium of Peace, declaring that:

There will not be Peace without Justice
There will not be Justice without Equity

There will not be Equity without Development

There will not be Development without Democracy

There will not be Democracy without respect for identity and Dignity of Peoples and Cultures.

In today's world, all of these are very scarce values and practices; nevertheless, the unequal manner in which they are distributed does little more than to fuel the impotence, the desperation and the hate. The role of your country in the actual world order is far from being neutral. Last night, we expected a sensitive speech, with reflection and self-criticism, but what we heard was an unacceptable threat.

I share with you that the "course of this conflict is not known", but when you declare that "its result is known", the only certainty which invades me is that of an enormous useless sacrifice, that of another colossal lie.

Before you give the cry for war, I would like to invite you to think about a different type of world leadership, one which must convince rather than conquer, in which the human species can show that in the last 1000 years we have overcome the idea of "an eye for an eye" which represented justice for the barbarians who took over humanity during the dark middle ages; in which we don't need new crusades to learn to respect those who have a different idea of a God and his work of creation; in which we share with solidarity the fruits of progress, we protect better the resources which remain on the planet and that no child lack bread or schooling.

With hope on a thread, I remain sincerely,

Rigoberta Menchú Tum

Nobel Peace Laureate

Ambassador of Goodwill and the Culture of Peace

Barbara Kingsolver

No Glory in Unjust War on the Weak

14 October 2001, *Los Angeles Times*.

TUCSON—I cannot find the glory in this day. When I picked up the newspaper and saw "America Strikes Back!" blazed boastfully across it in letters I swear were 10 inches tall—shouldn't they reserve at least one type size for something like, say, nuclear war?—my heart sank. We've answered one terrorist act with another, raining death on the most war-scarred, terrified populace that ever crept to a doorway and looked out.

The small plastic boxes of food we also dropped are a travesty. It is reported that these are untouched, of course—Afghanis have spent their lives learning terror of anything hurled at them from the sky. Meanwhile, the genuine food aid on which so many depended for survival has been halted by the war.

We've killed whoever was too poor or crippled to flee, plus four humanitarian aid workers who coordinated the removal of land mines from the beleaguered Afghan soil. That office is now rubble, and so is my heart.

I am going to have to keep pleading against this madness. I'll get scolded for it, I know. I've already been called every name in the Rush Limbaugh[1] handbook: traitor, sinner, naive, liberal, peacenik, whiner. I'm told I am dangerous because I might get in the way of this holy project we've undertaken to keep dropping heavy objects from the sky until we've wiped out every last person who could potentially hate us. Some people are praying for my immortal soul, and some have offered to buy me a one-way ticket out of the country, to anywhere.

I accept these gifts with a gratitude equal in measure to the spirit of generosity in which they were offered. People threaten vaguely, "She wouldn't feel this way if her child had died in the war!" (I feel this way precisely because I can imagine that horror.) More subtle adversaries simply say I am ridiculous, a dreamer who takes a child's view of the world, imagining it can be made better than it is. The more sophisticated approach,

---

1 Editors' note: Limbaugh is an extreme-right media commentator in the US.

they suggest, is to accept that we are all on a jolly road trip down the maw of catastrophe, so shut up and drive.

I fight that, I fight it as if I'm drowning. When I get to feeling I am an army of one standing out on the plain waving my ridiculous little flag of hope, I call up a friend or two. We remind ourselves in plain English that the last time we got to elect somebody, the majority of us, by a straight popular-vote count, did not ask for the guy who is currently telling us we will win this war and not be "misunderestimated". We aren't standing apart from the crowd, we are the crowd. There are millions of us, surely, who know how to look life in the eye, however awful things get, and still try to love it back.

It is not naive to propose alternatives to war. We could be the kindest nation on Earth, inside and out. I look at the bigger picture and see that many nations with fewer resources than ours have found solutions to problems that seem to baffle us. I'd like an end to corporate welfare so we could put that money into ending homelessness, as many other nations have done before us. I would like a humane health-care system organized along the lines of Canada's. I'd like the efficient public-transit system of Paris in my city, thank you. I'd like us to consume energy at the modest level that Europeans do, and then go them one better. I'd like a government that subsidizes renewable energy sources instead of forcefully patrolling the globe to protect oil gluttony. Because, make no mistake, oil gluttony is what got us into this holy war, and it's a deep tar pit. I would like us to sign the Kyoto agreement today, and reduce our fossil-fuel emissions with legislation that will ease us into safer, less gluttonous, sensibly reorganized lives. If this were the face we showed the world, and the model we helped bring about elsewhere, I expect we could get along with a military budget the size of Iceland's.

How can I take anything but a child's view of a war in which men are acting like children? What they're serving is not justice, it's simply vengeance. Adults bring about justice using the laws of common agreement. Uncivilized criminals are still held accountable through civilized institutions; we abolished stoning long ago. The World Court and the entire Muslim world stand ready to judge Osama Bin Laden and his accessories. If we were to put a few billion dollars into food, health care and education instead of bombs, you can bet we'd win over enough friends to find out where he's hiding. And I'd like to point out, since no one else has, the Taliban is an alleged accessory, not the perpetrator—a legal point quickly cast aside in the rush to find a sovereign target to bomb. The word "intelligence" keeps cropping up, but I feel like I'm standing on a playground where the little boys are all screaming at each other, "He started it!" and throwing rocks that keep taking out another eye, another tooth. I keep looking around for somebody's mother to come on the scene saying, "Boys! Boys! Who started it cannot possibly be the issue here. People are getting hurt."

I am somebody's mother, so I will say that now: the issue is, people are getting hurt. We need to take a moment's time out to review the monstrous waste of an endless cycle of retaliation. The biggest weapons don't win this one, guys. When there are people on Earth willing to give up their lives in hatred and use our own domestic airplanes as bombs, it's clear that we can't out-technologize them. You can't beat cancer by killing every cell in the body—or you could, I guess, but the point would be lost. This is a war of who can hate the most. There is no limit to that escalation. It will only end when we have the guts to say it really doesn't matter who started it, and begin to try and understand, then alter the forces that generate hatred.

We have always been at war, though the citizens of the US were mostly insulated from what that really felt like until September 11. Then, suddenly, we began to say, "The world has changed. This is something new." If there really is something new under the sun in the way of war, some alternative to the way people have always died when heavy objects are dropped on them from above, then please, in the name of heaven, I would like to see it. I would like to see it, now.

Union of Australian Women

Statement

16 October 2001. These resolutions were passed by members of the UAW at a meeting in Melbourne.

Bombing of Afghanistan

The Union of Australian Women condemns, in the strongest possible terms, the US and British military attacks on the people of Afghanistan and the Australian Government and Opposition's unequivocal support of these attacks.

We do not believe that this is an effective nor humane way of combating terrorism. In our view the bombing of Afghanistan will cause considerably more suffering for the Afghan people who already live under unbelievably appalling conditions and will do nothing to end future terrorist attacks.

We believe that the only to deal with terrorism (and germ warfare) is to use the power of international controls under the auspices of the United Nations. We urge the Australian Government and Opposition to use their efforts to persuade the United States and Great Britain to find a peaceful approach to solving the issues that result from the tragic events of September 11.

Asylum Seekers

The Union of Australian Women condemns in the strongest possible terms the Australian Government's treatment of asylum seekers and in particular opposes:

- the shameful treatment of those who arrived in the *Tampa* (and others who have since come by boat seeking asylum) and the appalling waste of public money in this heartless exercise
- the incarceration of asylum seekers in Australia's inhuman detention centres
- the new refugee legislation that makes it harder for women to be accepted as refugees
- the Government's policies and rhetoric on asylum seekers that has led to a rise in racism in Australia and has impacted adversely on Australia's international reputation.

The Union of Australian Women expresses support for a review of the number of asylum seekers being admitted into Australia with the aim of significantly increasing our annual intake. This is felt to be particularly urgent given the current bombing of Afghanistan.

Finally the Union of Australian Women urges the Australian Government to adopt a humane and speedy process of assessment for asylum seekers with immediate release into the community for mothers and their children.

Kalpana Sharma

A War ... by Men

21 October 2001, *The Hindu*.

By the time this appears in print, that pile of rubble that is Afghanistan might have been pulverised into a finer mound of rubble by the relentless shower of American and British bombs. In a war in which there can be no winners, and many losers, pause for a minute and ask yourself—what will be the future of those faceless women you occasionally see on your television screen? If and when this war ends, who will speak for the women of Afghanistan?

In all the hours of footage on Afghanistan, there is little about women. Playing the leading roles in the current theatre of war within Afghanistan are men—regardless of whether they are Taliban or Northern Alliance. And on the other side, the Bush and Blair Brigade also consists mostly of men. Both sides speak the language of war. But what of the men, women and children who are the recipients of an endless spiral of violence? People who had no role in the events of September 11. And for whom there is little in the foreseeable future that presages peace.

On the BBC, *Panorama* had some chilling reminders of life under the Taliban—shots of women being beaten with a cane by a Taliban moral policeman because their ankles and wrists were showing from under the voluminous burqas, and of a woman being publicly executed. Even worse were the hauntingly beautiful faces of the children maimed by previous wars, by the estimated 10 million landmines that cover 725 square kilometres of the country. What a ghastly irony that the first civilian casualties were the four United Nations workers who were clearing these mines.

For several years before the current crisis enveloped all of us, an appeal on the fate of women in Afghanistan has been circulated by e-mail. It would turn up with great regularity; its contents told us what we had already heard about the terrible depredations that women in Afghanistan had to bear under the Taliban.

One of the groups spearheading the struggle for women's rights in that country is the Revolutionary Association of the Women of Afghanistan (RAWA). At this present juncture, when we see darkened screens and flickering lights to indicate that a country is being pounded virtually out of existence, it is instructive to visit the RAWA website (www.rawa.org).

The women behind this organisation launched their fight for women's rights long before the Taliban appeared on the horizon. Founded in 1977, RAWA campaigned for these rights even as their country was convulsed with violent struggles between different groups, ending in the Soviet occupation in December 1979. This did not stop these brave women. Even when a number of them were arrested and their leader, Meena, was murdered, allegedly by KGB agents in Pakistan in 1987, they persisted. RAWA worked with women in Afghanistan as well as the millions in the refugee camps across the border in Pakistan. They ran schools, created jobs for women, ran a hospital and counselled their traumatised and displaced sisters.

The advent of the Taliban brought in a whole new dimension to their struggle. They could not operate freely in Afghanistan any more as women were forced to wear the burqa and banned from most jobs. But despite this they found ways to continue to work amongst Afghan women. Their website has a slide show that is not meant for the faint-hearted. It gives you an unedited view of life as it was in Afghanistan.

But the important point that RAWA makes is that those opposing the Taliban are not much better in their attitude towards women. Nor do they respect human rights. While RAWA has emphasised its commitment to democracy and secularism, they point out that none of the groups fighting to displace the Taliban have any commitment to these values. In other words, the chances that women might be better off if the Taliban is replaced with another group is not at all a given in Afghanistan.

The twenty years of conflict that have preceded the current war have already taken a huge toll on the health—both physical and mental—of Afghan women living in the country and in refugee camps outside. According to a 1998 study published in the *Journal of the American Medical Association* (vol. 280, 5 August 1998), women and children form three-quarters of the refugee population, which numbered 2.7 million in 1996. In addition, an estimated 1.2 million were internally displaced (that is they were refugees in Afghanistan) at the end of 1996. In other words, close to four million Afghans were refugees inside or outside their country in 1996.

The study surveyed 160 women, of whom half lived in Kabul and the other half in Pakistani refugee camps. It opens up a small window into the lives of these women. The majority of the women said that their mental and physical health had deteriorated during the two years they had lived in Kabul after the Taliban took over. A high 42 per cent were diagnosed with post-traumatic stress disorder, 97 per cent suffered from depression and 86 per cent exhibited anxiety symptoms.

More than half these women were employed before the Taliban took over on 26 September 1996. After that, only one-third held on to their jobs. In the pre-Taliban days, 70 per cent of the teachers in Kabul, 50 per cent of the civil servants and 40 per cent of the physicians were women. All this changed almost overnight with the Taliban's ban on women working outside their homes. The loss of income had a direct impact on health and nutrition levels in many families.

Worse still, in September 1997 the government stopped women's access to health services in Kabul. Only one "poorly equipped clinic" was available to women. Following the intervention of the Red Cross, around 20 per cent of the beds in hospitals were kept for women. The study found that a large number of women refugees streaming into Pakistan mentioned the absence of medical care as one of the important reasons for leaving their country. It is important that we know such facts. It is essential that we understand the conditions in which the majority of women lived. But it is also crucial that we realise that the future for the most vulnerable and abused in Afghan society, the women, is not at all guaranteed by a rain of bombs, by political machinations that bring about a change of government, or by painting Islam as being anti-women.

Afghan women were part of a Muslim society where they had rights. They were deprived of their democratic rights when the Soviets took over. They were deprived of their rights as women when the Taliban took over. Will they get their rights as human beings some day in the future?

Federation of Uganda Women

Letter to Kofi Annan

22 October 2001

His Excellency, Kofi Annan
The Secretary-General
United Nations
New York, NY10017

Your Excellency,

Re: Proposal for UN Women Strategies for Civil Conflict Resolution

The Federation of Uganda Women of Business Organizations, Industry and Agriculture is proposing an international brainstorming of strategies for:

- Civil Conflict Resolution
- An International Criminal Court
- A UN Conflict Resolution Council
- A World Security Council of Women.

Your Excellency, we have a dream. The dream, of a just world without Terrorism, State Terrorism, War, Conflicts and civil warlords. Hence urgent need to instill the culture of Tolerance. We are calling for Justice instead of Terror and War! Because Terrorists must be punished by an International Tribunal. We are calling for justice because war is state terrorism.

We are calling for justice because two-thirds of mankind lives in misery and oppression, and the globalized strategies of multinational companies and their political supporters ensure that the number of those suffering globally is growing steadily.

Women, Mothers of the world, are saying to survive as one world, we need global brainstorming for new strategies of conflict resolution and de-escalation. We need the cooperation of our countries and the United Nations and the power of Women and Universal Human and Civil Rights Organizations, Environmental and Peace Groups against Racism, Discrimination and Globalization of Conflicts.

We need Economic Strategies that will eliminate the terrible polarization between rich and poor, redistribute resources in a just manner, and enable us all to become independent of begging, and self-sustaining. We need new Political Strategies ensuring that human lives and human rights have the same value all over the world regardless of race, nationality, religion, sex, tribe, region, colour or any other sectarian considerations.

We urge countries, especially the United States of America, to no longer block the establishment of an international criminal court. It is the proper place to punish individuals and state terrorism.

We are demanding a world security council of women, for women are generally not part of logic of thinking in military terms as they are mothers of Peace, Justice, reconciliation and architects of tolerance. We call on women who are writers, scholars and independent individuals, to set up the world security council of women as symbolic site for global debate that will bring forth recommendations to resolve this international super crisis.

We support the initiative to form a UN council for conflict resolution affiliated with the world security council with the following duties:

- To identify peace-threatening situations
- To de-escalate conflicts
- To establish rules for the post-conflict period.

Your Excellency, this demand was formulated at the 1995 International Women's Conference in Beijing, and today it is more necessary in action than ever before.

The UN council for conflict resolution should convene to look at and repeal the right of veto or the option of military aggression and this council should be run by NGOs, civil society half of who are women.

We are saying one cannot pick and choose among human rights, ignoring some while insisting on others. Only as rights equally applied can they be rights universally accepted. Nor can they be applied selectively or relatively as a weapon with which to punish or suppress others.

The Universal Declaration of Human Rights enshrines and illuminates global pluralism and diversity. It is the standard for an emerging era in which communication and collaboration between states and people will determine their success and survival of all global citizens. It is the great power and it is the only tool of lasting value.

- It has been the struggle against all forms of tyranny and injustice, against slavery, colonialism, apartheid and civil rights violations. It is nothing less and nothing different today! The current trend is more scientific and hi-tech to warrant a decisive international action.
- It calls for the elimination of all forms of discrimination against women.

- It emphasises the indivisibility of all human rights and fundamental freedoms.
- It insists that the full realization of civil and political rights was not possible without the enjoyment of economic, social and cultural rights.

Your idealism inspires your faith in our common future, and your determination to make it more just and more merciful than the past.

Our special solidarity is with the oppressed, suffering and starving women and children of Afghanistan and United States of America.

FUWOBOIA is a network and movement of women of Diverse Women for Diversity, the bridge of the astute, grassroots, developed and developing women on earth. Therefore, stands with all vulnerables no matter where they live.

Your Excellency, Women in the world will be very glad if this proposal is considered within the purview of the Beijing Conference.

Yours faithfully,
Stella B. Nambuya
President

Ameena A. Saeed

Telling It Like It Isn't

23 October 2001, *The Hindu*.

In a country where time is of the essence, the American people get their information from the electronic media. Television has taken on the role of covert instrument of indoctrination, American-style. The American public, a consumerist society that is daily bombarded with poignant messages to buy, save, and be happy, is also kept insulated from events unfolding in the world.

Those who perished and the survivors in the wake of the September 11 tragedy are victims not just of desperadoes but also of the US media, which kept readers and viewers deliberately ignorant of unjust and unfair American foreign policies. The American media, instead of acting as a vigilante, has offered itself for decades as a mouthpiece for the administration with regard to foreign policy. The American viewers, hardworking, honest and annoyingly gullible, are rarely given non-partisan news and rational analysis. They are never informed of where their tax dollars are being funnelled by their representatives on Capitol Hill, the Pentagon, the State Department, and lobbyists (it is estimated that the last-named earn US$20,000–30,000 a month).

Here are some examples of media subversion in the past decade. The American is today horrified to learn about contemporary atrocities by Uncle Sam such as "the huge slaughter of Iraqi civilians by means of a particularly vicious form of biological warfare". "A very hard choice," Ms Madeleine Albright commented on national TV in 1996, when asked for her reaction to the killing of half a million Iraqi children in the last five years because of sanctions. "But we think the price is worth it," she said. Current estimates remain about 5000 children killed a month, and the price is still "worth it". Denis Halliday, a highly respected UN official, resigned under protest because he was being compelled to carry out what he called "genocidal acts", as did his successor Hans von Sponeck. It is agreed on all sides that the effect of the sanctions has been to strengthen Saddam Hussein and to devastate the population. The US media systematically misinformed the public of the opposite. There is no disagreement among policy-makers and the American taxpayer does not know he has blood on his hands. The American viewer is also not informed of continued bombing campaigns over Iraq, a mundane occurrence, since the war ended in 1991. When the US admitted that it had made a mistake in bombing a factory in Sudan, the domestic media showed indifference. Non-American news outlets thought otherwise. The BBC said, "Washington Didn't Have the Evidence", the London *Independent* said, "US Admits Sudan Bombing Mistake" and again the BBC reported, "US Backs Down on Sudan Factory" (all on 4 May 1999). In the US, the headlines were a remarkable lesson in obscurity. Americans hardly knew it from reading the news.

> In a tremendous reversal on the part of the US Government, the Treasury Department decided to unfreeze the assets of Saleh Idris, the owner of the El Shifa factory that was destroyed in last August's attack. Idris' assets had been frozen while the US Government tried to prove charges that he was linked to alleged terrorist mastermind Osama Bin Laden.

An implicit admission from the US Government that it had no justification for bombing Idris' factory. The *New York Times* followed suit in further confusing the readers: "The Government's justification for attacking the Sudanese plant remains a matter of dispute." The world comes full circle in its irony when it comes to Afghanistan, now being carpet-bombed by the US. Bombs and landmines are the only expensive items found in that country today. In a series of articles, Janet Wilson in the *New York Post* (1987) charged that Dan Rather and Mike Hoover, anchor and cameraman of CBS, had repeatedly "aired fake battle footage and false news accounts" of the Afghan War in which Afghan Mujahideen performed as actors in sequences purporting to show rebel advances against the Soviet invaders, such as blowing up electric lines leading to Kabul. It was revealed that scenes of Mujahideen stalking enemy positions and blowing up a mine were acted out and filmed in the safety of a Pakistani training camp.

On 26 December 1991, in Algeria, the first round of the general and presidential multi-party elections was held with fifty-nine political parties in the running. The Islamic Salvation Front (FIS) won 188 seats out of 231. With the help of the US that had earlier encouraged the need for "democracy" in Algeria, the military intervened before the second and deciding round could be held on 16 January 1991, fearing a landslide victory for the FIS. Tanks and soldiers were deployed on the streets of Algiers. The US media that called the democratically elected FIS party "Islamic militants" summarily supported this blatant infringement of democratic process engineered by US politicians.

The mainstream US media has marginalised the sane voice of Noam Chomsky because he dared to call Israel a "terrorist state". According to Chomsky,

We can express justified horror or listen to the words of the British journalist Robert Fisk, whose knowledge and insight into the affairs of the region are unmatched. Describing "the wickedness and awesome cruelty of a crushed and humiliated people", he writes, "This is not a war of democracy versus terror that the world will be asked to believe in the coming days. It is about American missiles smashing into Palestinian homes and US helicopters firing missiles into Lebanese ambulances in 1996 and American shells crashing into a village called Qana and about a Lebanese militia, paid and uniformed by America's Israeli ally, hacking and raping and murdering their way through refugee camps."

It is troubling that for truth Chomsky had to quote an honest British journalist. Is it a coincidence that he could not find one in the US?

The American media so far has feigned ignorance of General Assembly Resolution 31/34 of 30 November 1976, which reaffirms "the legitimacy of the peoples' struggle for independence, territorial integrity, national unity and liberation from colonial and foreign domination and alien subjugation by all available means, including armed struggle". Now in the wake of September 11, Mr Tony Blair had to remind the media and reaffirm UN resolutions to be in place so that a viable Palestinian state could exist besides Israel.

Robert Fisk in the English journal *Independent* bemoans the culture of censorship. He adds,

Last week, in a national European newspaper, I got a new and revealing example of what this means. I was accused of being anti-American and then informed that anti-Americanism was akin to anti-Semitism (anti-Jew). You get the point, of course. I'm not really sure what anti-Americanism is. But criticising the US is now to be the moral equivalent of Jew-hating. It's okay to write headlines about "Islamic terror" or my favourite French example "God's madmen", but it's definitely out of bounds to ask why the US is loathed by so many Arab Muslims in the Middle East.

The US media is happy to follow the American administration's line. It has been keeping the readers in a knowledge vacuum, subverting the truth from time to time and even offering itself to be muzzled in the line of "patriotic duty" as it did during the Gulf War in 1991 and now in America's campaign for revenge by reducing Afghanistan's debris to dust.

Cynthia Peters

What Does Feminism Have to Say?

23 October 2001

Cynthia Enloe, feminist scholar and author of several books and articles about women and the military, suggested that it is useful to ask, "Where are the women?"

A casual observer of recent events might be justified in responding: There aren't any. Or at least not too many.

True, there is Condoleezza Rice, in her tailored skirt, struggling to match Bush's stride, and properly keeping one pace behind. But she is mostly surrounded by men in suits spouting macho rhetoric about "ending states" (Under-Secretary of Defense, Paul Wolfowitz) and using cowboy metaphors to describe how we will catch Osama Bin Laden "dead or alive" (President Bush). In his nationally televised speech to Congress, Bush issued the Taliban-directed ultimatum, "They will hand over the terrorists or they will share in their fate."

Congressional leaders fell into fraternal lockstep, celebrating Bush's threats with genial supportive words: "I'll tell you, I think the terrorists and the leaders of the countries that are harboring them aren't going to sleep very comfortably tonight, and that's good news" (Senator Joseph Lieberman, Democrat, Connecticut, Armed Services Committee).

The Taliban, of course, is all men. The terrorists are all men. All the main players in the unfolding tragedy are men—including (at least according to the pictures you see in the papers) the heroic firefighters who rushed into a burning building to save people they did not know. Not to mention the brave men working to get the much needed food aid into Afghanistan.

The whole terrible tragedy seems to be about men—the terrorists, the ones who trained them and financed them, the leaders of the warring and feuding nations, and those who are providing the humanitarian aid.

But of course the women are there. You just have to look beneath the surface to find them.

In Afghanistan

Before the Taliban took control of Kabul, many Afghan women played important roles in public life. Since 1996, when the Taliban took power, they are not even allowed to leave their homes unless they are accompanied by a male relative. They are forbidden to work or go to school.

Banned from the job market but forced to eke out a living due to the death or incapacitation of their husbands, many Afghan women turn to prostitution. A report on the web site of the Revolutionary Association of the Women of Afghanistan (RAWA) reminds us of the conundrum of an Afghan woman navigating public life, employing different identities to sustain her life and avoid death.

> The women who work in a [brothel] usually carry three types of identity cards. One ID, showing them as a widow with children, is used to get aid from UN offices or Red Cross. These IDs are not used a lot as they change place quickly and don't want to get involved with the local officials. Another ID, showing them as a married woman, is used for renting houses and so on. If Taliban arrests them for *Zena* (crime of sex outside marriage) they use their third ID showing them as a single women. Being single helps them avoid being stoned to death.

Even such ingenuity used by Afghan women to scrape together an existence may fail when it comes to avoiding impending starvation. With every passing week it becomes less likely that food for the winter will reach the necessary distribution points in the mountains—putting millions at risk for starvation. Because women have primary responsibility for their children, they are less mobile and have more mouths to feed. For them, starvation poses a particular threat.

Assuming they don't starve to death, there is another "grave health emergency now facing Afghan women", according to the United Nations Population Fund (UNFPA).

> Thousands of pregnant women are among the Afghan civilians who have fled their homes in recent days and are massed along the country's borders. The lack of shelter, food and medical care, and unsanitary conditions pose a serious risk to these women and their infant children. Even before the current crisis, poor health conditions and malnutrition made pregnancy and childbirth exceptionally dangerous for Afghan women.

Beyond starvation and the health risks associated with pregnancy, Afghan women will face the usual wartime weapon of rape, assuming the United States uses the Northern Alliance as its foot soldiers. Robert Fisk argues in London's *The Independent* that Alliance "gangsters" are known rapists and murderers. In the 1990s, they "looted and raped their way through the suburbs of Kabul ... They chose girls for forced marriages [and] murdered their families."

"I haven't seen Osama. I don't know Osama. Why when things happen in the east, the west or the north of the world, do the problems have to come here and hit straight at the people of Afghanistan?" asked Farida, a 40-year-old widow and mother of four who was begging Tuesday on the streets of Kabul, the Afghan capital.

"I pray to my God that as soon as America attacks the first cruise missile hits my house and kills me and my family," the former teacher said from behind her all-encompassing veil. She recited a long list of woes including hunger and a lack of water and sanitation in her ruined home, according to an Associated Press article (25 September 2001).

Is this the female version of the suicide mission? The conditions that produced steel-willed men who choreographed their own and thousands of others' instantaneous deaths also produce this, the wretched and hopeless Aghan mother praying for a fiery death for her and her children?

Farida and women like her have become what Cynthia Enloe calls "womenandchildren"—the West's evocation of innocent, helpless, voiceless victims.

Yet despite pressures from sequential oppressive governments, the women of Afghanistan have not been voiceless. The pro-democracy, pro-women's rights organisation RAWA has worked diligently to make their plight known. Currently, Afghan women risk the death penalty for their organizing work. Yet, according to Kathleen Richter writing for Z Magazine, it has about 2000 members, half in Afghanistan and half in Pakistan. RAWA runs clandestine home-based schools for girls and boys in Afghanistan, operates underground mobile health teams in Afghanistan and Pakistan, and organizes income-generating projects for Afghan women. It also provides human rights organizations with reports about violations carried out by the Taliban and other fundamentalists, and produces educational cassettes, holds poetry and story nights, and publishes the quarterly magazine Payam-e-Zan (Women's Message).

However victimized Afghan women are by government and religious rules, they have cobbled together a peace and justice movement even as they cobble together a fragile day-to-day existence. Yet the international attention recently turned to them doesn't yield a picture of Afghan women as full complex human beings but rather as Third World "womenandchildren"—lump-sum victims of uncivilized domestic policies, and recipients of bene-volent aid from the supposedly civilized West.

Previously not on the West's radar screen, Afghan women are now showing up as "pregnant", "fleeing", "starving", and "widowed". All true,

I suppose, but such adjectives reduce Afghan women to nothing more than the sum of their most desperate parts.

Afghan women and men, not Western rulers, contain the seeds of their own liberation. Their insights, their agency, and their participation are key to solving the problem of terrorism, addressing the context that gave rise to the September 11 attacks, and bringing democracry to Afghanistan.

In the United States

One thing feminism has taught us is to watch out for that word "unity". Since that's all we're hearing these days ("United We Stand"; "America United", etc.), it's worth taking a moment to see what gets collapsed out of existence when we are all "one".

When Senate Majority Leader Tom Daschle (Democrat, South Dakota) bridged the gap between the major parties, saying, "We are resolved to work together, not as Democrats or Republicans, but as Americans", some might argue it wasn't much of a stretch anyway. But he added, "Tonight, the president asked for our unity ... We will do whatever is needed to protect our nation. Nothing is more urgent."

Calls for unity and assertions that there is one set of interests to protect in "our nation" dismiss in one fell swoop the huge divides that exist in this country—across race, class, gender, geography, ethnicity, sexuality and religion. Many social movements that have as their focus the dismantling of institutions that generate racism, sexism, classism and homophobia are aggressively silenced and marginalized as everything about the "American way" is promoted as the equivalent of freedom and democracy.

Jerry Falwell expressed the fundamentalist Christian version of Tom Daschle's insistence on unity when he sputtered that the terrorist attacks were caused by

> pagans, and the abortionists, and the feminists, and the gays and the lesbians who are actively trying to make that an alternative lifestyle, the American Civil Liberties Union, People for the American Way, all of them who have tried to secularize America. I point the finger in their face and say, "You helped this happen."

Because his statement was so absurd and his finger-pointing included enough mainstream elements to be considered impolite, Falwell had to retract and apologize for his statement. Yet it revealed something about what is behind the calls for unity. Falwell was wrong that feminists and gays and lesbians caused the terrorist attacks, but he's right that those of us who contest institutionalized white sumpremacy, patriarchy and the marketplace challenge US unity and thus destablize US power.

Whether they use Falwell's extreme words or Daschle's polite ones, US leaders are using the terrorist attacks as an opportunity for the United States to consolidate power, and that includes further marginalizing the social movements that have contested the workings and end-products of US institutions.

While pagans and abortionists are not welcome, women do have a special role to play in helping consolidate US power. Laura Bush role-modeled the necessity of giving up "our" men as they do the brave public deeds required of them during the crisis. During a recent interview with Larry King, the First Lady lamented that "she may have lost a little of him [her husband] because he gave more of himself to the country", according to a United Press International report.

"It's unbelievably stressful," she continued. "I thought today he looked a little tired." A moment's lament is acceptable, but only if it quickly morphs into cheerleading. "But he's doing great," the First Lady added. "He's very resolved. He's doing very well."

"The fact is," she said at one point, "is that most of us are safe. Nearly all of us are safe. Our children are safe in their schools. We need to reassure them of that.

"We're safe in our homes. We're safe. ... I know that people are getting back on planes and flying again, which I'm glad about," she said.

She ended the interview with an encouraging note: "I want to get across the message that I think people need to go about their daily lives and start feeling secure again, and certainly help make their children feel secure as they go about their daily lives."

The wifely and motherly role during a time of crisis is to admire our men, bravely suffer their understandable preoccupations, reassure the children, and breathe a sigh of relief for the return of our daily routines. We can celebrate the little things, like "getting back on planes and flying again," and not concern ourselves with the bigger issues like whether the US/UK bombing is itself terrorist in nature, whether our policies will lead to mass starvation in Afghanistan, and how US retaliation might further destabilize the region, making conditions even worse for local populations and increasing the chances of further terrorist attacks against the United States.

An important aspect of women's domestic work is to shop, and now it is her patriotic duty as well. "Go shopping," commands Rudolph Giuliani. "Buy that car," says Tom Daschle. "Take that trip," pleads John Kerry. The *New York Times* dedicated a whole page to high-end accessories in red, white and blue, noting that "the recovery effort must include shopping". Whether you choose a $42 flag-themed leash for your dog or a stars-and-stripes belt ($198) and matching handbag ($297) for yourself, the message is "the civic-minded can now buy a little guilt-free pleasure, in style".

For those with less disposable income, "here's how you can help", says a link on WalMart's top page. "Go to your local Wal-Mart store," is what they suggest, "and donate to the national relief effort." Playing off your sympathy, compassion and desire to help, WalMart just wants to get you in the store.

Never mind that stockholders are divesting, airlines are laying off people by the tens of thousands, and the rich are scaling back and protecting their wealth. Never mind that millions of Americans don't have disposable incomes and millions more get along every day without the benefit of health or life insurance (though they can now live secure in the knowledge that if a skyscraper collapses on them, they and their families will at least be eligible for basic social services).

Never mind all this, it's women's patriotic duty to go to the mall.

When we ask, where are the women in the United States, we see they are being coaxed to consume, minister to their tired-looking husbands, obsess about the minutia of daily routines, and stand united with the rest of the country as if it were one big family and the women are the loyal moms and daughters. In his 7 October 2001 war announcement, Bush shamefully showcased the ideal feminine gesture during this tragic time—literally to be willing to sacrifice our men. He said,

> I recently received a touching letter that says a lot about the state of America in these difficult times, a letter from a fourth-grade girl with a father in the military. "As much as I don't want my dad to fight," she wrote, "I'm willing to give him to you."

Women of color and working-class women, having never really been part of the great big American family, must continue as the invisible servants— bearing the brunt of economic downturn, continuing to function with less of a social safety net, being targeted by heightened racism, and losing a dispro-portionate share of their family members to the military. Only the privileged can relate to Laura Bush's luxuriating in the security of regular routines. For many people of color and working-class people, daily life is marked by the insecurity of low-paying and unrewarding jobs, higher rates of imprisonment, inadequate health care, and poor schooling.

Feminism should help us identify how the war cry is partly dependent on particular definitions of masculinity and femininity. Feminism can help us see how gender politics reinforces isolation and asks us to bypass thoughtful responses in the name of unity, which translates into mostly male decisions about how the country will go forward.

There are exceptions to the war cry, and we should note them. Barbara Lee, African-American congressperson from California, said in her 14 September 2001 speech to the House, "There must be some of us who say, let's step back for a moment and think through the implications of our actions today—let us more fully understand their consequences."

Peace groups and ad hoc coalitions have sprung up all over the United States and the world—responding rapidly and incisively to US rhetoric and activity. "We strongly believe the urge to vengeance must be resisted," says the activist group Women in Black. "A war waged by the US and its allies will cause the death of many innocent people, will de-stabilize many governments and societies, and its longterm effects on relations between countries and regions of the world will be disastrous."

In New York City, Laura Flanders reports that 75 people crammed into a Greenwich Village Gay and Lesbian Community Center to hear Tahmeena, a member of RAWA, talk about conditions in Afghanistan and possibilities for the future. Participants debated and shared ideas about how events will unfold. In the process, they learned something about where the women are. And not just that. But also: What are they saying? What are they doing? What do they think? The answers to these questions are critical elements of a peaceful and just response to the current crisis.

Cilocia Zaidi

Life of Afghan Refugee Women

27 October 2001, *The Nation*, Pakistan.

ISLAMABAD—There is probably more international concern about women of Afghanistan than there is for women in any other country of the world today. Much of this concern has been prompted by the shock of whatever the world heard or saw of the plight of Afghan women, living a life devoid of all contact with the outside world.

In December 1979, Afghanistan was invaded by the Soviet Union, and millions fled to Pakistan and Iran. The peak occurred in 1981, when 4700 people crossed the border into Pakistan seeking refuge and shelter.

The rural women, who were used to freedom of movement within their villages, suddenly found themselves confined in the refugee camps with no space of their own. Many of them complained of physical hardships, with intolerable heat and insufferable chilly nights, no water, or shade to protect them from the onslaught of the weather. They had to suffer shortage of food, non-existent health facilities, unhygienic conditions, dust and filth, and shortage of fuel and medicines.

The worst was the psychological need to have a privacy and someone kind to share their trauma of tortures, having left all their belongings back home, their loved ones being killed or lost, and their pain of being away from their homeland.

At the height of the exodus, there were 3.5 million Afghan refugees living in three provinces of Pakistan.

The refugees and the local inhabitants competed for water, firewood, and grazing ground for their herds of animals.

Eventually these refugees created large villages that were just a vast area of mud shanties, much different from their homes back in their country. The women, especially the young ones, built these mud shanties, which gave them a sense of confidence and security. But with many of their men away fighting, these refugee women had to face many problems and learnt to cope with things in different ways.

Too much free time and an uncertain future has created a conducive atmosphere for drug culture in the refugee camps. Male and females were drawn to addiction due to their frustrations. Under the cover of these mud dwellings, a spurious drug trade flourishes, which is difficult even for the authorities to check.

When bourgeois urban women became refugees, many found themselves leaving modern houses and apartments for cramped quarters of refugee camps or crowded sections of Pakistani cities. Living conditions in exile were especially hard for these urban women. Instead of one family per house, there were sometimes five to six families, with fifteen to thirty people living in a house designed for five to six persons. Rural women may have been able to recreate something of their own home atmosphere in the camps, but this was not possible for many urban women.

There are many refugees who would like to go back, but are staying because of their children, particularly girls. They do not trust the situation in Afghanistan, as there is practically no education for girls. And even if peace returns, much of Kabul and other cities are destroyed and these families have no homes to return to.

What Afghanistan now faces is that a very conservative attitude towards women has emerged.

There are greater numbers of disabled Afghan refugees. To become disabled is something that changes one's life. And for Afghan refugee women, it is a terrible tragedy. It is therefore, important for those claiming to work for humanitarian assistance to come up with ideas that will give these women a place in the society that is not necessarily charity.

It has been over twenty years these refugee women have been coping with living a decent life, without much help from the much publicized multibillion-dollar donor alerts being ringed out again and again.

Visiting the mud dwellings of Afghan Basti in Sector H-8 is enough to know the plight of these poor refugee women, who wait all day for their children to return with trash foods collected from garbage dumps. There are no clothes, no shoes, no hope for a better meal, let alone schooling. What future these women could think of for their children?

Vandana Shiva

Globalisation and Talibanisation

30 October 2001, *Outlook India*, Web.

The conflicts which were expressed in the tragedy of September 11 are being looked at through lenses coloured by mono-cultures—the monoculture of "a universal Western civilization" or the monoculture of an equally universal Islamic terrorism. In the Samuel Huntington paradigm, this is leading to the clash of civilizations. In the Francis Fukuyama paradigm, we are seeing the end of history—the ultimate conquest of the West over the rest. Yet both Huntington and Fukuyama are constructing fictitious worlds—removed from our diverse histories, and our plural pains.

Firstly, there is no such thing as a Western civilisation. The dominant West has extinguished its own diverse cultures—of women in the witch hunts, of native Americans in the genocide of colonisation. And Seattle, Washington, Gothenburg, Genoa were voices of other cultures, other visions from within the West which are being attempted to be silenced, including with bullets. Remember Gandhi's response when asked what he thought of Western civilization. "It would be a good idea", he said.

Just as dominant Western culture is not universal, terrorism is not necessarily linked to Islam. In India we experienced it as Sikh terrorism in Punjab during the 1980s. The farm crisis fuelled violent Sikh nationalism, as unemployed and angry youth took guns exported by the same global powers that had destroyed Indian agriculture and who looked on India as a market for their overpriced, non-essential, often hazardous products and technologies.

The Oklahoma bombing was a result of the rise of Christian militias in the mid-west of the US. And terrorism within the US, like that in Punjab, was also linked to the farm crisis, the growing dispossession of American family farmers which made them accept the new gospel of violence and hatred. As Joel Dyer says in *Harvest of Rage*: "Why Oklahoma City is only the Beginning." America's innocence lay in the rubble of the Murrah building as surely as the crumpled bodies of the victims. The deadly Oklahoma City bomb was just the first shot in the collective suicide of the nation. Some Americans—some of them our neighbors—have declared war on the powers that be, and those of us who stand unknowingly in between these warring factions are paying the price. And we will continue to pay the price—one building, one pipe bomb, one burned-down church at a time—until we come to understand, first, that the nation is holding a loaded gun to its head and, second, why so many among us are struggling to pull the trigger.

Terrorism has no religion—it is not restricted to any region. It is now global—and terrorisms everywhere share the culture of hate and hopelessness, victimhood and violence. In a discussion of September 11 at the Forum 2000 in Prague, Nobel Prize Winner Elie Wiesel asked, "What happened? Why did it happen? Could it have been avoided? In other words, what is the ecology of terrorism?

Over the past two decades, I have witnessed conflicts over development and conflicts over natural resources mutate into communal conflicts, and into extremism and terrorism. My book *Violence of the Green Revolution* was an attempt to understand the ecology of terrorism. The lessons I have drawn from the growing but diverse expressions of fundamentalism and terrorism are the following:

- Undemocratic economic systems which centralise control over decision-making and resources, and displace people from productive employment and livelihoods, create a culture of insecurity. Every policy decision is translated into the politics of "we" and "they". "We" have been unjustly treated, while "they" have gained privileges.
- Destruction of livelihoods and jobs, and erosion of democratic control over the economy and systems of production also leads to a mutation of cultural identity. With identity no longer coming from the positive experience of being a farmer, a craftsperson, a teacher, a nurse, culture is reduced to a negative shell, positive identities give way to negative identities, each, in competition with every "other", contesting for the scarce resources that define economic and political power.
- Centralised and undemocratic economic systems also erode the democratic base of politics. In a democracy, the economic agenda is the political agenda. When the former is hijacked by the World Bank, IMF, WTO, democracy is reduced to an empty shell with room only for fundamentalism and extremism, both because race, religion, ethnicity are the only cards left in the hands of politicians to garner votes and because the extremist can more effective fill the vacuum left by the decay of democracy.
- Globalisation is contributing to the Talibanisation of the world. Economic globalisation is fuelling economic insecurity, eroding cultural diversity and identity, and assaulting political freedoms of citizens.
- It is therefore providing fertile ground for the growth of fundamentalism and terrorism. Globalisation fuels fundamentalism at multiple levels: fundamentalism is a cultural backlash to globalisation, as alienated and

angry young men of colonised societies and cultures react to the erosion of identity and security.

- Dispossessed people robbed of economic security by globalisation cling to politicised religious identities and narrow nationalisms for security. Politicians, robbed of economic decision-making as national economic sovereignty is eroded by globalisation, organise their vote banks along lines of religious and cultural difference on the basis of fear and hatred. Imperialist forces, using the divide and rule strategy, also exploit religious conflicts to fragment the opposition to globalisation.

The survival of people and of democracy needs a simultaneous response to the double fascism of globalisation—the economic fascism that destroys people's lives, economic freedoms and economic security, and the fascism of fundamentalism that feeds off people's economic insecurities and fears. The "war against terrorism" will not contain terrorism because it does not address the roots of terrorism. It is in fact creating a chain-reaction of violence and spreading the virus of hate. Just as pests multiply and grow resistant with pesticides, the war effort will increase the numbers and resilience of terrorists. Pests can only be controlled by making plants resilient and maintaining pest-predator balance in ecosystems. The ecology of terror shows us the path to peace. Peace lies in nourishing democracy and nurturing diversity.

Democracy is not a shell but the lifeblood of free society. It is not merely an electoral ritual but the power of people to shape their destiny, and influence their lives, policies and conditions which destroy democratic control of people over how their food is produced and distributed, what health and education systems they have, how their natural resources are managed, owned and utilised.

Terrorism is born from the death of democracy and can only be responded to by giving the power back to people. This is why the anti-globalisation movement is an anti-terrorist movement. It is giving peace and democracy a chance. If it is stifled by the brute force of militaries and global markets, our worlds will disintegrate into vicious cycles of violence and chaos. And no one will be immune.

Tahmeena Faryal

Testimony Before the Subcommittee of the US House of Representatives on International Operations and Human Rights

31 October 2001

The basics of Afghanistan's situation have become more known in the past weeks, in the US and across the world. After years of neglect, the desperate situation of the Afghan people is receiving much-needed attention. However, the people's voices are rarely heard, and are at risk of being drowned out entirely by the horrific crash of war and global geopolitics.

Formed in 1977, the Revolutionary Association of the Women of Afghanistan is the oldest women's humanitarian and political organization in Afghanistan. Based inside Afghanistan and in neighboring Pakistan, RAWA is an independent, all-volunteer, non-violent organization calling for multilateral disarmament and the establishment of a secular democratic government in which women may once again participate fully in public life. Currently, RAWA provides refugee relief, underground medical care and education, income-generating projects, orphanages, documentation of Taliban and other jihadis' atrocities, protest demonstrations and events, and other initiatives in both countries. RAWA members in Afghanistan have stayed to continue our work during many past crises, and we remain there today. RAWA's work is also aimed toward giving voice to our downtrodden people, especially the women—and empowering women and men not to forget that they—we all—deserve human rights and freedoms and to look towards a day when the guns and rockets will stop and we can begin to rebuild. The current humanitarian situation is grave, and being made worse each day by the continued fighting, the US bombing, and the destruction and fear both continue to cause. Winter is coming and starving people are, of necessity, fluid in their alliances.

The political situation is made ever more precarious by what many Afghans perceive to be US aggression against our country and our civilians, even as we cheer the possibility of the Taliban's demise. And, continued and increasing foreign assistance to the reviled Northern Alliance has plunged our people into a horrific anxiety and fear of re-experiencing the dreadful years of the jihadis' "emirate" of the 1990s. In the words of one refugee in Peshawar, many, many of the people say that, "All of them, Taliban and Taliban opposition, are criminals, and we don't want them ruling Afghanistan. For the past twenty years they have all given the people only bullets instead of food and graves instead of houses."

The Afghan people want what any people on this earth would want—the cessation of wanton violence and establishment of basic stability so that we may re-establish civil society. What is going on now, and has for decades, is *not* our religion, our culture, nor our traditions—it is an abomination of Islam and all other peaceful religions, and a violation of our people who are being held hostage by fanatics. As another long-time Afghan refugee said this October, "the people of Afghanistan want peace, security, and the opportunity to rebuild under a government established by legitimate elections where the people vote without a gun to their heads."

RAWA sees the former king, Zahir Shah, as a viable non-monarchical central figure around which an interim government could form. However, if he comes to the scene while relying on the Northern Alliance and so-called "moderate" Taliban elements, he will not only betray his reputation among the Afghan people, but will also undermine the stability and viability of whatever structure he forms.

So many of those now involved in what has come to be called the Northern Alliance have the blood of our beloved people on their hands, as of course do the Taliban. Their sustained atrocities have been well documented by independent international human rights organizations such as Amnesty International and Human Rights Watch, and others. Those in the Taliban and the Northern Alliance have also proved themselves to be incompetent and corrupt as governing forces. Our people have not forgotten the years after the collapse of the Soviet puppet regime of Najib—the most horrible years of terrorism and unchastity—and as well we don't forget the time not so long ago when the Jihadis themselves were the cheap servants of Abdullah Ezam and Osama Bin Laden as the Taliban are today.

Currently, RAWA and many other Afghans fear that the "Northern Alliance" groups now lie in ambush, waiting to ride the guns of the US into Kabul and working to gain Western backing to establish their second "emirate". They have yet to prove, or even to offer, a single shred of reason or credible evidence suggesting that they would not repeat their prior atrocities. In its 1995 report on the Mujahideen wars that followed the Soviet withdrawal, Amnesty International documented that

Thousands of unarmed civilian women have been killed by unexpected and deliberate artillery attacks on their homes ... They have been blown up or hit by rockets or bullets while walking in the streets, waiting at bus stops, working in their houses, or sheltering in large buildings. Many have died or been injured in attacks aimed at mosques, schools, and hospitals. These attacks were justified on the grounds of fighting rival groups, but the nature of the attacks, especially on residential buildings, revealed a deliberate policy of terror by the Mujahideen against Afghans.

In addition, Mujahideen forces, armed and trained by the US government and now part of the Taliban and the Northern Alliance, waged a brutal war against women, using rape, torture, abduction, and forced marriage as their weapons. Many women committed suicide during this period as their only escape. Given their past record, we see no possibility that any of these jihadis will change their nature.

Therefore, any US, "Rome process", or multi-lateral initiatives to establish a broad-based government, must exclude all Taliban and other criminal jihadi factions from political power, unless and until a specific faction or person has been absolved of war crimes and crimes against humanity. Else the people will again be plunged into the living hell that engulfed our country from 1992 to 1996 under elements now involved in the Northern Alliance and continues to the present under the Taliban and other factions.

RAWA, on behalf of more than half of the population of Afghanistan, also must insist that any Loya Jirga or interim-government development process is not legitimate unless it includes and heeds women's voices from beginning to end in substantial and meaningful ways. We ask the unequivocal support of the US and other democracy- and justice-loving countries for this and our other standpoints.

Afghanistan of course needs substantial help from the international community, but we cannot tolerate external control, and even starving Afghans will resist foreign domination. RAWA as an organization does support the intervention of a multi-national UN or other peacekeeping force to assist in disarming the warring factions, establishing basic securities, and setting the stage for the establishment of an interim government. We know that such an interim government will likely fall short of democracy, and we strongly insist that the world community assist our people in making certain that such an interim government is only that—a temporary stepping stone towards full establishment of citizenship rights—including equal rights for women in all spheres—and democracy in a new Afghan constitution and governmental structure.

Based on historical evidence, we gravely fear that continuation of the US attacks and the resulting civilian lives lost give excuses to the Taliban and

Northern Alliance to wage war, and will also empower and embolden fundamentalist forces in the region and across the world—endangering not only Afghans, but further American lives, and the citizens of many countries.

After the horrific terrorist attacks of September 11 here in the US, Afghans and Americans, like too many other peoples across the globe, share a common experience of living under the rule of fear and death. Let us make the best of this tragic commonality: join us in advocating for US and international policies and initiatives that will help build a lasting peace in our country, re-establish internationally recognized human rights for the women, children and men of Afghanistan, pave the way directly to a secular, broad-based, democratic government welcoming to all who are innocent of crimes against our people, and bring all fundamentalist and other terrorists to justice under the rule of international law. Thank you.

References

Amnesty International. (1995). *Women in Afghanistan: A Human Rights Catastrophe*. AI Index: ASA 11/03/95.

RAWA. (2001). *Marginalised Women: Documentation on Refugee Women and Women in Situations of Armed Conflict*. Asian and Pacific Development Center.

Christina Gombar

Weekday Warriors

2 November 2001, *Women's Review of Books*, USA.

It always felt like a war zone to me. The huge, monolithic buildings. The dearth of sunlight, the vast barren stretches of concrete, and above all, the foreign, giant-scale money culture. It was all a far cry from my liberal arts degree, the left-wing weeklies and glossy literary magazines I wanted to work for that were so progressive they couldn't pay junior people anything at all, with the result that only the sons and daughters of the wealthy could afford to hone their skills there.

But I needed cash, so I went where the money was. Like the army, Wall Street will take anyone. They don't care what school you went to, or who your father was. They will find you a job. When I signed on, I quickly discovered a sense of camaraderie, of opportunity—if not quite equal opportunity—lacking in more prestigious academic and creative fields.

Civil rights are abridged in the war zone. There is no racial profiling. Everyone gets fingerprinted, drug tested, hooked up to wires and interrogated upon being hired and at random intervals thereafter. Criminal intention is assumed. Pages-long questionnaires about personal habits, violations of drug and securities laws: only indicted, but never convicted? indicted more than three times?

The first Wall Street company I worked for, back in the mid-1980s, was a huge, mysterious international conglomerate, its ranks filled with ex-army men, "spooks" from the CIA and FBI. We did business with "bad" countries —Chile, Yugoslavia and Arab nations I'd never even heard of before. When I told people this—people who worked at left-wing weeklies, in academia, at literary magazines—they said it was impossible; you can't do business with countries the US government doesn't recognize.

You can. We heard strange stories we didn't know whether to believe: that the company was behind Third World coups and had a sideline in sex tours to Thailand. The top secret organizational chart showed over four hundred subsidiaries. It was said the company was kept deliberately complicated, so no one could tell how much money it actually made.

The company was its own fortress, the buildings a self-contained world, with a lower concourse full of shops and services, its own bars and restaurants, and in the upper echelons of its tower, a private dining room that opened its doors to the sky. Here the company chief, in whose presence you swiftly understood the seductive charisma of history's great dictators, showcased photographs of himself flanked by then-President Reagan and the Chinese Premier. The other executives—many of whom had landed at Okinawa and Normandy—were so afraid of him that when he entered a room they would disperse as if a smoke bomb had landed in their midst. At meetings, they couldn't laugh at his jokes.

No one I knew who worked in journalism, or in book publishing, or at left-wing weeklies, had heard of the company. In fact, if you told most people in my circle then that you worked downtown, worked on Wall Street, they'd look at you like you were suddenly speaking a foreign tongue, or you were a Nazi sympathizer.

Wall Street gave me my first inkling that there was another point of view. A Cuban-born Chilean executive explained, quite convincingly, why his adopted country's dictatorship was preferable to Castro's Cuba, which he had been driven from as a child. A girl who interned in my department, the daughter of a Middle Eastern executive, told me exactly what it was like to grow up sleeping in the hallway every night, a pillow over her head to block out the sound of mortar shells showering her native Beirut, what it was like to see her beautiful city destroyed, building after building by her twentieth birthday.

I liked the company, but left for mercenary reasons. The second Wall Street company I worked for put itself up for sale the day I arrived. A demagogue gathered us in a room and told us there would be no mass firings, not in 1987. Two days later the company announced five thousand people would be laid off after Christmas. The acquiring company looked each of us over to decide who would stay, and who go.

Though we knew we would likely be fired, we worked till midnight at a downtown printing press to get our salesletter for the field brokers out on time. One of my co-workers was twenty-three years old and seven months pregnant with twins. "Maria's a real trooper," our boss said, because Maria could have got her doctor to write her out at six months but soldiered on through this crisis. I remember eating with her in the cavernous Orwellian cafeteria in Two World Trade Center, at ten pm on New Year's Eve. She was so ill I had to fetch her her food, and looked so dreadful I couldn't swallow my own. It was my last night with the company. I remember looking at my ill, pregnant co-worker, and thinking, This is no place for women. We got our newsletter out, and before dawn my co-worker gave birth to her twins, each dangerously underweight. She was so ill she doesn't remember any of it, or anything that happened at all for the next two days.

My third and last Wall Street job made *me* sick. I left just when Anita Hill was hitting the scene, and in lieu of filing a law suit, took a little hush money. Before they'd give it to me they made me sign a piece of paper swearing never to tell what happened.

The job wasn't all bad. During the last Gulf War, my co-workers, Vietnam vets all, would cluster in my office to listen to Desert Storm on my transistor, whose usage was otherwise restricted to hourly stock market updates. They recalled their own battles, glory days or otherwise, and discussed artillery makes and the pros and cons of various bombers.

At our company, the enemy was internal—the surprise attacks coming from above, a side effect of the prolonged bear market. When I was forced out, my male colleagues considered me lucky—they were equally abused, and a rash of cardiac disease was sweeping the building. But their harassment had no framework of accountability, no legal classification nor protection. It was just business as usual.

When I left that company, I swore I would never go back downtown again. I felt like a wounded veteran, exempt from future service. This is how I always explain myself to people: when I was young, I ruined my health working on Wall Street. It was my own fault. I should have evaded the draft, I should never have gone down there. There's a reason people avoid places like that.

People who've worked there understand. They know about the eleven-hour days, the seventy-hour weeks, the two weeks off a year. It takes a certain kind of person to stick out those conditions, people unafraid of either risk or sacrifice in the name of company, capitalism, the American dream. I wasn't one of them. What I do know is that everyone in those World Trade Towers, hard at work at 8.30 am, was already a warrior, long before any planes hit.

Sudha Ramachandran

Behind the Veil of Oppression

4 November 2001, *The Hindu Sunday Magazine.*

It is hard to believe that barely six years ago, most professionals in Kabul, Afghanistan, were women. Under the Taliban, their oppression has been systematic and has official sanction. Now faceless, anonymous and invisible, a range of edicts has severely restricted their mobility and access to health-care, education and employment. Afghan women, says Sudha Ramachandran, will tell you that they are the "living dead', targets of gender-specific abuse in the name of "honour', tradition and religion.

Long, ugly scars run down Hafisa Rashid's back. Scars of the twenty lashes she received from the Taliban four years ago for dressing "promiscuously". "I was wearing the prescribed burqa," Hafisa recalls. A member of the Taliban Ministry for the Propagation of Virtue and Suppression of Vice stopped her on the road and arrested her. Her crime? Her ankles were visible. Hafisa was then lashed in public. "I cannot tell you what they did to me after that," she whispers and looks away. The 40-year-old woman from Herat now lives in Delhi. She has built a new life for her family. The wounds have healed. But the scars remain.

Ask Afghan women to describe their lives and the overwhelming majority will tell you that they are "the living dead". Two decades of civil war have inflicted unimaginable suffering on them. In addition to the hardships all Afghans have had to endure because of the fighting—death of family members, disability and displacement—women have suffered in particular as targets of gender-specific abuse. Innumerable restrictions have been imposed on women in the name of "honour", Afghan tradition and Islam. As in other societies, notions of honour and shame are linked with a woman's chastity. Over the last two decades and especially between 1992 and 1995, warring mujahideen used rape as a weapon of war, to dishonour entire communities and to weaken their capacity for resistance. Women were often treated as the spoils of war, and leaders condoned rape as a method of rewarding their soldiers. Under the Taliban, the oppression of women has been systematic and has official sanction. They have imposed the tent-like burqa on women, rendering them faceless, anonymous and invisible. More damaging for women and society, however, have been the range of edicts that have restricted physical mobility of women and their access to health facilities, education and employment. The literacy rate for women in Afghanistan stands at a dismal 4 per cent. The Taliban announced a ban on schooling for girl children in 1996. Subsequently, limited school facilities for girls between the ages of six and ten were provided, but none for older girls.

"Women in Afghanistan are dying of treatable illnesses," says a French doctor who worked until recently with a non-government organisation in Kabul. "The Taliban prohibited women from being treated by male doctors and since women doctors were not allowed to practice, sick women had nowhere to go."

In the last couple of years, women have been allowed to go to male doctors but have to be accompanied by a male relative. According to United Nations statistics, the maternal mortality rate in Afghanistan is among the highest in the world. Radhika Coomaraswamy, the UN's Special Rapporteur on violence against women, observes in the *Report of the Special Rapporteur on Violence against Women*, its causes and consequences that women are discriminated against in the services provided. The Rabia Balkhi Women's Hospital in Kabul did not have even the minimum infrastructure, except for an X-ray machine. "The limited health resources that do exist are pumped into the male hospitals," she says. The Taliban have banned women from working outside their homes (this was later amended to allow them to work in the health and social service sectors). This has created a huge problem, especially for widows who need to provide for the family but are restricted from seeking employment. Large numbers of women have taken to begging on the streets of Kabul and there has been a dramatic increase in prostitution. "Many of the women who today roam the streets seeking alms were some years ago qualified teachers and engineers," points out Hafisa, who taught history to high-school students till the Taliban closed down schools for girls.

There are edicts that control the way a woman behaves. She must not laugh loudly. She must remained confined to her home and if she steps outside she must wear a burqa, be accompanied by a male relative, not loiter around, and have a specific destination to go. When she walks, her footwear must not make any noise and attract attention.

Non-compliance with the edicts, even if unintentional, can invite public flogging with an instrument that looks like a leather cricket bat. Women have been lashed for not being properly clothed—for wearing thin socks or brightly coloured shoes—and jailed for speaking to men on the streets. In their 1998 report, *The Taliban's War on Women: Health and Human Rights Crisis in Afghanistan*, the Physicians for Human Rights pointed out that 94 per cent of the Afghan women they interviewed in Kabul were depressed. An increasing number of women are choosing suicide, once rare in Afghanistan, as a means of escape. According to doctors who have worked in Kabul, there has been a sharp increase in cases of oesophageal burns. Women are swallowing battery acid or poisonous household cleansers, which are easily accessible.

It is hard to believe today that barely six years ago, 70 per cent of the teachers, 40 per cent of the doctors and 50 per cent of the civil servants and students in Kabul were women. During the 1980s, women were present in the ranks of the ruling People's Democratic Party of Afghanistan and its Central Committee. There were women in the government (although not in the Council of Ministers) and in the Loya Jirga (traditional council). In 1989, Parliament had seven women members. Women held prominent positions— Dr. Soheila, chief surgeon of the military hospital, held the rank of general— and were employed in areas that were male bastions. Hafisa's mother, a qualified engineer, did electrical wiring at the Kabul Construction Plant and was a member of the Central Trade Union. All this was possible because of the social reforms introduced by the Marxist government in 1978 and thereafter. It is a fact that the communists were responsible for the torture, death and disappearance of thousands of Afghan women. But with regard to legislation and social reform on issues of concern to women, they made a significant contribution. Decree No. 7, for instance, banned bride price, which the Marxists believed made marriage a monetary transaction between families that ignored the wishes and wellbeing of the woman. Women were granted greater freedom of choice in marriage. In a society where girls were usually married off upon puberty, the government decreed the minimum age for women and men at sixteen and eighteen years, respectively. The government also embarked on an aggressive literacy campaign for women. Soraya Palwasha, a lawyer who worked in Kabul during the 1980s, recalls that family courts, mostly presided over by female judges, provided hearings for discontented wives. "These courts protected women's rights to divorce, alimony, child custody and child support," she says. Traditional sections deeply resented the changes. They pointed out that the "godless Communists" were outlawing the Islamic practice of bride price and that the reform measures were making women vulnerable. But below their supposed concern for women and Islam lay hard material and political interests. Fathers of daughters resented their access to large bride price payments being cut off. Other men opposed it for weakening the elaborate patriarchal system and their hold over their wives and daughters. The core of the opposition to the pro-women legislation came from those who subsequently became the mujahideen and are today part of the Northern Alliance. Western writers have said that women played important roles in the "holy war" and that the mujahideen respected the women. The truth was that unlike most liberation movements, the Afghan mujahideen prohibited the participation of women.

In fact, they threatened and even killed Afghan women, like the founder and other members of the Revolutionary Association of the Women of Afghanistan (RAWA) who protested the violence and oppression of the last two decades. Following the exit of the Soviets, the Peshawar-based mujahideen "government-in-exile" issued a fatwa forbidding women from wearing Western clothes, bangles or perfumes. Veils had to cover the body at all times and clothing was not to be made of material that was soft or rustled. "Women were not to walk in the middle of the street or swing their hips; they were not to talk, laugh, or joke with strangers or foreigners," recalls Soraya. When they took over Kabul in 1992, the mujahideen factions began to fight each other. But the men all agreed on the question of women. The first order of the new government was that all women should wear the burqa. However, given the unstable nature of the alliance that made up the interim government, the enforcement of the restrictions on women was inconsistent. Consequently, women were able to study and work to some extent, but they did so under constant threat. The Taliban completed what the interim government had left undone. Systematically, they killed the spirit of women. Most Afghan women will welcome the likely fall of the Taliban. But the possible return of the mujahideen, now the Northern Alliance, to Kabul is hardly the positive change they have been waiting for.

Lesley Garner

Before the Bombs: My Beautiful Afghanistan

6 November 2001

Imagine a country where mountain walls of rose and terracotta soar above green valleys of sweet-smelling beanflower and clover.

Imagine sitting in the shade of mulberry and apricot trees, listening to the song of water running through the little canals that irrigate the fields.

At night, you hear the music of the nightingale. By day, the song of the muezzin from a distant mosque harmonises with the flute music of the shepherd herding his small flock along the paths.

Horsemen cross the high, green pastures beneath the snow-white peaks, and nomads from the east lead their camel trains through the deserts of the south. In the summer the valleys are full of yurts, the herdsmen's round shelters.

The old caravanserai for travellers still offer shelter by the waters of the Hari Rud. In winter the children fly kites, and on the steppes of the north wild riders, fur-hatted and booted, whips between their teeth, wheel and thunder in a mad game called *buzkashi*, the forerunner of polo.

As you sit with the men on the carpet-strewn platforms of the teahouses, breaking fresh hot bread and looking up at the mountains from the shade of the vines, you could be in a story from the Arabian Nights. But you are not.

You are in Afghanistan. Or were.

How much of this magic will be left, I wonder, when the bombing stops?

I flew into Kabul twenty-three years ago to live with my doctor husband and our four-month-old baby daughter. It was the kite-flying season.

It was enchanting to stand at my window and look through the poplar trees, over the huddled flat roofs which climbed the lower slopes of the mountains, and watch hundreds of little kites jerking on long strings. The air above the city seemed to dance. This playful scene wasn't at all what I had expected.

I expected what you would expect if you knew nothing about Afghanistan except what you had read in the papers in the past few weeks.

I expected a hell-hole of fierce, impassable landscape and fiery, impossible people. I expected brutality and hostility. I expected desert, ice and rock.

I expected, as a woman, even pre-Taliban, to be kept in my place and generally despised. What I didn't expect was everything I found. On my first day I bravely walked out through the streets with my baby and met only respect, curiosity and genuine kindness.

I didn't expect to find that the houses in Kabul were built with a special room for flowers, to house their geraniums against the winter cold. I didn't expect to find the fruit market piled with luscious grapes, melons and pomegranates the size of grapefruits.

I didn't expect to find that this supposedly barren and uncivilised country would be casually littered with the remains of great cities and lost cultures, an archaeologist's paradise.

When the bombs fall, they do not fall on a stone-age culture of mud huts and caves. They fall on more than 2000 years of civilisation. The Taliban blew up the great carved Buddhas of Bamian, 50 miles from Kabul, but what have Western bombs destroyed since then? As I desperately scan news bulletins, trying to reassemble the country that has haunted my imagination for twenty-three years, I wonder if they are talking about somewhere else.

The language of the military communiqués talks grandly about command and control centres, but the roads are horse tracks, the command and control centres are mud shacks, and the cities are medieval huddles of mud buildings, surrounded by trackless mountains and steppes.

As the bombing continues night after night, I remember the turreted mud houses, the wash of green valleys at the foot of waves of gold and red mountains.

I close my eyes and I can see the translucent green waters of the Hari Rud, rippling with silver trout. I can see the drying towers for turning luscious grapes into fat raisins, the carpets laid out on the streets of Kabul to age beneath the wheels of cars and buses.

I remember the magical bazaars which sold carpets and kettles, silver and saddles, cradles and caged birds, and I wonder: is this what they are bombing?

I was there when they bombed Kabul in 1978. Out of the blue, a communist coup turned the city into a war zone.

MiG fighters circled the presidential palace, tanks rolled down the main roads, machine-gunners wandered round our gardens. Electricity was down, phones were cut, the airport was bombed. All night, we hid in our houses, not daring to move until daybreak brought silence, a change of government and a chance to see the devastation.

It was the beginning of the end for modern Afghanistan. Russian advisers filtered in and Western aid ground to a slow halt.

But until the entry of the Red Army a year later there was a lull, and during it we were lucky enough to travel through this astonishing country and get a sense of its timelessness, its endurance, its layers of history and its ability to ride out invasion. The people in the countryside were indifferent to the political turmoil.

We travelled north, into the Panjshir valley and over the Salang Pass. We sat and watched the horsemen of the *buzkashi* create a dust storm with the horses' flying hooves.

We travelled west to find the twelfth-century Minaret of Jam, at the confluence of two rivers deep in the Hindu Kush, all that remains of a lost city. We camped by the green waters of the Hari Rud, on white beaches shaded with red rocks.

We climbed high on to the heads of the now-demolished giant buddhas and looked out over an idyllic valley whose inhabitants were slaughtered by the armies of Genghis Khan. We walked at dawn by the unforgettable chain of blue lakes of Band-i-Amir, while the sun lit up the golden pinnacles and mesas all around.

Afghanistan has learnt over the centuries how to take punishment, how to survive and endure.

In the West, we expect the quick fix. A country which has outlasted Alexander's armies, the Mongols, the Moghuls, the British and the Russians knows there is no quick fix.

I pray that, once the bombs have stopped, the singular beauty and pride of Afghanistan will rise from the rubble, as it has for 2000 years.

Women Living Under Muslim Laws
Urgent Action Alert: Include Afghan Women in Transition Processes

7 November 2001

Dear friends,

Women Living Under Muslim Laws (WLUML) has been trying to ensure that the voices of Afghan women are heard by as broad an audience as possible. We are doing this by making available their understanding and articulation, as women, of what is happening, the impact that this is having, and their demands.

WLUML believes that international efforts for the reconstruction of Afghanistan must promote a process guided by the Afghan people. Afghan women are half of the Afghan people—a fact too often and too easily forgotten. It is not enough to call merely for the representation of various ethnic communities and/or factions in the decision making and transition processes around Afghanistan. The presence of Afghan civil society, most particularly women, at the negotiation table and decision-making of any peace process is vital.

More than fifty Afghan women from different NGOs and organisations met at the call of the Afghan Women's Network on 7 November 2001 in Peshawar, Pakistan. We attach below the appeal they drafted, addressed to the concerned warring parties and countries. They would like the endorsement and support of other organisations for the demands in the appeal.

We call upon the UN, that is better-positioned than any other entity, to support and facilitate Afghan women's involvement in the decision-making and transition processes in the coming months. We appreciate that the Special Representative of the Secretary General for Afghanistan, Mr Lakhdar Brahimi, has been specifically interacting with Afghan women's groups to discuss ways of including women in the transition processes led by the UN.

We therefore urge you to endorse the statement and write to the following people involved in the UN transition and peace processes.

In solidarity,
WLUML

For more than two decades the Afghan nation has been passing through the most difficult experiences of war, human rights violations and brutality. While we struggle to survive, we are scared for life, losing our dear ones, seeing our children traumatized, our neighbors killed, our husbands disabled by a war fought under different banners but yet with the same tragic consequences. In whatever name the war might be fought, jihad, justice, terrorism etc. We ask you to stop it.

The waging and continuation of the war affects us more deeply every passing day by hearing that someone else has been added to the list of victims.

Perhaps a million Afghans are in movement facing closed borders, a hostile reception and already jammed camps with the most miserable conditions of life.

Stop this war in the name of the Afghan child, the Afghan mother, and a nation who have sacrificed more than enough. The continuation of war will not only be adding to the existing misery of the Afghan nation, but will hinder the chances of a peaceful solution in the future. We call upon the international community and the countries and groups involved in this war to support us by listening to us and ensuring our rights as citizens of the world are respected. Help us in seeking our right to survival.

We request the following:

- The military action in Afghanistan be stopped immediately.
- The anti-terrorism campaign should not be fought at the expense of restricting or violating human rights of Afghans. It should be dealt with in accordance with international law and procedures by an international tribunal.
- The neighboring countries of Afghanistan should open their borders to Afghan families fleeing the war.
- Afghans should be supported in the peace process and nation building effort in such a way, which ensures the respect of its diverse ethnic groups and religious sects, women and children.
- Afghan women's participation in the peace process must be assured.

Jennie Ruby

Is This a Feminist War?

November 2001

The war against terrorism is posing a difficult dilemma for feminists. On the one hand, the Feminist Majority, headed by Ellie Smeal, says that "the United States has a unique obligation to end the Taliban's atrocities toward women". On the other, the feminist Worldwide Sisterhood Against Terrorism and War denounces the US bombing and invasion of Afghanistan. Meanwhile, Katha Pollitt is making fun of the aging hippie war protestors in New York, and a popular feminist salon series in Washington, DC, failed to attract a crowd to discuss "Women as Peacemakers". Should feminists be taking a position in favor of the US bombing, then? Is this a feminist war?

It should be. Feminism as a social justice movement certainly demands justice for the attacks on the World Trade Center and the Pentagon. Undoubtedly one of the things the terrorists hate about the United States and the entire Western world is the relative freedom of women, so in some small sense the attacks themselves were specifically anti-feminist. And feminists do want the Taliban out of power in Afghanistan. The Taliban removed Afghan women's civil rights, forbids women health care and education, forbids women to move about outside their homes without a male relative, requires women to completely cover themselves with the burqa, which physically hampers movement and impairs women's health, and enforces these oppressions with barbarous punishments such as stoning and amputating hands. Oh, yes. Feminists want the Taliban done away with. Feminist groups like the Feminist Majority have been lobbying for political action against the Taliban for some time.

But does that make the US attack on Afghanistan feminist? In the public rhetoric and the stated goals of the government, sadly no. At what should be a time for the United States to be proudly feminist, this country is instead reverting to our own version of male-dominant patriarchy.

The public obsession primarily with the male firefighters who died in the collapse of the World Trade towers reflects a reactionary feeling. In the media and in the hearts of thousands of Americans, we valorize not just those truly outstanding and altruistic individuals, but the masculine ideal of man as the strong, brave rescuer. The US president's rhetoric has evoked the hypermasculinity of the cowboy in a western: "Smoke 'em out ...", and, in the *Wall Street Journal*, former Reagan aide Peggy Noonan gushed, "Men are back ... I'm speaking of masculine men, men who push things and pull things and haul things and build things." This return to the glorification of masculinity is also expressed in a kind of God, guts, and guns patriotism in which we thank God we have these valiant, dedicated men willing to go to war to save our country from the evil ones who have attacked us.

While some experiences can be radicalizing, apparently having your country attacked can be conservatizing: making us retreat to outdated illusions of safety in our own patriarchal past. It seems that when the chips are down, we collectively revert to the same basic patriarchal model that we should be trying to subvert: men as warriors, women (and children) as "innocent victims".

Pollitt has also observed this trend:

> You can see the gender skew everywhere—in the absence of female bylines in Op-Eds about the war, in the booing of Hillary Clinton during the Concert for New York at Madison Square Garden, in the slavish eagerness of the media to promote the callow and inadequate Dubya as a strong leader whose "cockiness" [interesting word] and swagger are just what Americans need in the hour of crisis.

So when it comes down to it, this war is between Islamic fundamentalist patriarchy and American Christian capitalist patriarchy. Like two men fighting over a woman in a barroom, neither side has the woman's own humanity and freedom to heart. As currently constituted, this is not the war to empower the women of Afghanistan.

Where should feminists stand, then? Alice Walker says Osama Bin Laden should "be reminded of all the good, nonviolent things he has done", and that "the only punishment that works is love". Her statement has been widely derided. But I believe that if this were the kind of world we ultimately do want, Alice Walker would be right on. In the long view, I am a pacifist feminist. I don't believe anyone should be in any military. And I don't believe violence can ultimately stop violence.

But in the short term, that seems a little like believing that we should dispense with police while violent crime is still rampant. What do we do while we have not yet reached a world where there is no need for policing anyone through force? Are feminists ready to say we don't need police right now, because we envision a world where people are so caring that the threat of social disapprobation is enough to prevent rape, murder, wife abuse, kitchen deaths and mugging?

If we are not done with police on our streets, then it seems we cannot dispense with the need for force in our world, at least as an interim strategy.

But we need a force that is accountable to the citizens through trial by jury, to laws that are created in democratic process. We do not need a macho vigilante group gunning for the criminal, no matter how sure we are that he did it. We need a process of law.

Of the various solutions being proposed or enacted in Afghanistan, the one that makes the most sense from this standpoint is intervention not by the US and the UK but by the United Nations acting in conjunction with a broad coalition of countries. And the stated goals should be extradition of Osama Bin Laden for trial at a world tribunal for crimes against humanity; humanitarian aid to prevent mass starvation and human misery; and the establishment of a new government in Afghanistan that incorporates the full civil rights of women from the outset. Instead of a John Wayne-style war, we should see a coordinated and judicious use of minimal force, with plenty of women working alongside men.

The radical feminist analysis remains: patriarchal masculinity and the oppression of women are the common root of terrorism and of war. Using the masculinist posturing and aggression of war without true legal justice will never get us to the world we envision. And in the world we envision, Alice Walker's statement will make perfect sense.

Nikki Craft

A Call on Feminists to Protest the War against Afghanistan

8 November 2001

Stop the presses, the feminist revolution is finally happening! Some liberal and moderate American feminists are actually calling for war to end women's oppression. In light of the crimes committed against Afghan women by the Taliban, they say, decisive military action is the only recourse. Some are even chiding their more radical sisters (those, say, who are participating in peace marches and anti-militarism protests) for their lack of enthusiasm.

The newly militant liberal feminists say that, under the circumstances, the radical feminists have misplaced their loyalty—their "pacifism" is incomprehensible and indefensible. It almost looks as if the radicals and the moderates have switched places: all of a sudden it's the mainstream feminists who are ready to defend women's lives, rights, and dignity with armed force.

Some feminist leaders are offering very public support for the US government invasion of Afghanistan. On C-Span,[1] I recently saw Feminist Majority president Ellie Smeal testify before Congress about the oppression of women in Afghanistan. She spoke eloquently of the need for women to have a role in the reconstructed post-war government. Mavis Leno, another Feminist Majority representative, reiterates that the Taliban must be "collapsed," that women must have a place at the table to form the new government. Neither of these women calls for an end to the US bombing of Afghanistan. Nor in any of their frequent TV appearances have I heard either one even acknowledge that their government is terrorizing and dropping bombs on the heads of the same women they care so much about. Nor have I heard either one acknowledge the brutal rape and other terrorism against women practiced by the warlords in the Northern Alliance, the faction the US is currently backing. Look who all else is talking about women's rights now! Newt Gingrich, a self-proclaimed "hawk", says that to win the military war, first the US must win the "moral arguments"; among other things, he says, we must show that "we

---

1   Editors' note: C-Span is a public affairs website that carries information about the US House of Representatives: www.c-span.org.

are against the side who would oppress women." On the Fox evening news, Haron Amin, a spokesman for the Northern Alliance, accused the Taliban of practicing "misogyny", "gender apartheid", and the "feminization of poverty". The next day, a Fox talking head threw his arms up right in the middle of a broadcast and cried out in frustration, "Don't you see what they are doing to women?!" Later the same commentators, so concerned about women being excluded in Afghanistan, defended the overall invisibility of women in most discussions about the war; that it's only rich, white, all male generals and militarists being showcased by the US media. With the exception of token Condoleezza Rice, our government's recent global round-table meetings look as segregated as the Taliban's. Then there's George W. Bush's expressed concern. I never even knew his limited vocabulary included the word "oppression" until he used it several times last week when talking about the "evil-doers" oppressing women. But I don't trust him to have any real compassion for, or comprehension of, women's oppression in Afghan-istan—or anywhere. When Bush said women in this country shouldn't have to be afraid, he was speaking against racism, against harassment of Muslim women. But when he added that women shouldn't be afraid to be under the veil in this country, it sent a shudder down my spine. Among the millions of propaganda flyers the US is scattering over Afghanistan there is one that shows the Taliban hitting a woman with a stick. It reads, "Do you want *your* [emphasis mine] women to live this way?"

All this government and media hand-waving about "women in Afghan-istan" is a day late and a dollar short after such a conspicuous, and lengthy, lack of concern; the Taliban has been murdering, imprisoning and dispossessing, disenfranchising and dehumanizing Afghan women for almost a decade. It's also manipulatively, transparently selective: we're all upset about the oppression of women by the Taliban "bad guys", but similar restrictions and abuses are fine when it's the Saudi "good guys" who are doing it. In the propaganda carnival surrounding Mr Bush's war, women are being used for a specific agenda, not defended in their own right and for their own sake.

Show me how bombing Afghanistan has thus far improved, or is likely to improve, the material conditions of life for any Afghan woman. Show me how Bush's closing of the country's borders helps women—it keeps them trapped in Afghanistan between American bombs and two armies of male thugs. Show me how the US, with its fundamentalist and patriarchal allies, is challenging "fundamentalism" in this campaign—particularly, how are we challenging the oldest fundamentalism of all?

Systematic male privilege is the first fundamentalism. Has anyone wondered where the women firefighters and cops were in all that "brotherhood" in the aftermath of September 11? Why were, according to Red Cross, 80 per cent of those killed in the World Trade Center men? Didn't Cantor Fitzgerald, and the other corporations in the upper echelons of those buildings, hire very many women? It's not just the burqa and the Taliban that can make women invisible.

The ill-treatment of women occurs not only in "radical Islamist" countries, but in most countries on Earth. Women are statistically about 50 per cent of the world population, but they work two-thirds of all the world's working hours, receiving only one-tenth of world income, and owning less than 1 per cent of all world property. When was the last time any US politician made changing these conditions a top national priority? Are we sending in the Marines to enforce land reform? To protect women's right to unionize? To bust the traffickers who betray refugee women's hopes of a better life, steal their passports, reduce them to indentured sexual servants?

Filipina and Bangladeshi migrant laborers work as "maids" under conditions described as "modern-day slavery" in Kuwait, Saudi Arabia, Qatar, Lebanon and worldwide, but we never hear about them on Fox news. The World Health Organization estimates 200,000 to 400,000 women die worldwide every year from illegal, incompetently performed abortions. The women in Nigeria who are stoned to death in the streets weren't mentioned by the press, or anyone else, during the recent visit there by George W. Bush. Female infanticide, rigorously suppressed by Mao's regime, has made a comeback in China. We don't notice US politicians getting all bent out of shape about it.

Millions of women in Africa are infected with AIDS, not because they are promiscuous or careless, but because their husbands or boyfriends are promiscuous and refuse to use condoms, or because they are raped by male acquaintances or strangers who are infected. There are insurance companies in South Africa which sell "rape insurance" because the incidence of rape is so high. Rape in an AIDS-infected country is not just about pain and humiliation—it can be a death sentence. But we don't hear US politicians railing about this, or demanding that South African women have representation in government.

Many women come to the US, the "land of freedom", only to be used as indentured, captive labour in sweatshops no different from the ones they worked in back home. You can find captive women in the US—women afraid of a husband's fist or of the sweatshop boss, women who have to ask permission to go to the bathroom, who are threatened with violence if they complain about health hazards in their workplace, who can't get their passports back from the thugs who run the operation. Even women born here might merit our attention. Our tens of thousands of prostituted women and girls—in Des Moines IA, Los Angeles CA, Portland OR, Your Town USA—beaten and threatened by their pimps, abused by their "customers", what about them? Their deaths go uninvestigated, their lives undocumented—when did the US government last get all concerned about these oppressed and endangered women? In New York City, the cops traditionally don't even start to investigate until numerous prostitutes are killed in one month. We apply a different standard to ourselves and our allies, and not just the brute squad that calls itself the Northern Alliance. Women are not allowed to drive cars in Saudi Arabia, but we don't hear men lamenting about this discrimination on the news every night.

In 1987 the Turkish government enacted its so-called "Anti-Terror Laws". Amnesty International informs us that under these laws, women prisoners and detainees in Turkey have been subjected to genital electroshock, "virginity testing", rape (including rape with objects), and other forms of torture and sexual assault while in offical custody. Now that Turkey is "with us" against the Taliban—are we likely to hear criticism of these atrocities against women any time soon? Don't hold your breath. Bearing all this in mind, can anyone really believe the US is invading and bombing yet another country, threatening millions of refugees with starvation and who knows what else, just because Afghan women are being subjected to patriarchal persecution and violence?

When our boys drop airline meals into minefields, or intentionally target Red Cross hospitals, is it all in the service of our grand humanitarian mission to liberate the women of Afghanistan? To free the women of Afghanistan from those stifling garments so frighteningly similar to body bags? Of course it isn't. Our national leaders, the ones aching to be the policemen of the world and most recently the great protectors of womankind, won't be the ones to liberate the women of Afghanistan. They aren't the "good guys". In war (and peace) these gentlemen will rape and plunder women as their war booty, strip them in "gentlemen's clubs", and buy and sell them in prostitution. A goodly number of them beat their girlfriends and wives. They write sexist, misogynist messages on the heads of their bombs. Eight per cent of female Persian Gulf War veterans in one survey reported being sexually abused during Desert Shield and Desert Storm. That's how much US soldier-boys care about women. They beat, rape and sexually harass even their wives, their lovers, and their sisters-in-arms; consider what Afghan women have to look forward to, under US occupation. Ask the women and girls of Okinawa, if you can't figure it out for yourself.

Let's get real here. Women don't matter now any more than they did when the Northern Alliance was raping them. The US media paid no attention to the abuse of women then. Along came the Taliban, our "freedom fighters" against the Godless Commies, and what they did to women still didn't matter much—except in the frantic e-mail petitions feminists were spamming each other with on the Internet. Now the US is buying the rapists guns, dropping them ammo, feeding them, training them to be even more effective killers and helping them to regain control of "their country"—does anyone imagine this won't include regaining control of "their women"?

The human rights of the women in Afghanistan don't matter any more now than they did when CNN showed, for the first time in the beginning of September, the extraordinay documentary *Beneath the Veil*. It appeared briefly and sank without a trace; only outraged feminists reviewed it, made videotape copies, and mentioned it in their petitions and letters to editors. It's one of the most brave and important documentaries I've ever seen in my life, but it made the very tiniest splash on the slick surface of US media culture. It wasn't until we needed some wartime propaganda that *Beneath the Veil* suddenly started being aired multiple times per day on CNN, over several weekends. All of a sudden, in October, it re-emerged and became terribly important that everyone in America see this essential documentary—if not on CNN, then excerpted on all their affiliates many times over. One article referred to it as "heavy rotation".

Though they may be temporarily first in the soundbites, women are the very last item on the agenda. If the US could still "make the Taliban obey" like a kept woman or an obedient wife, we would still be funding the Taliban. If the US could "own" the Taliban, their treatment of women would have remained irrelevant, as it has been for the last several years; as it has been for every other dictator, king, shah, sheik, geek, tyrant or tinhorn terrorist we've ever backed.

But the Taliban is biting the hand that fed it for so long, and now its misdeeds are suddenly all hand-wringingly shocking and dreadful, where before they were mere boyish pranks or temporary rough spots in the transition away from Godless Communist rule. In fact, Afghani women will be fortunate if they get any say in the new government at all. By the time the war is over and the Great Powers once again sit down to impose a government on the defeated party, a focus on women's rights will no longer be strategically advantageous to the US. No nation on earth has ever gone to war for women's rights. We are not likely to be the first.

Judith Gardam

International Law and the Terrorist Attacks on the USA

10 November 2001

The September 11 terrorist attacks against of the World Trade Center in New York, the Pentagon in Washington and the hijacking and destruction of four civilian US airliners clearly constitute a "threat to the peace" within Article 39 of the United Nations Charter, the treaty that sets out the powers and purposes of the United Nations. As a consequence the Security Council is seized with jurisdiction under Chapter VII of the United Nations Charter, that part of the Charter which contains the enforcement powers of the Security Council. Under Chapter VII of the Charter the Council has the power to authorise States, individually or collectively, to use the force necessary to restore international peace and security. The Security Council acted promptly in relation to these events, condemning them in the strongest terms. The Council, however, stopped short of authorising the use of force in response to these acts of terrorism.

The legality of any unilateral State action that may be carried out by the United States with the participation of any other States such as Australia, through such self-defence pacts as NATO and ANZUS, will fall to be determined under the law relating to reprisals involving the use of force. Since the adoption of the United Nations Charter, retaliatory action involving the use of force against States has been outlawed. States are nowadays restricted to the use of proportionate non-forceful measures such as economic sanctions in such circumstances.

Moreover, it is not clear that the terrorists' activities against the United States can be attributed to any particular State, in which case there is no State-based responsibility for these acts under international law. Even if it can be established that the terrorists concerned were harboured by a State or States, actions which do constitute a breach of the United Nations Charter, there is no right thereby conferred on the injured State to use force in self-defence or by way of forceful reprisal action. As far as criminal proceedings are concerned, it appears that those individuals who sponsored and supported the terrorist actions may have committed crimes against humanity for which there is individual criminal responsibility in international law. The commission of such a crime confers universal jurisdiction on any State which has custody of the alleged offender(s). This means that any State may make such acts criminal offences under its own laws and prosecute such individuals in its domestic courts.

The United Nations Charter is based on a system of the peaceful resolution of disputes and a collective security system. The unilateral right of States to use force is extremely limited, as history indicates that such actions are not conducive to the long-term resolution of disputes and the maintenance of international peace and security. The appropriate method by which terrorism should be countered is through the United Nations collective security system. Declarations of war are not only inappropriate and, moreover, meaningless under international law, but unnecessarily inflame a situation that requires measured and careful responses that accord with international law.

Australia, as a country that upholds the rule of law in international relations, must ensure that any support it offers to the United States to assist it in countering the threat of ongoing terrorist activities and in obtaining justice for the terrible injuries inflicted on the American people is in accordance with international law. Moreover, it should encourage the United States and all other members of the international community to rely on the existing framework of the collective security system established after World War II to resolve this problem.

At the same time, if it appears that the United States is resolved on military action, Australia should urge that any such action complies strictly with the requirements of necessity and proportionality and with the international humanitarian law rules protecting civilians and civilian objects.

Delhi Women's Petition

Women Oppose War

10 November 2001

....

> As a woman I have no country. As a woman my country is the whole world.
>
> Virginia Woolf.

With most of the world, we the undersigned women's organisations, condemn both the tragic events of September 11 and the war unleashed by the US on the people of Afghanistan as deplorable acts of terrorism. We condemn the slaughter of thousands of Afghans, the destruction of cities, the bombing of hospitals and old people's homes, and most of all the trauma, horror and suffering caused by this war to ostensibly avenge the crimes committed by Osama Bin Laden and the Taliban. Victimising thousands of poor ordinary people who have already suffered twenty-three years of the destruction and devastation of war in no way can wipe out the roots of terrorism.

It is common knowledge that the terrorist groups the US is trying to eliminate were its own creation. In addition, the US has trained, supported, and supplied with arms various groups, invasions, and dictators all over the world. The millions killed in Korea, Vietnam and Cambodia, in Israel's invasion of Lebanon, the 200,000 Iraqis killed in Operation Desert Storm, the thousands of Palestinians who have died fighting Israel's occupation of the West Bank, the millions who died in Yugoslavia, Somalia, Haiti, Chile, Nicaragua, El Salvador, the Dominican Republic, Panama—are all victims of such state terrorism. Nor has the US been alone in this, for in Afghanistan, if the killing squads were financed by the US, the Russian occupation too was responsible for colossal death and destruction.

And it is well known too that wherever fundamentalism has taken root, women are among its first victims. In Afghanistan, after the Taliban came back to power with CIA support, it unleashed a reign of terror whose first victims were its own people, particularly women. It closed down girls' schools, dismissed women from government jobs, and enforced Sharia laws under which women deemed to be "immoral" are stoned to death, and widows assumed to be guilty of being adulterous are buried alive.

Oppose Religious Fundamentalism across the Globe

Religious fundamentalism and military aggression are two sides of patriarchy that aim to seek control and wield power over women and other oppressed sections. The struggle for abortion rights by women in the US and other parts of the Western world is a struggle against such fundamentalist governments and policies. The denial of education to women in Afghanistan, acid-throwing attacks on young women to impose the burqa in Kashmir, the attacks by the Hindu Right in India on films depicting lesbian love or the travails of widowhood, are all part of the same orchestrated campaign of religious fundamentalists to terrorise and control women. The women's movement opposes the forces of religious fundamentalism, whether they are from the US or Afghanistan or from India or Pakistan, because fundamentalist forces in essence trample upon all democratic and women's rights and seek to reverse the gains made by women's liberation movements.

War Is Patriarchy

We see the violence, death and destruction caused by wars as an extension of the violence we confront daily within the family, in the community, and by the state. We have seen the aftermath of war and related crimes; thousands of women have lived through the burden of bearing the "honour" of the community and nation in war after war. Bruised minds and battered bodies: that is all war achieves. In 1992, more than 20,000 women and girls were raped in the Balkans, followed by 15,700 in Rwanda. The disruption of normal life in military situations adds additional burdens and dangers to women's continuing responsibility for subsistence and household provisioning. The militarisation of our societies has made brutalisation a way of life. War films, war toys and video games, and daily violence in films and on television have created a militaristic chauvinistic macho culture. For women, this means an increase in violence within the home and by the "custodians of law". As women, we are deeply concerned about the increased regional hostility, fanning of communal hatred and violence, and the deepening of inequality and prejudices being caused by this war.

The Politics of Militarisation

The increasing communalisation of politics can lead to more violence and war and in both India and Pakistan. In the name of "security", the state is already becoming more repressive and intolerant of dissent in both these countries. National security is being used as an excuse for both Pakistan and India to increase their levels of militarisation. National and religious chauvinism built on mutual hostility becomes the binding force to maintain the nation-state. It becomes possible, even commendable, to kill, humiliate, maim and threaten citizens of another country, religious or ethnic group, or nationality in the name of preserving the unity of one's own country. The existence of any manufacturing base for armament production in India creates a demand for more and more wars and lays the material basis for Indian dominance in the South Asian region. In the 1980s, India's defence expenditure shot up from Rs 4329 crores to 14,500 crores in 1989–90.[1] It is 66,382 crores today (2000/01), which is more than what the central government spends on health, education, women and child "welfare" and other social services put together!! This is also 89 per cent higher than the entire country's expenditure on primary education!! The doubling of the defence expenditure in just the last five years in India, the biggest-ever increase since independence, shows the priorities of our warmongers in a country in which people continue to die of starvation deaths.

The global arms export market is valued at $54.2 billion, of which the US controls 50 per cent while Britain and France together control 30 per cent. Russia, China, Germany, Israel, South Africa, Belgium etc. control the rest. It is only because weapons of war, huge military machines, exist everywhere that genocides/wars take place. If organised violence, terror, genocide, war have to end, the military establishment and also the monstrously big police and torturing apparatuses have to be abolished from the face of this. But can one hear even faintly about any such measures from the US and other big powers or any states anywhere?

Whose Freedom, Whose Justice, Whose Democracy?

While claiming to fight for freedom, justice and democracy, the USA is itself behaving in the most unjust and undemocratic manner. Their President has the audacity to threaten the world at large with the words, "If you are not with us, you are against us." No nation, organization, or individual has the freedom to even express a contrary opinion, let alone act on it. The USA seeks to avenge the tragic loss of 5000 lives through bombing Afghanistan. But if the rest of the world were to live by the same logic, then who shall we destroy for the 16,000 who perished at the hands of the US multinational Union Carbide in Bhopal, the 500,000 Iraqi children who died due to US sanctions, the thousands killed in Vietnam by the US military ...? Even after victory was already assured for US in World War II they dropped the horrific nuclear bombs on the people of Hiroshima and Nagasaki to demonstrate their awesome killing power to the world. Generations bear the torture and the scars of such irreparable damage. And yet, if this were a concern about peace and democracy, it should start by destroying its own monstrous stockpile of

---

1   Editors' note: one crore equals 10 million.

nuclear, chemical and biological weapons. All peace-loving people will welcome such a move. But in spite of tens of millions of people around the world, especially in Western Europe, demanding total nuclear disarmament, the US and other nuclear countries have turned a deaf ear to this. Western powers and US have used every violent means to keep their stranglehold over all resources of the world, particularly oil. Often they have used the weapon of economic blockade to starve people to death, to strangulate them economically. This is almost like a permanent class war waged by the rich and the powerful against the poor and the powerless. Hundreds of millions died and are dying in just over five decades after World War II due to hunger, disease, wars, genocide, violence and due to the poisoning of the biosphere and ecological disasters.

Large sections of the media everywhere are of course part of the apparatus to manufacture and force consent for the war in the name of democracy, to spread misinformation, to wage campaigns for the rulers, to whip up war hysteria, rabid nationalism, and hatred of the "other". To speak the truth is to invite the wrath of the local global rulers.

We believe that armed conflict can never be, and will never be, a substitute for dialogue. The failure to pursue democratic dialogue is to betray the aspirations of millions, to jeopardise the future and to put into question the very existence of democratic institutions and mechanisms. If we want to end terrorism we need to address all the structured sources of injustices that are increasingly widening the gap between the rich and the poor, men and women, nature and humans, and create the pauperization and hopelessness that lead to terrorism. The women's movement seeks to challenge the structures of oppression that people all over daily face:

- the fear of domestic violence within the home
- persistent poverty and the desperation it leads to such as to the sale of body and life organs
- the loss of our children to a culture of violence and to all kinds of conflicts and wars
- the loss of jobs, home, homeland, family and community and becoming a refugee
- the invisibility and violation that comes along with being lesbian, gay, bisexual and transgendered in a predominantly homophobic and patriarchal society
- the fear of enforced prostitution as a means of survival
- the fear of living in a society where rape, molestation, female infanticide, widow-burning and witch-hunting are daily realities
- the authoritarianism of having our voices silenced whenever we dare to protest.

This is not our war. We reject it unequivocally. We do not believe in this war for it snatches away from us the most basic right: the right to live.

We represent forces that are engaged in struggles and processes based on respect for human life, on yearnings, desires, and dreams for a pluralistic peaceful egalitarian world. We raise our voice for peace and freedom against repression, war, terrorism, and pogromist politics to make the world a better place to live in. We are protesting against this war along with thousands and thousands from the US, Britain, France, Germany, Pakistan, Indonesia, Nigeria, Indonesia, Korea, Japan and India.

For love, peace, freedom, egalitarian values against death, terror and war!!!

Ankur, Action India, Campaign for Lesbian Rights,
Forum against Sexual Harassment (DU), Jagori,
Kali for Women, Saheli, Sangini, Stree Adhikar Sangathan

Revolutionary Association of the Women of Afghanistan
Appeal to the UN and World Community

13 November 2000

The people of Afghanistan do not accept domination of the Northern Alliance!

Now it is confirmed that the Taliban have left Kabul and the Northern Alliance has entered the city.

The world should understand that the Northern Alliance is composed of some bands who did show their real criminal and inhuman nature when they were ruling Afghanistan from 1992 to 1996.

The retreat of the terrorist Taliban from Kabul is a positive development, but entering of the rapist and looter NA in the city is nothing but a dreadful and shocking news for about 2 million residents of Kabul whose wounds of the years 1992–96 have not healed yet.

Thousands of people who fled Kabul during the past two months were saying that they feared coming to power of the NA in Kabul much more than being scared by the US bombing.

The Taliban and Al-Qaeda will be eliminated, but the existence of the NA as a military force would shatter the joyful dream of the majority for an Afghanistan free from the odious chains of barbaric Taliban. The NA will horribly intensify the ethnic and religious conflicts and will never refrain to fan the fire of another brutal and endless civil war in order to retain in power. The terrible news of looting and inhuman massacre of the captured Taliban or their foreign accomplices in Mazar-e-Sharif in past few days speaks for itself.

Though the NA has learned how to pose sometimes before the West as "democratic" and even supporter of women's rights, but in fact they have not at all changed, as a leopard cannot change its spots. RAWA has already documented heinous crimes of the NA. Time is running out. RAWA on its own part appeals to the UN and world community as a whole to pay urgent and considerable heed to the recent developments in our ill-fated Afghanistan before it is too late.

We would like to emphatically ask the UN to send its effective peace-keeping force into the country before the NA can repeat the unforgettable crimes they committed in the said years. The UN should withdraw its recognition to the so-called Islamic government headed by Rabbani and help the establishment of a broad-based government based on the democratic values.

RAWA's call stems from the aspirations of the vast majority of the people of Afghanistan.

Montserrat Boix

Women's Networks: Islamists' Violence and Terror

November 2001

Europe and the United States seem at last to be resolved to fight against Islamists' terror and bring an end to some networks, which they themselves have been nourishing. From the sphere of feminist networks and political activism for women's rights we know a lot about the situation that we have been denouncing over the last decade concerning the aggressions of these radical fundamentalist groups against countless women in different Muslim countries (Afghanistan, Sudan, Algeria, Saudi Arabia, Pakistan) who have been brutally assaulted and on numerous occasions killed.

Up until now the West had been deaf to these denunciations. Thousands of people in the heart of Western civilization (New York) have had to die in order for the international community to react and consider putting an end to these situations of privilege, which these fundamentalist leaders have enjoyed and continue to enjoy.

For over four years the international organization WLUML (Women Living Under Muslim Laws) has been denouncing the presence, and in some instances the protection by the West, of certain individuals such as Anuar Haddam, first of all member of FIS (Islamic Salvation Front) and afterwards member of the Algerian GIA (Armed Islamic Group)—a group which at the moment is being investigated due to its links with Bin Laden and is responsible for countless terrorist attacks in Algeria—who today is processing his political asylum papers in the USA.

It was in 1993 after the first terrorist attack on the Twin Towers when for the first time the United States began to fear that the "monster" which in the 1980s they had been feeding—via Pakistan in the fratricidal Afghan fighting—was beginning to turn against them in an uncontrollable manner. The United States reacted by cutting off funding and mobility of numerous groups that made up the Islam International, but the USA did not act in a decisive way, perhaps because they hoped to overcome difficulties and continue to manipulate such movements that could be very "useful" in their actions on the ground.

France had to bear the hijacking of a plane in Algeria and afterwards become the victim of a bombing campaign on the Paris metro (July 1995) before it was able to weigh up and gauge the real threat posed by maintaining such networks on its territory. Up until then it had always seemed worth France's while. Indeed, France maintained excellent relations with the Sudan regime in spite of the fact—documentation exists—that it was in this country that the first meeting of Islam International took place and that Sudan in the last decade had been one of the focal points for the training of Islamist terrorists and one of the last countries before Afghanistan to play host to Bin Laden and his entourage.

But Sudan paid France dearly for its ambiguity and tolerance towards the radical Islamic movement, allowing the secret services to hunt inside Sudanese territory for "Carlos", one of the most historic and most sought-after terrorists. The arrest of "Carlos" was considered to be one of the greatest successes of the French secret services in recent years. It seems nobody worried about the price that would have to be paid for this.

And it was France who after the terrorist attacks of 1995 alerted the Spanish about the movement of Islamist radicals in Spain. Up until now Spain did not consider these Islamic networks to be particularly dangerous, given that they only used Spanish territory for "passing through" and not as their base.

One could continue with numerous examples of hypocrisy in international politics where these networks, which finally seem to be severely castigated, have been used as common currency. The Israeli security services for years stoked up Hamas because they considered the PLO and Arafat to be the "true enemy", a view that is very far from the one held now. Both Europe and the United States were ambiguous towards and tolerant of the radical Islamic movement in Algeria so that they could exert pressure on the Algerian government.

Great Britain is at present the key European centre of Islamic networks where Pakistanis and Saudi Arabians have established their main communications headquarters (press, radio, television). This country and Germany have harboured many of those expelled from France and Belgium in recent years.

And what is to be said about Saudi Arabia, directly responsible for the funding of many Islamist groups who under the cover of offering supposed humanitarian aid to the poorest of Muslim countries have been working to reinforce some of the most recalcitrant fundamentalist Islamic movements in the world? Is it just coincidence that Saudi Arabia and Pakistan are two of the only three, until yesterday, defenders of the Taliban in international politics?

Countless documents drawn up by international women's groups bear witness to the denunciations of all of this in recent years. Denunciations that not only fell on deaf ears but also suffered attempts of being silenced through the use of pressure and threats.

Western governments are the prime responsible ones for the creation of these big and small monsters that now it is attempting to fight against. The West never cared when the Taliban attacked Afghan women's rights, when they assaulted them, when they killed them. It has looked in the other direction while in Algeria the radical Islamic groups have kidnapped, raped, killed and ripped to pieces scores of women—the latest aggressions taking place barely two months ago—when in Bangladesh many women have to live with their faces scarred by the acid thrown in their faces by fundamentalists.

And now. Is an end to Western hypocrisy going to come with the resounding measures being taken against the terrorism of the radical Islamic networks? Will they be compatible with measures of justice? It does not seem that the carpet-bombing of a people, the Afghan people, who in the last years have been the prime victim of a regime which has been indirectly tolerated and harboured. There must be another way of achieving justice and the ones who have all the information to hand know that there is.

Candide's documents drawn up by international women's groups bear witness to the depredations of all of them in recent years. Depredations that not only fell on the soldiers but also suffered attempts at being silenced through the use of pressure and threats.

Western governments are the prime responsible ones for the creation of the cruelty and small monsters that power is attempting to fight against. The West never cared when the Taliban attacked Afghan women's rights, when they assaulted them, when they killed them; it has looked in the other direction while in Algeria the radical Islamic groups have kidnapped, raped, killed and ripped to pieces scores of women—the latest aggressions taking place barely two months ago, when in Bangladesh angry women have to live with their faces scarred by the acid thrown in their faces by fundamentalists. And now it is an end to Western hypocrisy going to come with these recommitment states being taken against the terrorism of the radical Islamic networks. Will they be compatible with measures of justice? It does not seem that the easier bombing of a people, the Afghan people, who in the last years have born the prime weight of a regime which has been indirectly tolerated and harboured. There must be another way of achieving justice and the ones who have all the information to hand now that there is.

Whose Peace?

14 November to 8 March

Ani di Franco

Self Evident

(inspired by the WTC disaster)

yes,
us people are just poems
we're 90% metaphor
with a leanness of meaning
approaching hyper-distillation
and once upon a time
we were moonshine
rushing down the throat of a giraffe
yes, rushing down the long hallway
despite what the p.a. announcement says
yes, rushing down the long stairs
with the whiskey of eternity
fermented and distilled
to eighteen minutes
burning down our throats
down the hall
down the stairs
in a building so tall
that it will always be there
yes, it's part of a pair
there on the bow of noah's ark
the most prestigious couple
just kickin back parked
against a perfectly blue sky
on a morning beatific
in its indian summer breeze
on the day that america
fell to its knees
after strutting around for a century
without saying thank you
or please

and the shock was subsonic
and the smoke was deafening
between the setup and the punch line
cuz we were all on time for work that day
we all boarded that plane for to fly
and then while the fires were raging
we all climbed up on the windowsill
and then we all held hands
and jumped into the sky

and every borough looked up when it heard the first blast
and then every dumb action movie was summarily surpassed
and the exodus uptown by foot and motorcar
looked more like war than anything i've seen so far
so far
so far
so fierce and ingenious
a poetic specter so far gone
that every jackass newscaster was struck dumb and stumbling
over 'oh my god' and 'this is unbelievable' and on and on
and i'll tell you what, while we're at it
you can keep the pentagon
keep the propaganda
keep each and every tv
that's been trying to convince me
to participate
in some prep school punk's plan to perpetuate retribution
perpetuate retribution
even as the blue toxic smoke of our lesson in retribution
is still hanging in the air
and there's ash on our shoes
and there's ash in our hair
and there's a fine silt on every mantle
from hell's kitchen to brooklyn
and the streets are full of stories
sudden twists and near misses
and soon every open bar is crammed to the rafters
with tales of narrowly averted disasters
and the whiskey is flowin
like never before
as all over the country
folks just shake their heads
and pour

so here's a toast to all the folks who live in palestine
afghanistan
iraq

el salvador

here's a toast to the folks living on the pine ridge reservation
under the stone cold gaze of mt. rushmore

here's a toast to all those nurses and doctors
who daily provide women with a choice
who stand down a threat the size of oklahoma city
just to listen to a young woman's voice

here's a toast to all the folks on death row right now
awaiting the executioner's guillotine
who are shackled there with dread and can only escape into their heads
to find peace in the form of a dream

cuz take away our playstations
and we are a third world nation
under the thumb of some blue blood royal son
who stole the oval office and that phony election
i mean
it don't take a weatherman
to look around and see the weather
jeb said he'd deliver florida, folks
and boy did he ever

and we hold these truths to be self evident:
#1 george w. bush is not president
#2 america is not a true democracy
#3 the media is not fooling me
cuz i am a poem heeding hyper-distillation
i've got no room for a lie so verbose
i'm looking out over my whole human family
and i'm raising my glass in a toast

here's to our last drink of fossil fuels
let us vow to get off of this sauce
shoo away the swarms of commuter planes
and find that train ticket we lost
cuz once upon a time the line followed the river

and peeked into all the backyards
and the laundry was waving
the graffiti was teasing us
from brick walls and bridges
we were rolling over ridges
through valleys
under stars
i dream of touring like duke ellington
in my own railroad car
i dream of waiting on the tall blonde wooden benches
in a grand station aglow with grace
and then standing out on the platform
and feeling the air on my face

give back the night its distant whistle
give the darkness back its soul
give the big oil companies the finger finally
and relearn how to rock-n-roll
yes, the lessons are all around us and a change is waiting there
so it's time to pick through the rubble, clean the streets
and clear the air
get our government to pull its big dick out of the sand
of someone else's desert
put it back in its pants
and quit the hypocritical chants of
freedom forever

cuz when one lone phone rang
in two thousand and one
at ten after nine
on nine one one
which is the number we all called
when that lone phone rang right off the wall
right off our desk and down the long hall
down the long stairs
in a building so tall
that the whole world turned
just to watch it fall

and while we're at it
remember the first time around?
the bomb?

the ryder truck?
the parking garage?
the princess that didn't even feel the pea?
remember joking around in our apartment on avenue D?

can you imagine how many paper coffee cups would have to change their design
following a fantastical reversal of the new york skyline?!

it was a joke, of course
it was a joke
at the time
and that was just a few years ago
so let the record show
that the FBI was all over that case
that the plot was obvious and in everybody's face
and scoping that scene
religiously
the CIA
or is it KGB?
committing countless crimes against humanity
with this kind of eventuality
as its excuse
for abuse after expensive abuse
and it didn't have a clue
look, another window to see through
way up here
on the 104th floor
look
another key
another door
10% literal
90% metaphor
3000 some poems disguised as people
on an almost too perfect day
should be more than pawns
in some asshole's passion play
so now it's your job
and it's my job
to make it that way
to make sure they didn't die in vain
sshhhhhh ...
baby listen
hear the train?

Fariba Nawa
Demanding to Be Heard
14 November 2001

As diplomats at the United Nations continue to lay out plans for a post-Taliban government in Afghanistan, advocates for the country's women are increasingly worried that the rights and freedoms of women will once again be left off the negotiating table.

"Of course, we're angry," says Khorshid Noori, head of the Afghan Women's Network, a coalition of relief agencies based in the northwestern Pakistani city of Peshawar. "Anyone would feel angry if they were forgotten, especially in that we have ... endured the suffering throughout so many years."

Spurred on by the rapid military gains made by anti-Taliban forces, diplomatic efforts to produce a framework for a transitional government are gaining momentum. Appearing recently before a hastily called meeting of the United Nations Security Council, the UN's envoy to Afghanistan, Lakhdar Brahimi, outlined plans for a political transition in the country. Representatives from the US, Russia and the six nations bordering Afghanistan had earlier approved a draft statement calling for the formation of a coalition government to replace the Taliban.

Brahimi's plan calls for the UN to convene a meeting of Afghan representatives to negotiate "the process of political transition" and to convene a Provisional Council "drawn from all ethnic and regional communities". While Brahimi did not directly call for women to be included on the council, he did note that the "credibility and legitimacy of the Provisional Council would be enhanced, if particular attention were to be given to the participation of individuals and groups, including women, who have not been engaged in armed conflict."

Even if Brahimi's recommendations are supported by diplomats at the UN, it remains unclear whether the emerging powerbrokers in Afghanistan, particularly the leaders of the anti-Taliban Northern Alliance, will follow suit. Afghan women's rights activists say they are not going to wait quietly as the diplomatic process unfolds.

"The players in Afghanistan, including the US and United Nations, all talk about women's rights but when it comes to action, there is nothing," says

Zieba Shorish, a Washington-based Afghan exile and veteran women's rights activist.

The co-founder and executive director of the Women's Alliance for Peace and Human Rights in Afghanistan, Shorish had been helping to organize a December meeting of Afghan women's rights leaders, which she hopes will result in a unified message which all Afghan women's groups can support.

"We've got to push on this issue," says Shorish. "We need to be involved. We need to have our rights fully restored."

The last time women had any significant say in Afghan affairs was when they were included in a 1963 constitutional drafting committee. That committee was convened by Mohammed Zahir Shah, the former king of Afghanistan, who has emerged as a possible figurehead around whom a multi-ethnic coalition government could be formed.

The Afghan constitution, enacted in 1964 but disregarded during the past twenty-two years of war, guarantees equality for men and women under the law. The Taliban regime, which seized Kabul in 1996, has ignored that constitution completely. Its laws are made by Islamic clerics. Under Taliban law, women have been forced to wear the burqa, a full-body veil which covers the face in a thick mesh, have been all but barred from working outside the home, and barred from attending state schools.

As they have seized territory across northern Afghanistan, Northern Alliance officials have announced that women would no longer be forced to live under such severe limitations. Women, they announced, are free to return to work and girls would be allowed to attend schools once more. Still, it remains unclear whether the Alliance will actively protect and ensure women's freedoms.

Given that most women's groups have little if any political clout, their political concerns may be largely ignored by foreign diplomats and Afghan politicians alike. Some moderate female activists, however, could find themselves thrust into the negotiations—particularly as the UN searches for Afghans untainted by the nation's bloody conflict.

If women are given a role in a transitional government, one of the likeliest candidates is Fatana Gailani, director of the moderate Afghanistan Women's Council. A member of a politically powerful Afghan family—she is the daughter-in-law of Sayed Salman Gailani, an adviser to Zahir Shah—Fatana Gailani says she does not expect deeper issues of women's rights and social change to be addressed until after a stable government is in place.

"Let the men get along first, then we will get involved," she says. "Until our country has been rescued, the women's issue is a non-issue."

Supporters of the deposed king have proposed the formation of a broad-based council, known as a Loya Jirga, to choose members of a post-Taliban

government. Advisers to Zahir Shah say they plan to include women in the
120-member Loya Jirga, but are still searching for representatives.

Leading women's activists, however, are unimpressed by the promises.
They have reason. Led by Pir Sayed Ahmad Gailani, the politically powerful
clan's patriarch, some 1200 men representing Afghanistan's diverse ethnicities, religious sects and political factions convened for a peace and unity
conference in Peshawar three weeks ago. No women were invited.

With little coordination among the various women's activists, the emergence of a unified, broad-based women's movement appears unlikely. While
united in their concern about the future of women's freedoms in Afghanistan
and their frustration over their exclusion from the ongoing negotiations,
Afghan women's groups are deeply divided on numerous other issues.

There remain deep disagreements between those activists pursuing a
radical transformation of Afghanistan's male-dominated society and those
wanting protection of women's freedoms without significant changes in
traditional gender roles.

Zelda D'Aprano

What Do You Do When You Are Fed up with Men's Mismanagement of Our Planet Earth and Their Wars?

17 November 2001

Today we are here to summarise our past, our present, and plan for our future.

I lived the past, and the present, but exactly how much future I have at my age remains to be seen.

Through my mother's commitment, I was, at an early age, involved in the peace protests during the Italian Abyssinian war, the invasion of China by the Japanese and the war in Spain. When older, it was World War II, the Korean War and Vietnam, and during all these wars the armaments and means of killing improved, with women and children becoming the greatest victims. There have been over fifty wars since the end of World War II in 1945.

The last Palm Sunday Peace March I participated in was several years ago at Port Macquarie and the words on my banner read, "I can accept men killing men but I object to men killing women and children."

The response to my banner by those gathered was varied. Some were shocked, some pretended not to see it and one man called me sexist.

The truth of the matter is, I am fed up with patriarchy, and world poverty; I am fed up with trying to stop men from producing armaments of mass destruction, of being super-nationalistic egotists while competing with each other, of creating enemies, of seeking to maintain total control of the world, and of causing so much bloodshed of women and children. This is my past and present.

When dealing with the future, I wholeheartedly believe that unless we use new methods, our situation will only deteriorate. Wars involving super-powers have become armament-driven to prevent loss of life on their own side while at the same time curtailing too much opposition from developing at home; also being curtailed are democratic rights and civil liberties. Poorer countries too are quite prepared to sacrifice the lives of their males. All sides in these wars accept deaths of women and children as collateral damage, a by-product of war.

The time has come for women to take dynamic action and this may require more than marching through the streets with banners. We need to be innovative. We need to create new ways of dealing with patriarchy. New methods are absolutely necessary.

Let me return to that Palm Sunday Rally. When I suggested to several participants that perhaps the best solution to man's aggression would be for the UN to take control of several uninhabited islands around the world and organise war games or war sports, the response from one old man who dedicated most of his life to campaigning for peace was "They wouldn't agree to that." He didn't define who "They" were and he didn't appear to be too thrilled by my suggestion.

What arguments could opponents of this proposal put forward to justify war as people experience it today? Would they say we need to show we are superior beings, we want your oil and mineral deposits, we need more land because of our growing population, we cannot have you as an economic competitor, we have the one and only true god, we need to be rid of all our idle young men who could be troublesome, and because of all these needs, its unfortunate, but women and children have to die..

Let's think about the suggestion ... These uninhabited islands could accommodate all those who wished to play out their greed, patriotism or religious fervor in war and perhaps also include those who were guilty of murder or violence. Women who wished to be with their men could join in the fray.

It would be important for these modern-day heroes to have the latest in conventional weapons and show the world just how brave and heroic they were with their flags, bugles and medals while their exploits could be viewed on TV nightly with each side egging their warriors on. The organisation, provisions and logistics of these war sports would need to be financed by the governments of the combatants or the UN.

I believe that, apart from carrying banners in future demonstrations, we do have to seriously propose alternative ways and means of protecting women and children. This suggestion of mine may be seen by some to be farcical and impractical but there is much to be said for taking wars and aggression away from women and children. It is up to each and every one of us to come up with methods of how this can be done. I am sure that many men would support our methods but we need to take the initiative and lead this campaign. Wouldn't it be wonderful if the women of the world rallied behind a proposal to take wars away from women and children?

Let us hear what all the patriarchal leaders of our world have to say in justifying the need to kill women and children.

I believe that if there is to be any future, the aggression of patriarchy has to be dealt with.

Gayle Forman

Women in War

18 November 2001, *The Nation*, Pakistan.

United Nations resolutions don't usually warrant birthday commemorations, but on 30 October, women from three war-torn regions—Afghanistan, Kosovo and East Timor—honored the first anniversary of Resolution no. 1325, which seeks to address the particular problems faced by women in conflict zones, by testifying before the Security Council. Their stories, which were imbued with new urgency by the current crisis in Afghanistan, described a variety of abuses they and their countrywomen suffer on a daily basis. Sexual exploitation, in the form of rape, trafficking, forced prostitution and early marriage, has become as commonplace in modern conflicts as mines and sniper fire, as Haxhere Veseili, a 21-year-old from Kosovo, attested. "Thousands of children have been born of rape. I have friends who were raped," she said. "I know other girls who have relations with peacekeepers just so they can have some safety. Other young women exchange sex for money."

Women and children constitute 75 per cent of war refugees. "And yet widows and single mothers in East Timor have received little or no aid," says Natia Godinho-Adams of East Timor. Unfortunately, even after fighting ceases, all too often such dilemmas are disregarded or swept under the rug once the ink has dried on a peace accord, prolonging instability and misery for millions. Which is why perhaps the most important component of Security Council Resolution 1325 is the call for governments and international agencies to include women in peace negotiations and nation-building.

The progress in East Timor shows just how much difference some feminist consciousness can make. This past August, two years after East Timor ended its 25-year civil war by passing a referendum to establish an independent state, the country held national elections. Women captured 27 per cent of elected seats and were subsequently appointed to two of ten Cabinet positions. Moreover, the progressive East Timorese constitution contains women-friendly provisions dealing with slavery and trafficking, forced prostitution and paid maternity leave. "Not even the United States goes this far," noted Godinho-Adams.

East Timorese women not only had a role in the UN-brokered referendum, but were also very active in the transitional administration. In the two years between the referendum and national elections, local grassroots NGOs and UN agencies lobbied the political parties to run female candidates. These groups also identified women community leaders who would make strong potential candidates and provided leadership training and assistance. Now East Timor has twice the level of nationally elected female representatives as the United States, who in turn are more likely to address women's issues. In Kosovo the situation for women is not as hopeful. In the two years since the war ended, the area has become a hotbed for sexual trafficking—a problem that seems to be growing worse. Last year the country held municipal elections, and in spite of quotas set up to insure women's presence in government, some of the women who were elected resigned their posts to men, in part due to a lack of the kind of support or leadership training that went on in East Timor. It remains to be seen how things will change after the 17 November national elections, in which 358 of the 1281 candidates are women.

If ever there were a time and place to invite women into the negotiating fray, it is in Afghanistan today. Now that Kabul has fallen, plans for a post-Taliban provisional government have assumed a new urgency. Lakhdar Brahimi, the UN's Special Representative for Afghanistan, is working to assemble a broad-based coalition that will apparently include the various tribal factions—the Pashtun, Tajiks, Hazaras and Uzbeks—as well as the spectrum of political persuasions. In spite of their repeated requests, women, who constitute 54 per cent of Afghanistan's population, have yet to be invited to the table.

Considering how women's subjugation in Afghanistan has become the political totem of the Taliban's repression, women's absence from these negotiations makes for bad symbolism—and even worse policy. Before the Taliban hid a nation full of females under house arrest and cover of the burqa, Afghan women were lawyers, judges, doctors, professors and government ministers. While the mujahideen were off fighting the Soviet invasion in the 1980s and the civil war of the early 1990s, women were keeping the shops, the hospitals and the courts going. "Do they think that because women wear veils we do not have a voice?" Jamila, an Afghan human rights worker, asked. They may be invisible now, but those women have the experience and brainpower that will be necessary to rebuild what is now a thoroughly decimated country. Women's participation in the peace process is not just a matter of symbolic equality; it is a matter of insuring peace and stability for all of Afghanistan.

Rinku Pegu

Interview with Mary Robinson

19 November 2001

....

Mary Robinson, United Nations Commissioner for Human Rights and former president of the Republic of Ireland, received the Indira Gandhi Prize for Peace, Disarmament and Development for 2001 on 19 November, the birth anniversary of Indira Gandhi. Robinson has, in recent years, emerged as the suave but firm face and voice of human rights across the world. At the Durban Conference against Racism, in response to loud Arab protests against Israelis and Zionists, she asserted, "I am a Jew" because she felt that the Jewish delegates were being obstructed and intimidated by the protestors. She has travelled to trouble spots like Kosovo, and to conservative countries like Iran to discuss human rights.

The Revolutionary Association of Women in Afghanistan (RAWA) has demanded that individuals and factions of the Northern Alliance (NA), responsible for the 1992–96 atrocities in Afghanistan, should first be absolved by the international community before participating in any government formation in Afghanistan. In such a context, what role do you envisage for UNHCR?
I would be open to such a process as I am very keen to have accountability. I am also aware that Afghanistan has been in a very difficult situation. For the past many years, our colleagues inside Afghanistan have been consistently reporting about the extent of human rights abuse to the UN General Assembly, again and again, first by the Taliban, then by the Northern Alliance, and again by the Taliban. We did not care about them. Here we have to be very honest with ourselves in acknowledging the fact that how little we care about civilians in Afghanistan.

Now is the time to care about the long-term [situation of the] Afghans. We have to address the issue of accountability, and we have to do it in a way that makes sense. We have to acknowledge the need for accountability, but also acknowledge that human rights violations were tolerated in the past by the international community. What I am more concerned about is that from now on there are no more massacres, no more rapes of women, no more pillaging of property, no more bullying because you are the strong guy in the town [or the] city.

What about the political will to make it happen?
We can do that if we wish. The military campaign in Afghanistan cost billions and summoned extraordinary resources. My contention is we can have the same resources build-up for the people in Afghanistan, for their homes, for their future and their country. That's what we should be concerned about doing now.

What specific framework do you have in mind?
It goes without saying that any government formation in Afghanistan will have to ensure the participation of women, who form 60 per cent of the population. They have to have access in governance. Women there are definitely not in positions of power. This is obvious because they cannot turn themselves into warlords or power brokers. But we have to identify thirty to fifty Afghan women to be given responsibility of governance in any power structure for stability and peace.

Right now, I am not saying that the UN has geared itself both in the Executive Committee on Peace and Security and in the core Special Council in the road map that is presumably being laid out for the Security Council. But in the choice of person by the Secretary-General to head the UN-led reconstruction in Afghanistan is a clear indication of the priority UN is giving. And the UN is forcefully saying that it wants an Afghan approach to any government formation, which is the only way forward in terms of a solution in a country like Afghanistan, one that will be able to govern the country effectively.

In that context, today in New York there is a meeting about Afghan women. And I will be participating in a major conference in Brussels early next month that will highlight the issues of Afghan women. These might seem far away, but there is no doubt that there is an alliance of women's groups worldwide forged for our sisters in Afghanistan. ...

Consequent to September 11, several democratic countries, including India, are implementing strong legislation that militates against the basic tenets of human rights. How do you combat such deviations?
I agree that we have to combat terrorism. But, in such a context, it is incumbent upon all democratic nations to balance anti-terrorist measures with the implementation of the pledges of anti-discrimination taken at the recently concluded Conference against Racism held at Durban. We must take care to remind ourselves of the fact that the attacks of September

11 happened because our laws (democratic) and the ideas behind those laws have not been implemented to the very deep extent that is required. With regard to the Prevention of Terrorism Ordinance in India, the measures will be closely monitored by our office, as well as the final outcome. If need be, we will take up the matter with the government.

Working Group on Women and International Peace and Security

Call for Action

21 November 2001

Mr Lakhdar Brahimi
Special Representative of the Secretary-General for Afghanistan

cc: Mr Francesc Vendrell
Personal Representative of the Secretary-General
and Head of the Special Mission to Afghanistan

United Nations Headquarters
New York, NY 10017

Dear Mr Brahimi:
This letter is being sent to you as a matter of great urgency on behalf of the Working Group on Women, International Peace and Security.

At a press conference yesterday, it was confirmed that a meeting of various Afghan groups and other interested players is set for next week in Germany. On hearing the news, the Security Council President Ambassador Patricia Durrant of Jamaica was quoted as saying that this was "an indispensable first step towards the establishment of a broad-based representative government in Afghanistan". She added that the members of the Security Council encouraged all parties to participate in this meeting "in good faith and without preconditions".

We urge in the strongest terms that women be represented at this most important meeting of "various Afghan groups and other interested players" in Germany. To leave women out of any stages in the rebuilding of this devastated country is to cripple that development irrevocably. Women represent 60 per cent of the population of Afghanistan. In the decade before the 1990s, women represented 70 per cent of the teachers, 40 per cent of the doctors, 15 per cent of the legislation and 50 per cent of the government workers. Women were engineers and scientists, media professionals, community leaders and small business owners, and the full involvement of women in the total development and life of Afghanistan was obvious. In recent years, women have helped to sustain their community by providing essential health care, education, relief and other humanitarian services in refugee camps and in Afghanistan.

In October 2000, the United Nations Security Council went on record as recognizing the essential role played by women in all aspects of a nation's development. In adopting unanimously a resolution of women, peace and security, the Security Council stressed in no uncertain terms "the importance of [women's] equal participation and full involvement in all efforts for the maintenance and promotion of peace and security, and the need to increase their role in decision-making with regard to conflict prevention and resolution."

In its Resolution 1325, the Security Council "Urges Member States to ensure increased representation of women at all decision-making levels in national, regional and international institutions and mechanisms for the prevention, management, and resolution of conflict." It calls on all actors involved, when negotiating and implementing peace agreements,

> to adopt a gender perspective, including, *inter alia*: a) The special needs of women and girls during repatriation and resettlement and for rehabilitation, reintegration and post-conflict reconstruction; and b) Measures that support local women's peace initiatives and indigenous processes for conflict resolution, and that involve women in all implementation mechanisms of the peace agreements.

Experienced and highly capable women are available to work for the disarmament of their country and the formation of a democratic government. In fact, leaders in the Afghan women's movement have made these two things, i.e. disarmament and a democratic government, essential goals if they are to be part of any negotiations. They have spoken passionately of the need for regional representation by people who played no role in the armed conflict and harsh rule that have devastated their country over the past twenty years. Women of Afghanistan want peace, security, justice and a sustainable development that is only possible if a democratic government is at the core. Yesterday, in Kabul, women demonstrated for human rights, demanding peace for the country, education for their children and power for themselves.

We have attached to this letter a list of Afghan women's groups for your action. Precedence for the involvement of women at all stages in the prevention and resolution of conflict and in peace-building has been established in Northern Ireland, Somalia and Burundi. We demand nothing less than this for Afghanistan. To deny the participation of women is to go against everything that women of the world fought for and won in Security Council Resolution 1325.

Mr Brahimi, the eyes of the world are now upon you. This is the moment for the United Nations to take its stand on behalf of peace, democracy, human rights and the full participation of women at every level of negotiations towards that end.

Yours sincerely,
Christelle Matou
Co-ordinator

Barbara Ehrenreich

The Fundamental Mystery of Repressing Women

23 November 2001

Feminists can take some dim comfort from the fact that the Taliban's egregious misogyny has finally been noticed. For years, the oppression of Afghan women was a topic for exotic Internet list serves and the occasional forlorn Internet petition. As recently as May, for example, President George W. Bush congratulated the ruling Taliban for banning opium production and handed them a cheque for $43 million—never mind that their regime accorded women a status below that of livestock.

In the weeks after September 11, however, you could find escaped Afghan women on *Oprah* and longtime anti-Taliban activist Mavis Leno doing the cable talk shows. CNN has shown the documentary *Behind the Veil*, and even Bush has seen fit to mention the Taliban's hostility toward women—although the regime's hospitality to Osama Bin Laden is still seen as a far greater crime.

Women's rights might play no part in United States foreign policy, but we should perhaps be grateful that they have at least been important enough to deploy in the media mobilisation for war.

On the analytical front, though, the neglect of Taliban misogyny—and beyond that, Islamic fundamentalist misogyny, in general—remains almost total.

If the extreme segregation and oppression of women do not stem from the Koran, as non-fundamentalist Muslims insist, if it is in fact something new, then why did it emerge when it did at the end of the twentieth century? Liberal and left-wing commentators have done a thorough job of explaining why the fundamentalists hate America, but no one has bothered to figure out why they hate women.

And "hate" is the operative verb here. Fundamentalists might claim that the sequestration and covering of women serves to "protect" the weaker, more rape-prone sex. Or that they "protect" men from having unclean thoughts.

But the protection argument hardly applies to the fundamentalist groups in Pakistan and Kashmir that specialise in throwing acid in the faces of unveiled women. There's a difference between protection and a protection racket.

The mystery of fundamentalist misogyny deepens when you consider that the anti-imperialist and anti-colonialist Third World movements of forty or fifty years ago were, for the most part, at least officially committed to women's rights.

Women participated in Mao's Long March; they fought in the Algerian revolution and in the guerilla armies of Mozambique, Angola and El Salvador. The ideologies of these movements—nationalist or socialist—were inclusive of women and open, theoretically anyway, to the idea of equality.

Bin Laden is, of course, hardly a suitable heir to the Third World liberation movements of the mid-twentieth century, but he does purport to speak for the downtrodden and against Western capitalism and militarism. Except that his movement has nothing to offer the most downtrodden sex but the veil and a life lived largely indoors.

Of those commentators who do bother with the subject, most explain the misogyny as part of the fundamentalists' wholesale rejection of "modernity" or "the West". Hollywood culture is filled with images of strong or at least sexually assertive women, hence, the reasoning goes, the Islamic fundamentalist impulse to respond by reducing women to chattels.

The only trouble with this explanation is that the fundamentalists have been otherwise notably selective in their rejection of the "modern". The nineteen terrorists of September 11 studied aviation and communicated with each other by e-mail. Bin Laden and the Taliban favor Kalashnikovs and Stingers over scimitars. If you're going to accept Western technology, why throw out something else that has contributed to Western economic success— the participation of women in public life?

I don't know, but I'm willing to start the dialogue by risking a speculation: maybe part of the answer lies in the ways that globalisation has posed a particular threat to men.

Western industry has displaced traditional crafts—female as well as male— and large-scale, multinational-controlled agriculture has downgraded the independent farmer to the status of hired hand. From West Africa to South-East Asia, these trends have resulted in massive male displacement and, frequently, unemployment.

At the same time, globalisation has offered new opportunities for Third World women—in export-oriented manufacturing, where women are favored for their presumed "nimble fingers", and, more recently, as migrant domestics working in wealthy countries.

These are not, of course, opportunities for brilliant careers, but for extremely low-paid work under frequently abusive conditions.

Still, the demand for female labor on the "global assembly line" and in the homes of the affluent has been enough to generate a kind of global gender revolution.

While males have lost their traditional status as farmers and breadwinners, women have been entering the market economy and gaining the marginal independence conferred even by a paltry wage.

In Sri Lanka, according to anthropologist Michele Ruth Gamburd, where many women find work in factories or as migrant domestics, the decline of the male breadwinning role has led to male demoralisation, marked by idleness, drinking and gambling.

Add to the economic dislocations engendered by globalisation the onslaught of Western cultural imagery, and you have the makings of what sociologist Arlie Hochschild has called a "global masculinity crisis". The man who can no longer make a living, who might depend on his wife's earnings, can watch Hollywood sexpots on pirated videos and begin to think the world has been turned upside down. This is *Stiffed*—Susan Faludi's 1999 book on the decline of traditional manhood in America—gone global.

Or maybe the global assembly line has played only a minor role in generating Islamic fundamentalist misogyny.

After all, the Taliban's home country has not been a popular site for multinational manufacturing plants. There, we might look for an explanation involving the exigencies—and mythologies—of war.

Afghans have fought each other and the Soviets for much of the past twenty years, and as Klaus Theweleit wrote in his brilliant late-1980s book *Male Fantasies*, long-term warriors have a tendency to see women as a corrupting and debilitating force.

Hence, perhaps, the all-male madrassahs in Pakistan, where boys as young as six are trained for "jihad", far from the potentially softening influence of mothers and sisters. Or recall terrorist Mohamed Atta's specification, in his will, that no woman handle his corpse or approach his grave.

Then again it could be a mistake to take Islamic fundamentalism out of the context of other fundamentalisms—Christian and Orthodox Jewish. All three aspire to restore women to the status they occupied—or are believed to have occupied—in certain ancient nomadic Middle Eastern tribes. Religious fundamentalism in general has been explained as a backlash against the modern capitalist world, and fundamentalism everywhere is no friend to the female sex.

To comprehend the full nature of the threats we face since September 11, we need to figure out why. Assuming women matter, that is.

Afghan Women's Summit for Democracy

The Brussels Proclamation

4–5 December 2001. The meeting of the Afghan Women's Summit for Democracy came up with the following demands with respect to the reconstruction of Afghanistan.

Education, Media and Culture

Infrastructures in Afghanistan for the past twenty-three years have been destroyed. People of Afghanistan lost their basic human rights—including the right to live, to be educated and to work—as well as their culture. Two generations of Afghans are illiterate and there was no adequate schooling available due to the war and the repressive regime, which banned girls from school and taught boys only about "political" Islam so that these boys were brainwashed and became extremists. These ideas are contrary to Islamic values.

Afghan women are in dire need of education and information through the media. Education, information and culture empower women. Women are the shapers of society; they have to be educated and have access to information in order to raise responsible children. Women should participate fully in the current and future development of Afghanistan.

We need to reopen the schools in major cities of Afghanistan, starting from Kabul the capital, and bring back to the people our cultural heritage. Particular attention should be given to orphans living in the streets, both in respect of shelter and education.

We need to bring hope and a bright future to our people. It is our duty as Afghan women to help and support our people in order to bring to the fore the important contribution of Afghan women as the torch-bearers of a culture in peril.

For the past twenty-three years, Afghan people have been living in the dark. We the Afghan women should join our efforts to establish a civil society in our country and bring back democratic values through education and culture. Education and culture transcend the reality of our lives. Their healing power and creative energy could act as a catalyst for peace and as an antidote to our national wounds by safeguarding our cultural heritage from disappearance. By reviving education and culture, we Afghans can all have something common to share and be united.

Recommendations

- sending a group of women to Afghanistan for assessing the schools' condition
- developing an emergency plan for re-opening schools by March 2002 for both girls and boys and reconstruction of the schools that have been damaged or destroyed
- reopening of institutes of higher education
- provision of all the necessary means for schools so that they will be able to function properly
- transfer of students taught at home to schools
- provision of a comprehensive school curriculum based on international standards and the relevant supplies
- provision of teachers' training including refresher courses for teachers
- creation of structures for sheltering and educating orphans
- ensuring fair salaries for all staff in education
- inclusion of educational professionals in the Ministry of Education
- ensuring inclusion of conflict-resolution courses in education
- Afghan journalists living abroad to assess the situation in Afghanistan
- reconstruction of TV satellites and radio stations, in particular in the major cities of Afghanistan that were already equipped
- provision of cameras and necessary equipment
- provision of training for personnel in the area of technical backing and production
- recuperation and repurchase of the ancient literary works which have been dispersed around the world, with the help of UNESCO and private donors
- reprinting of rare books of literature, poetry, etc.
- translation of Afghan literature into English and other languages so that the Afghan children living abroad will be able to regain their cultural identity
- establishment of a prize-award system in literature for young writers, poets and artists.

Health

Women should participate fully in the current and future development of Afghanistan, particularly in the field of health. We volunteer to do a comprehensive survey in order to specifically identify and point out the needs, if concrete support is provided. In order for the group members to conduct a comprehensive survey in the following areas, the group members request the European Commission and the donor agencies to provide the means for a team to conduct a survey of the medical needs of Afghans.

Recommendations

- provision of critical medical equipment, medicines and vitamins
- rebuilding of water and sanitation systems
- restarting of the food program
- vaccination programs
- medical teams be sent to Afghanistan to provide hands-on training and mentoring to Afghan doctors and other medical staff
- Afghan doctors and other medical staff be provided with the opportunities to get training abroad
- scholarships be provided to medical students to study abroad
- awareness-raising through media, distribution of health-related material, including but not limited to mother and child health, malnutrition, hygiene, contagious diseases, AIDS and other sexually transmitted diseases
- re-establishment of health centers in urban and rural areas
- re-establishment of training centers and training programs for the medical personnel
- rebuilding of medical faculties in Kabul, Herat, Nengrahar and Mazar-e-Sharif
- rehabilitation of psychological hospital in Kabul
- expansion of orthopedic centers for handicapped people
- expansion of clinics and treatment centers for malaria and leishmaniasis
- establishment of counselling and health centers in schools
- provision of family planning programs
- establishment and rebuilding of medical laboratories
- reintroduction of health insurance
- provision of centers for HIV/AIDS patients and drug addicts
- provision of blood banks.

Human Rights and the Constitution

Recalling the United Nations Universal Declaration of Human Rights, the Beijing Platform for Action, the Convention on the Elimination of all Forms of Discrimination Against Women (CEDAW), the Cairo Programme of Action, and the UN Convention Against Torture, we the participants of the Afghan Women's Summit for Democracy make the following recommendations.

Recommendations

- making all support, including monetary, from the international community conditional on the rights and treatment of women
- the cessation of using Pakistan as a proxy for Afghanistan and the sub-

sequent recognition of Afghanistan as an independent state in reconstruction negotiations

- guaranteed recognition of the returnees to Afghanistan as legitimate citizens of Afghanistan
- central inclusion of women in the Loya Jirga (Grand Assembly) and all peace processes and matters related to reconstruction
- inclusion of Afghan women lawyers in the development of a new constitution based on the 1964 constitution and resulting legal frameworks
- critical focus on disarmament in all areas of Afghanistan and a wide demining campaign
- ensuring that the principles of non-discrimination according to gender, age, ethnicity, disability, religion, and political affiliation in all aspects of political, social, cultural, civil and economic rights are central to the new legal system
- ensuring the protection of women from forced/under-age marriages, sexual harassment, trafficking in people and all other types of abuse
- ensuring a safe and secure environment for women and girls
- ensuring equal rights for women including the right to vote, equal pay and equal access to education, health care and employment
- elimination of child labor and child soldiering
- wide utilization of Afghan women experts, their knowledge and experiences
- establishment of an umbrella coalition under which a number of organizations will jointly work on projects or programs
- donor funding to be channeled through local Afghan non-governmental organizations and a transparent system of accountabilities be established
- ensuring examination of the economic involvement of regional actors in the context of promoting sustainable peace.

Refugees and Internally Displaced Women

According to UNHCR in the past two decades Afghan refugees constitute the largest refugee population in the world. Due to the current war in Afghanistan, approximately 300,000 more refugees have been added to the refugee population. More than 65 per cent of refugees are women and children. Afghan refugees in the first country of asylum, especially in neighbouring countries, including Central Asian countries, have very limited rights. The safety and security of most refugees, especially women, is extremely limited. Under the current circumstances, due to the presence of landmines and destruction of infrastructure in residential areas, Afghanistan does not have the capacity to provide sustainable living conditions. The political and security conditions in Afghanistan are not considered to be safe for some refugees. For those refugees who cannot return and are in need of international protection according to the 1951 Geneva Convention, resettlement should be provided as a tool of protection.

Recommendations

- avoidance of forced repatriation of refugees as it violates basic human rights according to UNHCR guidelines on repatriation
- provision of a durable resettlement solution for those refugees who cannot return to Afghanistan for security reasons
- increase of educational, training, capacity building and income generating programs to enhance the special needs of refugees and internally displaced women and children
- provision of basic needs of internally displaced and refugee women required for human existence. These needs include: security and protection; health-care services; education on prevention of sexually transmitted diseases; education on birth control and family planning.

Eve Ensler

Letter from Brussels

6 December 2001. Eve Ensler, author of *The Vagina Monologues*, initiated V-Day, a global movement to stop violence against women.

I am on an airplane leaving Brussels where I have been for the last four days at the Afghan Women's Summit. The sky is pink, shattering pink. I remember someone once telling me that pink was a crucial color, as it is the color of healing.

I wanted to write down some thoughts, so that you could share these last extraordinary days in Brussels. They have been miraculous, productive, and full of extremes. I think when people have suffered for a long time, they learn how to cope, manage, and contain. It is only later, when kindness or safety comes, that they are able to experience their suffering. This summit allowed Afghan women to collectively experience their terrible years of oppression, and to find their voices and dreams for the future.

The Summit was, first of all, a gathering. I mean that in the deepest sense— a gathering, a joining, a building. Forty Afghan women came from countries all over the world, including Afghanistan, Iran, Pakistan, Kyrgyzstan, Tajikistan, Russia, Germany, France, the Netherlands, Switzerland, the United Kingdom, the United States, Canada, and Australia. They were there with a common purpose and project—to let the world know what they wanted and needed for the future of their country. Most of these women had never met before. Even the women from inside Afghanistan were strangers to one another, as travel is so difficult and women were so isolated under the Taliban.

On the first day, women shared amazing stories—stories of survival, subversion, and brilliance. One woman who was a teacher told of how she asked students to always keep the Koran on top of their desks. They would study every other kind of subject. When she saw the Taliban approach, she would quickly tell them to turn to page 15 of the Koran and read. Another participant had organized fifty women in resistance—her community had been left defenseless after its men had either gone off to fight or had been taken by the Taliban. Any time the Taliban approached to harm them, the women would stand on their roofs and pour buckets of boiling water on their attackers' heads. They had many other surprises.

There were also about twenty-five non-Afghan human rights activists there from Belgium, Croatia, France, India, Italy, Jordan, Morocco, the Netherlands, Pakistan, Palestine, Somalia, Tajikistan, Tunisia, Turkey, the United Kingdom, and the United States (including our own Executive Director of V-Day, Willa Shalit). These women had come to show solidarity with the women of Afghanistan. Many were there from war-torn countries themselves, so they had practical experience to share. One activist, Maha Abu-Dayyeh Shamas, arrived on a day when there were bombings in her own country, Palestine. Although she was deeply worried about her family and friends, she stayed at the summit and devoted herself to the Afghan women.

During the three days, there were meetings and meals, canvassing, workshops, tears, and dancing. The Afghan women met on their own, superbly chaired by Judge Navanethem Pillay of South Africa, and facilitated by Hibaaq Osman of the Center for Strategic Initiatives of Women. The Afghan women were from diverse ethnic, class, age, tribal, and political backgrounds. There were huge chasms to cross and there were dangerous turns in the road. What most impressed me was the Afghan women's hunger for community and unity, the willingness in each woman to reach over the places of difference and go deeper into their common humanity. It was a result of their reaching and great thinking that this excellent Brussels Proclamation (this volume: 192–196) was born.

These Afghan women proved what women prove again and again—that because our interests are not primarily focused on gaining and maintaining power, we are in the profound position of being able to create peace and insure a humane, civil society. Because women have children, because we are connected to the earth, we have the ability to conceive of and insure the future. These Afghan women suffered the worst atrocities. Every human right was denied to them—jobs, education, personal freedom, medical care. They have been violated in every way. They have lived in the deepest poverty and deprivation. And yet "defense" was mentioned nowhere in their document, building weapons or instruments for retaliation was not called for in any category. Instead, they wanted education, health care, and the protection of refugees, culture, and human rights.

This Proclamation is a fantastic document. I believe it will lead the way for women everywhere. It outlines a list of demands that could and should be demanded in every country. It is the result of courage; the participants were brave enough to stop fighting, to sit with each other and listen, to honor difference and find the working places of commonality.

There were no guns at this summit, no machetes. Rarely was a voice raised.

There was a deep and central desire for peace, for transformation, for children to grow up fed and educated, for the terrible violence to stop. That desire was present in everything, as was the sorrow. It was so close to the surface that when one woman cried, all the women cried. I felt privileged to be at a summit of such vision and feeling.

This V-Day, as most of you know, we had planned to do an action in support of the women of Afghanistan. We asked all worldwide V-Days and College V-Day, to give a percentage of money raised to this effort.

An idea emerged at the summit and was heartily endorsed by the Afghan women: to declare on International Women's Day 2002 (8 March) that for women "Afghanistan is Everywhere". This means that we are all joined in solidarity with the women of Afghanistan not only because we all identify with their suffering but also because we understand that the same conditions of violence, oppression, invisibility, and other forms of inequality that plagued Afghanistan are universal. On 8 March 2002, we want the women of the world to endorse, promote, and insist that the Brussels Proclamation be implemented in every country. We urge you to circulate it everywhere. We urge you to create educational events, marches, speak-outs, and fora to discuss the proclamation and bring it as much attention as possible. We urge you to help people understand that the time of women has come. That our rights can no longer be denied. That what we value must become manifest and that the violence has to end. That when some women are hurt on this planet, all women and all men are hurt because "Afghanistan is Everywhere".

We are obviously in the early stages of organizing this 8 March reality. We will have posters soon and more updates. In the meantime, please spread the word. In terms of funding this year, money raised will be split between RAWA (whom we will continue to support) and new groups that will emerge in Afghanistan to implement the Proclamation, particularly focusing on the component that calls for an end to violence.

In closing, I want to say that I think you would be very proud of V-Day's involvement as a convenor of the summit. Your money and support made this possible. Along with the European Women's Lobby, Equality Now, and the Center for Strategic Initiatives of Women, we were able to make this all happen in less than six weeks.

We particularly want to acknowledge and applaud our partners from Equality Now—Jessica Neuwirth, Taina Biene-Aime, and Jacqui Hunt—for their leadership and tireless dedication to this effort.

We would also like to thank the European Women's Lobby for hosting this event in such a generous way, and for all their incredible work. We would like to acknowledge Angela King, the Gender Advisor to the United Nations Secretary-General, for attending the summit and giving such important guidance; and Noeleen Heyzer, the Executive Director of UNIFEM, for her great generosity and strength.

We want to bless Jane Fonda for her remarkably generous donation of $50,000 and Kristina and Allison Kiehl for their fantastic support. We thank the Ford Foundation, the Open Society Institute of the Soros Foundations, UNIFEM, and Kavita Ramdas of the Global Fund for Women. We thank Pearl Jam for sponsoring all costs associated with three of the attendees. We thank Gloria Steinem, Robin Morgan, and Ellie Smeal for their guidance. And we thank Lifetime Television, Bobbi Brown Cosmetics, Tony & Tina Cosmetics, Teen People and Delia's for providing gifts for the Afghan women.

We want to bless the truly fierce and devoted group of non-Afghan activists who gave their time and continue to give their lives for human rights. We particularly bless Sima Wali for organizing and bringing these women together.

Mainly, though, we want to bless the Afghan women for creating this glorious Proclamation and for breaking through their trauma and sorrow to keep their country alive.

This is a momentous occasion and a brilliant, hopeful document. We hope you will circulate it far and wide and insist that it become a framework for women everywhere.

Anuradha M. Chenoy

Forever Victims

7 December 2001, *The Times of India*.

Media and eminent persons the world over have recounted the horrors inflicted by the Taliban on women in Afghanistan. The injustices levelled against Afghan women became symbolic justification for military intervention several times.

Now that the UN-led peace process is on, what is in store for these very women who fought this regime, sustained the voices and sanity of thousands of women in despair, risked their own lives to give some relief and political vision to others behind closed doors, barred windows and veils?

Although there has been the token inclusion of two women in the newly constituted interim government, UN negotiator Lakhdar Brahimi called only the Northern Alliance and three other groups, including one that supports former King Zahir Shah, for the talks in Bonn.

Women's groups as independent, responsible, political bodies were not included. Mr Brahimi only added the caveat that the groups called must include women. Can the very same groups which excluded women from public vision and citizenship rights call women as equal negotiators?

Women have no more than token representation in the peace talks as relatives or sympathisers of those who held the guns in war and in peace. Civil society is thus being excluded from the very start of the process itself.

The UN negotiator has said that it is the Afghan people themselves that must decide their future. Does "Afghan people" mean excluding women's organisations?

The purpose of the Bonn meeting was to try and work out a truly representative and broad-based government that will take Afghanistan from civil war to civil coexistence. Women make up 60 per cent of Afghanistan's population.

The international community has acknowledged that they are the most oppressed women in the world. Despite the abuse heaped on them for years, unknown to the rest of the world, they organised themselves as vibrant underground groups like the Revolutionary Association of Women in Afghanistan (RAWA), Negar support group, Afghan Women's Association and others.

RAWA has intervened politically in all major issues during the civil war since its inception in 1977. Its founder member Meena was assassinated in Quetta before the Taliban came to power.

Many other RAWA members have been killed first by the jihadis who made up the Northern Alliance and then by the Taliban, for upholding women's rights and speaking for secularism and democracy.

RAWA is not dear to any of the groups in Afghanistan or outside it that will now dictate the terms of peace. Its members have long been critics of the Northern Alliance, its opportunistic politics, the pillage and rape that it indulged in when it was in power between 1992 and 1996.

RAWA documented the abuses it meted out to women and its curbs on women's rights after the Soviet withdrawal and civil war. RAWA's appeals to the international community to take note of these atrocities have fallen on deaf or embarrassed ears.

During the oppressive Taliban rule, it was RAWA that brought succour to women lashed by the regime for showing their ankles, who held secret classes for Afghan girls and more.

It also distributed leaflets against fundamentalism, did not side with any faction on the basis of ethnicity or religious preference, calling for secularism and pluralism all along. RAWA criticised UN economic sanctions against Afghanistan as harmful for a starving population.

RAWA was attacked when it took out political demonstrations in Pakistan. It called for a halt to US bombing and labelled it an act of aggression, criticising the US for its earlier support to the Taliban. It saw the fight against the Taliban as the fight of Afghan people for a secular and equal society.

Women's organisations are the only ones that have spoken out against the Taliban since 1996. These were times when US presidents and vice-presidents were making deals with the Taliban over the oil and gas pipe routes from the Central Asian and Caspian Sea reserves through Herat to Kandahar and then to Multan.

These routes planned by US companies like Unocal, Halburton and Carlyle are associated with big names in US politics who negotiated with the Taliban until a few months before the September attacks.

A friendly regime in Afghanistan will re-start these lucrative deals. Women's groups that would like to engage in nation-building and keep out of the great games of that region would be inconvenient for such deals.

If the terms of peace are written by the very people who wrote the terms of war and have been indicted for war crimes and gender abuse, then for many in Afghanistan, war will continue under the cloak of an unjust peace.

In these circumstances, ethnic and religious rivalries will influence popular politics, political culture and processes. The demands made by women's organisations for a just peace, human rights and transformatory politics that will change unfair relations between genders and peoples will be overlooked.

Peace like war is not gender-neutral, and will have interests that will affect men and women differently. The history of wars and post-war settlements has shown repeatedly that when women and civil society actors are left out of the peace process, it is yet another step to leave them out of the political process.

Once someone else appropriates the right to speak for civil society or women, they take away the right of an entire people and rob them of their future.

Women's organisations the world over, including from India, and other civil society groups have begged that Afghan women be included in this process. Most feel that by including only representatives of armed factions, the UN and the international community risks endorsing violence as the only legitimate means for people to participate in shaping their country's future.

Feminists have written reams to show the multiple roles that women play in war and peace. They analyse how women combine the social, the economic and psychological with the political to address issues of post-conflict rebuilding, which is not dissimilar to what UNDP and others call human security.

Yet in the first peace process of the twenty-first century, where are the women? Within the peace process or outside it, RAWA and other civil society groups like them will continue their work. Their place and role in history has already been established. Now it is up to the rest of the international community to decide which side it is on.

Revolutionary Association of the Women of Afghanistan

Declaration on the Occasion of International Human Rights Day

10 December 2001

The "Northern Alliance": The Most Murderous Violators of Human Rights! The medieval Taliban have been shredded to pieces in a few days of bombing by United States forces who until a couple of years ago were "engaged" with them. This ignominious end is despite all the Taliban's nauseating lying and bragging, and the bombastic fatwas of Mullah Omar and Osama to carry on their jihad to the very end. This is the result of the sheer disgust and revulsion the Taliban were so successful in garnering from inside Afghanistan and around the world. The Taliban, like their loathsome Golbodin brethren of the Hezb-i-Islami before them, saw so convenient—at the end of their shameful careers—to shave off beards and whiskers, throw away their turbans, drop their baggy pants, and scatter away like mice for dear life. This is the ultimate fate of all executioners in history who tyrannise a people under the guise of religion, traditions and ethnicity. Some people in Kabul and elsewhere opine that, instead of killing Mullah Omar and Mr Osama Bin Laden, it would be much worthier and befitting to house them in specially made cages until they wither away, and put them up for exhibition around the world as an example to all Islamic and non-Islamic fundamentalists who nurture fond dreams of building and running religio-fascist prison-regimes for entire peoples.

The ignominious pulverisation of the illiterate and ignorant Taliban should, first and foremost, be an indelible brand of shame on the foreheads of their ideologues, of the kind of Messrs Isshaq Negargar, Dr Khalilullah Hashimian, Nabi Mesdaq *et al.*, who wrote, bawled and howled—to the utmost of their capabilities—in defence of the Taliban and what they stood for. If these panegyrists and polished agents of the Taliban lack the sense of honour to commit suicide or to forego residence in the "infidel and decadent" West, they should at least have the decency to give themselves up to the counter-terrorism organisations of the United States and Britain in order to spell out how and at what level they were associated with the perpetrators of the September 11 infamy. In fact, if the Western anti-terrorism coalition partners had been serious in their anti-fundamentalist struggle, they should by now have gathered all these big and small "brains" and masterminds of the Taliban and Al-Qaeda from their sties in different Western countries, put them on a plane and despatched them to the hideouts of Mullah Omar and Osama to give comfort and guidance to their local Arab and Pakistani heroes in the moment of truth of their "jihad against the infidels"!

The Revolutionary Association of the Women of Afghanistan this year fervently hoped to be able to celebrate International Human Rights Day inside Afghanistan. But the re-emergence of the "Northern Alliance" criminals in different parts of our country, dangling as they are from American bayonets, crushed all such hopes. The "Northern Alliance" need to remember the years 1992 to 1996 when they were in power; when the execrable Golbodin Hekmatyar gang (Hezb-i-Islami) turned Kabul to rubble with their daily indiscriminate bombardment and rocketing; when the infamous Mazari-Khalili gang (Wahdat-i-Islami) were gouging out the eyes of non-Hazaras; when the vile Sayyaf gang (Ittehad-i-Islami) were driving 6-inch nails into the heads of Hazaras and broiling them alive in metal containers; when the perfidious Rabbani-Massoud gangs (Jamiat-i-Islami and Shorai Nazar) slaughtered the inhabitants of Afshar and other residential areas in Kabul and whitewashed the faces of all murderers, rapists and looters in history in terms of the barbarity and infamy they perpetrated against countless innocent and defenceless women, girls and young boys. The "Northern Alliance" should know that the bleeding wounds they have inflicted upon the people of Afghanistan during all the years of their jihadi rule of gore and infamy are too open, too painful, to allow any posturing of democratic baptism and conversion to belief in human rights on their part to be taken as anything but an added insult to the people who have suffered so much at their hands. Such posturing and talk of "democracy" and "women's rights" cannot wash away or hide their innate fundamentalist-terrorist nature. Watching the suave, polished appearance of certain jihadi leaders on TV, a still-mourning mother, shrivelled from years of suffering and agony, commented: "I see the blood of my sons on the immaculate suits and ties of these 'Northern Alliance' leaders." Such is the gut reaction of the overwhelming majority of our grieving people. The people of the world need to know the "Northern Alliance" criminals. These are the very people who declared democracy and elections to be blasphemous, heretical concepts. These are the very people who immediately, upon usurping power after the bursting of the bubble of the puppet Najib regime, and prior to any vitally pressing action in regard to the restoration of peace and well-being of the scourged people of Afghanistan, targeted their pious wrath against women and in a joint declaration of all allied jihadi parties proclaimed—amongst other sordid restrictions—the compulsory veiling of all women. The people of the world need to know that, long before the Taliban, it was Mr Mullah Younis Khalis (a confederate of the victorious jihadis) who "executed" the Buddha statutes at Bamiyan by firing volleys of artillery against them. The people of the world need to know that in terms of widespread raping of girls and women from ages seven to seventy, the track record of the Taliban can in no way stand up against that of these very same "Northern Alliance" associates. The people of the world need to know that with their track record of numerous massacres, looting national assets and archaeological riches, extorting vast amounts of money from defenceless people and perpetrating other crimes and atrocities too numerous to list here, the leaders of the "Northern Alliance" only deserve to sit in the dock in international tribunals beside other war criminals, and not at the helm of a government for Afghanistan.

Due to the presence of incorrigible fundamentalists at the talks in Bonn—especially the arch-criminal Homayoun Jarir, whose master Golbodin recently shifted his allegiance to the Taliban—RAWA from the outset regarded the Bonn gathering with mistrust. The composition of the interim government which includes jihadi vampires and two women, one of them a leader of the mercenary criminal Hezb-i-Wahdat party and the other a known Parchami traitor, has proven that very unfortunately the United Nations has failed in aiding our people get rid of the rancid remains of the "Northern Alliance" hellhounds. The United Nations needs to know that, even if all the cabinet posts of a government for Afghanistan were to be filled with such women, they can never be regarded as emblems of freedom and deliverance from oppression for Afghan women.

Jihadi leaders in yesteryears solemnly pledged their "honour", swore on the Koran in the heart of their holiest of holies—Mecca and Madina—in the presence of their Pakistani, Iranian and Arab masters to desist from bloodshed (and, of course, broke their pledge before the ink was dry). Do the United Nations think that those who are capable of such perfidy would honour their signatures on a piece of paper signed in Bonn? Do the United Nations not understand that these sold-out warlords will have no scruples in once again putting themselves up for sale at a cheap price to old and new proxy-seeking powers, and consequently will once again invite the interference of their foreign masters if their sordid parochial and personal ambitions and interests are fundamentally compromised? These parvenu felons have an unquenchable thirst for power and status, irrespective of the price; and it is for this reason that they cannot but conspire against each other and slit each other's throats. Do the United Nations not understand that members of the "Northern Alliance"—who not once but tens of times looted convoys of United Nations aid goods, and none other than Mahmoud Mistry, the then representative of the Secretary-General of the United Nations in Afghanistan, truthfully called them "bands of bandits"—can never be trusted to handle billions of dollars to be given to Afghanistan for reconstruction and rehabilitation?

RAWA once again serves warning to the United Nations and the world community that any delay in despatching UN peace-keeping forces to Afghanistan will in effect be leaving the way open for inevitable bloodbaths and repetition of the unparalleled horrors and atrocities of the 1992–96 years. The current dog-fighting between Dostum and Hezb-i-Wahdat gangs will not remain restricted to Mazar-e-Sharif. If the United Nations is sincerely concerned in regard to the independence, unity and democratisation of Afghanistan, it must under no name or pretext continue its support to the "Northern Alliance" and swiftly and unequivocally condemn and punish any country which tries to supply funds and arms to these murderers. It will only be then that a government devoid of terrorist-fundamentalist contamination and based on democratic values can be set up in Afghanistan, succeed in restoring peace and stability to this blighted land and address the challenge of its rehabilitation in earnest. The mere end of the forced misery and humiliation of the burqa is in no way an indication of attainment of women's rights and liberties. The Revolutionary Association of the Women of Afghanistan, as the only feminist anti-fundamentalist organisation in Afghanistan, believes that only with the establishment of a secular and democratic government in Afghanistan will Afghan women be able to unburden the deadweight of centuries of oppression and stand their full stature on a par with men.

Our devastated motherland, draped in unending mourning, escaped the talons of Taliban criminality only to find itself in the dead-end of jihadi murderers; a "dead-end" which eludes description and definition, except perhaps in the potent and glorious words of Ahmad Shamlu. But RAWA, together with the Afghan people who bore it, will never desist from struggling to break out of this "dead-end":

In This Deadend
They smell your breath.
You better not have said, "I love you."
They smell your heart.
These are strange times, darling ...
And they flog
love
at the roadblock.
We had better hide love in the closet ...

In this crooked dead end and twisting chill,
they feed the fire
with the kindling of song and poetry.
Do not risk a thought.
These are strange times, darling ...
He who knocks on the door at midnight
has come to kill the light.
We had better hide light in the closet ...

Those there are butchers
stationed at the crossroads
with bloody clubs and cleavers.
These are strange times, darling ...
And they excise smiles from lips
and songs from mouths.
We had better hide joy in the closet ...

Canaries barbecued
on a fire of lilies and jasmine,
these are strange times, darling ...
Satan drunk with victory
sits at our funeral feast.
We had better hide God in the closet.

Sonali Kolhatkar

By Any Standard, This Is a War Against Afghans

16 December 2001, *Z Magazine*. This article was written before research demonstrated that 3500 Afghans had been killed in seven weeks of incessant US bombings.

The bombing of Afghanistan by the United States is being reported in the press as "The War Against Terrorism". That war was never initiated by ordinary Afghans whom we are reportedly saving from terrorism (and yes, they are certainly the victims of Taliban and Mujahideen terrorism). Even American citizens were not included via their congressional representatives, to decide if the US should initiate a war in Afghanistan. It was an executive decision, made with only the justification that it was a War Against Evil, a War Against Terrorism. Let's call it what it is, not a War Against Terrorism, but a War Against Afghans.

Let me explain why this is a more appropriate title. More and more reports are coming out each day about "errant" bombs destroying whole villages full of Afghans. As early as 22 October, reports of US bombing of whole villages were surfacing. Human Rights Watch reported that the village of Chowkar Karez, 40 kilometres north of Kandhahar, was bombed at night by US planes. According to that report, "Many of the people in the village ... ran out of their homes, afraid that the bombs would fall on the homes. All witnesses stated that aircraft then returned to the area and began firing from guns"—they were bombed and then gunned down.

When asked to respond to this report, the Pentagon spokesperson said on 2 November, "The people there are dead because we wanted them dead". These people had nothing to do with the Taliban or Al-Qaeda—the ruins of the leveled village revealed nothing of military value. This pattern continues with the one difference—Pentagon officials have taken to completely denying the existence of Afghan civilians. The British media recently published an eyewitness report of the village of Kama Ado being destroyed by US bombs in which at least forty people were killed. When asked to respond, a Pentagon spokesperson vehemently said it simply didn't happen.

He said, "Nothing happened"—those were the exact words (*The Independent*). We are told "nothing happened" when evidence of the war's real victims is presented. Afghan civilians do not even have the distinction of being called collateral damage anymore—they are now non-existent, simply standing in the way of our war.

On 5 December we heard—once more in the British press—"For the fourth consecutive night, American warplanes targeting Al-Qaeda fighters in the White Mountains also bombed nearby villages, killing and injuring unknown numbers and forcing thousands to flee to the regional capital, Jalalabad" (*The Independent*). There is not enough room to detail all the reports of Afghan deaths from bombs here. And you can be sure that we do not hear about all of them, given the restrictions on the press in Afghanistan.

Every day thousands are forced to leave their homes in at least three major cities, Kabul, Jalalabad and Kandhahar, and become refugees for fear of their lives. A refugee who left Kandahar said of the victims of US bombing: "There are a lot of casualties, they are martyrs, and they are mostly civilians" (*Christian Science Monitor*). If the West can claim responsibility for the joy of the citizens liberated from the Taliban in Kabul, then it must also admit responsibility for the misery of the civilians fleeing the bombs into dismal refugee camps in southern Afghanistan.

One American government adviser, Richard Perle, said of US responsibility: "I don't think any outside power has a responsibility in Afghanistan. People have to take responsibility for their own destiny"—as though the people whose villages had been leveled should have known better, anyway, than to live in downtown Kandahar or Jalalabad or Kama Ado or Chowkar Karez. Would we have held those who were killed in the World Trade Center responsible for their fates? Of course not. Then why are Afghans responsible for the bombs dropping on them, for the starvation inflicted on them?

Global Exchange's Medea Benjamin reported back from her recent trip to Afghanistan and Pakistan:

> Everywhere we went, both in Afghanistan and in the external refugee camps, we met people who lost loved ones or were injured by US bombs ... Little is known about the actual numbers of innocent civilians killed. The US says the casualties are few. Afghans we spoke with said there are probably thousands of dead.

Sadly, this War Against Afghans is very much in line with the US's historical role in Afghanistan. In the 1970s, the US hired seven different political parties of fundamentalist men called mujahideen. These were extremists hired by the CIA during the Cold War, to "draw the Soviets into the Afghan trap" as expressed by former National Security Advisor for Carter, Zbignew Brzezinsky. The CIA empowered the mujahideen, many of whom now comprise the Northern Alliance, with billions of dollars of weapons, including American-made Stinger missiles, knowing well their fundamentalist and misogynist nature. Using these weapons and sophisticated training in the art of terror, these men successfully drove out the Soviets, but also waged a terrible war on their own people. Their fight for power over Afghanistan initiated a bloodbath in the early 1990s before the Taliban took over, during the so-called civil war. 45,000 innocent Afghans were killed in Kabul alone between 1992 and 1996, by men who now comprise the Northern Alliance, with guns and training bought and paid for by the United States. I think President Bush said it best: "If you feed a terrorist or fund a terrorist, you're a terrorist" (*The Guardian*).

The pursuit of destruction in Afghanistan continues with the bombing campaign. There are reports of the US intention to invade Afghanistan months before 11 September 2001. The CIA had been in Afghanistan for three years before September 11 as reported by the *New York Times*. As BBC reported on 18 September, Niaz Naik, a former Pakistani Foreign Secretary, was told by senior American officials in mid-July "that military action against Afghanistan would go ahead by the middle of October". For ordinary Afghans, the bombing campaign was the worst thing that could have happened.

On the one hand, they were living under the most fundamentalist regime in recent history, who were legalizing their oppression especially for women, not to mention the hideous accompanying disasters such as landmine infestation, eradication of agriculture, a terrible drought, a destruction of infrastructure from previous wars, and the largest refugee population in the world. And now on the other hand, they have to contend with the most powerful country in the world waging a war against them.

But the War Against Afghans has an additional dimension to accompany the bombing from above: starvation from below. Several weeks ago, international humanitarian organizations such as Oxfam International made a public plea to the United States to pause the bombing in order to allow food supplies to be taken into Afghanistan while winter drew ever closer. UNICEF had estimated that an additional 100,000 Afghan children would die of starvation and cold this winter because of the effects of the bombing. The response of the US government was stubborn refusal to let little things like civilian deaths come in the way of their "War on Terrorism". Soon afterward, Red Cross warehouses storing food and other supplies were "inadvertently" bombed, not once but twice, a week apart. Twice.

When five countries (including Britain and Canada) recently offered to send multinational troops to Afghanistan to provide security to ensure the delivery of humanitarian aid to Afghans, the only thing that stood in their way was the US government. Not Taliban, not the Northern Alliance, but the US government, who claims that these troops could interefere in their military campaign in Afghanistan. It seems that Afghans and their rumbling empty bellies are too much of a nuisance in our War Against Terrorism. Instead of at least providing the troops needed themselves, the US unbelievably declared that it would not provide security and not allow anyone else to do so either. So there is now food and other aid on the ground but the US is ensuring that it doesn't reach Afghans—somehow feeding innocent hungry people interferes with our efforts to target terrorism.

Conclusion: the military operation which we are told is saving Afghans from the Taliban, is more important than saving Afghans. One of the leaflets being scattered over Afghanistan by the United States says, "We do not want to take over your nation; we want to give it back to its rightful owners, the people of Afghanistan." Am I the only one who sees the gruesome hypocrisy of this operation? If deliberate starvation from below and deadly bombings from above is not pure terror, I don't know what is. Somehow this strategy will give back Afghans their nation.

To add to the US War Against Afghans, Afghans are seeing a new terrible stage of the conflict developing with the regaining of control by the Northern Alliance. Having worked with the Revolutionary Association of the Women of Afghanistan (RAWA), I had the privilege of being educated about the Afghan situation by people who experienced daily the realities of fundamentalist-dominated life. RAWA warns us consistently of the crimes committed by those who now comprise the Northern Alliance, contrary to what we read about in the US media. Human Rights Watch and Amnesty International have detailed their crimes, especially in regard to women's rights (see HRW report *Crisis of Impunity*). In Northern Alliance-controlled territory, women had little access to education, little access to decent jobs, and were treated very similarly to women under the Taliban (*New York Times*). This is in addition to the earlier mentioned record of tens of thousands of civilian murders during the civil war, which accompanied rapes, and forced marriages which drove women to mass suicide and depression. Recently, the Northern Alliance prevented a march by women in Kabul, apparently because they couldn't provide security, a hollow claim.

Of thirty members of the cabinet of the new so-called government in Afghanistan, which came out of closed-door talks in Bonn, Germany, eighteen are affiliated with the Northern Alliance, which bodes ill for demo-cratic forces in Afghanistan. How can a group responsible for death and destruction, rape and women's oppression before, during and after the civil war, espousing similar ideologies as the Taliban, be taken seriously as a step toward peace in Afghanistan? They simply joined forces to fight off the

Taliban but are an ever-defecting set of men who opportunistically lust for power. Even now, while the whole world is watching them, they are resorting to power grabs, dividing up the country into slices and encouraging lawlessness, looting and pillaging. Anuradha Chenoy said on 7 December in the *Times of India*: "If the terms of peace are written by the very people who wrote the terms of war and who have been indicted for war crimes and gender abuse, then for many in Afghanistan, war will continue under the cloak of an unjust peace." How ironic that the Taliban were initially welcomed in Afghanistan by the majority of the Afghan people because they were seen as an alternative to these groups that the UN and US are now presenting as leaders in a new Afghan government.

The Northern Alliance representatives in Bonn may appear to be a highly sophisticated set of men dressed smartly in dark suits and red ties. The token women appear happy and smiling. In this war, they have all gotten what they always wanted. Benjamin says, as part of her report back from Afghanistan,

> While it is a positive development that several women were asked to participate in the Bonn talks on the transition government, the women were selected by the male delegates in a completely undemocratic fashion. We met many women who felt that several of the women delegates were selected primarily due to family connections. Women's groups that have been on the forefront of defending women's rights under the reign of the Taliban were not invited.

Such groups include the women of RAWA, who have had over two decades of experience in community building, educating, organizing, who are pro-democracy, pro-women's rights, and non-violent. There is no scarcity of experienced, able women to help run the country. It is not that ordinary Afghans are not ready for women to run the country—General Suhaila Siddiqui, who is heading the interim Department of Public Health, is being warmly received (despite her connections with the past Afghan pro-Soviet government of Najibullah). She too is affiliated with the Northern Alliance, of course.

By any international definition, the men comprising the Northern Alliance are guilty of war crimes. Their illegitimacy in a majority representation in the delegation at Bonn makes a mockery of international law. Let us not forget that these negotiations happened in the context of the US's active bombing campaign. Ordinary Afghans suffer the consequences of the bombs and deliberate starvation, while powerful Afghans with dirty pasts are put forward to represent their government. In fact, the chairman of this new government, Hamad Karzai, was once working for the mujahideen and then closely working with the Taliban before defecting back.

There is little hope left for ordinary Afghans to regain their dignity and their nation. In a recent interview with a local channel, the reporter asked me what the US should do to end the suffering of Afghans. My response was "What has the US not done to ensure that Afghans suffer?" His retort, the standard one, was "Well, that was done in the past. We make mistakes and it's no use crying over spilt milk; what can we do now?" If what's in the past does not deserve accountability, why are we lamenting the fact that thousands of innocent Americans were killed in terrorist attacks? Is that not in the past? Yes it is, but it is a horrible crime that must be accounted for, whose perpetrators must be brought to trial. By the same standards—and here I make the leap that the same standards be applied to Americans as to others—the US's crimes, past and present, in Afghanistan, must be accounted for and addressed.

What can we do about it now? Stunningly simple in its logic but fully within our power to do so: end the War Against Afghans. Stop bombing them, stop facilitating their starvation, stop promoting criminals in the interim government. Why is that so difficult? "Oh, but there will be a power vacuum now if the US just leaves", said the same reporter. Well, it was quite convenient that the US created a situation where their bombs would be an adequate replacement for peace and democracy in Afghanistan. There is an alternative which groups like RAWA have proposed for years and which has been completely ignored—the intervention of a UN peace-keeping force—one which will disarm all the armed factions in Afghanistan and set the stage, as it did in East Timor (no thanks to the US which was actively selling arms to Indonesia to continue their massacres of Timorese) a few years ago. Afghans who are not armed, Afghan women and the elderly, freedom-loving Afghans, need to be actively playing a role in rebuilding their country and lifting it from the ashes of foreign-sponsored destruction. They need the help of the United Nations for that. But I'm being idealistic here, am I not? Madeleine Albright said, "We will act multi-laterally when we can, and uni-laterally when we must". This reflects the US's position toward the UN and, while we may harbor hopes of a UN-sponsored peace, it is not likely they will play out because of the active efforts of the US to thwart international law and UN legitimacy. There are solutions to ending this conflict. They involve changing the very nature of US intervention and engagement in the world. In the meantime, let's listen to what Afghans are saying to us: On 4 December, tribal and village leaders near Jalalabad, in a signed declaration, said: "Our demand to the United States government and its coalition: stop the bombing in the name of humanity" (*New York Times*).

Let's end this War Against Afghans.

Naomi Klein

Buying a Gladiatorial Myth

2 January 2002, *The Guardian*, London.

Since the Pentagon released its own Osama Bin Laden video last month, the Al-Qaeda leader's every gesture, chuckle and word has been dissected. But his co-star, identified in the transcript only as "Shaykh", has received little scrutiny. Too bad, since he offers a rare window into the psychology of men who think of mass murder as a great game.

A theme that comes up repeatedly in Bin Laden's guests' monologues is the idea that they are living in times as grand as those described in the Koran. This war, he observes, is like "in the days of the prophet Mohammed. Exactly like what's happening right now." He goes on to say: "It is the same, like the old days, such as Abu Bakr and Othman and Ali and others. In these days, in our times."

It's easy to chalk up this nostalgia to the usual theory about Bin Laden's followers being stuck in the Middle Ages. But the comments seem to reflect something more. It's not some ascetic medieval lifestyle that he longs for, but the idea of living in mythic times, when men were god-like, battles were epic and history was spelled with a capital H.

"Screw you, Francis Fukuyama," he seems to be saying, "history hasn't ended yet. We are making it, right here, right now!"

It's an idea we've heard from many quarters since September 11, a return of the great narrative: chosen men, evil empires, master plans, and great battles. All are ferociously back in style. The Bible, the Koran, "the clash of civilisations", *The Lord of the Rings*—all of them suddenly playing out "in these days, in our times". This grand redemption narrative is our most persistent myth, and it has a dangerous flip side. When a few men decide to live their myths, to be larger than life, it can't help but have an impact on all the lives that unfold in regular sizes. People suddenly look insignificant by comparison, easy to sacrifice in the name of some greater purpose.

When the Berlin Wall fell, it was supposed to have buried this epic narrative in its rubble. This was capitalism's decisive victory. Ideology is dead, let's go shopping. The end-of-history theory was understandably infuriating to those whose sweeping ideas lost the gladiatorial battles, whether it was global communism or, in Bin Laden's case, an imperial version of Islam.

What is becoming clear since September 11, however, is that history's end also turned out to be a hollow victory for the United States' cold warriors. It seems that since 1989, many of them have missed their epic narrative as if it were a lost limb. Without ideology, shopping was ... just shopping. During the Cold War, consumption in the US wasn't only about personal gratification; it was the economic front of the great battle. When Americans went shopping, they were participating in the lifestyle that the Commies supposedly wanted to crush. When kaleidoscopic outlet malls were contrasted with Moscow's grey and barren shops, the point wasn't just that we in the West had easy access to Levi's 501s. In this narrative, our malls stood for freedom and democracy, while their empty shelves were metaphors for control and repression.

But when the Cold War ended and this ideological backdrop was yanked away, the grander meaning behind the shopping evaporated. The response from the corporate world was "lifestyle branding": an attempt to restore consumerism as a philosophical or political pursuit by selling powerful ideas instead of mere products. Ad campaigns began equating Benetton sweaters with fighting racism, Ikea furniture with democracy, computers with revolution.

Lifestyle branding filled shopping's "meaning" vacuum for a time, but it wasn't enough to satisfy the ambitions of the old-school cold warriors. Cultural exiles in a world they had created, disgruntled hawks spent their most triumphant decade not basking in their new uncontested power but grouching about how America had gone "soft", become feminised. It was an orgy of indulgence personified by Oprah Winfrey and Bill Clinton.

But since September 11, history is back with a capital H. Shoppers are once again foot-soldiers in a battle between good and evil, wearing new stars-and-stripes bras by Elita and popping special-edition red, white and blue M&Ms.

When US politicians urge their citizens to fight terrorism by shopping, it is about more than feeding an ailing economy. It's about once again wrapping the day-to-day in the mythic.

Kalpana Sharma and Ayesha Khan

Peace Is the Only Option

7 January 2002, *The Hindu*.

It is strange to welcome the New Year with the imminence of war staring us in the face. As planes drone over Karachi and newspapers in Mumbai throw out images of Indian soldiers standing ready at the border, we are compelled to make this argument for peace. As journalists from India and Pakistan, we collaborated on a project on peace when both our countries went nuclear in 1998 and simultaneously spouted the rhetoric of war. Today, our arguments for peace and dialogue hold an even more urgent relevance. Hence our need to repeat them jointly.

With the global community of nations' appetite newly whetted for the waging of war, preferably for war with vague moral purposes fought with murderous accuracy and vengeance, our very own India and Pakistan are now on the brink of jumping into the fray again.

The mood of madness began with the September 11 attacks in New York and Washington. As the United States like a bewildered dumb giant rubbed its bruised head and wondered why it inspired such hatred, there was even then little hope that the giant would exercise restraint and choose the remedy of politics over the remedy of violence. It has now applied its brutal salve to Afghanistan, installed the Northern Alliance, despite its dodgy human rights record, into power and refused to count or acknowledge the number of "the enemy's" dead. India is pleased with the new regime in Afghanistan, for its enemy's enemy is its friend and Pakistan's new impotence in the affairs of its Western neighbour suit it well. Now that the US and Israel have exercised their self-assumed right to wage war against Afghanistan and Palestine based on charges of terrorism, India sees its turn next.

But this mad logic will not lead to a solution of the outstanding issues between India and Pakistan, and a war will not bring to an end covert violence sponsored by intelligence agencies within each other's countries. There will be no true winners in such a war, only yet another brutal "solution" imposed by one enemy on another and yet another refusal to count each other's dead.

We have just a few days left to recall some words of sanity that have been raised since the world decided to go to war against "terror". Michael Lerner, a rabbi in the United States, wrote just days after the September 11 attack that it was a world based on violence, inequity and injustice that produced the killers, and that the United States needed to recognise its own role in perpetrating the roots of such violence. "We may need a global day of atonement and repentance dedicated to finding a way to turn the direction of our society at every level, a return to the notion that every human life is sacred, such that violence becomes only a distant memory." He described a world that has lost the capacity to recognise the sacred in its people, the essential humanity of everyone.

In the past decades, South Asia has been victim of ruthless acts of violence, sponsored by intelligence agencies, foreign governments, its own governments, and even some of its own extremist political parties. In all cases, innocent people die, the sacred and humane within us get buried in the earth or burnt at the pyres. Can the leaders of India and Pakistan dare to take their people out of this darkness and refuse to violate their humanity yet again?

Peter Mahoney, a veteran of America's dirty war in Vietnam, wrote cautionary words after September 11 that our leaders would do well to heed. Vietnam, he stated, had taught him an essential lesson:

> Soldiers are required to do their jobs because politicians fail to do theirs. Make no mistake, the war on terrorism is the desperate act of politicians who failed miserably in the leadership responsibilities to those who elected them, and who, by the very act of starting the war, have failed us even again.

Indians, even those who may harbour bitter hatred for Pakistan and resent its belligerent Muslim identity and the very fact of its creation, and are deeply angered by its obsession with Kashmir and support for the militancy in that state, should ask themselves today whether they elected the Bharatiya Janata Party and its allies for the purpose of leading their country into war or into an age of peace and prosperity.

And Pakistanis, particularly its disgraced political cadres, must also consider whether the lack of clear foreign policy objectives in its leaders and their obsession with matching India's might as well as their reliance on the sinister ISI for achieving domestic and regional objectives have brought them anything better than chronic insecurity and the tattered dreams of a true democracy. Indeed, it is the failure of our politicians on both sides of the border that will lead us into a new war.

Let us not succumb to the distorted and sanitised view of war as projected in the Western media through its coverage of the war in Afghanistan. As we face our new potential war, let us be honest about the essentials. Innocent people will die by the thousands. Maybe our children will die. Can anyone countenance the death by violence of their children, or even those of their enemy? Our over-burdened exchequers will be further depleted in pursuit of these violent objectives, and even less money will be spent on the people. Hence our so-called leaders, on both sides, need war propaganda to banish from our imagination any thought of the humanity or the sacred in us all that should be nurtured, not destroyed.

As troops mass along the border, land mines are laid, and anti-aircraft missiles placed upon our apartment buildings, we need to remember one last thing. The US President, George W. Bush, and Israel's Prime Minister, Ariel Sharon, are still hedging their bets as they go after their terrorist enemies. As Nicholas Kristof of the *New York Times* pointed out in a recent article:

> One study found that foreign terrorists struck America 2400 times between 1983 and 1998, but that the United States hit back militarily only three times: for Libya's bombing of a nightclub in 1986, Iraq's attempt to assassinate former President Bush in 1993, and Al-Qaeda's bombing of American embassies in Africa in 1998. Quite responsibly, we pick fights only with 97-pound countries.

Israel, too, can wipe out Palestine when and if it desires to do so.

But the balance of power between India and Pakistan is not the same, and as India considers a similar remedy for the scourge of terrorism as its American and Israeli predecessors, it has to remember this reality. A conventional war, even a limited one, can devastate large swathes of one or both countries, while a nuclear war is too unthinkable to countenance.

South Asia must not go the way of the West, a region that has led the world in a culture of violence, global inequality, and a series of unjust wars in the last fifty years where only the mighty stand a chance to get out alive. The humanity has been taken out of the human, particularly the one who lives in the developing world. We need not follow suit like good post-colonial subjects. Let our leaders remember that their job as politicians is to find political solutions to intractable problems. Our role as citizens is to insist on preserving the humanity in us all, and protecting the future for our children.

Women Making Peace and Women's Peace Action against War

Statement following US President Bush's Hard-line Rhetoric directed at North Korea

7 February 2002, Seoul, South Korea.

We absolutely cannot accept words threatening war on the Korean peninsula.

Last year when President Bush declared war on Afghanistan, he demanded that every nation stand on his side. President Bush has now announced the second stage of the war on terrorism. In doing so he has called North Korea, Iran and Iraq an axis of evil with an implied threat of war on the Korean peninsula. A sensation of fear and anxiety is upon us.

The US administration's hard-line rhetoric directed at North Korea is a threat to Koreans who have worked so hard for peace and peaceful reunification on the Korean peninsula.

Bush's pronouncement has come at a point in time when many active non-governmental exchanges have been revived among South Koreans and North Koreans, building again a spirit of trust between the South and the North. This also occurs just ahead of the South Korea–US Summit in February. Bush's words mean that South Korea–North Korea and North Korea–US relations are not going to be easy. Furthermore, dividing the world into two parts of good and evil and increasing the likelihood of military arms deployment throw the world into a semi-war state. We women, who have suffered militarism, are greatly worried that physical and mental violence coming from militarism can devastate the world and humankind. Therefore, we women for the sake of peace and security on the Korean peninsula and moreover for a peaceful world, make known our demands as follows:

First, we strongly protest Bush's promotion of an atmosphere of war and creation of a pervasive sense of terror while seeking to gain hegemony. We demand that Bush renounce his bellicose words.

Second, we reject any kind of military action that increases tension and conflict on the Korean peninsula. We women know from experience that military action brings violence around the world and amplifies it towards women, children and innocent civilians. Also growing tension and military action will surely ruin the whole economy on the Korean peninsula. There have been talks between North Korea and the US about restraining the spread of weapons of mass destruction. We women urge the US to solve problems by continuing to talk and negotiate with North Korea, not through military action.

Third, we insist that the US stop forcing arms purchases and cease using alleged threats from North Korea as an excuse to justify the Missile Defence program. We are deeply concerned about the US Missile Defence. US talk of Missile Defence has built up tension in North-East Asia and also made an arms race a near certainty. North Korea has expressed its moratorium on missile tests until 2003. In the wake of September 11, North Korea condemned the terrorist attacks and signed several key UN anti-terrorism pacts. We women sincerely urge that advanced science, technology, and huge material resources, rather than being used to hasten hostile military confrontations, be employed to improve the welfare, human rights, and environmental conditions of the weak.

Fourth, we request that the Kim Dae Jung administration protest and clearly draw back from hostile US policy targeting North Korea. South Korea, which has maintained a military alliance with the US, requires skillful political leadership in carrying out a peaceful reunification process with North Korea. How can South Korea now accept seeing North Korea become a target of war in US sights? This is an issue entwined in our livelihoods and our very lives. We women insist that the South Korean government be the driving force behind a Reconciliation and Cooperation Policy and that it carry out the policy with positive action and wisdom.

Fifth, the press must realize that this crisis is directly connected with the fate of our nation and the people. We plead that this matter be carefully dealt with in order to serve the national interest and to promote peace on the Korean peninsula.

Lastly, we fervently hope that students, politicians, religious leaders, Women's Organizations, and Peace Organizations in the US will take steps to halt the spread of war rhetoric and the threat of military action. With them and all the peace-loving women and people in the world we may strongly oppose war together. We promise to continue our efforts to uphold and keep peace. We also declare that sustaining peace on the Korean peninsula is essential to maintaining and advancing the peace of the world. Living together in harmony is the imperative choice for our world.

Women Making Peace, Women's Peace Action against War, Korea Women's Associations United, Kyungki Korea Women's Associations United, Kwangju, Chonnam Korea Women's Associations United, Taegu, Kyungbuk Korea Women's Associations United, Pusan, Korea Women's Associations United, Chonbuk Korea, Women's Associations United, Kyungnam Women United, Christian Women Minjung Association, Taegu Women's Association, Taejon Women's Association, Pusan Sexual Violence Counseling Center, Pusan Women's Social Institute, Korean Catholic Women Association, Aaewoomtuh, Suwon Women's Association, Korean Women's Center For Social Research, Ulsan Women's Association, Korean Women Farmers Association, Cheju Women's Association, Chonbuk Women's Association, Pohang Women's Association, Korea Daycare Center Teachers' Association, Korea Sexual Violence Relief Center, Korea Women Worker Association, Women Link, Korean Women's Studies Institute, Korean Women Theologian Association, Korean Women's Hot Line, Korean Differently Abled Women's United, Taegu Housewives Association for Environment, Korean Catholic Women's Community for a New World, My Sister's Place, Peace Mother, The Korean Council For the Women Drafted for Military Sexual Slavery by Japan, Korean Church Women United, Committee of Women of the Korean Federation for Environment Movement.

Women's International League for Peace and Freedom, Australia

Letter to the Deputy Leader of the Opposition

8 February 2002

Ms Jenny Macklin MP
Deputy Leader of the Opposition
Parliament House
Canberra, ACT 2600

Dear Ms Macklin

We are writing to exhort you to reject the so-called Anti-Terrorism legislation when it is introduced into the Parliament. We believe that existing laws are perfectly adequate to deal with suspected and actual criminal activities, including acts of terrorism.

We are aware that this legislation in large part replicates the legislation which has been adopted in the United States and the United Kingdom hastily late last year. As an international organisation, WILPF does not believe that Australia should follow suit. We believe that the decisions made by the US and UK governments were misguided and driven by grief at the tragic events of 11 September. If we are committed to a future peace and to the principles of democracy we must not overreact to our grief, anger and fear at the deplorable terrorism which took place on 11 September 2001.

Of particular concern to us is the prospect that the proposed legislation will give the Australian Security and Intelligence Organisation (ASIO) the power to hold a suspect under arrest for up to forty-eight hours. We do not believe that ASIO should be given these new powers. We believe that the powers of arrest and questioning that already exist in our criminal justice system, those which the Police have, are perfectly adequate.

We are very concerned that the legislation will have the effect of reducing many of the freedoms we as a democracy hold dear. These freedoms relate to freedom of speech and of association, the idea that people who are arrested are "innocent until proven guilty" and that individuals have the "right to remain silent" while in custody. We do not think this legislation is at all constructive in helping to avoid acts of terrorism (similar to what happened in mainland US on September 11 last year) occurring in future. For this reason we ask that you totally reject the legislation. We believe that the best ways to combat terrorism are the same as they were before September 11—a commitment to social justice and human rights for the world's people as a whole. These human rights include freedom of speech and association.

Yours sincerely
Mary Ziesak and Elena Marchetti
Joint National Coordinators

Zubeida Malik

Better the Devil You Know?

February 2002, *The Ecologist*.

Suhail sits in the dust, surrounded by two of his six remaining children; he seems oblivious to the flies, the dirt, the hunger and misery of what remains of his family. Any hope and energy has been used up making it to the border with Pakistan.

He's walked all the way, occasionally hitching a lift, from Mazar-e-Sharif to Peshawar in Pakistan. Suhail's voice is emotionless as he describes how his wife and two daughters were kidnapped and raped by men fighting for local warlords, his sons were killed because they were men. Asked why this should happen to him, he says, "Because I am a Pathan".

His is not an isolated story. Many other refugees I spoke to had chillingly similar tales to tell, of incidents that had happened to themselves or friends and family. Afghanis are now making their way to the border with Pakistan at Peshawar and Quetta in their thousands. It's not just US bombing they are trying to escape, but the looting, killing and rape that has been unleashed upon them. The retreat of the Taliban has led to the return of the warlords and of ethnic rivalries.

Over 60 per cent of the population in Afghanistan is Pashtun, known locally as Pathan, who by and large support the Taliban. The rest is Tajik, Uzbek and Shi'ite. The Northern Alliance is made up of these minority groups. The Soviet withdrawal and the onset of civil war in Afghanistan laid bare these ethnic divisions. The five-year rule of Kabul by the Northern Alliance saw robbery, murder and rape as an everyday occurrence, and ended once and for all any possibility of the Pashtuns accepting Northern Alliance rule ever again.

With the Northern Alliance in power once again, controlling most of the country, stories are beginning to filter out of Pashtuns being killed by warlords and anti-Taliban forces. Refugees tell stories of men being rounded up and killed, women being taken away and raped, children being mutilated. The numbers may be small but in any other war this would be called ethnic cleansing.

Jamshaid, a refugee in Quetta, tells of how he saw soldiers in Herat kill a group of Pashtun men, and then tell people that they were Taliban fighters.

As he says, "They were just ordinary men, yes they had guns, but everyone has guns here ... by calling them Taliban it makes it easier for no one to ask why they were killed." His friend Abdullah nods in agreement. He talks of a similar incident when three men were killed in the bazaar for no apparent reason.

Many of the ordinary people I spoke to in Jalalabad said they were already tired of the fighters, they didn't pay for their food and lodgings, and roamed around the city harassing people. One shop-owner said he was frightened of asking the men for money because they would kill him. Another was telling me how he missed the law and order that the Taliban ensured. While he was talking to me a Northern Alliance soldier came up to him and started shouting and pushing the man for saying anything positive about the Taliban. The man quickly changed his story.

The "soldiers" that we met were not disciplined in any way and were capricious in the way they enforced law and order, demanding money from people and truck drivers at checkpoints. As for the women, they were terrified of going out on their own for fear of being raped. Those that I met in Kabul still wore the burqa. When asked how they felt about the Northern Alliance being in control of Kabul again, they were horrified and begged the West to send in the UN or an international peace-keeping force ... anything, they said, but Burhanuddin Rabbani and the Northern Alliance. Noor, a doctor in a women's hospital told me, "It isn't safe for women to go out now, the Taliban were strict but at least they didn't touch us." I asked if she had heard of women being attacked, she nodded yes, but said it was "shameful" to talk of these things.

Southern Afghanistan is now in anarchy, a patchwork of fiefdoms controlled by warlords. Elsewhere, armed gangs roam the land, backed by local warlords who in turn have the tacit support of the US. Mazar-e-Sharif is under the control of the Uzbek warlord General Abdul Rashid Dostum, who has made his hatred of Pashtuns clear. Eastern Afghanistan is under the control of a "shura", or council. We heard stories from refugees from all these areas; all of them spoke of random killings, rape and mutilations.

No wonder neighbouring Pakistan is worried. It has a substantial Pashtun population and over two million Afghan refugees. If these stories of ethnic cleansing spread then there is real concern that the conflict will widen. And so the bombing raids go on. The hunt for Al-Qaeda and Osama Bin Laden continues, but no one wants to talk about the ethnic cleansing that is gradually being unleashed in Afghanistan.

Bat Shalom

Declaration on the Occasion of International Women's Day 2002

8 March 2002. Bat Shalom, an Israeli feminist peace organisation, presented this declaration to twenty foreign embassies and consulates.

International Women's Day commemorates the human rights of women world-wide. But as history testifies, those rights are never achieved in isolation. They are embedded in the complex of universal rights, and their realization reflects and measures a society's commitment to justice, equality and democracy.

Israel's military occupation of Palestinian land and its continued rule over more than a million Palestinians severely violate the individual and national rights of another people, and turns Israelis into both perpetrators and victims of violence. Today we see that the most basic threat to the rights and well-being of Israeli and Palestinian women is the perpetuation of the occupation.

We Israeli women, Jewish and Palestinian, working to build the conditions for peace and reconciliation, are dismayed and revolted by our government's policies. We refuse to silently bear witness to the destruction of the hope and future of Israelis and Palestinians. And we need your help.

The Israeli government's flagrant violation of international law and moral norms present a great challenge to the international community, and we are appealing to you and your government to meet that challenge.

In view of the current situation, an immediate international humanitarian response is needed. We therefore request your support for the dispatching of international monitors to the area, whose presence may provide some measure of protection for Palestinian civilians.

Ending the occupation is the prerequisite to securing peace. In view of the Israeli government's obdurate refusal to commit itself to ending the occupation, we call upon you and your government to initiate urgent diplomatic efforts to convince Israel to make that commitment.

On this 8 March 2002, thousands of women around the world are presenting similar declarations to both their government representatives, as well as to Israeli foreign diplomats in their region. It is our greatest hope that you will elect to commemorate International Women's Day by honoring women and addressing our concerns.

UNIFEM: United Nations Development Fund for Women

Afghan Women's Consultation Concludes Today in Kabul

7 March 2002

KABUL—A three-day Afghan Women's Consultation concluded today in Kabul, Afghanistan. It brought together sixty Afghan women from seven provinces with policy-makers, representatives of key ministries, UN agencies and donors. The consultation was organized by UNIFEM, in collaboration with the Afghan Ministry of Women's Affairs (MOWA) and UN agencies, including UNDP, ILO, UNFPA, UNESCO, Habitat and UNICEF.

Held on 5–7 March at the Ministry of Women's Affairs, the consultation was designed to include women as active partners in rebuilding their communities and their country. It provided a unique opportunity for Afghan women to articulate their priorities, concerns, perspectives, and needs.

"Six months ago I could not have envisioned having such a unique, historical event in Afghanistan," said Noeleen Heyzer, UNIFEM Executive Director. "Afghan women are ready to rebuild their nation, but they want to be recognized, valued and supported."

Participants discussed issues of security, women's rights, education, health, political participation, the need for representation, protection, governance, capacity-building, economic security, and employment. The women emphasized their need to participate in decision-making processes for each of these issues.

The consultation was inaugurated by Dr Sima Samar, the Minister of Women's Affairs. Dr Samar highlighted the support of the international community, UN agencies, and NGOs as important players in rebuilding Afghanistan. She said that security is not only about ending the war and silencing the weapons, but it is about ensuring women and girls could live in safety and dignity. She also noted that women's concerns for their families are a universal concern for all women in the world.

Dr Samar added that she is working with the Interim Authority to make sure that women are issued national identification cards all over the country to ensure their right to engage in the political process as voters and representatives. She stressed that women must have the right to vote and she urged participants to be united and work closely with her. She also emphasized that she cannot tackle this enormous task single-handedly.

The consultation is a first step towards the full and equal involvement of Afghan women in shaping their country's future. Ms Heyzer urged the group to continue to support the Ministry of Women's Affairs She also acknowledged the heroism of women who continued to work under the Taliban and said that it was indicative of the strength and skills of Afghan women.

GABRIELA Network

Persevere in the Struggle against US Reoccupation of the Philippines

8 March 2002

International Women's Day, 2002, comes to women of Philippine ancestry in the United States with an added duty. It is the duty to:

1. oppose the presence of US military troops in the Philippine archipelago
2. insist on the validity of the sovereign decision by the people of the Philippines to forbid, constitutionally, the presence of foreign troops in the country
3. affirm the correctness of the Filipino people's victory in throwing out US military presence after nearly a hundred-year campaign.

By insisting on a return to the Philippine archipelago, the United States chose to show its utter contempt for the sovereign will of the Filipino people. Under the pretext of chasing the 100-man Abu Sayyaf band, as part of an allegedly global campaign against terrorism, and using the fiat of an unelected Philippine president, Gloria Macapagal Arroyo, the US has steadily increased its military presence in the archipelago. By establishing its headquarters in Cebu and Mindanao islands, the US military has effectively truncated the Philippine archipelago, subjecting its central and southern parts to military occupation and recolonization.

Ignored in the hype about the war against terrorism is the fact that the Philippine Armed Forces is nearly a quarter of a million strong, with all of its components integrated, and that it has received the lion's share of the national budget for the last thirty years. In addition, it has received aid from the US, in monies and equipment. Macapagal-Arroyo, who slandered those opposing US troops in the Philippines as "lovers of terrorists", would have done better had she dismissed the entire Philippine military establishment for incompetence. It was bad enough that the Philippine Navy couldn't protect Philippine territory in the matter of the Spratly Islands; how much worse is this state of military cowardice when, to pursue a hundred men, the Philippine military has to rely on US troops?

But the Abu Sayyaf is not the sole objective of, but rather the excuse for, US reoccupation of Philippine territory. The return comes at the heels of the overthrow of the corrupt pro-US president Joseph Ejercito Estrada and the increasing exercise of political power by the masses of Filipino people. To pre-empt the development of true democracy in the Philippines, to frustrate the increasing awareness among Filipinos of what constitutes national interest and national vision, to render safe once more the archipelago for the neo-liberal policies of liberalization, deregulation and privatization, the US insisted on this reoccupation of the Philippines.

What the return of US troops to the Philippines means for Filipinas is immediately discernible. Prostitution and the sex trade, whose large-scale origins are rooted in US military presence in the Philippines, are beginning to increase and flourish. A repeat of the historical experience of women of the Philippines with the US military is already guaranteed: girls and young women conscripted via poverty into prostitution; communities warped and deprived of traditional livelihood resorting to the sex trade; criminality, narcotics and sexually transmitted diseases; Amerasian children abandoned by their fathers ...

In a world beset by war and conflict and the prevalence of super-power tyranny, by aggressive neo-liberal globalization, GABRIELA Network asks all American women and men to support GABRIELA Philippines in its commitment to struggle against US presence in the archipelago. GABRIELA Network asks all women of Philippine ancestry to persevere in the struggle to remove this vestige of colonialism from the Philippines and to support the Filipino people's quest for genuine freedom, lasting peace and social justice. GABRIELA Network demands that Gloria Macapagal Arroyo withdraw her agreement to allow US troops in the Philippines as they represent a far greater and longer lasting threat to Philippine sovereignty than the paltry hundred-man band of the Abu Sayyaf. GABRIELA Network chooses to honor the Filipinos who died in the September 11 attacks on the World Trade Center by continuing its commitment to support the just cause of the struggle for true independence for the Philippines and a US foreign policy premised on justice and peace.

Revolutionary Association of the Women of Afghanistan

Let Us Struggle Against War and Fundamentalism and for Peace and Democracy!

8 March 2002. Statement on International Women's Day, Peshawar.

Partisans of freedom, sisters and brothers,

When celebrating 8 March last year, RAWA expressed the fond hope that in the coming year, i.e. 2002, we will be celebrating International Women's Day inside a free and liberated Afghanistan. During the course of the past year the world community was shocked by events emanating from Afghanistan and contemporary history has been drastically changed by them. Many things have come to pass in Afghanistan—not the least of which is the fumigation of the Taliban pestilence and their Al-Qaeda carriers—but it is with bitter disappointment that despite all these momentous changes our unhappy land is still far from enjoying freedom and liberty. The women of the world celebrate International Women's Day with spirit and enthusiasm; in Afghanistan women still don't feel safe enough to throw away their wretched burqa shrouds, let alone raise their voices in the thousands in support of freedom and democracy. There is still a wide chasm between us and the glorious future we have fixed our eyes, hearts and minds upon. It is as if Fate has decreed that this most pauperised nation on earth should not be able to throw the chains and shackles of despots and vampire fundamentalists away so easily.

To give voice to such agonised musings is by no means an indication of despair or lack of faith in a better tomorrow. For over two decades, RAWA has intrepidly and steadfastly been treading a precipitous path of tears and blood. We know full well the perils and the dangers of the road ahead of us, and we will not for an instant falter in our resolve to continue to fight crazed religious fundamentalism and its patrons who stand in our way of reaching our goals of peace, democracy, progress and women's emancipation. And in the course of this travail we will succumb neither to misgivings nor to delusions.

Despite the fact that in the course of the months after the horrendous attack of religious fanatics on New York and Washington we have on several

occasions set forth our views and stances on pertinent issues, we avail ourselves of the present opportunity to once again reiterate our principled
positions on key issues. We hope that by so doing we will have responded to
numerous queries posed by RAWA supporters inside Afghanistan and
abroad.

1. RAWA and the US Military Campaign against the Taliban and the Osama Band

RAWA has consistently emphasised the fact that the Taliban, Osama & Co.,
and other fundamentalist bands in Afghanistan are creatures of myopic US
policies vis-à-vis the Afghan war of resistance against Soviet aggression. As
long as such Frankenstein monsters were useful for the pursuance of US
policies, successive US governments supported them and persistently turned a
blind eye to the higher interests of the people of Afghanistan and to the
consequences of such support for freedom and democracy in our country and
the region. RAWA takes great pride in the fact that we persistently condemned this US policy and never caved in to pressure nor "circumspection",
nor to the lure political or financial opportunism.

We look upon the American nation as a great people who have made
immense contributions to human civilisation, social and scientific progress. It
is the conscience of the people of the United States that is scourged first and
foremost by the slaughter of innocent Afghans in consequence of US bombardment in Afghanistan. Proof of this is amply shown in demonstrations
against the war in Afghanistan in most American cities. RAWA has been
inundated by thousands of e-mails from across the United States expressing
sympathy with our people and condemning the US bombardments which
claim innocent victims. Visits to Afghanistan by groups of bereaved Americans who have lost dear ones in the September 11 tragedy to sympathise and
commiserate with the victims of the bombardments are a shining example of
the humanism and love of peace typical of the people of the United States.
Such gestures will never be forgotten by the people of Afghanistan. The tears
of anguish of thousands of mourning Americans and grieving Afghans will
give rise to a fountain of love and sincere bonding of the peoples of the two
countries.

We take greater pride in the fact that our organisation, ever marginalised
and sidelined by successive US administrations and US government institutions, has enjoyed immense moral support and the unbounded material
generosity of thousands of American men, women and children. The implementation of many of our diverse projects would not have been possible
without such generous American aid. Our heartfelt gratitude to the American
people is our response to allegations that "RAWA is anti-American".

We look upon the US military campaign in Afghanistan not as an aggression against Afghanistan or a war on the Afghan people, or as an aggression against Islam or the Muslims but as a fracas between patron and ex-protégés. In contradistinction to some mealy-mouthed, colluding women's organisations, the total obliteration not only of the Taliban and their Al-Qaeda props but also of the criminal Jihadis is a top RAWA political priority. The bloodshed and misery visited upon our innocent fundamentalism-scourged people—the euphemistically called "collateral damage"—in consequence of the US punishment meted out to its rebellious former agents cannot but incite our opposition to America's war in Afghanistan. We had many a time in the past proclaimed that a meaningful, decisive and timely UN injunction on all countries in regard to supplying funds and arms to the Taliban, coupled with a loud and clear call to all countries to support anti-fundamentalist and pro-democracy forces in Afghanistan were the means to contain the Taliban and Al-Qaeda and to shorten the life span of these vermin.

2. RAWA and the War on Terrorism

One fundamentalist band cannot be fought by siding with and supporting another. In its war on the Taliban and Al-Qaeda, the US has taken the "Northern Alliance" into service through wooing and arming certain infamous warlords. By so doing, the US is in fact abetting the worst enemies of our people and is continuing the same tyrannical policy against the people and the destiny of Afghanistan which successive US administrations adopted during the past two decades. The Taliban and Al-Qaeda cannot be eradicated through military and financial might alone. War on the Taliban and Al-Qaeda is not only a war on the military and financial fronts, it is a war on the ideological front too. Until such time as mindsets and thoughts characteristic of the Taliban and Osama & Co. remain, it is inevitable that we shall witness their trademark barbarism erupt yet once again, be it in Afghanistan or in any other part of the world. The den of these evil criminals in Afghanistan is under siege. Democratic and anti-fundamentalist forces in Afghanistan need to fight the Taliban, Al-Qaeda and their fundamentalist brethren relentlessly and resolutely until total eradication of terrorism and fundamentalism in all its forms in our country. Only with the taking root of democracy in Afghanistan with the unreserved support of the international community can final victory over terrorism and fundamentalism be achieved.

3. The Situation after the Fall of the Taliban

The Bonn gathering on Afghanistan was convened with the aim of forming a transitional administration and deciding what needs to be done in the long term after the pulverisation of the Taliban and Al-Qaeda. With the exception of supporters of the former king, over three fourths of the participants of the gathering were comprised of ignominious representatives of the "Northern Alliance" and affiliates of the infamous terrorist organisation of Golbodin Hekmatyar. Therefore, despite the vociferous benedictions of the Western media, the Bonn gathering cannot be a harbinger of peace and democracy for our people. The parcelling out of key ministries amongst figures whose horrendous crimes still haunt our people, and the worsening of the security situation in Kabul and in other provinces, have borne out for the umpteenth time the veracity of our predictions based on the track record of the "Northern Alliance". The existence of one or two showpiece women in the transitional administration (one belonging to a party infamous for being a lackey of the Iranian regime and the other a former high-ranking member of a party which epitomises treachery to the motherland) is more an insult to Afghan women than a symbol of the restoration of their status and legal rights. The women of Afghanistan have not been liberated. This fact has been most succinctly summed up by the *New York Times* in its issue of 19 November 2001, when writing about an Afghan widow with eight children to feed: "Now, at lest she is free to beg"!

RAWA has repeatedly and consistently asserted that under the prevailing circumstances no power except the Afghan people themselves can or will succour them against fundamentalism, and there is no precedent in history wherein a foreign nation or nations who have themselves been patrons and abettors of agents of bondage and fundamentalist affliction have granted liberty to a nation held in thrall by those very same agents. It was for this reason that RAWA persistently called on our people to rise up against the Taliban, Al-Qaeda and other fundamentalists. Such was the precondition for averting the circumstances which have brought about US bombardment and the slaughter of innocent people, and for preventing any group of religious vampires from having a share in power in post-Taliban Afghanistan.

Mr Karzai, who does not have the backing and support of any indigenous organisation or armed force, together with a number of his like-situated colleagues, are hostages in the hands of "Northern Alliance" criminals. Mr Karzai, not a fundamentalist himself, has a history of colluding and hob-nobbing with Burhanuddin Rabbani and his band, and has therefore deluded himself into thinking that putting up with the criminals he has around him and honouring arch-warlords like Rabbani would bring him political dividends. Unfortunately he either does not know or does not want to know that his key ministers are perpetrators of heinous crimes against our people— infamies which are manifold times more unpardonable and inexpiable than those of the Taliban. Mr Karzai can rest assured that the Rabbani gang he has around him, having already had a taste of a number of years of power and government and unfettered drug trafficking and legendary hoarding of wealth under the cloak of diplomatic immunity, will never be content with the simple usurpation of key government posts. They will bide their time to once again seize undivided and uncontested power.

The revolting efforts by the Rabbani group to canonise their icon, Ahmad Shah Massoud, and their fervid political ululations under his portraits are all in preparation for conspiracies in the offing. The "gentlemen" of the Rabbani gang, ex-fundamentalists and reborn "democrats", have worn the collar of fealty to the ilk of Abdullah Ozzam and Osama Bin Laden much more than the Taliban, and have fed much longer on the crumbs falling from their tables. With their ridiculous newly acquired obsession with their "civilised" appearance and their aping of the latest European menswear fashions, they may succeed in masking their real political and ideological features and backgrounds from the eyes of superficial people, particularly in the West, but they will never succeed in hiding their bloodstained sleeves from the eyes of our people.

The recent falling upon each other of fundamentalist Jihadi predators in Paktia and Ningarhar provinces, the growling and snarling of Karim Khalili in the Hazarajat region, the thuggeries of Rashid Dostum and his gang of scoundrels in the north of Afghanistan, the most recent political whorings of Ismael Khan in the Herat area, and the intrigues of Rabbani and his murderous band in Badakhshan, etc. etc., all show the cloven hoof and are prodromal signs of more treacheries to come. With the establishment of peace and democracy and the beginning of the march towards development and progress, all these "gentlemen" will find themselves out of the sovereignty-through-infamy-and-religion-hustling business and will lie in wait to once again drench Kabul in blood and extend their rule over the country.

The murder of the aviation minister, Dr Abdurrahman, is a not-too-subtle hint to the ex-King, Mr Karzai, and his friends; it is a small glimpse of the intrigues and infamies which the most depraved enemies of our people Mr Karzai has around him are capable of, in order to protect their criminal interests. Dr Abdurrahman was done away with because his murderers did not trust him to keep the shameful secrets he knew about Ahmad Shah Massoud, Dr Abdullah, General Fahim and other leaders of Jamiat-i-Islami. Any spilling of the beans by Dr Abdurrahman would have torn away the shreds that remain of the masks they continue to don and hope to fool everyone with.

Mr Karzai: It may be that the Afghan people will forbear from naming you a second Shah Shuja or a second Babrak Karmal because you were placed in the position you are in exigency circumstances and as an alternative to murderers of the kind of Golbodin Hekmatyar, Sayyaf, Khalili and their ilk; but they will not forgive the indefinite continuation of your spineless leniency, or your concurrence with Jihadi cutthroats—a concurrence that will ultimately stand you in no good stead. The litmus test of your—or any other Afghan leader's—worth, competence and honesty is your political conduct towards fundamentalists and their foreign masters, and your fidelity to the principles of democracy.

There are some who raise the issue of the need for national reconciliation in Afghanistan and cite the pardon of the Nazis in Germany and in other countries by way of an example. If such allegorisation is not a product of ignorance in regard to the nature and track record of Afghan fundamentalists, it can have no other meaning short of requesting Afghans to be jubilant and festive at the funeral of their most beloved ones. How can the Afghan nation be expected to pardon and reconcile themselves with bands and individuals who from 1992 to 1996 perpetrated such heinous atrocities and treacheries, and brought about so much devastation? To boot: not only do these "gentlemen" not show the slightest compunction in regard to their past, they recline in their ministerial and ambassadorial portfolios with unspeakable haughtiness and disdain for the people they have wronged so much. To take up the Nazi simile: firstly, there may be no Nazi of leadership calibre who has not received or been sentenced to capital punishment; secondly— and more importantly—second-rank Nazis who were not killed or brought to justice were not given the reins of government and the destinies of the people neither in Germany nor in any other country of the world. Would that the world community know that the atrocities perpetrated by Afghan fundamentalists are not paralleled either by the Nazis or Fascists or any other inhuman political entity; even the Afghan fundamentalists' Algerian brethren-in-creed who think nothing of cutting the throats of newborn babies would shrink from raping their compatriot mothers, sisters and sons, a favourite practice of the "Northern Alliance" predators who first rape their victims before killing them and plundering their belongings. There can be no reconciliation with such depraved criminals, especially as long as they are in a dominant position. Until such time as such criminals are brought to justice, the trial of lesser criminals by international tribunals at The Hague or elsewhere on charges of war crimes or crimes against humanity are at best defective, biased and travesties of justice. Serbian and non-Serbian criminals are innocent children when compared with their Afghan confreres. If deployment of troops and military action against the Taliban and Al-Qaeda is a just cause, prosecuting the bone-chilling crimes of the "Northern Alliance" is the *sine qua non* for peace, democracy and justice in Afghanistan.

There are some who ask, "Why can't RAWA finally approve of any government in Afghanistan?" The answer is simple: because we do not deem any present or past political force coming to power as democratic and believing in the inalienable rights of women. We can have no understanding with hellhounds who have the brand of years of atrocious criminality against the people on their features.

4. The Establishment of Peace

In conditions when—even with the presence of several thousand foreign troops in Kabul—the capital cannot be deemed a safe and secure place, there is no alternative to the deployment of an effective UN security force across the country to ensure secure conditions for the convocation of a Loya Jirga and, more importantly, countrywide suffrage. Despite all the criticism that is being levied against the UN *modus operandi*, RAWA much prefers the presence of UN troops to the unleashing of Jihadi psychopaths on the Afghan population. Such UN troops should not, however, comprise troops from countries who have hitherto aided and abetted fundamentalists and brutal warlords, e.g. Turkey, which has been a prime supporter of the criminal Dostum.

5. Neighbouring Countries

It seems that the Iranian regime, after years of cuddling Golbodin Hekmatyar and setting up the "Cyprus process" for the furtherance of his interests, is now divorcing him. Such a break-up, however, can fool no one. The sole aim of the blood-drenched Iranian regime from this Split-Up-With-Golbodin show is a smokescreen to hide its dangerous, deceitful manoeuvres to prevent —through strengthening and supporting its trusted lackeys, Ismael Khan and Karim Khalili—the reunification of Afghanistan. With the collapse of their Taliban cousins-in-creed, the Vilayat-e-Faqih regime in Iran shook to its foundations, and in order to keep the waters muddy in Afghanistan, did not desist from granting safe haven to Taliban and Al-Qaeda escapees to Iran.

If it is a dire misfortune for our ill-fated country to have as bloodthirsty a regime as the Iranian one incumbent in our neighbouring country to the west, it has the double misfortune to have incumbent to the east—a neighbour with which we share a border stretching for hundreds of miles from the northeast to the southwest—Pakistani regimes that during the past twenty-three years have based their Afghan policies on blueprints in which leaders, intelligence services and Islamic fundamentalist parties have worked hand in glove to create, nurture and train criminal Jihadi and subsequently Taliban bands and unleash them on the people of Afghanistan. The current Pakistani government has taken steps to muzzle terrorist Pakistani fundamentalist parties, but as stated in a RAWA declaration, such steps cannot be adequate to secure the trust of the Afghan people unless:

1. hundreds of assassination, abduction, extortion, torture, and other criminal cases against leaders and key members of terrorist Jihadi organis-

ations, including first and foremost Golbodin Hekmatyar's criminal band —created in response to suits brought up by families of the victims—have been processed and justice meted out

2. leaders and members of the Jamiat-e-Khoddam al-Furqan (Association of the Servants of the Koran) including Mullah Abdul Hakim Mujahed, who are none but a re-cast Taliban band, are arrested, tried and punished.

Likewise, the governments of Russia, Tajikistan and Uzbekistan can gain the trust and goodwill of the Afghan people only by releasing documents pertaining to the assistance they have given over the years to the "Northern Alliance" terrorists and pledging to desist from any form of further support to their erstwhile protégés.

6. Afghan Reconstruction

The pouring in of billions of dollars into a country where the fundamentalist mafia are still in power can little benefit the Afghan people. Under the circumstances, the only result from the flow of money will be the filling of the coffers of the religious Cosa Nostra and consequently funding their terrorist agendas inside and outside Afghanistan. In a country like Afghanistan, where there is no trace of a legal infrastructure or even a quasi-democratic government, most social and economic issues must be addressed as political issues. The satisfactory management of social and economic problems in Afghanistan and their resolution in the interests of the people of Afghanistan depend first and foremost on the formation of a democratic Afghan government. We draw the serious attention of all countries interested in contributing to the rehabilitation and reconstruction of Afghanistan to the point we have highlighted above.

7. Loya Jirga (Grand Council)

RAWA does not consider a Loya Jirga a democratic institution compatible with the exigencies of national political life in the contemporary world. However, we believe that under the current circumstances in which the shadow of the fundamentalists' beards and bayonets fall tall and ominous on the land, the anachronistic Loya Jirga can still play a positive national historical role. We have our strong reservations, though, in that none of the 21-member Preparatory Committee for the Convocation of the Loya Jirga has any background of struggle against Jihadi criminals, and some of them have records of spineless silence and compromise vis-à-vis the Taliban. With such a preparation committee, the nature and competence of the Loya Jirga come into question. It is "amusing" to note that one of the women members of the above-mentioned committee, in addition to being a former member of the Parcham faction of the disgraced PDPA (Soviet quisling party), was brought into the limelight by the international media simultaneously with the entry of the Rabbani band into Kabul. Whom does she represent?

As is evident, Mr Lakhdar Barahimi's indigenous advisers have unfortunately, in the matter of selecting members of the Preparatory Committee for the Convocation of the Loya Jirga, advised him in a direction contrary to the aspirations of the Afghan people. Mr Barahimi needs to know that, should the stench of fundamentalist composition rise from the Loya Jirga—as it does from the Transitional Administration—the UN and the UN only will be held responsible for the renewed Afghan tragedy, as no one will ascribe the blame to his indigenous advisers. Selection of players for any role or function in any institution solely on the basis of their religious or ethnic affiliation is highly inadequate and totally misguided. The crucial issue needs to be freedom from fundamentalist contamination for representatives of each and every religious or ethnic denomination. Otherwise, it is highly likely that the composition of the Loya Jirga will comprise representatives from all tribal, ethnic and religious groups in Afghanistan, but most or all of them will be carriers of the fundamentalist contagion. The outcome is in need of no elaboration.

One of the women members of the Transitional Administration, who deceitfully denies belonging to the leadership of an ethno-chauvinistic fundamentalist party, has rightfully admitted that she does not represent the people of Afghanistan. Not to be representative of a people for having lived away from them for long periods of time is not crucial; what is crucial is to have a mindset free of fundamentalist filth which would allow one to stand steadfast in the patriotic, democratic, progressive front in the sanguinary ideological war against Jihadi and Taliban treachery. If the Loya Jirga is not made into such a front, it will merely be a vile instrument for adoption of decisions along fundamentalist and anti-democratic lines.

8. The Constitution

The 1964 Afghan Constitution can, with the following amendments, be acceptable to the majority of the people of Afghanistan (except the fundamentalists):

- Expunction of references to official religion and schismatic religious branch. Constitutions of many Islamic countries have no such references. Why should the Constitution of Afghanistan be void of such a democratic characteristic? Why, through recognising one religion and one religious branch, should adherents of other religions or religious branches be marginalised? In order to forge the Constitution itself into a formidable barrier against the emergence of fundamentalism and religious strife, it must be stipulated that use of religion for furtherance of political objectives is strictly prohibited and prosecutable by law.

- Secularism and separation of religion from politics and the State: RAWA has repeatedly asserted that the only way for preventing our nation from being blighted by fundamentalism or any other pestilence in the garb of religion, whether now or in the future, is separation of religion from politics and the state. The inclusion of this explicit provision in the Constitutions of other Islamic countries has not been deemed alien or anti-Islamic. There is no reason why the Constitution of Afghanistan should be void of such a central democratic tenet. Those who consider calls for secularism as an "anti-religious penchant" do so, if not out of sheer ignorance, in order to wittingly or unwittingly serve fundamentalist interests.
- Establishment of a constant allotment of seats for women deputies in any future parliament.
- Abrogation of torture and execution under whatever name or excuse.

RAWA will present its more elaborate proposals at a future opportunity.

9. The Future Afghan State

In view of the composition of the Transitional Administration, RAWA does not deem it fit and competent to perform on the basis of democratic principles. Even if Mr Karzai and a select few of his team sincerely pledge their faith in democracy and their adherence to its tenets, they are enmeshed and paralysed in the tentacles of the avowed enemies of democracy who have them encircled.

RAWA calls for a future Afghan State which will be based on the following principles:

- Unqualified adherence to the principles and criteria of democracy and its major tenet, secularism.
- Strict prohibition of all forms of decrees, fatwas, etc. in regard to women and what they should wear, etc. (Isn't ten long years of suppression and waging of a savage and vile war on women enough?)
- Total and absolute abrogation of political police organisations or other institutions of civil espionage, torture or harassment, be it of the type of the Parchami, Khalqi, Jihadi or Taliban regimes, or in any other form. (A museum of shame should be established to record the totality of the infamies perpetrated by these successive regimes.)
- Prosecution of all individuals who, during the past twenty-three years, have committed high treason, war crimes, blatant violations of human rights and plunder of national assets.
- Abolishment and proscription of all religious madrassahs and other terrorist dens where Jihadi and Taliban mindsets are promoted and trained.

- Investigation and extraction of hundreds of millions of dollars' worth of funds embezzled and misappropriated by Jihadi and Taliban thieves from public coffers or from international financial assistance funds. (Such investigation and extraction should include the $10 million given by the then Pakistani Prime Minister Nawaz Sharif to Sebghatullah Mojadedi, the first Jihadi "President" of Afghanistan. This sum is inconsequential when compared with misappropriations of hundreds of millions of dollars by other Jihadi leaders, but fortunately it is well documented.)
- Debarment of higher-echelon individuals of Jihadi and Taliban parties from holding high public office. Likewise, debarment of intellectuals who, whether inside or outside Afghanistan, shamelessly put their talents, pens and voices at the service of Jihadi and Taliban criminals. The extradition of such Taliban and "Northern Alliance" ideologues should be requested from US, Canadian, European and Australian authorities, and authorities of all other countries of refuge of such elements. Legal proceedings should be initiated against such individuals for their venal servitude to Jihadi and Taliban scoundrels.

Let RAWA opponents and antagonists level any base accusation they wish against RAWA. Let so-called intellectual lackeys of Jihadi and Taliban criminal bands not desist from any sort of vile foul-mouthing of RAWA. Let imbeciles arise to claim that Afghan women, because of religious and cultural conditioning, consent to medieval Jihadi or Taliban despotism and are not worthy of freedom and democracy. The Revolutionary Association of the Women of Afghanistan is veteran of over two decades of intrepid struggles in the face of death and worse for democracy, women's emancipation and empowerment. We will not flinch from reactionary and misogynist defamation and vituperation levelled against us. We rely on the masses of bereaved, agonised Afghan women; and together with all other pro-democracy forces in our homeland will not desist for a moment nor take one step back from the pursuance of our lofty objectives.

Inspired by the blood Meena shed on this path, and with a resolve steeled as never before to create a free, prosperous and democratic Afghanistan, we shall march forward and fight at the vanguard of our country's legion of women. As a battalion of the great army of women partisans of freedom around the world, the women of the world will find us at our posts.

Let the succour and support for the fight of the women of Afghanistan against war and fundamentalism and for freedom and democracy strengthen and expand as never before!

Long live RAWA's solidarity with freedom-loving women and women's organisations around the world!

PART TWO

REFLECTIONS

Bronwyn Winter

Dislocations

Peshawar 2000

We are in a Sikh palace in the old city
Renovated and priced for tourists by Americans
Its carved arches handrails balconies
Polished to perfection. Starshaped windows
The signature image of a forgotten affluence
Intricate lampshades ripple the walls with light
The damp sewage smell from the bathrooms
The only reminder of when and where we are

We are in a street of Sikh palaces
Washing draped over rotting wood sagging walls
Electric wires like the branches of wintertrees
Shutters missing slats, corrugated iron doing the rest
Bright painted signs beneath star windows
Ghazal Paints, Brother's Pharmacy
Not owned by Americans
But translated for them

It is the end of the kite festival
Shreds of kite caught on the wintertree wiring
Flutter on occasion in the halfhearted March breeze
Yesterday, boys flew kites from the roofs
Colour and movement against the stagnancy of years
I did not see the girls
Peshawar carries its traditions well

Incongruous in local dress with Blundstone boots
Seated in a carvedwoodenchair in our palacefortourists
You stare half-bored, half-defiant from a photograph
How peculiar we are in this place

One morning from the balcony
We watch the town pass in bright painted buses
And draped in folds of heavy cotton
A woman wearing her portable tent
Looks up and waves. I imagine her smile

In three days I count six bareheaded little girls
The rest already playing at grownups

Walking through the bazaar
Jostled by men, avoided by women
We are offensive in our foreign femaleness
Some stare at us through the grilles of their tents
I imagine their eyes

In the hotel restaurant I eat Afghan food
And imagine the camps
Impossible not to feel like a fraud
Tasting the daytoday of others
And I know I can leave tomorrow

On the outskirts of the old city
The Hindu temple weeps
An abandoned car has settled in
In front of the abandoned temple
Ancient and modern obsolescence in beige and brown
This is an unpeopled place
A place to traverse quickly, a shortcut from there to there
Atop the crumbling ramparts of the old fortress
Homes of sticks and canvas and barbed wire
A television antenna perched on a treebranch
Stakes a claim to modern luxuries
This urban wasteland like so many others
Variations on a theme of dilapidation

In the central bazaar
Where gold jewellery and cameras
Glisten in glassed shopfronts
The mosque shines whitewhitewhite
Beautiful and loved
Beautiful because loved

I did not see the camps
What business had I there
Even a refugee deserves privacy
This was Before The War
Before The World Changed
Before New York realised It Too was Vulnerable
Before People Were Killed

Women were only women then
Not yet needed to salve consciences
Imagined faces beneath ambulatory tents
A breath, a whisper amidst the cacophony
Of more pressing concerns elsewhere

Kabul 2002

Kabul seizes your eyes your throat
Hangs heavy in the air
The mountains a vague background suggestion
Los Angeles on a bad day
Minus Venice Beach and Santa Monica

Kabul invades your nostrils
Heat dust petrol daysold oil
Sides of meat in the market buzzing with flies
The runoff dries and cakes in the gutters
Kabul smells of Peshawar

Kabul wakes you at 4am
The discordant stridency of busy dawn cars
Frenetically bound around a roundabout
The policeman parasol-protected
Against the sun heat dust no rain tospeakof
Blows his whistle on occasion
As the cars buzzbuzzbuzz like flies

Kabul greets you with destruction
Plane carcasses lined up along the runway
Ghosts of military welcomes past
Bombed out hangars house bombed out planes
Office buildings conduct business as usual
Next to gaping holes in their façades

Kabul marks its memories
In the middle of the main bazaar
An embarassed and cloaked-in central square
A former Taliban place of execution
We photograph the landmarks
"The Taliban soldiers were here" CLICK
"The United Front shot from here" CLICK
In between, a street full of saplings
Newly cut timber for rebuilding

Kabul teaches its children
In halfremaining rooms
Tarpaulins make up the difference
UN protection from the June sun
Classroom posters show the alphabet numbers landmines
The basics of Afghan literacy
The girls proudly recite their lesson
"The value of sharing water"
And jostle to smile for our cameras
The teachers invite us for tea
Later under their burqas
Screens muffling their voices their eyes
I remember their smiles

Kabul drinks tea
Delicate with cardamom
And the warmth of gentle hospitality
Incongruous and optimistic
Like the womenandgirls smiles
In this bleak and savage place

Kabul goes about its business
Salwar kameez driving donkeys
And burqas towing children
One day things will be better
In the meantime we have to eat

Parwan

Shamari stretches in the sun
The highway a red-dotted line to the Kush
Red for landmines
Remnants of villages, ghost towns elsewhere,
Less romantic here, they are Ruins Remains Rubble

The tanks are everywhere
Lined up along the highway
Like the planes along the runway
But the planes were orderly
Corpses laid out after battle
The tanks are everywhichway
Caught in suspended animation

But Afghanistan Is Rebuilding
Spanking new petrol stations
Smile at passing cars vans trucks
Prettily painted, almostready for customers
Gleaming new mosques
Dazzling in the midday heat
Prettily painted alwaysready for customers
Transport and religion
Priorities for national reconstruction

The women teach the value of sharing water
And the children memorise written words
No books to write in or pencils to write with
Water and words are precious things
To be savoured relished devoured
But only in moderation
While the men guzzle petrol and prayer

Water and words are precious
The children collect words like jewels
Their mothers stumble over the letters
And dream of becoming seamstresses

Panjshir

The road turns to rubble
And the mountains become visible
The rapids rush brown over rock
Heady excitement of leftalone wildness

Climbing high rounding rock water rock
A tank perched impossibly on an outcrop
Like some alien spaceship
Abandoned to an earthly fate

Abandon abandoned abandonment
Words to characterise a country

The Panjshir villages huddle in the valleys
They have managed to stay in hiding
Put their heads down until the battlefire passed
One survives how one can

I saw Massoud's house
Opulence and running water
Next to the running river
I saw Massoud's grave
A killer killed becomes a martyr
A Protector of the People
I shudder in the summer afternoon

Driving home after nightfall
An injured tank points its gun
Directly into our headlights
Sudden and frightening in the Panjshir moonscape

Peshawar 2002

It takes time to cross University Road
No such thing as a break in the traffic
Men lean out leering from buses
Rickshaws and taxis slow enquiringly
Their drivers incredulous to be waved away
A lone western woman crossing the road
Is not a concept here
Westerners ride in taxis rickshaws 4wheeldrives
And women do not venture alone
Through the streets of Peshawar
Peshawar is not a safe place

In pairs trios with children
The women are never alone
But always isolated
Covered heads faces bodies
The women are never invisible
But always anonymous
Threading through the marketplace
The women are never still
But always constrained
Bonded jailed burqaed
Bosses police landlords husbands children
Everyone stakes a claim gets a cut
Peshawar is not a gentle place

In the backstreets of University Town
The traffic thins people disappear
Into the grounds of whitewalled residences
As pristine as Pakistan gets
The trees gardens 4wheeldrives
Clumps of beggars at gateways
Universal giveaways of a city's rarefied space
Where bourgeoisie meets NGOs and UN
Peshawar's protected places

Those who liveandwork here are nervous
On Friday a carbomb in Karachi
Pedestrians unlucky enough
To be near something American
Already on Thursday a danger warning
Stay within University Town
Unless Absolutely Necessary
I do not stay in University Town
In the dusty lateafternoon
The city stirs from hot stupor
Traffic thick again on University Road
Sudden alertness of shopkeepers
As the bazaar bustles and jostles
University Town at a nearby distance
Draws its walls closer around
Peshawar is unsafe

Accompanied by radio antennae and guns
The UN and I climb the frontier mountains
"Welcome to the Khyber Pass"
Tourists greeted by signs and soldiers
Welcome to wildness and romantic imaginings
Beautiful breathtaking spectacular magnificent
Words accurate and inadequate
For this seductive and intimidating place
The road winds ribbons round the rockface
No tanks here, just 4wheeldrives and guns
And bustruckloads of those returning
The War Is Over Now
Two hours and fifty-four kilometres
A journey to the edge of lives
Peshawar is a long way away

Shalman sits like a surprise in the valley
A sudden peopling amidst barrenness
A clearing in the mountains
A flat place to pitch tents
Twenty thousand people in a holiday camp
Latrine enclosures like green marshmallows

And shalegrey gravestones like menhirs
Punctuate the beige monotony
Where water and hope are rare
Where Kabul Kunduz Mazar are memories
And Peshawar only a thought

Shalman's fortunes are those of war
Open in January overflowing in March
In April the men line up
There are eight nine ten in our family
One tent is not enough
In May the womenchildren line up
For medicines and extra flour
In June the families pack up
We can go back now
The War Is Over
Memories picked up where left off
But Kabul Kunduz Mazar are not the same
Do not have buildings jobs homes
Do not have food do not have water
And only the women have tents
Blue like the screened-off sky
The returners return again across mountains
Peshawar is a gentler and safer place

Cynthia Enloe

Masculinity as a Foreign Policy Issue

This article first appeared in *Foreign Policy in Focus* 5: 36 (October 2000).

The militarization of any country's foreign policy can be measured by monitoring the extent to which its policy:

1. is influenced by the views of Defense Department decision-makers and/or senior military officers,

2. flows from civilian officials' own presumption that the military needs to carry exceptional weight,

3. assigns the military a leading role in implementing the nation's foreign policy, and

4. treats military security and national security as if they were synonymous.

Employing these criteria, US foreign policy today is militarized.

A feminist analysis can help reveal why US foreign policy has become so militarized—and at what costs. Since 1980, due to the growth of the women's movement, it has become almost commonplace in many domestic US policy circles to ask: "Will this proposed solution have disproportionately negative impacts on girls and women?" and "Does this policy option derive from unspoken assumptions about men's employment, men's health, or men's supposed abilities?" Notable strides have been made in domestic policy arenas, even if there is still a long way to go before such intelligent questioning produces equally smart policy outcomes.

By contrast, in foreign policy, progress toward a more sophisticated—realistic—understanding of the causes and costs of policy options has been sluggish. In the 1970s and 1980s, women activists and feminist analysis did help drive popular protests against US wars in South-East Asia and Central America. Yet, generally, US foreign policy has been tightly controlled by the president and Congress, limiting a genuinely public debate. Stalling progress toward bringing feminist analyses into foreign policy decision-making processes has been the conventionally naive belief that international affairs—trade, immigration, high-tech weapons sales—have nothing to do with gender. They do.

Feminist foreign policy analysis is not naive. It derives from a systematic, eyes-wide-open curiosity, posing questions that nonfeminists too often imagine are irrelevant or find awkward to ask. For starters:

- Are any of the key actors motivated in part by a desire to appear "manly" in the eyes of their own principal allies or adversaries?
- What are the consequences?
- Which policy option will bring women "to the negotiating table"?
- Does the alleged reasonableness of any foreign policy choice rest on the unexamined assumption that women's issues in the target country can be addressed "later", that it is men's anxieties that must be dealt with immediately?

American feminist analysts and strategists have had the strongest impact on international political debates in recent years when they have worked in concert with women's advocates from both developed and developing countries, and when the US military and its congressional allies have not felt that they had a stake in the outcome. Feminist networks have had success, for example, in putting trafficking in women on the agenda of international agencies, making systematic wartime rape a distinct prosecutable charge in the Yugoslavian and Rwandan international war crime tribunals, making women refugees' interests administratively visible, and defining women's control over their reproductive processes as warranting the status of an internationally recognized human right.

However, when Defense Department officials have weighed in, the Democratic-controlled White House and Republican-controlled Senate have shied away from feminist analyses. Consequently, the US government either has invested energy in watering down new international treaties designed to roll back militarism, or has refused outright to ratify such agreements as, for instance, the treaty to ban landmines, the UN convention acknowledging the rights of children in war, and the treaty establishing the International Criminal Court, the first permanent international war crimes tribunal.[1]

In each instance, it has been the Pentagon's ability to persuade civilian officials that the military's own goals would be compromised—its desire to maintain landmines in South Korea, its desire to enlist and deploy teenage recruits, and its prioritizing the protection of American soldiers stationed

---

1 See *Foreign Policy in Focus* briefs: "The Mine Ban Treaty", 5: 21; "Use of Children as Soldiers", 4: 27; "International Criminal Court", 3: 4.

abroad when they are charged with criminal acts—that has carried the day in Washington. Civilian representatives' repeated privileging of military concerns over other important US international goals is due in part to the nervousness that many male civilian executive and congressional officeholders feel when confronted with military resistance. This is not about hormones. It is about the male politician's angst over not appearing "manly". This, in turn, is about American political culture.

Problems with Current US Policy

Many observers have remarked on the peculiar American contemporary political culture that equates military experience and/or military expertise with political leadership. It is this cultural inclination that has made it very risky for any American public figure to appear less "manly" than a uniformed senior military male officer. It is a culture—too often unchallenged by ordinary voters—that has given individuals with alleged military knowledge a disproportionate advantage in foreign policy debates.

Such a masculinized and militarized culture pressures nervous civilian candidates into appearing "tough" on military issues. The thought of not embracing a parade of militarized policy positions—that increase the defense budget, make NATO the primary institution for building a new European security, expand junior officer training programs in high schools, insure American male soldiers' access to prostitutes overseas, invest in destabilizing anti-missile technology, maintain crippling but politically ineffectual economic sanctions and bombing raids against Iraq, accept the Pentagon's flawed policy of "don't ask, don't tell, don't pursue", and finance a military-driven anti-drug policy—would leave most American public officials (women and men) feeling uncomfortably vulnerable in the political culture that assigns high value to masculinized toughness. The result: a political competition to appear "tough" has produced US foreign policies that severely limit the American capacity to play a useful role in creating a more genuinely secure international community. That is, America's conventional, masculinized political culture makes it unlikely that Washington policymakers will either come to grips with a realistic analysis of potential global threats or act to strengthen those multilateral institutions most effective in preventing and ending conflicts.

A feminist analysis turns the political spotlight on the conventional notion of manliness as a major factor shaping US foreign policy choices. It demonstrates that popular gender presumptions are not just the stuff of sociology texts. Every official who has tried not to appear "soft" knows this. For example, early in his administration, Bill Clinton made known his abhorrence of landmines and his determination to ban them. But by 1998, he had caved in to military pressure and stated, instead, that the US would not sign the widely endorsed international landmines treaty until the Defense Department came up with an "alternative".

Feminist questioning also produces a more realistic accounting of the consequences of macho policies. Despite slight increases in the number of women in policy positions, US militarized policies in the post-Cold War era have served to strengthen the privileged positions of men in decision-making, both in the United States and in other countries. For instance, the US government is currently promoting NATO as the central bastion of Western security. Although it is true that there are now women soldiers in all NATO governments' armed forces (the Italians were the most recent to enlist women), NATO remains a masculinized political organization. The alliance's policies are hammered out by a virtually all-male elite in which the roles of masculinity are silently accepted, when they should be openly questioned. Thus, to the extent that the US succeeds in pressing NATO to wield more political influence than the European Parliament (where women have won an increasing proportion of seats), not only American women but also European women will be shunted to the wings of the political stage.

Consider what feminist analysis reveals about the consequences of militarizing anti-drug policy. The American government's new billion-dollar-plus aid package to the Colombian military will, as its critics have noted,[2] further intensify the civil war and human rights abuses. But less discussed is the fact that this policy will serve to marginalize women of all classes in Colombia's political life. This—the obsession of America's politicians and senior appointees with not appearing "soft" on drugs—militarizes drug prevention efforts and, in so doing, disempowers women both in the US and in the drug-producing countries. Women—both as grassroots urban activists in American cities and as mobilizers of a broad, cross-class peace movement in Colombia—have offered alternative analyses and solutions to the problems of drug addiction and drug trade. However, their valuable ideas are drowned out by the sounds of helicopter engines and M-16 rifles.

This example illustrates a more general phenomenon. When any policy approach is militarized, one of the first things that happens is that women's voices are silenced. We find that when the US touts any military institution as the best hope for stability, security, and development, the result is deeply gendered: the politics of masculinity are made to seem "natural", the male grasp on political influence is tightened, and most women's access to real political influence shrinks dramatically.

---

1 See *Foreign Policy in Focus* brief, "Colombia in Crisis", 5: 5.

Toward a New Foreign Policy

Asking feminist questions openly, making them an explicit part of serious foreign policy discussion, is likely to produce a much more clear-eyed understanding of what is driving any given issue debate and what are the probable outcomes of one policy choice over another. Precisely because the United States currently has such an impact on the internal political workings of so many other countries, we need to start taking a hard look at American political culture. If this globalizing culture continues to elevate a masculinized "toughness" to the status of an enshrined good, military needs will continue to be assigned top political priority, and it will be impossible for the US to create a more imaginative, more internationally useful foreign policy.

Cultures are not immutable. Americans, in fact, are forever lecturing other societies—Indonesia, Russia, Mexico, France—on how they should remake their cultures. US citizens, however, have been loath to lift up the rock of political convention to peer underneath at the masculinized presumptions and worries that shape American foreign policies.

What would be the most immediate steps toward unravelling the masculinized US foreign policy knot? A first step would be to muster the political will to congressionally ratify the International Criminal Court treaty, the anti-landmines treaty, and the Convention on the Rights of the Child. A second step would be for Democrats and Republicans to halt their reckless game of "chicken" regarding both the anti-missile defense system and increases in US military spending. A third step would entail daring to own up to the consequences of making the military Colombia's most potent institution and opting, instead, to join European countries in supporting Colombia's peace process and adopting anti-narcotics policies that treat drugs largely as a medical and social problem rather than a military problem. A fourth step would be to shelve US efforts to remilitarize Europe and Japan. Together, these four policy steps would amount to a realistic strategy for crafting a less-militarized, less-distortedly masculinized foreign policy.

A feminist-informed analyst always asks: "Which notions of manliness are shaping this policy discussion?" and "Will the gap between women's and men's access to economic and political influence be widened or narrowed by this particular policy option?" By deploying feminist analytical tools, US citizens can clarify decisions about whether to foster militarization as the centerpiece of the post-Cold War international system. Moreover, by deploying feminist analysis, Americans are much more likely to craft a US foreign policy that will provide the foundation for a long-lasting global structure of genuine security, one that ensures women, both in the US and abroad, an effective public voice.

References

Enloe, Cynthia. (2001). *Bananas, Beaches and Bases: Making Feminist Sense of International Politics*. Berkeley: University of California Press. 2nd edition (first published 1990).

—— (2000). *Maneuvers: The International Politics of Militarizing Women's Lives*. Berkeley: University of California Press.

International Campaign to Ban Landmines: http://www.icbl.org/.

International Criminal Court (ICC) Caucus: http://www.iccnow.org/.

The International Feminist Journal of Politics. New York: Routledge Publishers.

Moon, Katherine. (1998). *Sex Among Allies*. New York: Columbia University Press.

Ms. Magazine. New York: Liberty Media for Women Publishers.

Seager, Joni. (1997). *The State of Women in the World Atlas*. New York: Penguin Books.

Women's Rights Watch, Kosovo. (2000). *Rape as a Weapon of "Ethnic Cleansing"*. Washington: Human Rights Watch, March.

Youth and Military Online News: http://www.afsc.org/youthmil.htm.

Valentine M. Moghadam

Women, the Taliban, and the Politics of Public Space in Afghanistan

First published in *Women's Studies International Forum*, 25(1), 2002.

Introduction

Women and gender issues hold a special place in the politics of public space. Historically, the public rights of men—their prerogatives, privileges, and power—were formulated in contradistinction to the disempowerment of women and women's relegation to the private sphere and to domesticity. This was, indeed, one of the paradoxical outcomes of the Enlightenment and of the democratic revolutions of the West (Pateman 1988; Applewhite and Levy 1990). In more recent times, Western women have made considerable gains in their access to full citizenship—including rights to public space, social participation, and their own sexuality—the result of both their own activism and broader socio-economic change.[1]

Even though Western societies were once organized in thoroughly patriarchal ways and women's rights and their access to public space were historically circumscribed, the idea of women's equality continues to be associated with the West. This misunderstanding is shared by a rather peculiar mix of Islamists, certain Westerners whom Edward Said (1978) would call Orientalists (that is, those who trumpet the superiority of the West), and postmodernists, whose one-time shrill denunciations of the Enlightenment, of progress, of colonialism and of everything Western shifted into an approval of any "indigenous", "non-Western", "Third World", or "authentic" practices and institutions (see Moghadam 1989a).

---

1 Of course, even in today's modernized and post-industrial societies such as the US, women's access to public space is circumscribed. An example is the hostility that women face in non-traditional places of work, study, or duty, such as in the industrial sector and in the military.

It is my view that during the 1980s, Afghan women were held hostage to the notion that women's rights were Western and that the modernizing government of Afghanistan was merely replicating the so-called bankrupt Western (or Soviet) model. The idea that there might be something inherently wrong with enshrouding women in a burqa, confining them to their homes, denying them the right to schooling, and excluding them from any form of public decision-making—in contrast to the visibility, mobility, and power of Afghan men—was totally eclipsed by the widespread indignation over the Soviet invasion and the equally widespread denigration of the social policies and reform program of the so-called Soviet puppets in Kabul (see Moghadam 1989b, 1993).

But Afghan women were held hostage by something else—the persistence of a particularly entrenched form of patriarchy and a tribal-based social structure in which only men have rights, equality, and unlimited access to public space. There are very few places left in our increasingly integrated world where women have been as excluded from the public sphere as in Afghanistan.

Gregorian (1969) has described the travails of nationalists and modernizers in the first half of the twentieth century, when small groups of educated Afghans tried, often unsuccessfully, to institute political reform, socio-economic development, and the advancement of women. A feminist lens reveals that at least three times in the twentieth century, women's rights and divergent conceptions of "women's place" became highly politicized and central to political conflicts in Afghanistan. In the 1920s, efforts by reformers, nationalists, and modernizers to improve the status of women, to establish an education system, and to modernize the economy and society met with the fierce resistance of traditionalists and *ulama* (Islamic clergy). In the 1980s, two opposing movements—one Marxist-modernizing and the other Islamist-traditionalist—fought a long and bloody war over divergent political agendas, cultural understandings, and conceptions of "women's place". And in the 1990s, a new group, the Taliban, gave new meaning to "social exclusion"—a term popular in European social theory and development studies (e.g., Appasamy *et al.* 1996; de Haan 1999)—when it instituted draconian policies against not only women's public participation but their very visibility.

Why have women's rights been such vexed issues in Afghanistan?

I argue that the issue of women's rights in Afghanistan has been historically constrained by two factors:

- the patriarchal nature of gender and social relations, deeply embedded in traditional communities

- the existence of a weak central state, which has been unable, since at least the beginning of the twentieth century, to implement modernizing programs and goals in the face of "tribal feudalism", especially among the Pashtuns.

The two are interconnected, for the state's weakness is correlated with a strong (if fragmented) society resistant to state bureaucratic expansion, civil authority, regulation, monopoly of the means of violence, and extraction— the business of modern states (see, e.g., Rubin 1995). These factors were behind the defeat of the modernizing efforts of King Amanullah in the 1920s, the defeat of the Marxists and their attempt to implement a social program in the 1980s, and the disintegration and defeat of the short-lived Mujahideen government in the early 1990s. These factors also explain why the Taliban regime was unable and unwilling to implement a program for social development, much less for women's rights.

A patriarchal social structure, the absence of a centralized and modernizing state, and the problematical stance of the international and feminist community (of which more below) relegated Afghan women to a status far worse than second-class citizenship. It was the status of an outsider, without legal rights and excluded from decision-making; the status of an object, on whom pronouncements were made and punishments inflicted; the status of a prisoner, confined to the home and darkened windows, or enveloped in an all-encompassing tent-like veil, while men roamed freely, unencumbered by anything but their guns. In Afghanistan, the public/private distinction has been highly gendered in a most exaggerated way.

Patriarchal Social Structure

Contemporary Afghanistan is situated in what the demographer John Caldwell (1982) has called "the patriarchal belt", and is an extreme case of what Deniz Kandiyoti (1988) terms "classic patriarchy". Here the patriarchal extended family is the central social unit, in which the senior man has authority over everyone else, including younger men. Women are subject to forms of control and subordination that include restrictive codes of behavior, gender segregation, and the association of female virtue with family honor.[2] Young brides marry into large families, gain respect mainly via their sons, and late in life acquire power as mothers-in-law. Patriarchal societies are characterized by an adverse sex ratio, low female literacy and educational

---

2 Anthropological studies on the Mediterranean during the 1960s identified an "honor–shame" complex governing women's behavior and male/family honor in countries such as France, Italy, Spain, Greece, and Portugal. See, for example Pitt-Rivers (1977).

attainment, high fertility rates, high maternal mortality rates, and low female labor-force participation in the formal or modern sector of the economy.

Afghan patriarchy is tied to the prevalence of such forms of subsistence as nomadic pastoralism, herding and farming, and settled agriculture, all organized along patrilineal lines. Women and children tend to be assimilated into the concept of property and to belong to a male. This is particularly the case among Pashtuns, whose tribal culture, Pashtunwali, is highly masculinist. Anthropologist Nancy Tapper, who studied the Durrani Pashtuns of north-central Afghanistan in the 1970s, has written: "The members of the community discuss control of all resources—especially labor, land, and women—in terms of honor" (1984: 304). Note that "community" is the community of men, and that "women" are assimilated in the concept of "resources". Census and surveys undertaken in 1967, 1972–74 and 1979 revealed a very high ratio of males to females, which even exceeded the expected under-reporting of females in a conservative Islamic society. The adverse sex ratio is a function of the subordinate status of women and girls and the privileged status of men and boys (Moghadam 1992).

In a patriarchal context, marriage and brideprice are a transaction between households, an integral part of property relations and the exchange system, and an indicator of status. In Afghanistan, marriage, forced or voluntary, has been a way of ending feuds, cementing a political alliance between families, increasing the family's prestige, or accumulating wealth. Mobility and migration patterns have revolved around the brideprice; Tapper (1991) has described how in the 1970s men from one region would travel to another to find inexpensive brides, while other men would travel elsewhere because they could obtain a higher price for their daughters. The heaviest expenses any household had to bear were connected with marriage. The choice of bride, the agreed brideprice, and the time taken to complete a marriage could visibly confirm—or, indeed, increase—a household's poverty. Tapper's description accords well with Gregory Massell's discussion of the importance of *kalym* (brideprice) to overall property relations in early-twentieth-century Central Asia (see Massell 1974). It reveals the extent to which the exchange of women for brideprice or in compensation for blood treats women exclusively as reproducers and pawns in economic and political exchanges, in a patriarchal context. It also suggests that there was a very real material interest on the part of men in resisting the marriage reforms that the Marxist government sought to institute in the late 1970s.

Afghanistan is a prototypical "weak state" (see Migdal 1988), inasmuch as the central authorities have been unable to realize their goals, or to regulate social relations and use resources in determined ways (Urban 1988). The existence of a weak modern state in a predominantly patriarchal and tribal society has had adverse implications for reform and development, as well as for the advancement of women. With the onset of the modernization process in the mid-nineteenth century, various governments and rulers sought to discourage excessive expenditure on brideprice and marriage celebrations as a way of preventing rural indebtedness; and they tried to extend education to girls. State initiatives during the twentieth century invariably resulted in tribal rebellion against government authority. Although Afghanistan was not immune to the general process of social change enveloping Muslim countries, it saw far less transformation than did neighboring countries (Gregorian 1969).

In examining King Amanullah's reform program of the 1920s and the organized resistance to it, one discovers parallels with the Democratic Republic of Afghanistan some fifty years later. Amanullah's general program to improve the position of women was promoted by his wife, Queen Soraya (who founded the first women's magazine, *Ershad-e Niswan*), the reformer Mahmud Tarzi and his wife, the small intelligentsia, and the modernist and nationalist "Young Afghans", impressed by developments in Turkey, Iran and Egypt (Gregorian 1969; Nawid 1999). In 1921 Amanullah enacted the Family Code, which undertook to regulate marriages and to establish the state's interest in the welfare of women and girls. Child marriages and inter-marriage between close kin were outlawed as contrary to Islamic principles. In the new code Amanullah stipulated that a widow was to be free of the domination of her husband's family; he placed tight restrictions on wedding expenses, including dowries, and granted wives the right to appeal to the courts if their husbands did not adhere to Koranic tenets regarding marriage. In the fall of 1924, Afghan girls were given the right to choose their husbands, a measure that incensed the traditionalists.

By the late 1920s, Afghan legislation pertaining to women and the family was among the most progressive in the Muslim world. No other country had yet addressed the sensitive issues of child marriage and polygamy. Afghan family law on these issues became the model for similar reforms in Soviet Central Asia in 1926. It is not surprising that the family law of 1921 was a major cause of the uprising instigated by the clergy in 1924.

King Amanullah's most audacious act was to begin a study-abroad program for Afghan students, and to open the first schools for girls. By 1928 there were about 800 girls attending schools in Kabul and several Afghan women studying abroad, notably in Turkey, France and Switzerland. Amanullah had plans to build five more schools for girls and intended his planned compulsory education system to apply to girls as well as boys (Gregorian 1969). The Association for the Protection of Women's Rights (Anjoman-i Hemayat-i Neswan) was established to help women fight domestic injustice and take a role in public life. The Queen presided over several committees to strengthen the emancipation campaign (Nawid 1999).

These unprecedented measures violated traditional norms and offended the religious leaders and their following, especially in rural areas. Reaction against the campaign for women's emancipation was a major factor in the outbreak of violent disturbances in November and December of 1928. When the King banned the practice of polygamy among government officials it caused an uproar among the religious establishment. A tribal revolt ensued, led by Bacha-i Saqqo, a Tajik rebel claiming Islamic credentials. The rebels attacked Kabul; Amanullah abdicated and left Afghanistan (Gregorian 1969).

Not until the 1950s were reforms attempted again. In 1950 a law attempted to ban ostentatious life-cycle ceremonies, prohibiting many of the expensive aspects of birth, circumcision, marriage and burial rituals. But the law proved difficult to enforce. The Marriage Law of 1971 once again tried to curb the indebtedness arising from the costs of marriage. The Civil Law of 1977 abolished child marriage and established sixteen as the minimum age of marriage for girls. But the law remained weak and was ignored. Furthermore, the law left the husband's right to unilateral divorce untouched (Tapper 1984; Kamali 1985). According to one analyst, the record of Afghanistan's leaders until 1978 was a pitiful one: they had failed to give the country any of the attributes of the modern centralized state, including a nation-wide school system (Urban 1988: 204).

The Interregnum: Space and Confinement

In 1965, while Afghanistan was still a monarchy with Zahir Shah at its helm, a group from the small Afghan intelligentsia formed the People's Democratic Party of Afghanistan (PDPA). Evoking the Amanullah experiment, the PDPA envisaged a national democratic government to liberate Afghanistan from backwardness. Among its demands was primary education for all children in their mother tongue and the development of the different languages and cultures of the country. Its social demands included guarantees of the right to work, equal treatment for women, a 42-hour work week, paid sickness and maternity leaves, and a ban on child labor (Halliday 1978). That same year, six women activists formed the Democratic Organization of Afghan Women (DOAW). The DOAW's main objectives were to eliminate illiteracy among women, forced marriages, and the brideprice. The 1964 Constitution had granted women the right to vote, and thus, four women from the DOAW were elected to parliament. Both the PDPA and the DOAW were eager for profound, extensive, and permanent social change.[3]

---

3 Author's interviews with Massoumeh Esmaty Wardak, head of the Afghan

In 1968 conservative members of parliament proposed to enact a law prohibiting Afghan girls from studying abroad. Hundreds of girls demonstrated in opposition. In 1970 two mullahs protested against "public women", including women teachers and schoolgirls, by shooting at the legs of women in Western dress and splashing them with acid. Among those who joined in this action was Gulbuddin Hekmatyar (who went on to be a leading figure in the Mujahideen, one of the "freedom fighters" hailed by US President Reagan during the 1980s, and a guest of the Islamic government in Iran during the 1990s). This time there was a protest demonstration of 5000 girls (Dupree 1984).

Zahir Shah was overthrown in 1973 by the former prime minister, also a cousin, Mohammad Daud, and went into a long exile in Rome. Despite attempts at reform on the part of the Daud government and the presence of unveiled and professional women in Kabul, for the vast majority of Afghan women, illiteracy, ill-health, seclusion, and immobility characterized their lives. According to World Bank figures, in 1975 only 8 per cent of girls (compared with 44 per cent of boys) were enrolled in primary school, while a mere 2 per cent of girls (compared with 13 per cent of boys) were enrolled in secondary school. Life expectancy was a mere 37 years; the total fertility rate was 8 children per woman; and the infant mortality rate was 35 deaths per 1000 births (World Bank 1988; Moghadam 1992, 1993: 224).[4]

Veronica Doubleday (1988), who lived in the city of Herat on and off between 1972 and 1977, explains that women's complaints focused around two issues, which she came to see as related: sickness and the restrictions imposed by their seclusion. The women complained of backaches, lack of energy and many other ailments, and said that sometimes their husbands would not allow them to visit a doctor. Some women complained specifically about their seclusion, which they called *qeit*, or confinement, imprisonment. Doubleday describes how, despite her desire to avoid Western ethnocentrism, she had to conclude that purdah was not simply about being segregated and veiled; it meant that men had complete control over the mobility of their women, and it gave men ultimate power. Anthropologist Micheline

Women's Council, and Soraya, head of the Red Crescent Society (the Afghan Red Cross) and a founding member of the DOAW, in Kabul in February 1989. Soraya identified three of the four women parliamentarians: Anahita Ratebzad, Massouma Esmaty Wardak, and Mrs Saljugi.

4   In a fact sheet provided to me by the Office of the Permanent Mission to the United Nations of the Democratic Republic of Afghanistan, in New York in October 1986, literacy on the eve of the Afghan revolution was estimated at 30 per cent for males and a mere 4 per cent for females.

Centlivres-Demont, who also spent time in Afghanistan in the 1970s, writes of the time that

> the roles and status of [Afghan] women are, before everything else, based on women's reproductive functions: physical reproduction and social reproduction. At the center of a system of exchange that is based not on the individual but on entire families, wives are acquired by a transfer of goods from the husband's family to the bride's, a transfer that ensures to the former the young women's reproductive functions (Centlivres-Demont 1994: 334).

When women are viewed as resources, they are restricted from access to resources and entitlements themselves. In addition, the extremely patriarchal and masculine nature of Afghan society meant that only men engaged in decision-making. This too reinforced women's social exclusion.

Creating Space for Women: The Marxist Experiment

In April 1978, the PDPA seized power in what came to be called the Saur (April) Revolution, established the Democratic Republic of Afghanistan (DRA), and introduced a reform program to change the political and social structure of Afghan society. Three decrees—Nos. 6, 7, and 8—were the main planks of the program of social and economic reform designed to assist peasants, poor households, and women and girls. Decree No. 6 was intended to put an end to land mortgage and indebtedness; No. 7 was designed to stop the payment of brideprice and give women more freedom of choice in marriage; No. 8 consisted of rules and regulations for the confiscation and redistribution of land. Whereas girls were usually wed immediately upon puberty, the new government set a minimum age of marriage of sixteeen years for women and eighteen years for men (Beattie 1984). The DRA also embarked upon an aggressive literacy campaign that was led by the DOAW, whose function was to educate women, bring them out of seclusion, and initiate social programs. Cadres established literacy classes for men, women, and children in villages, and by August 1979 the government had established 600 new schools (Halliday 1978; Katzikas 1982; author's interviews with Soraya in 1989).

This was clearly an audacious program for social change, one aimed at the rapid transformation of a patriarchal society and a power structure based on tribal and landlord authority. Revolutionary change, state-building, and women's rights subsequently went hand-in-hand. DRA attempts to change marriage laws, expand literacy, and educate rural girls met with strong opposition. Fathers with unmarried daughters resented Decree No. 7 most because they could no longer expect to receive large brideprice payments, and because it represented a threat to male honor (Beattie 1984; Dupree 1984).

The right of women to divorce, a measure introduced by the DRA, was also very controversial. Although the divorce law was never officially announced, owing to the outbreak of tribal Islamist opposition to the regime, the family courts (*mahakem-e famili*), mostly presided over by female judges, provided hearing sessions for discontented wives and sought to protect their rights to divorce and on related issues, such as alimony, child custody, and child support.[5]

The DRA's attempts to institute compulsory education—initially planned by King Amanullah in the 1920s and provided for in the Constitution of 1964 but ignored by the population—were opposed by traditionalists and by fathers keen to maintain control over their daughters. Believing that women should not appear at public gatherings, villagers often refused to attend classes after the first day. PDPA cadres viewed this attitude as retrograde, and, thus, the cadres resorted to different forms of persuasion, including physical force, to make the villagers return to literacy classes. Often PDPA cadres were either kicked out of the village or murdered. In the summer of 1978 refugees began pouring into Pakistan, giving as their major reason the forceful implementation of the literacy program among their women (Dupree 1984; Centlivres-Demont 1994). In Kandahar, three literacy workers from the women's organization were killed as symbols of the unwanted revolution. Two men killed all the women in their families to prevent them from "dishonor" (Dupree 1984). An Islamist opposition began organizing and conducted several armed actions against the government in spring 1979. Meanwhile, the Carter Administration of the United States, in an initiative by National Security Adviser Zbigniew Brzezinski, authorized use of American intelligence services to aid the Islamist opposition and undermine the government of Noor Mohammad Taraki.[6]

Internal battles within the PDPA, especially between its two wings, Parcham and Khalq, exacerbated the DRA's difficulties. In September 1979 President Taraki was killed on the orders of his deputy, Hafizullah Amin, a ruthless and ambitious man who imprisoned and executed hundreds of his own comrades in addition to further alienating the population. The Pakistani

---

5 Author's interviews with Massouma Esmaty Wardak and with Soraya, Kabul, February 1989.

6 The official US line was that support for the Mujahideen began in the 1980s, and only in response to the invasion by Soviet troops in December 1979. We now know, through an admission by Zbigniew Brzezinski in the 15–21 January 1998 issue of *Le Nouvel Observateur* of France, that in July 1979 President Carter signed the first directive for secret aid to the opponents of the DRA, which was seen as "an opportunity of giving to the USSR its Vietnam war". See also Mishra (2001).

regime of Zia ul-Haq was opposed to leftists next door, and began to extend support for the Mujahideen armed uprising. In December 1979 the Soviet army intervened, beginning a long military engagement in the country's civil war on the side of the DRA. Amin was killed and succeeded by Babrak Karmal, who initiated what was called "the second phase" (*marhale-ye dovvom*). The civil war continued, and was internationalized, with the Mujahideen receiving support not only from the United States and Pakistan but also from Saudi Arabia, the Islamic Republic of Iran, and China. In addition, numerous "Islamic internationalists" from Algeria, Egypt, Iran, and other Muslim countries fought alongside the Mujahideen, who based themselves in the northwest city of Peshawar in Pakistan.[7] This continued through the administrations of Babrak Karmal (1980–86) and Dr Najibullah (1986–92). The US/CIA funding of the Mujahideen during the 1980s was the largest and most expensive covert operation in history, and one scholar estimates that Saudi and US funds allocated to the Mujahideen may have amounted to as much as five billion dollars (see Rubin 1995).

Women and Public Space in Kabul and Peshawar: A Comparison

During the 1980s in areas under government control, and especially in Kabul, women's access to public space increased.[8] At the University of Kabul, according to 1985 official statistics, fully 65 per cent of the 7000 students were women.[9] Special programs existed to render financial aid to outstanding students through a collaborative effort of Kabul University and the Democratic Youth Organization. Under one program, students received a stipend of 1500 afghanis per month to facilitate their studies. Among the recipients were female students in the Faculty of Construction—an interesting point, because construction is a field of study usually off-limits to women in Muslim societies. During my visit to Kabul in January–February 1989, I saw

---

7 One such fighter was Osama Bin Laden, who later became an arch-enemy of the United States. Others who fought in Afghanistan on the side of the Mujahideen, notably Algerians, went on to carry out terrorist actions against their own governments.

8 In January 1989, during a postdoctoral year at Brown University's Pembroke Center for Teaching and Research on Women, in Rhode Island, USA, where I was researching revolution, the state, and gender politics in Iran and Afghanistan, I travelled to Kabul for observations and interviews regarding the status of women and the situation of the government.

9 See, for example, *Afghanistan Today* 5 (September–October 1987) and 6 (November–December 1988).

that a number of "social organizations" had considerable female participation and visibility. Apart from the PDPA itself, they included the Council of Trade Unions, the Democratic Youth Organization, the Peace, Solidarity and Friendship Organization, the Women's Council, and the Red Crescent Society. Two of these organizations were led by women: the president of the Afghan Red Crescent Society was Soraya, and the Afghan Women's Council also had female leadership. In the late 1980s the Afghan Women's Council (AWC) was run by Massouma Esmaty Wardak and her staff of eight women (Moghadam 1993, 1994).

Women were present in the different ranks of the party and the government, with the exception of the Council of Ministers. The Loya Jirga—the traditional parliament—included women delegates; in 1989 the parliament had seven female members. In 1989, women in prominent positions included Massouma Esmaty Wardak, president of the Women's Council; Shafiqeh Razmandeh, vice-president of the Women's Council; Soraya, director of the Afghan Red Crescent Society; Zahereh Dadmal, director of the Kabul Women's Club; Dr Soheila, chief surgeon of the Military Hospital, who also held the rank of general. The Central Committee of the PDPA had several women members, including Jamila Palwasha and Ruhafza (alternate member), a working-class grandmother and "model worker" at the Kabul Construction Plant, where she did electrical wiring.

During my stay in Kabul I saw women employees in all the government agencies and social organizations that I visited. Ariana Airlines employed female as well as male flight attendants. An employee of the Peace, Solidarity and Friendship Organization told me that he was thirty-seven and a man, yet had a supervisor who was ten years his junior and a woman. There were women radio announcers, and the evening news on television, whether in Pashtu or Dari, was read by a male announcer and a female announcer (unveiled). There were women technicians as well as reporters working for radio and television, and in the country's newspapers and magazines. Women worked in factories and many were members of the Central Trade Union. I was told that there were women soldiers and officers in the regular armed forces, as well as in the militia and Women's Self Defense (Defense of the Revolution) Units. There were women in security, intelligence, and the police agencies, women involved in logistics in the Defense Ministry, women parachutists and even women veterinarians—an occupation usually off-limits to women in Islamic countries. In 1989 all female members of the PDPA received military training and arms. These women were prominent at a party rally of some 50,000 held in Kabul in early February 1989 that I attended.

Above the primary level, schools were now segregated, and middle-school and secondary-school girls were taught by female teachers—this was a concession made to traditionalist elements. In offices and other workplaces, however, there was no segregation. Nor were buses divided into male and female sections.

In Peshawar, where the Mujahideen were based and where refugee camps were established and administered by various humanitarian agencies, the situation of women and the opportunities afforded them were very different. Unlike liberation, resistance, and guerrilla movements elsewhere, the Afghan Mujahideen never encouraged the active participation of women. In Cuba, Algeria, Vietnam, China, Eritrea, Oman, Iran, Nicaragua, El Salvador, and Palestine, women were/are active in the front lines, in party politics, and in social services. It is noteworthy that the Mujahideen had no female spokespersons. Indeed, women in Peshawar who became too visible or vocal were threatened and sometimes killed (e.g., Mina Kishwar, founder of the Revolutionary Association of the Women of Afghanistan, or RAWA). The group responsible for most of the intimidation of women was the fundamentalist Hizb-e Islami (Islamic Party), led by Gulbuddin Hekmatyar, who received considerable US diplomatic and military support.

The educational situation in Peshawar was extremely biased against girls. In 1988, some 104,600 boys were enrolled in schools, compared to 7800 girls. For boys there were 486 primary schools, 161 middle schools and 4 high schools. For girls there were 76 primary schools, 2 middle schools, and no high schools. A UNICEF study indicated that there were only 180 Afghan women with high-school education in the camps.[10]

Disciplining Women, Covering Bodies

Despite Mujahideen repression, some women in Peshawar continued to work with the aid agencies, or attend literacy classes, or engage in political activities. RAWA staged a demonstration by women and children in Rawalpindi on 27 December 1988 on the occasion of the ninth anniversary of the Soviet military intervention in Afghanistan. The demonstrators distributed pamphlets attacking the KGB, Khad (the Afghan political police), and the Hizb-e Islami in the strongest terms. They claimed that the majority of Afghans stood for an independent and democratic Afghanistan, where social justice and women's rights were guaranteed. In a communiqué distributed that day, RAWA deplored "The reactionary fanatics [who] are savagely suppressing our grieved people, specially [sic] the women".[11] It continued:

10 Cited in the *New York Times*, 2 April, 1988: A22. See also Moghadam (1993, 1994).

11 The communiqué was given to me by Selig Harrison, to whom I am most grateful.

Killing the innocent men and women, raping, marrying forcefully young girls and widows, and hostility toward women literacy and education, are some customary cruelties committed by the fundamentalists who have made the life inside and outside the country bitter and suffocating.

The communiqué decried the "anti-democratic and anti-woman" activities of the fundamentalists and warned of "fundamentalist fascism". Those fears were well-founded. In 1990 a group of eighty Afghan mullahs in Peshawar—all of whom were from the seven parties that made up the Western-backed Mujahideen "government-in-exile"—issued a fatwa (a holy writ) stating that women were not to wear perfume, noisy bangles, or Western clothes. Veils had to cover the body at all times and clothes were not to be made of material which was soft or which rustled. Women were not to walk in the middle of the street or swing their hips; they were not to talk, laugh or joke with strangers or foreigners. These pronouncements, it should be noticed, had no effect whatsoever on US policy toward the Mujahideen or toward the Kabul government, which was desperately trying to wage peace.

Although the government of Dr Najibullah stayed in power for nearly four years after the withdrawal of the Soviet troops, it could not withstand the unceasing onslaught of the Mujahideen, who continued to receive support from the US, Pakistan, Saudi Arabia, and Iran. The intransigence of these countries toward a negotiated settlement that would include the Kabul government, along with the incompetence of the UN negotiator, Benon Sevan, undermined Dr Najibullah's position, led to the collapse of the Kabul government, and hastened the assumption of power by the Mujahideen in April 1992.[12] Once their takeover of Kabul was complete, the Mujahideen factions began to fight each other, but the men all agreed on the question of women. Thus the very first order of the new government was that all women should wear the burqa. As one journalist wrote from Kabul:

> The most visible sign of change on the streets, apart from the guns, is the utter disappearance of women in western clothes. They used to be a common sight. Now women cover up from ankle to throat and hide their hair, or else use the burqa. Many women are frightened to leave their homes. At the telephone office, 80 per cent of the male workers reported for duty on Saturday, and only 20 per cent of the females (Brown 1992).

Rather than establishing a stable government and offering security to Afghans, the Mujahideen set about fighting among themselves. The government of President Burhanuddin Rabbani was ineffectual and corrupt, and the

---

12 For a detailed examination of these events, see Cordovez and Harrison (1995) and Halliday (1996).

countryside came to be controlled by marauding warlords whose revenues came from the drug trade, from cross-border smuggling, and from tolls and taxes they coerced from traders and hapless Afghans. According to Amnesty International (1995, 1996), tens of thousands of civilians were killed and numerous girls and women—as well as boys—were kidnapped and raped between 1992 and 1996.[13] In response to this state of affairs, a group of religious students called the Taliban formed an opposition army, and in September 1996 they captured Kabul after a bloody two-year campaign.

The Taliban's Gender Regime

The Taliban were an unconventional army of Pashtun men, raised in the refugee camps of Peshawar, Pakistan, during the 1980s. They adhered to a particularly orthodox brand of Islam, one that opposed education for girls and employment for women and that called for compulsory, and very heavy, veiling. The Taliban's only education came from poorly equipped religious schools in Peshawar espousing a very conservative doctrine partly inspired by the Wahhabi ideology of Saudi Arabia (Rashid 2000). They had no conception of modern governance, democratic or participatory rule, human rights, or women's rights. Nonetheless, the Clinton Administration was very close to recognizing the Taliban regime, partly because of its disappointment with the Mujahideen's corrupt and ineffectual rule, and partly because of the opportunity for a lucrative oil pipeline deal involving a California-based corporation, Unocal (Burns 1996; Rashid 2000).[14]

As early as February 1996, when the Taliban controlled some parts of Afghanistan, they had decreed that women would be forbidden to work outside their homes, except in hospitals and clinics, and then only to treat women and girls. But given that there were so few Afghan women health-workers, and given that the Taliban did not allow male healthworkers to treat females, women and girls were not receiving medical treatment. In areas under Taliban control, girls had been expelled from schools and young women from colleges; it was announced that, for the time being, education

---

13 For details see also Hassan (1995); Shirkat Gah/Women Living Under Muslim Laws (1996).

14 Non-recognition of the Taliban by the international community is largely a feminist success story, well documented in WLUML (1998). The Taliban were recognized by only three governments—those of Pakistan, Saudi Arabia, and the United Arab Emirates. The Clinton Administration in the US was pressured by US feminists to refrain from recognizing the Taliban, and subsequently developed a strong anti-Taliban stance when the terrorist Osama Bin Laden was given safe haven in Afghanistan.

was for males only. Women were also told that if they went shopping in the bazaars, they had to be accompanied by male kinfolk and wear the traditional burqa (Moghadam 1999).

It should be noted that, before the Taliban took control, Mujahideen infighting and the Rabbani government's inability to exert its authority had created an opportunity for educated Afghan women to return to their jobs, seek employment (often teaching, whether at the primary, secondary, or tertiary levels), or otherwise generate income for their households. Thus, in Kabul and Mazar-e-Sharif, some women were able to complete their studies, obtain teaching certificates, and be employed in the professions. Many of the younger women, in particular, had been beneficiaries of the educational and employment opportunities afforded them during the "communist" era. As soon as the Taliban entered Kabul in the fall of 1996, however, they worked quickly to defeat their rivals and establish a strong central authority. Terror and repression were part of their arsenal. Unlike the Mujahideen's Islamic state, which was weak and chaotic, the Taliban's Islamic state became strong, unified, and centralized, with the capacity to carry out its peculiar interpretation of Islam and institutionalize the subordination and subjugation of women.

Taliban enforcement of the new rules regarding compulsory veiling was brutal. Women who did not conform—perhaps they showed a little leg, or their burqa wasn't made of heavy enough fabric—were publicly beaten, in a few cases by men wielding chains, and in at least one case in front of the women's crying children.[15] In addition to the disruptions and destruction of services caused by war, many women healthworkers were too frightened to work. This despite a Taliban ruling that they could work provided they saw only women patients and had no conversations with male doctors except to discuss diagnosis and treatment. Only one woman general practitioner was running her practice in Kabul in October 1996, and most of her patients could not pay her. The lack of running water and adequate heating in Kabul forced people to attend public baths to wash, but a Taliban edict ordered that the women's section had to close, ostensibly to avoid moral corruption.

In March 1997, the Taliban ordered Kabul residents to screen windows in their homes to ensure that women could not be seen from the street. The regulations, announced on Taliban-controlled radio, told householders to paint clear glass in their upper windows or replace it with opaque glass up to a height of six feet from the floor. The Kabul city council rules referred to "second-floor windows on both sides of the house, which pose a threat to

---

15 Information above from various news accounts of the time, as well as from Physicians for Human Rights (1998).

neighbors as far as the women's dress code is concerned". A Taliban official said that women's faces corrupt men. The Taliban's Office for the Enforcement of Islamic Virtue and the Prevention of Vice implemented and enforced these and other new laws. A 1998 report by Physicians for Human Rights described the horrendous health conditions of Afghan women. In May 2001, the United Nations complained that the Taliban refused to allow women to be hired for a survey to continue bread supplies for about 300,000 poor persons in Kabul. The Taliban blocked the poverty survey because it claimed that hiring women would violate Islamic principles.

The power of the Taliban and the harsh manner in which they enforced their brand of Islam and patriarchy made it impossible for all but the most determined women to engage in such basic human endeavors as education, work, and travel. Small groups of such resilient women held classes in their homes for young girls, tried to obtain jobs with international humanitarian agencies in the country, organized income-generating projects for other women, or traveled to Peshawar to make contact with women activists.[16] These women did so at tremendous risk to themselves and their families; the Taliban took such an extreme position on the domesticity of women and their relegation to the private sphere of the home that they considered any infringement of their policy on women's roles to be tantamount to treason and apostasy.

Apart from the severe oppression of women, the Taliban also practiced ethnic discrimination. They decreed that all men must wear beards; the fact that some Afghan men of Uzbek origin cannot easily grow beards did not prevent the Taliban from punishing those men.

Resistance to the Taliban's gender regime emerged among expatriate Afghan women scholars and activists, such as those involved with the Afghan Women's Council (AWC), the Women's Association for Peace and Human Rights in Afghanistan (WAPHA), and the Revolutionary Association of the Women of Afghanistan (RAWA). They worked with feminists in various countries (e.g., the Feminist Majority in the United States, as well as feminists in Italy, Spain, France, and elsewhere) to raise international awareness about the plight of Afghan women.[17] The international solidarity network Women Living Under Muslim Laws issued numerous action alerts on the plight of Afghan women and produced a compendium of documents (WLUML 1998).

---

16 Information from the RAWA website and from discussions with three expatriate Afghan women at a conference at Harvard University, November 2000. See also Physicians for Human Rights (1998, 2001).

17 In the US the Feminist Majority initiated its very vocal and visible "Gender Apartheid" campaign, and sometimes worked with RAWA and WAPHA.

The South Asia branch of WLUML—Shirkat Gah in Lahore, Pakistan—was especially active in publicizing the repressive regime of the Taliban and in calling for the restoration of Afghan women's human rights.

The Slippery Slope of Cultural Relativism

Clearly the Taliban instituted the harshest and most bizarre theocratic dictatorship in the world, with a gender regime that was particularly severe on women. But the Taliban did not arise out of nowhere, and my narrative has stressed the role and responsibility of the United States (as well as Pakistan, Iran, and Saudi Arabia) in the subversion of a reformist, modernizing regime and the human rights tragedy that followed. But my critique would not be complete without reference to the curious silence of feminists during the 1980s and early 1990s. International feminists, including the Feminist Majority in the US, became quite vociferous in their denunciation of the Taliban after 1996. But they were strangely silent during the 1980s and early 1990s.

One would have thought that feminists around the world, including American feminists, would have rallied around the idea of equality for Afghan women, criticized the Mujahideen and even the Kabul government, and come to the aid of Afghan women, as they did in the mid-1990s in the case of Bosnia (e.g., Stiglmayer 1994; see also Bunch and Reilly 1994). Unfortunately this did not occur. Western feminists seem to have "discovered" the plight of Afghan women only in 1996, when the Taliban came to power. Prior to that, although the Mujahideen's Islamist movement was explicitly anti-feminist and its misogyny quite evident, it received more international support (even from European social democrats and some Western feminists) than did the modernizing government.[18] Why was this? One reason was certainly because the Mujahideen were perceived as attempting to liberate their country and culture from Soviet domination. Thus the journalist Jan Goodwin wrote a book during the 1980s in support of the Mujahideen and in denunciation of the DRA (Goodwin 1987).[19] The well-known author Doris Lessing did the same (Lessing 1987).

Another reason for the absence of support for the women's rights and reform program of the DRA was a widespread perception that this was

---

18 For example, at the annual Socialist Scholars' Conference in New York in 1986, I attended a panel discussion on the civil war in Afghanistan and was dismayed to hear three Swedish social democrats speaking in support of the Mujahideen. When I pressed them on the Mujahideen's opposition to women's rights, they replied: "Those are not our values, but we cannot impose our values on other cultures."

19 Goodwin later wrote articles decrying the oppression of women under the Taliban.

somehow inappropriate in a developing Muslim context. It should be recalled that, during the 1980s, debates raged around issues of universalism versus cultural relativism, women's rights and community rights, orientalism and neo-colonialist discourses, the nature of Islamist movements, and the meaning of development (see, e.g., Moghadam 1989a). Feminists from around the world had not yet found common ground, and there existed a notion that there was a feminism for the West, but different priorities for the women of the South. Thus, in the mid-1980s, Nancy Tapper could denigrate the DRA's reform program by claiming that it was "casting the issues of poverty and women's status into a basically First World perspective", and that "this perspective has many critics in the Third World and elsewhere" (1984: 291). For many, in a misguided version of anti-orientalism, veiling and seclusion were regarded as cultural artifacts not to be criticized. Thus Kathleen Howard-Merriam (1987: 104) wrote:

> The Mujahideen leaders recognize women's importance to the jihad (holy war) with their exhortations to preserve women's honor through the continued practice of seclusion. The reinforcement of this tradition ... serves to strengthen the men's will to resist ... *Purdah* provides the opportunity for preserving one's own identity and a certain stability in the face of external pressures ...

Today, these misguided notions are behind us. In more recent years, feminists from around the world have come to converge on issues pertaining to women's rights and interests. Transnational feminist networks such as Women Living Under Muslim Laws (WLUML), the Sisterhood is Global Institute (SIGI), and Development Alternatives with Women for a New Era (DAWN) link feminists and women's groups in developed and developing countries alike (Moghadam 2000). It is no longer possible to speak of a feminism for the West versus a different set of priorities for the developing world. Feminists from around the world are now agreed on the basic issues of education, income, and reproductive rights for women, no matter what the cultural context, and they are struggling for greater political representation and participation in economic decision-making. Feminist movements have proliferated in the Muslim world—for example, in Algeria, Turkey, Morocco, Iran, and Pakistan—and they have taken strong objection to discourses of cultural relativism (Afkhami 1995; Peters and Wolper 1995; WLUML 1998). Cultural relativism and the "hands off" approach of the past are explicitly rejected by feminist networks such as WLUML, as well as by Afghan women's groups such as RAWA and WAPHA.

Patriarchy, Public Space, and Women's Place

A number of scholars have taken issue with the public/private distinction that was originally established by feminist anthropology in the early 1970s (e.g., Rosaldo 1974; Reiter 1975). Cynthia Nelson (1974), for example, objected to the dichotomization of public and private and attempted to re-orient the approach to separate worlds. Although she acknowledged that ethnographic studies supported the idea of segregated social worlds, her suggestion was that

> rather than seeing this as a severe limitation on women, the evidence suggests that the segregation of women can alternatively be seen as an exclusion of men from a range of contacts which women have among themselves. ... women form their own exclusive solidarity groups and ... these groups exercise considerable social control. Also, by seeking alliance and support from other women in the community, certain women achieve high social status in the community and consequently exercise political influence (Nelson 1974: 556).

Nelson provided no empirical evidence for this statement and her research on Egypt did not support this.

In my view, we should continue to view gender-segregated social worlds (like racially segregated social worlds) as a severe limitation, an expression of unequal power, an indication of exclusion, and a form of social control by men over women. It cannot be denied that males in patriarchal societies such as Afghanistan continue to control not only their female relatives' access to public space, but also the access of women as a social group. What are the mechanisms of such control? They are varied and include: familial and household rules and constraints; compulsory veiling; laws that restrict women's mobility and travel; the appropriation of coffee shops and tea houses by men; and men's tendency to stare, leer, or touch women. Why the need to control and confine women? Certainly there is an ideological interest. Women's segregation has often been seen as central to the honor–shame complex, about which so much has been written for the Mediterranean context (e.g., Pitt-Rivers 1977). The honor–shame complex, a key element of classic patriarchy, rests on women's behavior and the control of their sexuality. But this ideological interest in controlling women and confining them to the private sphere derives from material interests, such as the marriage market and the exchange of women that I have described in connection with Afghanistan. Furthermore, controlling women's access to public space reduces men's competition over public goods and economic resources. It is perhaps no accident that, precisely when Middle Eastern and Muslim women were beginning to become "visible" through educational attainment and entry into the paid labor-force, fundamentalist Islamist movements appeared, with their demands that women retreat to domesticity, that they appear in public only when veiled, and that they work in segregated environments. Fundamentalists seek, among other things, to redefine the boundaries between the public and private and to put women "in their place" partly to reinforce their control over women's sexuality and partly to reinforce male ownership over the means of production. As such, the fundamentalist project threatens to reproduce patriarchal power relationships and male privilege, and to reinforce gender inequalities. The case of Afghanistan illustrates this perfectly.

The patriarchal project does have the support of some women, who find security and status in family life and who prefer not to have to negotiate in the public sphere. Other women, however, challenge the public/private distinction in subtle but subversive ways: they take in home-work; they use nearby empty plots of land to raise vegetables and fruits; they organize community festivals. Another category of women, usually those with higher education or secular worldviews, reject the idea of their relegation to the private sphere; they actively seek employment, join women's organizations, and agitate to change family and personal status laws that restrict women's mobility.

The concepts of public space and private space are perhaps nowhere more relevant than in Afghanistan, where women's access to public space has long been politicized, contested, and denied. The disciplining and exclusion of women in Afghanistan has been a reflection of the tribal, patriarchal nature of Afghan society and of Afghanistan's peripheralization from late-twentieth-century global developments, including emancipatory social movements such as feminism. When the patriarchal code and social structure restrict women to the role of producer of carpets and reproducer of children, women who do not conform to the communitarian ideal are viewed as a threat. The greatest threat to the patriarchal community and the power of men is posed by "public women"—those who work, or go to school, or even walk from one place to another.

All of this should be understood as the result of the patriarchal social structure and persistent tribal rivalries—in addition to interventions by foreign powers—which have precluded the implementation of projects of nation-building, citizenship, and the advancement of women in Afghanistan.

Postscript

As this article was being revised for publication (November–December 2001), the Taliban regime was collapsing in the face of US air raids. The government of US President George Bush Jr initiated the bombardment in the wake of the 11 September 2001 terrorist plane crashes into Washington DC's Pentagon and the twin towers of New York City's World Trade Center, which resulted in over 3000 deaths and considerable property and financial damage. The attacks were allegedly carried out by a network headed by Osama Bin Laden, who had been given safe haven in Afghanistan by the Taliban. The US government launched air raids into Afghanistan when the Taliban allegedly refused to turn over Osama Bin Laden.

The air raids allowed for the mobilization of the Northern Alliance, a regrouping of former Mujahideen forces. For some, this was alarming, given that not a single Mujahideen leader had been made accountable for the crimes committed during 1992–96. Nor had the Northern Alliance shown itself to be concerned with women's rights or human rights. At this writing, one can only hope that as plans are being made for a post-Taliban government, elections, and a new constitution, women's voices will not be muted and women's rights will not be sacrificed again. Instead, the institutionalization of women's civil, political, and social rights should be at the top of any diplomatic agenda and political settlement. It is encouraging that the interim government that was formed at the December 2001 meetings in Bonn, Germany, included two women, one of whom was Dr Soheila (mentioned above), who was given the post of Minister of Health. But the welfare and rights of Afghan women depend very much on the success of peace-building and the reconstruction and development of the country's social and physical infrastructure.

Given Afghanistan's underdevelopment and patriarchal social structure, a long-term strategy is needed for peace-building, reconstruction, and development in Afghanistan in which women's rights (and ethnic rights and human rights more generally) are central. This could be accomplished through at least two strategic initiatives. One would be the formation of an Afghan Fund for Peace, Reconstruction and Development, to which all states-parties to the conflicts of the 1980s and since should contribute. This fund would be administered by the United Nations toward peace-keeping, reconstruction, and social and economic development, keeping women's security, participation, and empowerment at the forefront of all programs, projects, and policies. The second strategic initiative that I would recommend is the formation of a Roundtable on Afghanistan—to consist of Afghan intellectuals, women activists, former civil servants, representatives of Afghan organizations and political groups, academics with expertise on Afghanistan, and others with experience in similar cases of conflict. This Roundtable would meet regularly and engage in dialogue, diplomacy, and planning with respect to conflict resolution, peace-building, reconstruction, state-building, human rights, women's empowerment, and socio-economic development in Afghanistan. The Roundtable could constitute one of the building blocks of a modern civil society in Afghanistan.

As this article has shown, Afghan women have suffered oppression, exclusion, and deprivation for a very long time. Any post-Taliban political arrangement must guarantee the allocation of resources toward social investments in women and girls. Investing in the women of Afghanistan and ensuring that women's groups participate in negotiations and decision-making are necessary steps to bring about development, modernization, and women's rights in Afghanistan.

References

Afkhami, Mahnaz, Ed. (1995). *Faith and Freedom: Women's Human Rights in the Muslim World*. Syracuse, NY: Syracuse University Press.

Amnesty International. (1995). *Women in Afghanistan: A Human Rights Catastrophe*. New York: Amnesty International.

———. (1996). *Focus*, 12.

Appasamy, Paul, S. Guhan, R. Hema, M. Majumdar and A. Vaidyanathan. (1996). *Social Exclusion From a Welfare Rights Perspective in India*. Geneva: ILO.

Applewhite, Harriet B. and Darline Levy, Eds. (1990). *Women and Politics in the Age of the Democratic Revolution*. Ann Arbor: University of Michigan Press.

Beattie, Hugh. (1984). "Effects of the Saur Revolution in Nahrin." Nazif Shahrani and Robert Canfield, Eds. *Revolutions and Rebellions in Afghanistan*. Berkeley: University of California Press.

Brown, Derek. (1992). "New Afghanistan Carries on Grisly Game of the Old." *Guardian* (UK). 4 May: 7.

Bunch, Charlotte and Niamh Reilly. (1994). *Demanding Accountability: The Global Campaign and the Vienna Tribunal for Women's Human Rights*. New Brunswick, NJ: Center for Women's Global Leadership.

Burns, John. (1996). "Roots of Repression: A Special Report. How Afghans' Stern Rulers Took Hold." *New York Times*. 31 December: p. A1.

Caldwell, John. (1982). *Theory of Fertility Decline*. London: Academic Press.

Centlivres-Demont, Micheline. (1994). "Afghan Women in Peace, War, and Exile." Myron Weiner and Ali Banuazizi, Eds. *The Politics of Social Transformation in Afghanistan, Iran, and Pakistan*. Syracuse, NY: Syracuse University Press: 333–65.

Cordovez, Diego and Selig Harrison. (1995). *Out of Afghanistan: The Inside Story of the Soviet Withdrawal*. New York: Oxford University Press.

De Haan, Arjan. (1999). *Social Exclusion: Towards a Holistic Understanding of Deprivation*. London: Department for International Development.

Doubleday, Veronica. (1988). *Three Women of Herat*. Austin: University of Texas Press.

Dupree, Nancy Haztch. (1984). "Revolutionary Rhetoric and Afghan Women." Nazif Shahrani and Robert Canfield, Eds. *Revolutions and Rebellions in Afghanistan*. Berkeley: University of California Press: 306–40.

Goodwin, Jan. (1987). *Caught in the Crossfire*. New York: Dutton.

Gregorian, Vartan. (1969). *The Emergence of Modern Afghanistan*. Stanford University Press.

Halliday, Fred. (1978). "Revolution in Afghanistan." *New Left Review 112* (November–December).

——. (1996). "The Un-Great Game," *The New Republic*. 25 March: 38–42.

Hassan, Habiba. (1995). "Women in Afghanistan." *Pakistan Journal of Women's Studies: Alam-e Niswam 2* (2): 105–10.

Howard-Merriam, Kathleen. (1987). "Afghan Women and their Struggle for Survival." Grant Farr and John Merriam, Eds. *The Afghan Conflict: The Politics of Survival*. Boulder, CO: Westview Press: 103–14.

Kamali, Mohammad Hashim. (1985). *Law in Afghanistan: A Study of the Constitutions, Matrimonial Law and the Judiciary*. Leiden: E. J. Brill.

Kandiyoti, Deniz. (1988). "Bargaining with Patriarchy." *Gender and Society*, 2 (3): 274–90.

Katzikas, Suzanne Jolicoeur. (1982). *The Arc of Socialist Revolution: Angola to Afghanistan*. Cambridge, MA: Schenkman Publishing Co.

Lessing, Doris. (1987). *The Wind Blows Away our Words*. New York: Vintage.

Massell, Gregory. (1974). *The Surrogate Proletariat: Moslem Women and Revolutionary Strategies in Soviet Central Asia, 1919–1929*. Princeton, NJ: Princeton University Press.

Migdal, Joel. (1988). *Strong Societies and Weak States: State–Society Relations and State Capabilities in the Third World*. Princeton, NJ: Princeton University Press.

Mishra, Pankaj. (2001). "The Making of Afghanistan." *The New York Review of Books*. 15 November: 18–21.

Moghadam, Val. (1989a). "Against Eurocentrism and Nativism: A Review Essay on Samir Amin's *Eurocentrism* and Other Texts." *Socialism and Democracy* (The Graduate Center, City University of New York) 9, Fall–Winter: 81–104.

——. (1989b). "Revolution, the State, Islam and Women: Sexual Politics in Iran and Afghanistan." *Social Text 22* (Spring): 40–61.

——. (1992). "Patriarchy and the Politics of Gender in Modernizing Societies: Iran, Pakistan and Afghanistan." *International Sociology 7* (1): 35–54.

——. (1993). "Women and Social Change in Afghanistan." In Valentine E. Moghadam, Ed. *Modernizing Women: Gender and Social Change in the Middle East*. Boulder, CO: Lynne Rienner Publishers.

——. (1994). "Building Human Resources and Women's Capabilities in Afghanistan: A Retrospect and Prospects." *World Development* 22 (6): 859–76.

——. 1999. "Revolution, Religion and Gender Politics: Iran and Afghanistan Compared." *Journal of Women's History 10* (4): 172–95.

——. (2000). "Transnational Feminist Networks: Collective Action in an Era of Globalization." *International Sociology 15* (1): 57–85.

Nawid, Senzil K. (1999). *Religious Response to Social Change in Afghanistan, 1919–29*. Costa Mesa, CA: Mazda Publishers.

Nelson, Cynthia. (1974). "Public and Private Politics: Women in the Middle Eastern World." *American Ethnologist 1* (3): 551–63.

Pateman, Carol. (1988). *The Sexual Contract*. Cambridge, UK: Polity Press.

Peters, Julie and Andrea Wolper, Eds. (1995). *Women's Rights Human Rights: International Feminist Perspectives*. New York and London: Routledge.

Physicians for Human Rights. (1998). *The Taliban's War on Women: A Health and Human Rights Crisis in Afghanistan*. Boston and Washington, DC: Physicians for Human Rights.

——. (2001). *Women's Health and Human Rights in Afghanistan: A Population-Based Assessment*. Boston and Washington, DC: Physicians for Human Rights.

Pitt-Rivers, Julian. (1977). *The Fate of Shechem or the Politics of Sex: Essays in the Anthropology of the Mediterranean*. Cambridge, UK: Cambridge University Press.

Rashid, Ahmed. (2000). *Taliban: Militant Islam, Oil and Fundamentalism in Central Asia*. New Haven: Yale University Press.

Reiter, Rayna. (1975). "Men and Women in the South of France: Public and Private Domains." In Rayna Reiter, Ed. *Toward an Anthropology of Women*. New York: Monthly Review Press.

Rosaldo, Michelle. (1974). "Theoretical Overview." M. Z. Rosaldo and L. Lamphere, Eds. *Woman, Culture, and Society*. Stanford University Press: 17–43.

Rubin, Barnett. (1995). *The Fragmentation of Afghanistan*. New Haven: Yale University Press.

Said, Edward. (1978). *Orientalism*. New York: Vintage.

Shirkat Gah/Women Living Under Muslim Laws. (1996). *Newsheet 8* (3), November.

Stiglmayer, Alexandra, Ed. (1994). *Mass Rape: The War Against Women in Bosnia-Herzegovina*. Trans. Marion Faber. Lincoln: University of Nebraska Press.

Tapper, Nancy. (1984). "Causes and Consequences of the Abolition of Brideprice in Afghanistan." In Nazif Shahrani and Robert Canfield, Eds. *Revolutions and Rebellions in Afghanistan*. Berkeley: University of California Press: 291–305.

——. (1991). *Bartered Brides: Politics, Gender and Marriage in an Afghan Tribal Society*. Cambridge, UK: Cambridge University Press.

Urban, Mark. (1988). *War in Afghanistan*. New York: St Martin's Press.

Women Living Under Muslim Laws [WLUML]. (1998). *Women's Situation in Afghanistan/La situation des femmes en Afghanistan: Compilation*. Montpelier: WLUML.

World Bank. (1988). *Social Indicators of Development, 1988*. Baltimore: Johns Hopkins University Press.

Karen Talbot

Afghanistan, Central Asia, Georgia: Key to Oil Profits

An earlier version was published in *Global Outlook*, Spring 2002.

By putting various pieces of the puzzle together we begin to get a picture of what really is behind Bush's "war on terrorism". We see that the groundwork for the current US military actions in Afghanistan was being built up for several years.

What comes into focus is that the horrific September 11 terrorist attacks have, among other things, provided a qualitatively new opportunity for the US, acting especially on behalf of giant oil companies, to permanently entrench its military in the former Soviet Republics of Central Asia and the Caucasus, where there are vast petroleum reserves—the second-largest in the world. Strategically, this also positions US armed might on the western doorstep of China, posing an unprecedented threat not only to those countries but to South Asia and the entire world. Particularly, the way is now open to jump-start projects for oil and gas pipelines through western Afghanistan and Pakistan, including to Karachi on the Arabian Sea—the most feasible and cheapest route for transporting those fuels to market. Afghanistan itself has untapped oil and gas, as does Pakistan.[1] So too, the recent deployment of US military personnel in the Pankisi Gorge of Georgia, ostensibly to fight terrorists, is aimed at guaranteeing and protecting the projected Baku–Tbilisi–Ceyhan (Turkey) pipeline designed to bypass Russia and Iran. Meanwhile, US energy companies have been feverishly exploring a section of the Caspian Sea, flouting the legalities and disputes surrounding jurisdiction over these sectors, especially between Azerbaijan and Iran.[2]

---

1 "Massive untapped gas reserves are believed to be lying beneath Pakistan's remotest deserts, but they are being held hostage by armed tribal groups demanding a better deal from the central government," reported Agence France Presse just days before September 11, says Nina Burleigh for TomPaine.com.

2 Armen Georgian (2002), "US Eyes Caspian Oil in 'War on Terrorism.'" *Foreign Policy in Focus*, 30 April.

Some pundits say Washington merely seeks to guarantee supplies of oil for US consumers, which explains why it claims Central Asia to be in its zone of "national interests". In reality, the US relies heavily on domestic sources and on Venezuela, Canada, and Africa.[3] No, this is about oil corporation profits which can be greatly enhanced, especially by selling to energy-hungry South, East, and South–East Asia, and by outflanking China and Russia for those Central Asian–Caspian Sea Basin energy resources and for the pipelines to transport them to market.

Supplies of natural gas and oil, including those from newly discovered huge oil reserves in Kazakhstan, can easily be piped through existing conduits traversing Russia. But bypassing, and thus hindering, Russian petroleum operations which rely heavily on European customers, would provide Western corporations another benefit. They would gain greater access to the European market. Building the Afghanistan pipelines would also mean spurning an even more direct route to the Arabian Sea through Iran. This would thwart the growing cooperation between Iran, Russia and the European oil companies which have invested heavily in Iran's oil and gas sectors, all of whom are pursuing that pipeline corridor. This is a major factor in the growing rivalry between the US and Europe in the ongoing imperial quest for corporate expansion.

The Great Oil Game

Frank Viviano, in an article in the *San Francisco Chronicle* asserts:

> The hidden stakes in the war against terrorism can be summed up in a single word: oil … It is inevitable that the war against terrorism will be seen by many as a war on behalf of America's Chevron, Exxon, and Arco; France's TotalFinaElf; British Petroleum; Royal Dutch Shell and other multinational giants, which have hundreds of billions of dollars of investment in the region … developing nations [are] already convinced … of a conspiratorial collaboration between global capital and US military might.[4]

Writing in the Hong Kong-based *Asia Times*, a business-oriented publication, Ranjit Devraj states: "Just as the Gulf War in 1991 was about oil, the new conflict in South and Central Asia is no less about access to the region's abundant petroleum resource."[5]

---

3 US National Security Council (1998), *A National Security Strategy for a New Century*. Washington, DC: White House, October: 32, as reported by Michael T. Klare, *Resource Wars*. New York: Metropolitan Books, Henry Holt.

4 Frank Viviano (2001), "Energy Future Rides on US War: Conflict Centered in World's Oil Patch." *San Francisco Chronicle*, 26 September.

5 Ranjit Devraj, *Asia Time*.

The very nature of the system inevitably drives corporations to expand or die. This will be done at any cost, no matter the suffering it may bring to human beings or the devastation it unleashes upon the environment. Such are the characteristics of today's imperialism, the main source of war, terrorism and violence. Commerce in oil remains paramount in this process. More than ever, these imperial foreign and military policies are being carried out by top US government leaders, from the President and Vice-President to CIA officials who have direct ties to the corporations and banks which stand to derive super profits from them. This is particularly true of the oil, energy, banking, and military–aerospace sectors.

Unocal and Afghanistan

A consortium headed by Unocal had for years sought to build a gas pipeline from Turkmenistan's Dauletabad gas field through Afghanistan and Pakistan to the Arabian Sea. Later they put together a larger consortium, the Central Asia Pipeline Project, to carry oil from the Chardzhou oil field, essentially following the same route.[6]

John J. Maresca, vice-president of Unocal, in testimony before a House of Representatives committee (12 February 1998), spoke of the tremendous untapped hydrocarbon reserves in the Caspian region and promoted the plan to build a pipeline through Afghanistan as the cheapest route to transport the oil to Asian markets. He stated that the Taliban controlled the territory through which the pipeline would extend. Pointing out that most nations did not recognize that government, he emphasized that the project could not begin until a recognized government was in place.[7]

Yet, a major reason for Washington's support of the Taliban between 1994 and 1997 was the expectation that they would swiftly conquer the whole country enabling Unocal to build a pipeline through Afghanistan. Pakistan, the US, and Saudi Arabia "are responsible for the very existence and maintenance of the Taliban".[8]

In his book *Taliban*, Central Asian expert Ahmed Rashid said:

---

6 Ishtiaq Ahmad (2001), "US–Taliban Relations: Friend Turns Fiend." Lecturer in International Relations, Eastern Mediterranean University, North Cyprus, Nicosia, 3 October, www.tehelka.com/channels/currentaffairs/2001/oct/3/ca100301usl. htm.

7 John J. Maresca, vice-president of Unocal, in testimony before a committee of the US House of Representatives, 12 February, 1998.

8 Larry P. Goodson (2001), *Afghanistan's Endless War*. Seattle and London: University of Washington Press: 81.

Impressed by the ruthlessness and willingness of the then-emerging Taliban to cut a pipeline deal, the State Department and Pakistan's Inter-Services Intelligence agency agreed to funnel arms and funding to the Taliban in their war against the ethnically Tajik Northern Alliance. As recently as 1999, US taxpayers paid the entire annual salary of every single Taliban government official.[9]

Unocal had even secured agreement from the Taliban to build the pipeline, according to Hugh Pope, writing in the *Wall Street Journal*.[10]

The *Washington Post* on 25 May 2001 reported that the US government "pledged another $43 million in assistance to Afghanistan, [the Taliban government] raising total aid this year to $124 million and making the United States the largest humanitarian donor to the country".[11] This was less than four months before the September 11 attacks. In an article in the British *Daily Mirror*, John Pilger stated:

> When the Taliban took Kabul in 1996, Washington said nothing. Why? Because Taliban leaders were soon on their way to Houston, Texas, to be entertained by executives of the oil company, Unocal. With secret US government approval, the company offered them a generous cut of the profits of the oil and gas pumped through a pipeline that the Americans wanted to build from the Soviet Central Asia through Afghanistan ... Although the deal fell through, it remains an urgent priority of the administration of George W. Bush, which is steeped in the oil industry. Bush's concealed agenda is to exploit the oil and gas reserves in the Caspian basin ... Only if the pipeline runs through Afghanistan can the Americans hope to control it.[12]

Taliban Wanted More

An Argentine oil company, Bridas, was also in the bidding to build a pipeline. The same month Taliban representatives were being given red-carpet treatment by Unocal in Texas, another delegation went to Buenos Aires to meet with Bridas executives. There was an intense campaign by Unocal and Washington to out-maneuver Bridas. The Taliban played one company against the other.[13]

---

9 Ted Rall (2001), "It's About Oil." *San Francisco Chronicle*, 2 November: A25.

10 Hugh Pope (1997), "Unocal Group Plans Central Asian Pipeline," *Wall Street Journal*, 27 October.

11 *Washington Post*, 25 May 2001.

12 John Pilger (2001), "This War is a Fraud." *Daily Mirror*, 29 October.

13 Rall, "It's About Oil".

The Taliban and Osama Bin Laden were demanding as part of the deal that Unocal rebuild the infrastructure in Afghanistan and allow them access to the oil in several places. Unocal rejected this demand.[14]

Nevertheless, the Bush Administration held a series of negotiations with the Taliban early in 2001, despite the developing rift with them over the pipeline scheme. Laila Helms, who was hired as the public relations agent for the Taliban government, brought Rahmatullah Hashimi, an adviser to Mullah Omar, to Washington as recently as March 2001. (Helms is the niece of Richard Helms, former chief of the CIA and former Ambassador to Iran.) One of the negotiating meetings was held on 2 August, just one month before September 11, when Christina Rocca, in charge of Asian Affairs at the State Department, met Taliban Ambassador to Pakistan Abdul Salem Zaef in Islamabad. Rocca has had extensive connections with Afghanistan, including supervising the delivery of Stinger missiles to the mujahideen in the 1980s. She had been in charge of contacts with Islamist fundamentalist guerrilla groups for the CIA.[15]

"At one moment during one of the negotiations, US representatives told the Taliban, 'either you accept our offer of a carpet of gold, or we bury you under a carpet of bombs'," said Charles Brisard, co-author of *Bin Laden, the Forbidden Truth*.[16]

When Washington decided to break with the Taliban, they took advantage of the fact that that the UN had continued to refuse to recognize their government. Then, of course, the Taliban suddenly became more vulnerable after September 11, for "harboring" Osama Bin Laden; thus it became much easier to win international support for bombing them. Another compelling reason may have been that the Northern Alliance forces, with whom the US would have to join forces, controlled the portion of the country near Turkmenistan, Tajikistan and Uzbekistan, whose governments were helping to support the Alliance. This offered a way for the US military to base troops in those countries. The Northern Alliance consists largely of ethnic Uzbeks and Tajiks, whereas the Taliban is made up of Pashtun tribesmen in addition to large

---

14 Ahmad, "US–Taliban Relations."

15 Ibid.

16 Charles Brisard and Guillaume Dasquie, *Bin Laden, La Vérite Interdite* (Bin Laden, the Forbidden Truth). Brisard had worked for the French secret service (DST) and wrote a report for them in 1997 on the al-Qaeda network. Dasquie is a journalist and publisher of the "Intelligence Online". As reported by V. K. Shashikumar, New Delhi, 21 November 2001, www.tehelka.com/channels/currentaffairs/2001/nov/21/call2112101america.htm.

numbers from Pakistan, Arab countries, and elsewhere, who had come to be trained and to fight in Afghanistan as well as in Chechnya, Kashmir, Bosnia, Kosovo, and former Soviet republics in Central Asia.

CIA Spawns Taliban

All of these disparate mujahideen forces led by feudal landholders and warlords and Osama Bin Laden's organization were incubated by the CIA in the 1980s when the largest-ever covert operation was carried out in Afghanistan. It was directed against the newly born government of the Saur Revolution (which gave equal rights to women and set up healthcare, literacy, housing, job creation and land reform programs) and then against the Soviets. The mujahideen who had been trained and armed by the CIA murdered teachers, doctors, and nurses, tortured women for not wearing the veil, and shot down civilian airliners with US-supplied Stinger missiles.[17]

The story sold to the public by the media is that the US and some Islamic countries began supporting the mujahideen to help them repel the Soviet invasion of Afghanistan which began on 24 December 1979. Actually, President Jimmy Carter secretly approved CIA efforts to try to topple the government of Afghanistan in July 1979, knowing that the US actions were likely to provoke Soviet intervention. Zbigniew Brzezinski, National Security Adviser in the Carter Administration, confirmed this in an interview with the French publication *Le Nouvel Observateur*.[18]

A remarkable description of CIA operations in Afghanistan can be found in the book *Victory: The Reagan Administration's Secret Strategy that Hastened the Collapse of the Soviet Union*.[19] The book carries many boastful accounts by William Casey, Director of the CIA under President Reagan. It paints a vivid picture of how Casey himself convinced the Saudi Arabians to match CIA funding of the mujahideen, and how all the money, arms and training were funneled through the Pakistan Intelligence Service (ISI).

According to the book,

> The strategy [to bring down the USSR under Reagan] attacked the very heart of the Soviet system and included ... [among several other key operations] substantial

---

17 Phillip Bonosky (2001), *Afghanistan: Washington's Secret War*. New York: International Publishers, 2nd ed.

18 *Le Nouvel Observateur*, 15–21 January 1998. (This is not included in the edition sent to the US.) Reported by and translated from original French by Bill Blum, author of "Killing Hope".

19 Peter Schweizer (1994), *Victory: The Reagan Administration's Secret Strategy that Hastened the Collapse of the Soviet Union*. New York: Atlantic Monthly Press.

financial and military support to the Afghan resistance [*sic*], as well as supplying the mujahideen personnel to take the war into the Soviet Union itself ... [and a] campaign to reduce dramatically Soviet hard-currency earnings by driving down the price of oil with Saudi cooperation and limiting natural gas exports to the West ...

We learn about the quantities of weapons that were delivered and how—including Stinger missiles and increasingly sophisticated armaments. One account states: "Tens of thousands of arms and ammunition were going through ... every year", rising to 65,000 tons by 1985. Approximately 100 Afghans living abroad were schooled in the "art of arms shipping ... Two-week courses in anti-tank and anti-aircraft guns, mine laying and lifting, demolitions, urban warfare and sabotage were offered for thousands of fighters ... Twenty thousand mujahideen were being pumped out every year by these schools dubbed 'CIA U' by some wags."

Concerning incursions into the USSR, the book relates: "Specially trained units working inside the Soviet Union would be equipped with ... rocket launchers and high-tech explosives provided by the CIA. They were to seek out Soviet civilian and military targets for sabotage."

This is just a small taste of the details revealed in *Victory*.[20]

New Made-in-the-USA Government

The disparate warlord-led factions, including the Taliban, all part of the CIA-financed mujahideen, have continued to fight each other for years. As always, the ascendancy of one group over another inevitably leads to more fractious-ness and warfare.

The newly established "interim" government of Afghanistan, conjured up by George W. Bush and his entourage, purports to include all of these militias, along with various Pashtun warlords who are linked with the Taliban.

Unocal Emerges Again

This "interim" government is headed by Hamid Karzai. According to the Saudi newspaper *Al-Watan*, Karzai has been a CIA covert operator since the 1980s, when he helped the CIA in Afghanistan. Karzai supported the Taliban and was a consultant for Unocal.[21] George W. Bush's envoy to the new government, Zalmay Khalilzad, also worked for Unocal. He drew up the risk analysis for the pipeline in 1997, lobbied for the Taliban and took part in negotiations with them. After acquiring US citizenship, Khalilzad became a special adviser to the State Department during the Reagan administration and

---

20 Ibid.

21 Tim Wheeler (2002), "Bush Calls for Wider War, Is Silent on Enron." *People's Weekly World*, 2 February.

THE EURASIAN CORRIDOR

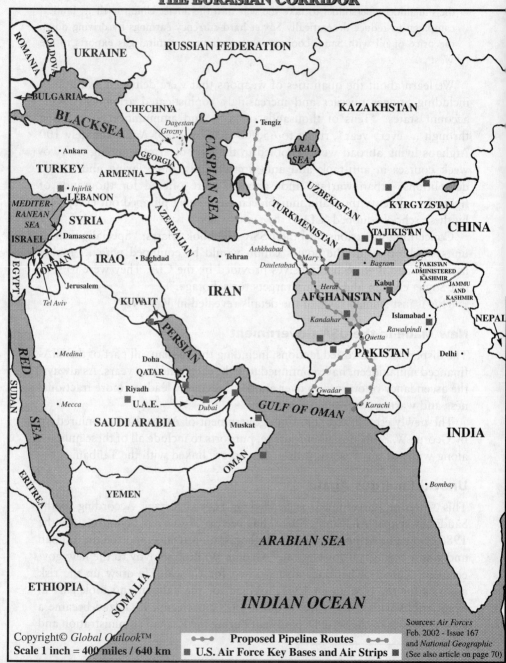

Copyright© *Global Outlook*™
Scale 1 inch = 400 miles / 640 km

→●→●→ **Proposed Pipeline Routes** ←●←●←
■ **U.S. Air Force Key Bases and Air Strips** ■

Sources: *Air Forces*
Feb. 2002 - Issue 167
and *National Geographic*
(See also article on page 70)

a key liaison with the mujahideen in the 1980s. He was under-secretary of defense in the administration of the elder George Bush; headed the Bush–Cheney transition team for the Defense Department; worked for the right-wing think-tank Rand Corporation; and was placed on the National Security Council where he reports to National Security Adviser Condoleezza Rice.[22] Rice is an expert on Central Asia, and a member of the Board of Chevron. Both Khalilzad and Rice had long advocated the establishment of US military bases in the region.

Enron and other Bush Connections

The direct connections between Bush Administration personnel and the oil, energy, and military-industrial corporations and with intrigues in Central Asian and the Caucasus are very intimate ones. Here are only a few: The proposed Baku–Ceyhan pipeline is represented by the law firm of Baker & Botts. The principal attorney is James Baker, former secretary of state and chief spokesman for the Bush campaign in the struggle over Florida votes.[23] In 1994, Cheney, as CEO of Halliburton, was a member of Kazakhstan's Oil Advisory Board and helped broker a deal between Chevron and Kazakhstan. Enron Corporation, closely linked with Bush and Cheney, conducted the feasibility study for the $2.5 billion Trans-Caspian pipeline—a joint venture with Turkmenistan, Bechtel Corp and General Electric.[24]

Moreover, Enron had a $3 billion investment in the Dabhol power plant near Mumbai, India, one of its largest-ever projects, constituting the single biggest direct foreign investment in India's history. There was massive public opposition to the project in India, including ultimately by the Indian government, due to the huge costs to consumers (700 per cent more than from other sources). Enron's survival depended on getting a cheap source of gas and oil to save the project. This could be solved by the building of a branch of the proposed natural gas pipeline from Turkmenistan through Afghanistan to terminate in Multan near the Indian border. In addition, in 1997, Enron announced it was going to spend over $1 billion building and improving the lines between the Dabhol plant and India's pipeline network. In other words, the gas would be piped from Multan, Pakistan, to New Delhi, thence to Mumbai and the Enron plant.[25]

---

22 Patrick Martin (2002), "Oil Company Advisor Named US Representative to Afghanistan." 3 January, World Socialist Web Site.

23 Salim Muwakkil (2002), OutlookIndia.com, 21 March.

24 Ibid.

25 Ron Callari (2002), "The Enron–Cheney–Taliban Connection?" *Albion Monitor*, 28 February.

Enron was expecting also to cash in on the main spur of the pipeline ending on the Pakistan coast, from which hydrocarbon supplies would be exported to the other vast Asian markets. Clearly, developments in Afghanistan were critical to Enron. George W. Bush became president just at the point when the India project was in serious trouble. One month later, Vice-President Dick Cheney moved into action and held his first secret meeting with Enron CEO Kenneth Lay. The Bush administration is refusing to reveal the details of this and subsequent consultations with Lay, even in the face of a suit by the General Accounting Office suit against Cheney for release of the papers. Nevertheless, it has been documented that the Vice-President's energy taskforce did change a draft energy proposal to include a provision to boost oil and natural gas production in India in February 2001. The amendment was clearly targeted to help Enron's Dabhol plant. Later, Cheney stepped in to try to help Enron collect its $64 million debt during a 27 June meeting with India's opposition leader Sonia Gandhi. These are but some revelations concerning the machinations by Bush and his cohorts to help Enron regarding the India deal.[26] Some of the negotiations with the Taliban, such as those led by Christina Rocca, to promote the trans-Afghan pipeline and thus also to help save Enron, coincidentally transpired just prior to the September 11 terrorist attacks.

Brown & Root—a business unit of Halliburton Company, where Vice-President Cheney was CEO until taking office—will be upgrading the US air base in Uzbekistan. According to an article in *Stars and Stripes*,

> Brown & Root scouts traveled to Central Asia [including Afghanistan] to check out US bases … By mid-June the contractor is expected to take charge of base camp maintenance, airfield services and fuel supplies. For troops' welfare the company will run the dining halls and laundry service and will oversee the Morale, Welfare and Recreation program.[27]

Brown & Root perform similar lucrative services at other bases including those in Bosnia and Kosovo, most notably the giant and permanent Camp Bondsteel in Kosovo, located conveniently—along with satellite bases—near the soon-to-be-constructed trans-Balkan Albanian–Macedonian–Bulgarian oil pipeline.

---

26 Ibid.

27 Rick Scavetta (2002), *Stars and Stripes*, 2 May.

US Bases in Afghanistan and Former Soviet Republics

"If one looks at the map of the big American bases created for the war in Afghanistan, one is struck by the fact that they are completely identical to the route of the projected oil pipelines to the Indian Ocean," says Uri Averny, a former member of the Israeli Knesset (parliament), writing in the daily *Ma'ariv* in Israel.[28]

In the name of conducting the war, the US also won agreement to station troops at former Soviet airfields in Uzbekistan and Tajikistan and to build a long-term base in Kyrgyzstan. Kazakhstan is next.[29] The big payoff for the Bush Administration is the entrenchment of a permanent US military presence in oil-rich Central Asia—which is also wide open to another coveted resource-rich region, Siberia. Thus, realization of other goals could be closer at hand—the further balkanization of Central Asian and trans-Caucasus nations into easily controlled emirate-like entities, lacking any real sovereignty—and further military encirclement of China. All of this is icing on the cake—the "cake" being the trans-Afghanistan pipelines with their access to and dominance of the South, South-East and East Asian markets.

Another major goal of Bush Administration policies appears to be to obstruct or control China's access to the oil and natural gas of Central Asia. China has a rapidly increasing need for those sources of energy. It has relatively few reserves within its borders, the largest being in Tibet. China has joint partnership with US companies for the development of its oil. Nevertheless, as is always the case, those US-based oil conglomerates would much prefer to get their hands on the whole pie and not just a large slice. That includes unfettered access to Chinese consumers.

Potentially vast sources of petroleum and natural gas have been discovered in the South China Sea. A struggle is looming among the littoral states regarding jurisdiction over these offshore reserves, with China laying claim to a large portion of the sea including the Spratly and Paracel Islands. The Philippine government is one of the disputants over this territory. The Philippines are strategically located in this region and adjacent to the critically important sea lanes through which oil and other goods are shipped to and from Japan, China and Korea. Kellogg Brown & Root just built the largest offshore oil platform in the world for Shell Philippines.[30] The current US

---

28 Uri Averny (2002), *Ma'ariv*, Israel, 14 February.

29 Michael R. Gordon and C. J. Chivers (2001), "US, Tajikistan Make a Deal on Military Cooperation." *San Francisco Chronicle*, 5 November: A4.

30 "Malampaya Topsides Installed in the South China Sea." Kellog Brown & Root, Press Release, 28 March 2001, http://www.halliburton.com/KBR/KBRNWS/ KBRNWS_032801.

"war on terrorism" military operations in the Philippines are clearly linked to major oil considerations. Bush's perpetual war is already headed towards Iraq, Somalia, Yemen, and Iran—not so coincidentally, these are all rich in petroleum. So too, the ongoing US-backed brutal Israeli war against the Palestinians continues to be about maintaining US hegemony over the oil-rich Middle East. US military support to Colombia is now openly admitted by the Bush Administration to be aimed at protecting pipelines and putting down the peoples' insurgency. Similarly, the recent US-backed coup attempt against the Chavez government of Venezuela had much to do with controlling that country's petroleum riches.

Increasingly, US and world public opinion is awakening to the hidden agenda of the "war on terrorism" earmarked by the corporate frenzy to plunder oil and other resources, particularly in the petroleum-rich arch stretching from the Middle East to South-East Asia. The war in Afghanistan is central to reaping super profits from all that "black gold".

Update

A two-day summit meeting began on 29 May by President General Pervez Musharraf of Pakistan, Hamid Karzai of Afghanistan and Saparmyrat Niyazov of Turkmenistan. The purpose of the sumit was to conclude a tri-partite agreement to proceed with the construction of the parallel oil and gas pipelines from the Dauletabad fields in Turkmenistan via Afghanistan to Multan in Pakistan. With an additional 6000 million dollars, the pipelines might be extended to India, according to the Pakistan newspaper *Dawn*. Afghanistan is to provide security for the lines through its territory.

According to *Dawn*, US companies were trying to "block entry" of Argentinian firm Bridas and Russian Gazprom from landing contracts for the project. (From Deutsche Presse-Agentur, 27 May 2002.)

Farida Akhter

Huntington's "Clash of Civilisations" Thesis and Population Control

10 May 2002, Dhaka, Bangladesh.

The author of the *The Clash of Civilizations and the Remaking of World Order*,[1] Samuel P. Huntington, is very worried about the increased Muslim population in the world (1997: 117). His most recent article, "The Age of Muslim Wars", published in *Newsweek*, is a continuation of his earlier thesis of the clash of civilisations. According to him, "Muslim wars have replaced the cold war as the principal form of international conflict. These wars include wars of terrorism, guerrilla wars, civil wars and interstate conflicts" (Huntington 2001: 14). Although Huntington traces the start of Muslim wars to the last two decades of the last century, i.e. the 1980s, those were all on US set-ups in other countries. Attacks were outside the US. But now,

---

1 Editors' note: Samuel Huntington's thesis on "the clash of civilizations" suggests that in the post-Cold War era it is not the struggle for a political ideology—capitalism, communism or non-aligned—that determines world politics, but rather that the "fault line" falls instead between what Huntington calls "the world's major civilizations". He argues further that civilizational identities are now the major force shaping "patterns of cohesion, disintegration and conflict" (1997: 20). His thesis emphasises the likelihood of conflict rather than suggesting the possibility of dialogue.

The clearest statement of Frances Fukuyama's "end of history" thesis occurs in his introduction to *The End of History and the Last Man*. The thesis, he argues, is "that liberal democracy may constitute the 'end point of mankind's [*sic*] ideological evolution' and is the 'final form of human government,' and as such constituted the 'end of history'" (1992: xi). Fukuyama takes Western institutions as the pinnacle of human achievement. Both Huntington and Fukuyama obliterate women and indigenous peoples, as well as the vast majority of peoples who throughout history have lived in completely different ways. Their theories represent the views of the dominant culture which suggests that globalisation and its attendant institutions are *the* model for "progress and prosperity". Neither asks, For whom?

Huntington says, "The age of Muslim wars had come home to America" (2001: 16) after the attack on the World Trade Center on September 11, 2001. Although he is a political scientist, not a demographer, now he is looking more closely at the birth rate in Muslim countries.

War is essentially a population policy, or to look from the reverse side, population policies are essentially war policies aiming to terminate the people considered as enemy. Population policies have always been promoted in the areas of conflict and resistance. Population policies as war strategies are always aimed at controlling the number of people of a certain class, colour, religion, sect, sex, etc. with very systematic and targeted planning. Needless to mention that tactical interventions of such war strategies are always pro-filed in disguised format. For example, termination of the targeted population at the level of the field of human reproduction is called "family planning". Such tactical intervention has always confused mainstream liberal feminists who take sides with the population terminators, believing that it is indeed family planning. Hardly do they realise that "family planning" and "popula-tion control" are not the same thing. Taking sides with the population terminators is to engage in war against women, particularly women of colour and poor women and the women from the Third World.

The United States of America is the leader in promoting such programmes in the remotest corners of the world. While it takes too long a time for the food to reach the poor in the distressed areas, jungles, refugee camps, etc., it is much easier to get injectables like Depo-provera, IUDs and even Norplant. For these services money is never a problem. The US looks at the Third World and sees only children or young people under thirty years of age. They all look like "guerrillas". The kids who are fighting against Israel with stones in their hands are all "terrorists", but the big tanks and guns aiming at them by the Zionist state of Israel are legitimate defence. Kids throw stones. And Sharon uses the most modern war weapons against them. The US government helps all the repressive governments around the world to kill the rebels. It is not only the US government who is worried about them, the Ford and Rockefeller Foundations have nightmares about millions of children advancing like locusts over the horizon from the Third World. Therefore, terminating them under the guise of a family planning programme is a very useful war strategy. Population theory can be used effectively to blame the victims. Eduardo Galeano in his book *Open Veins of Latin America* pointed out: "While intrauterine devices compete with bombs and machine-gun salvos to arrest the growth of the Vietnamese population, in Latin America it is more hygienic and effective to kill *guerrilleros* in the womb than in the mountains or the streets" (Galeano 1973: 16). Imposed and coercive family planning programmes in Latin America, particularly forced sterilisation, are very well known. Various US missions have sterilised thousands of women in Amazonia, although this was the least populated habitable zone on the planet. But people were considered enemy in the light of the rich biological and other resources they own. Indigenous communities must be depopulated to take control of their wealth and resources.

Huntington has underscored four major reasons for getting worried about the Islamic resurgence. The first one is that the present-day Islamic resurgence is a result of modernisation and globalisation. The second is that there exists a grievance, resentment, envy and hostility toward the West and its wealth, power and culture. Third, tribal, religious, ethnic, political and cultural divisions within the Muslim world stimulate violence between Muslims. Fourth is that the Islamic Resurgence has coincided with and been invigorated by high birth rates in most Muslim societies, which have produced a "youth bulge" with large numbers of people between the ages of sixteen and thirty. Huntington's concern is: "Young males are the principal perpetrators of violence in all societies; they exist in overabundant numbers in Muslim societies."

The implication of Huntington's thesis is that the conflict within the Muslim world could have been a way for the West to get rid of the attacks from the "youth bulge" without the West doing anything against them. But Huntington's latest prophecy says: "September 11 produced Western unity; a prolonged response to September 11 could produce more Muslim unity" (Huntington 2001: 19). This is a dangerous forecast, which implies that something must be done. He seems to take the demographic aspect more seriously than other factors. Even though the Muslim world is not very united at the moment, US actions, aided by barbaric Israeli attacks on Palestinian civilians, may create common sympathy among Muslims. For Huntington, "Muslim disunity is unlikely, while the demographic is very optimistic. Although the birth rate in many Muslim countries is declining, in some countries it is still high." In his article in *Newsweek*, the two pictures featured were of militant Muslim youths and a third was of innocent children reading the Koran. What does this mean? Is it not to target them to kill? These children are going to be the "youth bulge".

Statistics show that, out of 133 countries in the world, 39 (or 29 per cent) have over 80 per cent Muslim population. Bangladesh is one of them. Another 16 countries have a Muslim population of more than 50 per cent. Huntington must have all this information in hand and therefore he is worried. Those Muslims who are already born are facing wars, and are dying. These deaths are becoming visible and brutal. But family planning can help the West in hiding such killings. The US must target the unborn.

Francis Fukuyama, the author of *The End of History and the Last Man* and a professor at Johns Hopkins University, USA, elaborated on Huntington's "clash of civilisations" theory. The present conflict and the war against terrorism is not against terrorists of all kinds. He writes:

> While the Bush administration has been correctly asserting that the current struggle is against terrorists, not a war between the West and Islam, there are clearly cultural issues at play … (Fukuyama 2001: 117)

He continues,

> The basic conflict we face is much broader, and concerns not just a small group of terrorists, but a much larger group of radical Islamists and Muslims for whom religious identity overrides all other political values (2001: 121).

Fukuyama also believes that at the present time, there is a resistance against the Western lifestyle and modernity. "Islam is the one major world culture that arguably does have some very basic problems with modernity" (Fukuyama 2001: 120). This, however, is not entirely true. The attacks on McDonald's, a symbol of youth modernity, happened in France; the big demonstrations against the WTO, the World Bank, the IMF and so on, were all organised by "Christians" or non-believers in the US and in Europe. The resistance against globalisation is happening all over the world, but somehow the US political analysts find only Islam to be against modernity.

In the middle part of the last century, Bonnie Mass wrote that American social planners were concerned with the notion of a permanent "communist threat" to capitalist interests. In the mid-1930s, studies of migration movements, census and population growth trends were directly related to British interests in India, where the independence movement was developing under Gandhi. Similar studies were carried out in Puerto Rico, where a strong nationalist movement had arisen. In 1939, a meeting of the International Union of Scientific Study of Population was held in Nazi-ruled Berlin. Here population arguments were used to justify anti-Semitic policies. To study the international aspects of demographic problems, the prestigious Princeton Office of Population Research was created in 1936, funded by the Rockefeller Foundation and the Milibank Memorial Fund (Mass 1976).

Now there is no such threat of communism. The Cold War is over but globalisation has created discontent among many nations. Most people are becoming poorer day by day, most nations are becoming powerless. Wealth and power is being concentrated only among a few corporations and among a tiny fraction of the world's population. Before the events of September 11, there were many other global militant resistances. Huntington cannot see any problem in these clashes. He can only see the *tupi*—the white cap and beard. I am not sure if he saw the burqa, as there was no mention of it in his writing.

His concern is with young males! His concern is only to defend capitalism and therefore, after communism, he wants to get rid of any other threat to capitalism that may appear. Islam is therefore targeted. Huntington's clash is with the Muslims. The war is indeed against Islam in order to defend capitalism.

References

Fukuyama, Francis. (1992). *The End of History and the Last Man*. London: Penguin Books.

———. (2001). "Their Target: The Modern World." *Newsweek*. (138) 25, 17 December: 114–24.

Galeano, Eduardo. (1973). *Open Veins of Latin America: Five Centuries of the Pillage of a Continent*. New York and London: Monthly Review Press.

Huntington, Samuel P. (1997). *The Clash of Civilizations and the Remaking of World Order*. New York: Simon and Schuster.

———. (2001). "The Age of Muslim Wars." *Newsweek*. (138) 25, 17 December: 14–19.

Mass, Bonnie. (1976). *Population Target: The Political Economy of Population Control in Latin America*. Brampton, Ont.: Charters Publishing.

Christine Delphy

A War for Afghan Women?

Translated from French by Bronwyn Winter.

It would appear today that since Kabul was captured, the Coalition against terrorism has waged war against Afghanistan in order to liberate Afghan women. But if one casts one's mind back over the sequence of events, this is the fourth declared objective, and the third change, since the beginning of the war. The war was declared by Bush on 11 September 2001, on no-one in particular and on everyone in general. Even though this corresponded to what was really happening, it constituted too great a development for the press and the public to be able to be maintained. The very next day, a specific enemy was chosen: it was Bin Laden, whom the US enjoined the Taliban to hand over. To them, to the Americans. Faced with the Taliban's response— standard in cases of extradition—asking for evidence of Bin Laden's guilt, the US repeated its ultimatum. Two weeks later it rejected a new offer by the Taliban to hand Bin Laden over to a neutral country, calling this offer "negotiations", and God forbid that the US negotiate.[1]

"Smiles from Kabul"

Then Rumsfeld, US Secretary of Defense, declares that Bin Laden will perhaps never be found; second change and third objective: from now on, the enemy is the Taliban regime. There is no lack of arguments against this regime. I would go even further: there has been no lack of arguments for the last six years, and for the last six years they have not been enough to justify

---

1 On 22 September, the Taliban offered to hand over Bin Laden if the US could provide evidence against him, which the US refused to do. But on 1 October, Mullah Omar offered to extradite Bin Laden to Pakistan, where he would be kept under house arrest in Peshawar before appearing before an international tribunal, and this time, without asking for evidence. The US contemptuously rejected this offer, reiterating what Ari Fleischer, spokesperson for the White House, had several times repeated: "there will be neither discussions nor negotiations with the Taliban". If there was no other solution apart from war, it is because the US did not want there to be: it blocked the way in advance and refused the alternative path of diplomacy, even when its enemies asked for it: http://www.wluml.org/english/new-archives/september-2001.htm.

a war. But all of a sudden, they are enough. Not on their own, of course: on top of being odious, the Taliban have given shelter to Bin Laden, suspected of being responsible for the September 11 attacks. After a month of bombing, the Alliance troops enter Kabul, the West cries "Victory" and feels it has accomplished a very good thing at little expense. The newspapers publish photos of women's smiles—no, sorry, of one woman's smile—and the war finds its fourth reason: women's liberation.

But it is not the right reason, because the people that the Allies have brought to power are no better than the Taliban. The truth about the Northern Alliance can no longer be hidden. Given the number of reporters on the ground, the distrust of the citizens of Kabul and Jalalabad with regard to the Alliance can no longer be hidden.[2] It is a distrust that comes from experience: between 1992 and 1996, the Northern Alliance troops (or "United Front") perpetrated massacres and gratuitous killings of prisoners and of the wounded, terrorised civilians and held them to ransom. Neither the massacres nor the gratuitous killings of prisoners and of the wounded can now be hidden. It can no longer be hidden that what is happening today is almost exactly the same as what happened between 1992 and 1996, in an Afghanistan newly carved up into fiefdoms where warlords are forever on the brink of the multiple civil wars which ravaged the country between the departure of the Soviets and the arrival of the Taliban.[3]

Taliban and Mujahideen: Two of One and a Pair of the Other

It is not the right reason because the US is no friend of Afghan women. Women's rights have never been a US preoccupation, and no more in Afghanistan than in Kuwait or Saudi Arabia or elsewhere—one could even say that it is the exact opposite, that the US has knowingly and deliberately sacrificed Afghan women to its own interests.

How far do the Mujahideen—whose current regrouping is called the Northern Alliance—go back? Even before the Soviet Army invaded the country in 1979 in order to replace one Marxist president (Hafizullah Amin) with another (Babrak Karmal), the tribal lords and religious author-ities had declared holy war against the Marxist leadership of Nur Mohammed Taraki.[4] So even before fighting the foreign invasion, in 1978 the

---

2 Patrice Claude (2001), "Le pouvoir désordonné des Moudjahidins s'installe sur Jalalabad en proie à toutes les terreurs", *Le Monde*, 25–26 November.

3 At the end of January, for example, Sharzai was fighting Khan over the town of Herat (*Globe and Mail*, 22 January 2002).

4 Ahmed Rashid (2001). *Taliban*. London: Pan: 12–13.

khans[5] and the Mullahs had taken up arms against a government that forced girls to go to school, that prohibited the levirate[6] and the sale of women. For that was what shocked, scandalised and disgusted them. Women's rights were worth a war for them, were worth a fight—*against* them. The fighters became Mujahideen: God's soldiers against impious Marxism, the ensuing Soviet invasion giving a patriotic dimension to that combat. The US helped the Mujahideen, for its enemies' enemies were its friends. What did it matter what they did or wanted? The US knew what the Mujahideen wanted: to put women in their place. But they thwarted Moscow's plans, and that's what counted for the US. It was also, alas, what counted for our romantic French pioneers, the "French doctors" (including Médecins Sans Frontières and Médecins du Monde): anti-Soviet was for them a synonym of "for freedom". Whose freedom? They did not ask themselves that question: they found the berets becoming and the adventure exciting. Doing good in magnificent countryside, all the while contributing to the fight against totalitarianism, what more could a young Western man of our times ask? As for women's rights: well, it's their custom, and custom is sacred, especially when one does not suffer from it personally.

Media Whitewashing of the Western Coalition's Mercenaries

In 1988 the Soviet army left. The only remaining enemy for the Mujahideen was Najibullah's government. The Mujahideen fight everyone in the name of Islam, for an Islamic state and the application of the sharia law, hence their name. In Pashtun, Urdu (and all the other local languages), they are called "Jihadi", which is clearly derived from "Jihad". They have never hidden the fact that they are fundamentalists. Since the war against the Soviets, however, the French have pretended that the name means "freedom fighters". We have been plagued by even more TV disinformation since the "events". In September 2001, the hagiographic film *Massoud l'Afghan* was broadcast,[7] along with a documentary made by unnamed Afghan women who had filmed, with a hidden camera, executions carried out by the Taliban in the Kabul stadium. After the capture of Kabul, some information on the conduct of the "allied"

---

5 The name *khan* derives from that denoting the ruler or monarch of a Mongol tribe. It subsequently became attached to the name of any property owner, particularly in Afghanistan, Pakistan, India and Bangladesh. In modern Afghanistan the khans are the tribal lords or warlords (usually both).

6 Levirate: custom requiring a widow to marry the brother or nearest kinsman of her late husband.

7 This film, by Christophe de Ponfilly, irresponsibly idealises its subject, unless it was made as a deliberate work of disinformation.

troops started to filter through. The French media clearly indulged in self-censorship, and blocked any objective and balanced information from reaching the French public. The media had no lack of information, for even if their knowledge of the region is extremely poor—no French newspaper has a permanent correspondent in Pakistan—foreign press agencies, press, television and websites are at their disposal. They deliberately kept the public in the dark, and refused the articles that the French Coalition Internationale Contre la Guerre (International Coalition Against the War) sent them containing this information. We had to wait until 23 January 2002 for the film on the executions in the Kabul stadium to be rebroadcast in full (on Arte, a European cultural TV network), in *Sorties de ténèbres?* (*Beneath the Veil*) by Saira Shah, to learn that the filmmakers belonged to the Revolutionary Association of the Women of Afghanistan (RAWA) (see this volume: 70). We had to wait for another documentary, *Women of Kabul* by Antonia Rados, also made thanks to RAWA, to show the reality of women's lives following their supposed "liberation", and finally to allow Afghan women to explain what the journalists had hidden for four months: that the repression of women had started with the Mujahideen, and not with the Taliban. Recently, the television magazine *Télérama* broke with the "politically correct" to the point of interviewing an Afghan musician who said: "When the Communists came to power in 1979, opportunities for concerts increased significantly and it even happened that I went to do demonstrations for music classes in girls' schools ... The difficulties commenced when the Mujahideen arrived in 1992."[8] (This does not of course mean that the Communist regime was entirely one of halcyon days, that there were not other problems—notably as concerns the functioning of democracy. There was, however, definitely a policy striving toward a measure of equality between the sexes, which disappeared with the Mujahideen.)

This withholding of information could appear anodyne: it is, however, one of the major mechanisms of the conditioning of public opinion. On one hand, Western powers could not admit that they had attached themselves to such dubious allies on the ground; because the Mujahideen were the allies of the Western Coalition, "we have so idolised these gunmen ... that we are now immune to their history".[9] On the other hand, in order to justify the war in

---

8   Rahim Khushnawas (2002), *Télérama* 2714, 16 January: 50.

9   "The Northern Alliance is advancing, meanwhile, with all its baggage of massacres and looting and rape intact. We have so idolised these gunmen, been so infatuated with them, supported them so unquestioningly, pictured them on television so deferentially that we are now immune to their history": Robert Fisk (2001), "What Will the Northern Alliance Do In Our Name Now?" *The Independent*, London, 14 November.

the eyes of public opinion, it was necessary to promise that its aim was to "improve" the fate of Afghans, and not just to avenge the US or consolidate Western power. Public opinion, however, would not have believed in the promise of improvement had it known the truth about the Northern Alliance. It was necessary to oppose—through action (the barefaced lies told by the usual propagandists) but especially through omission—the "bad" Taliban and the "good" Mujahideen, at least as long as the latter hadn't won.

Why the Taliban Came to Power in 1996

The media thus "drew a veil over the glorious (and well-known) past" of the Mujahideen: from the time of the Soviets' departure in 1989, the commonalities among them no longer sufficed to silence their rivalries. The cupidity and the hunger for power of all these warlords pushed them to fight incessantly among themselves, within alliances that were hardly formed before they were overthrown. At the end of four years, in 1992, they took Kabul and overthrew Najibullah, the last Marxist prime minister; but this did not stop the civil war, and especially not the war against civilians. The Northern Alliance soldiers looted houses and raped women. Local chiefs demanded ransoms from lorries every 50 kilometres, transport became impossible, and corruption and disorder prevented application of the sharia law.

Certain Mujahideen, and especially the youngest, who took Islamic ideas seriously, left in disgust to study in Pakistan. They were the students: the Taliban, the spiritual and sometimes physical sons of the Mujahideen. They were as anti-communist as their fathers but more disciplined, more earnest, and yet more fundamentalist: in short, good candidates for aid from the US, which handed out dollars to Pakistani madrassahs (Koranic schools) via Saudi Arabia.[10] And within a year, formidably armed Taliban had conquered a great part of the country and entered Kabul. When the Mujahideen beat a retreat in 1996, they left 50,000 dead in Kabul alone and the city was in ruins. Four years of inter-factional war had accomplished what six years of anti-Soviet war had not succeeded in doing.

And Women in Amongst All That?

So, has the US always fought for women's rights? No. Has it ever fought for women's rights? No. Has it, on the contrary, trampled on women's rights? Yes. For women's rights were promoted and defended in Afghanistan between 1978 and 1992, but by Marxist or pro-Soviet governments. It is from this period, that of Presidents Amin, Karmal, Taraki and Najibullah,

---

10 For an account of US bankrolling of Islamists, and in particular of the Taliban, see Richard Labévière (1999), *Les Dollars de la terreur: Les États-Unis et les islamistes*. Paris: Bernard Grasset.

that astonishing statistics can be drawn concerning the large number of women doctors, teachers, lawyers. But that was bad luck for Afghan women: for since they were being defended by governments allied to an enemy of the US, it was necessary to sacrifice them. One cannot allow people's rights, especially when those people are only women, to interfere with the pursuit of world hegemony. Women's rights are like Iraqi children: their death is the price of US power, and Americans pay that price all the more easily because in the end, they are not the ones paying it.

The fathers of the Taliban, the Mujahideen, this time armed by the Russians that they had chased out twelve years previously, returned under the shadow of American bombs; they had hardly changed, if one is to judge by their way of waging war: "the Northern Alliance is advancing, meanwhile, with all its baggage of massacres and looting and rape intact".[11] Why would they change with regard to women, why would they become feminist, these men who, before fighting the Soviets, then amongst themselves, fought against women's rights? Like feminists the world over, who have waged an international campaign for some years against the fate of Afghan women at the hands of the Taliban, I hope that the government that is being put in place in Afghanistan will guarantee women's human rights, and that it will make sure at least some of these rights are respected.

Better status for women could be one of the unexpected results of a war: a collateral gain of sorts. One can hope. But without dreaming. The Tajik party led by Rabbani, who was president of the legal government and recognised by the international community until the Bonn accords, instituted sharia law in Kabul in 1992. This is the party of Massoud, who was its military commander; its troops gave themselves over to an orgy of rapes and murders when it occupied the Hazara area of Kabul during the struggles between it and other factions in 1995.

But in February 2002, the American war is not over, the Northern Alliance is coming undone as the warlords that make it up reconquer the fiefdoms that they had lost. Rabbani's Jamiat-i-Islami, which was the first to enter Kabul, is, with every passing day, increasing its power on the ground. Supported by the Russians, who are once again in Kabul, the Jamiat-i-Islami has scooped up the majority of portfolios in the provisional government, in spite of the US. While the US has succeeded in having Karzai, a Pathan, rather than Rabbani, Russia's man, placed at the head of the provisional government, Karzai wields no real power.[12] Two women are part of the provisional government, two exiles, one from the Hezb-i-Wahdat party and the other

---

11 Fisk, "What Will the Northern Alliance Do in Our Name Now?"

12 Human Rights Watch (2000), *Military Assistance to the Afghan Opposition*, October.

from the Parchami party, both of which—like the other components of the Northern Alliance—are contested by RAWA. RAWA activists have been working clandestinely for years with Afghan women refugees in Pakistan; in particular, they have provided schooling for the girls. They have also returned to Afghanistan, at risk to their lives, to make films on the state of the country under the Taliban. In the face of death threats from all fundamentalists, they denounce both the Mujahideen and the Taliban; they have also protested energetically against the US bombings of their country.[13]

The Jamiat-i-Islami, in response to urging by the international organisations that all the factions in Afghanistan still need, has made some concessions concerning women. Here is an indication of that. One week after the fall of Kabul, a spokesperson for Rabbani declared on *BBC World*: "The Taliban's 'restrictions' will be lifted [no details were provided], and the burqa will no longer be compulsory; the hijab will suffice." The hijab will suffice: now there's something to dream about.[14]

But if it had been more, would this have justified a war? And if the defence of women's rights had been the real reason behind the US bombings, would that have justified these bombings?

A Tale (with a Moral) and a Question: Does One Have the Right to Bomb People for Their Own Good?

Once upon a time there was a country where women still did not have the right to vote, despite thirty years of feminist struggle, years and decades after they obtained it in neighbouring European nations. How did these other

---

13 Contrary to this, Negar, an association of "Support for Afghan Women" based in France, is supportive of both the Northern Alliance and the US bombings. According to this association, a "Charter of the Fundamental Rights of Afghan Women" was supposedly signed by Massoud as well as, more recently, by Karzai. (cicg.free.fr: "Afghanistan: droits des femmes", interview with Shoukria Haidar by Christine Delphy). This association attributes the horror of the situation of Afghan women only to the Taliban, and never mentions the Mujahideen (*Lesbia* 208, December 2001: 33). A possible explanation of this partisanship—which is, in the case of Negar, pro-Northern Alliance—resides in the fact that, according to Sippi Azerbaijani-Moghadam, technical adviser to the UN Commission on women and children refugees and specialist on the region, "women's organisations are formed from the Pathan, Tajik and Hazara ethnic groups": Sharon Groves (2001), "Report from Afghanistan", *Feminist Studies* 27: 3 (Fall).

14 In Afghanistan, "hijab" means "Iranian chador", that is, a cloak covering the entire body and head, including the face, and not just a headscarf. The term *chadri* is also used; it is synonymous with burqa.

nations treat this country? Did they declare war on it? Did they impose an embargo? Did they withdraw their confidence and their alliance? On the contrary, they defended this country when it was attacked; and following victory, in 1945, they gave financial assistance to its reconstruction, and asked it to go back to the drawing board and give women the vote, which it did.

The right to vote is fundamental. And yet, am I sorry that the USA, Great Britain and the USSR did not bomb France between 1918 and 1939? No. For however precious this right is, if it had had to be won at the cost of a war, I wonder whether its value would ever have equalled its cost. And I am all the less sorry because this example proves that there are peaceful and efficient means of putting pressure on states.

In the end, where women's rights—that is, human rights—are concerned, the question to be asked with regard to a war is always the same one: What evils are worse than war for a population? At what point does a war become preferable? To say that war is beneficial for Afghan women is to decide that it is better for them to die from bombs, from hunger, from cold, than to live under the Taliban. Death rather than servitude: that is what Western public opinion has decided for Afghan women. A decision that was almost heroic. What would have been needed for it to be so? Well, Rumsfeld, for example, would have needed to say "I prefer to die rather than see Afghan women in the Taliban's clutches for a minute longer"; Westerners would have needed to put their own lives at stake and not those of Afghan women.

A decision that would be heroic in the first case is, in the second, a morally repugnant way of playing with the lives of others. Here, we are dealing with the second case. The irresponsible tokenism of the Western take on "the liberation of Afghan women" is an illustration of the fact that Western lives are worth more—infinitely more—than other lives, and of the fact that the West, not content with placing an extremely low price on these other lives, considers that it has the right to make use of these lives as it will.

The Assumptions behind the Tokenism of "Women's Liberation", or the Missionary Paradox

Until recently, one could only deduce from the number of speeches and acts what decision had been made in the place of Afghan women. But some days after I had written the first version of this article, this decision and its colonialist assumptions were explicitly formulated by Peter Schneider: "Can Franz Kroetz not conceive of Afghan women ... seeing American soldiers [sic] as liberators rather than as hostage-takers? The idea that freedom can come at a high price, that it can even be worth risking one's own life, seems to be incomprehensible to more than one friend of peace."[15] Contrary to appearances, the "own life" of which Schneider speaks is not his. At the very moment when he says that the freedom of Afghan women is worth sacrificing their lives, he denies them this freedom: he is the one making that "choice" for them. This contradiction is not only Schneider's; it permeates the whole Western attitude towards Afghan women, because it is, more generally, the organising principle of the attitude of the dominant towards the dominated.

I would like to suggest a simple rule for an international ethic which could also hold between individuals: one does not have the right to make decisions, especially heroic ones, when others apart from oneself are to bear the consequences. The only population that can decide that a war is worth the cost is the one that bears this cost. Here, however, those who decided on the war are not themselves subjected to it, and those who are subjected to the war did not make the decision to be.

For the moment, the humanitarian war has not kept its promises. Afghan women are on the roads, in tents, in camps, in their millions. Before the war, 4.5 million Afghans lived in refugee camps in Pakistan and Iran. Since the war, yet more have fled the US bombings. Their exact number is unknown, for many go into hiding for fear of being sent back, but it is estimated that 700,000 more have arrived in Pakistan and 300,000 more in Iran. But those most in danger, and the hardest to count, are the "internally displaced persons", who, simply trying to flee the bombs, have followed the front line within the country and are now in improvised camps, without food and without protection against armed men. To this day, because of the partition of the territory into fiefdoms controlled by the warlords' underfed troops, "soldiers by day and bandits by night", international aid is not getting to these people. When organisations don't give up on transporting it, it is hijacked by armed groups.

Many refugees—especially among the "internally displaced" and the populations of the high plateaus, who have, since September, been deprived of food aid because of the war and who are now isolated by snow—are dead or are going to die.[16] As in all wars and all famines, these dead will include a

---

15 *Le Monde*, 5 February 2002. The use by the press of the term "liberation" probably evoked for Schneider the image of French women kissing American soldiers when Paris was liberated. But the action is not taking place in France in 1944. In 2001 and in Afghanistan, the American soldiers are not visible. It is the troops of the Northern Alliance, whose reputation is not exactly that of "liberators", who entered Kabul. Sorry, Mr Schneider, it's not the same film!

16 There is no more information on the numbers of these dead than on the numbers of direct victims of the US bombings.

disproportionate number of women. And without any guarantee that this "sacrifice" will win them rights. Should we in any case be speaking of sacrifice, when they did not choose it? No. We should be speaking here of bad treatment imposed by others, and even of torture.

But this is temporary, we will be told; with the return of peace, food aid will recommence and the country will be rebuilt. We are still far from this, first because the reconstruction of the country would necessitate peace, and peace has not returned.

The US has used the warlords who had spread ruin in Afghanistan before 1996; 700,000 armed men now roam through a country that is even more ravaged than before. Ethnic divisions, already accentuated by the first civil war (1992–96), have been further accentuated by the Taliban, who hold anyone who is not Pathan in contempt. Following their defeat, desire for vengeance on the part of the Hazara, the Tajik and the Uzbek has added itself to the traditional rivalry among warlords. On 10 January 2002, RAWA called for an international force "to protect the Afghan people against the criminals of the Northern Alliance".[17] Some days later, Karzai began to denounce reprisals against the Pathan in regions where they are in the minority. He then used the occasion of a visit to New York to request that the UN send an international police force, when he had previously only asked for money.[18]

The resumption of the civil war, already on the cards during the fight against the Taliban (for example, during the overthrow of Kunduz), is now being openly declared. Shirzai, the Pathan governor of Kandahar, backed by a force of 20,000 men, is fighting the Tajik Ismail Khan for control of Herat.[19] Fighting has broken out to the north, in the Kunduz region, and to the south-east, in the Khost region. Confrontations have taken place at Mazar-e-Sharif between the troops of Dostum (Uzbek) and Atta Mohammed (Tajik), while at Gardez, in the south-east, the governor appointed by Karzai, Pacha Khan Zadran, has been fighting the local chief, Haji Saifullah, resulting in sixty deaths.[20] Even the most protected of the towns, Kabul, is prey to insecurity. A diplomat posted to the city has declared that residents no longer go to certain areas of the city because "Kalashnikov culture reigns there".[21]

But the US is busy flattening the Tora-Bora mountains, and has on several occasions reiterated its dislike for "nation-building"; clearly, the US destroys

17 Letter on RAWA website: www.rawa.org.

18 *BBC World*, 30 January 2002.

19 *Globe and Mail*, 22 January 2002.

20 AP and *Time Magazine Newsletter*, 1 February 2002.

21 *Hindustan Times*, via AFP, 25 January 2002.

but does not repair the damage. An international force that might be enough to protect the whole country will thus not see the light of day: there will only be a force of 4500 stationed around Kabul and only for six months.[22] An estimated 30,000 are needed, but the US wishes neither to immobilise soldiers within Afghanistan nor to leave it up to other countries (which would necessarily include Russia) to do it. The Taliban, now "ordinary citizens" (they only need to tie their turbans a little differently, as an Afghan man showed a Western reporter), will go back to serve the Pathan lords to whom they will bring their taste for war—all they know—and their hatred for the Uzbek and the Tajik.

The West has not brought peace and prosperity: it has destroyed what was left to destroy, it has caused even more people to flee from a country already bled white, it has finished off the job of starving a people already dying from hunger, and it has re-armed tribal leaders who dream only of conquests, emoluments and massacres. Before the war, it was inconceivable that Afghanistan could fall into an even worse state than it was in already: but it is possible, we have done it.

The New "Duty to Intervene" and the Old "White Man's Burden"

The smallest modicum of decency would have necessitated that the Allies cease to proclaim that it is for their own good that Afghan women (and men) are being made to suffer, and above all that they abstain from claiming that it is in the name of the Afghans' freedom that their right to choose their fate, and even the right to life, is being taken away from them. But it is the contrary that is happening: indeed, one may well fear that this little ditty will become a smash hit; the Coalition of Allies against evil already has a long list of countries to which it has promised to bring good through the sword.[23] And of course, any resemblance with past historical events (so far past that even

---

22 Ibid, 20 January 2002.

23 On 31 January, George Bush reiterated for the fifth time since 11 September his assurance that the US would wage war worldwide, and named new countries: Iran and North Korea, along with Hamas, Hezbollah and the Islamic Jihad, three fundamentalist groups combating Israeli occupation. Two days previously, the first US soldiers arrived in the Philippines. The media and Western public opinion had for three months brushed aside these declarations as so much hyperbole. No doubt another country will have to become the target of a bombing campaign (which is no doubt imminent), for Bush's declcarations to be taken for what they are: the announcement of a program, and not mere rhetorical devices.

to refer to them seems old hat), any resemblance, that is, with colonial wars is pure coincidence.

War waged in the interests of control and exploitation will never progress human rights. For, apart from the men and women of Afghanistan, this war in the name of civilisation has in two months sent a sizeable parcel of that civilisation into oblivion. The Geneva Conventions have been declared invalid by the Allies, who were first accessories to the crimes of the butcher of Mazar-e-Sharif ("General" Dostum, Vice-Minister for Defence in Karzai's government) and the others,[24] and are now accessories to the manœuvres of the Americans, who are inventing new pseudo-legal categories: the "illegal fighters" imprisoned at Guantanamo, who are covered by no law, either national or international, common or of war![25] Public freedoms, the pride of our democracies, are thus wiped out, and international law is mortally wounded—the great dying body of the UN is there to testify to this.

Only true and peaceful cooperation among nations will progress human rights. But this is not on the agenda. Not only do the real goals of the war have nothing to do with the arguments used to "sell" it to public opinion, but these "humanitarian" or "humanist" arguments are themselves vitiated at the outset. Those of P. Schneider, for example, are typical of those used by Spanish monks towards the Indians of the New World: they postulate that we Westerners know what is good for everybody, and that we have the right, and perhaps the duty, to suggest it to or impose it on others. These others, who are intellectually and morally inferior to us, do not have the same value as we do: consequently, their lives are also less valuable than ours.

Civilian populations in the alliance countries have no direct interest in imperialist wars. The real motives of their governments do not motivate

---

24 Robert Fisk 2001, "We are the War Criminals Now", *The Independent*, London, 29 November; Human Rights Watch www.hrw.org, 1 December 2001; Coalition Internationale Contre la Guerre, cicg.free.fr/dirafghna/news11.htm, 29 November 2001.

25 www.hrw.org, 21 January 2002; Lettre de la CICG, cicg.free.fr/diractu/lettres.htm, 23 January 2002; Amnesty International, Letter to George Bush, 21 January 2002, web.amnesty.org; 11/01/2002, Amnesty International, memorandum to the government, amnesty.org, 15 April 2002.

More precisely, in January see: web.amnesty.org/aiusf/recent/AMR10532002, Amr51/009/2002; hrw.org/press/2002/01/us011102.htm; iacenter.org/geneva_usrefuse.htm.

Letter, 15 April, from Human Rights Watch to: hrw.org/press/2002/05/pentagon-ltr.htm.

them: as soon as economic motivations are invoked, the legitimacy of wars immediately diminishes in the eyes of the public. Governments always provide impartial and even noble motives for wars, if not as the only reasons for the wars, at least as an adjuvant or excipient. The Gulf War was perceived by public opinion as a war "for oil", but also as a war "for right"—the latter making the former easier to swallow. The Serbian war—the most popular one—is reputed to have prevented genocide. It is possible that public opinion is duplicitous, that it is really in agreement with the self-interested and selfish motives for war. But certainly it is not this that is pushed to the forefront of public opinion: this cynicism is left to governments.

As concerns the Afghan war, French public opinion has accepted an assortment of reasons, including some that are hardly ethical, such as vengeance. But this shameful motivation needs to be "balanced" by something else. It is impossible to provide as the sole reason for this war the increased torture of one of the poorest and longest-suffering populations in the world; the war needs to carry a promise of good, or at least of something better, for the Afghan people, in order to "compensate" them, as it were, for their suffering.

Which is why the motive of liberating Afghan women, which appeared late on the scene, is nonetheless crucial, for it gives the conflict its necessary "altruistic" and "moral" dimension. But, as we have seen, this motive in fact conceals the denial of free will and even life to the people it targets. To what ethical structure does this "moral" motive belong, then, and to what extent is it truly "altruistic"?

The moral motive—in this case, the "liberation of Afghan women"—calls on values which appear to be progressive; but they only appear to be, for on closer examination, they consist of a more or less conscious belief in the West's "mission". We only consider ourselves to have such a mission because we consider ourselves to be the carriers of "civilisation". No journalist, politician or intellectual criticised the equating of the West and civilisation by George W. Bush and his epigones following the attack on the World Trade Center—on the contrary, a complete consensus emerged concerning "attacks on civilisation". The action of Western powers in the non-Western world relies on the opinon of a public whose vision of the world has hardly changed in depth since the end of colonisation. The belief in Western superiority is intact. This more or less stated racism is today allied with a type of paternalistic compassion; their combination produces a potentially very dangerous ideology for non-Westerners and more generally for all dominated groups, for it provides as much justification for military intervention as for humanitarian action, and sometimes justifies them both at once, as we saw when American public opinion approved both the parachuting in of parcels and the dropping of bombs. Feed and punish, such is the definition of the role of parents in relation to children. The vocabulary used by George W. Bush is very revealing; whether it is to his allies or his enemies, he speaks the language of a father who is strict but fair, who, in relation to the behaviour of his children, distributes gold stars and black marks, punishments and rewards. Equally revealing is the fact that Western opinion does not seem to have been shocked by this condescension, which would appear to indicate that it identifies with the position taken by Bush.

Without attempting for the moment to link these attitudes to the concrete actions of Western governments over the last fifty years, one has to note that the ideological changes heralded by decolonisation, the UN Charter, the right of peoples to self-determination, and all the other international conventions, seem neither to reflect nor to influence commonly held feelings in the slightest. The words have changed, but it is not difficult to recognise behind this new phrase, "the right to intervene", the same old white man's burden, still as lethal, for it incorporates the missionary's paradox: "We will save their souls (their freedom) even if we have to kill them to do it."

Rosalind P. Petchesky

Phantom Towers: Feminist Reflections on the Battle between Global Capitalism and Fundamentalist Terrorism

Presentation at Hunter College Political Science Department Teach-In, 25 September 2001.

These are trying times, hard times to know where we are from one day to the next. The attack on the World Trade Center has left many kinds of damage in its wake, not the least of which is a gaping ethical and political confusion in the minds of many Americans who identify in some way as "progressive"—meaning anti-racist, feminist, democratic (small d), anti-war. While we have a responsibility to those who died in the disaster and their loved ones, and to ourselves, to mourn, it is urgent that we also begin the work of thinking through what kind of world we are now living in and what it demands of us. And we have to do this, even while we know our understanding at this time can only be very tentative and may well be invalidated a year or even a month or a week from now by events we can't foresee or information now hidden from us.

So I want to try to draw a picture or a kind of mapping of the global power dynamics as I see them at this moment, including their gendered and racialized dimensions. I want to ask whether there is some alternative, more humane and peaceable way out of the two unacceptable polarities now being presented to us: the permanent war machine (or permanent security state) and the regime of holy terror.

Let me make very clear that, when I pose the question whether we are presently facing a confrontation between global capitalism and an Islamist-fundamentalist brand of fascism, I do not mean to imply their equivalence. If, in fact, the attacks of September 11 were the work of Bin Laden's Al-Qaeda network or something related and even larger—and for the moment I think we can assume this as a real possibility—then most of us in this room are *structurally positioned* in a way that gives us little choice about our identities.

(For the Muslim-Americans and Arab-Americans among us, who are both opposed to terrorism and terrified to walk in our streets, the moral dilemma must be, I imagine, much more agonizing.) As an American, a woman, a feminist, and a Jew, I have to recognize that the Bin Ladens of the world hate me and would like me dead; or, if they had power over me, would make my life a living hell. I have to wish them—these "perpetrators", "terrorists", whatever they are—apprehended, annulled, so I can breathe in some kind of peace. This is quite different from living at the very center of global capitalism—which is more like living in a very dysfunctional family that fills you with shame and anger for its arrogance, greed, and insensitivity but is, like it or not, your home and gives you both immense privileges and immense responsibilities.

Nor, however, do I succumb to the temptation of casting our current dilemma in the simplistic, Manichean terms of cosmic Good versus Evil. Currently this comes in two opposed but mirror-image versions: the narrative, advanced not only by the terrorists and their sympathizers but also by many on the left in the US and around the globe, that blames US cultural imperialism and economic hegemony for the "chickens coming home to roost"; versus the patriotic, right-wing version that casts US democracy and freedom as the innocent target of Islamist madness. Both these stories erase all the complexities that we must try to factor into a different, more inclusive ethical and political vision. The Manichean, apocalyptic rhetorics that echoed back and forth between Bush and Bin Laden in the aftermath of the attacks— the pseudo-Islamic and the pseudo-Christian, the jihad and the crusade— both lie.

So, while I do not see terrorist networks and global capitalism as equivalents or the same, I do see some striking and disturbing parallels between them. I picture them as the phantom Twin Towers arising in the smoke clouds of the old—fraternal twins, not identical, locked in a battle over wealth, imperial aggrandizement and the meanings of masculinity. It is a battle that could well end in a stalemate, an interminable cycle of violence that neither can win because of their failure to see the Other clearly. Feminist analysts and activists from many countries—whose voices have been inaudible thus far in the present crisis—have a lot of experience to draw from in making this double critique. Whether in the UN or national settings, we have been challenging the gender-biased and racialized dimensions of *both* neoliberal capitalism and various fundamentalisms for years, trying to steer a path between their double menace. The difference now is that they parade onto the world stage in their most extreme and violent forms. I see six areas where their posturing overlaps.

1. Wealth

Little needs to be said about the US as the world's wealthiest country nor the ways in which wealth-accumulation is the holy grail, not only of our political system (think of the difficulty we have even in reforming campaign finance laws), but of our national ethos. We are the headquarters of the corporate and financial mega-empires that dominate global capitalism and influence the policies of the international financial institutions (IMF, World Bank, WTO) that are its main governing bodies. This reality resonates around the globe in the symbolic pantheon of what the US stands for—from the McDonald's and Kentucky Fried Chicken ads sported by protestors in Genoa and Rawalpindi to the World Trade Center towers themselves. Acquisitiveness, whether individual or corporate, also lurks very closely behind the values that Bush and Rumsfeld mean when they say our "freedoms" and our "way of life" are being attacked and must be defended fiercely. (Why, as I'm writing this, do unsolicited messages about Wall Street investment opportunities or low fares to the Bahamas come spewing out of my fax machine?)

Wealth is also a driving force behind the Al-Qaeda network, whose principals are mainly the beneficiaries of upper-middle-class or elite financing and education. Bin Laden himself derives much of his power and influence from his family's vast fortune, and the cells of Arab-Afghan fighters in the 1980s war against the Soviets were bankrolled not only by the Pakistani secret police and the CIA—$3 billion writes Katha Pollitt in *The Nation*, "more money and expertise than for any other cause in CIA history" (2001)—but also by Saudi oil money. More important than this, though, are the values behind the terrorist organizations, which include—as Bin Laden made clear in his famous 1998 interview—defending the "honor" and "property" of Muslims everywhere and "[fighting] the governments that are bent on attacking our religion and on stealing our wealth". Political scientist Paul Amar (2001), in a recent talk at Hunter College, rightly urges us not to confuse these wealthy networks—whose nepotism and ties to oil interests eerily resemble those of the Bush family—with impoverished and resistant social movements throughout the Middle East and Asia. There is no evidence that economic justice or equality figure anywhere in the terrorist program.

2. Imperialist Nationalism

The Bush administration's initial reaction to the attacks exhibited the behavior of a superpower that knows no limits, that issues ultimatums under the cover of "seeking cooperation". "Every nation in every region has a decision to make," pronounced Bush in his speech to the nation that was really a speech to the world; "Either you are with us or you are with the terrorists." "This is the world's fight, this is civilization's fight"—the US, then, becoming the leader and spokesman of "civilization", relegating not only the terrorists but also those who refuse to join the fight to the ranks of the uncivilized. To the Taliban and to every other regime that "harbors terrorists", he was the sheriff stonewalling the cattle rustlers: "Hand over all the terrorists or you will share in their fate." And a few days later we read "the American announcement that it *would* use Saudi Arabia as a head-quarters for air operations against Afghanistan". As the war campaign progresses, its aims seem more openly imperialist: "Washington wants to offer [the small, also fundamentalist, drug-dealing mujahideen mostly routed by the Taliban] a role in governing Afghanistan after the conflict," according to *The New York Times* of 24 September, as if this were "Washington's" official role. Further, it and its allies are courting the octogenarian, long-forgotten Afghan king (now exiled in Italy) to join in a military operation to oust the Taliban and set up—what? a kind of puppet government? Nothing here about internationally monitored elections, nothing about the UN, or any concept of the millions of Afghan people—within the country or in exile—as anything but voiceless, downtrodden victims and refugees.

Clearly, this offensive involves far more than rooting out and punishing terrorists. Though I don't want to reduce the situation to a crude Marxist scenario, one can't help wondering how it relates to the longstanding determination of the US to keep a dominant foothold in the Gulf region and to maintain control over oil supplies. At least one faction of the Bush "team", clamoring to go after Saddam Hussein as well, is clearly in this mindset. And let's not forget Pakistan and its concessions to US demands for cooperation in return for lifting of US economic sanctions—and now, the assurance of a sizeable IMF loan. In the tradition of neo-imperial power, the US does not need to dominate countries politically or militarily to get the concessions it wants; its economic influence backed up by the capacity for military anni-hilation is sufficient. And, spurred by popular rage over the World Trade Center attacks, all this is wrapped in the outpouring of nationalist patriotism and flag-waving that now envelops the American landscape.

Though lacking the actual imperial power of the US, the Bin Laden forces mimic its imperial aspirations. If we ask, what are the terrorists seeking?, we need to recognize their worldview as an extreme and vicious form of nationalism—a kind of fascism, I would argue, because of its reliance on terror to achieve its ends. In this respect, their goals, like those of the US, go beyond merely punishment. Amar (2001) says the whole history of Arab and Islamic nationalism has been one that transcended the colonially imposed boundaries of the nation-state, one that was always transnational and pan-Arabic, or pan-Muslim, in form. Although the terrorists have no social base or legitimacy in laying claim to this tradition, they clearly seek to usurp it.

This seems evident in Bin Laden's language invoking "the Arab nation", "the Arab peninsula", and a "brotherhood" reaching from Eastern Europe to Turkey and Albania, to the entire Middle East, South Asia and Kashmir. Their mission is to drive out "the infidels" and their Muslim supporters from something that looks like one-third of the globe. Provoking the US to bomb Afghanistan and/or attempt ousting the Taliban would likely destabilize Pakistan and possibly catapult it into the hands of Taliban-like extremists, who would then control nuclear weapons—a big step toward their perverted and hijacked version of the pan-Muslim dream.

3. Pseudo-Religion

As many others have commented, the "clash of religions" or "clash of cultures" interpretation of the current scenario is utterly specious. What we have instead is an appropriation of religious symbolism and discourse for predominantly political purposes, and to justify permanent war and violence. So Bin Laden declares a jihad, or holy war, against the US, its civilians as well as its soldiers; and Bush declares a crusade against the terrorists and all who harbor or support them. Bin Laden declares himself the "servant of Allah fighting for the sake of the religion of Allah" and to protect Islam's holy mosques, while Bush declares Washington the promoter of "infinite justice" and predicts certain victory, because "God is not neutral." (The Pentagon changed the "Operation Infinite Justice" label to "Operation Enduring Freedom" after Muslim-Americans objected and three Christian clergymen warned that "infinite" presumed divinity, the "sin of pride".) But we have to question the authenticity of this religious discourse on both sides, however sincere its proponents. A "Statement from Scholars of the Islamic Religion", circulated after the attacks, firmly denounces terrorism—the wanton killing of innocent civilians—as contrary to sharia law. And Bush's adoption of this apocalyptic discourse can only be seen as substituting a conservative, right-wing form of legitimation for the neoliberal internationalist discourse that conservatives reject. In either case, it is worth quoting the always wise Eduardo Galeano, writing in Mexico's La Jornada: "In the struggle of Good against Evil, it's always the people who get killed."

4. Militarism

Both the Bush administration and the Bin Laden forces adopt the methods of war and violence to achieve their ends, but in very different ways. US militarism is of the ultra-high-tech variety that seeks to terrorize by the sheer might, volume and technological virtuosity of our armaments. Of course, as the history of Vietnam and the survival of Saddam Hussein attest, this is an illusion of the highest order. (Remember the "smart bombs" in the Gulf War that headed for soda machines?) But our military technology is also a vast and insatiable industry for which profit, not strategy, is the driving rationale. As Jack Blum, a critic of US foreign policy, pointed out recently in the Sacramento Bee, "the national defense game is a systems and money operation" that has little if any relevance to terrorism. Missiles were designed to counter hostile states with their own fixed territories and weapons arsenals, not terrorists who sneak around the globe and whose "weapons of mass destruction" are human bodies and hijacked planes; nor the famously impervious terrain and piles of rubble that constitute Afghanistan. Even George W. Bush, in one of his most sensible comments to date, remarked that we'd know better than to aim "a $2 billion cruise missile at a $10 empty tent". And yet, four days after the attack, the Democrats in Congress piled madness atop madness and withdrew their opposition to Bush's costly and destructive "missile shield", voting to restore $1.3 billion in spending authority for this misconceived and dangerous project. And the armaments companies quickly started lining up to receive their big orders for the impending next war—the war, we are told, that will last a long time, maybe the rest of our lives. US militarism is not about rationality—not even about fighting terrorism—but about profits.

The war-mania and rallying around the flag exhibited by the American people express desire, not for military profits, but for something else, something harder for feminist and anti-war dissidents to understand. Maybe it's just the need to vent anger and feel avenged, or the more deep-rooted one to experience some sense of community and higher purpose in a society where we are so atomized and isolated from one another and the world. On 25 September, Barbara Kingsolver wrote in the *San Francisco Chronicle* that she and her husband reluctantly sent their five-year-old daughter to school dressed in red, white and blue like the other kids because they didn't want to let jingoists and censors "steal the flag from us". Their little girl probably echoed the longings of many less reflective grownups when she said, wearing the colors of the flag "means we're a country; just people all together".

The militarism of the terrorists is of a very different nature—based on the mythic figure of the Bedouin warrior, or the Ikhwan fighters of the early twentieth century who enabled Ibn Saud to consolidate his dynastic state. Their hallmark is individual courage and ferocity in battle; Malise Ruthven's *Islam in the World* (1984) quotes one Arab witness who described them, foreshadowing reports of Soviet veterans from the 1980s Afghan war, as "utterly fearless of death, not caring how many fall, advancing rank upon rank with only one desire—the defeat and annihilation of the enemy". Of course, this image too, like every hyper-nationalist ideology, is rooted in a mythic golden past and has little to do with how real terrorists in the twenty-first century are recruited, trained and paid off. And, like high-tech militarism, terrorist low-tech militarism is also based in an illusion—that millions of believers will rise up, obey the fatwa, and defeat the infidel. It's an illusion because it grossly underestimates the most powerful weapon in global capitalism's arsenal—not "infinite justice" or even nukes but infinite Nikes and CDs. And it also underestimates the local power of feminism, which the fundamentalists mistakenly confuse with the West. Iran today, in all its internal contradictions, shows the resilience and globalized/localized variety of both youth cultures and women's movements.

5. Masculinism

Militarism, nationalism, and colonialism as terrains of power have always been in large part contests over the meanings of manhood. Feminist political scientist Cynthia Enloe remarks that "men's sense of their own masculinity, often tenuous, is as much a factor in international politics as is the flow of oil, cables, and military hardware" (1993: 173). In the case of Bin Laden's Taliban patrons, the form and excessiveness of the misogyny that goes hand in hand with state terrorism and extreme fundamentalism have been graphically documented. Just go to the website of the Revolutionary Association of the Women of Afghanistan (RAWA), at www.rawa.org, to view more photos of atrocities against women (and men) for sexual offenses, dress code offenses, and other forms of deviance than you'll be able to stomach. According to John Burns, writing in the *New York Times Magazine* in 1990, the "rebel" leader in the Afghan war who received "the lion's share of American money and weapons"—and was not a Taliban—had been reputed to have "dispatched followers [during his student movement days] to throw vials of acid into the faces of women students who refused to wear veils".

In the case of transnational terrorists and Bin Laden himself, their model of manliness is that of the Islamic "brotherhood", the band of brothers bonded together in an agonistic commitment to fighting the enemy to the death. The CIA–Pakistani–Saudi-backed camps and training schools set up to support the "freedom fighters" (who later became "terrorists") in the anti-Soviet war were breeding grounds not only of a worldwide terrorist network but also of its masculinist, misogynist culture. Bin Laden clearly sees himself as a patriarchal tribal chief whose duty is to provide for and protect, not only his own retinue, wives and many children, but also his whole network of lieutenants and recruits and their families. He is the legendary Arabic counterpart of the Godfather.

In contrast to this, can we say that the US as standard-bearer of global capitalism is "gender-neutral"? Don't we have a woman— indeed an African-American woman—at the helm of our National Security Council, the president's right hand in designing the permanent war machine? Despite reported "gender gaps" in polls about war, we know that women are not inherently more peace-loving than men. Remember all those suburban housewives with their yellow ribbons in midwestern airports and shopping malls during the Gulf War? Global capitalist masculinism is alive and well but concealed in its Eurocentric, racist guise of "rescuing" downtrodden Afghan women from the misogynist regime it helped bring to power. Feminists around the world, who have tried for so long to call attention to the plight of women and girls in Afghanistan, cannot feel consoled by the prospect of US warplanes and US-backed guerrilla chiefs coming to "save our Afghan sisters". Meanwhile, the US will send single mothers who signed up for the National Guard when welfare ended to fight and die in its holy war; US media remain silent about the activism and self-determination of groups like RAWA and Refugee Women in Development; and the US military establishment refuses accountability before an International Criminal Court for the acts of rape and sexual assault committed by its soldiers stationed across the globe. Masculinism and misogyny take many forms, not always the most visible.

6. Racism

Of course, what I have named fascist fundamentalism, or transnational terrorism, is also saturated in racism, but of a very specific, focused kind— which is anti-Semitism. The World Trade Center towers symbolized not only American capitalism, not only finance capitalism, but, for the terrorists, *Jewish* finance capitalism. We can see this in the reported misreporting of the September 11 attacks in Arabic-language newspapers in the Middle East as probably the work of the Israelis; their erroneous allegation that not a single person among the dead and missing was Jewish, so Jews must have had advance warning, etc. In his 1998 interview, Bin Laden constantly refers to "Jews", not Israelis, in his accusations about plans to take over the whole Arab peninsula. He asserts that "the Americans and the Jews ... represent the spearhead with which the members of our religion have been slaughtered. Any effort directed against America and the Jews yields positive and direct results." And finally, he rewrites history and collapses the diversity of Muslims in a warning to "Western governments" to sever their ties to Jews:

> the enmity between us and the Jews goes far back in time and is deep-rooted. There is no question that war between the two of us is inevitable. For this reason it is not in the interest of Western governments to expose the interests of their people to all kinds of retaliation for almost nothing.

(I cringe to realize I am part of the "nothing".)

US racism is much more diffuse but just as insidious; the pervasive racism and ethnocentrism that fester under the American skin always boil to the surface at times of national crisis. As Sunita Reddy (2001) put it in a recent teach-in, the targeting of Sikhs and other Indians, Arabs, and even tan Latinos and African-Americans in the wave of violent and abusive acts throughout the country since the disaster signals an enlargement of the "zone of distrust" in American racism beyond the usual black–white focus. Women who wear headscarves or saris are particularly vulnerable to harassment, but Arab and Indian men of all ages are the ones being murdered. The state pretends to abhor such incidents and threatens their full prosecution. But this is the same state that made the so-called Anti-Terrorism Act, passed in 1995 after the Oklahoma City bombing (an act committed by native white Christian terrorists), a pretext for rounding up and deporting immigrants of all kinds; and that is now once again waiving the civil liberties of immigrants in its zealous anti-terrorist manhunt. Each day *The New York Times* publishes its rogues' gallery of police photos of the suspects, so reminiscent of those eugenic photographs of "criminal types" of an earlier era and imprinting upon readers' minds a certain set of facial characteristics they should now fear and blame. Racial profiling becomes a national pastime.

If we look only at terrorist tactics and the world's revulsion against them, then we might conclude rather optimistically that thuggery will never win out in the end. But we ignore the context in which terrorism operates at our peril, and that context includes not only racism and Eurocentrism but many forms of social injustice. In thinking through a moral position on this crisis, we have to distinguish between *immediate causes* and *necessary conditions*. Neither the United States (as a state) nor the corporate and financial power structure that the World Trade Center symbolized *caused* the horrors of September 11. Without question, the outrageous, heinous murder, maiming and orphaning of so many innocent people—who were every race, ethnicity, color, class, age, gender, and some sixty-odd nationalities—deserve some kind of just redress. On the other hand, the *conditions* in which transnational terrorism thrives, gains recruits, and lays claim to moral legitimacy include many for which the US and its corporate and financial interests are directly responsible, even if they don't for a minute excuse the attacks. It is often asked lately, why does the Third World hate us so much? Put another way, why do so many people, including my own friends in Asia, Africa, Latin America and the Middle East, express so much ambivalence about what happened, both lamenting an unforgivable criminal act and at the same time taking some satisfaction that Americans are finally suffering too? We make a fatal mistake if we attribute these mixed feelings only to envy or resentment of our wealth and freedoms and ignore a historical context of aggression, injustice and inequality. Consider these facts:

1. The United States is still the only country in the world to have actually *used* the most infamous weapons of mass destruction in the nuclear bombing of innocent civilians—in Hiroshima and Nagasaki.

2. The US persists to this day in bombing Iraq, destroying the lives and food supplies of hundreds of thousands of civilian adults and children there. We bombed Belgrade—a dense capital city—for eighty straight days during the war in Kosovo, and supported bombing that killed untold civilians in El Salvador in the 1980s. In the name of fighting Communism, our CIA and military training apparatus sponsored paramilitary massacres, assassinations, tortures and disappearances in many Latin American and Central American countries in Operation Condor and the like in the 1970s and has supported corrupt, authoritarian regimes in the Middle East, South-East Asia, and elsewhere—the Shah of Iran, Suharto in Indonesia, the Saudi dynasty, and let's not forget the Taliban regime itself. September 11 is also the date of the coup against the democratically elected Allende government in Chile and the beginning of the 25-year Pinochet dictatorship, again thanks to US support. Yes, a long history of state terrorism.

3. In the Middle East, which is the microcosm of the current conflagration, billions in annual US military aid and the Bush administration's refusal to pressure the Sharon government are the *sine qua non* of continued Israeli government policies of attacks on villages, demolition of homes, destruction of olive orchards, restrictions on travel, continual human rights abuses of Palestinians and even Arab citizens, assassination of political leaders, building of roads and enlarging of settlements—all of which exacerbate Palestinian despair and suicide bombings. The US thereby contributes to deepening the illegal occupation and "bantustanizing" the Palestinian territories, and thus perpetuating hostilities.

4. Despite its pretense to uphold women's rights, the US is one of only around two dozen countries that have failed to ratify the UN Convention on the Elimination of All Forms of Discrimination Against Women, and the only country in the world (as of April 2002, when Somalia finally agreed to sign) that refuses to sign the UN Convention on the Rights of the Child. It is the most vocal opponent of the statute establishing an International Criminal Court as well as the treaties banning landmines and germ warfare; a principal subverter of a new multilateral treaty to combat illegal small arms trafficking; and the sole country in the world to

threaten an unprecedented space-based defense system and imminent violation of the anti-ballistic missile treaty. So who is the "outlaw", the "rogue state"?

5. The US is the only major industrialized country to refuse signing the final Kyoto Protocol on Global Climate Change, despite compromises in that document designed to meet US objections. Meanwhile, a new global scientific study shows that the countries whose productivity will benefit most from climate change are Canada, Russia and the US, while the biggest losers will be the countries that have contributed least to global climate change—i.e., most of Africa.

6. As even the World Bank and the United Nations Development Programme attest, two decades of globalization have resulted in enlarging rather than shrinking the gaps between rich and poor, both within countries and among countries. The benefits of global market liberalization and integration have accrued disproportionately to wealthy Americans and Europeans (as well as small elites in the Third World). Despite the presumed democratizing effects of the Internet, a middle-class American "needs to save a month's salary to buy a computer; a Bangladeshi must save all his wages for eight years to do so". And despite its constant trumpeting of "free-trade" rhetoric, the US remains a persistent defender of protectionist policies for its farmers and steel and textile manufacturers. Meanwhile small producers throughout Asia, Africa and the Caribbean— a great many of whom are women—are squeezed out by US imports and relegated to the informal economy or sweatshop labor for multinationals.

7. The G-8 countries, of which the US is the senior partner, dominate decision-making in the IMF and the World Bank, whose structural adjust-ments and conditionalities for loans and debt relief help to keep many poor countries and their citizens locked in poverty.

8. In the aftermath of the September 11 attacks, the US Congress was able to come up with an immediate $40 billion for "anti-terrorism" activities, another $40 billion to bail out the airlines, and a 20-year contract with Lockheed to produce military aircraft for $200 billion—enough to eliminate contagious diseases from the face of the earth. Yet our foreign assistance appropriations (except for military aid) have shrunk; we, the world's richest country, contribute only one-seventh of 1 per cent of our gross national product to foreign aid—the least of any industrialized country. A recent WHO report tells us the total cost of providing safe water and sanitation to all of sub-Saharan Africa would be only $11 billion, only no one can figure out where the money will come from; and

the UN is still a long way off from raising a similar amount for its proclaimed Global Fund to combat AIDS, malaria and tuberculosis. What kind of meanness is this? And what does it say about forms of racism, or "global apartheid", that value some lives—those in the US and Europe—far more than others in other parts of the globe?

And the list goes on, with McDonald's, Coca-Cola and CNN and all the uninvited commercial detritus that proliferates everywhere on the face of the earth and offends the cultural and spiritual sensibilities of so many—including transnational feminist travelers like me, when we find pieces of our local shopping mall transplanted to central Manila, Kampala or Bangalore. But worse than the triviality and bad taste of these cultural and commercial barrages is the arrogant presumption that our "way of life" is the best on earth and ought to be welcome everywhere; or that our power and supposed advancement entitle us to dictate policies and strategies to the rest of the world. This is the face of imperialism in the twenty-first century.

None of this reckoning can comfort those who lost loved ones on September 11, or the thousands of attack victims who lost their jobs, homes and livelihoods; nor can it excuse the hideous crimes. As the Palestinian poet Mahmoud Darwish writes, "nothing, nothing justifies terrorism". Still, in attempting to understand what has happened and think how to prevent it happening again (which is probably a vain wish), we Americans have to take all these painful facts into account. The United States as the command center of global capitalism will remain ill-equipped to "stop terrorism" until it begins to recognize its own past and present responsibility for many of the conditions I've listed and to address them in a responsible way. But this would mean the United States becoming something different from itself, transforming itself, including abandoning the presumption that it should unilaterally police the world. This problem of transformation is at the heart of the vexing question of finding solutions different from all-out war. So let me turn to how we might think differently about power. Here is what I propose, tentatively, for now:

1. The slogan "War Is Not the Answer" is a practical as well as an onto-logical truth. Bombing or other military attacks on Afghanistan will not root out networks of terrorists, who could be hiding deep in the mountains or in Pakistan or Germany or Florida or New Jersey. It will only succeed in destroying an already decimated country, killing untold numbers of civilians as well as combatants, and creating hundreds of thousands more refugees. And it is likely to arouse so much anger among Islamist sympathizers as to destabilize the entire region and perpetuate the cycle of retaliation and terrorist attacks. All the horror of the twentieth

century surely should teach us that war feeds on itself and that armed violence reflects, not an extension of politics by other means, but the failure of politics; not the defense of civilization, but the breakdown of civilization.

2. Tracking down and bringing the perpetrators of terrorism to justice, in some kind of international police action, is a reasonable aim but one fraught with dangers. Because the US is the world's only "superpower", its declaration of war against terrorism and its supporters everywhere says to other countries that we are once again taking over as global policeman, or, as Fidel Castro put it, a "world military dictatorship under the exclusive rule of force, irrespective of any international laws or institutions". Here at home a "national emergency" or "state of war"—*especially* when defined as different from any other war—means the curtailment of civil liberties, harassment of immigrants, racial profiling, and withholding of information (censorship) or feeding of disinformation to the media, all without any time limits or accountability under the dubious Office of Homeland Security and the "USA Patriot Act". We should oppose both US unilateralism and the permanent security state. We should urge our representatives in Congress to diligently defend the civil liberties of all.

3. I agree with the Afro-Asian Peoples Solidarity Organization (AAPSO) in Cairo that "this punishment should be inflicted according to the law and only upon those who were responsible for these events", and that it should be organized within the framework of the United Nations and international law, not unilaterally by the United States. This is not the same as the US getting unanimous approval from the Security Council to commandeer global security, which is a first step at best. Numerous treaties against terrorism and money-laundering already exist in international law. The International Criminal Court, whose establishment the US government has so stubbornly opposed, would be the logical body to try terrorist cases, with the cooperation of national police and surveillance systems. *We should demand that the US ratify the ICC statute.* In the meantime, a special tribunal under international auspices, like the ones for the former Yugoslavia and Rwanda, could be set up as well as an international agency to coordinate national police and intelligence efforts, with the US as one participating member. This is the power of international engagement and cooperation.

4. No amount of police action, however cooperative, can stop terrorism without addressing the conditions of misery and injustice that nourish and aggravate terrorism. The US has to undertake a serious re-examination of

its values and its policies with regard not only to the Middle East but also to the larger world. It has to take responsibility for being in the world, including ways of sharing its wealth, resources and technology; democratizing decisions about global trade, finance, and security; and assuring that access to "global public goods" like health care, housing, food, education, sanitation, water, and freedom from racial and gender discrimination is given priority in international relations. What we even mean by "security" has to encompass all these aspects of wellbeing, of "human security", and has to be universal in its reach.

Let me again quote from the poet Mahmoud Darwish's statement, which was published in the Palestinian daily *Al-Ayyam* on 17 September and signed by many Palestinian writers and intellectuals.

> We know that the American wound is deep and we know that this tragic moment is a time for solidarity and the sharing of pain. But we also know that the horizons of the intellect can traverse landscapes of devastation. Terrorism has no location or boundaries, it does not reside in a geography of its own; its homeland is disillusionment and despair.
>
> The best weapon to eradicate terrorism from the soul lies in the solidarity of the international world, in respecting the rights of all peoples of this globe to live in harmony and by reducing the ever increasing gap between north and south. And the most effective way to defend freedom is through fully realizing the meaning of justice.

What gives me hope is that this statement's sentiments are being voiced by growing numbers of groups here in the US, including the National Council of Churches, the Green Party, a coalition of 100 entertainers and civil rights leaders, huge coalitions of peace groups and student organizations, New Yorkers Say No to War, black and white women celebrities featured on Oprah Winfrey's show, parents and spouses of attack victims, as well as some 500 petitioners from women's peace groups here and across the globe calling on the UN Security Council to "Stop the War, Rebuild a Just Society in Afghanistan, and Support Women's Human Rights". Maybe out of the ashes we will recover a new kind of solidarity; maybe the terrorists will force us, not to mirror them, but to see the world and humanity as a whole.

References

Amar, Paul. (2001). Talk at Teach-In, Hunter College. New York: September.

Darwish, Mahmood. (2001). *Al-Ayyam*. 17 September.

Enloe, Cynthia. (1993). *The Morning After: Sexual Politics at the End of the Cold War*. Berkeley: University of California Press.

Pollitt, Katha. (2001). "Put Out No Flags". Subject to Debate column, *The Nation*. 8 October.

Reddy, Sunita. (2001). Talk at Teach-In, City University of New York Graduate Centre. New York: September.

Ruthven, Malise. (1984). *Islam in the World*. New York: Oxford.

Arundhati Roy
The Algebra of Infinite Justice

Saturday, 29 September 2001.

In the aftermath of the unconscionable September 11 suicide attacks on the Pentagon and the World Trade Center, an American newscaster said: "Good and evil rarely manifest themselves as clearly as they did last Tuesday. People who we don't know massacred people who we do. And they did so with contemptuous glee." Then he broke down and wept.

Here's the rub: America is at war against people it doesn't know, because they don't appear much on TV. Before it has properly identified or even begun to comprehend the nature of its enemy, the US government has, in a rush of publicity and embarrassing rhetoric, cobbled together an "international coalition against terror", mobilised its army, its air force, its navy and its media, and committed them to battle.

The trouble is that once America goes off to war, it can't very well return without having fought one. If it doesn't find its enemy, for the sake of the enraged folks back home, it will have to manufacture one. Once war begins, it will develop a momentum, a logic and a justification of its own, and we'll lose sight of why it's being fought in the first place.

What we're witnessing here is the spectacle of the world's most powerful country reaching reflexively, angrily, for an old instinct to fight a new kind of war. Suddenly, when it comes to defending itself, America's streamlined warships, cruise missiles and F-16 jets look like obsolete, lumbering things. As deterrence, its arsenal of nuclear bombs is no longer worth its weight in scrap. Box-cutters, penknives, and cold anger are the weapons with which the wars of the new century will be waged. Anger is the lock pick. It slips through customs unnoticed. Doesn't show up in baggage checks.

Who is America fighting? On 20 September, the FBI said that it had doubts about the identities of some of the hijackers. On the same day President George W. Bush said, "We know exactly who these people are and which governments are supporting them." It sounds as though the president knows something that the FBI and the American public don't.

In his 20 September address to the US Congress, President Bush called the enemies of America "enemies of freedom". "Americans are asking, 'Why do they hate us?'", he said. "They hate our freedoms—our freedom of religion, our freedom of speech, our freedom to vote and assemble and disagree with each other." People are being asked to make two leaps of faith here. First, to assume that The Enemy is who the US government says it is, even though it has no substantial evidence to support that claim. And second, to assume that The Enemy's motives are what the US government says they are, and there's nothing to support that either.

For strategic, military and economic reasons, it is vital for the US government to persuade its public that their commitment to freedom and democracy and the American Way of Life is under attack. In the current atmosphere of grief, outrage and anger, it's an easy notion to peddle. However, if that were true, it's reasonable to wonder why the symbols of America's economic and military dominance—the World Trade Center and the Pentagon—were chosen as the targets of the attacks. Why not the Statue of Liberty?

Could it be that the stygian anger that led to the attacks has its taproot not in American freedom and democracy, but in the US government's record of commitment and support to exactly the opposite things—to military and economic terrorism, insurgency, military dictatorship, religious bigotry and unimaginable genocide (outside America)?

It must be hard for ordinary Americans, so recently bereaved, to look up at the world with their eyes full of tears and encounter what might appear to them to be indifference. It isn't indifference. It's just augury. An absence of surprise. The tired wisdom of knowing that what goes around eventually comes around. American people ought to know that it is not them but their government's policies that are so hated. They can't possibly doubt that they themselves, their extraordinary musicians, their writers, their actors, their spectacular sportsmen and their cinema, are universally welcomed. All of us have been moved by the courage and grace shown by firefighters, rescue workers and ordinary office staff in the days since the attacks.

America's grief at what happened has been immense and immensely public. It would be grotesque to expect it to calibrate or modulate its anguish. However, it will be a pity if, instead of using this as an opportunity to try to understand why September 11 happened, Americans use it as an opportunity to usurp the whole world's sorrow to mourn and avenge only their own. Because then it falls to the rest of us to ask the hard questions and say the harsh things. And for our pains, for our bad timing, we will be disliked, ignored and perhaps eventually silenced.

The world will probably never know what motivated those particular hijackers who flew planes into those particular American buildings. They were not glory boys. They left no suicide notes, no political messages; no organisation has claimed credit for the attacks. All we know is that their belief in what they were doing outstripped the natural human instinct for survival, or any desire to be remembered. It's almost as though they could not scale down the enormity of their rage to anything smaller than their deeds. And what they did has blown a hole in the world as we knew it. In the absence of information, politicians, political commentators and writers (like myself) will invest the act with their own politics, with their own interpretations. This speculation, this analysis of the political climate in which the attacks took place, can only be a good thing.

But war is looming large. Whatever remains to be said must be said quickly. Before America places itself at the helm of the "international coalition against terror", before it invites (and coerces) countries to actively participate in its almost godlike mission—called Operation Infinite Justice until it was pointed out that this could be seen as an insult to Muslims, who believe that only Allah can mete out infinite justice, and was renamed Operation Enduring Freedom—it would help if some small clarifications are made.

For example, Infinite Justice/Enduring Freedom: for whom? Is this America's war against terror in America or against terror in general? What exactly is being avenged here? Is it the tragic loss of almost 7000 lives, the gutting of five million square feet of office space in Manhattan, the destruction of a section of the Pentagon, the loss of several hundreds of thousands of jobs, the bankruptcy of some airline companies and the dip in the New York Stock Exchange? Or is it more than that?

In 1996, Madeleine Albright, then the US secretary of state, was asked on national television what she felt about the fact that 500,000 Iraqi children had died as a result of US economic sanctions. She replied that it was "a very hard choice", but that, all things considered, "we think the price is worth it". Albright never lost her job for saying this. She continued to travel the world representing the views and aspirations of the US government. More pertinently, the sanctions against Iraq remain in place. Children continue to die.

So here we have it. The equivocating distinction between civilisation and savagery, between the "massacre of innocent people" or, if you like, "a clash of civilisations" and "collateral damage". The sophistry and fastidious algebra of infinite justice. How many dead Iraqis will it take to make the world a better place? How many dead Afghans for every dead American? How many dead women and children for every dead man? How many dead mujahideen for each dead investment banker? As we watch mesmerised, Operation Enduring Freedom unfolds on TV monitors across the world. A coalition of the world's superpowers is closing in on Afghanistan, one of the poorest, most ravaged, war-torn countries in the world, whose ruling Taliban government is sheltering Osama Bin Laden, the man being held responsible for the September 11 attacks.

The only thing in Afghanistan that could possibly count as collateral value is its citizenry. (Among them, half a million maimed orphans. There are accounts of hobbling stampedes that occur when artificial limbs are air-dropped into remote, inaccessible villages.) Afghanistan's economy is in a shambles. In fact, the problem for an invading army is that Afghanistan has no conventional coordinates or signposts to plot on a military map—no big cities, no highways, no industrial complexes, no water treatment plants. Farms have been turned into mass graves. The countryside is littered with land-mines—10 million is the most recent estimate. The American army would first have to clear the mines and build roads in order to take its soldiers in.

Fearing an attack from America, one million citizens have fled from their homes and arrived at the border between Pakistan and Afghanistan. The UN estimates that there are eight million Afghan citizens who need emergency aid. As supplies run out—food and aid agencies have been asked to leave—the BBC reports that one of the worst humanitarian disasters of recent times has begun to unfold. Witness the infinite justice of the new century. Civilians starving to death while they're waiting to be killed.

In America there has been rough talk of "bombing Afghanistan back to the stone age". Someone please break the news that Afghanistan is already there. And if it's any consolation, America played no small part in helping it on its way. The American people may be a little fuzzy about where exactly Afghan-istan is (we hear reports that there's a run on maps of the country), but the US government and Afghanistan are old friends.

In 1979, after the Soviet invasion of Afghanistan, the CIA and Pakistan's ISI (Inter Services Intelligence) launched the largest covert operation in the history of the CIA. Their purpose was to harness the energy of Afghan resistance to the Soviets and expand it into a holy war, an Islamic jihad, which would turn Muslim countries within the Soviet Union against the communist regime and eventually destabilise it. When it began, it was meant to be the Soviet Union's Vietnam. It turned out to be much more than that. Over the years, through the ISI, the CIA funded and recruited almost 100,000 radical mujahideen from forty Islamic countries as soldiers for America's proxy war. The rank and file of the mujahideen were unaware that their jihad was actually being fought on behalf of Uncle Sam. (The irony is that America was equally unaware that it was financing a future war against itself.)

In 1989, after being bloodied by ten years of relentless conflict, the Russians withdrew, leaving behind a civilisation reduced to rubble.

Civil war in Afghanistan raged on. The jihad spread to Chechnya, Kosovo and eventually to Kashmir. The CIA continued to pour in money and military equipment, but the overheads had become immense, and more money was needed. The mujahideen ordered farmers to plant opium as a "revolutionary tax". The ISI set up hundreds of heroin laboratories across Afghanistan. Within two years of the CIA's arrival, the Pakistan–Afghanistan borderland had become the biggest producer of heroin in the world, and the single biggest source of the heroin on American streets. The annual profits, said to be between $100 billion and $200 billion, were ploughed back into training and arming militants.

In 1995, the Taliban—then a marginal sect of dangerous, hardline fundamentalists—fought its way to power in Afghanistan. It was funded by the ISI, that old cohort of the CIA, and supported by many political parties in Pakistan. The Taliban unleashed a regime of terror. Its first victims were its own people, particularly women. It closed down girls' schools, dismissed women from government jobs, and enforced sharia laws under which women deemed to be "immoral" are stoned to death, and widows guilty of being adulterous are buried alive. Given the Taliban government's human rights track record, it seems unlikely that it will in any way be intimidated or swerved from its purpose by the prospect of war, or the threat to the lives of its civilians.

After all that has happened, can there be anything more ironic than Russia and America joining hands to re-destroy Afghanistan? The question is, can you destroy destruction? Dropping more bombs on Afghanistan will only shuffle the rubble, scramble some old graves and disturb the dead.

The desolate landscape of Afghanistan was the burial ground of Soviet communism and the springboard of a unipolar world dominated by America. It made the space for neo-capitalism and corporate globalisation, again dominated by America. And now Afghanistan is poised to become the graveyard for the unlikely soldiers who fought and won this war for America.

And what of America's trusted ally? Pakistan too has suffered enormously. The US government has not been shy of supporting military dictators who have blocked the idea of democracy from taking root in the country. Before the CIA arrived, there was a small rural market for opium in Pakistan. Between 1979 and 1985, the number of heroin addicts grew from zero to 1.5 million. Even before September 11, there were 3 million Afghan refugees living in tented camps along the border. Pakistan's economy is crumbling. Sectarian violence, globalisation's structural adjustment programmes and drug lords are tearing the country to pieces. Set up to fight the Soviets, the terrorist training centres and madrassahs, sown like dragon's teeth across the country, produced fundamentalists with tremendous popular appeal within Pakistan itself. The Taliban, which the Pakistan government has supported, funded and propped up for years, has material and strategic alliances with Pakistan's own political parties.

Now the US government is asking (asking?) Pakistan to garotte the pet it has hand-reared in its backyard for so many years. President Musharraf, having pledged his support to the US, could well find he has something resembling civil war on his hands.

India, thanks in part to its geography, and in part to the vision of its former leaders, has so far been fortunate enough to be left out of this Great Game. Had it been drawn in, it's more than likely that our democracy, such as it is, would not have survived. Today, as some of us watch in horror, the Indian government is furiously gyrating its hips, begging the US to set up its base in India rather than Pakistan. Having had this ringside view of Pakistan's sordid fate, it isn't just odd, it's unthinkable, that India should want to do this. Any Third World country with a fragile economy and a complex social base should know by now that to invite a superpower such as America in (whether it says it's staying or just passing through) would be like inviting a brick to drop through your windscreen.

Operation Enduring Freedom is ostensibly being fought to uphold the American Way of Life. It'll probably end up undermining it completely. It will spawn more anger and more terror across the world. For ordinary people in America, it will mean lives lived in a climate of sickening uncertainty: Will my child be safe in school? Will there be nerve gas in the subway? a bomb in the cinema hall? Will my love come home tonight?

There have been warnings about the possibility of biological warfare—smallpox, bubonic plague, anthrax—the deadly payload of innocuous crop-duster aircraft. Being picked off a few at a time may end up being worse than being annihilated all at once by a nuclear bomb.

The US government, and no doubt governments all over the world, will use the climate of war as an excuse to curtail civil liberties, deny free speech, lay off workers, harass ethnic and religious minorities, cut back on public spending, and divert huge amounts of money to the defence industry. To what purpose?

President Bush can no more "rid the world of evil-doers" than he can stock it with saints. It's absurd for the US government to even toy with the notion that it can stamp out terrorism with more violence and oppression. Terrorism is the symptom, not the disease. Terrorism has no country. It's transnational, as global an enterprise as Coke or Pepsi or Nike. At the first sign of trouble, terrorists can pull up stakes and move their "factories" from country to country in search of a better deal. Just like the multinationals.

Terrorism as a phenomenon may never go away. But if it is to be contained, the first step is for America to at least acknowledge that it shares the planet with other nations, with other human beings who, even if they are not on TV, have loves and griefs and stories and songs and sorrows and, for heaven's sake, rights.

Instead, when Donald Rumsfeld, the US defence secretary, was asked what he would call a victory in America's new war, he said that if he could convince the world that Americans must be allowed to continue with their way of life, he would consider it a victory.

The September 11 attacks were a monstrous calling card from a world gone horribly wrong. The message may have been written by Bin Laden (who knows?) and delivered by his couriers, but it could well have been signed by the ghosts of the victims of America's old wars. The millions killed in Korea, Vietnam and Cambodia, the 17,500 killed when Israel—backed by the US— invaded Lebanon in 1982, the 200,000 Iraqis killed in Operation Desert Storm, the thousands of Palestinians who have died fighting Israel's occupation of the West Bank. And the millions who died, in Yugoslavia, Somalia, Haiti, Chile, Nicaragua, El Salvador, the Dominican Republic, Panama, at the hands of all the terrorists, dictators and genocidists whom the American government supported, trained, bankrolled and supplied with arms. And this is far from being a comprehensive list.

For a country involved in so much warfare and conflict, the American people have been extremely fortunate. The strikes on September 11 were only the second on American soil in over a century. The first was Pearl Harbor. The reprisal for this took a long route, but ended with Hiroshima and Nagasaki. This time the world waits with bated breath for the horrors to come.

Someone recently said that if Osama Bin Laden didn't exist, America would have had to invent him. But, in a way, America did invent him. He was among the jihadis who moved to Afghanistan in 1979 when the CIA commenced its operations there. Bin Laden has the distinction of being created by the CIA and wanted by the FBI. In the course of a fortnight he has been promoted from suspect to prime suspect and then, despite the lack of any real evidence, straight up the charts to being "wanted, dead or alive".

From all accounts, it will be impossible to produce evidence (of the sort that would stand scrutiny in a court of law) to link Bin Laden to the September 11 attacks. So far, it appears that the most incriminating piece of evidence against him is the fact that he has not condemned them. From what is known about the location of Bin Laden and the living conditions in which he operates, it's entirely possible that he did not personally plan and carry out the attacks—that he is the inspirational figure, "the CEO of the holding company". The Taliban's response to US demands for the extradition of Bin Laden has been uncharacteristically reasonable: produce the evidence, then we'll hand him over. President Bush's response is that the demand is "non-negotiable".

(While talks are on for the extradition of CEOs—can India put in a side request for the extradition of Warren Anderson of the US? He was the chairman of Union Carbide, responsible for the Bhopal gas leak that killed 16,000 people in 1984. We have collated the necessary evidence. It's all in the files. Could we have him, please?)

But who is Osama Bin Laden really?

Let me rephrase that. What is Osama Bin Laden? He's America's family secret. He is the American president's dark *doppelgänger*. The savage twin of all that purports to be beautiful and civilised. He has been sculpted from the spare rib of a world laid to waste by America's foreign policy: its gunboat diplomacy, its nuclear arsenal, its vulgarly stated policy of "full-spectrum dominance", its chilling disregard for non-American lives, its barbarous military interventions, its support for despotic and dictatorial regimes, its merciless economic agenda that has munched through the economies of poor countries like a cloud of locusts. Its marauding multinationals who are taking over the air we breathe, the ground we stand on, the water we drink, the thoughts we think. Now that the family secret has been spilled, the twins are blurring into one another and gradually becoming interchangeable. Their guns, bombs, money and drugs have been going around in the loop for a while. (The Stinger missiles that will greet US helicopters were supplied by the CIA. The heroin used by America's drug addicts comes from Afghanistan. The Bush administration recently gave Afghanistan a $43 million subsidy for a "war on drugs" ...)

Now Bush and Bin Laden have even begun to borrow each other's rhetoric. Each refers to the other as "the head of the snake". Both invoke God and use the loose millenarian currency of good and evil as their terms of reference. Both are engaged in unequivocal political crimes. Both are dangerously armed—one with the nuclear arsenal of the obscenely powerful, the other with the incandescent, destructive power of the utterly hopeless. The fireball and the ice pick. The bludgeon and the axe. The important thing to keep in mind is that neither is an acceptable alternative to the other.

President Bush's ultimatum to the people of the world—"If you're not with us, you're against us"—is a piece of presumptuous arrogance. It's not a choice that people want to, need to, or should have to make.

Susan Hawthorne

Fundamentalism, Violence and Disconnection

Debates on issues about violence and responsibility, about fundamentalism and masculinity, have long been fare for feminists. They are debates which have surfaced and resurfaced continuously in different contexts, in different countries. The events of September 11 have created a new wave of debates, not just about private violence, or violence between communities or between men and women, but also about the impact of public violence, of violence which has erupted on a global scale, violence which affects people from the most powerful nation on earth as well as the most vulnerable. It is also violence which affects profits, hits at the heart of the economic and military complex of the US government. And so the debates have shifted. But many of the same themes remain.

In this essay I draw on a range of themes. There is the issue of identity and of identification. When I speak of "us" who do I mean? Where do I stand in relation to this question? Where does a US marine (male or female) stand in relation to this question? Where does a Muslim or a Christian or a Jew stand in relation to this question? These are central issues about standpoint and context.

Where is power located? is a related question central to the following discussion. Those with power tend to be less concerned with the impact of consequences since they are less directly affected by them. On the other hand, their degree of responsibility is often far greater than the less powerful people who implement policies and decisions. One of the outcomes of this discrepancy is the way that violence is structured into the socio-political architecture and violence becomes a tool for the powerful. Indeed, access to the means of wielding violence is a key to understanding how much power an individual or an institution wields. To acknowledge the existence of that power, however, is not in the interests of the powerful, so the powerful engage (through the mainstream media) in a public relations exercise of promoting the concept of "choice" in relation to violence. If one can choose violence, there is a good chance the individual or institution is a centre of power. The powerless face violence, and when they resort to its use, it is often not a matter of choice. The powerless represent the diversity matrix,[1] the broad group marginalised by the dominant culture. They are also the group most likely to be vulnerable to the violence of war and masculine aggression.

I argue that disconnection fosters a culture of violence as "choice" and that fundamentalism and masculinity play a central role in the development of this culture. I conclude that misogyny is a key driving force and that women are a major target of the masculinism that drives fundamentalism. I suggest that the battle has little to do with cultural difference and much more to do with men posturing for power and for profits.

"Us" and "Them"

They hate us because we champion a "new world order" of capitalism, individualism, secularism and democracy that should be the norm everywhere.

Ronald Steel, *New York Times*, 14 September 2001.

We welcome the combat against terrorism. In fact, this combat should have started years ago in terms of preventing incidents like September 11. But this combat against terrorism cannot be won by bombing this or that country. It should be a campaign to stop any country that sells arms or supports financially the fundamentalists' movements or fundamentalist regimes.

RAWA cited by Sonali Kolhatkar, 9 May 2002:
http://www.zmag.org/content/Gender/kolhatkarwomen.cfm

Haruki Murakami, in his examination of the sarin gas attacks on the Tokyo underground on 20 March 1995, writes that when the attacks first occurred he wanted to know nothing about the perpetrators who represented a "them" and this view was also the one reflected by the Japanese media. The US media and the US government together have portrayed very sharply defined depictions of "us" and "them". The "terrorists" are from somewhere else; they do not share the worldview of Americans; they represent a fear of the unknown; and they embody the terror of random acts of violence. But as Murakami goes on to argue, if we don't understand "us", we cannot understand "them". And although Murakami was speaking of violators from within Japanese culture, "they" are not dissimilar from the September 11 attackers. For "they" had imbibed US culture; "they" lived in the USA; and with globalisation spreading its tentacles around the world, it is not difficult for

---

1   The diversity matrix is a term I discuss at length in Hawthorne (2002). Those in the diversity matrix are poor, often women, mostly black. They are indigenous peoples, the "underclasses", as well as slaves, gypsies, nomads, refugees, political exiles. They also include among their number those who do not meet the expectations of the dominant culture: the disabled or the ill, lesbians, eco-activists and some radicals. The primary feature of the diversity matrix is its poverty.

people from many places to "know" American culture in a way that Americans cannot easily "know" other cultures.[2] If US citizens put the image of the attackers out of "their" minds as nothing to do with "us", or as Murakami comments, "if it is used to prop up this 'righteous' position of 'ours' all we will see from now on are ever more exacting and minute analyses of the 'dirty' distortions in 'their' thinking" (2000: 198, 197). And, he continues, in order to understand "the rationale and workings of 'them'" there is "a similar need for a parallel analysis of 'us'" (2000: 197). This essay underscores that analysis through examining the connections between September 11 and the forces of globalisation, as well as examining the structures of violence. Terrorism, as Arundhati Roy points out, "is the symptom, not the disease" (Roy 2001a; this volume: 336).

September 11, 2001, is seen as a watershed date by many. But the level of importance it is given tends to reflect where one stands in relation to the benefits of US globalisation. For those of us with friends in Washington or New York, the reaction was immediate. Are they all right? But what of those for whom the names Washington and New York conjure up (rightly or not) wealth, power, mobility, sophistication, communication, infrastructure, moral ineptitude and military might? Was September 11 an attack on the heart of capitalism? Was it an attack on US complacency? How the attack was framed was also influenced by where the commentator was geographically or politically located. Those outside the US sphere of influence drew parallels with other attacks and other disasters, some of them US-provoked. Those inside the US sphere of influence tended to see September 11 within the US political framework, and record it as an attack on "freedom" and the American way of life. There were many examples of this in US newspapers in the days following September 11. Serge Schmemann, for example, in *The New York Times* wrote, "The perpetrators acted out of hatred for the values cherished in the West as freedom, tolerance, prosperity, religious pluralism and universal suffrage" (2001: 1).

As Murakami asks, who constitutes "us"? Schmemann's "us" is clearly mainstream American. My own "us" is a very different one. As a feminist activist I rarely see my concerns reflected in the media. Indeed, I sometimes listen to radio talkbacks with some horror, realising that the ideas I have discussed with other feminists ten and twenty years ago are only just being aired by the mainstream now. My "us" is not represented by the US government, media and military; nor even by "their" Australian one. How does an "us" like mine get a chance to speak and to dissociate itself from the dominant "us" used by the mainstream media?

The homogenising of "us" is a useful tool for the forces of dominant

---

2   For a longer discussion of this phenomenon see Hawthorne (2002: 47ff).

culture. It turns a diverse, often fragmented, political culture into a mono-culture. And in times of war and conflict, the monoculture gets much more airtime than the forces of resistance. The gagging of discussion is obvious both in New York and Australia. In New York, a feminist tells me that she simply cannot speak among friends even of anything that is critical of Sharon's policies in Israel; and beyond her circle of friends criticising US policy on Afghanistan is difficult (see also Steele 2002: 15; Altman 2002: 17–18). In Australia, during the election campaign of 2001, the so-called left Australian Labor Party parroted the conservative views put forward by Prime Minister John Howard on immigration and on defence. The former Aus-tralian Labor Party leader, Kim Beazley, found himself effectively saying that, because he'd been a Minister for Defence, he too could play boys' war games. The monoculture of war is very seductive for those who value masculinity.

The homogenising of the enemy, of "them", is common to both sides. Although George W. Bush retreated from initial talk of Crusades and Infinite Justice, he persisted with the process of stereotyping and homogenising the attackers and anyone associated with them, and the passing of the USA PATRIOT Act (2002)[3] reinforces such stereotyping. His statement of 19 September, "Either you are with us or you are with the terrorists", is balanced by a similar statement, a fatwa, by a Saudi cleric in the week follow-ing 7 October, "that those who supported infidels against Muslims were themselves infidels" (cited in Mason 2001: 138).

The Americans and the Saudis have both fostered monocultures of ideology. For the USA, their monoculture is one of global capitalism driven by the profit motive. Corporate America imagines a world of "free trade" where America always has the upper hand. In order to achieve its ends it has bought off nations, leaders, companies, international institutions, or it has punished them through the power of the IMF, the World Bank and WTO rules (which apply to everyone except the USA). The foundation of this phil-osophy lies not in some notion of progressive liberalism, but rather in fascism. Kate Jennings, in her novel, *Moral Hazard*, about Wall Street, com-ments that Mussolini "admired American corporations". The main character who describes herself as a "bedrock feminist" gives us clues to the driving

---

3   The USA PATRIOT Act is an acronym for "Uniting and Strengthening America by Providing Appropriate Tools Required to Intercept and Obstruct Terrorism". It gives powers to the US federal government's agents to seize the assets of any organisation or individual aiding and abetting "terrorist activities". Foreign individuals can be arrested, detained indefinitely, deported, subjected to a military tribunal and they could also be shot. All of these can be done without any reference to the usual appeals processes of courts and juries. Attorney, Nancy Chang says that the USA PATRIOT Act is "the criminalization of legitimate political dissent" (cited in Zinn 2002: 40).

force of US capitalism. She muses, "The United States is a democracy, and yet it's powered by autocratic corporations. Its engines are fascist. Nothing democratic about them" (2002: 124, 11, 124–5).

Nor is Saudi Arabia a democracy. Far from it. Through the Wahhabi branch of Islam (a particularly fundamentalist and patriarchal group within Islam, not dissimilar from the role the far right Christian fundamentalists play in US politics) has also spread its ideology[4] through buying off nations,[5] leaders, religious institutions, and schools. Through these means the precepts of Wahhabi Islam have been spread to the poorest parts of the Islamic world. So, on the one hand there is Bush emerging from a fundamentalist Christian tradition with oil, politics and the military (including the CIA) as family careers. On the other hand there is Bin Laden emerging from a fundamentalist Islamic tradition with oil, business, the military (Al-Qaeda)[6] and the CIA as part of his individual career.[7]

Wahhabism is a philosophy derived from the works of Muhammad ibn Abd al-Wahhab (1703–1792). The doctrine "equates excess piety, and extrem ism with virtue ... [and] aims at purifying religion from all 'satanic' influences, including most facets of modernity" (Abu Khalil 2002: 62–3).[8] Such doctrines are familiar to most Western Christians with a smattering of knowledge about the Inquisition, and the burning of (overwhelmingly) women under charges of witchcraft during the so-called Renaissance period, or to anyone who has seen movies like The Exorcist.

The consequences of such a fundamentalist philosophy, set alongside the fundamentalist trappings of the Bush regimes in the USA, have severe consequences for all peoples of the world. Fundamentalist regimes are

5   Lest the reader think that Bin Laden is allied with the ruling family of the House of Saud, the reality is much more complex. Although the Saudi monarchy has directed funding and support to spreading Wahhabi fundamentalism, Bin Laden considered Saudi support for George Bush sr's attack on Iraq in 1991 as a betrayal. A further complexity is that Saudi Arabia is a major ally of the USA; indeed it has been propped up by US political and military support.

6   Al-Qaeda's structure reflects some of these priorities. Al-Qaeda comprises four main committees: the religious committee, the military committee, the finance committee, and the media committee (Corera 2001: 72).

7   Bin Laden is said to have given the Taliban regime millions of dollars (Simpson 2001: 112; Mason 2001: 136), while the CIA has channelled Western arms through Pakistan's ISI to the mujahideen (Wooldridge 2001: 119). Ironically, this too benefited the Taliban.

8   For an in-depth treatment of Wahhab's life and philosophy see Vassiliev (2000: 64–82).

particularly inimical to women: they are violent, and they dissociate from the real world to an ascetic world that privileges the next life.

Consequences and Responsibility

As the USA is now the most powerful nation on earth, its actions are no longer influenced by consequences of counteraction. It acts like the school playground bully with no restraint, and no sense of those whom he (I use the pronoun intentionally) violates. Prior to 1990 communism provided the *raison d'être* for the USA's foreign policy. Also, during the period when communism persisted, the USA supported regimes run by thugs or undermined regimes with some democratic impulses, including, most importantly, moves toward legal and social equality for women. Afghanistan was one such regime the USA undermined.

Afghanistan has undergone profound changes in the last fifty years. Under the rulership of Mohammed Daud, the cousin of King Zahir Shar, Afghanistan underwent a process of modernisation and Westernisation.[9] The effect of this was to shift Afghanistan from a feudally-oriented society to a relatively modern one. Such changes, however, do not occur in a political vacuum. Modernisation also made Afghanistan more attractive to foreign—that is, Western—investment. Given Afghanistan's geopolitical importance—a characteristic that goes back to at least the time of Alexander the Great and more recently to the needs of the British Empire—its regional importance cannot be underestimated. On the positive side, in Afghanistan religious tolerance was enhanced and women were given some opportunities for education (see Vogelsang 2002: 301). Daud was ousted by a coup in 1978 which brought in the People's Democratic Party of Afghanistan (PDPA), a Marxist government which, according to John Pilger (2002: 149), was not a puppet of the Soviet regime although this is usually how it is portrayed in mainstream media in the West.

As a Western reader, and someone not deeply versed in Central Asian history and politics, the period from the early 1970s to the present is a complex and vexed one, and it is difficult to untangle the web of heavily biased descriptions of the political changes in Afghanistan during that period. For example, the succeeding regimes of Nur Muhammad Taraki, Hafizullah

---

9   Huntington refers to this as one of three possible responses of non-Western societies to Western "civilization" (2002: 72–4). As Huntington never mentions women in his analysis of civilizations, it is worth noting that "Kemalism"—as he calls acceptance of modernisation and westernisation (after Mustafa Kemal Ataturk)—tends to increase the power of elites while increasing tolerance to some marginalised groups such as women.

Amin, Babrak Karmal,[10] and Najibullah are described variously as "lunatics" (Margolis 2001: 15) or as "tyrants" (Benard 2002: 180); John Pilger describes the coup as "popular" (2002: 149); Michael Parenti describes Taraki as "a poet and novelist" (2002: 56),[11] while Tariq Ali describes Najibullah as a "secular communist" (2002: 275). Part of the complexity of the recent history of Afghanistan is the competing claims of outsiders, many of whom are continuing to play what Lord Curzon, Viceroy of India, called in 1898 "the Great Game" (Pilger 2002: 98). The Great Game in every era excludes women's perspectives and priorities.

The Great Game has been replayed in Afghanistan since the late 1970s, and Washington was active in Afghanistan in 1979 before the Soviet Invasion (Brzezinsky cited in Talbot, this volume: 290). Although the PDPA appears to have extended some freedoms for ordinary people including increasing literacy and educational access for women, its time was marred by political violence culminating in the violent overthrow of Najibullah by the mujahideen in 1992.

That political freedom for women was not a central aim of the PDPA is borne out by Sonali Koltokhar who points out that it was a KGB operative who murdered Meena, the founder of RAWA, for her outspoken views on women (Kolhatkar 2002).

When fear becomes rife in a society—as it did under the PDPA in spite of the gains made by some women—and when social disconnection becomes the norm, it does not matter whether the regime is ruled by Western imperialist interests or by Soviet imperialist interests. Both result in fragmentation of society and the imposition of a political and economic monoculture.

Since 1992, Afghanistan has been further torn by political violence, war, civil war and conditions that threaten people's dignity, health and their lives, including widespread rape of women, brutalisation of men, as well as killing of women, children and men in the civilian population. Both the mujahideen and the Taliban represented those whose impetus was fundamentalist,

---

10 Taraki, Amin and Karmal were all active in the coup against Daud.

11 Sonali Kolhatkar gives another perspective: "At a recent anti-war forum, I spoke alongside well-known activist and writer Michael Parenti, who claimed that the Soviet Union was invited into Afghanistan in 1979, that it didn't really invade. After I contradicted him in my speech, citing that the vast majority of the Afghan population were fairly united against the foreign domination and imperialist motives of the Soviet Union, Michael angrily asked me after the talk why RAWA does not concede to some of the good that the Russians did in Afghanistan. Wow. Do we ever dwell on the good that the US may have done in Vietnam?" (9 May 2002 http://www.zmag.org/content/Gender/kolhatkarwomen.cfm).

woman-hating, violent, and potentially lucrative for the USA and its corporations. If the USA did not foresee the consequences of their support for individuals such as CIA-trained Osama Bin Laden,[12] nor temper their dealings with the Taliban in discussions with them over a Unocal-sponsored pipeline through Afghanistan, they were even less likely to pay any attention to calls by feminists about the violations of women's freedoms. The USA (government, military and corporations) sees itself as the earth's policeman, but it behaves more like the earth's Mafia: enforcing the rules upon others, while blithely disregarding the rules in its own actions. This is exemplified in several ways, firstly through the military, and secondly through economic might. What is clear is that the support given by the USA to hardline fundamentalists and thugs has backfired.[13]

The power wielded by the US military is excessive. Gore Vidal puts the figure at seven trillion dollars for "Defense" since 1950 (2002: 3); $3 billion worth of arms was given to the mujahideen in Afghanistan (Klare 2002: 33, see also Klare 2001); Parenti suggests that Saudi Arabia and the US together have spent $40 billion on the war in Afghanistan (2002: 60); and that the USA's annual expenditure on arms is seven times greater than that of Russia, the next largest military nation (Parenti 2002: 5). Furthermore, the military are implicated in a host of other violations, violences, as well as economic and ecological dispossession. I am thinking here of diamonds fuelling war in Angola, Sierra Leone and the Republic of Congo; of unwilling conscripts to wars, as well as the tragic loss of life through landmines, unexploded cluster bombs, and "collateral damage", all of which continue to be current problems in war zones around the world; of the impact of economic sanctions on Iraqi children; of the ecological impact of oil spills in Kuwait during the Gulf War. Those who bear the brunt of these violations are usually the poorest and have the least political and economic clout.

Military power sits alongside economic power in a globalised world, and while the benefits accrue to the powerful, the losses are concentrated on the poorest and most vulnerable. For the USA, globalisation has many benefits; key among them is increased profits. In the process some (thousands) of its

---

12 Ruppert (2001) argues that the CIA was perfectly aware of Bin Laden's activities and even met with him in the months just before September 11. Burbach makes the interesting point that George W. Bush's first business venture on graduating from Harvard Business School, was to set up Arbustos Energy in partnership with Salem Bin Laden, brother of Osama! (2002: 14).

13 In Iraq the US backed the Ba'ath Party, led by Saddam Hussein, against communists and trade unionists. Not only was Hussein encouraged in his actions, he was also rewarded with arms and trade contracts.

own workers are laid off while large corporations go off-shore, but these are minor hiccups in the achievement of ever-increasing profits for shareholders and company directors.

And it is not surprising to hear the repetition of names (companies and families) across military, political and economic terrains. Carlyle,[14] Halliburton Oil,[15] Unocal, Enron, Bush, Cheney, Bin Laden, the CIA, ISI. The common theme is oil, vast amounts of money, global investments, military hardware and intelligence, and violence. And the power of men.

Violence is Elitist

Theresa Wolfwood makes the interesting observation that "violence is elitist" (2001: 2; this volume: 44). This statement had me thinking—over and over I asked who is violent in this circumstance; in that circumstance? And each time the answer was—those with the most power in the particular context. This is no mere trifle to while away the hours; it is, rather, important to identify where violence comes from; where the ideology of violence is most forcefully defended.

As Catharine MacKinnon points out, "the number of women who die at the hands of men every year in the United States is almost the same as the number of people who died on September 11" (2002: 7–8; this volume: 426). Who here is the violator? Men who exercise more power and have access to the power of violence and institutionalised legal and financial power in any society deemed "patriarchal"?[16] Similarly, Cynthia Enloe remarks on the

14 George Bush Sr. joined the Carlyle Group soon after leaving the office of President of the USA. Carlyle has "extensive investments in the energy sector and the Middle East" (Burbach 2002: 14). Carlyle has investments in defence, and military conflicts and weapons are the basis of its profitability (Roy 2001b: 106). "Established in 1987, the Carlyle Group is a private global investment firm that originates, structures and acts as lead equity investor in management-led buyouts, strategic minority equity investments, equity private placements, consolidations and buildups, and growth capital financings. Since its inception, the firm has invested more than $6.4 billion of equity in 233 corporate and real estate transactions with an aggregate acquisition value of over $18 billion. As of September 30, 2001, the firm had more than $12.5 billion of committed capital under management." (2002: www.thecarlylegroup.com/profile.htm). John Pilger notes that "Bush Senior remains a paid consultant to the Bin Laden family through the Carlyle Group" (2002: 109).

15 A company with oil business links to the Gulf, it was also where Dick Cheney was CEO from 1995 to 1998 just before becoming Vice-President (Tirman 2002: 42; Roy 2002b: 107; Caldicott 2002: 35). In 2001 its worldwide revenues were $13 billion (2002: www.halliburton.com/about/history_new_phase.jsp).

predominantly male constituency of military decision makers. Male elites define the agenda and the policies of military power, never questioning the masculine ethos at its centre (Enloe 2000; this volume: 254–9). While men's agendas are given prominence, women are silenced (Enloe 2000; this volume: 257); see also Moghadam 2001; this volume: 260–84). and made invisible.[17] Militarisation silences the vulnerable. Valerie L. Kuletz writes of "deterritoriality" in relation to the impact of the military on land (1998: 7). Much the same effect can be seen on women. The specific territory of women is their bodies; women are "disembodied", objectified and raped; women's needs are defined as secondary (at best); and they become objects of sexual torture, just another kind of property belonging to the enemy which can be violated and destroyed. Robin Morgan points to the increase not only in civilian casualties of war, but the level of women's fatality in war. From 5 per cent in World War I, women's fatality jumped to 50 per cent in World War II, and to an alarming 80 per cent in the 1990s (2001: 415). Who is the target of war? The news reporters dwell on all the details of soldiers killed in battle. The casualties for the military have been relatively few on the US and allies side in Afghanistan; in the Middle East the ratio in 2001 was "one Israeli for every six Palestinians killed" (AbuKhalil 2002: 39). Who reports the deaths of women in Afghanistan? Who reports the deaths of civilian Palestinian women? Who reports the deaths of women in any theatre of war? Who benefits from violence?

Choosing Between Good and Bad Kinds of Violence

The powerful also engage in false options. One of the most pervasive is that "there are good and bad kinds of violence and that we must choose between them" (Wolfwood 2001: 2; this volume: 44). Another is that American loss and grief is more important than the loss and grief of other people. But neither of these can be measured; neither can be "calibrated" (Roy 2001a; this volume: 332).

The force used by the powerful is framed as responsible and rational. It emerges from a structure which is put in place in order to authorise it, thereby making it legally "right". The USA is able to drop bombs on Afghanistan, killing civilians, and call this good. It is not even categorised as violence, nor

16 For a full discussion of these issues see Hawthorne (2002: 64–85).

17 This was literally so for women living under the Taliban who were forced to wear the burqa. John Simpson expresses some surprise at his experience. He and another journalist, Peter Jouvenal, disguised themselves in burqas to cross into Afghanistan. "The effect was extraordinary: it was as though we had become invisible. No one gave us a glance, and we found ourselves occupying the worst and most humble places in vehicles" (Simpson 2001: 109).

are bodies counted as casualties. Marc Herold notes that "the only casualty reports considered 'real' by the mainstream US press are those issued by a Western enterprise or organization, or 'independently verified' by Western individuals and/or organizations" (2002: 116). Only what the West sees is real! This is the ultimate in arrogance; a restating of a very old feminist truism that only what the king sees counts as real (Frye 1983: 152–74). This failure to recognise diversity in a marginalised group is typical of Dominant Culture politics. It marks out the "despised" enemy and makes it appear that we can choose between good and bad violences. As AbuKhalil argues, the "violence of Muslims is terrorism, while Western violence is understood by a different set of standards and a different set of terms" (2002: 26).

In an international setting, violence is generally described either as terrorism (an illegal form of violence) or war (an international legalised form). The distinction between war and terrorism is a vexed one and depends a great deal on the political alignments between the speakers and the actions. To make an analogy at the individual level, it is like the distinction between a street rape (terrorism) and a legal rape in marriage (war).[18] In my view, none of these forms of violence, individual or international, is justifiable. Just as rape is backed by the generally greater economic and cultural power of individual men, so too is war backed by the economic power of the military-industrial complex. Many feminist theorists have analysed the intimate connections between institutional international violence (war) and individual male violence against women and children (rape), as well as mass rape of women and children in war.[19]

Michael Stohl makes a point not dissimilar from that made by Catharine A. MacKinnon when he says "the threat and often the use of violence for what would be described as terroristic purposes were it not great powers who were pursuing the very same tactic" (cited in Chomsky 2001: 16).[20] Noam Chomsky goes on to point out that discussion of such issues is almost impossible in the USA. I assume that is because the philosophy of liberalism accompanied by the structures of global capital and the politics of rising US nationalism is so strong. For all the talk of "freedom of speech" there is a great deal of muzzling of critical challenges going on (see Bell, this volume:

---

18 Enloe (1989: 195) makes this point and entitles her final chapter "The Personal is International".

19 See for instance Brownmiller (1976); Caputi (1987); Enloe (1989); Morgan (1990, republished 2001); Copelan (1994); Stiglmayer (1994); Kappeler (1995); Mladjenovic and Matijasevic (1996); Boric and Desnica (1996); Nenadic (1996).

20 The US was condemned in the World Court in 1986 for "unlawful use of force" (international terrorism) in Nicaragua (Chomsky 2001: 23).

432). Double standards are the norm when the powerful want something that the powerless are unwilling to give up (for example, their own autonomy, independence, sense of dignity and freedoms). Double standards are also the norm when the powerful speak about violence wielded by the less powerful. For example, the association between Muslim and terrorist is a problematic one. Robin Morgan's association between masculinity and terrorism is much more useful, while the connection between the conjunction of fundamentalism in all its forms and masculinity is especially predictive of violence. As AbuKhalil argues, no one protests to the "Pope or Protestant ministers to free their religion of terrorists when ... Christians carry out violent acts" (2002: 22).

Violence used by the vulnerable, either offensively or defensively, is categorised as violence, and it is almost always called bad. I am not suggesting that violence perpetrated by the powerless is good, since violence breeds violence. What is required is a reappraisal of the role of violence, from wherever it comes, as perpetuating *violence*. As Susanne Kappeler argues in relation to resisting violence: "Resistance to violence however cannot consist of violence. Violence may change the direction of violence, invert the roles of violator and victim, but it necessarily affirms the principle of violence, whatever else it may achieve" (1995: 258; emphasis in the original).

The problem of violence and resistance to it is an ongoing one. Here I am thinking of political violence and philosophically "choosing" to support violence. I might engage in violence if I am given no choice—that is if I have to defend myself or someone else—but choosing violence when other means are at hand is philosophically repugnant. It diminishes everyone.

When the powerful choose violence, the force used against the most vulnerable is given less importance. This can be seen in the case of Afghanistan: the force used by the USA and its allies against Afghans (including civilians as well as the Taliban) is diminished in importance. It is presented as less important than the loss of lives among groups deemed powerful. Crimes against the poor, the vulnerable, the women are normalised as daily fare, as not worth commenting on or feeling anything about. The devaluation of people's lives as bereft of emotional content, of relationship with others, and of having a place in the world is part of the process of homogenisation that reduces everyone outside the axis of the West to meaninglessness.

The cost of grief cannot be measured, but US policy-makers attempt to do just that. As Helen Caldicott argues, the response to September 11 from the US government and military has been to literally capitalise on the trauma of American civilians and on the rather insular view of the mainstream American public (2002: 184–5). Herold summarises the view that "the 'cost' of a dead Afghan civilian is zero (as long as these civilian deaths are hidden from the public) but the 'benefits' of preserving US military lives is enormous, given the US public's aversion to returning body bags" (Herold 2002: 120–1).

The women of the Revolutionary Association of the Women of Afghanistan (RAWA) provide the world with an interesting example of how to counter violence without falling into what Jeffner Allen has called the "patriarchal construct of non-violence" (1986: 29). What Allen means by this is a false duality which enables violence to continue because the weaker party, the victim, is non-violent in response to violence, and the cycle of violence relies on this non-response. RAWA has taken as its method for countering violence the power of connection and of relationship. This is resistance to violence rather than active non-violence. To this end the members of RAWA use a variety of strategies. One is "saying poetry against them" (Benard: 2002: 22), a method which brings groups of women together and connects them through the words of a poem; another is characterised as "undercover chatting" (2002: 48) which involves small groups talking with neighbours, creating links between the members of RAWA and the communities they live and work in. They build networks among women by running literacy classes spiked with political analysis (and sometimes classes for men too); they build networks among children and young people by establishing schools run in such a way as to encourage critical thinking and creativity; they make a point of taking care of widows, of orphans, of those injured physically or psychologically by the many years of war. Interaction, relationship-building, trust and connection between people in communities mark the foundation of RAWA's approach to resistance to violence.

RAWA also display a remarkable sense of humour. Cheryl Benard mentions that the website offers for sale "men's boxer shorts stamped with the RAWA symbol ... a socialist-realist image of five combative women raising a banner imprinted with the words 'Freedom, democracy, women's rights'" (2002: 227). And the website itself has contributed to making connections with like-minded people around the world.

By contrast, what the fundamentalists aim for is disconnection through rote learning, blind obedience, displacement of the self for the higher good— especially death as a martyr—and "deliberate and indifferent harshness" (Benard 2002: 177). Through social, religious and political separation of the self and of the people from one another through fear, fundamentalists propagate violence. In the schools boys are trained to be "unfeeling" (Benard 2002: 220) and tenderness has no part to play.

The training is not restricted to boys and men, and women are subjected to even harsher forms of disconnection. The use of the burqa is intended to break the possibility of community among women and to make women invisible and therefore worthless. One of the dictates of the Taliban for women was to order them *"to conceal themselves to the point of having no human form"* (Benard 2002: 205; my italics). This is an extreme demand upon women to self-separate and, as Benard argues, it amounts to torture.

Wahhabism has been mixed into an environment of violence and dispossession. It capitalised on the orphans of war, drawing them into schools which focused on obedience to strict Wahhabism. Combined with the hyper-masculinised mujahideen which RAWA characterises as rapists (RAWA 2001; this volume: 95–6) under the tutelage of the CIA during its war against the Soviet Union, this mix has become explosive. Indeed, one could argue that the forces at work represent the worst aspects of fundamentalist Christianity and Islam, while Israel's latest incursions represent the third in a fundamentalist unholy trinity of the world's three major monotheistic religions. All three religions are well known for their oppression of women, although the Taliban is the most overt about its oppression and its violations. It is only a matter of degree, and the other violations identified above are not justifiable either. There is no such thing as a choice between good and bad misogyny. Misogyny is hatred. Indeed, under fundamentalist regimes "being a woman is a crime" (Benard 2002: 74).

Fundamentalism can readily be applied to elements of the Republican party, especially that associated with George W. Bush, as well as with the Saudi regime of Wahhabism, from which the Taliban grew. Indeed, the intertwining dependences and links between the USA, Saudi Arabia, the Taliban, Pakistan, and (some argue) Israel, are very disturbing. Parenti relates that "as recently as 1999, the US government paid the entire annual salary of every single Taliban government official" (2002: 64; also see Rall 2002: 49); Mullah Omar, commander of the Taliban, was "on the direct payroll of the Pakistani regime" (Ali 2002: 212); Israeli advisers are reported to have played an important role in the government of Pakistan's ruler, General Zia-ul-Haq during the mid-1980s (Ali 2002: 209); while Hamid Karzai was a consultant for Unocal (Talbot 2002; this volume: 291).

In 1988 Zbigniew Brzezinski was President Carter's National Security chief. When asked in 1998 if he had any regrets about supporting and funding anti-Soviet fundamentalists, he answered in the negative. His response is full of contempt, and shows the anti-communist ideology which has driven US foreign policy for the last fifty years.[21] He answered with a series of questions: "What is most important to the history of the world? The Taliban or the collapse of the Soviet empire? A few crazed Muslims or the liberation of Central Europe and the end of the Cold War?" (cited in Ali 2002: 208).

Clearly, for profit-oriented US capitalism, the collapse of the Soviet empire

opened up markets in a new and exciting way. And globalisation, in particular drawing in a vast array of former Soviet countries and zones of influence,
has characterised the main areas of conflict since the fall of the Soviet Union.
The war in the Balkans, in Somalia,[22] and in the new independent countries
of Central Asia, as well as the profits to be made from oil and its distribution,
lie behind most of the conflicts of the past decade.

Disconnection

Fundamentalism aims for disconnection from the real world in its adherents.
Globalisation creates social, political and economic disconnection between
people on a massive scale (Hawthorne 2002: 363–8). Violence, especially
harsh and indiscriminate physical violence, creates social fragmentation and
personal dissociation (Hawthorne 2002: 69–74; Copelan 1994: 199–203).
Terrorism fills "all our emotional space with fear, rage, powerlessness and
despair" and disconnects us "from the sources of life and hope" (Starhawk
2002a: 166).[23] And, as Robin Morgan put it in 1990, "if I had to name one
quality as the genius of patriarchy, it would be compartmentalization, the
capacity for institutionalizing disconnection" (1990: 51).

Institutionalised disconnection is precisely the *modus operandi* of these
many forces, all coming together in the single global politic of the twenty-first
century. As I have argued in this essay through drawing together the threads
of connection between very different regimes around the world, the problem
is not a matter of conflict between civilisations as Samuel Huntington (1997)
argues; it is not by a long shot the end of history (Fukuyama 1992) nor the
only way of living in the modern world (Fukuyama 2001: 15). Indeed, I am
not even sure it is, as Tariq Ali (2002) argues, a "clash of fundamentalisms".
What all of these writers have missed is that it is always the most vulnerable
of citizens who lose the most in these battles. And it is women—and their
children—who are consistently the most vulnerable. It is women in
fundamentalist regimes who are the targets of the most vicious attacks, and
of dehumanisation. It is women's resistance which is ignored—RAWA is
barely mentioned in any of the indexes of the many books I have consulted
on terrorism, on fundamentalism, and on Afghanistan. When RAWA is
included, it is usually in the analyses of feminist writers.

---

21 For a good summary of the current operations, completed operations and Cold
   War Era military operations engaged in by the USA see Vidal (2002: 22–41); also
   see Talbot 2002, this volume: 285–296.

22 John Pilger states that "Somalia and part of the north-western Indian Ocean are a
   major oil and gas reserve, perhaps as large as the Caspian Sea" (2002: 105).

23 See also an extended version of this essay in Starhawk (2002b: 142–154).

The beneficiaries of disconnection are the powerful. They constitute what I have elsewhere called the transnational sector (2002: 387). They are immensely rich, highly mobile, they wield political and economic power. They may be corporations or countries. They may be the decision-makers, the CEOs, presidents and military men. It is not a clash between cultures or civilisations, but a conflict between the powerful in order to find out who will fill the role of the most powerful in the coming century. And the great majority of the powerful are men.

That women constitute a central place as enemy is clear in the statements and actions of fundamentalists (Winter 2001: 9–41). In the USA Jerry Falwell, speaking of September 11, said, "the pagans and the abortionists and the feminists and gays and lesbians ... You made this happen" (cited in Parenti 2002: 47). Also laying the blame for September 11 was Andrew Apel, a lobbyist for biotechnology and globalisation and editor of *AgBioNews*. He accused feminist and anti-globalisation activists of "having blood on their hands".[24] The Taliban, too, mark feminists as their enemy. In 2000, a Mr Hashemi visited the USA on a lecture and promotional tour. When asked the purpose of his visit, he replied to "do battle with the feminists" (in Benard 2002: 182). It is therefore my contention that this powerful coalition of religious, political and economic fundamentalists are not really in conflict with one another ideologically; they are, rather, battling for their men to gain the position as most powerful (Winter 1996, 1998).[25] The trouble is that women, children, the poor and other vulnerable peoples are the ones to suffer and die.

The pattern followed here is an ancient one. In Ancient Greece it is epitomised by the battles between succeeding generations of male gods: Ouranos is castrated by his son, Kronos, who then devours his own children, except Zeus who is protected and later rises up against Kronos and in turn puts him in chains. It is no longer generations of fathers and sons but the battles remain the battles of men.

Like the feminists who have fought for women over many centuries, like RAWA, like the imaginative and inspiring strategies of the powerless wherever they are, people from a diverse range of backgrounds and settings are

---

24 A brief extract of Andrew Apel's accusations can be found at: www.nowto.org/summit/call.html

25 Winter (1996, 1998) demonstrates the cross-cultural collusion of men against women. She writes of the headscarves affair in France in 1989 (1996), and extends this analysis to the appropriation of women of Maghrebian background in the name of various masculinist discourses (1998).

questioning the institutions and mechanisms of the powerful. Now is a time for imagination. It is time for the members of the diversity matrix—the powerless—to come together and develop ways to counter these ancient battles between the powerful in which the most vulnerable continue to lose their lives.

References

AbuKhalil, As'ad. (2002). *Bin Laden, Islam and America's New "War on Terrorism"*. New York: Seven Stories Press.

Ali, Tariq. (2002). *The Clash of Fundamentalisms: Crusades, Jihads and Postmodernity*. London and New York: Verso.

Allen, Jeffner. (1986). *Lesbian Philosophy: Explorations*. Palo Alto, CA: Institute of Lesbian Studies.

Altman, Dennis. (2002). "Letter from New York." *Australian Book Review*. June/July.

Baxter, Jenny and Malcolm Downing, Eds. (2001). *The Day That Shook the World: Understanding September 11th*. London: BBC; Sydney: ABC Books.

Bell, Diane. (2002). "Good and Evil: At Home and Abroad. In this volume: 432–49.

Benard, Cheryl with Edit Schlaffer. (2002). *Veiled Courage: Inside the Afghan Women's Resistance*. Sydney: Random House.

Boric, Rada and Mica Mladineo Desnica. (1996). "Croatia: Three Years After." In Chris Corrin, Ed. *Women in a Violent World: Feminist Analyses and Resistance Across "Europe"*. Edinburgh: Edinburgh University Press: 133–50.

Brownmiller, Susan. (1976). *Against Our Will: Men, Women and Rape*. Harmondsworth, UK: Penguin.

Burbach, Roger. (2002). "Globalization's War. " In Roger Burbach and Ben Clarke Eds. *September 11 and the US War: Beyond the Curtain of Smoke*. San Francisco: City Lights: 12–17.

Burbach, Roger and Ben Clarke Eds. (2002). *September 11 and the US War: Beyond the Curtain of Smoke*. San Francisco: City Lights.

Caldicott, Helen. (2002). *The New Nuclear Danger: George W. Bush's Military–industrial Complex*. Melbourne: Scribe.

Caputi, Jane. (1987). *The Age of Sex Crime*. London: The Women's Press.

Chapkis, Wendy and Cynthia Enloe, Eds. (1983). *Of Common Cloth: Women in the Global Textile Industry*. Amsterdam: Transnational Institute.

Chomsky, Noam. (2001). *September 11*. Sydney: Allen and Unwin; New York: Seven Stories Press.

Copelan, Rhonda. (1994). "Surfacing Gender: Reconceptualizing Crimes Against Women in Time of War." In Alexandra Stiglmayer, Ed. *Mass Rape: The War against Women in Bosnia-Herzogovina*. Lincoln and London: University of Nebraska Press: 197–218.

Corera, Gordon. (2001). "Inside the Terror Network." In Jenny Baxter and Malcolm Downing, Eds. *The Day That Shook the World: Understanding September 11th*. London: BBC; Sydney: ABC Books: 68–83.

Enloe, Cynthia. (1983a). *Does Khaki Become You? The Militarisation of Women's Lives*. London: Pluto Press.

———. (1983b). "We Are What We Wear—The Dilemma of the Feminist Consumer." In Wendy Chapkis and Cynthia Enloe, Eds. *Of Common Cloth: Women in the Global Textile Industry*. Amsterdam: Transnational Institute: 115–19.

———. (1989). *Bananas, Beaches and Bases: Making Feminist Sense of International Politics*. London: Pandora.

———. (2000). "Masculinity as a Foreign Policy Issue." *Foreign Policy in Focus(5)* 36 (October 2000). Republished, this volume: 254–9.

Frye, Marilyn. (1983). "To See and Be Seen: The Politics of Reality." In Marilyn Frye, Ed. *The Politics of Reality*. Trumansburg, NY: The Crossing Press: 152–74.

Fukuyama, Francis. (1992). *The End of History and the Last Man*. London: Penguin Books.

———. (2001). "History Beyond the End." Sydney: *Australian*. 9 October: 15.

Hawthorne, Susan (2002). *Wild Politics*. Melbourne: Spinifex Press.

Herold, Marc. (2002). "Who Will Count the Dead? Civilian Casualties in Afghanistan." In Roger Burbach and Ben Clarke Eds. *September 11 and the US War: Beyond the Curtain of Smoke*. San Francisco: City Lights: 116–122.

Huntington, Samuel P. (1997). *The Clash of Civilizations and the Remaking of World Order*. New York: Simon and Schuster.

Jennings, Kate. (2002). *Moral Hazard*. Sydney: Pan Macmillan.

Kappeler, Susanne. (1995). *The Will to Violence: The Politics of Personal Behaviour*. London: Polity Press; New York: Teachers College Press; Melbourne: Spinifex Press.

Klare, Michael T. (2001). *Resource Wars: The New Landscape of Global Conflict*. New York: Henry Holt and Company.

———. (2002). "The Geopolitics of War". In Roger Burbach and Ben Clarke Eds. *September 11 and the US War: Beyond the Curtain of Smoke*. San Francisco: City Lights: 31–5.

Kolhatkar, Sonali. (2002). http://www.zmag.org/content/Gender/kolhatkarwomen.cfm, 9 May.

Kuletz, Valerie. (1998). *The Tainted Desert: Environmental and Social Ruin in the American West*. New York and London: Routledge.

Lentin, Ronit, Ed. (1997). *Gender and Catastrophe*. London and New York: Zed Books.

MacKinnon, Catharine A. (2001). "State of Emergency". *Women's Review of Books (XIX)*6: 7–8. Republished, this volume: 426–31.

Margolis, Eric S. (2001). *War at the Top of the World: The Struggle for Afghanistan, Kashmir, and Tibet*. New York: Routledge.

Mason, Barnaby. (2001). "The Street, the State and the Mosque—a Middle East Dilemma." In Jenny Baxter and Malcolm Downing, Eds. *The Day That Shook the World: Understanding September 11th*. London: BBC; Sydney: ABC Books: 128–43.

Mladjenovic, Lepa and Divna Matijasevic. (1996). "SOS Belgrade July 1993–1995: Dirty Streets." In Chris Corrin, Ed. *Women in a Violent World: Feminist Analyses and Resistance Across "Europe"*. Edinburgh: Edinburgh University Press: 118–32.

Morgan, Robin. (1990). *The Demon Lover: On the Sexuality of Terrorism*. London: Methuen.

——. (2001). *The Demon Lover: The Roots of Terrorism*. London: Piatkus.

Murakami, Haruki. (2000). *Underground: The Tokyo Gas Attack and the Japanese Psyche*. London: The Harvill Press.

Nenadic, Natalie. (1996). "Femicide: A Framework for Understanding Genocide." In Diane Bell and Renate Klein, Eds. *Radically Speaking: Feminism Reclaimed*. Melbourne: Spinifex Press: 456–40.

Parenti, Michael. (2002). *The Terrorism Trap: September 11 and Beyond*. San Francisco: City Lights.

Pilger, John. (2002). *The New Rulers of the World*. London: Verso.

Rall, Ted. (2002). "Oil Politics in Central Asia". In Roger Burbach and Ben Clarke Eds. *September 11 and the US War: Beyond the Curtain of Smoke*. San Francisco: City Lights: 49–50.

Roy, Arundhati. (2001a). "The Algebra of Infinite Justice." *Guardian*. 29 September. Republished (2002). *Power Politics*. Boston: South End Press: 105–124; *The Algebra of Infinite Justice*. New Delhi: Penguin India; London: Flamingo. Republished, this volume: 331–8.

——. "War is Peace." *Outlook India* 29 October, "Frontlines." In Roger Burbach and Ben Clarke Eds. *September 11 and the US War: Beyond the Curtain of Smoke*. San Francisco: City Lights: 101–10. Republished (2002). *Power Politics*. Boston: South End Press: 125–145; *The Algebra of Infinite Justice*. New Delhi: Penguin India; London: Flamingo.

Ruppert, Michael. (2001). "Time Line Surrounding September 11th." *Global Outlook 1* (1): 7–10. Also available on websites, for example: www.guerillanews.com/intelligence/doc211.html.

Schmemann, Serge. (2001). "War Zone, What Would 'Victory' Mean?" *New York Times*: Section 4, 1.

Simpson, John. (2001). "Afghanistan's Tragedy." In Jenny Baxter and Malcolm Downing, Eds. *The Day That Shook the World: Understanding September 11th*. London: BBC; Sydney: ABC Books: 99–113.

Starhawk. (2002a). "Moving Forward After 9/11." In Roger Burbach and Ben Clarke, Eds. (2002). *September 11 and the US War: Beyond the Curtain of Smoke*. San Francisco: City Lights: 165–6.

——. (2002b). *Webs of Power: Notes from the Global Uprising*. Gabriola Island, BC: New Society Publishers.

Steel, Ronald. (2001). "The Weak at War with the Strong." Editorial. *New York Times*. 14 September: Section A, 27.

Steele, Jonathan. (2002). "New York, Where Public Debate is Tainted by 'Loyalty'." *Age*. 22 May: 15.

Stiglmayer, Alexandra, Ed. (1994). *Mass Rape: The War Against Women in Bosnia-Herzegovina*. Lincoln and London: University of Nebraska Press.

Talbot, Karen. (2002) "Afghanistan, Central Asia, Georgia: Key to Oil Profits". *Global Outlook (1)* 1: 19–21. Republished in a revised version, this volume: 285–96.

Talbott, Strobe and Chanda, Nayan. (2001). *The Age of Terror: America and the World after September 11*. New York: Basic Books and the Yale Center for the Study of Globalization.

Tirman, John. (2002). *September 11 and the US War: Beyond the Curtain of Smoke*. San Francisco: City Lights: 36–43.

Vassiliev, Alexei. (2000). *The History of Saudi Arabia*. New York: New York University Press.

Vidal, Gore. (2002). *Perpetual War for Perpetual Peace: How We Got to Be So Hated*. New York: Thunder's Mouth Press/Nation Books.

Vogelsang, Willem. (2002). *The Afghans*. Oxford: Blackwell Publishers.

Winter, Bronwyn (1996). "Learning the Hard Way: The Debate on Women, Cultural Difference and Secular Schooling in France." In *Europe: Retrospects and Prospects: Proceedings of the Australasian Association of European Histories Tenth Biennial Conference*. Manly: South End Press: 203–13.

——. (1998). "Adherence or Appropriation? Images of Maghrebian Women and the French Ideal of Nationhood." In Virginia Ferreira, Teresa Tavares and Sylvia Portugal, Eds. *Shifting Bonds, Shifting Bounds: Women, Mobility and Citizenship in Europe*. Oeiras, Portugal: Celta Editore: 149–63.

——. (2001). "Fundamental Misunderstandings: Issues in Feminist Approaches to Islamism." *Journal of Women's History 13(1)*: 9–41.

Wolfwood, Theresa. (2001). "Resistance is Creative: False Options and Real Hope." Draft for speech at Resisting Global Militarism conference, Victoria, BC, Canada. 27–29 September. Republished, this volume: 43–7.

Wooldridge, Mike. (2001). "Musharraf's Motives." In Jenny Baxter and Malcolm Downing, Eds. *The Day That Shook the World: Understanding September 11th*. London: BBC; Sydney: ABC Books: 114–27.

Zinn, Howard. (2002).*Terrorism and War*. New York: Seven Stories Press.

Bronwyn Winter
Who will mourn on October 7?

Friday, 29 March 2002

Today's headline straddles six columns. Bold 90-point lower case.

Terror war on Arafat

An exercise in tautology. All war is "terror war". By definition.

Above the headline, a quote from Arafat (26-point): "No Palestinian and no-one in the Arab nation will surrender or kneel."

Below the headline, a photograph of a tank beside broken terracotta tiles covering a pile of bricks and timber that was once a house in Arafat's compound.

Below this (18-point): "Arafat is the enemy and he will be isolated.—Ariel Sharon."

Beside this, a photo of Arafat on the phone with a gun on his desk.

In the left-hand column, beside the headlines, photographs and story on this latest escalation of the Israel–Palestine conflict, are teasers and photographs for news items inside: "Your new body"—"Australia's richest race day"—"Why the old estates vanished". Plus an article on Natasha Stott Despoja:[1] "Her long year as leader", and another on loyalty cards for shareholders. Surreal juxtapositions.

On page 30, an editorial condemns Israel's war, and a "special report" in the news review pages describes Palestinian martyrdom and the dubious role of the US. The Middle East is once again (still ...) described as being "on the brink", the atmosphere there as "explosive", Sharon's strategy "ill-advised".

There is some discussion of who "originally" owned land in the region. Very little owned by the Jews. But they owned very little land anywhere.

---

1   Natasha Stott Despoja is the leader of the centrist political party, the Australian Democrats. She achieved fame some years ago as the youngest person in federal parliament. She is part of the left wing of her party and is popular with some feminists, although the party, which has for some time held the balance of power in the Senate (Australian Upper House), has attracted considerable criticism for doing "deals" with the right-wing government, notably on privatisation, repressive industrial relations legislation and the introduction of a goods and services tax.

I shudder every time I think of the name "wandering Jew", the name we English-speaking goyim give to a noxious weed. Who was it that forced them to wander? How many times were they cast out, told or forced to move on for fear of extermination?

Arguing about land is a sterile debate. The "Middle East crisis" will not be solved by Palestinians claiming all but the 7 per cent of land that Jews "originally" owned in Israel,[2] no more than it will be solved by well-off US Ashkenazi immigrants or Sephardim from former French colonies in the Maghreb (North Africa) with some surplus weight to throw around and some sort of revenge to be had, claiming a stake to the occupied territories and chasing the Palestinian people who have lived there for hundreds of years.

Perhaps Nth-generation US citizens don't understand being colonised. It has never happened to them. Even if there is always a Jewish collective memory. The Maghrebian Sephardim, however, know about colonisation. Only too well. They got it from both sides: Arab and European. But if the experience of an oppression were enough to stop us oppressing others, what a different world we would live in. And how different the Israeli state would look.

This war is being fought over territory but it is not about land.

There are over fifty Christian states in the world, and close to fifty Muslim states. There is one Jewish state. And without Hitler and Uncle Sam, there probably wouldn't have even been the one. Whose war is this? Not the Jewish people's. Not the Palestinian people's. It is a politician's war, a businessman's war, a war of men with guns and something to prove. Which they can only prove through inflicting as much pain and destruction as possible. There will always be another death to avenge.

The Middle East has been "on the brink", "in crisis", for decades. It is a crisis that will never be solved, as too many have interests in it not being solved. The US state, some powerful fundamentalist Arab states, the fundamentalist wing of the Israeli state, and non-state fundamentalist actors, with varying degrees of influence, from both sides of the Israel–Palestine divide. Not to mention the odd business interest.

Tuesday, 2 April

News today from France. Car bomb and arson attacks on synagogues in Lyons and elsewhere, two individuals murdered in Villeurbanne, gunshots through the windows of a kosher butcher shop in Toulouse. A synagogue in Marseilles has been burned to the ground. In Sydney, so far no worse than

---

2   This is according to the *Sydney Morning Herald* report of 29 March.

graffiti. There has not yet been an Nth arson attempt on the Bondi synagogue. It is perhaps only a matter of time.

Thursday, 4 April

Five days ago I was wondering whether the Jewish cemetery in the southern
French town of Carpentras would once more be desecrated.[3] It is not
Carpentras this time, but it has happened. An acquaintance gives me similar
news from Germany. Synagogues, cemeteries, kosher eating places.

This evening I stood with Women in Black on the steps of Sydney Town
Hall. A small group of us, thirty at most. Silent and still in the autumn
twilight after rain. A woman, passing, took a leaflet from one of us, looked
at the banner "Women in Black Oppose War" and said incredulously: "But
surely, don't you think we *all* oppose war?" Response: "If that were true,
there would be no wars." Not all oppose war. Not even all women. But most
of those who wage it are men.

Saturday, 6 April

Daily, almost hourly, reports from Ramallah. No access to the outside world,
access to water and electricity limited then disappearing, no means of obtaining food. Widespread looting and intimidation by Israeli soldiers. Put a boy
in a uniform (or a turban, or a scarf, or a tunic), tell him he's important and
give him a gun. Tell him he's a hero. Tell him someone has to pay for every
wrong ever done to him; then tell him who the "someone" is. Give him a
reason (he won't need too many). Then watch him kill.

One week ago I anticipated that Jewish people the world over would again
be made to pay for the actions taken by Sharon and his acolytes. And they
are paying, and continue to pay. As Muslims in the US, Australia and
elsewhere are paying for the attacks on September 11. As French people living

---

3   On 10 May 1990, it was discovered that 34 graves in the Jewish cemetery at
    Carpentras, a town in the south of France, had been desecrated and one body
    exhumed and impaled. Four days later, 200,000 people demonstrated in Paris. The
    then President, François Mitterrand, was among their number. (Mitterrand was
    later implicated as having "protected" Nazi sympathisers during the Petainist
    régime in France.) The extreme-right party the National Front was suspected of
    involvement in the Carpentras affair, given the demonstrated anti-Semitism of its
    leader, Jean-Marie Le Pen, who has become notorious for the throwaway remark
    "the gas chambers are a detail of history". It took until 1996 to find the real
    culprits. They were members of the neo-Nazi group the National French and
    European Party. In the meantime Jean-Marie Le Pen and the National Front had
    exploited the affair to accuse various left groupings of having perpetrated the
    desecration to "set up" the National Front.

in Australia paid for the *Rainbow Warrior* bombing and Chirac's nuclear tests.

And many of the assailants are white Westerners.

Today in Sydney and France, demonstrations in support of Palestine. Tomorrow in France, the Zionist right is cynically using the attacks on Jewish people to call for a demonstration in support of the Israeli state. And large sections of the pro-Palestinian left assimilate "Jewish" and "right-wing Zionist". Obliterating with one thought the Jewish left. Obliterating Women in Black, obliterating the peace movement in Israel. They have short memories. They have also forgotten the many Islamist terrorist attacks in France. The Tati department store, Rue de Rennes, 1986. St Michel RER station 1995.[4] There are no angels in this war. Only those who have power and those who do not.

This is not the Jewish people's war. This is not the Palestinian people's war. But they are paying for it. Betrayed from both without and within. By men with uniforms and banners and guns. In the end, the Cause does not matter. Carnage becomes sexy and one's claim to status, even existence, is measured by the number of wounds one inflicts.

And those who rise up against the war pay its heaviest price. As do those who flee it.

Afghans imprisoned in detention centres in Australia are paying. For the crime of wanting to flee decades of war. For the crime of wanting to stay alive.

As if exile were an easy or joyful choice.

In 1997, I spoke with Algerian women exiled in France. Many of them journalists, members of left-wing political movements. Not all. But all targeted by the Islamic Salvation Front (FIS). Because they were women and would not be silent. It is difficult to write of their distress; I have no wish to portray them as snivelling victims. Objectively speaking, they *were* of course victims. Victims of both the FIS and the French government's refusal to grant them refugee status. This is despite 1995 guidelines issued by the UNHCR, according to which Algerian women refusing Islamist prescriptions were subjected to persecution because of their membership of a social group—that of women—and their political opinions—refusal of Islamism—and as such

---

4   Tati is a chain of department stores selling inexpensive goods. The stores are always extremely crowded. Rue de Rennes is on the left bank of central Paris, south-west of St Michel, which is in the heart of the Quartier Latin. "RER" means "Réseau Express Régional": the outer suburban train network. The Tati department store in rue de Rennes has since closed.

fitted the 1951 Geneva Convention's definition of a refugee.[5] The French government did not concur.

So, victims in that sense. But far from the passivity the Western media likes to attribute to women who are subjected to violence. The French press of the early 1990s was littered with articles, the television full of images, of the "terrible and distressing" situation of Algerian women. Algerian women in tears, Algerian women mourning. Every now and then, Algerian women fighting back, as they did, massively, in 1991–92, taking to the streets to demonstrate their opposition to the Islamists.

The women who talked with me all spoke of that resistance. And all spoke of the pain of exile. Their tears a difficult moment. Temporary loss of dignity on the one hand, invasion of privacy on the other. Grief is not easily communicable to strangers.

They did not choose to live in France. Did not choose to leave friends and loved ones. Their distress was the distress of separation, the distress of feeling they had betrayed those who were left behind. "What right do I have to be safe here when my friends, family, colleagues, sisters risk their lives on a daily basis?" Every single one of them spoke to me of betrayal. Every single one of them spoke of the difficult and ambiguous relationship with France, at once the former coloniser (oh how hard France hung on to Algeria, and at what cost), and the land of asylum.

Exile is not an easy choice. Never an easy choice. A choice between life and death is not a choice. A choice between shelter at night and exposure to bombs and dust and rubble is not a choice. A choice between hunger and having enough to eat is not a choice. A choice between suffering male violence and not suffering male violence is not a choice.

The oppressed do not choose. They flee. Or, if they find the strength and the means and the will, they fight. This is not a choice. It is a necessity for survival.

---

5   Section III.1.1:C of the UNHCR's May 1995 "Protection Guidelines on the Treatment of Algerian Asylum Seekers" reads as follows: "In view of the information provided in sub-para b of para 2.1.6 of section II above concerning the significant increase in the numbers of assassinations targeting the vulnerable group of women adopting 'western life-style' and not following the Islamic fundamentalist code, it has been deemed appropriate to consider this group of persons as a separate category of asylum seekers. The mere fact of not following the Islamic fundamentalist code can be considered an expression of a political opinion whereby women may be identified with the Algerian authorities and against the Islamic militant groups. Women intellectuals (teachers, journalists, etc) and wives of government officials encounter particularly high risk of being persecuted by the militant Islamic extremists" (WLUML 1996).

Afghan women do not choose. They are the alibi, the token, the banner to be waved when it is convenient for others more powerful to do so. Bombed for their own good. Starved for their own good. Throwing off the Taliban's burqa to don the Northern Alliance's hijab. Out of the frying pan ...

But George Dubbaya has proved his point now, shown the world that His Is Bigger. So the women can be left to their fate. Afghanistan was always a poor bit player in any case, a country that had to be reduced to rubble (and then have the rubble further reduced to more rubble) so Frankenstein-US could remind his Taliban monster of his might.

George Dubbaya hasn't got Bin Laden, but this war was never about getting Bin Laden. It was about letting the Islamists know that they're nothing without Uncle Sam. Syria and Pakistan just don't have as many dollars, and even Saudi Arabia, much as it likes to—and can afford to—bankroll Islamist groups (a study of Algeria's FIS is singularly illuminating of Islamic financial networks),[6] just does not have the same connections as the US, or the same history of expertise in covert operations. At the same time, it's got the oil, it's got Mecca: two firm guarantees of continued US friendship. (And now it is even playing Good Guy with a peace plan for the Middle East.) Which is no doubt why its Wahhabi state fundamentalism—the most fundamentalist form of "orthodox" Islam in the Muslim world—goes largely uncriticised, and indeed ignored, by the West in its demonising of Islam. It helps to have God, oil and the American Way on your side.

So Afghan women have never really mattered. Before George Dubbaya's war, Buddhist statues were more deserving of the US president's attention. During George Dubbaya's war, the women were a useful symbol—as women often are. Appropriating "their" women is the virile mark of the coloniser, the invader. Defending "our" women is the mark of an emasculated nation reclaiming its manhood. Women the emblems of an identity, the human demarcation lines of national boundaries. The Mothers Of Our Sons.[7]

Following George Dubbaya's war, Afghan women have ceased to exist, even symbolically. The Smiling Woman who throws off her burqa and gleefully partakes in The Delights of Fashion has marked the moment of closure for the West. She has served her purpose and now has become anew as faceless as any burqa could ever make her.

---

6   See Labévière (1999).

7   See Enloe (1990) and Lacoste-Dujardin (1985), among others, for elaboration of these arguments.

Monday, 8 April

Tahmeena Faryal from RAWA is giving a series of talks in Australia. This evening she spoke at the New South Wales Labor Council. She is tired and harassed today. The Afghan consul in Australia, representing the supposed "liberator", the Northern Alliance, has attempted to discredit RAWA to the Australian government, claiming it is funded by the Pakistani secret service, and the Northern Alliance is attempting to cut RAWA out of any official discussions concerning the future of Aghanistan. If the Pakistani secret service supports anyone, it is the Islamists. There is no way that it—that any secret service—has ever supported a feminist organisation.

It appears that the Northern Alliance has declared invalid all Afghan passports issued under the Taliban. Tahmeena's passport was issued under the Taliban.

The exclusion of RAWA is not exactly new: RAWA has always been excluded from such discussions; it was excluded from the Bonn talks and continues to be excluded, despite appeals from RAWA to the UN and the US. Tahmeena tells me, with black humour in her eyes and voice, that the main contribution of one of the women politicians in the Northern Alliance government to women's liberation appears to be to extol the virtues of pasta-making machines as a labour-saving device for women. Women in many parts of Afghanistan are frightened to leave their houses and the politicians give them pasta-making machines. Booby prizes for women who have been had.

To be had, however, you need to have believed in the first place. As some Iranian women believed. Nawal El Saadawi wrote in 1980 that Khomeiny's revolution sought "to emancipate the people of Iran, both men and women, and not to send women back to the prison of the veil, the kitchen and the bedroom" (1980: iii). The Shah was so hated, so strongly identified as a British puppet, that Khomeiny just had to be better. Didn't he? But "emancipation" in the public sphere is only part of the story. As Chahla Chafiq observed in 1991, women in Iran were at that time the best-educated and the most professionally active in the Muslim world. This did not make them "liberated" (Chafiq 1991: 96).

Have Afghan women truly believed that the Northern Alliance is better than the Taliban? Have the poor and illiterate women of rural Afghanistan, now internally displaced following civil war then US bombings, really had the information and the opportunity to even contemplate such a choice?

Tahmeena is to meet this week with Alexander Downer, Australian Foreign Minister. An exercise in diplomacy. Theatre of the absurd.

When I first heard on the radio, on the morning of 12 September 2001, that the twin towers of the World Trade Center had been demolished by two planes flying into them, I thought it was a monumental hoax, like Orson Welles' end of the world broadcast. No chance of remaining long in that shock of disbelief, with the pages and pages of photographs and hyperbolic headlines, the television footage with action replays of the towers' destruction repeated *ad nauseam* in the following hours, days and weeks. The footage was edited so that the work of destruction appeared to take just a few minutes, when in fact it took several hours. But the viewing public needs instant gratification. Needs its dose of kerboom-splat.

Over the days and weeks following the World Trade Center attack, I felt uncharacteristically inarticulate. Not through a sense of grief, although grief can be difficult to articulate. It was more because I simultaneously felt sorrow and a peculiar kind of vindication, even macabre glee. On the one hand, I deplored the tragedy of loss of life, and in particular the lives of those whom one might call "shitkickers": those secretaries, clerks and cleaners who were just trying to eke out a living in low-status and largely routine jobs (but jobs they probably clung to, as one clings to a lifeline), those who died suddenly and violently, without having any idea why. Not that the lives of these people are intrinsically more "valuable" than those of others who died, but the shit-kickers always matter less to the media and to governments. A diplomat or a captain of industry dies, the world mourns. His secretary or cleaner dies, no-one even knows. So for me, the shitkickers had to matter more.

At the same time, something in me secretly cheered, wanted to celebrate a victory that it seemed no-one else would see as such. One of the major edifices symbolising world capitalism had been destroyed. One of my many lifelong dreams of seeing these places blown to smithereens had been realised. Something in me wanted to dance for joy. Something in me wanted to say, Well Take That, Uncle Sam! How does it feel now, big guys? How does it feel to have a couple of your gigantic phalluses reduced to rubble and ash?

I even indulged in black and rather off humour. During the flurry of Bin Laden and George Dubbaya jokes following September 11, we had our own local version, concerning current right-wing Prime Minister John Howard. Howard was in the US at the time of the attack, following which, he had a little difficulty returning to Australia. Given that this was happening not long after the *Tampa* asylum-seeker incident, a joke started circulating in Australia that perhaps John Howard could be put on a ship and then put ashore on Nauru to be "processed" (the so-called "Pacific solution" Howard had arranged for asylum seekers). I added a variation to that joke: "I have a better idea: we could put him inside a monument to world capitalism and then aim a plane at it." I am not sure that all found my version funny ...

We all cope with the surreal as best we can.

The loss of thousands of lives at the World Trade Center was certainly tragic. To me, however, it was no less banal than the many tragedies of violence in the world, and significantly more banal than some. I did not need to wait for the World Trade Center attack for horror stories to disturb my sleep or reduce me to sobs or provoke me to cry out in frustration and rage: war in Vietnam, Biafra, Palestine, Rwanda, the Gulf, Chechnya, violence and repression in Soweto, Chile, Argentina, Haiti, war on women in particular in Algeria and Afghanistan, war of another kind on women in the sex-tourism industry in the Philippines and Thailand ... the story of destruction is massive and widespread.

Plus all the more familiar horror stories in the relatively privileged West. The homeless in cardboard lean-tos under the bridges of the Seine or on the benches in the Paris Metro, the decision taken many years ago to leave some Metro stations open all night in winter so the homeless would not freeze to death being a curiously circumscribed act of compassion. In US cities, where there are many many more homeless, they cope as they can in the public parks and doorways, or ride the night buses. To and fro, to and fro. Just to keep warm.

The *sans papiers*[8] in France. The Malian camp at Vincennes. The occupation of a Paris church. The protests at Villawood, Woomera and elsewhere in Australia, where asylum seekers are detained, where international treaty obligations are treated in as cavalier a fashion as they would be by any dictator.

Indigenous Australian people living in so-called Third World conditions. The unemployed subjected to the indignities of so-called "mutual obligation".

Plus the many many stories of violence against women. Less easily noticed in the general collective horror of the world. Because less public, less collective, less likely to be placed at the abnormal end of the spectrum of human (read male) behaviour.

If there were only women in the camps at Villawood and Woomera, would the Australian left have mobilised? If there were only women among the homeless, would the French group Droit au Logement (Right to Accommodation) have mounted its commando operation to break into the hundreds of empty Paris apartments and open them up to those without somewhere to live?

No end to the list of horror stories. But all banalised. Violence so systematic—and systemic—so everyday, that in the end it is just part of life.

---

8 *Sans papiers*: "without papers", i.e. clandestine immigrants, including asylum seekers.

Predictable, even "normal". One has to live after all. So one thickens one's skin as best one can. Wears earplugs to muffle one's world to bearable decibel levels, and blinkers to avoid being distracted by the agitation at the periphery.

But the World Trade Center attack? This was not predictable. This was not normal. This was not yet another tragedy on a list. This was not something one could muffle or blinker off—or even something one would want to push to the periphery. This was a centre-stage tragedy—the indestructible destroyed; the stuff Real Human Drama is made of. The stuff of which the Western world wanted to comb through the smallest details. The minutiae of death and destruction in a US city—in the financial and trade centre of the world, not to mention on Manhattan, a strip of land that is one of the primary cultural icons of the world's most powerful nation—fascinated the West as the minutiae of death and destruction in an Afghan town could never do. The West was aggrieved by all the small senseless losses in ways that the losses in Afghanistan do not touch us. Some hoped that this would mean we—we the West—would finally understand, that the US populace would feel the enormity of the violence done to others in its name. Unfortunately, however, it has even further banalised the violence done Elsewhere. Elsewhere is not Us. Elsewhere is not Home. Elsewhere Does Not Count. And Elsewhere Must Pay for destroying Us Here and Home.

And the women of Elsewhere count the least. If the women of Us and Here and Home do not count, if the US women raped and battered and humiliated and silenced by their millions, in a multitude of ways, every day, do not count, how can the women of Afghanistan count, with their unfamiliar names, women who are even faceless, shrouded in their burqas? ... or if they have a face, it is the eternally distraught face of the Universal Third World Refugee, a face one has seen before, too many times for it to continue to capture our interest.

What if only women had been inside the World Trade Center?

But then, of course, they would have been "our women", the tragic female face of (preferably white) Western middle-class victimhood attacked by the racialised other. An attack on "our women" is a symbolic castration, so protecting "our women" is about reaffirming "our masculinity". George Dubbaya would not then have had so great a need for Afghan women as an alibi. No loss of western masculine honour if they die or are otherwise discarded.

Only women died at Montreal Polytechnic in 1989.[9] But their male killer

---

9   On 6 December 1989, Marc Lépine, who earlier that year had been refused an engineering place at Montreal Polytechnic, burst into an engineeering class at the Polytechnic with an automatic gun in his hand. He ordered the male students to

(not an "other", one of "ours") was easy to dismiss as an aberration. (And female engineering students are also, no doubt, dismissable as an aberration.) In any case, the women died not because they belonged to the West and its men but because they were women. This is not important. Women are not important. And the guy was crazy anyway. No point making a fuss.

When the individual extremes of male violence become so dramatically visible they cannot be ignored, and cannot be represented as other than male violence against women (Marc Lépine made it plain that he murdered the women at Montreal Polytechnic because they were women), they must be sectioned off as abnormal. Individual not structural. Idiosyncratic not systemic.[10] Marc Lépine was abnormal. So are the Taliban. Fanatics. Lunatics. So the story goes: Marc Lépine was violent not because he was a man but because he was nuts. The Taliban are violent not because they are men but because they are Islamist (thus also nuts). Sharon and the Israeli right are violent not because they are men but because they are Zionist (thus presumably nuts as well). And George Dubbaya? John Howard? Tony Blair?

It was the public, orchestrated, Hollywoodised grieving following September 11 that nauseated me the most. Shades of Princess Diana's funeral. When will Tom Cruise and Julia Roberts give a benefit performance for Afghan women? Where are the flowers and photographs and ribbons with which New Yorkers will line the streets on 7 October 2002, the anniversary of the day the US started bombing Afghanistan? They will surely be there in abundance on September 11. But October 7? Who will mourn then?

And whom will the US people mourn on September 11, 2002? Those who died in the World Trade Center? Certainly. Those who died—and continue to die—in Afghanistan? Unlikely. Those who have died—and continue to die—in Israel and the occupied territories? Those who died—and may yet still die—in Iraq? Or those who live to suffer yet another day as the "demon lovers"[11] continue their "terror war"?

Who will mourn the women?

---

stand aside and then proceeded to murder fourteen women, aiming at their heads, while shouting abuse against feminists. He then turned the gun on himself, committing suicide. A letter he left constituting a sort of antifeminist manifesto, made it clear that the women had been shot because of Lépine's hatred of feminists. The letter was not made public by Montreal police until November 1990.

10 For an analysis of the Montreal massacre as an extreme manifestation of the social "norm" of male violence, see Guillaumin (1992).

11 This is a reference to Morgan (1989). This book has recently been published in a new edition with post-September 11 material, and with an interesting change in

And who will name the authors of this violence? It is not "people", it is not "the Muslims" or "the Israelis" or "the Americans" or "the Australians". It is men. Not all men. But many. Not only men. But mostly. Violence is masculine and violence is celebrated. Be a hero. Wield power. Inflict wounds. Kick the weak when they are already down. Or, if you help them, make sure they remain beholden to you. Keep the power. That is what makes you a man.

Who will rise up on September 11, 2002, in New York, Sydney, Kabul, Jerusalem, Paris, Baghdad ... and say "Enough! This is not my war and you will not wage it in my name!"? I can only hope that there will be hundreds of millions of us, and that our voices will be powerful enough. But somehow I doubt it.

References

Chafiq, Chahla. (1991). *La femme et le retour de l'Islam. L'expérience iranienne.* Paris: Le Félin.

El Saadawi, Nawal. (1980). *The Hidden Face of Eve*. Preface to the English edition. London: Zed Press.

Enloe, Cynthia. (1990). *Bananas, Beaches and Bases: Making Feminist Sense of International Politics*. Berkeley: University of California Press.

Guillaumin, Colette. (1992). "Folie et norme sociale. A propos de l'attentat du 6 décembre 1989." Colette Guillaumin, *Sexe, Race et Pratique du pouvoir. L'idée de Nature*. Paris: Côté-femmes.

Labévière, Richard. (1999). *Les dollars de la terreur. Les Etats-Unis et les Islamistes*. Paris: Grasset.

Lacoste-Dujardin, Camille. (1985). *Des mères contre les femmes. Maternité et patriarcat au Maghreb*. Paris: La Découverte.

Morgan, Robin. (1989). *Demon Lover: On the Sexuality of Terrorism*. New York: W.W. Norton & Company

——. (2001). *The Demon Lover: The Roots of Terrorism*. London: Piatkus.

UNHCR. ([1995]1996). "Protection Guidelines on the Treatment of Algerian Asylum-seekers", Geneva, May 1995, reproduced in Femmes Sous Lois Musulmanes, *Dossier d'information sur la situation en Algérie. Résistance des femmes et solidarité internationale*. No. 2. Grabels: WLUML.

---

title. Formerly *Demon Lover: The Sexuality of Terrorism*, it is now *The Demon Lover: The Roots of Terrorism* (Morgan 2001). I must say that I found the original title more eloquent.

Nahla Abdo

Eurocentrism, Orientalism, and Essentialism: Some Reflections on September 11 and Beyond

The warmongering discourses generated in the aftermath of September 11 have come, not surprisingly, as but another, albeit higher, phase of racist imperialism practiced by the US Empire.[1] While the criminal attack on Washington and New York could never be condoned, this heinous act demonstrated an unprecedented level of inhuman destruction conducted in the name of "Islam". The US policies and practices which followed seem to be equally racist, inhuman and arrogant. Most surprising in this discourse has been the crystallization of US imperial, racist, and most importantly hate-based attitudes towards the Third World, and most importantly the "Middle East". The return, with a vengeance, of Eurocentric Orientalism, expressed in a statement like "The West and the Rest", and in the exclusivist language of "us" and "them"—pronounced repeatedly by the Bush administration— warrants our utmost attention. It is to this aspect of the current imperialist discourse that my paper hopes to contribute.

The aim of this article is to demonstrate that Western, and most importantly North American, racist policies and practices towards the Middle East are not a new phenomenon, but rather, as old as the Western strategic needs and interests in the region. More importantly, such a phenomenon is not confined to the national/official patriarchal policy-makers. In fact it has been plaguing the Western feminist movement in general for several decades now. At the outset I would like to emphasize that the concept of the "Middle East" is itself a Western imperialist construct and not a unifying concept for any specific region. Depending on where the wind blows and the historically specific region in which the West, and particularly the US, finds its interest, the concept gets constructed accordingly. Thus, if by the Middle East we

---

1   The term Empire used in the context of the USA refers to the hegemonic role played by the US throughout the world. The concept encompasses the economic, political and cultural pressure exercised by the US government throughout the world, especially the Third World, in implementing the former's agenda and interest worldwide.

mean the current US reference point, namely, those who "breed" and "harbor" terrorists, then it means primarily the Arab world. Excluded from this definition are Israel and Turkey. Mind you, Iran and Afghanistan are added to the "Middle East" despite the fact that they do not form part of the region, not culturally, not linguistically and in no other factors, other than being targeted for attack! In other words, the concept of the "Middle East" is arbitrarily constructed to serve specific imperialist interests. I prefer to use clearer terms like Arab world or Muslim world, with full recognition that neither is a homogeneous or uncontested terrain.

The History which Started and Continues

It is possible to argue that Zionism was a multi-faceted ideological movement. Pro-Zionist Jews, for example, see this movement as a movement for the salvation of the European Jews from European persecution, hence, a salvation movement, or even a nationalist movement. This belief was further strengthened during the 1930s with the European, specifically German, atrocities and the Holocaust, which claimed the lives of many Jews, among others. While this is not an unfounded claim—particularly for European Jews whose experiences of the Holocaust will always stand as a mark of shame for Europe's history—this remains one face of Zionism only.

As a member of the indigenous people of Palestine, as a Palestinian, Zionism for me and for the people of Palestine is a different thing altogether. For Palestinians, Zionism meant *what it actually did in Palestine* and *not what it intended to do for the European Jews*. For the overwhelming majority of peasant Palestinians (about 1 million) during the first half of the twentieth century, Zionism meant the expropriation and grabbing of their lands, their expulsion from the land and the destruction of their social, cultural and economic livelihood. More importantly, what then—not unlike now—was considered necessary for creating an exclusively Jewish community, state and economy, namely, the *Judaization of Palestinian land, labor and market*, were deemed as exclusionary, racist and unacceptable practices, resulting in constant resistance, including the 1936 Palestinian revolution.

It is impossible for any one of us who adheres to anti-racist, anti-colonialist feminist analysis to fail to see the historical context which resulted in the establishment of the state of Israel in 1948. Most of us are aware of the fact that the establishment of the state of Israel was possible immediately after the UN resolution of 1947 which divided Palestine into a Jewish state and a Palestinian one. It gave the Jews, who at the time made up about 34 per cent of the total population, about 60 per cent of the best land in Palestine, which included the large cities on the coastal plain, while the Palestinians were given about 40 per cent of the inland area, resulting in the Palestinian refusal to accept such an offer. During 1947–48, the Zionist army in Palestine, made up of regiments such as the Lehi, Etzel and Hagana, also known as "terrorist gangs", waged what became known as "the war of Independence". This war of "Independence" for Israeli Jews was also the war of *ethnic cleansing* or Al-Nakba for the Palestinians. During this period, about 80 per cent of the Palestinians either were expelled by force or escaped out of fear for their lives. Several Israeli revisionist historians, including Benny Morris, Simha Flappan and Ilan Pappe, using Israeli Army classified information, have documented various atrocities and massacres committed by the Jewish army as means to expel Palestinians.

Al-Nakba or the catastrophe of 1948, which resulted in the "transfer" or *expulsion* of the overwhelming majority of the Palestinians, was accompanied by the further destruction of Palestinian material culture and the obliteration of Palestinian national identity. Israel sought to erase all Palestinian national memory from the map of Palestine, particularly by the erasure of about 500 Palestinian villages and their replacement with Jewish settlements.

After September 11

Leaving aside the broader context of the political economy for the emergence of forms of racist and ethnicist ideologies, Eurocentric Orientalism and essentialism since September 11 have stood at the core of "our civilization, freedom, democracy and ways of life" vis-à-vis "their barbarism, inhumanity, low morality and style of life", hence the legitimation of announcing a "crusade" for "hunting them", "sniping them" and "smoking them out of their holes".[2] This language, incidentally, is all too well known and has been in use since North American colonial genocide against the Natives. The newest version of this doctrine of racism was articulated in the Bush speech to the nation in February 2002, carrying the title "The Axis of Evil"!

There is little doubt that since September 11 Eurocentrism and Orientalism have essentialized all Muslims, Arabs and the Middle Easterners, turning "them" (and us living in North America) into one homogeneous and undifferentiated entity of an "other" which "produces", "harbors", and "protects" terrorists, and seeks to destroy "our civilization" (i.e., white, Christian). This has provided grounds for the re-emergence of Samuel Huntington's infamous thesis on "The Clash of Civilizations".

---

2   This language which referred to the US "ways" of dealing with Al-Qaeda, repeatedly used by George Bush, Dick Cheney and Donald Rumsfield, particularly during the early days of bombardment in Afghanistan, was captured by all US media, especially TV.

In the USA, Eurocentric essentialism has resulted in the harassment of and attacks on hundreds of Arabs and Muslims and those who look like them. Arrests and harassment of Arabs were reported throughout Europe as well. In one case in Holland, an apparently veiled woman was physically attacked, only be revealed later as an Orthodox Jewish woman wearing a headdress!

In Canada, similar attacks were made on young Arab men and women. For example, a Saudi female doctor was reportedly attacked in an elevator in a hospital in Montreal, while other young Arab and non-Arab Muslim students were harassed at schools, in the streets and in their neighborhoods. A couple of cases of attacks on young Arab students were reported in Ottawa; one in the area of Nepean and the other outside a shopping mall in the city.[3] Eurocentric essentialism was not only conducted at the individual level, but also found its way at the institutional levels of the state. In Canada, for example, the largest cultural institution, the Museum of Civilization, itself designed by a Native architect to symbolize "multicultural harmony", took an unprecedented decision to postpone indefinitely an art show which had been in the making for over five years and was to take place on 18 October. A fierce struggle mounted by Arabs and Canadian supporters forced the president of the museum to reverse his decision.[4] This case, which received widespread coverage in all national and local newspapers, radio and TV, was of particular significance because of the supportive role taken by the Canadian Prime Minister in the House of Commons, who basically stated that "what was good before September is good for now". After September, and following the footsteps of the USA, Canada also introduced a bill providing new regulations for immigrants: Bill C36, which has become law, is a mechanism to control all immigrants coming to Canada and particularly

---

3   It is interesting to note that, while some cases were reported in the press, most cases were communicated through other young children sharing the same schools or neighborhood. The first weeks of the attack had profound impact on many young children of Arab or Muslim origin here in Canada. The Canadian Arab Federation, the Council on Canadian Arab Relations and the Arab Community Center, for example, have documented ample cases of Arab and Muslim youth undergoing harassment and humiliation by fellow (white) students.

4   For more information on the decision to postpone the opening of the Art Show by 26 Arab Canadian artists, the intervention of the Prime Minister and the rescinding of the decision, see documentation gathered by the Canadian Museum of Civilization. My partner happened to be one of these artists and like other artists he has compiled a lot of data around this debate. The exhibition is entitled "The Lands within Me: Expressions by Canadian Artists of Arab Origin". See www.civilization.ca/cultur/cespays/payinte.html.

those from countries perceived as "supporters" of terrorism. Suspected immigrants, or those who are perceived to have any connection with "terrorists", according to the new law can be detained without any charge and interrogated. The Canadian legal system, which until then was based on the presumption that "the accused is not guilty until proven otherwise", has changed into "the accused is guilty until proven otherwise". Draconian measures known to be characteristic of dictatorial regimes have become the rule of law in liberal democracies!

The racialization of Arabs and Muslims within the domestic Western front was further heightened with the declaration of "war on Islam" and particularly on Afghanistan, suspected by the US administration and its "allies/ followers" (most importantly Britain) of being the center of terrorism. Today, several months after the bombardment of Afghanistan, and the killing of untold numbers of women, men, and children, and the creation of millions more refugees, US imperialism with the voluntary contribution of war-mongering Israeli officials, such as the war criminal Sharon, appear to be more determined than ever before to wage a devastating attack on more Arab and Muslim countries. The recent Israeli invasion and reoccupation of the Palestinian occupied territories by the Sharon-led government in late March 2002 and the ensuing war crimes and suspected massacres conducted by the Israeli army in Jenin and Nablus are just an example.

It is worth mentioning here that the similarity in language and discourse between the two regimes (the US and the Israeli) is striking, not just after the September 11 events. Like other colonial settler regimes, Israel has always treated Palestinians as less-than-human, colonial subjects. Such treatment has been true not only for Palestinians under Israeli occupation in the West Bank and Gaza Strip and East Jerusalem, but also for those who are officially considered as Israeli citizens (the Arab population of Israel). The general demonization, dehumanization and degradation of the "other", being an in-digenous population or perceived "enemies" of the colonial state, is an integral part of the racist ideological underpinning of all colonial or imperial rule. In the case of Israel, for example, Palestinians have always been targeted by state and institutional policies as the "perfect enemy" of the "democratic, civilized and cultured" Israel. As a means to strip from them their legitimate rights to their own land and history, Palestinians were invariably described as "cockroaches", "vipers", "crocodiles", etc. (Ashrawi, November 2001). Projecting the Palestinians as the "enemy" and treating them as sub-human is not a September 11 phenomenon. It is rather part and parcel of the very racist agenda on which the Zionist settler colonial movement has based itself since the late nineteenth century. Without dwelling on that history, it is important to remember that Sharon's current policies, while they might be openly and publicly abhorrent, and (due to the development of satellite TV) also widely exposed, are not an aberration in the whole history and experiences of the Palestinians at the hands of the state of Israel.

The most demonizing, dehumanizing and degrading description attributed to individuals, groups and nations that are deemed by the imperial or colonial power to be a "threat" or "obstruction" to the latter's interest is their depiction as "terrorists". The US campaign to "fight terrorism", initiated after September 11, has crystallized all the ideological underpinnings of colonial and imperial policies towards the constructed "other". The US's adamant refusal to provide, or allow other international bodies to work out, a definition of the notion of "terrorism"[5] is an intentional policy designed to facilitate present and future US incursions into any country deemed necessary for the latter's imperialist agenda.

Leaving the concept of "terrorism" wide open has served as a crucial device not only for the US but also for the Israeli government to conduct atrocities and inflict untold pain and destruction on the Palestinians. It is very telling how, immediately after September 11, Sharon found in the concept of "terrorism" the perfect excuse to attain his long dreamed-of objectives: killing as many Palestinians as possible and attempting to obliterate the whole Palestinian nation, by killing their leadership and making their lives unbearable in the hope that they would give up not just resisting, but also living in Palestine ... A well-known policy, known in Israel as "transfer", or elsewhere in the world as *ethnic cleansing*!

As the US administration was busy preparing for war in Afghanistan, the Sharon government had begun its own campaign of re-creating the Palestinians as terrorists, thus as people who must be "eliminated". The first analogy he tried came in his warning to the US not to "Sacrifice Czechoslovakia–Israel, to please Arafat–Hitler". But this one was *bad* and strongly resisted by Bush. Later, Sharon changed into "Arafat equals Bin Laden and the Palestinian Authority equals Taliban", while he, like Bush, is the force of Good fighting Terrorism! In his speech to the Knesset (parliament) session in memory of the assassinated minister, Zeevi, Sharon promised, "We will wage all-out war on the terrorists, those who collaborate with them and those who send them" and concluded: "As far as I am

---

5   One of the major concerns raised by many in the international community, particularly in the Arab world, is that the term "terrorism" lumps together all resistance movements, including national liberation movements still struggling against foreign colonialism and occupation of their land, such as in Lebanon, Syria, and most importantly the Palestinians, whose struggles against Israeli occupation have been internationally recognized as legitimate struggles.

concerned, the era of Arafat is over." His position was also echoed by his spokesman Raanan Gissin, who declared: "We are doing precisely what the US is doing in Afghanistan" (CNN, 24 October). Or, "the situation is different today, and will not again be like it was yesterday" (Ha'aretz, 18 October).

The similarity in the language used by Sharon and his men on the one hand, and Bush and his spokesmen and women on the other, is so stark that listening to one is tantamount to listening to the other![6]

But this is not about language or simple "academic" discourse. In fact, George W. Bush and Ariel Sharon are the personification of the ideology of war, colonialism and destruction, they are the very tools needed to implement the colonial and imperialist interests of both the USA and Israel. One needs only remember that the massacre in Jenin refugee camp and the old city of Nablus in April 2002 is but one of a series of massacres conducted directly (and indirectly) by Sharon, beginning with the village of Qibya in 1953 and the well-known massacre of Sabra and Shatila refugee camps in the summer of 1982.

Amidst the heightened campaign of war hysteria, the most cherished value traditionally associated with "Western civilization", namely, democracy or the freedom to speak or voice a different opinion, is being muted if not mutilated. The intensive campaign of "fear" and "loathing" of the "other" has deeply affected the voices of dissent, domestically and internationally. Any attempt at criticizing US foreign policies or hinting at the long history of terror it has been inflicting upon millions of people throughout the Third World, including Arabs and Muslims, is being hushed, silenced and even attacked. In a gathering of about 500 women delegates from all over Canada called by the National Action Committee on the Status of Women (NAC), Sunera Thobani, a previous president of NAC, addressed the gathering with a daring feminist speech, outlining among other things the need for the US to re-think its position concerning the poor throughout the world (see this volume: 64–9. Thobani stated that "the West for 500 years has believed that

---

6   It is important to add here that the most important similarity between the two regimes is the disregard for human life. After the first attacks in the West Bank and responding to the reports speaking of many civilian casualties, Israeli Defense Minister Benjamin Ben Eliezer said that "the harm to civilians has been minimal, but with Palestinians it's a procedure to hide behind civilians and shoot." We in the West were hearing similar statements in defense of the so-called "stray bombs" dropped on villages, wiping out whole villages, killing children, destroying roads, hospitals, UN buildings and Red Cross food depots. In both cases collateral damage and collective punishment are employed regardless of any moral or ethical concern.

it could slaughter people into submission and it has not been able to do so. And it will not be able to do so this time either", quoting among her examples the hundreds of thousands of Iraqi children who have been dying as a result of US bombing and embargo against Iraq, as well as the constant suffering of the Palestinians by from US-made missiles, planes and guns at the hand of the Israeli occupying forces. Although Professor Thobani was neither Muslim nor Arab (but not white either), and despite the fact that her speech received a standing ovation from all participants, she did not escape a fierce attack from two most significant symbols within the Canadian feminist or women's movement. The first was Alexa McDonough, the only female head of a major party in the Canadian parliament, the New Democratic Party, which was a close ally to NAC. (This is the same party which supposedly champions the rights of the working class and the poor, defends democracy and upholds human rights domestically and internationally!). McDonough announced that "This is a time to be building tolerance, to be building bridges not to create greater divisions", adding that Hedy Fry, Minister for Multiculturalism and Women's Affairs, should have offered "an unequivocal rejection of the kind of cheap sloganeering, of the excessive rhetoric". The second was Hedy Fry herself, who defended her position by saying: "People in this country are allowed to say what they want ... I did not support [Thobani's speech]. I did not applaud it. I got up and left immediately following ...", adding "I condemn that speech. I thought the speech that was made by the expert of NAC to be incitement"! (*The Citizen*, 2 October 2001: A5). In other words, the two most public and official symbols of Canadian feminism have caved in to the Bush campaign of silencing the voices of dissent. More importantly, they also tried to use their power in silencing other women as well—that the target was an "other" must not have come as a surprise! But the story was not over; several days later the police received a complaint from one anonymous citizen accusing Thobani of a "Crime Hate Crime" against the US.

George Bush's infamous statement "you are either with us or against us" was literally followed up by the American and Canadian police, resulting in the arrest of hundreds of Arab men. In Canada, for example, several hundred men in Toronto alone were questioned by the Royal Canadian Mounted Police. As one officer said: "many of the tips [received] concern individuals who reportedly have positive opinions of Osama bin Laden or who deny Mr. Bin Laden [is] responsible for the September 11 terrorist attacks in the US" (*The Citizen*, 11 October 2001: A7).

To these examples I would like to add my own personal experience. In one live radio interview, after strongly condemning the heinous attack on Washington and New York, I added a dissenting voice against the US racist warmongering discourse. My statements were taken out of context, seen as "inflammatory" and even deemed "dangerous", resulting in a barrage of phone calls and messages, some to me and some to the administration of my institution questioning my "employability and appropriateness as an educator to Canadian students". Although I have been a Canadian citizen for over twenty years now, the producer of my interview, without bothering to consult with me, had decided to introduce me as Palestinian, thus one of "them". These examples are indicative of the conflicting and contradictory nature of the feminist movement, as well as the shaky grounds on which the so-called "global feminism" or "sisterhood" stands! Such dynamics and problems have historically characterized the tensions which marred the relationship between West and East, especially in its feminist manifestation, whether this be in general politics, in academia, within the women's movement, or at the popular public level.

The Feminist Debate: Three Different Approaches

This paper is part of a research project in progress and therefore it is not complete, nor does it have answers to all of the questions it raises. All I will do is to try to set the conceptual or theoretical framework for understanding the tensions, contestations and conflicts between the West and the East by focusing on how feminists on both sides have perceived the "other". Let me emphasize here that my approach refuses to draw a separate and definite line between "West" and "East" and rejects the binary constructed between "them" and "us". As I will show here, the line separating the two is blurred: at many junctures, the "us" becomes "them" and the "them" become "us". After all, many Arabs, Muslims and Middle Easterners form part and parcel of the European and North American social fabric.

I argue that there are three major arenas or phases in the development of academic (and consequently political) approaches to studying/understanding women in the Arab world. These approaches are: Eurocentric Orientalism: essentialism (or ethnicism); and the Other or alternative feminism, which is more academically active and politically subdued. Although these three approaches have followed three different historical stages in the development of feminist academia, they are not fixed in time, nor are they exclusivist in terms of class, race or ethnicity. Instead, the different approaches are fluid in their nature and capable of crossing the boundaries of national, ethnic and racial identities. The elasticity of these approaches is highly determined by various local, national and international changes in the socio-economic, political and cultural conditions under which any approach or epistemological project operates.

The first approach, to which I refer as Eurocentric Orientalism, represents an amalgam of sociological and anthropological work, which has largely focused on an exoticized version of the Arab and/or Muslim woman. Characteristic of this approach is the Eurocentric or Orientalist essentializing of Arab and/or Muslim women. Literature here, which includes the works of Germaine Tillion (1958) and Juliette Minces (1982) among others, has taken up issues such as the "veil", the "harem", "hammam", and other forms of "bodily" features/behaviors or "cultural" symbols as its main research object, turning them into the only, or most important, issues in Arab/Muslim women's lives. In this approach, feminists (historians, sociologists, anthropologists, fiction writers and so on) expressed more interest in the "outer looks", the "superficial", the "sensual" and the "sexual" appearances of the Arab or Muslim woman, deeming them to be "different" or "other" to the Western "eye", "taste", or "lifestyle". Such approaches have also focused on the "other" as "less", "lacks", "under", "below"—yet exotic—rather than the other as in *different but equal*.[7]

The second approach, identified as Ethnicism or Essentialism, refers to a particularly interesting period in the women's or feminist movements, especially among Arab and/or Muslim scholars. During the 1980s and early 1990s, a rich literature and interesting debates largely produced by these women scholars have emerged, with the participation of indigenous as well as Diasporic Arab and/or Muslim women. Scholars identified with this stage include Hoodfar (1991, 1993, 1996), Mernissi (1986, 1988, 1992, 1994), Hessini (1994), Dirie (1996), and a long list of other contributors. This literature has undoubtedly contributed a wealth of information to existing debates; it has also made an especially important contribution to feminist epistemology. Yet, as a set of literature primarily concerned with responding to the existing Eurocentric Orientalist and basically essentialist literature, these approaches have ended up largely falling into the trap of the Orientalist feminists, fighting one form of essentialism with another. Much of these "responsive" or "reactive" approaches by feminists or women identified within this category was focused on issues that were similar to—if not the same as—those raised by their opponents. Once again, cultural symbolism, including the veil, polygamy and other religious/cultural markers were taken up, but this time with an "indigenous" "Eastern" or "native" flavor.

The third approach, which I refer to as the Other or alternative feminist approach, represents what I think is a new movement in feminism, one which is capable, not necessarily of bridging the gap, so to speak, but more importantly of challenging the "self" and the "other" simultaneously. Feminists here are not necessarily Arab and/or Muslim only. They are, instead,

7   For more on the line of thought of feminist Orientalists, see Alloula (1986); Lazreg (1994).

progressive women/feminists who have opted to provide an alternative approach to studying, understanding and presenting Arab women or Middle Eastern women by contributing to a more substantive body of research. This trend, which began in the late 1980s and flourished during the 1990s, has placed more emphasis on the lived actuality and daily life experiences of Arab and/or Muslim women. Issues raised in this body of literature deal with the real lives of women, being economic survival, political conditions, cultural complexities, internal and external patriarchies, and general legal context, as they affect the daily experiences of these women. This new feminist epistemology on Arab and/or Muslim women is identified with feminists such as Suad Joseph (1996, 2002), Lila Abu-Lughod (1986, 1993), Julie Peteet (1991), Rosemary Sayigh (1996), Deniz Kandiyoti (1999), and Annelise Moors (1995), to name just a few.

Eurocentric or Orientalist Feminism

The first feminist approach identified earlier corresponds to the wave of Western feminism of the 1960s and 1970s. It presents an environment where social sciences in general, and feminist approaches in particular, were tied to the grand design of the European imperial powers. During that historical period, social science disciplines, such as sociology and anthropology, were largely used as tools to gather practical information, which supported the purpose of feeding Western colonial interests with necessary background knowledge ultimately used to justify the decades-long colonial presence in these regions.

In the absence of a feminist movement independent of the existing state/official policies, which would go beyond domestic issues of patriarchy, it is not surprising that Western feminism then—and to some degree even now—has been heavily influenced by the official policies of the Western state. (Lazreg, 1988; Mohanty 1991). Eurocentric Orientalism, which informed—and continues to inform—the theoretical framework of the colonial policies, was reflected in the frameworks adopted by social scientists including feminist writers and academics.

Eurocentrism, Orientalism and the Making of Social Relations in the Middle East

Much of the dynamics of social relations within the "Middle East", including gender relations and women's positions, have historically been cast within the Orientalist and Eurocentric frame of thought. Eurocentrism and Orientalism as forms of racism practiced against the Arab and Muslim world have been eloquently criticized by social scientists and critics like Edward Said (1978),

Bryan Turner (1983), Samir Amin (1989), and Ella Shohat and Robert Stam (1994), to mention just a few.[8]

Feminist students of sociology and anthropology, among other disciplines within the social sciences, are well aware of the Orientalist approaches embedded in the works of major classical theorists, particularly those of Max Weber, in which he describes Islam (1978: 624–6). Still, they were not dissuaded from such approaches; instead, they continued to adopt patriarchal frameworks, following such racist schools of thought. Marx, for example, based his approach to studying the "Orient" and the Arab world on British imperial archives. His thesis on the "Asiatic Mode of Production" thus failed to escape the tendency of orientalizing the Arabs and the Middle Eastern cultures by describing them as "barbarians who can be civilized with Western imperialism".

The problem with the approach of Max Weber, on the other hand, goes beyond being erratic, abnormal or an aberration to his overall methodology. Marx's emphasis was on people's material existence under the clutches of capitalism, which he, at a later stage and in reference to the case of British colonialism in India, sought to oppose and even to overthrow. In contrast, Weber has vacillated on the question of capitalism, focusing instead on the role of cultures, religions and people's attitudes: an approach which made it easier to focus on the "other" as different and lacking what the Western or Christian spirit provides. It is in this sense—namely, the use of a culturalist approach, rather than a historical materialist one to describe West and East— that has resulted in replacing a scientific objective approach with one based on people's traits, behaviors and belief systems. In this approach, Weber has in fact crossed all scientific and moral boundaries of the social sciences insofar as loathing of Arabs and Muslims was concerned. This is most evidenced in his infamous treatise on what he referred to as the "Mohammedan faith" (sic) (see Abdo 1996: 14).

According to Weber, Islam is a "simplistic dervish faith" created by "a promiscuous sensual" Mohammad, ruled by an "irrational class of warriors" and motivated only by "booty and real estate gains" (1978: 444–626). Weber had the following to say:

> Islam was never really a religion of salvation; the ethical concept of salvation was actually alien to Islam ... An essentially political character marked all the chief ordinances of Islam: the elimination of private feuds to the interest of increasing the group's striking power against external foes; the proscription of illegitimate

---

8 Elsewhere, I have provided a detailed analysis of the critical and anti-racist approaches presented by above authors. See Abdo (1997).

forms of sexual behavior and the regulation of legitimate sexual relations along strongly patriarchal lines (actually creating sexual privileges only for the wealthy), in view of the facility of divorce and the maintenance of concubinage with female slaves ... (1978: 625).

Commenting on this, the Arab historian Albert Hourani rejected:

the idea that political encounter (enmity) between Christianity and Islam goes back to the beginning of the [twentieth] century. That encounter has been expressed in terms of holy war, of Crusade and Jihad. The first great Muslim expansion in Christian lands, Syria, Egypt and North Africa, Spain and Sicily; the first Christian reconquests, in Spain, Sicily and the Holy Land; the spread of Ottoman power in Asia Minor and the Balkans; and then the spread of European power in the last two centuries; all these processes have created and maintained an attitude of suspicion and hostility on both sides and still provide, if not a reason for enmity, at least a language in which it can express itself. (1980: 4)

Islam, Hourani suggests, is seen with the eyes of inherited fear and hostility. It is seen "not in itself" but as the symbol of some enemy nearer home" (1980: 10).

Eurocentrism and Orientalism are two faces of the same coin. Both are epistemological constructs used to distinguish the "self" from the "other". On the one hand, Eurocentrism constructs Europe and the West as a homogenous and unitary entity of cultural congruence and continuity, with uninterrupted growth and development since ancient Greece; hence the claim for the whiteness, and therefore superiority, of the "West". On the other hand, Orientalism casts the West's superiority onto the "Other", the "East", by describing the latter as lacking all the cultural traits and value-systems of the Western self; hence it legitimizes the inferiority of the East. By combining both faces of the racist coin, we get Eurocentric Orientalism as a manifest-ation of power relations of the superiority of the West and the inferiority of the East, an epistemology that has found its way to the Western feminist movement via various threads. Commenting on the notions of Eurocentric Orientalism, Bryan Turner argues that the reason for the survival of the claim for Western epistemological superiority over the Arab/Muslim Middle East is "closely tied to the crises of global politics and, in particular, to the location of Islam with respect to the energy requirements of industrial societies" (1983: 18–19).

As an ideological discourse with a clear political agenda, and a project constructed around more or less defined power relations, Eurocentric Orientalism is not concerned with scientific or historical facts; it is not concerned with objective facts, nor is it value-free. Instead it is a value-laden epistemology, which denigrates the Orient by homogenizing Arabs, Middle Easterners and Muslims and presenting them as an undifferentiated entity. In so doing, it constructs a mythical entity devoid of any historical or factual foundations and treats it as the "other". Othering which is constituted as a form of relations of domination and subordination has become the context within which Arabs and Muslims are viewed. In this view the "other" becomes "always seen as 'Not', 'lacks', 'void' and as lacking in the valued qualities of the society, whatever these values may be" (Hartsock 1987: 86).

It is within this context of Western epistemology, the epistemology of domination and Empire, of superiority of the West and inferiority of the East, that much of the feminist writings were produced and reproduced during the 1960s and the 1970s. Following the methodological approach adopted by Weber and the general epistemological mood prevalent, especially during the 1960s, at the height of Arab anti-colonial and national liberation struggles, it is not surprising to see the general obsession with body and sexuality being adopted by early Western feminists or female-centered approaches to Middle Eastern women. To put it differently, cultural imperialism, which is largely influenced by economic and political imperialism, has used women's bodies and sexuality as a terrain for colonial and settler colonial policies, as the cases of Algeria and Palestine demonstrate.

It is important to observe here that, despite all attempts at glossing over all that is West as "White" and "One" and the "Same" on the one hand, and all that is East as "Other" but also "One" and the "Same" on the other hand, Eurocentic Orientalist epistemology remains fraught with tensions and contradictions, as it fails to stand the check of reality. The Orientalist epistemology not only essentializes, misrepresents and constructs the "external" or "outside" Other as "one and the same", it also fails to take into consideration the diversified identities and differences within its own boundaries. The West, as we all know, is not all white, but rather, a diversi-fied entity with differences based on class, gender, race, ethnic, national and religious constituents. All these are at the core of the making of the Western or North American cultures. Yet racism and supremacist ideologies are blind. They are espoused mainly, but not exclusively, by men in patriarchal power positions—such as the current US administration, along with their "national" allies or supporters of different genders, classes and colors—who refuse to use the conscious eye in their perception of the world.

Essentialism as a Reactive Approach to Eurocentric Orientalism

The second approach to Arab or Middle Eastern women is characterized by the rich and diverse methodologies found mostly in the body of literature pro-duced mainly, but not exclusively, by Arab and/or Muslim feminist authors. I emphasize the term "mainly" and not "exclusively" because I also recognize the presence of Western feminists who in defense of the "other" sometimes go beyond the boundaries of critical thinking, and in blind support to the "other", end up legitimizing the latter's ways of presenting themselves. I refer to these as "apologetic feminists". There is no one unified theoretical perspective or methodological approach used in this body of literature; some have resorted to culturalist approaches; others have adopted an individualist social psychological method; a third group has even used economic and political factors as tools for explaining the "Arab" or "Muslim" woman phenomenon! Yet, most authors in this perspective have responded to the existing distorted vision and image of Arab and or Muslim women by employing research methods which focus equally on women's bodies and sexuality. Here again, the focus of these groups of feminists has been on issues of the veil, the harem, polygamy, symbols like saints and sanctuaries, and textual interpretations of the Canon (including the Koran, Hadith, and sharia law) in so far as Muslim women are concerned (see Abdo 1997). The only marked difference between most works produced in this category, such as the work of Mernissi, Hoodfar and Dirie, and the Eurocentric Orientalist literature discussed above, has been the different interpretation, or spin, placed on Muslim women's bodies, as seen within the context of different Islamic societies.

For example a large amount of literature was produced in defense of the veil as a means by which it provides security and freedom of mobility for women in the public sphere [Hoodfar 1991, 1996]. Other works have justified veiling as a means of modesty, necessitated by poverty and inability to follow the never-ending consumerist values which, some authors claim (Mernissi 1986, 1988, 1992, 1994), have characterized various Arab countries. Still another group of writers have legitimized veiling as a form of "cultural distinction" and resistance to Western encroachment in the Arab countries (Hessini 1994; Dirie 1996). Moreover, most such works have adopted one version or another of the postmodern methods, employing, as stated earlier, a variety of conceptual frameworks to explain such phenomena.[9]

Works that I classify as Arab and Muslim feminist essentialism have received adequate analysis and critique elsewhere (Abdo 1997). I suggest that most such works are conceptually poor and methodologically problematic. The term I employ to describe this school of feminist thought is *feminist legalistic opportunism*. This is

---

9   For an in-depth analysis and extensive references to such approaches, I refer the reader to Abdo (1997).

the claim that women's problems, oppression, and victimization, as well as their solutions and emancipation, can primarily be attained within the confines of the Muslim laws and the boundaries of the legal system. In other words, this approach entrusts all discussions of women's problems and prospects [to] the legal system, trusting the latter to be the ultimate savior or champion of women's emancipation. Additionally, this approach confines women's rights to religious jurisprudence, albeit with a call to reinterpret the sharia (Abdo 1997: 170–6).

Fixation on the legal sphere is characteristic of the work of the prolific scholar Fatima Mernissi, particularly in her book, *The Veil and the Male Elite: A Feminist Interpretation of Women's Rights in Islam* (1992a). While Mernissi's approach is more of a social-psychological one that, among other things, is heavily concerned with men's or the masculine perception of women's bodies, her solution to women's oppression within Muslim laws is similar to that adopted by other scholars in this approach. For Mernissi, the main problem for Muslim women is that the Koran, the sharia, and the Hadith have been interpreted by men in a manner to serve their own interests. Therefore, according to her, in order to change their conditions, Muslim women must engage in the work of reinterpreting the Family Laws, diverting them from a male-centered into female-centered interpretation. (Abdo 1997: 173–5).

Mernissi's approach is relevant here because of her insistence that it is not the "text" itself, but rather its interpretation, that is wrong. This claim is similar to the argument made by other authors identified in this approach, who consider the veil as a form of "subverting patriarchy" (Hoodfar 1993, 1996; Dirie 1996; Hessini 1994). For feminists with this approach, it is the details of the "symbol", rather than the wider socio-economic and cultural context within which women experience their lives, which have been made central to their arguments. In this sense, there is little difference between this approach and the Eurocentric Orientalist described above: both are essentialist, both are concerned with the outer looks or symbolism and not with the essence of life experience and conditions. The difference between the two approaches, perhaps, is that one is largely an "outsider" Orientalist approach and the second is an "insider"—or, more properly, an "insider-outsider"—approach claiming "authenticity". This latter approach has been referred to by the Arab author Sadeq Jalal al-Azem as "Orientalism in Reverse".

These "reactive" approaches, instead of challenging existing stereotyped and ahistorical depictions of women—instead of refusing the very premise of the Orientalist approach itself— help to maintain and reproduce existing inferior images of Arab and Muslim women. Despite the seemingly "liberating", "emancipatory" twist that they attempt to give to the symbols—for example, by using the notion of "subverting patriarchy" in (re)presenting and (re)constructing phenomena such as the veil—they remain nonetheless essentialist. Not unlike Eurocentric epistemology, such approaches produce Arabo-centrism and/or Islamo-centrism as a means to combat Western or Eurocentrism. Common to both Eurocentric epistemology and Arab or Muslim Essentialism is the fact that both systems of knowledge feed into conservative and reactionary political systems, with grave consequences to differential politics and democratic rights. Both epistemological constructs, the Eurocentric Orientalist and the "native" "legalistic" essentialist, help to maintain and reproduce the status quo. By producing an elaborate system of epistemology about the East, Eurocentric Orientalism contributes to a wealth of special (read, expert) knowledge placed at the service of the hegemonic imperialist interests in the region. These "expert opinions" are, in turn, used as a legitimizing source for political and practical decision-making by the West. In the same vein, "Islamist" or "nativist" epistemologies are used in the hands of the dependent and weak Arab and Muslim states as means to further silence voices of dissent or difference deemed by them as a threat to their entrenched social conflicts and already unstable positions.

It is not enough to be a "native", an "insider" or one of "them" to be guaranteed a position of authenticity and/or representation. What they fail to realize, instead, is that the point is one of approach, historical specificity, and critical thinking: it is not enough to be a secular or religious Muslim to understand and represent Muslim women. True expressions of the actuality of Arab and/or Muslim women do not lie in how they dress or how they don the veil or the chador, nor in why they present themselves as they do. Instead, it is in what they do, how they live, and under what circumstances they experience their daily lives.

Most claims about Orientalism have been associated with the West and North America. Very little, if any, work has been devoted, for example, to examining Eurocentric Orientalism as a primary ideological construct used by the Israeli state and the state-official or mainstream Israeli feminism towards Palestinians in general and women in particular. In much of the West, Israel, ironically, is associated with the West, with democracy, and is largely removed from the inferior connotations of the Middle East. There are many important questions which warrant further research: What are the Eurocentric and Orientalist foundations of the Israeli ideology of Zionism? How has Zionism been influenced by Eurocentrism and particularly by cultural imperialism? How has the Zionist settler project influenced the Israeli state perspective and treatment of Palestinians in general and women in particular? In this regard, notions such as "Land Without People for People Without Land" and "the Jewish state" can be used as vital analytical tools in disclosing the essentially racist basis of the Zionist Israeli establishment. Such notions will also aid us in understanding the dehumanization and demonization of the Palestinians by the Zionist settlers; the Zionist perception of gender relations, especially around issues of Palestinian women's position in the family; and the question of why Arab female citizens of the state of Israel are still killed today under the guise of "family honor". Along with these questions, we also need to examine the Palestinian feminist responses to Israeli Zionism, and the extent to which such responses are "essentialist", "nationalist" or "emancipatory".

Alternative Feminism: Critical Feminist Approaches

The third feminist approach to Arab and/or Muslim women refers to the increasing body of literature which began in the early 1980s and flourished throughout the 1990s. This literature, which is found in the works of feminists like Rosemary Sayigh, Laila Abu-Lughod, Annelies Moors, Judith Tucker, Deniz Kandiyoti and others, provides theoretical and methodological approaches which are characteristically different from those in the previous approaches to Arab and/or Muslim women. Although here as well one cannot identify a single method, but rather a multiplicity of approaches, most such approaches appear to have paid specific attention to the historical and the socio-economic and political contexts as the wider framework for understanding gender dynamics and the factors which shape and reshape women's experiences and modes of presentation.

The body of scholarship in this category provides alternative methodologies to both approaches described above. On the one hand, in contrast to the Eurocentric or Orientalist literature, scholarship in this category avoids the ahistorical and static approach to Arab and Muslim societies, refuses the fixation on the sensual or sexual, and opts for a more dynamic approach that accounts for the internal contestations, conflicts and contradictions among women. Most approaches in this category are experientially based analyses of the life and conditions of Arab women. On the other hand, in opposition to Arab- or Muslim-centered essentialist approaches, critical alternative feminism recognizes the diversity and heterogeneity of Arab and Muslim societies and avoids the trap of essentializing culture or identity.

This approach is clear in the work of, for example, Annelies Moors (1995), who locates gender relations and the subject of women, property and Islam in a historic, dynamic and inter-generational context, giving woman her voice and agency. In the same vein, Laila Abu-Lughod's research among Bedouin women in Egypt, regardless of what critiques one might have, is still an exposition of the actual experiences of these women as they go about their daily lives (Abu-Lughod 1986). In a similar way and with focus on the experience of Palestinian refugee women in Lebanon, both Rosemary Sayigh (1996) and Julie Peteet (1991) provide hands-on approaches to women's experiences in Palestinian refugee camps in Lebanon.

Briefly, alternative feminism is about the actual living reality of Arab and/or Muslim women. It is about turning Arab women from objects of research into subjects and real selves. By refusing to sensualize, sexualize or essentialize their subjects, Alternative Feminists recognize the diversity, dynamic and historical contextuality of the women they study, research, speak about, or represent. Alternative feminism is not a neutral approach. Although some feminists, particularly those interested in ethnographic accounts, might take up the position of "let the subject" speak herself, hence take an "objective distance" from the researched subject, other feminists seek to use their academic skills in a more active and political manner. Emancipatory research or research that seeks to challenge existing oppressive conditions under which women subjects find themselves must form an integral part of alternative feminism. The latter, I believe, would be the type of intervention needed or welcomed by women worldwide, including Iraqi, Afghani and Palestinian women.

References

Abdo, Nahla. (1992). "Racism, Zionism and the Palestinian Working Class, 1920–1947." *Studies in Political Economy* 37: 59–93.

——. (1991) "Women of the Intifada: Gender, Class and National Liberation." *Race and Class* (32), 4: 19–35.

——. (1996). "Orientalism, Eurocentrism and the Making of Theory." In Nahla Abdo, Ed. *Sociological Thought: Beyond Eurocentric Theory.* Toronto: Canadian Scholars Press. 1–31.

——. (1997). "Family Law: Articulating Gender, State and Islam." *International Review of Comparative Public Policy* (9): 169–93.

Abu-Lughod, Laila. (1986). *Veiled Sentiments: Honour and Poetry in a Bedouin Society.* University of California Press.

——. (1993). *Writing Women's Worlds: Bedouin Stories.* Berkeley: University of California Press.

Amin, Samir. (1989). *Eurocentrism.* Monthly Review Press: New York.

Dirie, F. (1996). "Female Circumcision and Islam", a Seminar presented at the Canadian Arab Women's Conference. Toronto, March 1.

Hartsock, N. (1987). "False Universalities and Real Differences: Reconstituting Marxism for the Eighties." *New Politics*, 1(2): 83–96.

Hoodfar, Homa. (1991). "Return to the Veil: Personal Strategy and Public Participation in Egypt." In N. Redclift and M.T. Sinclair, Eds. *Working Women: International Perspectives on Labor and Gender Ideology.* London and New York: Routledge.

——. (1993). "The Veil in Their Minds and On Our Heads: the Persistence of Colonial Images of Muslim Women." *Resources for Feminist Research* (22): 5–18.

——. (1996). "Reflections on Gender and Religion in the Middle East: Can Muslim Women Be Feminists?" Lecture, Carleton University. March, 15.

Hourani, Albert. (1980). *Europe and the Middle East*. London: Macmillan.

Joseph, Suad. (1996). "Gender and Citizenship in the Middle East." *Middle East Report*. (198): 4–10.

——. (2000). Ed. *Gender and Citizenship in the Middle East*. Syracuse University Press.

Kandiyoti, Deniz. (1996). "Contemporary Feminist Scholarship and Middle East Studies." In Deniz Kandiyoti, Ed. *Gendering the Middle East: Emerging Perspectives*. Syracuse University Press.

Lazreg, Marnia. (1988). "Feminism and Difference: The perils of writing as a woman on women in Algeria." *Feminist Studies* 14(1): 81–107.

——. (2001). "Decolonising Feminism." In Kum Kum Bhavnani, Ed. *Feminism and Race*. Oxford University Press. (281–96).

Mernissi, Fatima. (1986). *Beyond the Veil: Male-female dynamics in Modern Muslim Society*. London: al-Saqi.

——. (1988). "Muslim Women and Fundamentalism." *Middle East Report*. (153): 8–11.

——. (1992). *Islam and Democracy: Fear of the Modern World*. Reading, Mass: Addison-Wesley.

——. (1994). *Dreams of Trespass: Tales of a Harem Girlhood*. Reading, Mass: Addison-Wesley.

Minces, Juliette. (1982). *The House of Obedience: Women in Arab Society*. London: Zed Press.

Mohanty, Chandra. (1991). "Under Western Eyes: Feminist Scholarship and Colonial Discourses." In Chandra Mohanty and Ann Russo, Eds. *Third World Women and the Politics of Feminism*. Bloomington: University of Indiana Press. (51–80).

Moors, Annelise. (1995). *Women, Property and Islam: Palestinian Experiences 1920–1990*. Cambridge University Press.

Peteet, Julie, (1991) *Gender in Crisis: Women and the Palestinian Resistance Movement*. Columbia University Press.

Said, Edward. (1978). *Orientalism*. New York: Pantheon.

Sayigh, Rosemary. (1996). "Researching Gender in a Palestinian Camp: Political, Theoretical and Methodological Problems." In Deniz Kkandiyoti, Ed. *Gendering the Middle East: Emerging Perspectives*. Syracuse University Press.

Shohat, Ella and Robert Stam. (1995). *Unthinking Eurocentrism: Multiculturalism and the Media*. New York: Routledge.

Tillion, Germaine. (1958). *Algeria: The Realities*. New York, Knopf.

Tucker, Judith E., Ed. (1993). *Arab Women: Old Boundaries New Frontiers*, Indiana University Press in association with the Centre for Contemporary Arab Studies, Georgetown University.

Turner, Bryan. (1983). *Religion and Social Theory: a Materialist Perspective*. London: Heinemann Educational Books.

Weber, Max. (1978). *Economy and Society 1* (edited by Guenther Roth and Claus Wittich). Berkeley: University of California Press.

Ronit Lentin

Feminist Snapshots from the Edge: Reflections on Women, War and Peace Activism in Israel after September 11

Introduction: The Black and White Poetics of War

A random selection of snapshots from my "women and war" folder, collected as I was becoming increasingly obsessed by the ongoing jingoistic self-congratulatory discourses emanating from the Pentagon in the "war against terrorism" aftermath of the bombing of the New York Twin Towers on September 11, 2001, and from the Israeli media in the wake of the re-entry to West Bank cities in early 2002.

The first is a press photograph of Northern Alliance ground troops on their way to Kabul (*Guardian*, 5 November 2001: 5). In the foreground stands a veiled Afghan woman, her head bent, her burqa held to her chest. The pleats of her burqa blow in the desert wind softly, invitingly, almost sensually. The macho army sweeping past the feminine trope of the victimised nation: the dogs bark and the convoy rides by.

In another press photograph, a 26-year-old US Air Force woman pilot smiles from the seat of her jet fighter painted with thirteen missiles marked "Destination Kandahar". Is equality for women in combat a feminist achievement?

The third is a cartoon in the Irish satirical fortnightly *Phoenix,* showing an Irish woman soldier with the Irish Prime Minister, Bertie Ahern. The woman is holding a rifle cocked at 45 degrees. When the PM asks what she is aiming at, she says: "I am shooting the glass ceiling"…

The fourth, and most personal, is a portrait of Yaffa Yarkoni, the 75-year-old celebrated Israeli songstress whose songs accompanied all of Israel's wars since 1948, in the weekly edition of *Ha'aretz*, in May 2002. When Yarkoni, the *passionara* of Israel's wars, was shocked by accounts of Israeli soldiers writing numbers on the forearms of Palestinian prisoners, saying, "We are a people who survived the Holocaust; how can we do such things?"—the whole country protested. How could the nightingale of Israel's wars break the taboo of linking the Israel Defence Forces with the Holocaust? Yarkoni apologised to the soldiers, but her apology was not enough to revoke the cancellation of her seventy-fifth birthday concert; she was doomed, but in her photograph, although wrinkled, she is still beautifully majestic, towering above the mass patriotic hysterics (Klein 2002).

The black and white poetics of war.

In the light of the post-September 11 US "war against terrorism", there has been a growing conviction that "gender differences between men and women are thrown into sharp relief" by the conflict (Bunting 2001), in that men are perceived almost universally as the perpetrators of war and conflict, and women as their victims, but also as more capable than men to make peace and resolve conflicts. A similar gendered discourse has emerged in relation to another "war against terrorism", this time in the Middle East in the wake of the 2001–02 al-Aqsa Intifada. In particular this has been in response to the re-invasion of the West Bank and to the suicide bombings, carried out, according to the Israelis, by order of the Palestinian Authority against innocent civilians, and according to the Palestinians, by desperate people responding to the ongoing occupation and repression of the Palestinian population since the 1967 war.

More men than women were shown by opinion polls as supporting the US–British initiative against Afghanistan (Bunting 2001). According to *Observer* journalist Mary Riddel, women, whether bystanders or warriors, have been routinely portrayed in the Western media as "the conflict's losers". Riddel cites military historian Martin van Creveld as arguing, "ludicrously", that "one of the cardinal functions of warfare is a (positive) 'affirmation of masculinity'". In line with the position of women as both the producers of the next generations of ethnic and national collectivities, and their symbolic trope (Yuval-Davis and Anthias 1989; Yuval-Davis 1997), war is increasingly depicted as a masculine construction. Despite the fact that men usually make up the largest number of war casualties, women are universally constructed as its victims. The involvement of women as perpetrators in the Rwandan genocide, for instance, as argued by African Rights (1995), failed to attract national and international attention, precisely because of the construction of women as the universal victims of the Rwandan genocide.

Women are not merely war's main innocent victims. They are also positioned, by feminist theorists such as Ruddick (1990) and Papandreou (1997), as uniquely capable of making peace and resolving conflicts. In the Middle East context, according to the Israeli feminist peace activist Gila Svirsky,

[Israeli] women have consistently been a large part, if not the majority, of the rank-and-file peace activists, and have often led the pack in out-of-the-box thinking. ... Ever since 'Women in Black' began its first vigil in January 1988, women's peace activism in Israel has consistently been more varied, more progressive, and more courageous than the peace activism of the mixed-gender peace groups (Svirsky 2002).

This article combines two different, but linked, threads. On the one hand, I present some theoretical reflections on the gendering of war and peace activism, arguing that feminist writing about war has moved from excavating the gendered experiences of women towards theorising war, and peace, as themselves gendered. I begin the chapter with a re-rehearsal of some theoretical feminist positions on the construction of gender in relation of war and peace. On the other hand, since I have written extensively about the gendering of war and peace activism in the Middle East (e.g., Lentin 1982, 1997a, 1998; Abdo and Lentin 2002a), I illustrate my argument about the discursive gendering of war and peace with an examination of Israeli feminist peace activism. I argue that, welcome and necessary as it is, particularly against a backdrop of the almost total Israeli intellectual self-silencing since the beginning of the al-Aqsa Intifada (at least initially), Israeli feminist peace activism has tended to valorise and essentialise women as ultimately "more peaceful than men", a theoretically problematic position.

Stemming from the US-led attack on Afghanistan in the wake of September 11, I suggest that, while the enemy is by definition othered and its humanity erased in times of conflict (as has so obviously been done by the US in relation to Afghanistan, and by Israel in relation to the Palestinians), that Other is increasingly feminised, since wars are often being waged on the symbolic battlegrounds of women's bodies. I conclude by flagging several questions about women, war and peace, and propose we should reposition ourselves as feminist researchers beyond constructions of nation, but also beyond the voyeurism of "strollers" whose ethnocentrism and/or cultural relativism often construct their analyses as a series of blurred (even when gendered) snapshots of wartime rhetoric.

Women, War and Peace: Reflections on Some Feminist Debates

Feminist scholarship about women's role in war and conflict resolution has progressed from the realisation that women and men experience wartime violence and conflict differently, both as victims and as perpetrators (Moser and Clark 2001), to the understanding of war itself as gendered (Lorentzen and Turpin 1998; Jacobs, Jacobson and Marchbank 2000; see also Lentin 1997b for a discussion of the feminisation of catastrophe). Contexualising constructions of masculinities and femininities in times of war, the veteran feminist theorist and peace activist Cynthia Cockburn (2001) argues for the importance of a gender analysis of war and peace, since "gender power is seen to shape the dynamics of every site of human interaction, from the household to the international arena" (2001: 15), and highlights the gendered "features of armed conflicts and political violence that are otherwise overlooked".

Despite the recent proliferation of feminist analyses of the gendered aspects of war and conflict, the Israeli-American sociologist Simona Sharoni (2001) argues that much of the literature on political conflicts excludes women and gender issues from the arena of international politics. This exclusion is based on the public/private dichotomy (as proposed by, among others, Elshtain 1981, and Enloe 1983) across cultural contexts, and serves to emphasise the view that women have no power or political agency. Thus, the portrayal of women as the victims of armed conflicts overlooks their power and agency and the ways in which women can benefit from periods of conflict, particularly national liberation struggles (Sharoni 2001: 86).

Analysing the relations between militarism and sexism within broader feminist debates through her examination of the Israeli–Palestinian conflict, Sharoni (1992, 1994) presents three feminist positions on the relationship between women, war and peace.

The equity position encourages women to serve in the military so that they can transform it. However, not only do women not succeed in transforming the military's "hegemonic masculinity" (Connell 1987), but this liberal feminist assumption that serving in the military enables women to gain greater access to social power is countered by the lack of proof that female veterans enjoy a share of the political spoils of war equal to that of male veterans. Although Israel is one of the few states to conscript women, and despite the recent law sanctioning the equal access of women to all military positions, women are far from equal in the Israeli Defence Forces (IDF). Nor is access to political power, which often derives from service in the IDF, accorded to women to the same extent as it is accorded to men, as is evident from the long list of former and present prime ministers, ministers, parliamentarians, and other politically influential male IDF veterans. Moreover, the promotion of women to IDF commanding roles, despite the new law, is tinged with class and ethnic discrimination. According to contributors to the Israeli feminist magazine *Noga* (2000), most high-ranking female IDF officers tend to be Ashkenazi, while Mizrahi[1] women tend to perform service jobs in

---

1   The term "Ashkenazi" refers to Jews born in Europe or North America, the term "Mizrahi" to Jews born in Arab and North African countries. See Dahan-Kalev (2001) on the relationship between Ashkenazi feminism and Mizrahi women in Israel.

greater numbers. Gendered power in the military also means the prevalence of sexual harassment in the IDF, but harassed women soldiers are often afraid to complain (see, for instance, Goldberg 1995). Nevertheless, many Israeli feminists support the equity position, as illustrated by the enthusiastic response by feminists to the new law (*Noga* 2000), making me wonder whether liberal feminism is really about "shooting the glass ceiling".[2]

Secondly, *the essentialist position* argues that women, because of their mothering and nurturing roles, are more peaceful than men and are therefore more inclined to conflict resolution (e.g., Ruddick 1990; Papandreou 1997). This argument equates war with patriarchy, militarism with sexism, and peace with feminism. However, the belief that if women were leaders there would be no wars is negated by female leaders such as Margaret Thatcher and Golda Meir, who led their countries to war; by women who perpetrate war and genocide, for instance in Rwanda (African Rights 1995); and by women whose tacit support is crucial for war and genocide, as studies of women in the service of the Nazi regime reveal (e.g., Milton 1993; Eschebach, Jacobeit, and Wenk 2002). The extensive use of symbols of motherhood by women to protest against war and violence results from the belief in women's potential for conflict resolution and nurturance. In Israel the essentialist belief in the peaceful power of mothering has a long history, as will be argued later. Organisations such as Mothers against Silence and Four Mothers, which called to "bring the boys back home" during the 1982 Lebanon war, were also arguably premised on the "men equal war, women equal peace" principle.

Finally, Simona Sharoni posits *the social constructionist position*, which argues that military power itself must be understood as gendered (Enloe 1983). The gender "woman", indispensable to the conduct of wars, is central to the construction of wartime masculinities, and women have serviced warring armies not only as soldiers' mothers, sisters, wives, and sweethearts, as nurses and other service workers, and as prostitutes and "comfort workers" (e.g., Sancho 1997), but also as soldiers.

Gender, both femininities and masculinities, must be understood as a social construction (as argued by, among others, Kimmel and Messner 1998).

---

2 For example, after the opening of the "Jerusalem tunnel" by Prime Minister Binyamin Netanyahu in October 1996, resulting in Palestinian bloodshed, Yehudit Ben Natan, former commander of the IDF Women's Corps, protested the fact that women soldiers were not allowed to join their male counterparts in active combat. According to *Ha'aretz* journalist Orit Shohat, liberal Israeli feminism could apparently live with the occupation of Palestinian territories, but not with the fact that women were not allowed to join men in taking up arms against the occupied population (Shohat 1996).

Therefore social constructionism seems the most appropriate explanation of the link between militarism and sexism, and between violence against women and the general level of violence in society. In most societies in conflict the general level of political violence results in increased levels of violence against women, as argued, for instance, by Monica McWilliams and Joan McKiernan (1993) in relation to Northern Ireland, by Rada Boric (1997) in relation to Bosnia, and by Euan Hague (1997) in relation to Serbia.[3]

Another example is the upsurge of violence against women and children in Israeli society during the Gulf War, when Israeli men found their passive role during that war difficult and vented their frustration on women and children. *Noga* editor Rachel Ostrowitz links violence against women to the Israeli–Palestinian conflict during the 1987–93 Intifada:

> The similarity of treatment of oppressed human beings is clear to us. When we hear every day about nameless dead Palestinians, we remember that women are often treated as persons without names. 'Women are all the same', they tell us, 'and Palestinians are all the same'. The voices merge (1996: 11).

This analysis is, however, somewhat problematic: in equating "women" with "Palestinians", Ostrowitz ignores the power differentials between (Israeli) women, who, despite gender discrimination, have more power than all Palestinian people, women, as well as men. A similar increase in violence was observed in Palestinian society: during the 1987–93 Intifada, Palestinian journalist Souha Aref found that in Daheisha refugee camp five out of six women were battered: "it seems that Palestinian men, oppressed by the Israelis, oppress their wives in order to prove their manhood" (1993).

More generally, as I have argued elsewhere (Lentin 1999), wartime rape, used not merely as a metaphor for the penetration and colonisation of peoples and lands, is ethnicised in that war itself is discursively interpreted as the "rape of the nation". At the same time emasculation is used as a metaphor for male disempowerment through colonisation: re-appropriating and re-subjugating women, as argued, for instance, by Ashis Nandy (1983) in relation to post-colonial India, may become a metaphor for masculine re-affirmation (see also Meaney 1991 in relation to Ireland).

However, in the Israeli–Palestinian context, the image of the Israeli soldier as brutal occupier who shoots Palestinian children and brings violence home to his family sits uncomfortably with the Israeli national image of the post-

---

3 See also Lentin (1997a) for a comparative analysis of the link between political violence and violence against women in relation to Israel–Palestine and Northern Ireland.

Shoah[4] brave "new Hebrew" who fought for his country and protected women and children. Israel—like many colonised nations that reimpose rigid gender roles once they assume independence—constructed a new masculine, militant type of Jew, the antithesis of the weak, persecuted diaspora Jew, affirming the right of power of the male, privileging "national security" above all else (Lentin 2000). The Palestinians, colonised for centuries, also prioritise the national agenda, and in the process maintain rigid gender divisions. Palestinian–American sociologist Souad Dajani, calling to incorporate the "social agenda", including gender equality, into the Palestinian national struggle, prophesied in 1994 that, since Palestinian women have made significant advances towards a more equal role in a future Palestinian state, "perhaps ... the next Intifada will be the women's Intifada" (1994: 54). Dajani's prophecy has clearly not been fulfilled, but according to Palestinian journalist Muna Hamsa-Mahsein, the al-Aqsa Intifada may have contributed to the liberation of Palestinian women: "If all the women of the West Bank sat on the road, you could not get to the settlements ... the women here [in the Daheisha refugee camp] speak of nothing else" (Segev 2000: B12).

Feminisms and Nationalism: Israeli and Palestinian Feminists Working for Peace

Another theoretical debate in relation to the role of women in times of war is the intersection of feminism and nationalism. For me there is a conceptual contradiction between nationalism—an exclusivist ideology—and feminism, which in its ideal form ought to be an inclusive, transformatory ideology. At the same time, Black and Majority World feminists have challenged Western feminist analyses in this area, arguing that Western feminist priorities serve to mask the racism and imperialism of Western feminism itself (see, to cite but very few examples, Amos and Parmar 1984; Mohanty 1991; Abdo 2001). These feminists argue that the construction of a dichotomy between the universalism of (Western) feminism and the particularism of nationalism is the domain of the developing rather than the overdeveloped world—an assumption negated by the surge since September 11 of American nationalism, both "banal" and not so banal. This erroneous dichotomy is reminiscent of the binary construction of the "Third World woman" as a unitary, homogeneous, ahistorical subject, versus the supposed superiority and heterogeneity of Western feminists (Mohanty 1991). While many Western feminists

---

4 I use the Hebrew term "Shoah", meaning catastrophe or calamity, rather than the English term "Holocaust", to describe the annihilation of a third of the Jewish people by the Nazis because the term "Holocaust", which derives from the Greek "whole burnt", indicates the sacrifice of the Jews. (See Lentin 2000: 3.)

ought to be critiqued for conceptual exclusions,[5] many Majority World feminists support national liberation and nationalist ideologies. This has to be taken on board by (Western) feminist opponents of such ideologies, particularly in situations of national and military conflict, as the respective stances of Israelis and Palestinians serve to demonstrate. On the one hand Israeli nationalism, mostly articulated as "patriotism", is often disavowed; on the other hand, most Palestinian feminists understandably do not wish to relinquish the Palestinian national agenda while at the same time struggling for gender equality in Palestinian society, as argued by the Palestinian sociologist Nahla Abdo in the introduction to our joint book, *Women and the Politics of Military Confrontation: Palestinian and Israeli Gendered Narratives of Dislocation* (Abdo and Lentin 2002b).

The examples I quote below, from a research project on Israeli and Palestinian feminist peace activists (Lentin 1997a, 1998) demonstrate the link—for Palestinian feminists—between feminism, nationalism and peace. The Israeli Palestinian activist Aida Touma Souleiman, a member of Women in Black and director of a lobby against violence against women in the Israeli Palestinian sector, firmly links peace with Palestinian national rights:

> The first stage of real peace in our region is the recognition of the full rights of the Palestinian nation to establish a state side by side with Israel and for Israel to leave all the territories occupied in 1967. As an Israeli Palestinian, peace means ensuring the full equality of the Arab population in Israel. And as a woman, perhaps they will find another planet to dump all the armaments and then we women will begin achieving the equality we are dreaming about (personal communication 1994).

Israeli Palestinian academic Manar Hassan, a member of al-Fanar, the Palestinian feminist organisation, links peace with both national and gender equality:

> As a Palestinian woman, this "peace" means nothing to me. There is an old woman from a village destroyed in 1948, who lives in a refugee camp ... When this business of Oslo began, she was asked if she was pro-peace. She said, of course, we should be able to return home. For me, as a Palestinian and a woman, peace means being equal to Israeli women; and equal to my brother, a Palestinian man. If this does not exist, it is not peace (personal communication 1994; see also Hassan 1991).

---

5 It can also be argued that "Western women" are also often dismissively constructed as a homogeneous whole by Majority World women, ignoring differences of class, ethnicity, cultural/national backgrounds, sexuality, political allegiances, as well as theoretical differences between the diverse feminist stances.

Thus for Palestinian women, peace means equal national rights (and indeed for some of them this may include the dismantling of the state of Israel as a Jewish state, a position not necessarily shared by all Palestinian feminist peace activists). In contrast, Israeli Jewish feminist peace activism, while challenging the consensus of the military men, rarely challenges Zionism itself, despite the recognition by feminist activists, such as members of the Coalition of Women for a Just Peace, that the ongoing occupation, and the policies of closure, curfew, and house demolitions, are racist and oppressive.

In fact, Israeli feminist peace activism is far from univocal or homogenous as illustrated by the Israeli peace activist Erella Shadmi. She argued in 1992 that Women in Black, by holding weekly vigils and calling for an end to the occupation during the 1987–93 Intifada, negated and redefined traditional images of femininity. By using their bodies to express their protest; by dressing in black and ridiculing the image of women as "pure", and the traditional "white" of peace; and by breaking the public/private dichotomy and entering politics through the back door, women created new spaces and a new political discourse (Shadmi 1992). Eight years later, Erella Shadmi reworked her original evaluation of Women in Black. She acknowledged the difficulties the group faced when confronted by "hostile, sexist and violent responses from passers-by (such as being called 'whores of Arafat', and 'Lesbians', and being told 'go back to the kitchen', and 'you need a man to show you your proper place'), and ignorance from the mass media and traditional politics". Nevertheless, Shadmi (2000) argues that internal tensions in this supposedly non-hierarchical group, between Ashkenazi middle-class and Mizrahi working-class women, brought about its demise and ultimately rendered its work ineffective. Although Women in Black did not cease to exist, and in fact renewed its activities during the al-Aqsa Intifada, Shadmi's analysis puts paid to the perception of women as always essentially more peaceful than men, and demonstrates that ethnic and class divisions often destabilise notions of universal sisterhood.

The (Self-) Silencing of the Lambs: Between Essentialism and (Feminist) Silences

Understandably, a major tension within Israeli feminist peace activism is that between allegiance to the national cause and the opposition to war and oppression. The start of the al-Aqsa Intifada caught many Israeli intellectuals unawares. Trying to explain the intellectuals' initial self-silencing, Israeli academic Shlomo Sand (2000) argued already in October 2000 that

the fact that most of the important Israeli intellectuals—authors, poets and philosophy and literature professors—are supporting the Israeli government and blaming the Palestinian leader Yasser Arafat for the violence, is not particularly surprising. Apart from the Lebanon war, each confrontation between the Israelis and the Arab worlds saw the central intellectual players line up under the shadow of the establishment, giving it the necessary legitimacy. (Cited in Karpel 2000)

Similarly, many Israeli feminists initially preferred to join other Israeli intellectuals in nurturing Israeli victimhood and blaming the Palestinian leadership—and, implicitly, Palestinian women—for the al-Aqsa Intifada. At the time of writing, May 2002, after the siege of Jenin, Ramallah and other West Bank cities, and several massive suicide bombs, Israeli voices of peace and dialogue—many of them intellectuals, many of them feminists—keep struggling to overcome the near universal support for Ariel Sharon's government. Developments such as the letters by several high-ranking reserve officers who declared their refusal to serve in the occupied territories, and the growing, hitherto unprecedented, phenomenon of refusal to serve by young conscripts, as well as several large anti-occupation demonstrations, do indicate that the Israeli peace camp has rallied around and is alive and kicking. A sizeable minority consisting of Israeli academics, left-wing activists, and feminists bravely and assiduously continue to demonstrate, hold vigils and maintain contact with Palestinian women and men. Nevertheless, I would suggest that the Israeli feminist response has often vacillated between self-silencing and essentialist discourses about women being more adept than men at conflict resolution, as I demonstrate below, using examples mostly from email communications.

On 4 October 2000 I invited the Israeli feminist electronic mailing list (iff-l@research.haifa.ac.il) to discuss the implications of the al-Aqsa Intifada. Though the debate did not initially take place in that forum, the list has been posting daily notices from various feminist peace organisations, such as Bat Shalom—the Israeli part of the joint Israeli–Palestinian feminist peace organisations The Jerusalem Link and New Profile—the Movement for the Civilisation of Israeli Society, and the Coalition of Women for a Just Peace. At the same time, as mentioned above, Women in Black continues to hold silent weekly vigils, "to express horror at the killings and the extreme expressions of racism and brutality within Israeli society and police forces" and "to demand an end to the occupation". Other activities of the feminist peace camp include condolence calls to the families of Palestinians who were killed, humanitarian aid to Palestinian hospitals and refugee camps, joint Jewish–Muslim–Christian prayer services, email protests, and practical help to Palestinians whose houses have been demolished and whose olive groves were uprooted by the IDF, and in particular, crucial support for conscripts who refuse to enlist (conscientious objectors are not recognised in Israel), and to reserve soldiers who refuse to serve in the territories and are jailed.[6]

Thus some Israeli feminists continue to demonstrate, agitate and dialogue against the occupation, war and racism, but resist the essentialist equation of women with peace; nevertheless, the evocation of essentialism persists. For example, on 2 November 2000 a call for a demonstration emphasised the essentialist equation of women with peace and men with war:

> Women make peace, generals do not. We did not get our children peacefully out of Lebanon so that they kill or get killed in Judea and Samaria ... We, women call on the Israeli government to talk, not kill. Listen to the voice of feminine wisdom, because the era of the generals is over!

In the spirit of essentialism, the motherhood discourse is paramount, as demonstrated in Dorit Abramovich's December 2001 *Ha'aretz* article, "Four Mothers and More", in which she reports on "hundreds of mothers who object openly to their sons serving in the IDF in general and in the occupied territories in particular". Abramovich cites New Profile member Orit Degani, who joins other mothers in opposing her son's military service:

> Like many other Israeli mothers, I had wanted my son to be an army paratrooper. Today I do not want to desert my sons and I am finding more and more partners in this belief. These are mothers who don't want merely to save their son but also to change this terrible reality (Abramovich 2001: B6).

Degani's maternal narrative has progressed from nurturing the ultimate Zionist dream of "my son, the paratrooper" to the maternal counter-narrative of wishing to save her son from military service, while, at the same time, "changing this terrible reality".

The mothering discourse is also used by Palestinian women in protesting against the occupation. Diane Roe, member of the Christian Peacemaker Team, an initiative to support violence reduction around the world (CPT@igc.org), wrote to New Profile member Rela Mazali: "I have never had a child. What does a mother do when a child says he is ready to die? What does a mother do when she hears a child overcome with rage and she knows that her child may also be prepared to kill?" In reply, Mazali argued that the

---

6 The Women in Black vigils have grown substantially with men also joining them, and have reconvened in several cities where they had long closed. Extensive activity is also carried out by New Profile, Gush Shalom, Bat Shalom, Rabbis for Human Rights, Yesh Gvul (the conscientious objectors), ecumenical groups, and others. Human rights work continues at a more intensive level than ever by B'Tselem, the Moked, Adalah, Association for Civil Rights, Physicians for Human Rights, and others (see Svirsky 2002 and gsvirsky@netvision.net.il).

discourse of mothering can also be used in a non-essentialist way to oppose militarism and resist racism, occupation and war, the basis of New Profile's ideology. An important part of the group's work is keeping the pressure on parents of soldiers. On 12 October 2000, Rela Mazali posted the following letter on the New Profile email list (http://www.newprofile.org/):

> Letter to a Soldier's Mother and Father
> You know only too well: If your son or daughter takes part in the war in the occupied territories, he or she may injure or kill someone; he himself or she herself may be injured or killed.
> Do you support this war? Do you believe it justified? Necessary? Are you prepared to make such a sacrifice?
> Dear Parents—For long years you protected your son or daughter from seasonal flu, from unsafe games, from biking in heavy traffic because "it's too dangerous". And now? Are you still doing all you can to protect him or her?
> Make no mistake: You're personally responsible![7]

Palestinian women are fully aware of the moral dividend of their victim status when they remind Israeli women that "We are not afraid. We do suffer, we do cry and mourn our dead—but we're not afraid because unlike you, we have nothing to lose." In their appeal for protection for Palestinian children —who, some cynical Israelis have argued, are sent to demonstrate by manipulative politicians, but also by parents who do not care for their well-being—they too often essentialise motherhood. In an open letter (29 October 2000) to Queen Sylvia of Sweden, the Women's Affairs Technical Committee pointed out that most children were killed as bystanders; their worst "crime" was carrying stones "in front of one of the world's mightiest armies". The IDF, they pointed out, suffered no fatalities at the hand of Palestinian children. Children are not dispatched to the "front line"; they are killed near their homes or schools.

Another example of the perpetuation of the maternal discourse was an email sent by Bat Shalom titled: "They Shoot Pregnant Women, Don't They?" on 26 February 2002:

> Two days ago, a Palestinian pregnant woman who tried to reach a hospital to give birth, was shot in the back at the Israeli army roadblock at the entrance to Nablus. The woman was transported to the Nablus Hospital and had to be operated [on] while in the process of giving birth. The army published an official apology. But it

---

7 See also Hannah Safran's "Not a Soldier's Mother" (2000) in which she argues that, had women's voice been included in the peace process from the start, feminists would not have had to resort to maternal arguments; Israeli women are only listened to as the mothers of soldiers, not as political beings in their own right.

seems that it did not impress the soldiers who yesterday manned that same roadblock. Another Palestinian pregnant woman was shot there under much the same circumstances. This woman, too, had to be operated [on] while in the process of giving birth, and when recovering from the operation, was told that she is now a widow.

Later the same day, a highly pregnant Israeli settler woman was shot by Palestinian snipers while driving on one of the West Bank roads, south-east of Bethlehem. She was brought to the Hadassa Hospital in Jerusalem. She too had to be operated [on] and gave birth in the operation room (batshalo@netvision.net.il).

The tag line, "they are shooting pregnant women in the name of security, in the name of national liberation, the occupation is killing us all", not only expresses justifiable horror at the targeting of pregnant women, but under-pins the essentialist belief that women are the universal victims of wars (or, conversely, better suited than men to peaceful conflict resolution) as the underlying discourse in some feminist writings about women, war and peace. However, in order to further the debate, I believe that feminist researchers and activists refrain from the zero power assumption of the dichotomy of powerful men versus powerless women, and warring men versus peaceful women, and reposition ourselves beyond nationalism and the voyeurism of the researcher-stroller, as I suggest in the conclusion.

Conclusion: Snapshots from the Edge

Women are curiously positioned: not only are they the producers of the next generations of national and ethnic collectivities, and thus, the targets of various political projects including population and migration control mechanisms; but they are also seen as the symbolic tropes of the nation (Yuval-Davis 1997). The figure of woman is often the chosen representative image of genocide and war, as was demonstrated by the photograph of the "Madonna in Hell" published in October 1997 in the world press during the height of the crisis in Algeria. A beautiful, tearful, veiled Algerian woman, whose eight children had allegedly been massacred, mouth open and eyes hollow, comforted by another veiled woman, was selected to represent Algeria's grief over the ongoing massacres. Woman as universal victim, motherhood as the epitome of suffering, and shattered female beauty as symbol of "man's inhumanity to man", war's feminised images are served for media consumption as part of a gendered lexicon of victimhood (Lentin 1999).

In the war in Afghanistan, Afghan women have been positioned by the media as emblems of Taliban inhumanity, as if the war against Bin Laden and Al-Qaeda was waged mostly in order to liberate and protect Afghan women. According to a radio address on 17 November 2001 by the US president's wife, Laura Bush, the US "victory" meant, above all else, the rejoicing of Afghan women: "Afghan women know, through hard experience, what the rest of the world is discovering: The brutal oppression of women is a central goal of the terrorists" (www.state.gov/g/drl/rls/rm/2001).

Although this war has supposedly been discursively waged on the battleground of women's bodies, Valentine Moghadam, in an article titled "Patriarchy, the Taliban, and the Politics of Public Space in Afghanistan", reminds us that international feminists "seem to have 'discovered' the plight of Afghan women only in 1996, when the Taliban came to power", although they were "strangely" silent about the position of women in Afghanistan during the 1980s and 1990s (2002; this volume: 276). Since the Taliban's predecessors, according to Moghadam, were perceived as attempting to liberate the country from Soviet domination, Western feminists, like other intellectuals, were co-opted into the Western anti-Soviet rhetoric, and therefore blind to the oppression of women during the repressive Mujahideen rule.

Moghadam further cautions against Western feminist cultural relativism and reminds us that "feminists from around the world are now agreed on the basic issues of education, income, and reproductive rights for women, no matter what the cultural context" (2002; this volume: 277). Indeed, cultural relativism, as well as ethnocentrism, are two Western feminist stances we should guard against in our theorisations of the links between gender, war and peace. Feminist researchers, like city strollers (see Benjamin 1968), finding themselves among strangers and being strangers to them, often perceive strangers as mere "surfaces", "so that 'what one sees' exhausts 'what they are', seeing and knowing them only episodically" (Bauman 1998: 92). In the "universal otherhood" that rules modernity, stroller-researchers often take "snapshots", which, according to Erich Fromm (1974: 343), become a substitute for seeing. Snapshots, the "momentary link between the shooter and the hit", are unconnected pleasurable fragments of the stroller, that pioneer onlooker, the first practitioner of looking without seeing (Bauman 1998: 133). Inclusivist assimilation and exclusivist expulsion are, according to Zygmunt Bauman, the two strategies of managing strangers, those ubiquitous and irremovable "others" of modernity. These strategies, however, are not "solutions" to the "problem" of strangers, but rather ways of controlling the problem, and no administration of social spaces eliminates proteophobia. Bauman's Janus-faced stranger is both stroller, mysterious and inviting, and the face of infinite opportunity; and stranger proper, sinister and menacing, but also half-visible and blurred (1998: 138). Linking the stranger-researched—in this instance women as victims, but also as agents, of war—and stroller-researcher—in this instance feminist researchers anxious to make sense of the links between women, war and peace—should aim at the very

REFLECTIONS: RONIT LENTIN   407

least to make the complex intersections between gender, war and peace somewhat less blurred.

Rather than analyse the stereotypical random snapshots of women in wartime, I would like to end with some questions, because I don't really have any definitive answers. Reflecting on women, war and peace in the Middle East, and in light of the war on Afghanistan, I would like to question whether women—despite the fact that it is mostly young men who are casualties of war—are, on the one hand, the symbolic representations of a "raped nation" (Lentin 1999), and on the other, possess some essentialist privilege in doing peace work, which, we are often told, given half a chance, would bring about the resolution of all armed conflicts. This is often argued by Israeli feminist peace activists, who are often not cognizant of the power differentials between them—members of the occupying force—and Palestinian women—members of the occupied nation.

It is hard to engage in peace work without a deep conviction in our ability to bring about peace, or at least, an end to violence. In the case of Israeli feminist peace activists, this entails a belief in women's greater ability to make peace, while invoking discourses of motherhood, which, for example, imply —erroneously—that fathers are less concerned about their children's lives than mothers. In order to make sense of the obvious fact that wars are more often instigated by men than by women, feminist researchers have no option but to engage in the complex theorisation of wars as gendered, rather than resort to the essentialist portrayal of women as either universal victims or as more peaceful and more adept than men at conflict resolution.

This said, I would also like to question whether it ultimately matters what intellectuals, including feminist intellectuals, say or do while the killing continues. Is the self-silencing of Israeli intellectuals a sign of collusion, collaboration or merely confusion? Do national elites on both sides of the conflict ultimately need intellectuals only in order to confirm the institutions of ruling? Do intellectuals, in attempting to reformulate discourses such as national identity, racism, discrimination and state violence, not merely reaffirm them? The discussion on the role of intellectuals in general is beyond the scope of this paper, but at least we—Israeli feminist peace activists and Israeli feminist researchers alike—can no longer pretend that "we did not know" (see *Noga* 2001).

References

Abdo, Nahla. (2001). "Eurocentrism, Essentialism and the Other Feminism: The history of gender ethnography in the Middle East." Paper presented at Anthropology in the Middle East: Gendered Perpectives, Centre for Modern Oriental Studies, Berlin, 30 November–2 December 2001.

Abdo, Nahla and Ronit Lentin, Eds. (2002a). *Women and the Politics of Military Confrontation: Palestinian and Israeli Gendered Narratives of Dislocation*. New York and Oxford: Berghahn Books.

Abdo, Nahla and Ronit Lentin. (2002b). "Writing Dislocation, Writing the Self: Bringing (back) the political into gendered Israeli–Palestinian dialoguing." In Nahla Abdo and Ronit Lentin, Eds. *Women and the Politics of Military Confrontation: Palestinian and Israeli Gendered Narratives of Dislocation*. New York and Oxford: Berghahn Books.

Abramovich, Dorit. (2001). "Arba Imahot veyoter" (Four mothers and more). *Ha'aretz*, 28 December: B6.

African Rights. (1995). *Rwanda. Not so Innocent: When Women Become Killers*. London: African Rights.

Amos, Valerie and Prathibha Parmar. (1984). "Challenging Imperial Feminism." *Feminist Review 17*.

Aref, Souah. (1993). "Women and the Intifada." *Noga 26*: 18–21.

Bauman, Zygmunt. (1998). *Life in Fragments: Essays in Postmodern Morality*. Oxford: Blackwell.

Benjamin, Walter. (1968). *Illuminations: Essays and Reflections*. New York: Schoken Books.

Boric, Rada. (1997). "Against the War: Women Organising Themselves in the Countries of the Former Yugoslavia." In R. Lentin, Ed. *Gender and Catastrophe*. London: Zed Books.

Bunting, Madeleine. (2001). "Special Report: Terrorism in the US" www.guardian.co.uk, 20 September.

Cockburn, Cynthia. (2001). "The Gendered Dynamics of Armed Conflict and Political Violence." In Caroline O. N. Moser and Fiona C. Clark, Eds. *Victims, Perpetrators or Actors: Gender, Armed Conflict and Political Violence*. London: Zed Books.

Connell, Robert W. (1987). *Gender and Power*. Cambridge: Polity Press.

Dahan-Kalev, Henriette. (2001). "Tensions in Israeli Feminism: The Mizrahi–Ashkenazi rift." *Women's Studies International Forum 24*(6): 669–84.

Dajani, Souad. (1994). "Between National and Social Liberation: The Palestinian women's movement in the Israeli-occupied West Bank and Gaza." In Tamar Mayer, Ed. *Women and the Israeli Occupation*. London: Routledge.

Elshtain, Jean B. (1981). *Public Man, Private Woman: Women in Social and Political Thought*. Princeton: Princeton University Press.

Enloe, Cynthia. (1983). *Does Khaki Become You? The Militarisation of Women's Lives*. London: Pluto Press.

Eschebach, Insa, Sigrid Jacobeit, and Silke Wenk, Eds. (2002). *Gedächtnis und Geschlecht. Internationale Studien zur Rezeptionsgeschichte des*

Nationalsozialismus und seiner Verbrechen. Frankfurt am Main: Campus Verlag.

Fromm, Erich. (1974). *The Anatomy of Human Destructiveness*. London: Jonathan Cape.

Goldberg, Andy. (1995). "Sex Video Exposes Torment of Israel's Women Soldiers." *Sunday Times*. 23 April: 20.

Hague, Euan. (1997). "Rape, Power and Masculinity: The Construction of Gender and National Identities in the War in Bosnia–Herzegovna." In R. Lentin, Ed. *Gender and Catastrophe*. London: Zed Books.

Hassan, Manar. (1991). "Growing up Female and Palestinian in Israel." In Barbara Swirski and Marilyn P. Safir, Eds. *Calling the Equality Bluff: Women in Israel*, New York: Pergamon.

Jacobs, Susie, Ruth Jacobson and Jennifer Marchbank, Eds. (2000). *States of Conflict: Gender, Violence and Resistance*. London: Zed Books.

Karpel, Dalia. (2000). "Nefilato shel ha'intellectual haIsraeli" (The fall of the Israeli intellectual). *Ha'aretz Magazine*. 27 October: 50–4.

Kimmel, Michael and Michael A. Messner. (1998). "Introduction." In Michael Kimmel and Michael A. Messner, Eds. *Men's Lives*. Boston and London: Ally and Bacon.

Klein, Yossi. (2002). "Letif'eret Medinat Israel" (For the glory of the state of Israel). *Ha'aretz Magazine*. 3 May: 18–22.

Lentin, Ronit. (1982). *Conversations with Palestinian Women*. Jerusalem: Mifras (Hebrew).

——. (1997a). "Women, War and Peace in a Culture of Violence: The Middle East and Northern Ireland." In Biljana Kasic, Ed. *Women and the Politics of Peace: Contributions to a Culture of Women's Resistance*. Zagreb: Centre for Women's Studies.

——. Ed. (1997b). *Gender and Catastrophe*. London: Zed Books.

——. (1998). "Israeli and Palestinian Women Working for Peace." In Lois Lorentzen and Jennifer Turpin, Eds. *Women and War Reader*. New York: New York University Press.

——. (1999). "The Rape of the Nation: Women narrativising genocide". *Sociology Research Online* 4 (2) http://www.socresonline.uk/socresonline/4/2/lentin.html

——. (2000). *Israel and the Daughters of the Shoah: Reoccupying the Territories of Silence*. New York and Oxford: Berghahn Books.

Lorentzen, Lois A. and Jennifer Turpin, Eds. (1998). *The Women and War Reader*. New York: New York University Press.

McWilliams, Monica and Joan McKiernan. (1993). "Women, Religion and Violence in the Family." Paper presented at the Sociological Association of Ireland conference, May.

Meaney, Geraldine. (1991). *Sex and Nation: Women in Irish Culture and Politics*. Dublin: Attic Press.

Milton, Sybil. (1993). "Women and the Holocaust: The case of German and German Jewish women." In Carol Rittner and John K. Roth, Eds. *Women and the Holocaust: Different Voices*. New York: Paragon House.

Moghadam, Valentine M. (2002). "Women, the Taliban, and the Politics of Public Space in Afghanistan." *Women's Studies International Forum 25*(1). Republished, this volume, as "Patriarchy, the Taliban and the Politics of Public Space in Afghanistan": 260–84.

Mohanty, Chandra Talpade. (1991). "Under Western Eyes: Feminist scholarship and colonial discourses." In Chandra T. Mohanty, Anne Russo, and Lourdes Torres, Eds. *Third World Women and the Politics of Feminism*, Bloomington: Indiana University Press.

Moser, Caroline O. N. and Fiona C. Clark. (2001). "Introduction." In Caroline O. N. Moser, and Fiona C. Clark, Eds. *Victims, Perpetrators or Actors: Gender, Armed Conflict and Political Violence*. London: Zed Books.

Nandy, Ashis. (1983). *The Intimate Enemy: Loss and Recovery of Self under Colonialism*. Delhi and Oxford: Oxford University Press.

Noga. (2000). "Gam nashim rotsot lirot" (Women too want to shoot). *Noga* 38: 34–6.

——. (2001). "Do Not Say We Didn't Know: Testimonies of Palestinian women from al-Aqsa Intifada." *Noga* 40: 14–32.

Ostrowitz, Rachel. (1996). "Al hamatsav" (On the situation). *Noga* 30: 13.

Papandreou, Margarita. (1997). "Are Women More Peace-loving than Men?" In Biljana Kasic, Ed. *Women and the Politics of Peace: Contributions to a Culture of Women's Resistance*. Zagreb: Centre for Women's Studies.

Ruddick, S. (1990). *Maternal Thinking: Towards a Politics of Peace*. London: The Women's Press.

Safran, Hannah. (2000). "Lo imma shel hayal" (Not a soldier's mother). *Noga* 39: 15.

Sancho, Leila. (1997). "The 'Comfort Women' System during World War II: Asian women as targets of mass rape and sexual slavery by Japan." In Ronit Lentin, Ed. *Gender and Catastrophe*. London: Zed Books.

Sand, Shlomo. (2000). *Ha'intellectual, Haemet veHacoach* (Intellectuals, Truth and Power: From the Dreifus Affair to the Gulf War). Tel Aviv: Ofakim, Am Oved.

Segev, Tom. (2000). "The Diary of Muma Hamsa-Mahsein". *Ha'aretz*, 3 November: B12.

Shadmi, Erella. (1992). "Women, Palestinian, Zionism: A personal view." *News from Within 8* (10–11): 13–16.

——. (2000). "Between Resistance and Compliance: Feminism and Nationalism, Women in Black in Israel." *Women's Studies International Forum 23* (1): 23–34.

Sharoni, Simona. (1992). "Every Woman an Occupied Territory: The politics of militarism and sexism and the Israeli–Palestinian conflict." *Journal of Gender Studies 1* (4): 447–62.

——. (1994). *Gender and the Israeli–Palestinian Conflict: The Politics of Women's Resistance.* Syracuse, NY: Syracuse University Press.

——. (2001). "Rethinking Women's Struggles in Israel–Palestine and in the North of Ireland." In Caroline O. N. Moser, and Fiona C. Clark, Eds. *Victims, Perpetrators or Actors: Gender, Armed Conflict and Political Violence.* London: Zed Books.

Shohat, Orit. (1996). "Rak lo leshabesh et haseder" (Providing we do not destabilise order). *Ha'aretz,* 11 October: B1.

Svirsky, Gila. (2002). http://www.fire.or.cr./junio01/coalition.htm.

Yuval-Davis, Nira. (1997). *Gender and Nation.* London: Sage.

Yuval-Davis, Nira, and Floya Anthias, Eds. (1989) *Woman—Nation—State.* London: Macmillan.

Evelyne Accad

The Phallus of September 11

> Children here find refuge in their hopes to die. The fact that death is equated to life is horrifying me. How are we going to deal with this generation in the future, how could we talk about life?
>
> Message from Nadera Shalhoub-Kevorkian, working in the Palestinian Balata camp during the recent Israeli raids, March 2002

This passage from an email message I received from Nadera,[1] an extraordinary woman I met in Istanbul last September, who works with and for women in Israel and Palestine, very much sums up the place we have reached in our present world: children hope to die, the world offers them only despair, injustices are the order of the day ... How can it go on like this? How can we go on living in such a world?

The situation in the Middle East, which has been left to fester since the creation of the state of Israel in 1948, has degenerated, and is manifesting itself at many levels now, among which are the September 11 attacks. Israeli Prime Minister Sharon, who as Minister for Defense in the early 1980s spearheaded the invasion of Lebanon in 1982, and was cited as responsible for the massacres of Sabra and Shatila in the Palestinian camps that left upwards of 2000 Lebanese and Palestinian civilians dead, is now taking advantage of Bush's war cry, "war on terrorism", to once again massacre the Palestinian people, "to smoke them out" of their crumbling shacks, to crush and annihilate them, an extension of Bush's campaign against terrorism, or so he thinks. But the goals are different, and only the gullible are being fooled into thinking there is a single front to this war.

Lest we be taken in by this rhetoric, we must ask ourselves what is really at stake in all this. I cannot help but deeply feel the two events must be linked, even though I despise Sharon's politics and am loath to give his words any legitimacy. My linkage has less to do with a co-extensive war than with deferred, cumulative cause and effect, a point that many have tried to make, but these people were shouted down as being unpatriotic.

As I watched the news these last few weeks, the tanks and heavy artillery

---

1 Nadera Shalhoub-Kevorkian, PhD, School of Social Work, Institute of Criminology, Faculty of Law, Hebrew University, Jerusalem.

against the major cities of Palestine, against the camps and the civilians, I was reminded of 1991, the first air raids of the US forces against Iraq, and I was reminded of Beirut, the summer of 1982. That summer, I remember it so vividly; my sister was in West Beirut, spending most of her nights in the shelter. Israel was bombarding by air, land and sea civilian targets, an urban center, and innocent victims. Most nights were filled with the sounds of shells crushing, detonating, burning, with the Beirut sky going up in fires, flames, explosions and lights. The massacres in the Sabra and Shatila Palestinian camps were to soon follow, exactly in the same manner as today. The bodies of women, children, old people, young people, their throats slit, their stomachs open, blood flowing in the earth, holocaust repeated by the victims of the holocaust, just like today. But today, it is much worse, and the problems have reached proportions beyond words. Today, I feel a sense of urgency and doom I had not felt then.

Men slaughtered in shame
Silence of the Auschwitz ovens
Repeated in the silence of crucified Jenin
Dark smoke covering the world
Putrefaction of roasted skin
Hands tied-up above their heads
Humiliation of brave men
Their eyes fixed, glued,
Haunted and haunting
Numbers marked on their foreheads and arms
Yellow stars repeated all over again
At the point of possible reconciliation
At the world's holiest places
The same look, the same despair
The same helplessness, hopelessness
Similar deaths, different times.

The cries, tears, despair of someone as strong and beautiful as Nadera keep ringing in my ears and are haunting me day and night. How can the world remain so indifferent to those cries? Why should the tears and despair of the World Trade Center's orphans be more important than those of the Palestinian camps? I shall publish your words, Nadera (her email was sent to me in March of 2002); those wanting to hear shall hear them:

The situation here is very sad and bad. Despair is the general sense for most of us, and all we can do meanwhile is to keep the good faith, and keep on doing the work we need to do. It is very hard, for every day we face losses, and this past week I lost two people who worked with me in the Nablus area. It is hard to express the feeling; if you only spent the day with me yesterday you would have seen a different person. I spent the day crying, for there is a limit to this madness, and no one could keep on living such a hell. Women are suffering the most, the fear, agony, despair and helplessness is filling their lives, that in addition to all the other abuses: political, cultural, familial and other. I am sitting in my office writing my article on the effect of militarization on women, mainly the narratives and words of mothers of martyrs ... All I can say is that I am not sure how we will be able to heal those harsh memories, how can we bring hope in such a suffocating atmosphere? Any ideas??

On the plane between Paris and Beirut, 19 December 2001

I am sitting next to a man who works for United Airlines in Virginia and is coming to visit some relatives in Beirut. We talk about "the events"; he thinks people "love to fly" and will continue doing so no matter what. I tell him my American Airlines flight between Chicago and Paris a few days ago was two-thirds empty. He tells me he could not find a seat on United and had to fly Air France, which was also completely booked. He says: "Things will get back to normal after we get rid of the wrong-doers." I tell him: "But we are not going to the roots of the problems, so how can we really have long-lasting solutions?" He nods, but I wonder if the sign is in agreement or because he is tired. I also wonder what nationality he is ... probably half-Arab, half-American like me, but identifying more with his American side, unlike me.

This little exchange is indicative of how I feel about "the events", what I have been attempting to express, but which so few people are willing to listen to. Stated simply, there are huge problems in the world, especially in this part of the world, and they are not going to get solved by dropping bombs:

> Violence begets violence
> Vengeance repeats itself in blood
> Procession of all the innocents
> dying, dying, dying ...
> War conceives only war
> Hatred breeds only fear
> Anger of all the innocents
> Caught up in this chain of death.

These lines from one of my songs resurface and soothe the irritation I feel at my not being heard by this man, already asleep.

Last night I could not sleep. I was "afraid of flying". There had always been a little bit of that fear before, but now it has become a fear that grips me deeply and will not let me rest.

> Images of airhostesses' slit throats
> Arab men gone mad

manifesting their disgust and fear of women
through unspeakable sexual violence
Can I call them brothers, these men?
Images of young Arab men turned insane
Through which mechanisms I ask?
By what, by what?
I keep turning this question upside down
over and over again
The promise of a paradise with virgins
Remaining ever virgin, reflowering after deflowering?
What could be so appealing in such penetration?
A desire for unending purity?
A need for ultimate possession
unrelinquished property and propriety?
repeated sadistic thrive
with a call for spilled blood every time
slaughtered lamb,
innocence butchered at the altar
Or a mysticism giving much greater sensual pleasure than all the real orgasms
with real women in real equal tender sharing?
What could have gone wrong in the formative years
of their childhood, their adolescence
to produce such monsters?

Palestine torched with napalm
Palestine's slit throat
spilled blood all over again
Palestine made silent at nightfall
Palestine which haunts me more than words can express
Palestine crushed, starved, humiliated, abandoned
before the indifference of the West

Were they thinking of Palestine, these men?
They did not express it
They left no trace saying it was their cause
No mention of vengeance for more noble causes
The Gulf? Baghdad? Palestine?

No, the mere pleasure of entering a tower
a body through sick penetration
anger and oblivion
Bring down the rest of the world
Into nothingness

Their chiefs used Palestine only later
To try and calm things down
But nobody believed them.

I have just finished my meal on this Middle East Airlines flight. My neighbor tells me that the "terrorists" slit the throat of the pilots as well, in order to take their place and fly the aircraft into the World Trade Center. His descriptions make me shiver.

I notice that Middle East Airlines still uses "real" forks and knives, not the plastic ones found on American Airlines. He tells me those can be dangerous and become weapons, there is no reason to use them except aesthetic ones. He obviously does not appreciate aesthetics.

He has fallen asleep again (it is a long trip between Washington DC and Beirut).

The pleasure of entering a tower
Symbol of the male phallus
Symbol of the arrogance of Western civilization
Globalization also turned mad
Tentacular America devouring all the food
all the resources of a starving Third World

Fraternity gang rapes
Men who will not grow up
Needing male reinforcement for their sick sexuality
from which love has been evacuated
Group homosexuality erected like towers
Sexual drive of degraded men, degrading
No need for women except as objects
Plastic dolls one can penetrate and throw away later
Repeated rape through drugs and alcohol
Penetration until death
Vomiting sexuality,
thrown up and throwing up
sick view of themselves and of the world
Call for death and for oblivion
No love, no tenderness, no harmonious exchange
In these acts of ejaculation.

I think of the love of my life, of our love exchanges, of all our daily detailed love life for the last twenty-three years. This love which carries me through time and space and gives me courage and fortitude. The tenderness we share allowing the other to grow in beauty and harmony, encouraging the other to be, to become, to live, independent and in fusion. How to communicate the necessity of such love to the rest of the world? How to show that such understanding and communication can have huge political ramifications? How to demonstrate the strength of love in a world falling apart for lack of it? This love which is not mystical, nor narcissistic, nor idealized, but which seeks the growth of the other, the development and fulfillment of the other. How to show what such love can do?

A haunting Middle Eastern melody is being played right now on this plane and I am melting with emotions thinking about what this love means to me and how I wish other people could experience the beauty and strength of it. It can be mad also but not a sick madness, rather a creative, enlightening, enveloping madness, tender, illuminated and illuminating.

This is incredible: the film being shown on the television screen of this Middle East Airlines flight is the same Woody Allen movie screened on American Airlines between Chicago and Paris a few days ago. There is certainly globalization of the world and this is not its ugliest aspect even if I wish Middle East Airlines had dared show a Lebanese movie by one of our talented young Lebanese producers (and we do have quite a few).

On the plane between Beirut and Paris, 9 January 2002

I realize now that not all the world has been turned upside down by September 11, thanks to my travels, which give me some perspective and allow me to compare. I see now that only Americans felt that sense, the ground shaking under our feet, stripped of that sense of security we had so long taken for granted.

In Lebanon, people hardly talk about it any more and when they do, it is with derision or to express some "US plot". Many people here cannot believe that people without technology could have caused so much havoc and such spectacular destruction.

Lebanon has had its share of war and destruction in the last decades: between 1975 and 1992, it was torn apart by a civil war, fed by many countries worldwide that cashed in with sales of weapons to various militias, sometimes to both sides, regardless of alliance. Some militias in exchange for money and weapons buried nuclear waste products in various parts of Lebanon. The Lebanese population is now paying the price with a rise in cancers of all kinds. Cancers of the mind and heavy depressions plague the youth that have had to deal with the war. The wounds and scars are visible. It will take a long time for the country and its people to heal.

While in Beirut, I received the Phoenix Prize for my book on cancer and had to deliver a speech on that occasion. I am reproducing parts of it here because it was a special moment and because I spoke about some of the problems Lebanon and the rest of the world are facing today.

Beirut, Phoenix Prize Ceremony, 28 December 2001

I am very moved to be here in Lebanon to receive this prize, which I was not expecting and which came as a huge surprise. It is wonderful to be recognized in one's own country. I wish to thank all the people who contributed either to the edition or to the recognition of this book. They are so numerous that I will not be able to name them all here: friends, family, doctors, readers, etc., and of course I also wish to thank the members of the jury whose secret decision I do not know, but my gratitude goes to them because it is a difficult book ...

The Wounded Breast: Intimate Journeys through Cancer (Accad 2001) is a book written through suffering but also through joy, pains of the disease and of its treatment, fears of the after-treatment, joys of love, friendship, friendships discovered and manifested during the disease and expressed in these pages.

I wrote this book to exorcise my fears, my pain, but also in order to help others, all those who will have to travel on that road, and who are going to be more and more numerous, as you know. It is a difficult journey with its doubts, its questions, its analysis, its reflections on the disease, the plague of our century falling apart on all sides, the consequence of the violence done to nature and to human beings, the price we have to pay for modernity, the terrible price we must pay for all the pollutants and chemical products ejected into the atmosphere, the result of the wars we are subjected to, total wars which no longer spare civilians, the kind of war which Lebanon knows only too well.

One of the things that really struck me during my illness was the isolation of the patient. I wanted to express this malaise and got interested in this problem and particularly in the associations that dealt with it. And this is how I discovered with great joy, right here in Lebanon, the association Faire Face (Confronting It), founded by Dr Saade, whom I want to salute here since it is quite a rare thing in this world. As you may know, everywhere in the world, this disease is unnameable: "*Al marad illi ma btitsamma*" (in Arabic literally "the disease one does not name").

I lived my cancer a little bit as I had lived the war in Lebanon, a whirlwind of violence in the physiological as well as in the social body, the death of loved ones, unrelenting and unsolvable, unending despair in both cases.

I do not want to interpret here the decision of the jury but to me this prize is also the recognition of the seriousness of cancer in our societies, a tragedy that, in reality, is at the core of my literary expression.

Allow me to add here a word on this special day dedicated by Mediterranean women's associations to the memory of all the Palestinian–Israeli conflict's victims. Marches are taking place today in various capitals of the world to protest the violence and the victims on both sides. I would like to salute their courage here publicly.

Sexuality and War[2]

The importance of incorporating a discourse on sexuality when formulating a revolutionary feminist theory, which had been so evident to me when I started analyzing and writing about the Lebanese war in the 1980s, has become even more urgent today. Wars themselves seem closely connected with the way people perceive and act out their sense of love and power, as well as people's sense of relationship to their partners, to the family and to the general society. Usually the argument has been made that women's issues detract from the war effort, that wars create such conditions of despair that, within this context, women's issues are unimportant, and if the "right" side in a war were to win, women's problems would automatically be solved. I would like to argue the reverse. I would suggest that sexuality is centrally involved in motivations to war, and if women's issues were dealt with from the beginning, wars might be avoided, and revolutionary struggles and movements for liberation would take on a very different path. Justice cannot be won in the midst of injustice. All these levels are interwoven.

The gun, the machine-gun, the cannon—all masculine sexual symbols which are extensions of the phallus—are put forward and used to conquer and destroy. For Adam Farrar, there is a kind of *jouissance*—pleasure in a sexual sense, no equivalent word in English—in war:

> One of the main features of the phenomenology of war is the unique intensity of experience. War experience is exactly the converse of alienation. In war, the elimination of all the norms of intersubjectivity produces, not alienation, but the most intense *jouissance*. The machining of events on the plane of intensity (to use the Deleuzian image), the form of desire, is utterly transformed. Power no longer consists in the capacity to redeem the warrants of communicative intersubjectivity. It consists in the ability of the spear, the sword, the gun, napalm, the bomb etc. to manifest "in a blast of sound and energy and light" (or in another time, in the blood of a severed limb or a disembowelled body), the merest "wish flashing across your mind like a shadow". (1985: 66)

---

2   See Accad (1990). *Sexuality and War: Literary Masks of the Middle East*. New York: New York University Press.

Farrar continues, quoting an article by William Broyles in *Esquire* entitled "Why Men Love War", that it is at some terrible level, for men, the closest thing to what childbirth is for women: the initiation into the power of life and death (1985: 61).

Many important studies by women and men see a link between sexuality and national/international conflicts. In an article published in an important French review entitled *Alternatives Non-Violentes*, Jean-William Lapierre, well-known specialist on the subject, sees a real "deep connection between masculine predominance and the importance of war" (1981: 21). According to him, most civilizations are based on conquest and war. "The importance of hunting, then of war in social existence, in economic resources, in cultural models (which valorize the warrior exploits), are at the roots of masculine domination and of women's oppression" (1981: 21). He explains how in so-called "modern" societies, politics, industry, business, are always a kind of war where one (mostly men, and sometimes women imitating men's behavior) must be energetic, aggressive, etc., to be powerful. It is not only capitalist societies which "carry war like clouds carry the storm, but product-ivism in all its forms, including the so-called 'socialistic' one. In all societies in which economy and politics require a spirit of competition (while its ethic exalts it) women are oppressed" (1981: 22). And Bob Connell sees a relationship between masculinity, violence and war. He says that it is not by chance that the great majority of soldiers are men—of the 22 million people under arms in the world in 1976, 20 million were men.

> Most of the police, most of the prison warders, and almost all the generals, admirals, bureaucrats and politicians who control the apparatus of coercion and collective violence [are men]. Most murderers are men. Almost all bandits, armed robbers, and muggers are men; all rapists, most domestic bashers; and most people involved in street brawls, riots and the like. (Connell 1985: 4).

But such connection should not be attributed to biology, which would absolve masculine responsibility—men's violence associated to some human "destiny"—but rather to social and cultural factors.

Betty Reardon explains how the patriarchal system is not only happy with dividing women along loyalty lines, but also uses violence to train people into gender roles which reinforce the war system:

> The fundamental willingness to use violence against others on which warfare depends is conditioned by early training and continuous socialization in patriarchal society. All are taught to respect authority, that is, fear violence ... Boys and men are encouraged to become more fierce, more aggressive when they feel fear. Fear in men is channeled into aggression, in women into submission, for such behaviors are necessary to maintain patriarchal authoritarianism. Aggression and submission

are also the core of the basic relations between men and women, accounting, many believe, for women's toleration of male chauvinism. Some assert that these behaviors are the primary cause of all forceful exploitation, and account for perhaps the most significant common characteristic of sexism and the war system: rape. (Reardon 1985: 38–9)

Issa Makhlouf in his book, *Beyrouth ou la fascination de la mort* (Beirut or The Fascination with Death), analyzes rape in the war of Lebanon, a subject no one before him had been willing to expose. He says that it is another facet of the barbarism, frequently practiced by militias during massacres and occurring almost everywhere on Lebanese soil.

The fixation of militias on sexual organs did not only hit women. Several male cadavers were discovered with their sex cut off and sometimes pushed into their mouths; the simulation of fellatio, generally repressed by morality, is very revealing as a rejection of moral codes. On the other hand, numerous mutilations were practiced on victims, dead or alive. In rape, all forms of violence are combined. All possibilities of death and pleasure are present. All dreams of domination are fulfilled. The victim of rape is the toy of all phantasms and ambitions. Rape is the place of all experimentations. (Makhlouf 1988: 88–90)

The whole system must be changed and rethought. To use Betty Reardon's words:

What I am advocating here is a new world order value, reconciliation, and perhaps even forgiveness, not only of those who trespass against us, but primarily of ourselves. By understanding that no human being is totally incapable of the most reprehensible of human acts, or of the most selfless and noble, we open up the possibilities for change of cosmic dimensions. Essentially this realization is what lies at the base of the philosophy of nonviolence. If we are to move through a disarmed world to a truly nonviolent one, to authentic peace and justice, we must come to terms with and accept the other in ourselves, be it our masculine or our feminine attributes or any of those traits and characteristics we have projected on enemies and criminals, or heroes and saints. (1985: 94)

And as Andrea Dworkin put it: "To transform the world we must transform the very substance of our erotic sensibilities and we must do so as consciously and as conscientiously as we do any act which involves our whole lives" (1980: 6).

I would like to conclude with how some of my days are spent here in Beirut where I am presently teaching at the Lebanese American University and conducting research on women. I live on campus in an apartment located very close to the palace of Rachid Hariri, the Lebanese Prime Minister. The area is overrun with noisy, polluting construction equipment. As a child, I used to walk that way to go up to school, when it was still all fields of flowers and grass, where now it is all concrete and pollution with smelly diesel-fuelled cars and buses competing with the background din from construction.

Beirut, February 2002

When I first arrived, I went walking on the seashore with one of my nieces. A strong wind was blowing, the waves were unraveling with fury. I would have liked to sit in one of those little Arab cafés, as I remembered them, with a plate of hummus and a glass of beer, but all we could find were those horrible fast food places, and since my niece was very hungry (and I was too) we settled for a sandwich, unappetizing and not cheap. Then we went to see a film with one of my friends who had invited us. It was in one of those new theaters and we had to walk under torrential rain … We got soaked head to toe, because the roads suddenly turn into rivers whenever there is a heavy downpour. Another disappointment was in store, it was an American film in Hollywood fashion, the kind I hate, with violence, women with all the possible clichés, women for whom macho men fight, a huge screen bursting with special effects, falling towers, monstrous cities, bad guys who are able to triumph thanks to money and shrewdness … I told myself it was not surprising that America had engendered the monsters of September 11; the film was in the exact spirit of those terrible events. And what was even more surprising, the audience (with many women in Khomeini-inspired headgear) seemed to take it all in uncritically and were clapping by the end! Completely funky and grotesque … Where were the Art theaters I used to go to before the war, where those wonderfully engaging movies would be shown (often French)?

Beirut, March and April 2002

My Tunisian friend Amel and I went to the Cité Sportive (the Sport Stadium where so many massacres took place during the war). We listened to Mahmoud Darwish (the Palestinian poet who lived in Beirut during the war and now lives in Ramallah), to Majida al-Roumi (a well-known female Lebanese singer committed to various worthy causes) and to another male Lebanese singer who has composed a song everybody has been singing and that we hear all over the place these days, on TV, on the radio, etc. It is about the earth "*Aboussou al-arda* …" ("I kiss the earth …"—the Palestinian one of course). It was very moving to find ourselves in the midst of this crowd (I do not like—I even fear—crowds usually), this completely pacifist crowd, and to sing and listen to the words of this great poet hammering the rhythmical, beautiful Arabic language, with words on the condition of his people, their suffering, their martyrdom …

Last week, I interviewed a woman in the camp of Sabra. I went there with one of my nieces and Amel. The condition of the Sabra and Shatila camps is beyond words: one walks on garbage and sewers; the houses of *tanak* (tin) are crippled with bullets; many houses are in ruins, remnants of a war, of spilled blood, of massacres, blood that has flowed, still freshly present ... It is beyond any description ... And this week we went again to this camp where we interviewed a woman who had had breast cancer, and ten children (one of whom is retarded)! She was breast-feeding her latest newborn baby with her only breast (even though the doctor had told her not to bring another child into the world, that it would kill her!). She was carrying the baby like a trophy, a triumph over illness, a miracle of a renewed body! After telling us about her illness and how she was treated (mastectomy, chemotherapy and radiation) she talked mainly about the massacres (Sabra and Shatila) of which she is also a survivor. Her descriptions were chilling, and I still feel sick about them! And to think that the massacres taking place today in Palestine (Jenin in particular) are repeating the same horrors—real butchery, slaughters and collective rapes. (I had been under the illusion until then that there had rarely been rapes in Lebanon ... it shows how occulted such a problem is in our society.) She described the militias as young men heavily drugged and drunk, going from house to house to cut the throats of all living human beings, taking the young women to make them sit on bottles and then collectively raping them before slaughtering. The niece helping me with the translation and transcription of the interviews told me she would have a hard time working on it, the descriptions being so unbearable. The news about rapes taking place in Palestine are just beginning to come out, I received an e-mail to that effect today, in spite of the news blackout.

It was hard to listen to this Sabra woman's stories, her surviving the massacres and the cancer (two plagues of our century) ... But she was beautiful, so alive, and seemed happy with her good-looking husband; they looked as if they were in love and had a sensual relationship, but we could not ask her intimate questions because of the presence of her husband and of their eldest son, there with his wife, pregnant, who had already lost four children, still-born ... The hardest was misery, poverty, surviving ...

May 2002

I received another e-mail from Nadera Shalhoub-Kevorkian:

> I must confess that it is very hard for me to write, for no words could express what is going on here ... life became meaningless, human beings became commodities for the Israelis, and misery is the name of the game for us Palestinians. I was in Jenin ... I saw the most painful scenes that I never thought I would see. It was too painful to see, comprehend, or write about it ... but I will share some of the things I saw. Yes ... I have met the agony of my people, and our history of trauma through the

destruction. The fields … the place that once was a neighborhood in the Jenin refugee camp, was full of pain … full of women searching for their beloved ones among the destruction … and a small girl was telling me that they just found the body of a baby … and yes, I saw the hand of the baby … but not a regular hand … but a tiny little hand that was full of all the agonies of my nation. You could imagine what happened to a dead body after two weeks … and yes I saw it, and Shaima'a was looking with me … explaining to me why it looks so bad now … why? I saw the pain of my people but with so much disgust. While I was walking, with tears hidden in my eyes, trying to show some strength—for I should be strong—I heard a voice calling me "Doctora Nadera, Doctora Nadera". It was Rania, a previous student of mine. She started screaming and crying, "Why did you come now?" I always wanted you to see my house … and now I am standing on what was left from the house … some pillows… look at them, some books … and so many wounds." We cried and hugged for more than ten minutes … and I felt that I could barely walk … but how could I … for I need to be strong. We walked … talked to people, and mainly kids … when Huthaifa told me: "Do you know, Khalto (Aunt), you might be stepping on my Dad's bones." That was too hard on my heart … Yes, I walked on my people's bones … and needed to keep on walking, for there was no other way but to do so. I needed to show Shaima'a and Huthaifa and the other kids and women that walked and showed me around and I kept on telling them "we could make it". I needed to tell them that we need to keep on walking the walk. Do you know how could we keep on walking … stepping on the bodies of our beloved ones. I kept on walking … and saw a house half destroyed … all you could see is half a house … and half of its inhabitants were in prison, and one dead … so not only half a house … but so many stories of the ugly behavior of the soldiers … the way they pissed inside vases … the way they humiliated women and forbade them to go to the toilet … and you could imagine what happened next … the way they forbade girls who had their period to change … and they did not have any sanitary napkins … the filth was all over the place. But the most filthy thing was the occupiers' behavior. When I decided to leave the half house, I asked Um Subhi, "Where are you originally from?" Guess what … she is from my town Haifa … she used to live in my neighborhood … and she even knew my house … that was the harshest thing for me. Yes, she was from my home town … and now she is again a refugee … but in her own refugee camp?

Yes, I decided that I will start a group with children and women, and Rania is working with me. So we are moving, talking to people, helping them comprehend the trauma, and offering some coping strategies. The children's group is meeting on a weekly basis, in the camp itself … on the destruction itself … and they refused to put up a tent and sit in it. So we decided to build a kind of fence, made of Palestinian carpet, and we put it around us, so as to feel safer. They refused to use a tent, for tents mean that we are going back … back to the tents in 1948 … and the children refused to go back to the tents … for we are here sitting on this destruction of our beloved ones.

We are doing some work ... but the question is if this is what is needed, do you have a better idea for me?

Love you all, searching for more power to continue ... Nadera ...but with much more agony in my heart.[3]

References

Accad, Evelyne. (1990). *Sexuality and War: Literary Masks of the Middle East*. New York: New York University Press.

———. (2001). *The Wounded Breast: Intimate Journeys through Cancer*. Melbourne: Spinifex Press.

Connell, Bob. (1985). "Masculinity, Violence and War." In Paul Patton and Ross Poole, Eds. *War/Masculinity*. Sydney: Intervention: 3–10.

Dworkin, Andrea. (1980). *Marx and Gandhi were Liberals: Feminism and the "Radical" Left*. Los Angeles: Frog in the Well.

Farrar, Adam. (1985). "War, Machining Male Desire." In Paul Patton and Ross Poole, Eds. *War/Masculinity*. Sydney: Intervention: 66–86.

Lapierre, Jean-William. (1981). "Femmes: Une oppression millénaire." *Alternatives non-violentes: Femmes et violences* 40: 21–6.

Makhlouf, Issa. (1988). *Beyrouth ou la fascination de la mort*. Paris: La Passion.

Reardon, Betty. (1985). *Sexism and the War System*. New York and London: Teacher's College and Columbia University.

Catharine A. MacKinnon

State of Emergency

First published in *Women's Review of Books*, March 2002.

....

> The tradition of the oppressed teaches us that the 'state of emergency' in which we live is not the exception but the rule.
>
> —Walter Benjamin[1]

The atrocities of September 11 were gender-neutral on the victim side. Women were people along with men that day, jumping from upper floors, rushing up and up and up to help, crawling down and down and down being helped, fleeing covered with fear, becoming ash. And there they are, if fewer than men, one at a time on the special pages of *The New York Times* every day for months, their faces smiling, before. In remembrance, they are individual, are everyone, do everything, had every prospect. Then on one crushing day, they were vaporized without regard to sex.

On the perpetrator side, the atrocities were hardly gender-neutral. Animated by a misogynist extremism, this time in the guise of religion, which has silenced women, subordinated them in private and excluded them from the public for years, men bound for glory and pleasure, for virgins in a martyrs' paradise,[2] exterminated people by the thousands to make a point. Their propaganda by deed was exemplary male violence.

The number of women who die at the hands of men every year in the United States alone is almost the same as the number of people who died on September 11.[3] The war on women, as male violence against women is sometimes called, is also, of course, far from egalitarian; much of it, too, makes points. But to call it a war is thought to be a metaphor. It is not a real war, we are told, because states do not wage it against states. So no Geneva Conventions set limits. With no rules of combat, women get no quarter.

1 From Walter Benjamin. (1968). "Theses on the Philosophy of History." In *Illuminations* trans. Harry Zohn. New York: Harcourt, Brace & World: 243.

2 See "Excerpts from Letter Thought to Be Instructions," *New York Times*, 28 September, 2001: B4; Joseph Lelyveld. (2001). "All Suicide Bombers Are Not Alike," *New York Times* Magazine, 20 October: 49–53.

3 FBI Uniform Crime Reports for the United States report 3076 female victims of homicide in 2000.

These atrocities do not count as war crimes. No one has protected civilian status. Its combatants cannot be distinguished by their clothes or command structure. Force in response is not justified to the United Nations as self-defense. There are no tribunals set up for justice. Women who defend themselves forcefully are more likely to wind up on death row, convicted of murder and called criminals.

Osama Bin Laden and his Al-Qaeda network—assume they are behind the attacks—are private citizens. They were not working for any state. If anything, Bin Laden may have hijacked Afghanistan, so its illegitimate regime may have been working for him rather than the other way around. The World Trade Center was not, *pace* Bin Laden, an official target (the Pentagon was). However the Twin Towers may have symbolized the United States to some, they are not "the United States" in the sense that they embody the nation officially. In a war, they would be a civilian target, not a military one.

On September 11, non-state actors committed violence against mostly non-state (non-governmental and civilian) actors. Yet we were told "We are at war" at that moment[4] and have been ever since. So this is a war, complete with war crimes committed by the other side, military tribunals, justified acts of self-defense and (one would surely think) prisoners of war. The fact that the existing structure of international law was not created with a conflict of this sort in mind has not stopped the US from responding on a wartime scale, complete with military mobilization, finance, ordnance, rhetoric and allies. Nobody calls the months since the attacks "peacetime".

But when is a war? International law does not define it. It talks of armed conflict, which is seen to take place between—or, in the case of civil wars, within—states. If one side is armed and the other side isn't, or states are not the units of conflict in any sense, it may not qualify as an armed conflict under international law. Terrorism, too, has no settled international definition, although most people think the acts of September 11 fall within the meaning of the term. In the international legal order, the acts of that dreadful day are surely crimes against humanity, but that makes them illegal any time, not only in war, and it is hard to know where to go to enforce anyone's rights against them. (The International Criminal Court might become that place for any future such atrocities.) But terrorism as such is not a war crime; acts like those of September 11 are only war crimes in a war. In fact, these acts most closely fall into a legal category that no one has invoked: genocide, intentional killing of members of a national group with intent to destroy, in part, the group as such. It is the "war on terror" that is the metaphor, a legally mixed one at that.

---

4   So Utah Republican Senator Bob Bennett told the *Salt Lake Tribune* on September 11 (12 September 2001: A6).

When women contend that men's daily violence against women ought to be a violation of international law, as some of us who work with these issues have been arguing for years,[5] we are often told, essentially, that we do not know what we are talking about. International law is designed to control official acts and applies primarily to official entities, either state to state or individual to state (exceptions are mainly for genocide and crimes against humanity); or else it addresses internal armed conflicts called civil wars, as when guerrilla forces contest state power. Even then, when women are raped in wartime, it has taken years of work to begin to get a serious legal response. But nothing in international law seems to have in mind half the society being structured to dominate the other half all the time, world war on the basis of sex going on for millennia. Nothing in law imagines a war in which one side is trained and armed, the other side taught to cry and not to wield kitchen knives. We are not told why international law cannot address a configuration like this one; just that, for historical reasons, it can't.

Women have no state, are no state, seek no state. So, since "history" seems never to get around to including us, and genocide prohibitions do not cover women as women, and the concept of crimes against humanity has been largely unimplemented in law, women violated by men have to labor to get states on the hook by meeting, expanding, or weakening the requirements for proof of state action. Usually, this is done by trying to triangulate the connection between the so-called individual men, often armed, who assault and violate us, and the states who—what? What is it they do to make men's impunity for violence against women nearly total? How can we make that connection into the kind of affirmative, preferably intentional, backing that law requires before anything can be done? How to capture the men getting away with violence against women, knowing they can—a force that operates between the sexes like gravity? How to get at the endless doing of nothing that enables something, a pattern we are told is inaction, not action? Letting die, we are told, can be killing, but letting men abuse women seems virtually never to be acknowledged as abusing women. How to bring in, too, the pervasive support for "being men" in its countless guises that we are told is social and cultural, not political far less criminal, hence a form of freedom (theirs), not coercion (ours)? Then, on September 11, out of the mouth of

---

5   See, for example, Kathleen Mahoney and Paul Mahoney, Eds. (1992). "On Torture: A Feminist Perspective on Human Rights." *Human Rights in the Twenty-First Century: A Global Challenge*. Dordrecht, Netherlands: Martinus Nijhoff: 21; Hilary Charlesworth and Christine Chinkin, Eds. (1994). "Rape, Genocide, and Women's Human Rights." *Harvard Women's Law Journal* 5: 17; (2000) *The Boundaries of International Law: A Feminist Analysis*. Manchester, UK: Juris Publishing.

President Bush came: "We will make no distinction between the terrorists who committed these acts and those who harbor them."[6] There it is: the state harbors them.

If the Taliban had not existed, in other words, the United States would have had to invent them in order to have a state to bomb and invade, in order to turn what would otherwise be crimes against humanity responding to crimes against humanity, state terrorism retaliating for non-state terrorism, male violence against male violence, into this thing called war. Having demolished one state base, the United States now pursues the network worldwide. The fact that Al-Qaeda is not organized into a nation with armies and territory did not stop this response before it started. Yet the fact that male dominance is not organized as a state, being literally transnational, has kept male violence largely unopposed in the international system, and has even been used to argue that men as such have no power over women. (Actually, the organization of the pornography industry and other sex traffickers—sex their religion—is strikingly parallel to Al-Qaeda's.) Once the sources of September 11 are found to be located deep in social and economic life, in culture and belief and identity, its acts as expressive as they are masculine, will the war on terror stop short? Will we give up?

This is the question: when will opposition to terrorism include the daily terrorism against women as women that goes on day after day, worldwide? Not to assume that the only effective response to a war is a war, but when will the United States and the international order stop regarding that very condition as "peace" and move all at once, with will, to end it? Why does the whole world turn on a dime into a concerted force to face down the one, while to address the other squarely and urgently is unthinkable? That the configuration of parties of September 11 failed to fit the prior structure and assumptions of the international legal order did not deter the response one whit. That actions like those taken by the US and its allies since September 11 produce the structure and assumptions that become international law is, for better and worse, closer to the truth.

Asked another way, why didn't women's condition in Afghanistan, imprisoned in their homes and clothes, whipped if an ankle emerged, prohibited education or employment or political office or medical care on the basis of sex, subjected to who yet knows what other male violence, rank as a reason to intervene—yes, including militarily—on any day up to September 11? When men subordinate women within one country, does that make it non-international, hence no one else's business, even if women have no effective recourse at home? If nothing else, September 11 showed that the bounded

6   George W. Bush, Address to the Nation on the Terrorist Attacks, September 11, 2001.

view of sovereignty enshrined in international law is, among other things, an illusion, protecting the boundaries neither of women within national lines nor people across them.

Can it be that men inside each country are allowed to do to women what men from other countries are not allowed to do? What about the women incinerated in dowry killings, or living in fear that they could be, any day? stoned to death for sex outside marriage? dead of botched abortions or genital mutilations? the girls killed at birth, or starved at an early age? fetuses aborted because they are female? If foreign men did all this, would that make it a war? Why isn't sex tourism an invasion? What about the (conservatively counted) one in four women raped, one in three sexually abused in childhood, one in four battered in their homes, and the uncounted prostituted—the women living in non-metaphorical terror in the United States, who have no effective relief?[7] These are mass human rights violations, pervasively unaddressed. But are they not also violent, organized conflict? Do these women not count as casualties? Will the Marines of any country ever land for them? Why does no model—not war, not criminal law, not even human rights—yet intervene effectively in this anywhere?

It makes you want to look again at the smiling faces of the women on the special pages of the *Times* and wonder: who hurt her, before? If she had died from male violence on some other day, would the *Times* have noticed? Would her dying have had the dignity of politics? If she had lived, would she ever have been as full a citizen of the United States as she has been dead? Was she more equal that day than on any day in her life? (Or, with larger death benefits going to survivors of men than of women, than on any day since?)

So what is the real connection between how the men who created September 11 treated women and what they did that day? Not the moralistic one, that the way women are treated tells us how civilized we are. Nor quite the opportunistic (if accurate) one, that ignoring how these men treated women endangered everyone. It is this: what they do to women every day is what they did to both women and men on September 11. How men, in their roles and status as men, treat women is September 11's real context: who they are to women is who they are.

Really hard to take is the systematic hierarchical slaughter built into everyday life in quiet, ignored crises of normality that are effectively permitted by most authorities national and transnational, while crises from normality, exceptional counter-hierarchical acts like September 11, mobilize the world with outrage and determination to walk right through legal walls. (The situation of women is not alone in this.) Equally hard to avoid is the impres-

---

7   See Catharine A. MacKinnon (2000), *Sex Equality*, Foundation Press, for sources and discussion of data.

sion that men call "war" what they make against each other, and "everyday life" what they do to women—so that wars can be fratricidally fought and are then fraternally over, while everyday life never ends.

Shatteringly and indelibly clear is that the losses of September 11 are real to power in a way that women's extermination and terror by men have never been. Recall how a year ago, equal protection of the laws suddenly became a valid legal tool when men's access to something real—the presidency—was at stake, but wasn't a few months earlier, when women's equal access to justice for men's violence against them was at issue. The federalism (meaning states' rights) that had supposedly precluded women's access to equal protection of state criminal laws against rape and battering, invalidating the federal Violence Against Women Act, simply dissolved when some men's access to equal protection of state election laws was at stake, putting Bush into office.[8]

So, too, aggressive international intervention—not to mention multi-lateralism, nation-building, new federal departments, federalization of formerly private labor forces and sweeping executive authority, all formerly opposed—became no problem, necessary, legal after September 11. Once men, many white middle-class men at that, were victims (along with women) of foreign men, the fact that the violence took place between non-state actors—the same problem in international law as in constitutional law—did not reduce it to mass murder, a municipal crime. It did not produce a covert international police action leading to criminal trials. The unofficial status of the parties and the acts was barely publicly noticed.

Now, it seems, because women and men have a recognized common enemy, women have a foreign policy, or have become part of a pretext for one. But we also know this: the reasons we have been given for inaction in the face of atrocities committed by men against women are nothing but excuses, transparent reaffirmations that we don't count, smokescreens for our expendability, legalistic rationalizations for the systemic unreality of our lives. No one has made September 11 into sex; no one speaks of its victims in quotation marks; there is no talk, yet, of closure. Now after a century of increasing convergence between the civilian casualties of wars and the noncombatant casualties of peace, what will be done for the women whose own September 11 can come any day?

---

8   *United States v. Morrison*, 529 U.S. 598 (2000) held the federal Violence Against Women Act unconstitutional for exceeding Congressional power in an area traditionally regulated by states, rather than a remedy provided under the Equal Protection Clause. *Bush v. Gore*, 531 U.S. 98 (2000) found an Equal Protection Clause violation in the standards used for recounting votes in the US presidential election of 2000 in the state of Florida.

Diane Bell

Good and Evil:
At Home and Abroad

Of silence, symbols, and citizenship

*My car has been serviced. I am signing my credit card slip. The young man
who has already asked me to repeat answers to his questions because, he says,
he doesn't understand my accent, slams down a sticker on the counter and
says with real menace in his voice, "Put this on your car, lady." It is an
American flag. "God Bless America." I don't want this on my car. I want to
explain why but I bite my tongue. He knows where I live. He has access to
my car. I am momentarily silenced.*

A number of reports of silencing in the land of free speech give me pause.[1]
On 28 September 2001, University of South Florida Professor of Computer
Science in the College of Engineering, Sami Al-Arian, appeared on *The
O'Reilly Factor* on the Fox Network. He expected to speak in his role as a
leader in the local Muslim community, as one who could talk about Muslim
American responses to September 11; instead he was denounced as a
"terrorist" (Shapiro 2002).[2] Although tenured, he was suspended then fired
because, as University President Judy Genshaft explained, he didn't make it
plain he was speaking for himself and not on behalf of his university.[3] Florida
Governor Jeb Bush praised the move, but then Bill O'Reilly denounced it.
Who is protecting whose interests? Whence academic freedom?

"Beware of binaries," I routinely caution my students. The inter-relations

---

1 A number of excellent web sites chronicle the chilly post-September 11 environment in the media, schools, the work place and academe. Follow the links to
individual articles from http://www.ncac.org/issues/freeex911.html; http://www.
freedomforum.org; http://www.salon.com/news/feature/2002/01/08/professor/
index_np.html.

2 For a transcript see http://chronicle.com/colloquylive/2002/02/alarian/
http://www.usforacle.com/vnews/display.v/ART/2001/10/12/3bc6d8a0b00da.

3 The debates can be traced through the minutes of the Board of Trustees and press
releases on website of the university, www.usf.edu/search.html, See also Shapiro
2002.

of dichotomies such as culture/nature, objective/subjective, reason/emotion, impartial/partial, male/female are ones we discuss at length in class. The juxtapositions are not a matter of simple opposites but rather mask the power of one side of the binary to control the other. "Man" creates culture which controls nature through exercise of his reason, objectively and impartially expressed. "Woman", on the other hand, is at the mercy of her biology (nature), emotional, partial, and subjective in her reasoning. We discuss the logic of the binaries and whether it is better to deconstruct them or to revalue the devalued component. Does this help us understand the current situation?

Since September 11, I see the citizen/foreigner and good/evil binaries being evoked and fused. It certainly simplifies one's analysis and response. If evil emanates from "other", then there is no need to scrutinise "self". To prove one is a citizen and good, one must be loyal, and the flag says, "I am a patriot." To be a non-citizen is dangerous. One's patriotism cannot be assumed or tweaked. Even more important to fly the flag—that way there can be no question. Those who challenge or in some way destabilise the alignment of this cluster of meanings are immediately suspect and must be taught the rules of combat. This is war and the politics of free speech have moved to the right. If one is a citizen, the threat is being called unpatriotic. If one is a non-citizen, one can be tried before a military tribunal and shot.[4]

Thus we see Bill Maher, irreverent host of the ABC's late-night political talk show *Politically Incorrect*, being cautioned by White House spokesperson Ari Fleischer. In discussion with conservative Dinesh D'Souza on 17 September 2001, Maher had quipped: "We have been the cowards, lobbing cruise missiles from 2000 miles away … Staying in the airplane when it hits the building, say what you want about it, it's not cowardly."[5] With Fleischer's

---

4 See the USA PATRIOT Act (http://www.epic.org/privacy/terrorism/hr3162.html, www.netcoalition.com/keyissues/2001-11-30.200.doc). Civil Liberties groups have been highly critical of the Act (www.aclu.org/action/usa107.html).

5 abc.go.com/primetime/politicallyincorrect/transcripts/transcript_20010917.html Take a look at the actual exchange developed. This was Maher's first show after September 11.

Dinesh D'Souza, an author and former policy analyst during the Reagan administration, stated: "Bill, there's another piece of political correctness I want to mention … And, although I think Bush has been doing a great job, one of the themes we hear constantly is that the people who did this are cowards."

Maher: "Not true."

D'Souza: "Not true. Look at what they did. First of all, you have a whole bunch of guys who are willing to give their life. None of them backed out. All of them slammed themselves into pieces of concrete."

Maher: "Exactly."

response, "It's a terrible thing to say, and it's unfortunate ... They're reminders to all Americans that they need to watch what they say, watch what they do. This is not a time for remarks like that; there never is," the temperature dropped considerably (http://www.whitehouse.gov/news/releases/2001/09/20010926-5.html). Maher obviously understood this was not the time to deconstruct patriotism: "In no way was I intending to say, nor have I ever thought, that the men and women who defend our nation in uniform are anything but courageous and valiant, and I offer my apologies to anyone who took it wrong," Maher said in a statement. "My criticism was meant for politicians who, fearing public reaction, have not allowed our military to do the job they are obviously ready, willing and able to do and who now will, I'm certain, as they always have, get it done" (http://www.abc.abcnews.go.com/primetime/politicallyincorrect/index.html) A number of advertisers pulled their commercials. ABC held off until the end of the season. *Politically Incorrect* ended on 28 June 2002.[6]

Tom Gutting, city editor of the *Texas City Sun*, was fired after he wrote of President Bush as "flying around the country like a scared child seeking refuge in his mother's bed after having a nightmare" (http://www.ncac.org/issues/freex911.html). As an aside I would note the evocation of mother as security but the refuge of a coward. Is the implication that real men don't need mothers? In a much milder voice, Peter Jennings, respected ABC News anchor, ventured: "The country looks to the president on occasions like this to be reassuring to the nation. Some presidents do it well, some presidents don't" (Noyes 2001). He was besieged with e-mail. Raising the temperature considerably, syndicated talk show host Rush Limbaugh (variously described as infamous, reactionary, right-wing) told his listeners that Jennings had questioned Bush's character. Jennings apologised and Limbaugh issued an on-

---

D'Souza: "These are warriors. And we have to realize that the principles of our way of life are in conflict with people in the world. And so—I mean, I'm all for understanding the sociological causes of this, but we should not blame the victim. Americans shouldn't blame themselves because other people want to bomb them."

Maher: "But also, we should—we have been the cowards, lobbing cruise missiles from 2,000 miles away. That's cowardly. Staying in the airplane when it hits the building, say what you want about it, it's not cowardly. You're right."

6 Maher's defenders see him as the victim of his own personality and a witch hunt. Essayist and novelist Susan Sontag (2001) wrote of the terrorist attacks in *The New Yorker*: "Where is the acknowledgement that this was not a 'cowardly' attack on 'civilization' or 'liberty' or 'humanity' or the 'free world' but an attack on the world's self-proclaimed superpower, undertaken as a consequence of specific American alliances and actions?".

air retraction. Since September 11 conservative and reactionary voices have played the patriot card and played it with force.

The power to silence has been exercised through the deployment of symbols, in the legislature, and in policy shifts. In those first weeks the flag and singing of "God Bless America" dominate the landscape. It will be some time before measured critiques emerge in mainstream media. America may be bloodied but she is not bowed. Men and women in the police force and fire brigade become the heroes. Ordinary women and men are called upon to do the extra-ordinary. The American flag hangs from overpasses, is displayed on front porches, in shop windows, flies on tall buildings, is pinned to lapels. There are rules about the correct display and handling of the flag. It cannot be flown in a tattered state. It mustn't touch the ground. There is a passion in the debates regarding the legality and propriety of burning the flag. Reverence for the flag is learned in school, in Girl Scouts, in watching the rituals of state, at military funerals. The constitution may guarantee a separation of church and state but the flag is sacred. It is a sacrilege to mishandle it. It is saluted by loyal Americans. A hand is placed on one's heart out of love for the flag. This is a powerful symbol evoking nation, pride, unity, liberty, a shared history.

Symbols work because they are multivocal, a number of meanings are condensed in one simple icon—a cross, a swastika, a yellow ribbon. These symbols can be read at a number of levels, mean different things to different people, at different times. A burning cross in the south is different from the cross in the Easter mass and different again from the Apache ritual use of the cross symbol. To go into war under the flag evokes a different sort of solidarity than reciting the pledge of allegiance at a school assembly or placing the sticker on a car. At the level of the nation it stands for "country" and those who salute it are members of one big family, a family for which one will make sacrifices of the lives of loved ones and of certain parts of one's liberty for the security the flag offers. Some of the meanings are contradictory, but the power of the symbol is to make it unthinkable to read these meanings against one another. Teasing those meanings apart challenges the established order. It asks in whose interests are these meanings fused? Why can't a mother, lover, child, who is asked to "sacrifice" in the name of the nation, represented as the "American family", ask about their particular loved one? When the "sacrifice" is wrapped in the flag, it is a tight wrap shutting out critique. It is unravelled at one's own peril.

We've seen this before. In the Gulf War the Yellow Ribbons campaign made it impossible to think of the troops as anything other than members of the idealised and abstract "American family". The nation was grateful that their young men and women were over there fighting to protect liberty. To question the war was to put the troops in harm's way, it was traitorous, as it had been in Vietnam. To argue that one did not want the troops to die but also did not believe that war was the best approach was nigh on impossible. Symbols work because they conflate, compress and condense meanings.

Feminist Queries

Asking questions about September 11 is fraught. Yet such situations are exactly where feminists excel. We ask the awkward questions. We are less vested in "business as usual"—too often that business excludes us. We've had plenty of practice in dislodging dearly held beliefs about the "natural order" of things, of exploring the systemic relations of power which significantly limit the enjoyment of individual rights.[7] The idea that certain roles are "natural" keeps women in low-paid nurturing work while men are free to politic in the public domain. A feminist standpoint can yield fresh insights, particularly in the grounded nature of women's approaches to moral dilemmas (Jaggar 1989; Benhabib 1987).

Feminists, I suggest, are well positioned to ask awkward questions, and post-September 11 feminist critiques of war, peace, government policy have connected the nature of violence at home and abroad. Of course our questions are not always embraced for their clarity of vision. Rather, on the one hand, in tirades against feminists, conservatives like Jerry Falwell blame us for the nation's woes, including September 11 (surely a reason for paying closer attention to us). On the other hand, in carefully crafted appeals to protect the vulnerable, First Lady Laura Bush appropriates much of the feminist work on the ethic of care (http://www.whitehouse.gov/news/releases/2001/11/20011117.html, Noddings 1984). Suddenly saving women from the abuses of the Taliban regime is part of the war effort.

"You're either for us or against us," says President Bush. Can there be no middle ground, no nuanced reasoning? I want context. I want particulars. I want to know more of the history, the local politics and the global interests in the region. I want to explore the connections between an economic stimulus package at home and the economies of war. My questions concern the power of binaries at home/abroad, good/evil; the need to envision the particular other; to listen to what women say and have been saying of their situation in Afghanistan; to read this in terms of women and minorities in the USA.

---

7 Feminist interrogations of the root of liberal feminism point to the ways in which the privileging of individual rights masks class, sex, race, ethnicity (Waters 2000).

Moment One: Safe in DC?

September 11. *I am walking to work at the George Washington University past the Foggy Bottom Metro station in Washington, DC. One of the workers I see every morning on this route is on his cell phone. He looks up: "A plane just flew into one the Twin Towers in New York City." "An accident?" I ask. "Don't know," he says. It is just after nine. One more block and I am at work. With the assistance of Heidi Lindemann, my administrative aide, we set up our new television and with help from the telecom worker, who has come to work on connectivity in our new building, we rig up an aerial and watch open-mouthed as the second tower is hit, then the Pentagon. There is no emergency signal sounded. There are plenty of rumours about planes headed our way, and a threat to the nearby State Building. One more plane down in Pennsylvania. I figure we are six blocks from the White House and probably as safe in our basement as on the streets. We gather: faculty, students, administrators, significant others and cleaning staff. We watch Peter Jennings who becomes the narrator of the tragedy. We don't leave till late afternoon. By then the bridges are cleared and the city is deserted. The next morning as I walk to work there are camouflaged vehicles on every corner. The National Guard is abroad and armed. We have to carry ID. The dumpster which had been languishing outside our building for a month since we moved in has disappeared overnight. I have a class to teach that night.*

The classroom becomes a safe place to work through our fears, rage, incomprehension. Some students who have studied the region know a little of the politics of oil; something of the Northern Alliance, the Taliban and the war lords; one knows the name Osama Bin Laden. We all know of the treatment of women under the Taliban. But these are not their first questions. No, the first questions are about their conflicted emotions regarding responses. They don't know how to name the "enemy". They don't want to rush to judgement. They want to know what it will mean in their lives in very grounded ways. They all know students from the Middle East. They want background on the conflicts in the region. They don't want heavy-handed intervention. They see the parallels to interventions made in the name of protecting women, of family planning programs which target poor women and not the conditions which give rise to poverty. They have compassion for the citizens of Afghanistan who have suffered under the Taliban as innocents, who will be "collateral damage" if there is a war.

We have been reading Cynthia Enloe's *Maneuvers* (2000) and they like her advocacy of the exercise of "feminist curiousity". Who is making the decisions? On the basis of what information, beliefs, and interests? What/ who defines terrorism? Is a war on "terrorism" like a war on "poverty"? Both are ill-defined: both seem unwinnable. In whose interests are such "wars" waged? Can we talk about what it means to be an American but not want to see military retaliation? I love my boyfriend and don't want him to have to go into a war zone but he's in ROTC. I have relatives who are in the National Guard who will be called up. Yes, I know that is part of the bargain but the armed forces do not represent the American population. Minorities are over-represented. The sacrifice being demanded is not shared evenly. What would it mean if women were serving in a country where women are not seen in public? We have the Gulf War as history and we have Enloe's careful deconstruction of the ways in which nationalism, militarism and masculinities are fused. The students are asking about agency, a quintessentially feminist question.

Moment Two: Anthrax, women and minorities

Mid-October: *One of my students mentions in class that her organisation has received anthrax threats. Why aren't we reading about this? asks a journalism major. Isn't this intimidation of women? Don't women have rights in this country? We've been reading Patricia Hill Collins (1998) on the issue of visibility and invisibility—on what makes the story and what remains hidden. Clearly anthrax in a Senator's office is visible as terrorism: persistent threats against women's reproductive rights, it seems, are the work of deranged individuals.*

In mid-October 2001 more than 250 abortion clinics received letters containing a white powdery substance and the message: "You have been exposed to anthrax." The FBI met with the National Abortion Federation, Planned Parenthood and the Fund for the Feminist Majority. There has always been a reluctance to name these threats as a form of domestic terrorism, part of a war on women. Instead an individual such as Clayton Waagner, a man wanted by the FBI, is labelled as a lone nut-case. He is pursued on weapons violations, not because he has said "I'm an abortion bomber, that's what I do" (http://www.ArmyofGod.com). If the Justice Department were to pursue Waagner and his links to domestic networks with the same zeal that foreign terrorists are pursued, suggests Frederick Clarkson (2001), it could expose links ranging from the far-right fringe to right-wing politics, even to the attorney-general himself. Yet as feminists know, the power to name is the power to control (Rich 1980: 644).

There was no nation-wide reporting of the scope of the threats; few backgrounders where one can learn that abortion clinics have been the targets of anthrax threats since 1989; that they have established protocols for handling mail, which is routinely opened in a sealed room by gloved handlers. The Waagner hoax was detected because they had these safeguards in place. This is "business as usual" for abortion providers. Perhaps they possess expertise in handling terrorists on which the FBI might draw in the current crisis.

Waagner himself understood that he was engaged in acts of terrorism but claimed he had never really meant to kill the forty-two people he had targeted in his threats on the Army of God website. His shifting story can be traced through the press releases on http://www.Kaisernetwork.org. In summary: Waagner claims he decided to "terrorize them with death threats and with letters laced with fake anthrax powder". Waagner said that he mailed two sets of letters to the clinics: one set containing flour and another set containing a harmless substance that often tests positive for anthrax. Waagner said that he got the idea for mailing anthrax hoax letters after witnessing the anthrax scare that followed the September 11 attacks on the World Trade Center and the Pentagon. He said that he sent the hoax letters because he wanted to "close abortion clinics for a day, an hour, a week. Whatever I could."

How to understand Waagner, who as a member of the Army of God claims to act in the name of God, in relation to similar claims to have God on their side being made by the pilots of the September 11 planes? Is there a good God and a bad one? Is there one who looks after good women and allows bad women to be terrorised? One in whose name we may bomb the enemy but whose name is improperly invoked by the enemy? In class we talk about the generalised, abstract "other" and the particularised, concrete "other". The former can be imagined but is never known as a person. The Muslim "woman" is mute. The Muslim "man" a killer. What if we knew them as individuals? Part of the effectiveness of the local responses to the loss at "Ground Zero" in New York City was the personalising of the tragedy in the photographs, the mementoes, the tributes to individuals. These were not statistics: these were relatives, loved ones, friends, each with their own unique personality. It reminds me of Mothers of the Disappeared displaying images of their lost sons in the Plaza de Mayo (Agosín 1989).

In the USA the domestic anthrax threat added more urgency to the call for greater surveillance. When an anthrax-laced letter was opened in Senator Daschle's office on 15 October 2001, the response was immediate and prolonged. No-one was to be endangered. The place was decontaminated, tested and tested again. But the postal workers who handled the mail did not get such treatment. It took fatalities to focus attention on their exposure to anthrax. They lined up through the night for the antibiotics. The line snaked around the building. I watched on the late-night news. I didn't see one white person in line.[8] Increasingly, and in particular driven by critiques of women

8 http://www.nytimes.com/2001/09/29/arts/television/29TANK.html There is also the business of who had access to Cipro, the preferred drug, and the use of substitutes for the postal workers, and the period covered by the prescriptions (Baltimore 2001).

of colour, feminist analyses highlight the intersections of gender, race and class (Collins 1998).

Moment Three: Bombs Abroad, Legislate at Home

7 October 2001. *The bombing has begun. I am talking with a couple of colleagues. One says this is the right thing to do although it is hard on the civilians who live there. One says that the USA is right to retaliate and others should be grateful that they have moved so quickly. I venture that there might be other solutions, that I have some appreciation of why people may not like the USA: so powerful; able to mobilize for war so rapidly; so sure of its role on the global stage; so driven by its own national interests. I mention the call for the abandonment of the Anti-Ballistic Missile Treaty, which holds a promise of global security but represents a hindrance to the development of the Missile Defence Shield for the protection of America and its allies; the undermining of the Kyoto Protocol and its potential to slow global warming which could curb "growth" in the US economy; the US walk-out at the World Conference Against Racism held in South Africa which removes talk of reparations for slavery from the home agenda; the US failure to pay its way in the United Nations but its attempts to control key decisions in the national interest. I point out that the USA and Afghanistan share the distinction of not having ratified the Convention on the Elimination of All Discrimination Against Women. I am asked, "Are you a citizen?" "No, I am not."*

I have been asked this question many times since September 11. The question has an edge. I am out of line in offering a critique. I should mind what I say, but these are my colleagues. This is academe. I am not silenced. I argue back, but I am perplexed. When will it be the right time to raise doubts and who will do it? I am aware that I am vulnerable.

On Friday, 26 October 2001, President George W. Bush signed into law the anti-terrorism bill known as the USA PATRIOT Act, which stands for "Uniting and Strengthening America by Providing Appropriate Tools Required to Intercept and Obstruct Terrorism". It gives the US federal government the power to seize the assets of any organisation or individual aiding and abetting "terrorist activities".[9] Americans are being asked to trade some freedoms for

---

9 http://www.epic.org/privacy/terrorism/hr3162.html. Law enforcement agencies controlled by the federal government had been complaining that since the Watergate era their powers had been eroded and their effectiveness diminished. This new law restores many powers. It has a sunset clause of 2006. (http://www.eff.org/Privacy/Surveillance/Terrorism_militias/20011031_eff_usa_patriot_analysis.html). See President Bush on signing the Act (http://www.whitehouse.gov/news/releases/2001/10/20011026-5.html).

security. Certainly in the wake of September 11 one can see why people might need reassuring. But will the measures address the failure of intelligence?

Feminists have pondered the so-called trade-off of security against freedom. Is that not what marriage purports to offer? And is it not within marriage that women are abused? Remember, it took feminist critiques of the myth of the stranger rapist to draw attention to marital rape and incest; the symbol of the family as the locus of care was deconstructed and shown to mask unequal power relations within. These insights were not received with joy; indeed, they are resisted by many who promote "family values" which recall the happy family of the 1950s, a family that never was, but which is a powerful symbol to discuss feminist analyses.

Moment Four: Global Feminisms

23 October. *I have been invited to address the Clearing House on Women's Issues—a DC-based network of women—at their October meeting on the subject of "Global Feminisms: What's on the agenda". Prior to September 11, I probably would have offered a list of persistent problems: violence against women, trafficking, reproductive technologies, pornography, sexual harassment, militarisation, and environmental degradation. I would have argued that Women's Studies must retain its activist focus and that we are certainly not living in "post-patriarchy". Those matters are still on my agenda. But, on this occasion I ask: How might feminists, particularly in North America, begin to strategise around issues of "terrorism"?*

Here is part of what I said:

Certainly we have much to learn from those who have lived in war zones for decades. In the current situation for the USA, the terror is at home while the "enemy" is a shadowy "other" represented as living elsewhere. Bombs drop in Afghanistan while the domestic agenda is being rapidly transformed. The priority establishing bodies are male, mainly white, and definitely not attuned to the needs of minorities, working women and children. Programs concerning health, education and housing are on the back burner. Airlines which were already ailing prior to September 11 are being bailed out, while workers are being dismissed. Inequalities and injustices at home are rendered invisible, and critiques which seek to make them visible are drowned in appeals to patriotism unity and "business as usual". Women are being asked to shop to help the economy, to talk to their children, and to support the war effort. Women need to be asking: Why? In whose interest? With what consequences? For whom? On the basis of what input? How to move from being the "good mother" of the family and nation into active voice and how to move beyond the simplistic notions of good and evil to a more nuanced understanding of terrorism are on my agenda.

Women are a token at home and abroad. As loyal Americans, women were being asked to be part of the consumer society. No matter that at the same time we were also being told to avoid shopping malls as they were potential targets. No matter that few have the knowledge to explain the difference between bad fundamentalism and ethical Muslim beliefs. And what of those who can't afford a holiday at Disney World? Are they bad Americans because they are not helping to spend our way out of the slump but rather are in need of relief?

My analysis is not accepted wholeheartedly. One woman with a long history fighting for women's rights insists that it is all about religion. "Get rid of that and there would be no more fundamentalists," she declares. I demur. I argue that Islamic practices vary from region to region, even within regions. One needs to know the cultural and historical underpinnings to understand the various manifestations (Ahmed 1993). She dismisses me with "There is no difference between culture and religion." I hold off on exploring further the anthropological distinctions I am making. Others argue with some passion that any intervention is better than none. Am I advocating doing nothing? No, I'm not. I'm arguing for informed decision-making. I suggest that sincerity is not enough. Why not ask the local women? Why not look at the inequalities at home? Perhaps it is not US intervention that is needed but reform of US policy. Now I have said the unsayable. The most vocal of the women turns her back on me and talks loudly to her neighbour at the conference table.

Moment Five: Laura Bush and RAWA speak of women

17 November: *Good morning. I'm Laura Bush and I am delivering this week's radio address to kick off a worldwide effort to focus on the brutality against women and children by the Al-Qaeda terrorist network and the regime it supports in Afghanistan, the Taliban ... Only the terrorist and the Taliban threaten to pull out women's fingernails for wearing nail polish ... The brutal oppression of women is a central goal of the terrorists ... The plight of women and children in Afghanistan is a matter of deliberate cruelty carried out by those who seek to intimidate and control* (http://www. whitehouse.gov/news/releases/2001/11/20011117.html).

My immediate question is what would have happened had Hillary Clinton ever addressed the nation on her husband's radio time-slot? Laura Bush speaks in a different register. At the Clearing House in October I had asked, "Why suddenly is the treatment of women by the Taliban newsworthy? Why are the women rendered mute? Why do others speak for them?" Before a new regime is installed, I insisted, we need to hear from those women. A new regime is taking hold in the US and women need to be heard here also. How could the Bush administration not have known about the Taliban treatment of women? The petition regarding the treatment of women under the Taliban has been circulating for six years on feminist e-mail lists. Is this yet another massive "failure of intelligence", or is the surprise of the Bush administration regarding the treatment of women under the Taliban feigned? Certainly the purported ignorance masks the role the USA played in creating the Taliban.

For my students the sudden sympathy for Afghan women is infuriating. In one clean move the Bush administration has appropriated the shrouded, silenced woman and made her the symbol of all the evil being perpetrated in Afghanistan. Mrs Bush makes no mention of RAWA, the Revolutionary Association of the Women of Afghanistan, or any other feminist organisation. No, she has suddenly figured all this out herself. The treatment of women is an index of civilisation. Oh that she knew something of the plight of women in the USA. Can the lack of child care, pre- and post-natal care be considered the mark of a civilised country? If you desegregate the infant mortality statistics by race and ethnicity in the USA, you have a Third World statistic. Maybe she would give these women vouchers and let them choose! While the flag speaks for one nation, one family, we can't look inside at the violence within the family, structural or personal. Instead Laura Bush evokes the vulnerability of children elsewhere. There were similar images in the Gulf War and images of the oppressed women of Kuwait—there it was drivers' licences; here is it the wearing of nail polish. But what reporting do we have of the liberated Kuwaiti woman? What we do know is that after military interventions the vulnerable are more endangered as refugees, as displaced persons, as spoils of war. The bombing in Afghanistan destroyed roads used for peaceful purposes, disrupted food deliveries, and led to starvation. It was an intervention which imperilled the already vulnerable.

There are many sources to which we may turn for detailed knowledge, for past, present, and future strategising, regarding women in Afghanistan. RAWA has been working to empower women in Afghanistan and Pakistan since 1977 and in that time has amassed considerable expertise—surely more experts for intelligence-gatherers to consult, that is if the claim to place women's rights at the centre of the war on terrorism had any substance. RAWA has worked underground to provide literacy and health care for girls and women. Their goals include secular democracy, full participation in public life for girls and women, and respect for all human rights (http://www.rawa.org). Their work is no secret. They raise funds, organise, and travel the world with their message. They have cautioned against supporting the Northern Alliance whose history of abuse is not that much different from the Taliban. RAWA called upon the UN "to withdraw its recognition to the so-called Islamic government headed by the Rabbani and help the establishment of a broad-based government based on democratic values" (Groves 2001).

Further, RAWA is not the only organisation working in Afghanistan (see Groves 2002). There are non-government organisations such as the Afghan Women's Resource Centre and Afghan Women's Welfare Development, Shuhada, the Afghan Women's Education Centre, as well as a number of networks like RAWA, the Afghan Women's Network, and the Afghan Women's Council. There are local women's groups. Afghan women in exile have also been speaking out and organising. Within the USA a number of feminist organisations have been advocating for women's rights in Afghanistan (http://www.feminist.org; http://www.helpafghanwomen.com). This wealth of knowledge and expertise should be at the centre of any policies concerning future governance and service delivery in the region.

Moment Six: Voices for Peace

6 December 2001: *Students at Hampshire, an experimenting, small, liberal arts college in western Massachusetts, issue a statement condemning the war on terrorism and propose alternative solutions. They believe they are the first campus to do so. They state, "We refuse to fall into silent support for an unjust war that kills innocents overseas, and threatens our safety and civil liberties at home."*

Hampshire has often been at the forefront of political action, and the students recall the vote for the impeachment of President Nixon and their vote on divestment in South Africa under apartheid. In their December statement they called, amongst other things, for a "UN-led effort to establish in Afghanistan a democratic and multi-ethnic government, respectful of the rights of women" (http://www.freerepublic.com/focus/fr/586725/posts). The Hampshire President, Gregory Prince (2001), offered full support for the students' efforts to debate issues of war, terrorism and justice. "This is liberal arts education: it is democracy; it is patriotism," he declared. However, he chose to withhold his vote on their statement for two reasons. Firstly, the students had taken the vote before the Hampshire forum for such a vote, the "all-community meeting", was held. Secondly, he argued that their statement over-simplified a complex situation and contained exaggerated claims. His message was simple: "The goals of a liberal arts education are to encourage critical thinking; to encourage respect for diversity, human rights and human dignity; and to develop the courage of individuals to act on the basis of critical analyses in the pursuit of principles of human dignity and human rights" (Prince 2001).

Again we see the voice from the margins calling for nuanced, informed debate. This was not Stanford, Yale, or Harvard weighing in. The modelling for debate and a readiness to countenance dissent, test free speech, not curtail, it came from Hampshire. Several decades ago we might have looked to university and college presidents to act as public intellectuals, but most now must operate like CEOs and money raisers. Voices are coming out of academe but, as was seen at South Florida University and has been found in a number of other educational fora, debate is difficult when the talk is of war.

Moment Seven: An Invitation to Contribute to a Book

12 February 2002: *Would I be interested in contributing to a volume being put together by Spinifex Press with a publication date of September 11, 2002? asks Susan Hawthorne. We have already exchanged our immediate responses to September 11 and share an interest in the global ramifications of shifts in US policy. Of course I would like to contribute, but how to organise my reflections?*

Every day the media brings more to this complicated picture, but I like the idea of an international volume emanating from Melbourne, Australia. I think of bell hooks' *From Margin to Center* (1984), of the work I have been doing on feminist standpoint theory, and the epistemic privilege of those not at the centre of power, those not tainted by the power at the centre. As women and non-citizens we are certainly on the margins, albeit different margins—me as "resident alien" in the USA; Susan as an Australian citizen living in Australia but writing about globalism; and Renate Klein, as a Swiss-born Australian citizen writing about reproductive technologies. In November 2001, Susan, Renate Klein and I plan a session for the conference of the National Women's Studies Association in Las Vegas in mid-June 2002. As it turns out we are the only panel addressing September 11 and we are all "foreigners", a point not lost on the audience. Carol Anne Douglas in particular ponders aloud: "Have I been silenced?"

Feminists, it seems to me, have been at the forefront of making the relationship between the researcher and the researched explicit, of being reflexive, and of course they have been dismissed as lacking in objectivity for their troubles. I am not claiming that all women's voices are equal by virtue of being female. Rather I am arguing that positionality is critical. Thus, on the one hand, I would note the wisdom to be distilled from Representative Barbara Lee, a Democrat from California, the lone voice saying, "Far too many people have died already ... If we rush to launch a counter-attack, we run too great a risk that women, children, and other non-combatants will be caught in the crossfire", and her one vote against ceding Congress's authority to use military force to President George W. Bush (see this volume: 38). On the other hand, I would note the message being read into whistle-blower Coleen Rowley's testimony and thirteen-page memo to FBI Director Robert Mueller of 21 May 2002 (http://www.newsmax.com/archives/articles/2002/5/27/163915.shtml) Both raise questions regarding the trade-off between security and freedoms, but the former seeks security in more measured, compassionate decision-making, while the latter advocates greater surveillance in the name of security.

The number of voices in this volume, voices from so many different margins, it seems to me will map the centre nicely. Many of my reflections have been prompted by my students, colleagues and workplace—it is there I have chosen, or perhaps been forced, to articulate a position. As feminist educators we have an important role to play. My students complain that when they raise the matters we discuss in class, they are told not to be trivial. There are much more important things to be discussed than what impact gender has on a policy analysis. They need this book.

Moment Eight: Globalisation Week at George Washington University

15 March: *My colleague Cynthia Deitch, Associate Director of Women's Studies, e-mails me: "I can't stand this—the consistent absence of women and dissenting voices. I want to organize a panel on 'Gender and globalisation: Feminist responses'."*

The program for "Globalisation Week", hosted by the George Washington Center for the Study of Globalization, sets out a series of activities that are "designed to heighten awareness and understanding of globalization." Very quickly Cynthia pulls together a panel: Sarah Grusky, Co-Director of Global Challenge Initiative; Dan Moshenberg, Associate Professor of English; Njoki Njehü; Cynthia, Associate Director of Women's Studies, and myself. We all know that structural adjustment programs, when subjected to a gender analysis, indicate women fare badly (Sparr 1994). The speakers map the deterioration of women's health, education, and the increase in domestic violence as World Bank and IMF developments undermine women's security and impoverish communities. They critique gender-neutral approaches.

It is helpful to set these analyses beside the restructuring of the economy which is happening in the USA. Who will be better off after the economic stimulus package is delivered? Airlines will be bailed out, but the tens of thousands of service workers stood down as the economy took a nosedive are not part of this package. Dr Heidi Hartmann, a feminist economist, and the Institute for Women's Policy Research of which she is president, provide a steady stream of research papers which indicate gender matters in policy analyses. Hartmann (2001a) points out that the economic stimulus package is proceeding as if there had been no changes in the economy over the past decade. What of the nearly three million more working wives than there were in 1991, and nearly four million more working mothers (both married and single) than ten years earlier? she asks. Hartmann (2001b) summarises:

Any federal stimulus package should include grants to state and local governments to allow them to maintain crucial services and to ensure that their budget decisions do not worsen the recession. Not only are women a key part of any state's work force but many state-funded services are critically important to women and their families. Women need unemployment insurance reform and an economic stimulus package that will address their specific needs.

A Time to Speak

18 June 2002: "Let it not be said that people in the United States did nothing when their government declared a war without limit and instituted stark new measures of repression," begins the statement of conscience "Not in Our Name", signed by a number of leading American writers, actors and academics. It is both a critique and a rallying call to action.

> We believe that questioning, criticism, and dissent must be valued and protected. We understand that such rights are always contested and must be fought for ... President Bush has declared: "You're either for us or against us."' Here is our answer: we refuse to allow you to speak for all American people. We will not give up our right to question ... We say NOT IN OUR NAME. (Campbell 2002)

I am at work. I say these are hard times and having George W. Bush at the helm is extremely worrying. I am told, "We have lived through worse." There is no further conversation. Can an idea in the abstract be so secure? I am interested in the particulars, in the concrete, in the now. I have little faith in the "swings and roundabouts" and "checks and balances" approach.

The scope, texture and reach of responses to and analyses of September 11 and its aftermath are ripe for feminist reflections and rich in lessons for those schooled in feminist theory and practice. Many of the moves to contain and control debates resonate for feminists who know how easily histories of dissent and the non-dominant sectors of society are erased. I often say my guiding philosophy is "constant vigilance". We have seen much of this before. Deflection of domestic issues, the construction of a shadowy "other", the deployment of powerful symbols, and unwinnable wars. We know that to think concretely raises different moral and ethical questions regarding intervention. We know to ask in whose interests are women in Afghanistan suddenly on the agenda and to be curious about what isn't being said.

Acknowledgements: I thank my students and all those who attended the 2002 NSWA session where I delivered the talk on which this paper is based. In particular, thanks to Susan Hawthorne for her patience as I missed deadline after deadline and to Heidi Lindemann for all manner of assistance from the purely practical to her incisive critiques of American culture. Garnet Marsh, Genevieve Bell, Renate Klein, Suzanne Bellamy, thanks also. Jane Perkins—this is for you—may we live in a more just world.

References

Agosín, Marjorie. (1989). *Women of Smoke: Latin American Women in Literature and Life*. Canada: Williams Wallace.

Ahmed, Lila. (1993). *Women and Gender in Islam: Historical Roots of a Modern Debate*. New Haven: Yale University Press.

Baltimore, Chris. (2001). "Postal Workers Told to Take Doxy instead of Cipro." Main page, 29 October, www.rense.com.

Benhabib, Seyla. (1987). "The Generalized and Concrete Other: The Kohlberg-Gilligan Controversy and Feminist Theory." In Benhabib, S. and D. Cornell, Eds. *Feminism as Critique*. Minnesota: University of Minnesota Press.

Brownfield, Paul. (2001). "Troubled Timing takes Maher Beyond 'Politically Incorrect'," *Los Angeles Times*, 26 September.

Campbell, Duncan. (2002). "Not in Our Name: US Artists Damn 'War Without Limit'." 18 June: www.commondreams.org (Published *Guardian*, London, 14 June).

Clarkson, Frederick. (2001). "Our Own Terror Cells." Salon Online Exclusive, 7 January. www.salon.com.

Collins, Patricia Hill. (1998). *Fighting Words: Black Women and the Search for Justice*. Minneapolis: University of Minnesota Press.

Enloe, Cynthia. (2000). *Maneuvers: The International Politics of Militarizing Women's Lives*. Berkeley: University of California Press.

Groves, Sharon. (2001). "News and Views." *Feminist Studies* 27 (Fall): 753–9.

——. (2002). Afghan Women Speak Out. Unpublished paper.

Hartmann, Heidi. (2001a). "Placing Women Front and Center: New Family and Economic Realities." Press release for the Press Conference on "New Employment statistics: What they mean for African Americans, women, and the nation." 2 November, Rayburn House Office Building. www.iwpr. org.

——. (2001b) "Shrinking Job Market Hits Women and Families Hard." *Chicago Tribune Internet Edition*, 12 December. www.chicagotribune.com.

Hawthorne, Susan. (2002). *Wild Politics: Feminism, Globalisation, and Bio/diversity*. Melbourne: Spinifex Press.

hooks, bell. (1984). *Feminist Theory: From Margin to Center*. Boston: South End Press.

Jaggar, Alison. (1989). "Feminist Ethics: Some Issues for the Nineties." *Journal of Social Philosophy* XX (1&2): 91–105.

Noddings, Nel. (1984). *Caring: A Feminine Approach to Ethics and Moral Education*. Berkeley: University of California Press.

Noyes, Rich. (2001). "September 11, 2001: What Did Jennings Say?" 19 September. http://www.mediaresearch.org/realitycheck/2001/20010919.asp.

Prince, Gregory S. Jr. (2001). "Statement of Gregory S. Prince Jr., President, Hampshire College, Amherst, Massachusetts," 5 December.

Rich, Adrienne. (1980). "Compulsory Heterosexuality and Lesbian Existence." *Signs* 5 (4): 631–60.

Shapiro, Bruce. (2002). "Florida Witch Hunt." Salon Online Exclusive, 8 January. www.salon.com.

Sontag, Susan. (2001). "A Mature Democracy." *The New Yorker*. 24 September: 32.

Sparr, Pamela. Ed. (1994). *Mortgaging Women's Lives: Feminist Critiques of Structural Adjustment*. London: Zed Books.

Waters, Kristin. Ed. (2000) *Women and Men Political Theorists: Enlightened Conversations*. Malden: Blackwell.

Bronwyn Winter

If Women Really Mattered ...

"État des lieux"[1]

The first thing one notices on arriving in Afghanistan is destruction. It is apparent everywhere in the city, from the chewed-up planes alongside the runway at Kabul airport to the remains of bombed-out office and apartment buildings in the city.

But it is when one leaves Kabul that the full realisation hits: the country is in ruins. North of Kabul, and extending into Parwan province, lies the Shamari plateau, site of the front line. Everywhere one looks, villages in ruins and abandoned, abandoned tanks half shot away, containers, formerly used to house prisoners, so riddled with bullets that they resemble a surreal attempt at iron lacework. Some of the containers have small high window holes cut in them; the luckier prisoners had some access to light and air.

Containers are now used as housing for village shops. In Pakistan, these box-like structures are made of wood. In Afghanistan, they are made of recycled containers.

And then there are the endless minefields. According to a report of 15 January 2002 by the UN's Mine Action Programme for Afghanistan (MAPA), "Afghanistan is the most mine- and unexploded ordnance (UXO)-affected country in the world, with 732 km^2 of known mined area, of which an estimated 100 km^2 are mined in former frontline areas, and approximately 500 km^2 of UXO in contaminated battle areas." The report goes on to estimate at 200,000 the number of survivors of accidents with mines or unexploded ordnance. Prior to the US State's War on Afghanistan, the death and injury rate was estimated to be between 150 and 300 per month (MAPA 2002a). At the commencement of the US State's War in October 2001, mined areas were still being discovered at a rate of twelve to fourteen square kilometres per year (Human Rights Watch 2001a). Of the millions of mines in Afghanistan, of about fifty different types, most were laid by Soviet and pro-Soviet Afghan forces between 1979 and 1992, although according to a

---

1 Literally, this means "inventory". It is the inspection carried out when a property is rented or sold, to note the condition of fittings and fixtures. By extension, it is used, often figuratively, to describe any stocktaking of a situation.

Human Rights Watch background paper, "virtually all combatants in Afghanistan in recent decades are thought to have used mines ... The United States provided landmines to mujahideen fighters as part of US covert assistance in the 1980s" (Human Rights Watch 2001a).

The war declared on Afghanistan by the US State severely disturbed MAPA's operations, which had been ongoing since 1989, as airstrikes and looting threatened the safety of MAPA's workforce of 4800. Operations have since been resumed. The UN further notes that, although Afghanistan is not a party to any of the international instruments dealing with landmines, Hamid Karzai has committed his administration to accede to the Anti-Personnel Mine Ban Convention (MAPA 2002b).

The country is poor and hungry, not only because of the war but also because of the effects of five years of severe drought, but it is impossible to regenerate livestock farms and agriculture in much of Afghanistan because of the mines. According to a report by the UN Secretary-General, Kofi Annan, dated 7 December 2001, of the total of mined areas scattered throughout the country, "350 km^2 are assessed as being vitally important residential areas, commercial land, roads, irrigation systems and primary production land" (UN/Annan 2001).

As primary education, and particularly education for girls, is being revitalised in Afghanistan, much of it under the auspices of the UN (although some schools are already threatened with closure due to lack of funds),[2] landmine education is prioritised, as it is in refugee camps in Pakistan. Posters on landmines are visible in every classroom, and MAPA and non-government organisations such as Save the Children tour schools with education packages.

The second thing one notices on arriving in Afghanistan is illiteracy. Along with two NGO employees I had met on the plane, one of whom had learned a smattering of Dari (Afghan Persian), I spent my first quarter-hour on Afghan soil being a scribe, filling out disembarkation cards for Afghans returning to the country. All men. Only one other woman on the flight, and she was a member of the privileged literate class.

The noticing of the maleness of public space came earlier. This is not a new discovery anywhere.

According to the United States Fund for UNICEF (2001), between 1995 and 1999 the adult (over 15) illiteracy rate for women was estimated at 84

---

2   This is the case, for example, of a school in the destroyed village of Qarabagh, on the Shamari plateau, currently run by the UN under three large tents, pending reconstruction of the school building. Two of the tents are classrooms for boys and one is for girls. I estimated at upwards of 150 the number of children being educated in this makeshift school. Its future is uncertain at the time of this writing.

per cent, that of men being 54 per cent. The Revolutionary Association of the Women of Afghanistan (2002), however, puts the illiteracy rate for women at over 95 per cent, and suggests that even this may be an underestimation.

On 7, 8 and 9 June 2002, I attended a women's conference in Kabul, associated with the Loya Jirga and held immediately prior to it. The participants at this conference spoke again and again of the need for literacy classes for women. Literacy was related to everything: basic hygiene and health care (how can one administer medication to one's sick children if one cannot read the labels?), training for employment, access to social and economic independence.

In refugee camps in Pakistan, schooling, like most other services, is provided by NGOs, often with UN funding, with a focus on educating children. Girl children in particular have been disadvantaged by years of Taliban rule in Afghanistan. For example, the majority of pupils of both sexes in the four schools run by the Norwegian Refugee Council in Ashgharo Camp, south of Peshawar, are in Grade One (1215 boys and 1089 girls).[3] In the higher grades, there are very few girls indeed: only 47 in Grade Two (as against 163 boys) and 35 in Grade Three (as against 164 boys). There are no girls in Grades Four and up. (There are 55 boys in Grade Four and 15 in Grade Five.) As at June 2002, there are no children of either sex in Grade Six. The Norwegian Refugee Council does not run adult literacy classes.

Norwegian Church Aid, on the contrary, runs literacy classes for adults in Shalman refugee camp near the Pakistan–Afghanistan border in North-West Frontier Province. As at 17 June 2002, 855 adult men and women had registered for literacy classes, but Norwegian Church Aid was waiting on the second instalment of UN funding to implement them.

Feminist organisations such as RAWA and Shirkat Gah also run a number of literacy classes for Afghan women in Pakistan. As well, RAWA runs fifteen primary and secondary schools and five orphanages for refugee girls and boys. Inside Afghanistan, RAWA's operations are more covert, but the organisation manages to run home-based schools for girls and boys and literacy classes for girls and women (RAWA website 2002). What is specific and important about the literacy classes run by feminist organisations is that they also provide human rights and legal training for women alongside literacy (RAWA website 2002; Farida Saheed of Shirkat Gah, personal communication, 18 June 2002).

The third thing one notices on arriving in Afghanistan is poverty. Even the luxury hotels (there are only two remaining in Kabul to speak of: the

---

3   The NRC follows the newly developed Afghan curriculum. It is apparently, at present, one of the few aid agencies operating in Pakistan refugee camps to do so.

Intercontinental and the Kabul Hotel) are shabby relics of a Stalinist idea of upmarket accommodation. The Intercontinental has no hot water; the Kabul Hotel sometimes has. The hotels are dirty and dilapidated. But they have running water, flushing toilets and, apart from a destroyed shopfront next door to the Ariana Airlines office on the ground floor of the Kabul Hotel, are intact. Even the roses in the luxurious gardens of the Kabul Hotel continue to bloom, providing a touch of protected gentility behind iron railings. To confirm the knowledge that one has the protection of luxury, the hotels are fenced in and protected round-the-clock by military guards.

These, then, are the signs of privilege in Kabul: sanitation, gardens, barbed wire and guards. In the gardens of the French embassy, geraniums grow as vivid as anywhere in the Midi. Average rents are US$15,000 per month in these bourgeois areas. Someone mentioned one case of US$27,000 being charged. Outrageous even by any Western standard. Only embassies, the UN and aid agencies can afford the real estate.

But even the UN is close to broke. The aid agencies are broke. At the time of this writing at the end of June 2002, the UNHCR is cutting by two-thirds its monthly food ration to returning refugees, from 150 to 50 kilograms (this is in a situation where malnutrition is the most common problem affecting refugee children). As for aid agencies, like the UN agencies, they largely pulled out of Afghanistan after September 11, to protect the safety of their employees. Although they returned when Kabul fell to the United Front, major agencies are now scaling back their operations, because the crisis is past, money is short and they are more urgently needed elsewhere. But the notion of "crisis" is relative.

Afghanistan is one of the poorest countries in the world. It did not become poor following September 11, 2001, nor did it become poor under the Taliban. But it is certain that decades of war, compounded by five years of drought, have bled dry an already highly anaemic economy. According to a report by Médecins du Monde (2002), agricultural production fell by 65 per cent in the two years to 2001, and the country was at the brink of famine. The UN's 2001 *Human Development Report* ranks Afghanistan 89th out of 90 developing countries on its Human Poverty Index, between Ethiopia (number 88) and Niger (90). Two other countries generally considered as extremely poor, Haiti and Bangladesh, rank at 71 and 73 respectively (UNDP 2001: 151).

It is difficult to obtain reliable statistics on Afghanistan. The reference in the *Human Development Report* is virtually the only one. It would appear that the last census in Afghanistan was conducted in 1980. At that time, according to the UN and Afghan-Info, the population was some 15.8 million (including some 2.4 million nomadic), with 15 per cent or roughly 2 million living in the cities. Half of these were living in Kabul (Afghan-Info 1998). Subsequent statistics are generally cited as estimates. The CIA "World Fact Book" estimates the population at 26.8 million in July 2001, of which over 42 per cent were aged 14 or under (CIA 2001). The latest population statistic, reported by Associated Press on 26 June 2002, puts the Afghan population at 27 million. According to the latest available statistics, Afghan life expectancy at birth is 45.88 years for men; 45.1 years for women. The Afghan birth rate, at 41.82 per 1000 or 5.87 per woman, is the highest in the region. The infant mortality rate, also—by far—the highest in the region, sits at a staggering 149.28 deaths per 1000 live births, or close to 15 per cent.

Gross domestic product per capita is by far the lowest in the region, at $800 per person; as a point of comparison, it is $1470 in Bangladesh and $2000 in Pakistan (AsiaSource 2002). Ironically, as even the UN has noted, prohibition by the Taliban of the country's main cash crop, opium, while generally seen as one of the Taliban's few positive measures, also interfered with one of Afghanistan's major exports, causing severe economic hardship, particularly in the north. The UN report, by Secretary-General Kofi Annan, estimates at 480,000 the number of workers who have been deprived of earnings from opium poppies, "and the farm-gate income foregone is estimated to be in the region of $100 million". Despite this cutback, Afghanistan continues to produce 90 per cent of Europe's heroin. Annan goes on to suggest that "urgent action is required by the international community to support the rehabilitation and crop substitution efforts of the United Nations in those areas" (UN/Annan 2001). Given Karzai's recent commitment to end Afghanistan's drug trade, the need for such urgent action can only increase exponentially.

It is significant that, of the US$4.5 billion in aid committed by various governments at talks in Tokyo in January 2002 to assist the reconstruction of Afghanistan, only an infinitesimal proportion has to date dribbled through. A resolution by the UN Security Council on 26 June called for those commitments to be honoured; unfortunately, a resolution from the UN does not suffice to make things happen. The West rallied round to help the US in its "War Against Terrorism" and France, at least, has similarly rallied round to help the US train the Afghan army under the new transitional regime, but it seems that while the West can easily find the money to destroy lives, it is rather more hard-pressed to find the money to rebuild them.

Another issue facing Afghanistan, to which Moghadam (this volume: 279) has referred, is its ethnic factionalism, as political rivalries (notably among various versions of Islamism) compound the country's fierce tribal rivalries. There are more than thirty ethnic groups in Afghanistan, the main ones being Pashtun (38 per cent), Tajik (25 per cent—although some put this figure higher), Hazara (19 per cent), and Uzbek (6 per cent). Turkmen, Baloch and other small minorities make up the remaining 12 per cent. The huge ethnic diversity and attendant frictions, along with tribal social organisation, particularly among Pashtuns, have meant that Afghanistan has never really had an effectively operating centralised government. Local leaders have had a great deal of leeway to do as they wished.

This continues to be the case in the post-Taliban regime. Indeed, many doubt whether the US-supported Karzai regime, reconfirmed at the Loya Jirga in June 2002, will be able to exercise political authority beyond the Kabul province and surrounding regions. There have been numerous reports of violence against both Afghan citizens and UN and NGO workers in the north and west of Afghanistan, which according to a UNHCR representative, speaking on 15 June to BBC World, the local warlords show absolutely no political will to control.

The Taliban and National Psychosis

Sometimes, however, this virtual autonomy in the regions has had its advantages, as the following "success story" during Taliban times demonstrates. Abdul Wakil Hanifi, an Afghan national and currently Education Officer with the Norwegian Refugee Council, based in Peshawar, reports that when he was working alongside the UNDP, with the implementing agency Comprehensive Disabled Afghan Program, in the Kandahar province during the Taliban's reign, he was able to set up a girls' school. At that time, the UNDP provided training for teachers and stationery on the condition that the local community provide the premises and that girls be allowed to attend. The first breakthrough occurred when, after some negotiation in one local area, Hanifi was able to obtain written permission from local Taliban authorities for a burqa-clad woman teacher to be employed in a strictly segregated girls' school. It appears that the Taliban responded to local community pressure in this matter. In terms of funding the teachers' salaries, the UNDP originally paid these during the setting-up period, but in many communities UNDP-sponsored income-generating projects provided sufficient means to pay the teachers.

By 11 September 2001, there were eight UNDP-sponsored schools in Kandahar and Farah recognised and funded by the Taliban; Hanifi estimated that at that time there were 2000 girls and over 3000 boys attending school in those provinces. Farah authorities in particular were very cooperative. After September 11, the UN evacuated the region, but at last news in February many of the schools were still functioning, thanks to community support.

Even in Kandahar, which was the fiefdom of the Taliban's Defence Minister, there was considerable progress, with the Defence Minister's cooperation. At first, he agreed to schooling for girls on the condition that most of the resources went to boys and numbers of girls were limited. When the first UN-sponsored school in Kandahar opened, there were 25 girl pupils. Three months later, this number had grown to 104, compared to over 250 boys. The Minister even committed the equivalent of 5000 Pakistani rupiahs per month to hiring teachers.

After September 11, this particular village was the first in Kandahar province to be bombed by the US, being the Defence Minister's village.

Despite these small and idiosyncratic breathing spaces that NGOs, the UN and local communities were able to create under the Taliban regime, there is no doubt that the people of Afghanistan found the regime oppressive, even if at first it appeared to clean up some of the corruption that had become rife under the Jihadi (Mujahideen) regime of Rabbani. Farida Akram, one of the founders, in 1980, of the Franco-Afghan solidarity association Afrane, set up in response to the Soviet invasion, describes the progression of the Taliban regime as follows:

- *Year one, 1997:* People were almost relieved. No more shooting. No more corruption. People felt safer, there were no robberies. Shops were left unlocked. Even the incidence of rape initially appeared to diminish. (This would change quickly with forced marriages, which were rapes—and bashings—under another guise.)

- *Year two, 1998:* People started to feel oppressed. They had no right to do anything. Husbands were punished if their wives were heard laughing. People had no right to play music or dance, which deprived them of an important means of expression and social interaction; the impact of this was particularly severe on women in rural areas. Even the hammams (bath houses) were closed. Women had no social space. Nonetheless, the memory of the negative experience of the Rabbani regime remained so strong that people were still attempting to remain hopeful: "Maybe things will still work out."

- *Year three, 1999:* The psychiatric problems start. The suicides start. People are not coping, they are giving way to despair. They are saying, "Well, US, come and bomb us, that way there will at least be an end."

- *Year four, 2000:* The whole country is completely dysfunctional. Nation-wide psychosis.[4]

I will add a fifth year to Akram's chronlogy. Year five, 2001: The country enters its fifth year of drought and teeters at the edge of famine. Afghanistan is starving in every way: culturally, socially, politically, economically.

---

4   Personal communication, 9 June 2002.

Among other restrictions and mistreatment of citizens imposed by the Taliban were:

- a requirement that all people attend prayers in a mosque five times per day
- a requirement that all men grow beards
- a ban on certain games such as the traditional kite-flying
- the execution of anyone who carries "objectionable literature" or converts from Islam
- a requirement that all non-Muslim minorities wear a distinct yellow badge or piece of yellow cloth stitched to their clothing (which is reminiscent of another notoriously bleak moment in history)
- a ban on watching television, videos and movies and on use of the Internet.

For women, the bans were more comprehensive. Many are now common knowledge: women had no right to work, to go to school or even to leave the house unaccompanied by a close male relative—and even then they had to be shrouded in their *chadri* (burqas)—and were required to remain silent in public (there were bans on laughter and on high-heeled shoes, which were assumed to be noisier than other shoes). Other bans are perhaps less well known. Women showing their ankles or otherwise inappropriately dressed were to be publicly whipped. They were prohibited from gathering in public during Muslim festivals or indeed from attending any other public gathering. They were not allowed to wear bright colours, to wash clothes in a public place or use public baths. (All women's hammams were closed under the Taliban, which deprived women and girl children of access to basic hygiene, given how few homes have easy access to water. Some hammams are now reopening.) Even place names containing the word "women" were changed.

So extreme was the national psychosis experienced under the Taliban, so absolute the oppression of Afghan women, that, despite the devastating effect of the US State's war, many felt relieved at its advent, as the following anecdote demonstrates. An American member of the women's delegation with which I travelled to Kabul in June 2002 told me she felt tremendously guilty and ashamed because of what her country had done to Afghanistan. But she was surprised, and more than a little uncomfortable, to be thanked by so many Afghan women for getting rid of the Taliban. "Thank you for bombing us." Apparently, even a woman who had been widowed by a US bomb said thank you. This made us squirm and I found myself wondering if the widely-reputed Afghan politeness could possibly extend as far as thanking a Western rogue state[5] for compounding the havoc wreaked in Afghanistan since 1979.

---

5   This is the title of a book by William Blum (2000), who maintains that the world's primary "rogue state" is the US.

But that way, "at least there has been an end" to the Taliban regime. A country "bombed for its own good" as Christine Delphy ironically puts it (this volume: 308): the Western left is not buying this, but it appears some Afghans are. It is a savage and monstrous realisation. Were US bombs really the only way?

A decade previously, I had dealt with the same dilemma in relation to Bosnia. We wanted the torture of Bosnian women to stop. Was sending in the military the only way? Some fifteen years before that, I had asked myself the question in relation to South Africa after the 1976 Soweto uprising, brutally repressed by Apartheid troops. Is a feminist response as simple as blanket and intransigent pacifism? Judith Ezekiel has raised the same question, with relation to Nazism in Europe (this volume: 102), even as many—indeed, most—other contributors condemn violence, either that of "terrorists" or that of the US State. But who defines who are the "terrorists"? And is feminist recourse to violence, such as that of Angry Women who set fire to sex shops in the United Kingdom in the 1980s, always necesssarily and fundamentally "wrong"?[6] As Catharine MacKinnon points out, the US State has bombed Afghanistan with impunity while those few desperate women who take up arms against the war waged on them within the US now languish in US jails (this volume: 426).

Can one only stop violence with violence? It would appear that in relation to the Taliban, some have thought the answer to be "yes". Hamasa Maiwand, of RAWA's base in Peshawar, also appears to think so with relation to the Jihadi. She maintains that the Jihadi murderers (who continue to be represented in the post-Taliban regime), should be condemned to death (personal communication, Peshawar, 15 June). Indeed, the return of the Jihadi[7] is far from being the salvation of the Afghan people.

The Loya Jirga: From Uncontrolled Psychosis to Controlled Neurosis

"Loya jirga" simply means "grand council" in Pashtu. Loya Jirgas are the traditional form of governance in Afghanistan, with delegates being chosen by tribal elders. The Loya Jirga of June 2002 comes directly out of the Bonn Agreement of 5 December 2001, which created an interim administration in

---

6   The actions of Angry Women gave rise to a heated debate within the British feminist community at the time, on the justifiability of such "direct action": such debates were reported and waged in such fora as *Spare Rib* and the *London Women's Liberation Newsletter*.

7   I note in passing the darkly absurd resemblance between this phrase and the title of a *Star Wars* sequel.

Afghanistan and a timetable for setting up a future, elected government. The agreement provided for the convening of an emergency Loya Jirga to appoint a transitional administration within six months of the assumption of office by the Interim Administration on 22 December 2001. This transitional administration would in turn lead Afghanistan for up to two years, until a "fully representative government can be elected through free and fair elections" (Bonn Agreement 2001).[8]

The Loya Jirga held in June 2002 had 1575 delegates, including 200 women. There had been a quota set of 160 women; the fact that this quota was exceeded by chosen and elected delegates was seen to be highly positive. The June Emergency Loya Jirga differed from traditional Loya Jirgas in that, alongside the locally chosen representatives (who are not democratically elected but chosen by local councils of elders), there were places set aside for appointed representatives of refugees, women, and various professional and government groups. Under rules announced by the Loya Jirga commission, all delegates to the Loya Jirga were to sign an affidavit attesting that they had not taken part in criminal activities or human rights abuses in the past. In reality, many former Jihadi, directly responsible for crimes against the Afghan people following the withdrawal of Soviet troops in 1989, were present at the assembly, to the great disgust of many dissenting delegates, and now form part of the transitional government headed by Hamid Karzai.[9] Women delegates in particular were cynical about the possibility of a feminist voice or even any sort of democracy. One delegate, Mahba Noor Zai from Kunduz, is cited by French daily *Le Monde* as saying, "We cannot speak out against the commanders or their ideas, because we have to return to our villages. Who will protect us then?" (Chipaux 2002).

The "unity" achieved at the conclusion of the Loya Jirga has been widely acknowledged to have been brokered by the US through its envoy, Zalmay Khalilzad. It is understood to have been largely pressure from Khalilzad and various Jihadi factions that resulted in the former king, Mohammed Zahir Shah, recently returned from exile, relinquishing any claim to candidacy as head of state. Even Sima Samar, former Women's Minister who was not

---

8   Human Rights Watch has compiled a concise background briefing on the Loya Jirga: hrw.org/press/2002/04/qna-loyagirga.htm.

9   A list of cabinet members was provided by Associated Press on 23 June 2002. See www.myafghan.com/news2.asp?id=-570001411&seracg=6/23/2002. Together, the Cabinet ministries, special advisers and other Cabinet-level posts total 35 people (this is 15 more than the Bush Cabinet in the US), which demonstrates the difficulty of conciliating different factions to attempt to create national unity in Afghanistan.

renowned for distancing herself from the Jihadi, is cited as saying, "This is not a democracy. This is a rubber stamp. Everything has already been decided by the powerful ones" (cited by Clark 2002).[10] The stepping down of the king has in particular been considered by feminists such as RAWA, along with other progressives, (including a cousin of Karzai's who currently works as a researcher in Australia), as auguring ill for the country, as many believe the king provided the best chance for unifying the country and providing distance from the Islamists.[11]

In the absence of Zahir Shah, and under political pressure from the US, engineering national unity has largely involved providing a place for the different Jihadi factions and ethnic warlords. Karzai, who is Pashtun, was himself once close to the Taliban, but distanced himself from them in 1994. Robert Kaplan (2000) quotes him as saying:

> I had no reservations about helping them. I had a lot of money and weapons left over from the jihad. I also helped them with political legitimacy. It was only in September of 1994 that others began to appear at the meetings—silent ones I did not recognize, people who took over the Taliban movement. That was the hidden hand of Pakistani intelligence.

As Karen Talbot has pointed out, both Karzai and Khalilzad also have connections with Unocal (this volume: 291). Karzai has been a covert CIA operator since the 1980s and Khalilzad was during the 1980s a key liaison person between the US State Department and the Jihadi.

Karzai's Deputy Presidents are Mohammed Qaseem Fahim (Tajik), who is also Defence Minister, Karim Khalil (Hazara) and Abdul Qadir (Pashtun). Fahim, who is considered the most powerful man in Karzai's transitional government, formerly worked as deputy to Jihadi leader Ahmad Shah Massoud in military affairs and was commander of the Jihadi in the northern sector. After the fall of Kabul to the Taliban in 1996, Fahim was appointed the commander of Jihadi forces north of Kabul. Fahim heads the National Defence Commission, which includes the country's main warlords. Among them are the rivals Abdul Rashid Dostom (Uzbek), former Communist general, and Mohammad Ustad Atta (Tajik), member of the Jamiat-e Islami (Society of Islam) and former Jihadi fighter, who, a day after the media

---

10 Samar was subsequently passed over for the women's ministry (see below, page 464).

11 Tahmeena Faryal of RAWA, discussion in answer to questions from the floor following her speech at the Asia-Pacific Global Solidarity Conference, Sydney, 1 April 2002; Huma Haque, professor at Qaid-i-Azam University, Islamabad, and visiting scholar at Institute for Women's Studies Lahore, personal communication, 19 June 2002; Hashim Durrani, personal communication, 24 June 2002.

announcement of the new Cabinet, were already fighting in the north of the country. Dostom's supporters launched an attack against Atta's supporters in the village of Abdrang, 120 kilometres south of Mazar-e-Sharif, destroying the homes of 150 families (Agence France Presse, 27 June 2002).

Khalil, who was a key member of the United Front, is head of the Shia party Hezb-e Wahdat-e Islami (the Islamic Unity Party), and prior to the Loya Jirga had expressed dissatisfaction about the Bonn Agreement. He considered Hezb-e Wahdat-e Islami to be under-represented in the interim government, and claimed that Hazaras should be given 20 per cent of the posts in the army, police, government and civil service. Qadir is somewhat of the odd one out in the Vice-Presidential lineup, because of his former Soviet connections. He was a participant in Daud Khan's coup in 1973, and played a major role in the subsequent 1978 coup against Daud Khan, serving briefly at that time as the Minister of Defence. He was later arrested and accused of plotting a coup against the Khalqi government, which he had helped bring to power. He was freed from jail after the Soviet invasion of the country, and reappointed as Minister of Defence by Karmal. In 1986 he was sent to Poland as the Afghan ambassador.

Yunus Qanooni, Education Minister and special adviser on security, caused a media stir when he criticised the Karzai transitional government. There had been rumblings from many of the delegates that the powerful warlords were hijacking the discussions at the Loya Jirga, but Qanooni was the first of the powerful in-group to express dissent. He is a former close associate of Massoud, who was known as the "lion of Panjshir" because of his leading role in the Jihadi military opposition to the USSR. Massoud, who was assassinated by agents of Bin Laden on 9 September 2001, was a supporter of the fundamentalist Jamiat-e Islami and Rabbani's "military supremo", as William Maley puts it (1998: 6). He now appears to have been recycled as a martyr for the cause of democracy, and reconstructed by some as the liberator of women.

As for Qanooni, during the 1980s he was in charge of relations between the Jamiat-e-Islami and the Pakistani ISI (Inter Services Intelligence), which was itself closely connected to the CIA and provided money, weapons and ammunition to the Jamiat-e-Islami. After the fall of Kabul in september 1996, Qanooni took part in the meetings that led to the creation of the Supreme Council for Defence of the Motherland (Massoud, Khalil and Dostom also took part in the creation of the Council), and in 1997, after the fall of Dostom, he played a role in the creation of the United Islamic and National Front for the Salvation of Afghanistan. Despite his criticism of the government and his momentary hesitation in accepting the combined education and security portfolio, Qanooni remains a strong player in the transitional government. As Education Minister, his Islamist connections do not augur well for the future curriculum nor for the education of women.

This, then, is the "unity" government that the Loya Jirga has ostensibly chosen. But it would be more accurate to say that it is the government chosen by the mullahs, the warlords and the US, through the person of Khalilzad. Dissenting voices were marginalised or silenced, whether they criticised the absence of democracy in the process, as did Sima Samar, or stood up for women's rights, as did Abdul Nassim. On 14 June, Nassim, director of security in the Kabul muncipality, caused a stir with the following remarks made to the assembly:

> When a mullah says that women do not have the same intellectual capacity as men, I reply that neither do I, because I was born of a woman. The name of martyr was given to Commander Massoud and to Abdul Haq. But who gives this name to the women of Kabul, whose rights have been treated with scorn for years? (cited by Jaulmes 2002, my translation)

Following his speech, Nassim was threatened by mullahs and did not reappear at the Loya Jirga the following day. He was subsequently summoned to the Presidential Palace, where Karzai, Fahim and Qanooni all gave him to understand that he was lucky to be alive. At the time of this writing, he is under protection of the UN and seeking political asylum (*Le Figaro*, 28 June 2002).

Nassim is not the only one who fears for his safety. Hamasa Maiwand recounts that during Rabbani's regime, the Jihadi set fire to newsagencies and bookshops in Afghanistan that sold RAWA's magazine (personal communication, 15 June 2002). RAWA's premises in Peshawar are kept secret for security reasons, and Maiwand did not want to be photographed for the same reasons.

A Way Forward for Afghan Women?

On 7, 8 and 9 June 2002, a women's conference was held as an adjunct to the Loya Jirga. It was organised by a Franco-Afghan women's association called Negar, which is close to the Northern Alliance, which Negar prefers to call the United Front. A problematic political position to say the least, especially as the founders of Negar were either associates or admirers of Massoud. It is thus an organisation close to the Karzai regime; indeed, had it not been endorsed or at least tolerated by that regime, the conference would certainly not have been able to take place in Kabul at that time. At the same time, Negar is attempting to work strategically to ensure that women's rights are placed on the national agenda as Afghanistan (ostensibly) operates the transition to a modern democracy. In June 2000, a Franco-Afghan women's meeting orgnised by Negar in Dushanbe, Tajikistan, elaborated a *Declaration of the Essential Rights of Afghan Women*, which it is attempting to have appended to the new Afghan Constitution being elaborated between June 2002 and the end of 2003 by Karzai's transitional government (Negar 2000).

The regime's support for the conference was made evident by the fact that it was opened by Mohammed Ismael Qasemyar, appointed chairman of the independent commission for convening the Emergency Loya Jirga, and that guest speakers included Sima Samar, Women's Minister in the Karzai interim administration. (Qasemyar has been criticised for not abiding by the terms of the Bonn Agreement in keeping former Jihadi criminals out of the Loya Jirga, while Samar has been criticised for relative inaction during the six months of the interim administration.) Qasemyar's speech at the women's conference was full of the expected demagogic references to women's rights and to women as representing the values of peace, justice, honour and democracy. He also described them as men's "helpmates" in work and struggle. His speech contained numerous references to "Islamic values" and "Afghan values" as being synonymous with justice and democracy, and referred to women and men as "God's caliphs on earth".

Sima Samar's speech was brief and to the point: it was not the physical presence of the two hundred women participating in the Loya Jirga that was the most important. What mattered was that they speak for women's rights and insist on them being respected. She stressed that the road ahead remained long and that the women of Afghanistan needed to work together to achieve results. She also referred to the importance of international solidarity among women (given that Negar was founded in France and that a sizeable Western delegation—mostly French—was present, it would have been difficult for her not to make this allusion).

Within days of the close of the Loya Jirga, Samar was passed over as Women's Minister for the more moderate Habiba Sarabi. Already, Samar had been perceived as moderate by some, and in the six months of the interim administration had not done a great deal. With the odds stacked against her, however, it is entirely possible that she was not given much of a chance to do a great deal. One Afghan participant at the women's conference, who knew Samar quite well, commented that it was not so much that she did not want to do anything but that she didn't know what to do, where to start. The impression I was given was of a woman who was overwhelmed by the enormity of her task. According to RAWA's Hamasa Maiwand, Sima Samar was a puppet of the Jihadi, who had to say what the Karzai regime wanted her to (personal communication, 15 June 2002). She was probably not particularly combative in feminist terms; but if she had been, she never would have been a member of the interim administration in the first place. Which makes it all the more noteworthy that she was removed from the office of Women's Minister "after offending hardline religious elements" (Associated Press, 26 June 2002). This says a great deal about the allegiances of the new transitional government.

There were three workshop groups at the Negar conference: social policy issues, education, and constitution/human rights. The last of these workshops was largely educational: Afghan delegates were informed of international instruments such as the Convention on the Elimination of All Forms of Discrimination Against Women and studied the 1964 Afghan Constitution. The other two workshops discussed women's needs in the area of education in terms of access, recruitment and retraining, and curriculum, and their social policy needs in the areas of violence against women, health and the right to work.

I attended the social policy workshop. It proceeded laboriously at times, due to the heat, to the need for consecutive interpretation, sometimes directly from Dari to French and sometimes via English to French, and to the immense need of women to tell their stories. The workshops were expected to come up with five "outcomes", along the lines of procedures at UN-supported NGO international, regional and subregional fora. But "outcomes" in terms of broad umbrella human rights statements or demands were not the objectives of the participants. Above all, they wanted to be heard.

What they told us were infinite local variations on the same litany. We need affordable housing. (Rents in downmarket areas of Kabul are now at $50 per month. The average income, for those lucky enough to have stable employment, is $20 per month. So several families crowd into one house.) We need hygiene and health care. We need local clinics. We need hospitals, including mental hospitals for the drug-addicted and the distressed. We need sanitation and drinking water. We need schools. We need the means to train women for employment. We need safe green spaces for the children and the elderly.

We need to look after each other. We need to rebuild our lives.

The women have no lack of ideas. They know what they need, they have developed and costed projects. They are already working with women and children in the villages. But they have no money. Some projects are started up with funding from various aid agencies. Then three months later the money runs out. Back to square one.

Rebuilding lives is expensive. So the women, not surprisingly, were asking the French delegation for money, for assistance in obtaining money to support their projects. One women's group, the Freedom Messenger Association, had elaborated two detailed projects for making shoes and sambal bags, costed at US$5880 and US$4880 respectively, to train twenty-four women over three months. They had prepared typed-up copies of these projects to give to the French delegates.

The stated aim of the projects, in its original wording, is:

> Provision for availability of work for the women and girls who has the obligation of supplying living facilities for their families. This will enable them to pick-up and to learn profession so that could be able to provide and make ready a piece of bread.

The "Preface" or background statement to the project reads as follows. I am reproducing it in full here, in its original wording and without further comment. This is done not with any condescending intent, but rather because I believe that part of the force of the appeal made by these women is in the very words—foreign, unfamiliar and difficult: hence both awkward and devoid of the reassuring niceties of pseudo-objectivity—that they are obliged to use. I am unable to find words to express more forcefully the extent of deprivation from which Afghan women and children are suffering at this point in time.

> You and all the world knows that 23 years war destroyed all finance & moral of our Country. Inaddition a big number of famillies lost their Bread supplier "means their". The mother together-with some childrens of small age and year without Guardian with empty-hand, World of poverty, empty hand with tear and groan carried the Life. There was no ear for listening to their groan and Clamour. The mother and daughter are compelled either to cleaning and washing the cars and are wild-rue.[12] If they find the bread the night by said work, they are hungry during the day, if they do it for the day, will sleep the night hunger. This condition of the famillies will harm the heart of every human who has sense and pain.
>
> In addition to that despite that world is the system of computer of Education and Training but the children of this family mainly has no news of education and school, and they are only thinking that how to find a piece of bread. With no doubt the future of these children is dark and will be sad.
>
> In view to feel such problem the Freedom Messenger Association which is a basic for the women and its aims is to serve the Women and Children of the Country.
>
> We have taken in view to establish Courses for young Orphan and Widow Women and poverty for 3 months to enable them to learn the profession & work from one side and to assist their family in the future and on other side to avoid them from deviation so that they will be honest, Healthy and educated individuals in the future.
>
> Therefore we are respectfully requesting your esteemed Organisation to help

---

12 It is possible that this means something like "running wild in the streets" as *rue* is French for street. But this is pure conjecture on my part.

and assist us in this humanitirians and politely action in establishing this project to help us in financial and materials required as your aim and programme is stands and based to help the human in such occasion.

The Holy and the Highest Service to the Humen is the approval of this Project.

Violence against Women in Afghanistan: Physical, Economic, Symbolic

Many feminists have pointed out that women are both universal symbols of masculinist ideals of culture, identity, honour, nation, even justice and liberty,[13] and universal targets, both for nationalist appropriation and manipulation (and resulting disempowerment of women and distortion of their struggle for their rights), and for fundamentalist, extreme-right and ethnicist violence (which in itself indicates the importance men attribute to women as symbols and guardians of identity). Feminists have pointed time and again to this masculinist construction of women (e.g. Hélie-Lucas [1987] 1990; Enloe 1990; Winter 1994, 1995; Howard 1995, esp. ch. 6; Yuval-Davis 1997), in particular within fundamentalist movements (e.g. Allami, 1988; Hélie-Lucas 1991; Moghadam 1993: 146, 1994; Moghissi, 1999). Some have suggested that women are being "instrumentalised" as the means by which particular masculinist political factions exert pressure or gain control, but I have suggested elsewhere that such attention paid to controlling women is not a means to an end but *an end in itself* (Winter 2001). If one maintains—as I do—that woman-hatred is a cornerstone of the societies in which we live, then it is logical that doing damage to women should constitute a major element of a society's economic, social, cultural and political structures, and naive to assume that men—with some partial and relatively rare exceptions—are going to take women's well-being seriously unless they are forced to do so.

It is thus unsurprising, in a country such as Afghanistan, where women are acknowledged by various human rights organisations to be among the most oppressed in the world, to find these scenarios acted out in extreme and violent ways. Indeed, the Taliban's targeting of women as primary objects of hatred and instruments of control is widely considered—including by feminists—to be one of the most extreme, sustained and violent manifestations of

---

13 It is significant that the symbols of justice and liberty in the first two Western nations—setting aside Cromwell's England—to embrace republican, democratic and human rights values that subsequently became the template for the UN's Universal Declaration of Human Rights, are women: a statue of Marianne, symbol of the French Republic, watches over the Place de la République in Paris, while a female Statue of Liberty, a present from France to the US, watches over the waters of New York.

woman-hatred in the modern world. But we would be seriously mistaken in assuming either that women suddenly became severely oppressed under the Taliban or that the US State's "War Against Evil" has liberated them. Indeed, many of the contributions to this book demonstrate the contrary, and Christine Delphy's article in particular unmasks the odious opportunism of the US State in brandishing "women's rights" as a pretext for declaring war on Afghanistan (this volume: 306). Similarly, the demagoguery of Qasemyar's speech to the Negar women's conference, cited above, shows clearly that for the current regime, "women's rights" are necessarily to be filtered through masculinist understandings of women, religion, culture, honour and nation.

We would also be seriously mistaken, however, in assuming that the violence from which Afghan women have suffered is *necessarily* more systematic, or more systemic, or always more extreme than violence from which women suffer elsewhere. Certainly, the oppression of Afghan women must be combated, and indeed, many have been combating it for decades. (Not all, thankfully, were dupes to the anti-communist discourse of the US and the fundamentalist agenda of the Mujahideen, constructed as resistants for liberation at the time and subsequently, in their reinvention as the United Front, as heroes or martyrs for the cause of freedom and justice.) At the same time, it is imperative that we do not see the situation of Afghan women in isolation, either from that of women elsewhere in the world or from a globalised continuum of violence from which the poor and relatively powerless—and especially women—suffer the most.

When I say "violence", I am referring not only to the extremes of male physical violence against women, but also to psychological and economic violence. To paraphrase a conference paper I gave in 1996 on outcomes from the UN Fourth World Conference on Women held in Beijing, 1995, when I use the term "male violence", I mean that we live in a world structured around the violent domination—physical, psychological, and institutional (political, economic, cultural)—of one half of the human population by the other half (Winter 1996). It would appear that this understanding of violence against women has gained increasing currency among feminist researchers, and it is certainly a common understanding among feminists who work with the economically disadvantaged and/or themselves come from such backgrounds.

Women are murdered, raped, mutilated, humiliated, imprisoned, impoverished, appropriated, manipulated, marginalised and any one of a number of other acts of violence, all over the world. The examples I could list would fill several volumes, although I have referred briefly to some in my earlier article (this volume: 360–371). In any case, such acts of violence against women have been well-documented by many feminist and human rights

organisations—one does not need to look further than the UN, Human
Rights Watch or Amnesty International, although the most detailed
information and telling analysis is often provided by feminist organisations[14]—as well as by a plethora of individual feminist writers and scholars.
This violent domination of women is not "specific" to any particular religion
or any particular national economic or political context. In other words,
violence against Afghan women is not caused by "Islam" *per se*. It is not
caused by "poverty" *per se*. It is caused by a violent system of domination in
which religion and global capital both play their part. But even these are not
the whole story.

It is tempting, for Western feminists, in looking at the situation of Afghan
women, to focus immediately and primarily on male physical violence against
women: rape, beatings and so on. Such a focus certainly has a logical justification: Afghan women *have* been subjected, and continue to be subjected, to
male physical violence. A Human Rights Watch briefing paper prepared in
May 2002 provides a picture of post-Taliban violence against women. In the
north of the country, particularly in and around Mazar-e-Sharif, women have
become the targets of ethnically related violence, especially rape. Pashtun
women are particular targets but women of other ethnic groups are also being
attacked. Human Rights Watch reports that women feel compelled to limit
their movement and expression and continue to wear the burqa so as to avoid
becoming targets, especially of men aligned with the three main ethnically-
(and religiously-) based parties. In the Kandahar region, women who are not
conforming to Taliban prescriptions concerning dress and behaviour are
being targeted. It is significant that the interim administration did not repeal
the Taliban edicts, which thus still remain in place at the time of this writing
(Human Rights Watch 2002).

It is not, however, only the threat of physical violence that constrains
women's movement. It is also the lack of money and of public transport.
Most of the regionally-based participants at the Negar women's conference in
Kabul, all of whom formed part of the literate minority of Afghan women
and some of whom were university-educated, spoke of the financial hardship
they had had to incur to attend the conference and requested some financial
compensation. All also spoke of women's and children's difficulties in circulating due to the almost complete lack of affordable public transport. Even
in Kabul, I noticed the virtual non-existence of public buses, while the more
expensive taxis are plentiful.

---

14 These include, for example, RAWA as concerns Afghanistan and Shirkat Gah, the
   Aurat Foundation, Asr and Women Workers' Helpline as concerns Pakistan—
   including, in some cases, Afghan women in exile.

If even literate and thus relatively privileged women are experiencing financial hardship, the immobilising effect of poverty on the majority of the country's women can only be imagined. If one adds to this the threat and the reality of physical violence, and the apparent lack of political will, by either the interim administration or the newly chosen, US-supported transitional administration, to effect legislative and infrastructural change, then it becomes painfully obvious that very little has changed for the majority of Afghan women.

What the participants at the Negar conference stressed was not so much male physical violence but the economic, cultural and social violence from which women and children are suffering. The appeal from the Freedom Messenger Association underscores this clearly. When one does not have money to pay rent, does not have enough food for the children and has no access to clean water or medical care, when no family member knows how to read, particularly in the case of female-headed households, the bottom line is survival.

A Nigerian NGO campaigner against female genital mutilation once told me: "If I had a million dollars tomorrow to spend on Nigerian women, I would not spend it on combating female genital mutilation. I would spend it combating poverty. I would spend it to ensure that women had the means to earn an income, have enough to eat. I would spend it on their education." At the Negar women's conference, Afghan women were not telling us: "We have been raped and beaten." They were telling us: "Our children need to eat, need health care, need an education. We need to work: we need an education."

Some talked of the violence of the Taliban. But only some. And only because it was the Taliban. The Taliban are the vanquished enemy, the universally recognised oppressor. One can take distance. But even here, the aspect of the Taliban's violence against women that was stressed the most was the socio-cultural impact for young women who had been married by force to Taliban militants and who now find themselves either widowed or abandoned by their husbands who fled the US and Northern Alliance armies. At the age of twenty or younger, many of these women, who now have young children by their Taliban husbands, are social outcasts because of their intimate connection with the former oppressor. Most of them live with parents or other relatives, and are socially isolated and economically disempowered. As in the case of the ethnic violence in the north, women are paying the price of a quarrel not of their making. And, as in the case of many women who are raped the world over, the Taliban wives are paying doubly: the violence of rape compounded by the violence of social ostracism.

Clothing and Symbolic Violence

Much was made, following the post-September 11 war, of the newfound liberty being discovered by Afghan women, with news reports of them gleefully throwing off their burqas. The Human Rights Watch report on violence against women and the continuation of Taliban prescriptions, cited above, rather gives the lie to that rosy picture. As does my own observation. Despite reports by, for example, Valérie Rohart (a journalist working for Radio France Internationale) and Farida Akram (founder of Afrane, which works closely with the French Embassy in Kabul), that between March and June 2002, Kabul had relaxed just a little and more women were discarding their burqas,[15] I saw no evidence of this latter claim. I saw not one woman who was not burqa-clad in the streets of Kabul, apart from Western women or Afghan women who either lived in the West or spent considerable time there. Perhaps they are there, in the more bourgeois areas, although driving through those areas, one sees barely anyone at all on the streeets. Except the military. When you have money, you do not have to walk. Perhaps the women inside the cars are not wearing burqas.

I did see an occasional woman, in a semi-secure public situation (in her local village community, or inside a van or a shop), with the veil of her burqa flipped back over her head. But the burqa itself was not removed. The veil remained, ready to be flipped down as needed, or, as I often saw, drawn quickly across the women's faces like a scarf or shawl. Afghan women are not comfortable with being looked at in public. Anonymity is always a safer option when one is a member of a group under threat. Indeed, participants at the Negar women's conference and other women cited in the Human Rights Watch report (2002), have reported cases of harassment when they attempted to discard their burqas.

What I found particularly significant, however, about women's use of the burqa in Kabul, was that it was not ultimately to do with being invisible but with controlling women's behaviour in space demarcated as "public". The Negar conference took place in the Park Cinema in the centre of Kabul (indeed, the only cinema in Kabul at present). The building reminded me of old country cinemas or theatres that one might find in Australia. It was surrounded by a large yard, fenced by iron railings, through which people inside the yard were perfectly visible from the street. Pedestrian and vehicle access to the compound was policed by armed guards hired for the conference. The Afghan women participants all arrived in the morning, virtually without exception, dressed in their burqas, which they removed the moment they were inside the compound. Most of them wore headscarves under their

15 Personal communications, 7 June 2002.

burqas, and most of these women kept their headscarves on once inside; a minority did not. At the end of the day, the same process in reverse: the women would exit into the yard, and don their burqas just before passing through the gate into the street.

The covering of women is thus demonstrably not to do with not being seen by men, as the women were visible from the street through the iron railings. It is to do with the requirement that women, once they have crossed the symbolic barrier into that space designated by men as public and thus male, must tailor their appearance and behaviour to masculinist prescriptions.

One can find similar clothing prescriptions and restrictions on women in the West. For example, women in professional and political life are expected to dress in close-fitting suits with skirts and high heels that limit their ability to walk, stand and sit comfortably, they must carry handbags which encumber them, they must wear jewellery and makeup which make them conform to a masculinist image of a "well-groomed woman"—and which require considerable financial outlay. I do not see such Western prescriptions as being qualitatively different from the requirement to wear a burqa. The constraint imposed by a burqa relative to that imposed by a tight skirt and high heels is simply a matter of degree. The intent—controlling women's behaviour, making them physically uncomfortable and limiting their freedom of movement—is the same.

It is thus most unfortunate that Western dress and Western versions of female adornment, beauty and "coquetry" are set up as an emancipating alternative to Islamist or Jewish fundamentalist dress codes. Even the French feminists present at the Negar conference spoke of the fact that they had brought makeup as presents for the Afghan women, and even went as far as suggesting a "makeup table" on the last day of the conference. I was most relieved to see that this did not eventuate. But of the Afghan women present at the conference, the most highly educated professional women were indeed often heavily made up, heavily bejewelled, coiffed with ribbons and bows and shod in high heels. Many of the women I saw walking in the streets of Kabul also wore high heels. I remember in particular a woman walking along a hilly and unevenly surfaced dirt road on the outskirts of Kabul in black patent-leather high heels, the limited visibility and encumbrance of material imposed by her burqa compounded by the difficulty in walking on such a surface in such footwear.

Swapping one form of control for another will not liberate Afghan women.

Be that as it may, however, it is clear that the imposition of the burqa (or the hijab, or the Hasidic wig, and so on) is not about "women's modesty" (as a response to men's seeemingly uncontrollable "sexual" urges),[16] but about preventing women from confidently and freely occupying space designated by men as "public".

Afghanistan, Refugees and the Global Political Economy: Where Are the Women?

In the preceding pages, I have offered a brief and no doubt incomplete overview of the current situation in Afghanistan and in particular of the current situation for Afghan women. One cannot appropriately finish such an article, however, or bring this book to its conclusion, without locating that discussion within the global post-September 11 context.

The very first element of that context, and the one that appears most immediately and urgently connected to Afghanistan, is the world refugee crisis. As Western governments toughen their policies towards asylum-seekers,[17] as has been spectacularly and most shamefully demonstrated in Australia, the country where I currently live,[18] the world's refugees are ever-increasing in number. At the start of 2001 the UNHCR put the number of people "of concern" at 21.8 million, "or one out of every 275 persons on Earth". This was slightly down on the previous year's figure of 22.3 million (UNHCR 2001). After September 11, however, the number was once again on the rise with Afghan refugees fleeing to neighbouring Pakistan and Iran (an estimated 20,000 to 30,000 fled to Pakistan in the five weeks to 15 October), forcing those countries to re-open their previously closed borders. In 2002, the UNHCR estimated the number of refugees under its protection at 22 million, with an additional estimated 25 million displaced people in the world who live in dangerous and vulnerable situations within their own

---

16 I place the word "sexual" in inverted commas to denote that we are dealing here with a narrowly defined masculinist construction of sexuality as being synonymous with violence against women.

17 "Strengthening of borders" was once again the refrain at the recent European summit held in Spain. It has been the refrain since the EU was formed. Observe, for example, the Schengen accords, specifically designed, among other things, to keep non-European immigrants, including asylum-seekers, out. For once, however, France was loth to follow the Ibero-British hard line on foreigners. This runs contrary to its stance during the Algerian crisis of the 1990s (partly taken, it must be acknowledged, in response to an appeal from Bouteflika, the then President of Algeria, to curb the "brain drain" from Algeria as journalists and intellectuals fled the Islamic Salvation Front).

18 A Human Rights Watch report notes: "Following the September 11 attacks, the Australian Defense Minister Peter Reith justified his government's refusal to allow

countries (Pittaway 2002). Women and children make up 80 per cent of the world's refugees, and the single largest national group of refugees comes from Afghanistan.

In October 2001, the time of the last available reliable statistics, there were close to 5 million Afghan refugees across the world (although Arundhati Roy, this volume: 334, puts at 8 milllion the number of Afghan citizens in need of emergency aid as at the end of September 2001). Most Afghan refugees are currently in Pakistan (over 2 million, although decreasing since April 2002 with repatriations), Iran (1.5 million), or internally displaced (an estimated 1 million) (Human Rights Watch 2001b). At the end of January 2002, the UNHCR was operating thirteen refugee camps along the Pakistan border, and estimated the numbers of refugees housed there at 151,000 (UNHCR media release, 29 January 2002). In addition, local estimates put at 50 per cent the Afghan population of the North-West Frontier Province town of Peshawar, situated some 55 kilometres from the Afghan border: many of these Afghan residents have been there for upwards of twenty years, with adult children who have grown up in Pakistan. Many are unable to leave in any case because the women and children have been sold as bonded labour to local Pakistani captains of industry, notably in brickworks.[19]

By the third week of June 2002, the numbers of refugees returning to Afghanistan had exceeded 1 million, most (920,000) returning from Pakistan, and UN High Commissioner for Refugees Ruud Lubbers anticipated that up to 2 million might return by the end of 2002 (Europa World 2002). The number of refugees either in other countries or internally displaced remains high, however, as new refugees arrive on a daily basis, many of them "recyclers". Recyclers are those refugees who, following voluntary

---

the asylum seekers entry, arguing that it should reserve the right to refuse entry to "unauthorized arrivals" on security grounds. Ironically, Australia granted refugee status to 93 per cent of the 1431 Afghans whose cases were decided in 2000" (Human Rights Watch, 2001b). It would appear that before September 11, Afghans were not a security risk. After September 11, they all got dipped in a "terrorist" solution, if we are to believe Peter Reith. For more on Australian treatment of refugees, see Mares (2001).

19 Bonded labour is one of the main forms of child slavery in Pakistan, as well as one of the main means of putting sexual and economic pressure on women. This is despite the fact that Pakistan's Supreme Court declared bonded labour anticonstitutional in 1989 and that bonded labour violates International Labour Organisation Convention No. 29. See Anti-slavery (1999) and Ercelawn and Nauman (2001) for more information. An estimated 40 per cent of workers in brick kilns are women.

repatriation (for which the UNHCR provides transport or assistance with transport, some money, bedding and food), find that Afghanistan is not ready to receive them, and return across the border. Both Pakistani and UNHCR authorities are becoming increasingly strict in policing recyclers, some of whom are perceived to be knowingly "rorting the system". To some extent, the UNHCR has no doubt little choice but to be strict, given its straitened financial circumstances. That said, when one considers the still unstable and often violent situation in Afghanistan, the accusation that recyclers are rorting the system seems spurious. A number of observers have reported that Afghanistan, including its UNHCR refugee transit camps, has neither the means nor the infrastructure to support returning refugees. Already, those who are neither refugees nor internally displaced are facing enormous hardship and risks of disease and violence; the return of refugees is placing increased pressure on an already fragile nation.

Official discourses on refugees, including those by the UNHCR and various humanitarian organisations, take care to separate "economic" from "political" refugees, the argument being that only "political" refugees are *bona fide*. Western governments have increasingly used the "economic" tag to justify exclusion of refugees, claiming that these people are not escaping persecution but "merely" escaping poverty. Which rather begs the question of how one defines persecution in situations such as the current one in Afghanistan. Now the US State's war is over, there is pressure from Western governments, and indeed a desire from many refugees themselves, to return. But when one is returning to a nation that is devastated by twenty-three years of war, largely fuelled and manipulated by the US with the assistance of Pakistan, as well as by the USSR for some of that time; where reconstruction is difficult because of landmines, lack of money, lack of national and international political will and the persistent agitation of Islamists of all persuasions; where women are under constant threat of violence in many parts of the country—how is it possible to suggest that Afghan refugees' need for asylum has passed?

Feminists have often argued that systematic male violence or the threat thereof should be grounds for women being granted asylum. This has happened in some isolated cases of female genital mutilation, and has been recommended in others (such as the case of Algerian women I cite earlier in this book: 363–4). If such grounds were fully acknowledged, however, then all countries would be persecutors and no country would be able truly to offer asylum to women.

Putting aside such arguments, however, even the current narrow definition of "refugee" afforded by the 1951 Geneva Convention is not being respected by most governments of the world. And many of the main creators of situations that cause people to become refugees are not being brought to account. The US readily comes to mind, but it is not alone.

Some of the contributors to refugee-creating situations are also, paradoxically, lands of asylum for the victims. Thus Pakistan, which is one of the major players in the rise to power of the Jihadi, and thus must necessarily be seen as a co-persecutor, is now the main country of asylum for Afghan refugees. That Pakistan can with alacrity and not a little cynicism set itself up as a land of asylum and assist the UNHCR in maintaining refugee camps,[20] at the same time as it has substantially contributed to the conditions that caused the Afghan refugee crisis in the first place, shows just how unimportant the lives of "ordinary people" are when governments collude to assert power and consolidate earnings. The word "pawns" is often used to describe such manipulations of the powerless to serve the agendas of the powerful. I would argue, however, that pawns in a chess game have more freedom of movement than most of the population of Afghanistan, particularly its women. And they are not "pawns" that can ever possibly reach the other side of the chessboard, the side where they might become transformed into powerful "queens".

The many contributions to this book have almost unanimously denounced the cynical exploitation by the US State of the World Trade Center attacks to impose its will on the world, and in particular on Afghanistan. One could, irony intended, characterise the US State's actions as "overkill". As both Arundhati Roy and I have emphasised (this volume: 334, 365), US bombs were not particularly necessary to transform Afghanistan to a graveyard, reduce it to rubble. It was already a mess. And the mess was largely of the US State's making.

This in itself is unsurprising. Like a greedy and spoilt little boy, the US State has created messes all over the world, leaving others (the surrogate "mothers" of the so-called Third World, as well as some from the First and Second), to clean up the chaos as best they are able.

It would, however, be manichean in the extreme to render the US solely responsible for the world's ills and in particular of those of the world's women. Islamists, including all of Al-Qaeda, the Taliban and the Jihadi, have certainly benefited from US money and arms, but they were not "created" by the US. The US has simply fanned a fire that others ignited. Moreover, it has

---

20 The Pakistani Commission for Afghan Refugees (CAR) has, however, come under criticism from some NGOs for not doing its job particularly well. But the UNHCR itself has come under similar criticism from some quarters, particularly as concerns ensuring the security of refugees in UNHCR camps in North West Frontier Province.

not been the sole capitalist state to plunder and control elsewhere in the world. France has come in for its share of criticism in relation to Africa, for example, while Japan's track record in Asia as well as, increasingly, in some Western countries, leaves a great deal to be desired.

What has been perversely noteworthy, however, about the US manipulation of crisis situations in the non-West is that the US State has found ways of channelling *anti-Western* cultural particularism into conservative expressions that support (a) global capitalist systems and (b) global male supremacism. In other words, the ostensible "enemies" of the US have in fact been its *allies*. This has frequently been pointed out in relation to the world economic system; although the existence of an Afghan privileged class has been pointed out more in relation to Islamism and various acts of political and military thuggery than it has been pointed out in relation to economics. The Afghan khans and urban bourgeoisie, the landed gentry if you will, are doing very well. The US$15,000-per-month rentals in Kabul are going into someone's pocket: it may not be the pockets of the Afghan "people" but it is certainly the pockets of Afghan citizens.

The alliance between the US and its ostensible "enemies" has been less frequently pointed out in relation to a world political system that is predicated on the construction of the fiction of "national identity".[21] US-driven globalisation is widely assumed to depend on the undermining of non-Western nation-states and more generally on the weakening of state control, both as concerns their "cultural identity" and as concerns their national legislative and political apparatus. A number of observers, however, have maintained that the existence of a strong state, as both a political and cultural entity and as an economic regulatory entity, is in fact essential to the smooth workings of a so-called "free-market", globalised economy (see e.g. Sassen 1998; Quiggin 2001; Winter 2002), and, ultimately, to the strengthening of the US State.

Finally, this alliance is hardly ever pointed out in relation to the global domination of women. The US waved Afghan women's rights like a banner when it decided to declare war on Bin Laden, but prior to that moment, it had done nothing to attempt to combat the Taliban's treatment of Afghan women. And it could not care less about the well-documented abuses of women's rights by the Jihadi warlords. The domination of women is not something the US has any particular interest in addressing. On the contrary, it has a vested interest in *maintaining* it, and in supporting those who use and abuse women, whether those people are labelled "fundamentalists" or "captains of industry". Diane Bell has commented that the US and Afghanistan

---

21 See Anderson (1991) for a discussion of the nation as an "imagined community".

share the shame of not having ratified the Convention on the Elimination of All Forms of Discrimination against Women (this volume: 440). It is arguably not the only thing that the US and Afghanistan have in common, but it is highly significant.

Susan George (1999) has suggested that "human rights" are merely a sop to the powerless. How much more of a sop to the powerless, then, are "women's rights"? The rights of Afghan women do not matter. They do not matter to the US State, nor do they matter to the Afghan State. Nor do they matter to the so-called "international" so-called "community".

Women's rights matter only when they can be used and manipulated. Women themselves matter mostly when they need to be controlled. If there is one lesson to be learned from the events of September 11 and their aftermath, it is this.

In case we had not already understood.

References

Afghan-Info. (1998). "Afghanistan Profile by Afghanistan Educational Web Site." 1 November: www.afghan-info.com/GENINFO.HTM.

Allami, Noria. (1988). *Voilées, dévoilées: Etre femme dans le monde arabe.* Paris: L'Harmattan.

Anderson, Benedict. (1991). *Imagined Communities: Reflections on the Origin and Spread of Nationalism*, rev. edn. London and New York: Verso.

Anti-slavery. (1999). "Bonded Labour in Pakistan: submission to the United Nations Economic and Social Council Commission on Human Rights: Sub-Commission on Prevention of Discrimination and protection of Minorities: Working Group on Contemporary Forms of Slavery: 24th Session." Geneva, 23 June–2 July 1999: www.antislavery.org/archive/submission/submission1999-08Pakistan.htm.

Asia Source. (2002). "Afghanistan." www.asiasource.org/profiles/ap_mp_03.cfm?countryid=32.

Blum, William. (2000). *Rogue State: A Guide to the World's Only Superpower.* Monroe, ME: Common Courage Press.

Bonn Agreement. (2001). UNICBonn, "Agreement on Provisional Arrangements in Afghanistan Pending the Re-Establishment of Permanent Government Institutions" www.uno.de/frieden/afghanistan/talks/agreement.htm.

Central Intelligence Agency. (2002). "CIA World Fact Book 2001: Afghanistan." June. www.cia.gov/cia/publications/factbook/geos/af.html.

Chipaux, Françoise. (2002). "Les Afghans déçus et amers après la Loya Jirga". *Le Monde*, Paris. 21 June. www.lemonde.fr/recherche_resultats/1,9687,,00.html.

Clark, Kate. (2002). "Afghans Protest over US Manipulation of Summit." *The Independent*, London. 12 June: 13.

Enloe, Cynthia. (1990). *Bananas, Beaches and Bases: Making Feminist Sense of International Politics*. Berkeley: University of California Press.

Ercelawn, Aly and Muhammad Nauman. (2001). "Bonded labour in Pakistan: An overview". Pakistani Institute of Labour Education and Research. June. www.ilo.org/public/english/standards/ decl/publ/papers/piler.pdf.

Europa World. (2002). "One Million Afghans Have Gone Home." 21 June. www.europaworld.org/week87/onemillion21602.htm.

George, Susan. (1999). *The Lugano Report: On Preserving Capitalism in the Twenty-first Century*. London: Pluto Press.

Hélie-Lucas, Marie-Aimée. ([1987] 1990). "Women, Nationalism and Religion in the Algerian Liberation Struggle." In Margot Badran and Miriam Cooke Eds. *Opening the Gates: A Century of Arab Feminist Writing*. London: Virago.

——. (1991). "Les stratégies des femmes à l'égard des fondamentalismes dans le monde musulman." *Nouvelles Questions Fémnistes* 16–17–18: 29–62.

Howard, Rhoda. (1995). *Human Rights and the Search for Community*. Boulder, CO: Westview Press.

Human Rights Watch. (2001a). "Landmine Use in Afghanistan: Human Rights Watch Backgrounder." October. www.hrw.org/backgrounder/arms/landmines-bck1011.htm.

——. (2001b). "No Safe Refuge: The Impact of the September 11 Attacks on Refugees, Asylum Seekers and Migrants in the Afghanistan Region and Worldwide." 18 October. http://www.hrw.org/backgrounder/refugees/afghan-bck1017.htm.

——. (2002). "Taking Cover: Women in Post-Taliban Afghanistan: Human Rights Watch Briefing Paper." May. www.hrw.org/backgrounder/wrd/afghan-women-2k2.htm.

Jaulmes, Adrien. (2002). "Kaboul peine à s'ouvrir à la politique." *Le Figaro*, Paris. 28 June. www.lefigaro.fr/dossiers/archives_lefigaro/frameset.htm.

Kaplan, Robert D. (2000). "The Lawless Frontier". *The Atlantic Online*. September. www.theatlantic.com/issues/2000/09/kaplan.htm.

Maley, William. (1998). "Interpreting the Taliban." In William Maley, Ed. *Fundamentalism Reborn? Afghanistan and the Taliban*. London: Hurst & Company: 1–28.

MAPA, *see* United Nations Mine Action Programme.

Mares, Peter. (2001). *Borderline: Australia's Treatment of Refugees and Asylum Seekers*. Sydney: University of New South Wales Press.

Médecins du Monde. (2002). *Afghanistan: levons le voile sur une catastrophe humanitaire*. www.medecinsdumonde.org/afghanistan/index.html.

Moghadam, Valentine. (1993). *Modernizing Women: Gender and Social Change in the Middle East.* Boulder, CO, and London: Lynne Reiner Publishers.

Moghissi, Haideh. (1999). *Feminism and Islamic Fundamentalism: The Limits of Postmodern Analysis.* London and New York: Zed Books.

——. Ed. (1994). *Identity Politics and Women: Cultural Reassertions and Feminisms in International Perspective.* Boulder, CO, San Francisco and Oxford: Westview Press.

Negar. (2000). *Declaration of the Essential Rights of Afghan Women.* 28 June. http://perso.wanadoo.fr/negar/anglais/declaration.htm.

Pittaway, Eileen. (2002). "Refugees in the Twenty-first Century, a Humanitarian Challenge." *Mots pluriels 21.* www.arts.uwa.edu.au/MotsPluriels/MP2102edito1.html.

Quiggin, John. (2001). "The Fall and Rise of the Global Economy: Finance." In Christopher Shiel, Ed. *Globalisation: Australian Impacts.* Sydney: University of New South Wales Press: 19–34.

RAWA. (2002). "On the Situation of Afghan Women." rawasongs. fancymarketing.net/wom-view.htm.

Sassen, Saskia. (1998). *Globalization and its Discontents.* New York: The New Press.

United Nations / Kofi Annan. (2001). "Report of the Secretary-General—Emergency international assistance for peace, normalcy and reconstruction of war-stricken Afghanistan", document A/56/687. 7 December. www.mineaction.org/countries/_refdocs.cfm?doc_ID=470&country_id=1.

United Nations Development Program. (2001). *Human Development Report 2001: Making New Technologies Work for Human Development.* New York and Oxford: Oxford University Press.

United Nations High Commissioner for Refugees. (2001). "Refugees by Numbers: 2001 edition." www.uhcr.ch/cgi-bin/texis/vtx/home/+cwwBme LqZw_wwwwMwwwwwwwmFqtFElfglhFqoUflfRZ2ItFqtxw5oq5zFqt FelfghAFqoUflfRZ21Dzmxwwwwwww1FqtFelfgl/opendoc.htm

United Nations Mine Action Programme. (2002a). "Afghanistan—Preliminary needs assessment for recovery and reconstruction." 15 January. http://www.mineaction.org/countries/_refdocs.cfm?doc_ID=463&country _id=1.

——. (2002b). "Afghanistan." 2 May. www.mineaction.org/countries/ countries_overview.cfm?country_id=Afghanistan.

United States Fund for UNICEF. (2001). "Country Statistics for Afghanistan." September. www.unicefusa.org/alert/casia/statistics.html.

Winter, Bronwyn. (1994). "Women, the Law and Cultural Relativism in France: The Case of Excision." *Signs: A Journal of Women, Culture and Society 19*(4): 939–74.

——. (1995). "Symboles, moteurs et alibis: l'identification culturelle et nationale des femmes d'origine maghrébine en France". University of Sydney: Unpublished doctoral thesis.

——. (1996). "Down the River: The Political Marketing of Women's Rights". Paper presented at 6th International Interdisciplinary Congress on Women. University of Adelaide. April. Unpublished conference paper.

——. (2001). "'Fundamental Misunderstandings: Issues in Feminist Approaches to Islamism." *Journal of Women's History* 13(1): 9–41.

——. (2002). "Women's Rights, Globalisation and the Nation-state: Are Human Rights and Democracy Enough?" *Australian Feminist Law Journal*, forthcoming. December.

Yuval-Davis, Nira. (1997). *Gender and Nation*. London: Sage.

Contributors

Nahla Abdo is an Arab feminist activist and Professor of Sociology at Carleton University, Ottawa, Canada, She has published extensively on women and the state in the Middle East with special focus on Palestinian women. Among her books are *Sociological Thought: Beyond Eurocentric Theory* (1996) and *Women and the Politics of Military Confrontation: Palestinian and Israeli Gendered Narratives of Dislocation* (with Ronit Lentin, 2002). She contributed to the establishment of the Women's Studies Institute at Birzeith University and founded the Gender Research Unit at the Women's Empowerment Project/Gaza Community Mental Health Program in Gaza.

Evelyne Accad was born and raised in Beirut, Lebanon, and is a professor at the University of Illinois, Champaign-Urbana, in French, Comparative Literature, African Studies, Women Studies, and Middle-East Studies. Her publications include: *The Wounded Breast: Intimate Journeys through Cancer* (2001), *Sexuality and War: Literary Masks of the Middle East* (1990), *Contemporary Arab Women Writers and Poets* (1986), *Veil of Shame: The Role of Women in the Modern Fiction of North Africa and the Arab World* (1978), as well as five edited volumes and fifteen book chapters. Other activities include writing and composing songs and performing in the USA and abroad.

Farida Akhter is the Executive Director of UBINIG—the Policy Research for Development Alternative—based in Dhaka, Bangladesh. She has been an activist against population control and is the author of numerous articles, pamphlets and books, including *Women and Trees* (1990), *Depopulating Bangladesh* (1992), and *Resisting Norplant* (1995). She also runs a feminist bookstore and the publishing company, Narigrantha Prabartana.

Amber Amundson is the 28-year-old widow of Craig Amundson who was killed at the Pentagon on September 11, 2001. Soon after, Amber wrote an open letter to President Bush asking that they not take military action in her husband's name. She immediately became the focus of controversy over the place of dissent during times of war. She is working with the families of other victims of the September 11 attacks to create an organisation of families who do not want their grief used to justify war.

Kathleen Barry is a sociologist and Professor of Human Development in Penn State's College of Health and Human Development. She has campaigned and written extensively on sexual slavery and is author of many books, including *The Prostitution of Sexuality: The Global Exploitation of Women* (1995) and *Female Sexual Slavery* (1979).

Bat Shalom is a feminist peace organisation of Israelis. They work toward a just peace between Israel and its Arab neighbors that includes recognition of a Palestinian state side-by-side with Israel, and Jerusalem as the capital of both. For more information, visit http://www.batshalom.org.

Diane Bell is a feminist anthropologist who has written with passion and courage of women in Aboriginal society, land rights, law reform, human rights and violence against women. She is Professor of Anthropology and Director of Women's Studies at George Washington University. Her books include *Daughters of the Dreaming* (1983/2002), *Radically Speaking: Feminism Reclaimed* (with Renate Klein, 1996) and *Ngarrindjeri Wurruwarrin: A World That Is, Was, and Will Be* (1998).

Monserrat Boix is an Arab world journalist, a specialist in Islamist movements and the Coordinator of Women in Black Network.

Janelle Brown is a freelance writer and has written widely on Afghanistan including in Salon.com and *Ms Magazine*.

Madeleine Bunting is a columnist and leader writer for *The Guardian*, London.

Urvashi Butalia is the co-founder of Kali for Women publishing house in India, a writer and an activist. Her published works include *The Other Side of Silence: Voices from the Partition of India* (1998), and edited volumes, *Speaking Peace: Women's Voices from Kashmir* (2002) and *Women and the Hindu Right: A Collection of Essays* (co-edited, 1995). She is currently working on a project on gender and conflict in South Asia, focusing on oral narratives of women impacted by conflict. She has had long involvement in the women's movement in India and writes on issues relating to fundamentalism, communalism, media, communications, gender and literature.

Dr Anuradha M. Chenoy is Professor in International Studies, Jawaharlal Nehru University, New Delhi. She was born and educated in Delhi, and was recipient of a Fulbright Fellowship at Columbia University, New York. She is an activist on gender and social issues and has written articles and books. Her books include *Militarization and Women in South Asia* (2001), *The Making of New Russia* (2001) and *India Under Siege: Challenges Within and Without* (co-authored, 1994).

Jen Couch grew up in Adelaide and moved to Melbourne ten years ago after spending much of her twenties in India. She has worked with a broad spectrum of community, activist and social justice organisations, both in Australia and South Asia. Jen currently teaches community development at Victoria University and is undertaking a PhD, "This is what democracy looks like: Capturing the culture of anti-globalisation resistance". Her study has involved extensive interviews with activists in the USA, Australia and India. She has published in *Arena Magazine, Communal Plural Journal* and a variety of newsletters. Jen lives with her partner Namgyal, travels to India as much as she can and has recently had her first baby.

Nikki Craft has been a prominent feminist activist for many years who has in particular challenged the pornography and prostitution industry. More recently she has developed a number of feminist activist websites. For more information, visit http://www.nostatusquo.com.

Zelda D'Aprano renowned Women's Liberation Movement activist, was born in Melbourne in 1928. She took direct action for equal pay by chaining herself to the Commonwealth Building in Melbourne in 1969 and was a founding member of the Women's Action Committee in 1970. She has written two books: *Zelda*, her autobiography and early history of the 1970s Women's Liberation Movement, and *Kath Williams, the Unions and the Fight for Equal Pay*. In April 2000, she received an honorary doctorate from Macquarie University, Sydney.

Christine Delphy studied sociology and anthropology at the Universities of Paris, Chicago and Berkeley. She is currently Director of Research at the National Center for Scientific Research in France, and was among those who founded the Women's Liberation Movement in 1970. She co-founded the first feminist journal in France, *Questions Féministes,* in 1977, and is now co-editor of *Nouvelles Questions Féministes,* founded in 1980.

Ani di Franco was born in Buffalo, NY, in 1970. A singer, songwriter and poet, she has written a lifetime's worth of songs exploring both the politics of love and the personal dimensions of political issues, grounded in her own experience and her percussive, no-holds-barred approach to the acoustic guitar. Since 1990, she has toured internationally, building a dedicated grassroots following and releasing fourteen self-produced solo albums on her own Buffalo-based indie label, Righteous Babe Records. The latest of these is the 2002 double live CD, *So Much Shouting, So Much Laughter*. For more information, visit http://www.righteousbabe.com.

Diverse Women for Diversity is a Southern initiative to build an international coalition of women to respond to globalisation and its impacts by creating diverse solutions at the local level and a common defence at the global level.

Carol Anne Douglas is a radical lesbian feminist who lives in Washington, DC. She has been on the collective that produces *off our backs: a feminist news journal* since 1973. She has written over 200 reviews of feminist books for *off our backs*, and has interviewed many feminist writers and activists. Her book, *Love and Politics: Radical Feminist and Lesbian Theories*, was published in 1990. She has a wonderful lover named Mandy and a wonderful cat named Posey. Other than radical lesbian feminism, nature is Carol Anne's chief passion. She can be found bird-watching most weekends.

Barbara Ehrenreich is a political essayist and social critic who tackles a brave and diverse range of issues in books and magazine articles. She is the author or co-author of twelve books, including *Fear of Falling: The Inner Life of the Middle Class* (1989), and, most recently, *Blood Rites: Origins and History of the Passions of War* (1997). She has written for dozens of magazines, including *Ms.*, *Harper's*, *The Nation*, *The Progressive*, *The New Republic*, *The Atlantic Monthly* and the *New York Times Magazine*. Her forthcoming book is called *Nickle and Dimed: Surviving in Low-Wage America*.

Cynthia Enloe received her PhD in political science from the University of California, Berkeley. She serves on the editorial boards of several feminist journals including *Signs*, *Women's Studies International Forum*, and *International Feminist Review of Politics*. She has been teaching at Clark University since 1972.

Eve Ensler is an award-winning playwright, poet, activist, and screenwriter, and the 1999 recipient of the Guggenheim Grant in Playwriting. She is best known as the author of *The Vagina Monologues*, which won a 1997 Obie Award and was nominated for Drama Desk and Helen Hayes awards. The world tour of *The Vagina Monologues* (1998) initiated V-Day, a global movement to stop violence against women. She is also the author of *Necessary Targets* (2001) and a new book, *Points of Reentry* (2001). Eve Ensler is currently writing a screenplay on women in prison for Glenn Close.

Judith Ezekiel is the author of *Feminism in the Heartland* (2002) and articles in journals such as *Les Temps Modernes, Nouvelles Questions Féministes* and *Women's Studies Quarterly*. She teaches women's history and social movements at the University of Toulouse-le-Mirail, is a member of the Simone-SAGESSE feminist studies research centre, associate editor of *The European Journal of Women's Studies*, co-founder of Women's Studies International Europe (WISE) and the Worldwide Organization of Women's Studies, and created and runs the electronic discussion lists WISE-L and etudesfeministes-l. She has been active in the feminist movements in the USA and France for over thirty years.

Tahmeena Faryal was born in 1978 in Afghanistan. She began primary school in Kabul. Her family and other relatives who were patriotic and freedom-loving migrated to Pakistan. As a schoolgirl in Pakistan she became involved in RAWA. For the last two years she has travelled widely, speaking to governments and other representational bodies, trying to gain support and aid for rebuilding Afghanistan—which includes instituting democratic reform and human rights. She has represented RAWA in the UK, Italy, Spain, Canada, Thailand and the USA. In 2001 she addressed the UN General Assembly, and the New York-based collective of non-government organisations working within the UN for the equal rights of women. In March and April 2002 she made a speaking tour to Australia to raise awareness.

Gayle Forman is a freelance journalist who writes about social justice issues pertaining to young people. She recently returned from Quetta, Pakistan, where she reported on Afghan refugees, and is currently at work on a book about subcultures and community.

GABRIELA Network is a US-based women's solidarity organisation working with GABRIELA Philippines. GABRIELA Philippines is an alliance of 105 women's organisations. It is the largest and only multi-sectoral women's assembly in the archipelago. GABRIELA Network organises around issues such as the global traffic in women, world trade and the sex industry, the mail-order bride industry, First World and Third World perspectives on the women's movement, and gender relations in the Asian-American community. GABNet operates a speakers' bureau which offers lecturers who lead in-depth discussions on these issues, and also publishes the bimonthly newsletter, *kaWomenan*.

Dr Judith Gardam teaches international law at the University of Adelaide, Australia. She has a longstanding interest in the area of women and humanitarian law and was appointed in 2001 to write the expert brief on "International Humanitarian Law and Human Rights Law as they Relate to Women and Girl Children" for the study commissioned by the Secretary-General of the United Nations. Publications include *Non-Combatant Immunity as a Norm of International Humanitarian Law* (1993), editor, *Humanitarian Law* (1999) and co-author, *Women, Armed Conflict and International Law* (2001).

Lesley Garner is a travel writer who lived in Afghanistan before the Soviet invasion.

Christina Gombar once worked in the World Trade Towers and has a best friend who escaped them. Like her piece in this book, Christina's work follows no political creed but is rather based on first-hand experience, often going against the grain of contemporary American thought. An extended post-September 11 diary, "War Zone", of which this piece is an opening excerpt, won the Red Hen Press prize in creative non-fiction. As well as having worked in finance for over fifteen years, Christina is the author of *Great Women Writers, 1900-1950* (1996). She has been a fellow of the New York Foundation for the Arts in creative non-fiction. Her work has appeared in business, consumer and literary journals. Christina lives just outside New York City, and in Rhode Island, and has recently completed her first novel, *Theft*, based on her Wall Street experience.

Suheir Hammad, "Poet Laureate of the People's Republic of Brooklyn", is of Palestinian heritage. She edits the journal *Butter Phoenix*, is author of the poetry collection *Born Palestinian, Born Black* (1996), and is featured in *Listen Up! An Anthology of Spoken Word Poetry* (1999). A film producer, she is working on a film based on her memoir.

Susan Hawthorne has been a feminist activist for thirty years. She is the author of *Wild Politics* (2002), based on her PhD, which looks at issues around feminism, globalisation and bio/diversity. She is also the author of a novel, *The Falling Woman* (1992); *Bird* (1999) a collection of poems; and (co-)editor of numerous anthologies including *CyberFeminism* (with Renate Klein, 1999).

Ayesha Khan is a freelance journalist and researcher based in Islamabad, Pakistan. She is General Secretary of Bangla Desh Mahila Parishad and is serving a Fellowship with the *Bulletin of the Atomic Scientists*.

Barbara Kingsolver has written extensively for a variety of publications, including *The Nation*, *The New York Times*, and *Smithsonian*. In 1986 she won an Arizona Press Club award for outstanding feature writing, and in 1995, after the publication of *High Tide in Tucson*, she was awarded an Honorary Doctorate of Letters from her alma mater, De Pauw University. For Kingsolver, writing is a form of political activism. Her publications include poetry, *Another America: Otra America* (1992, 1998), *The Poisonwood Bible* (1998), *Prodigal Summer* (2000) and *Small Wonder* (2002). For more information visit http://www.kingsolver.com/.

Naomi Klein is an award-winning journalist and author of the international best-selling book, *No Logo: Taking Aim at the Brand Bullies* (2000). Translated into twenty-five languages, it was described by *The New York Times* as "a movement bible". Naomi Klein's articles have appeared in numerous publications including *The Nation*, *The Guardian*, *The New Statesman*, *The New York Times*, and *Ms. Magazine*. She writes an internationally syndicated column. She is a frequent media commentator and has been a guest lecturer at Harvard, Yale and New York universities. In December 2001, she was named as one of *Ms. Magazine*'s Women of the Year. For more information visit http://www.nologo.org.

Sonali Kolhatkar is a radio broadcast journalist in Los Angeles. She is also Vice-President of the Afghan Women's Mission. She has degrees in physics and astronomy and a master's degree in astrophysics, and until recently, worked as a software developer at the California Institute of Technology. Sonali has spoken out about women's rights and human rights in Afghanistan as well as the responsibility of the USA to the people of Afghanistan. Her paper "The Impact of US Intervention on Afghan Women's Rights" is in publication at the *Berkeley Women's Law Journal*.

Congresswoman Barbara Lee (Democrat) was first elected to the House of Representatives for the Ninth District of California in a 1998 special election. She came to Washington after serving in the California State Assembly 1990–96 and the California State Senate 1996–98. Throughout her political career, Congresswoman Barbara Lee has sought to bring her training as a social worker to bear on the problems and challenges that confront the nation and the world. She has worked to build bipartisan coalitions to provide for the basic and inter-related needs of all people: health care, housing, education, jobs, and the quest to create liveable communities in a peaceful world.

Ronit Lentin is director of the Master of Philosophy degree in Ethnic and Racial Studies, Trinity College Dublin. Her books include *Conversations with Palestinian Women* (1982), *Israel and the Daughters of the Shoah: Re-occupying the Territories of Silence* (2000), *Gender and Catastrophe* (1997), *Racism and Anti-racism in Ireland* (with Robbie McVeigh, 2002), and *Women and the Politics of Military Confrontation: Palestinian and Israeli Gendered Narratives of Dislocation (*with Nahla Abdo, 2002).

Catharine A. MacKinnon is a lawyer, teacher, writer, activist, and expert on sex equality. She has a BA from Smith College, a JD from Yale Law School, and a PhD in political science from Yale University Graduate School. She has been Professor of Law at the University of Michigan Law School since 1990, and Visiting Professor of Law at the University of Chicago Law School since 1997. Professor MacKinnon is involved in litigation, legislation, and policy development on women's human rights domestically and internationally. Her publications include: *Women's Lives, Men's Laws* (collection of writings, speeches, and briefs from 1980-1997) and *In Harm's Way: The Pornography Civil Rights Hearings* (1988), edited and introduced (with Andrea Dworkin).

Betty McLellan is a feminist psychotherapist with more than twenty years' experience. She works with women and men in individual and couple counselling. She is the author of *Overcoming Anxiety* (1992), *Beyond Psychoppression* (1995) and *Help! I'm Living with a ~~Man~~ Boy* (1999).

Zubeida Malik is the reporter on Islamic issues for BBC Radio 4's *The Today Programme*. She was the first British broadcaster, and the only woman, to interview the Taliban during the war on terrorism. She has been studying Islamic terrorist movements such as Al-Qaeda since the 1990s. In November 2000 Zubeida Mailk was named Young Journalist of the Year by the Foreign Press Association, and in April 2001 was named Best Radio News Journalist in the Ethnic Multicultural Media Awards.

Susanne Martain was born in April 1954 in Western Australia. Growing up in many different places in Australia, she attended nine primary schools, and after three years of high school, began work in Port Pirie, South Australia. Soon Susanne was back on the road and worked her way around Australia. After living on the Nullarbor Plain, Susanne travelled through the Centre to Darwin, from which she departed for Eora Country (Sydney) for six weeks. One daughter, some more education, varied income generation, mind-boggling experiences and thirty years later, Susanne is wondering just how long six weeks is. http://www.isis.aust.com/win/godside.htm.

Rigoberta Menchú Tum was born in 1959 at Chimel, a small Guatemalan village located in Quiche. Like her ancestors, she dedicated herself to cultivate the soil and to caress animals. Witnessing the oppression, the discrimination and the exploitation of the indigenous people, she decided to follow the labour of her father, who was a peasant leader. In 1980, when terror was stretching over her country, she went to Mexico into exile to denounce the atrocities committed in Guatemala and to defend the indigenous cause. In 1992 the Nobel Committee awarded her the Nobel Peace Prize. One year later, the Rigoberta Menchú Tum Foundation was born. The institution, whose mission is to bolster the recognition of indigenous peoples' rights and identity, promote respect for human rights through justice and fight against impunity, support a Culture of Peace and contribute to self-managed initiatives, has offices in Guatemala and Mexico City. Rigoberta Menchú now lives in Mexico City due to the reign of terror that still prevails in Guatemala. Among her publications are *I, Rigoberta Menchú* (1984) and *A Girl from Chimel*.

Valentine M. Moghadam is Director of the Women's Studies Program and Associate Professor of Sociology at Illinois State University. Her research interests include sociology of gender, comparative development, social change, sociology and political economy of the Middle East and North Africa, Afghanistan, and women and social change in the Muslim world. Her publications include *Gendering Economic Reform: Women and Structural Change in the Middle East and North Africa* (1997), *Gender and National Identity: Women and Politics in Muslim Societies* (1994), *Gender and Development in the Arab World: Women's Economic Participation, Patterns and Policies* (co-editor with Nabil Khoury, 1995).

Robin Morgan is an award-winning writer, feminist leader, political theorist, journalist and editor, and has published seventeen books, including six of poetry, two of fiction, and the now-classic anthologies *Sisterhood is Powerful* (1970) and *Sisterhood is Global* (1984). A founder of contemporary US feminism, she has also been a leader in the international women's movement for twenty-five years. Her latest books include *A Hot January: Poems, 1996–1999* (2001), *Saturday's Child: A Memoir* (2000) and (reissued and updated) *The Demon Lover: The Roots of Terrorism* (1989/2001).

Fariba Nawa is an Afghan-born journalist who lives in the USA.

Stella Birah Nambuya is the President of the **Federation of Uganda Women of Business Organisations, Industry and Agriculture**. She is a women-human rights activist and advocate, consultant in the private sector on policy and planning, an economist, manager and writer. She has advocated for the release of women prostitutes from Luzira prison in Uganda and founded the women's network of businesses Globally, she co-ordinated the world women's conference in Washington, DC, as a follow-up to Beijing, and belongs to the network Diverse Women for Diversity.

Rinku Pegu is a journalist who writes for the Indian web magazine http://www.tehelka.com.

Rosalind Petchesky is Distinguished Professor of Political Science at Hunter College and the Graduate Center, City University of New York.

Cynthia Peters is a political activist, freelance editor, and writer for progressive publications such as *Z Magazine*, *ZNet* http://www.zmag.org *Dollars and Sense*, and *Sojourner*. She is the editor of *Collateral Damage: The "New World Order" at Home and Abroad* (1992), and homeschooling mother of two daughters. Her writing and speaking focus on a wide range of topics including organising, the media, parenting, and sex and sexuality. She currently works with the East Timor Action Network and United for Justice with Peace, where she supports neighborhood groups to form in response to the "war on terrorism" and its concurrent rollback of civil liberties.

Sudha Ramachandran is an analyst based in Bangalore, India. She writes for several publications and until recently, was Assistant Editor at the *Deccan Herald*. She has a doctoral degree from the Jawaharlal Nehru University, New Delhi, and teaches at the Asian College of Journalism (Chennai). She received a fellowship from Women in Security, Conflict Management and Peace (WISCOMP) and has contributed a chapter "Dying to be Equal", in *Women, Security, South Asia: A Clearing in the Thicket*, edited by Farah Faizal and Swarna Rajagopalan (in progress).

RAWA, the Revolutionary Association of the Women of Afghanistan, was established in Kabul, Afghanistan, in 1977 with the objective of involving an increasing number of Afghan women in social and political activities aimed at acquiring women's human rights and contributing to the struggle for the establishment of a government based on democratic and secular values in Afghanistan. Despite the suffocating political atmosphere, RAWA very soon became involved in widespread activities in different socio-political arenas, including education, health and income generation as well as political agitation. For more information visit http://www.rawa.org.

Mary Robinson was appointed the United Nations High Commissioner for Human Rights by UN Secretary-General Kofi Annan in June 1997. She trained in law and from 1969 to 1989 was a member of Seanad Éireann, the Upper House of Parliament in Ireland. In 1990 she was elected President of Ireland.

Arundhati Roy trained as an architect and is the author of the Booker Prize-winning novel *The God of Small Things* (1998). She has authored collections of essays including *The Cost of Living* (1999), *The Algebra of Infinite Justice* (2001) and *Power Politics* (2001). She has been active in protesting the building of dams on the Narmada River in India.

Jennie Ruby is a lesbian feminist writer and editor and a long-term collective member of *off our backs: a feminist news journal,* which has been published out of Washington, DC, since 1970. She has a master's degree from George Washington University. She is a computer nerd, loves to play electric guitar, and dotes on her partner's children (and her little dog, too). She passionately believes that another world is possible.

Ameena A. Saeed teaches sociology at California State University.

Azra Talat Sayeed is the executive director of Roots for Equity, editor of *Resistance/Muzehamat* and *Challenge* and holds positions as Visiting Faculty at the University of Karachi and the Institute of Women Studies, Lahore. She manages several projects regarding women and children's education and awareness-raising and is a member of the Task Force for Women and Environment, Asia Pacific Forum on Women, Law and Development.

Kalpana Sharma is currently a deputy editor with *The Hindu*, one of India's important national English-language daily newspapers. She has been a journalist and writer for thirty years and has held senior positions in prominent Indian newspapers. She has concentrated on writing on developmental and environmental issues in addition to the issues related to women and gender. She has won many awards for her outstanding journalism, for her service to the cause of women and for spread of education and knowledge.

Vandana Shiva is a world-renowned environmental leader and thinker. She has devoted her life to fighting for the rights of the ordinary people of India while challenging globalisation of the food system worldwide. Dr Shiva is director of the Research Foundation for Science, Technology and Ecology, dedicated to independent research to address significant ecological and social issues in close partnership with local communities and social movements. She is also the founder of Navdanya, a national social movement for biodiversity conservation and farmers' rights.

Mythily Sivaraman is a women's rights activist and working president of the Tamil Nadu unit of the All-India Democratic Women's Association.

Makere Stewart-Harawira is of both Maori and Scots descent and her tribal affiliations are Waitaha and Kati Mamoe. She is in the final stages of her PhD (Education) at the University of Auckland in the School of Education where her doctoral research topic is "Globalisation and Indigenous Peoples: resistance and integration". She has a particular interest in issues of world order and global governance and is actively involved in socio-economic issues involving indigenous peoples, including ecological issues, biodiversity, traditional knowledge and the impact of international trade and investment regimes.

Patricia Sykes is a poet and storyteller and is currently a non-performing member of the Women's Circus, Melbourne, for whom she co-edited *Women's Circus: Leaping Off the Edge* (1997). She has performed her poems and stories in various venues, is the author of a collection of poetry *Wire Dancing* (1999), and won the Tom Collins Poetry Prize in 2002.

Karen Talbot is the director of International Council for Peace and Justice. She speaks and writes extensively on a range of issues with articles appearing in publications in the United States and many countries around the world. She has a long history of work in the women's peace movement and leadership in the movement against the war in Vietnam and continues to serve on the board of the SF-Women's International League for Peace and Freedom and the WILPF national disarmament committee. For many years she was an NGO representative to the UN and she has also worked closely with the labour movement having, among other things, helped build international labour solidarity as well as community–labour coalitions, including for actions against the North America Free Trade Agreement, and a 10,000-strong march across the Golden Gate Bridge: "Health Care is a Human Right". She is a recipient of the Martin Luther King Jr award for peace. The website of ICPJ is: http://www.icpj.org.

Dr Sunera Thobani is cross-appointed to the Centre for Research in Women's Studies and Gender Relations and the Women's Studies program at the University of British Columbia. She is Past President of the National Action

Committee on the Status of Women (1993–96), and the first woman of colour to hold this position. Her doctoral research at Simon Fraser University examined the impact of globalisation on women's citizenship rights in Canada.

Transnational Feminists. The authors of this statement are faculty members at various universities around the USA. They share interests in transnational culture, postcolonial and ethnic studies, and contemporary politics of gender and sexuality.

Union of Australian Women is a national organisation, formed in 1950 to work for the status and well-being of women in a peaceful and environmentally safe world. They have been leaders in a wide variety of campaigns, including the demand for equal pay, campaigns for control of prices and profits, health issues, abortion law reform, opposition to nuclear testing and mining, and for peaceful settlement of international disputes. The UAW networks with women's groups, community and union organisations on these and other issues concerning women.

The United Nations Development Fund for Women (UNIFEM) is the women's fund at the United Nations. Established in 1976, UNIFEM provides financial and technical assistance to innovative programmes and strategies that promote women's human rights, political participation, and economic security worldwide. UNIFEM works in partnership with UN agencies and non-government organisations to link women's issues and concerns to national, regional and global agendas. UNIFEM assists women in over 100 countries in Africa, the Arab States, Asia and the Pacific, Central and Eastern Europe and the Commonwealth of Independent States, Latin America and the Caribbean. For more information, visit http://www.unifem.undp.org.

Bronwyn Winter is a Senior Lecturer in the Department of French Studies at the University of Sydney, where she is also President of the National Tertiary Education Union. Her work on feminist theory, feminism in France, women and the idea of "culture", Islamism, women and politics, liberalism and women's human rights has been widely published in international journals and anthologies. Her main objective in writing, apart from survival, is to stir up feminist debate in the hope of realising what Somer Brodribb (1992) has called "the feminist potential to make sense".

Theresa Wolfwood is the director of the Barnard-Boecker Centre Foundation, Victoria, Canada. She is active in many local and global citizen organisations and has organised and spoken at rallies, conferences, workshops and meetings in Canada and abroad. Her articles and photographs appear in many Canadian and international publications, and she is a contributor to *There is an Alternative* (2001). Her poetry collection, *Porphyry*, was published in 2000. Theresa and her husband hand-built a house in the forest. She bakes bread in a handcrafted clay oven and makes banners for all occasions. She lives by the motto of her late friend, Kay Macpherson: When in doubt, do both. For more information visit http://www.islandnet.com/~bbcf.

Women Living Under Muslim Laws (WLUML) was formed during the years 1984-85. WLUML is an international network that provides information, solidarity and support for all women whose lives are shaped, conditioned or governed by laws and customs said to derive from Islam. The Network aims to increase the autonomy of women by supporting the local struggles of women from within Muslim countries and communities and linking them with feminist and progressive groups at large; facilitating interaction, exchanges and contacts and providing information as well as a channel of communication. More information can be found at http://www.wluml.org.

Women's International League for Peace and Freedom (WILPF) was founded in 1915. WILPF empowers women to work for peace and justice in every Australian state and territory, and in forty-five countries around the world.

Cilocia Zaidi writes for *The Nation*, Pakistan, and *The News International Islamabad*.

Permissions

The editors are grateful to the following individuals and organisations for their generosity in allowing us to reproduce the following images and texts:

Patricia Sykes for "Log of Impacts: As It Happened", © 2001, permission from the author.

Robin Morgan for "NYC: The Day After", Copyright © 2001 by Robin Morgan, all rights reserved. Reprinted by permission of the author from her "Letters from Ground Zero", appearing as the Afterword to the new, updated edition of her book *The Demon Lover: The Roots of Terrorism* (Judity Piatkus Books, UK, Washington Square Press/Pocket Books, US, 2002).

Revolutionary Association of the Women of Afghanistan (RAWA) for "Afghani Women's Resistance Organization: Bin Laden Is Not Afghanistan", permission from RAWA.

Kathleen Barry for "Nono-Selective Compassion", © 2001.

Suzanne Martain for "Rancid Social Soup", first published on Ausfem-Polnet email list, 18 September 2001, permission from the author.

Robin Morgan for "Week One: Ghosts and Echoes", Copyright © 2001 by Robin Morgan, all rights reserved. Reprinted by permission of the author from her "Letters from Ground Zero", appearing as the Afterword to the new, updated edition of her book *The Demon Lover: The Roots of Terrorism* (Judith Piatkus Books, UK, Washington Square Press/PocketBooks, US, 2002).

Madeleine Bunting for "Women's Voices Silenced in the Enthusiasm for War", © 2001, first published in *The Guardian*, 20 September 2001.

Women Living Under Muslim Laws (WLUML) for "Statement on Attacks in the USA", permission from WLUML.

Susan Hawthorne for "Terrorism, Globalisation, Bio/diversity, Survival: A Feminist Perspective", © 2001, first published on Diverse Women for Diversity list, permission from the author.

Barbara Kingsolver for "A Pure, High Note of Anguish", originally published in *The Los Angeles Times*.

Barbara Lee for "Why I Voted Against War", first published in the *San Francisco Chronicle* on 24 September 2001, permission from the author.

Amber Amundson for "A Pentagon Widow Pleads for Non-violence", © 2001.

Rigoberta Menchú Tum for "Letter to President George W. Bush", permission from the author.

Barbara Kingsolver for "No Glory in Unjust War on the Weak", originally published in *The Los Angeles Times*.

Union of Australian Women for "Statement", permission from Union of Australian Women.

Kalpana Sharma and *The Hindu* for "A War … By Men", first printed in *The Hindu*, 21 October 2001, permission from the author.

Uganda Federation of Women, for "Letter To Kofi Annan", permission from the authors.

Ameena A. Saeed for "Telling It Like It Isn't", first printed in *The Hindu*, 23 October, 2001, permission from the author.

Cynthia Peters for "Where Are the Afghan Women?", first printed in *Sojourner*, November 2001, www.sojourner.org. Permission from the author.

The Nation for "Life of Afghan Refugee Women" by Cilocia Zaidi, first printed in *The Nation*, 27 October 2001, permission from *The Nation*.

Vandana Shiva for "Globalisation and Talibanisation", © 2001, permission from the author.

Revolutionary Association of the Women of Afghanistan (RAWA) for Testimony of Tahmeena Faryal, permission from RAWA.

Christina Gombar for "Weekday Warriors", first printed in *London Review of Books*, 2 November 2001, and *Women's Review of Books*, January 2002. Permission from the author.

Sudha Ramachandran for "Behind the Veil of Oppression", first printed in *The Hindu*, 4 November 2001, permission from the author.

Lesley Garner for "Before the Bombs: My Beautiful Afghanistan", © 2001.

Women Living Under Muslim Laws (WLUML) for "Urgent Action Alert", permission from WLUML.

Jennie Ruby for "Is This a Feminist War?", first printed in *off our backs: a feminist news journal 31*(10), November 2001, permission from the author.

Nikki Craft for "A Call on Feminists to Protest the War against Afghanistan", © 2001, permission from the author.

Judith Gardam for "International Law and the Terrorist Attacks on the USA", © 2001, permission from the author.

Ranjana Padhi for "Women Oppose War", © 2001, permission from the authors.

Revolutionary Association of the Women of Afghanistan (RAWA) for "Appeal to the UN and World Community", permission from RAWA.

Bronwyn Winter for "Who Will Mourn on October 7?", © 2002, permission from the author.

Nahla Abdo for "Eurocentrism, Orientalism and Essentialism", presented at Anthropology and Gender in the Middle East Conference, November–December 2001.

Ronit Lentin for "Feminist Snapshots from the Edge", © 2002, permission from the author.

Evelyne Accad for "The Phallus of September 11", © 2002, permission from the author.

Catharine A. MacKinnon for "State of Emergency", first printed in *Women's Review of Books*, March 2002, permission from the author.

Diane Bell for "Good and Evil: At Home and Abroad", © 2002, permission from the author.

Bronwyn Winter for "If Women Really Mattered ...", © 2002, permission from the author.

We would also like to thank De Clarke for the website www.ucolick.org/~de/WTChit/, where we first saw many of the pieces published herein.

In some instances it has proven to be impossible to contact copyright holders. Any copyright holders not acknowledged here or acknowledged incorrectly should contact the publishers.